The Routledge International Handbook of Dyscalculia and Mathematical Learning Difficulties

Mathematics plays an important part in every person's life, so why isn't everyone good at it? *The Routledge International Handbook of Dyscalculia and Mathematical Learning Difficulties* brings together commissioned pieces by a range of hand-picked influential, international authors from a variety of disciplines, all of whom share a high public profile. More than fifty experts write about mathematics learning difficulties and disabilities from a range of perspectives and answer questions such as:

- What are mathematics learning difficulties and disabilities?
- What are the key skills and concepts for learning mathematics?
- How will IT help, now and in the future?
- What is the role of language and vocabulary?
- How should we teach mathematics?

By posing notoriously difficult questions such as these and studying the answers *The Routledge International Handbook of Dyscalculia and Mathematical Learning Difficulties* is the authoritative volume, and essential reading, for academics in the field of mathematics. It is an incredibly important contribution to the study of dyscalculia and mathematical difficulties in children and young adults.

Steve Chinn is an independent consultant, researcher and writer who presents papers and contributes to conferences world-wide. He has delivered training courses for teachers, psychologists, parents and support assistants in over thirty countries. Among his other books are the award-winning *The Trouble with Maths* (now in its second edition, 2011) and *More Trouble with Maths* (2012), both published by Routledge.

The Routledge International Handbook Series

The Routledge International Handbook of Dyscalculia and Mathematical Learning Difficulties

Edited by Steve Chinn

LONDON AND NEW YORK

First published 2015 by Routledge

2 Park Square, Milton Park, Abingdon, Oxfordshire OX14 4RN
711 Third Avenue, New York, NY 10017

Routledge is an imprint of the Taylor & Francis Group, an informa business

First issued in paperback 2017

British Library Cataloguing in Publication Data
A catalogue record for this book is available from the British Library

Library of Congress Cataloging in Publication Data
The Routledge international handbook of dyscalculia and mathematical learning difficulties / edited by Steve Chinn.
pages cm.—(Routledge international handbooks of education)
Includes bibliographical references.
1. Acalculia. 2. Mathematical ability. 3. Learning disabilities. 4. Math anxiety. I. Chinn, Stephen J.
RJ496.A25R68 2015
618.92'85889—dc23
2014021426

ISBN: 978-0-415-82285-5 (hbk)
ISBN: 978-1-138-57731-2 (pbk)

Typeset in Bembo
by Swales & Willis Ltd, Exeter, Devon, UK

Contents

Contents

Contents

Figures

Tables

Contributors

Gabriel A. Allred is pursuing a Ph.D. in the interrelationships among mathematics anxiety, working memory, performance in novel mathematics tasks, and embodied effects related to performance at the University of Nevada, Las Vegas.

Mowafak Al-Manabri Ph.D. is Assistant Executive Director for Training and Assessment and an Educational Consultant at the Centre for Child Evaluation & Teaching in Kuwait. His primary interests are in mathematics learning disabilities, and as such he is part of the Arabic Dyscalculia Screener and an Arabic Multisensory Intervention Program to teach mathematics. His other interests are teacher training and processes of inclusion across mainstream and special schools.

Daniel Ansari Ph.D. is a Professor and Canada Research Chair in Developmental Cognitive Neuroscience in the Department of Psychology and the Brain & Mind Institute at the University of Western Ontario in London, Ontario, Canada. Ansari and his team (www.numericalcognition.org) investigate the typical and atypical development of numerical and mathematical cognition using both behavioural and brain-imaging methods. Ansari has published over 80 papers in peer-reviewed journals as well as numerous book chapters and commentaries.

Mark H. Ashcraft is Professor of Psychology at the University of Nevada Las Vegas. He earned his PhD in Experimental Psychology in 1975 from the University of Kansas. His primary area of research is mathematical cognition, with interests in both the basic cognitive processes involved in performance and in the development of those processes in children. Since the mid-1990s, he has also investigated how cognitive processing is influenced by mathematics anxiety and factors related to mathematics ability and achievement.

Robert B. Ashlock taught in the elementary grades and served as an administrator. He completed his doctorate at Indiana University. While at the College Park campus of the University of Maryland he taught courses about teaching mathematics to children, and developed a graduate programme for teachers who had students experiencing difficulty learning mathematics. He also had a clinic programme for children and youth who needed help learning mathematics. He is now retired from Covenant College in Lookout Mountain, GA, USA.

Jai Astilla completed her Bachelor's degree in Elementary Education, majoring in Special Education, at the University of the Philippines in 2006. She has been a member of the Wordlab (Manila) faculty since 2006 and is currently the Programme Director of the primary level. She continues to be involved in the testing and diagnosis of children with mathematics difficulties. She provides individualised remedial programmes for children struggling in mathematics. She is also highly involved in training teachers and educating parents about learning difficulties and ADHD.

Remegious Baale is a Senior Specialist in Mathematics Education at the National Curriculum Development Centre (NCDC) of Uganda. He joined the NCDC in 2001, after teaching mathematics in secondary schools in Uganda for 15 years. At the NCDC, Remegious has been involved in the development of the mathematics syllabus for primary schools. Currently, he is working on the programme to reform the learning and teaching of mathematics in secondary schools in Uganda.

Brian R. Bryant Ph.D. lives and works in Austin, Texas. He is currently a Research Professor and Fellow for the Meadows Center for Preventing Educational Risk at The University of Texas in Austin. Dr Bryant is the Co-Editor-in-Chief of *Learning Disability Quarterly*. His research interests are in reading, writing, and mathematics learning disabilities; support provision for persons with intellectual and/or developmental disability; and AT applications across the life span.

Diane Pedrotty Bryant Ph.D. is a Professor in the Department of Special Education, University of Texas. She holds the Mollie Villeret Davis Professorship in Learning Disabilities and is the project director for the Mathematics Institute at the Meadows Center for Preventing Educational Risk. She is the principal investigator on an algebra readiness project, which is funded by the Institute of Education Sciences. Dr Bryant is the Co-Editor-in-Chief of *Learning Disability Quarterly*. Her research interests include instructional strategies and assistive technology for students with learning disabilities and she is the co-author of textbooks and educational tests.

Stephanie Bugden M.Ed. is a Ph.D. candidate at The Numerical Cognition Laboratory, The University of Western Ontario, London, Canada. Stephanie obtained her Masters of Education focusing on special education and educational psychology in 2010 from the University of Western Ontario and, at the time of this book's publication, is completing her Ph.D. under the supervision of Dr Daniel Ansari. Her research interests include uncovering the neurobiological mechanisms that contribute to poor arithmetic abilities in children who have a specific mathematics learning disability known as developmental dyscalculia.

Danilka Castro Ph.D. serves as collaborator researcher in the developmental cognitive neuroscience lab from the Cuban Center for Neuroscience, where she has been on staff since 2006. Dr Castro received her doctorate in psychology in 2012 from Havana University in Havana, Cuba. She has published articles on the normal development of the basic skills in learning maths and mathematical disabilities. She is currently focused on mathematical cognition and developmental dyscalculia.

Sara Caviola is a post-doctoral researcher in the Department of Developmental Psychology and Socialization, University of Padova since 2012, the year she received her Ph.D. in Developmental Psychology at Padova under the supervision of Professor Lucangeli. She has spent several study periods abroad working under the supervision of Professor Jo-Anne LeFevre at Carleton University, Canada and under the supervision of Professor Brian Butterworth at the Institute of Cognitive Neuroscience, UCL, London. Her main areas of research are mathematical cognition, calculation abilities, the relationship between working memory and calculation, learning disabilities, developmental dyscalculia and non-verbal learning disability.

Winnie Wai Lan Chan obtained her doctorate degree at the University of Hong Kong and is a registered educational psychologist. She is an Assistant Professor in the Department of Psychology at the University of Hong Kong. Her research area is children's mathematical learning and difficulties. She is particularly interested in how children understand numbers and why some children have difficulties doing so. Her research projects have examined basic numerical processing as well as mathematical difficulties among Chinese children.

Dazhi Cheng is a Ph.D. candidate at the School of Brain and Cognitive Science, Beijing Normal University, supervised by Professor Xinlin Zhou. The topic of Mr Cheng's Ph.D. research is the cognitive mechanism and intervention of dyscalculia.

Tandi Clausen-May is an independent consultant for mathematics education and assessment. After teaching mathematics in mainstream and special schools for 13 years, Tandi joined the National Foundation for Educational Research in the UK. She left in 2009 to become an independent consultant, and has since been involved in a range of projects. In 2012 she joined the National Curriculum Development Centre (NCDC) in Kampala to support the Curriculum, Assessment and Examination (CURASSE) programme to reform the secondary school mathematics curriculum in Uganda.

Anny Cooreman holds a Master's degree in Educational Sciences from the University of Leuven Belgium. She is the Founder and Director of Eureka Leuven Belgium and the author of several books about learning disabilities. She is an expert with a long and broad experience in the different areas of effective education of students with Special Educational Needs. She had done research in dyslexia and effective intervention. Her innovative techniques in maths are widely used both in individual interventions as well as class settings.

Annemie Desoete is Professor in the research group Learning Disabilities of the Department of Experimental, Clinical and Health Psychology – Developmental Disorders, of Ghent University (Belgium) and at the Artevelde University College of Ghent. She has extensive experience in research in early characteristics of mathematical learning disorders (dyscalculia) and reading learning disorders (dyslexia). In addition she has conducted studies on subtypes of MLD, executive functions (working memory, inhibition, etc.), comorbidity with DCD, mathematics and ASS.

Chris Donlan started his career as a teacher in special education, working with children with Specific Language Impairments (SLI). He was Deputy Head of ICAN's John Horniman School in Worthing, and opened a Language Unit in north-west London, before taking a Ph.D. in Psychology at the University of Manchester, studying mathematical development in children with SLI. He is currently Deputy Head of the Division of Psychology and Language Sciences at University College London, and continues to study the development of language and mathematical skills.

Ann Dowker is University Research Lecturer at the Department of Experimental Psychology, University of Oxford. She has carried out extensive research on mathematical development and mathematical difficulties. She is the lead researcher on the Catch Up Numeracy intervention project. She has published numerous academic articles and produced two reports for the British government on 'What works for children with mathematical difficulties?' She is author of *Individual Differences in Arithmetic: Implications for Psychology, Neuroscience and Education* (Psychology Press, 2005).

Danielle N. Dupuis is a doctoral candidate in the Quantitative Methods Education programme in the Department of Educational Psychology at the University of Minnesota. She has over ten years of experience as a methodologist in educational research. Her substantive research interests include secondary mathematics curricula and teacher effectiveness.

Gad Elbeheri is the Dean of the Australian College of Kuwait. He is also a consultant at the Centre for Child Evaluation and Teaching, Kuwait. An applied linguist who obtained his Ph.D. from the University of Durham, UK, Dr Elbeheri's research focuses on cross-linguistic studies of dyslexia and other specific learning difficulties, and their manifestations in Arabic.

Jane Emerson is founding Director of Emerson House in London, a specialist centre for dyslexia, dyscalculia and dyspraxia for primary age children. She is a speech and language therapist, as well as a trained literacy and numeracy specialist teacher. She is recognized as a leader in the field of dyscalculia and lectures widely as well as running training courses for teachers. Jane is co-author of the books, *The Dyscalculia Assessment* (winner of the BESA Best Special Education Resource; Bloomsbury, 2011) and *The Dyscalculia Solution* (Bloomsbury, 2014).

John Everatt is a Professor of Education in the College of Education, University of Canterbury, New Zealand. He received his Ph.D. from the University of Nottingham and, before moving to NZ, he lectured in Psychology at the Universities of Wales and Surrey, UK. His research focuses on developmental learning difficulties, and potential cross-language/multilingual influences on such disabilities.

Lynn Fuchs Ph.D. is the Nicholas Hobbs Professor of Special Education and Human Development at Vanderbilt University. She has conducted programmatic research on assessment methods for enhancing instructional planning, on instructional methods for improving mathematics and reading outcomes for students at risk for and with learning disabilities, and on the cognitive and linguistic characteristics associated with mathematics development. She has been identified by Thomas Reuters as one of the 250 most frequently cited researchers in the social sciences in the United States.

David C. Geary is a Curators' Professor at the University of Missouri. He has wide ranging interests but his primary areas of research and scholarly work are children's mathematical cognition and learning and Darwin's sexual selection as largely, but not solely, related to human sex differences. The former includes directing a ten-year longitudinal study of children's mathematical development from kindergarten to ninth grade, with a focus on identifying the core deficits underlying learning disabilities and persistent low achievement in mathematics.

Russell Gersten is Professor Emeritus in educational research with the College of Education at the University of Oregon. He currently directs the Instructional Research Group in Los Alamitos, California. He has done extensive research on the topic of teaching mathematics to students who struggle, and written extensively on tools for teachers to use to increase their effectiveness in teaching mathematics, particularly in the areas of fractions and number sense. He recently served on the presidentially appointed National Mathematics Advisory Panel.

Gowramma I.P. is Associate Professor in Education, RIE, Bhubaneswar (NCERT) India. M.Sc. (Psychology), M.Ed., Ph.D. (Education), PG Diploma HI. Her main experience is in developing teaching experience in elementary and secondary schools through B.Ed., M.Ed. and M.Phil. courses, providing support to students with disabilities, their parents and teachers to enable them to cope in an inclusive setting. She has published books, contributed articles, presented papers, delivered Key Note addresses and has been an invited speaker at international, national and state levels. She has conducted and provided consultancy for many research projects.

Sarah Gray works at the Royal Children's Hospital, Melbourne and is a Ph.D. candidate at the Melbourne School of Psychological Sciences, University of Melbourne, Melbourne, Victoria, Australia.

Sherlynmay Hamak completed her Bachelor's degree in Elementary Maths Education at the University of the Philippines in 2001. She has since provided classroom-based and individualised mathematics teaching at Wordlab School, Manila. Sherlynmay is currently part of a team of specialists that conducts reading and mathematics assessments and designs remediation programmes. She is also involved in the curricular planning and supervision of mathematics teaching and the assessment and remedial instruction of students experiencing difficulties in learning mathematics.

Egbert Harskamp is Professor of Educational Sciences at the University of Groningen, the Netherlands. His main interest is the development and research of digital learning environments. He has conducted research in the field of computer-supported problem solving in secondary and primary education and the effects of learning environments on mathematics strategies and achievement of students.

Garron Hillaire Ed.M., Educational Software Architect, contributes to the formative development and research of the technology-based universally designed environment. With a primary focus on technical implementation, his interest in Learning Analytics bridges his activity into both instructional design and research design. He holds an Ed.M. in Technology, Innovation, and Education from the Harvard Graduate School of Education and a B.A. in Mathematics – Philosophy Option from the University of Washington.

Connie Suk-Han Ho, is a Professor at the Psychology Department of the University of Hong Kong, and has authored over 100 publications on mathematics learning and disabilities, literacy development, assessment and intervention, reading disabilities, and genetics of language and reading development. She is also an editorial board member of the *Scientific Study of Reading* journal and the *Reading and Writing* journal, and an associate editor of the *Asian-Pacific Journal of Developmental Differences*.

Judy Hornigold BSc, PGCSpE, AMBDA is an independent educational consultant specialising in dyscalculia and dyslexia. She is particularly passionate about the teaching of maths and finding ways to support learners with dyscalculia and general maths learning difficulties. Consequently, Judy has written the PGCert in Dyscalculia and Maths Learning Difficulties for Edge Hill University and an accredited dyscalculia course for the BDA. Judy lectures on Inclusion for Edge Hill University and is an Associate Tutor for the BDA. She also delivers lectures and workshops throughout the UK and internationally. She has written two books of lesson plans for learners with dyscalculia as well as a guide for parents of children with dyslexia.

Asha K. Jitendra Ph.D. is the Rodney Wallace Professor for the Advancement of Teaching and Learning at the University of Minnesota. Her research focuses on evaluating the variables that impact children's ability to succeed in school-related tasks. Jitendra has developed both mathematics and reading interventions and has tested their effectiveness with students with learning difficulties. Also, she has scrutinised theoretical models that deal with the coherent organisation and structure of information as the basis for her research on textbook analysis.

Mindy Johnson is an Instructional Designer and Research Associate at CAST in Wakefield, MA. She participates in the formative development and research of technology-based universally designed learning environments and coordinates the social media efforts of CAST, the National Center on Universal Design for Learning, and the National Center on Accessible Instructional Materials. She is a former special education teacher and holds a Master's degree in Technology in Education from the Harvard Graduate School of Education.

Sue Johnston-Wilder is a chartered mathematics teacher, supervisor and colleague of mathematics teachers and learners at all levels. She has published widely with a range of co-authors, on areas such as the use of ICT and history of mathematics to enhance teaching and learning of mathematics and the design of mathematical tasks. She is currently Associate Professor of Mathematics Education at the University of Warwick. Working with Clare Lee, she has developed the construct Mathematical Resilience to tackle mathematics anxiety.

Nancy Jordan is a Professor at the School of Education at the University of Delaware. Dr Jordan's research interests are in children's mathematical development, mathematics learning disabilities, and early interventions. She received her doctoral degree in education from Harvard University and completed a post-doctoral fellowship at the University of Chicago. Recently, Professor Jordan served on the Committee on Early Childhood Mathematics sponsored by the National Research Council of the National Academies and on the IES Early Math Practice Guide.

Giannis N. Karagiannakis is a Ph.D. student of the Research Centre of Psychophysiology and Education of the National and Kapodistrian University of Athens (NKUA). His interest is in the scientific fields of Mathematical Learning Difficulties (MLD). He holds M.Ed. and Mathematics degrees from NKUA as well as a scholarship on a programme for training professionals at Harvard University. He has many years experience in the assessment, planning and application of individualised programmes of intervention in Mathematics for MLD students (third to twelfth grade) as well as in supervision of other maths teachers. He gives lectures and training courses all over the world.

Karin Landerl is Professor of Developmental Psychology at the University of Graz (Austria). From her neuro-cognitive perspective, she is doing research on typical and atypical development of numerical processing, arithmetic, reading and spelling. She is particularly interested in learning disorders (dyscalculia, dyslexia) and their comorbidities.

Clare Lee leads on the Mathematics PGCE for the Open University. She has published widely on Assessment for Learning, the role of language in learning mathematics and mathematical resilience. She is currently working internationally on teacher development and, working with Sue Johnston-Wilder, she has developed the construct Mathematical Resilience to enable students to overcome barriers that present themselves when learning mathematics.

Amy E. Lein is a doctoral candidate in the Special Education programme in the Department of Educational Psychology at the University of Minnesota. She has over ten years of experience teaching middle and high school special education and mathematics. Her research interests include educational interventions for struggling students and professional development for teachers.

Daniela Lucangeli is a Professor of Developmental Psychology in the University of Padova. She has a Ph.D. in Developmental Psychology from the University of Leiden (1997) following an international project (Erasmus/Socrates). She has spent many periods abroad to study and collaborate with several European universities, such as the Faculty of Social Sciences of Leiden, the Faculty of Psychology of Ghent and the Institute of Cognitive Neuroscience (UCL) of London. She teaches at the Faculty of Educational Science, Psychology and Medicine at the University of Padova in graduate courses, Ph.D. courses and specialisation courses. She has delivered several lectures at the Faculty of Psychology at the University of Valencia on Developmental Psychology and the Psychopathology of Learning. Her main areas of research are mathematical cognition, metacognition, developmental dyscalculia (assessment and treatment) and learning disabilities.

Amy J. McAuley is pursuing a Ph.D. in the interrelationships among mathematics anxiety, working memory, performance in novel mathematics tasks, and embodied effects related to performance at the University of Nevada, Las Vegas.

Caroline McGrath is a lecturer for the Early Childhood Studies Foundation Degree, in partnership with Plymouth University, at City of Bristol College. She has a particular interest in children's mathematical development, and is author of *Supporting Early Mathematical Development: Practical Approaches to Play-Based Learning* (Routledge, 2010) and *Teaching Mathematics through Story: A Creative Approach for the Early Years* (Routledge, 2014). She writes for the education journal *Early Years Educator*. Caroline draws from her experience as an early years teacher, lecturer and as a researcher for a doctorate.

Abdessatar Mahfoudhi Ph.D. is the Head of the English Department at the Australian College of Kuwait and an educational consultant at the Centre for Child Evaluation and Teaching in Kuwait. His research interests are in language, literacy and language-based disabilities, with a focus on Arabic as a first language and English as an additional language. His work has appeared in many international journals. He co-edited four volumes, the latest of which is a special issue of *Reading and Writing* on literacy in Arabic. He has also co-authored books and tests, including a comprehensive Arabic intervention programme, 'I Read and Write!' (Grades K-9). Together with colleagues from Kuwait, the UK and New Zealand he is currently finalising a comprehensive Arabic intervention programme, 'I Am Part of the Equation', to teach students with dyscalculia and mathematics difficulties.

Alex M. Moore completed his Ph.D. in Experimental Psychology at the University of Nevada Las Vegas in 2014, with a concentration in mathematical cognition. His current research investigates the role of attention and working memory in simple mathematical tasks like subitising and number comparison.

Peter Morris is a visiting academic at the Department of Experimental Psychology, and an associate of the Computational Linguistics group in the Department of Computer Science, both at the University of Oxford. His background is in computer science, mathematics/statistics and software engineering.

Kinga Morsanyi graduated from Lorand Eotvos University, Hungary, and subsequently obtained a Ph.D. in Experimental Psychology from the University of Plymouth. She has worked as a post-doctoral fellow with Professor Pierre Barrouillet at the University of Geneva, and with Dr Denes Szücs at the University of Cambridge. In 2012 she was appointed as Lecturer in Psychology at Queen's University Belfast. Her research has been funded by the ESRC, the British Academy and the Higher Education Academy Psychology Network.

Elizabeth Murray Sc.D. is a Senior Research Scientist and Instructional Designer at CAST where she applies her technical skills, mathematics background, special education experience, and clinical specialties to the research and development of universally designed materials to support students in maths and science.

Rob Ochsendorf Ed.D. is a Research Scientist at the National Center for Special Education Research within the Institute of Education Sciences at the U.S. Department of Education. In this role, he oversees research focusing on improving maths and science outcomes for students with or at risk of disabilities, including the National Research and Development Center for Improving Learning of Fractions. Dr Ochsendorf completed his doctorate at George Washington University and was previously a high school science teacher in New York.

Kathleen Hughes Pfannenstiel Ph.D. is currently a project manager for the Meadows Center for Preventing Educational Risk at The University of Texas, Austin. She is also a Lecturer for the Department of Special Education at The University of Texas, Austin. Kathleen's research interests are in the area of special education, specifically students with learning and behaviour disorders. In addition, Kathleen is interested in the areas of mathematics, intervention, response to intervention, pre-service teaching, and self-determination.

Hazelle R. Preclaro completed her M.A. in Reading Specialist Education in Teachers College, Columbia University. She is currently an Assistant Professor at the University of the Philippines, teaching courses on classroom-based and individualised reading instruction with a particular focus on students with learning difficulties. She has extensive experience teaching children, adolescents and adults who have been diagnosed with learning disabilities and other comorbid conditions. Currently, she is involved in research focused on literacy learning and inclusive education.

Ramaa S. Ph.D. has been Professor of Special Education in the National Council of Educational Research & Training (NCERT), India, since 2001. She was the recipient of a British Council Fellowship for Post-Doctoral Research, Manchester University, UK. She is a professionally qualified psychotherapist. She has conducted several research projects and guided doctoral students on diverse learners and has contributed invited articles to the journals of the BDA and IDA, published many articles, chapters, diagnostic tests and instructional materials and has written books on dyslexia and autism. She has presented papers at many world conferences and is a member of the National Level Panel of Experts and a member of the Editorial Board of the BDA's *Dyslexia – An International Journal of Research and Practice*.

Gabrielle Rappolt-Schlichtmann Ed.D. is Co-President and Chief Learning and Science Officer at the Center for Applied Special Technology (CAST). She holds expertise in the developmental neuroscience of at-risk children, especially the impact of children's experiences of stress on their emotional development and performance in the context of school. At CAST she works with her colleagues to research the role of emotion in learning, and to develop technology that instantiates the engagement component of Universal Design for Learning.

Robert A. Reeve Ph.D. is Associate Professor at the Cognitive and Neuropsychological Development Laboratory, Melbourne School of Psychological Sciences, University of Melbourne, Australia. His research area is cognitive psychology and behavioural neuroscience.

Vivian Reigosa-Crespo Ph.D., is a Research Professor and serves as Director of Research at the Cuban Center for Neuroscience Havana, Cuba. Dr Reigosa-Crespo received her doctorate in psychology from Havana University, Cuba. She is a member of the Research Council of the Cuban Biotechnology Group. Her research interests include the typical and atypical development of mathematical cognition. She is developing screening and diagnosis tools and interventions for use in schools.

Mahesh C. Sharma is the President of the Center for Teaching/Learning of Mathematics, Framingham, Massachusetts. He is the former President and Professor of Mathematics Education at Cambridge College. Sharma edited and published *Focus on Learning Problems in Mathematics*, and *The Math Notebook* for more than thirty years. He provides evaluation and tutoring services for students who face learning difficulties due to learning disabilities such as dyscalculia, and works with schools in designing strategies and curriculum to improve mathematics instruction.

Mikyung Shin Ph.D. is currently a high school mathematics and special education teacher in the Round Rock Independent School District. Her research interests are in mathematics instruction for students with learning disabilities, instructional technology, and teacher preparation programmes in special education.

Robert Siegler is Teresa Heinz Professor of Cognitive Psychology at Carnegie Mellon University, as well as Director of the Siegler Center for Innovative Learning at Beijing Normal University. His research focuses on numerical development, including how children discover new strategies, how they learn to choose strategies adaptively, and how they learn (or fail to learn) fractions. He was awarded the American Psychological Association's Distinguished Scientific Contribution Award in 2005 and was elected to the National Academy of Education in 2010.

Denes Szücs is a cognitive neuroscientist doing both behavioural and neuroimaging research on number cognition, dyscalculia, working memory, attention and cognitive control. Denes has been a lecturer and then a senior lecturer at the University of Cambridge, UK since 2004 where he is the Deputy Director of the Centre for Neuroscience in Education and official Fellow of Darwin College. Acknowledging his research performance he was the recipient of the prestigious scholar award of the James S. McDonnel Foundation in 2013.

Clare Trott is a Mathematics Support Tutor in the Mathematics Education Centre at Loughborough University. She specialises in the provision of one-to-one mathematics support for students with additional needs or who are low in mathematical confidence. Clare is interested in mathematics and specific learning differences in Higher Education, particularly dyscalculia and dyslexia in STEM subjects. She has developed a first-line screener for dyscalculia. She is a member of The Association for Dyslexia Specialists in Higher Education and the BDA Dyscalculia committee.

Terry Tin-Yau Wong obtained his doctoral degree in Educational Psychology in the University of Hong Kong. He is a registered educational psychologist. He is currently a Lecturer in the Department of Psychological Studies at the Hong Kong Institute of Education. His research area is mathematical cognition. In particular, he is interested in the process of number acquisition in children and the cognitive profiles of children with developmental dyscalculia (or mathematics learning disabilities). He is also interested in the relationships between mathematical skills and other aspects of people's life (e.g., decision making, psychological well-being).

Xinlin Zhou Ph.D. is a Professor in the State Key Laboratory of Cognitive Neuroscience and Learning, Beijing Normal University, focusing on mathematical cognition and learning with behavioural and neuroimaging approaches. He has been directing the Brain and Mathematical Cognition Laboratory affiliated to the Key Lab.

Acknowledgements

Editing a book requires a team of people. I have been extremely lucky with everyone who has contributed to this book.

I wish to thank the Routledge personnel, especially Alison Foyle who commissioned the book and Sarah Tuckwell who guided and supported me as the project took shape. Also I thank Rachel Hutchings and Tom Newman from Swales and Willis who dealt so efficiently, effectively and calmly with the proof reading, never my own strong point.

My thanks to my wife, Carole Stott, who managed to show genuine interest in my constant questions, comments and, as my USA friends would say, my 'sharing' of many fascinating snippets of information gleaned from the contributing authors. Maths is not a topic that is the top of her list of engrossing conversations.

My gratitude to Professor Brian Butterworth, who provided me with introductions to many of the authors who wrote chapters for the book.

I am indebted to John Pasmore and "The Estate of Victor Pasmore" for granting me permission to use Victor Pasmore's wonderful work, 'Blue Ocean' for the cover of this book. A print (90/90) hangs in my dining room.

Finally, and most significantly, I thank the authors who agreed to contribute to the book and then had to suffer my demands on their busy lives as I asked them to meet deadlines at the various stages of production. Thank you all for your contributions and your patience with me. It has been both a pleasure and an honour to work with you. We have met the scheduled date for publication!

Steve Chinn

The Routledge International Handbook of Dyscalculia and Mathematical Learning Difficulties

An overview

Steve Chinn

Mathematics plays an important part in our lives, from basic trading at a market stall in Marrakesh or Beijing to the complex algorithms that guide international banking, from working out the time of a journey to see a friend in a nearby town to the time it takes a sub-atomic particle to travel around CERN's Large Hadron Collider.

But, not everyone is good at mathematics. Of course, we have to define what being 'good' means (and maybe what 'mathematics' means) and that might depend very much on where you live and the work you do. For example, in the UK there is now an expectation that all students will reach a basic level of competency in mathematics, confirmed by passing an examination by the age of 18 years, despite our recent history of innumeracy levels of over 20 per cent for adults (Rashid and Brooks, 2010).

So, do we know about 'being bad at mathematics'? And will this help us to address the problem? In this book over fifty experts from around the world write about mathematics learning difficulties and disabilities from a range of perspectives. From their work, and their references to work from others in this field, we are taken a little closer to answering what I consider to be sixteen key questions.

Compared to research on language difficulties, this field is in its infancy, but knowledge is growing and there is a great deal of pertinent information available now that can inform us as to how education can adapt to address difficulties and disabilities in learning mathematics.

At the heart of this problem is a three-way relationship between the learner, the mathematics and the teacher (Figure I.1). The three are always interlinked, such that any change in one will influence the other two and any gaps in our knowledge of one will depress our knowledge of the other two. For example, if we are a

1

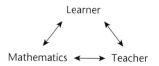

Figure I.1 The inter-relationships between the three key factors for teaching

teacher (which is the role exclusively played by the parents when children are very young), we need to know and understand both the mathematics we are teaching and the child we are teaching. It may be that the 'parent as teacher' knows the young child intimately, but is less knowledgeable about mathematics. At school it may be that the teacher knows the mathematics, but is less knowledgeable about the child. It is, of course, more complicated than that, but the overview is a useful aide memoire.

It would be quite astonishing if one book could suggest solutions for the many problems that are generated by mathematics and the ways in which it is taught. This book, wisely I like to think, does not claim to do that. However, it contains a collection of pertinent wisdom from those fifty leading researchers and teachers from around the world, which could suggest that it has something to contribute to the field.

In this overview I pose sixteen key questions about difficulties in learning mathematics. Each is addressed by at least one of the chapters in this book.

1   *What is dyscalculia/mathematics learning disabilities (MLD)?*
This book is not the place to discuss the relevance of labels for learning disabilities, but labelling remains an on-going issue for dyslexia and will undoubtedly become an issue for dyscalculia. I suspect that by using the joint term 'dyscalculia/mathematics learning disabilities' some of the debate will be pre-empted.

It seems reasonable to assume that there will be a spectrum of performance levels in mathematics. The data collected for any standardised test would support this assumption. Will dyscalculia/MLD be similar to Ellis's (1985) explanation of dyslexia as being more like obesity than measles, where the former is a spectrum with 'obesity' defined as an arbitrary place on that spectrum and the latter is an illness that you either have or do not have?

Not surprisingly in a book with the title *The International Handbook for Mathematical Difficulties and Dyscalculia*, several of the chapters directly address the topic of dyscalculia (mathematics learning disabilities). Incidentally, the word 'International' is validated in that the contributing authors are from the UK, India, Canada, USA, China, Hong Kong, Austria, Italy, the Netherlands, Uganda, Australia, Kuwait, Cuba, Greece, the Philippines and Belgium. Difficulties and disabilities in learning mathematics are international.

Trott's chapter, 'Dyscalculia in Higher Education: systems, support and student strategies', looks at the financial and other implications of a label for various accommodations (assistance) for students in Higher Education.

Emerson's chapter, 'The enigma of dyscalculia', is comprehensive in its discussion about the issues of definitions, co-occurrence with other disorders, diagnosis and intervention.

Karagiannakis and Cooreman's chapter, 'Focused MLD intervention based on the classification of MLD subtypes', proposes four subtypes of MLD and interventions that are informed by the nature of the subtype.

Zhou and Cheng's chapter, 'When and why numerosity processing is associated with developmental dyscalculia', considers the early stages of learning about numbers, suggesting that dyscalculia is a problem for children during the acquisition of basic arithmetical skills. Among other observations from their comprehensive research they note that neither numerosity processing nor figure-matching ability were predictors for later success in curriculum-based mathematical achievement. This may also be an indirect observation on the nature of mathematics and the way it is taught in schools.

Ramaa's chapter, 'Arithmetic difficulties among socially disadvantaged children and children with dyscalculia', notes that, in her study, each child with dyscalculia exhibited a unique profile of strengths and weaknesses in different criteria measures. The heterogeneous nature of learners is a frequently made observation throughout this book.

Reeve and Gray's chapter, 'Number difficulties in young children: deficits in core number?', observes that 'a defensible account of developmental dyscalculia awaits a better understanding of the significance of the core competences in the early years'. Geary's chapter, 'Preschool children's quantitative knowledge and long-term risk for functional innumeracy', also has highly pertinent comments to add to Reeve and Gray's observation.

Partly as an acknowledgement of a research subject that is in its infancy, cautions on our current state of knowledge are made in three chapters. Morsanyi and Szücs in their chapter, 'The link between mathematics and logical reasoning: implications for research and education', comment on dot patterns, the use of which is key to many research papers on dyscalculia, that 'nothing is straightforward'. Reigosa-Crespo and Castro in their chapter, 'Dots and digits: how do children process the numerical magnitude? Evidence from brain and behaviour', write that there is a need for validity and reliability checks on data and that nothing is simple even at this fundamental level of mathematics.

Bugden and Ansari's chapter, 'How can cognitive developmental neuroscience constrain our understanding of Developmental Dyscalculia?', provides a detailed overview and critique of the current state of knowledge of dyscalculia from a neuroscience perspective. They note that the precise parts of the brain disrupted in Developmental Dyscalculia (DD), how they interact, change over time and are affected by education is a formidable challenge for the next forty-five years of research into DD using a Developmental Cognitive Neuroscience approach.

The concept of a specific learning disability in mathematics is generally assumed to be of recent interest, but it is interesting to note that Buswell and Judd (1925) quote Bronner (1917) as proposing the hypothesis that there are special disabilities in subjects such as arithmetic.

Together the chapters mentioned above offer a comprehensive and realistic overview and a current answer to the question, 'What is dyscalculia/MLD?'

2   What are mathematics learning difficulties?

Changing the word disabilities for difficulties creates a significant difference in the construct. It could also support the implication that there is a spectrum of difficulties in mathematics where, at the extreme end, the difficulties become severe enough to be classified as a disability.

Whatever the future debates may be about the nature of dyscalculia/MLD it will always be an unarguable fact that a significant percentage of children and adults underachieve in mathematics to the point of being functionally innumerate, for example, Rashid and Brooks (2010) and Chinn (2013).

Commenting on low achievement in mathematics, usually taken to be an achievement level below the 25th (and sometimes 35th percentile), Geary (2004) alludes to the difference between difficulties and disabilities when he notes that a cut-off at the 25th percentile on a mathematics achievement test does not fit with the estimation that between 5% and 8% of children have some form of mathematics learning disability.

In their chapter, 'Representing, Acting, and Engaging: Universal Design for Learning and Mathematics', Murray, Hillaire, Johnson and Rappolt-Schlichtmann take a broader conceptualisation of what the term 'disability' means. 'Under UDL [Universal Design for Learning], disability represents one form of variability within a given domain. In essence, students with learning disabilities are representative of a set of outliers on a continuum where all students experience difficulty in mathematics to some degree.' Murray et al. suggest that: 'Students identified with mathematics disability represent one extreme of students who struggle with mathematics, and we believe these students can inform the ways in which approaches to mathematics education should be designed for all.'

It is a spectrum.

3   What about co-occurrence with other difficulties and disabilities?

Some thirty years ago it was unlikely that, unless autism was your specialist research topic, you would have heard of Asperger Syndrome. Some thirty years ago the term dyscalculia was not widely known or used. Along with co-author Richard Ashcroft I wrote *Mathematics for Dyslexics: A Teaching Handbook* (1993) which, by its third edition (2007), had become *Mathematics for Dyslexics, Including Dyscalculia*. Across most of the world, awareness of disabilities and learning difficulties has grown dramatically over those thirty years.

I like to relate the concept of 'specific learning disabilities' to Gardner's (1983) theory of multiple intelligences. Disabilities may not be absolute in their impact on an individual in much the same way that the levels of intelligence for the many intellectual (and physical) skills are not homogeneous.

The key chapter for a clear exposition of our current knowledge on comorbidity is Landerl's 'How specific is the specific disorder of arithmetic skills?' Landerl notes that multiple-deficit models of dyscalculia can explain the heterogeneity of the disorder and thus the need for the availability of a range of compensatory methods.

Emerson also includes some discussion on comorbidity issues in her chapter, particularly with regard to dyslexia and dyspraxia, while in his chapter, 'Numbersense: a window into dyscalculia and other mathematics difficulties', Sharma suggests that there are parallels in the development of numeracy and literacy.

Gowramma's fascinating chapter, 'Arithmetic difficulties of children with hearing impairment', brings a little-studied area to our attention.

4   *What about early identification?*

This is, of course, a key question. If problems can be identified as early as possible and appropriate interventions put in place, then far fewer children will fail. Singapore identifies children at risk before they enter school and provides special classes for them. Singapore is a country that takes a pragmatic and effective approach to education.

One of the findings I quote frequently is from almost 100 years ago. Buswell and Judd (1925) commented on the powerful influence of a child's first learning experience: 'errors made in the initial stages of a pupil's contact with the various processes tend to become fixed. Initial errors persist and repeat themselves even after periods of apparently full mastery.' It is critical to make the first learning experiences successful if at all possible. This places a great onus on the teachers of early-years children and suggests that they need effective skills, and thus thorough training, for teaching early number work.

Since mathematics has many components, it would be optimistic to find a predictor that worked for all aspects of the mathematics that children will experience as they progress through school. For example, in Desoete's chapter, 'Predictive indicators for mathematical learning disabilities/dyscalculia in kindergarten children', she states the value of seriation and classification (logical thinking skills) as well as procedural and conceptual counting knowledge as predictive indicators for dyscalculia/MLD in kindergarten. However, she has found that procedural counting knowledge and seriation are related to fact-retrieval skills whereas conceptual counting knowledge and classification correlate with mathematical calculation skills in elementary school.

Reeve and Gray also take a detailed look at the predictors for later achievements in mathematics. Like Desoete, they find that there can be different predictors for different future achievements. They note that pre-schoolers' non-symbolic magnitude comparison abilities predict informal mathematics abilities, whereas symbolic number skills better predict mathematics learning abilities. Similar observations are noted by Reigosa-Crespo and Castro, that is, 'performance on symbolic comparison tasks is strongly and significantly associated with current and prospective mathematics achievement'.

Geary's research found that first graders who are more than one standard deviation below average in understanding numerals are more than four times more likely to be functionally innumerate adolescents than children with average understanding. He also summarises the situation for early learning: 'At this time, the key foundational competence appears to be cardinal value; knowing the exact quantities represented by number words and Arabic numerals. Preschool children's learning of this concept is related to parental background, their intuitive number sense, effortful attentional control and intelligence.'

Zhou and Cheng found that neither numerosity processing nor figure-matching ability were important for curriculum-based mathematical achievement and cautioned that, 'mathematical competence is a constellation of abilities which might have different origins and disabilities in mathematics would be diagnosed with different screening measures and successfully intervened by using different approaches'.

Finally, Reeve and Gray observe that 'we are at the beginning of a critical research agenda designed to better understanding the origins of children's mathematics difficulties and much remains to be done'.

5   *What other factors might be involved, for example, low socio-economic status, working memory, slow processing?*

In addition to issues with the co-occurrence of other disorders, there are many issues that might impact on mathematics learning difficulties. Some are 'within' the child, such as working memory and some are 'without', such as socio-economic status. Some are an issue as a consequence of the demands that the culture of mathematics and mathematics curricula make of students, for example, the need to answer quickly in activities such as recall of basic facts. In their chapter, 'Mathematical resilience: what is it and why is it important?', Lee and Johnston-Wilder suggest that asking learners to perform tasks that require rapid feats of memory is cognitive abuse. Speed of processing and recalling facts are domain general skills, but demands on these abilities are especially prevalent in mathematics. Lee and Johnston-Wilder note that making children perform tasks rapidly causes (additional levels of) anxiety.

At the early stages of development, speed of processing might be a learning factor. Zhou and Cheng suggest that the speed of visual perceptual processing as measured by a figure-matching task, rather than the processing of numerical magnitude, might be the mechanism underlying that close relationship between numerosity processing and computational fluency.

The role of working memory in learning has received a significant level of attention, for example, Baddeley and Hitch (1974) and Baddeley and Logie (1999). Ashcraft's work (for example, Ashcraft, Kirk and Hopko, 1998) on the influence of anxiety on working memory was highly influential on the way I taught mathematics, particularly in trying to address influences from the affective domain.

Desoete identifies working memory ability in kindergarten as a predictor of future achievement in mathematics and, more specifically, states that the central executive component of working memory is the most important predictor for dyscalculia/MLD. Reeve and Gray's work identifies working memory as contributing to abilities with subtraction.

Computations that are more complex, particularly in the number of steps required to achieve a solution will be more affected by working memory capacity. This is especially relevant for mental arithmetic as comprehensively discussed in Caviola and Lucangeli's chapter, 'Lights and shadows of mental arithmetic: analysis of cognitive processes in typical and atypical development'. They raise, among many other factors, the issues of metacognition and the development in children of strategies that can compensate for poor abilities to retrieve facts from memory.

There will always be, of course, an interaction between the demands of particular topics in mathematics and the characteristics of learners, such that this fact alone can make achievement profiles uneven. Severe problems with anxiety may well level out (downwards) those spikes of achievement.

While training working memory by itself might or might not transfer to performance in mathematics, it is likely that adjustment of lesson structures to accommodate weak working memories will have a positive impact on learning.

Ramaa's chapter, 'Arithmetic difficulties among socially disadvantaged children and children with dyscalculia', is a fascinating study of children from India, identifying the role of socio-economic background on achievement in mathematics and comparing the impact of this disadvantage with the influence of dyscalculia on learning mathematics.

Clausen-May and Baale's chapter, 'Meeting the needs of the "bottom eighty per cent": Towards an inclusive mathematics curriculum in Uganda', introduces other aspects, attitudes and influences. For example, the perception that education is an investment that expects swift returns is not such a frequently encountered influence in Western culture.

It is possible to identify many individual factors that contribute to mathematics learning difficulties, but this complexity is greatly compounded by the many interactions between these factors, thus creating the heterogeneous nature of mathematics learning difficulties and disabilities.

6   *What about heterogeneity?*

It is more difficult to explain a specific learning difficulty when the profile of learners presenting with difficulties is so varied. It is worth acknowledging, while we are discussing the heterogeneous nature of children, that teachers, too, are a heterogeneous group. For example, the construct of different cognitive styles in mathematics (Skemp, 1986; Chinn, 2012b) applies to both learner and teacher.

This heterogeneity makes the diagnosis of mathematics learning difficulties a far from formulaic, one-test procedure. Sharma notes that no single explanation adequately addresses the nature of learning difficulties in mathematics, and in Dowker and Morris's chapter, 'Targeted interventions for children with difficulties in learning mathematics', they comment that 'although the components [that contribute to mathematics learning difficulties] often correlate with one another, people can show weaknesses in virtually any component'.

Ramaa notes that for the ten children with dyscalculia in one of her studies, each exhibited a unique profile of strengths and weaknesses in different criterion measures.

7   *What are the key skills and concepts for learning mathematics?*

The Hindu-Arabic number system uses the placing of ten digits in different sequences to convey the value of any number. It is a sophisticated system and thus it is not surprising that a poor understanding of the place-value system of numbers is a common phenomenon. This poor understanding will have far-reaching implications for children learning mathematics.

In her studies on children with and without hearing impairment from environmentally disadvantaged environments, Gowramma notes that most of the errors in computations could be due to a poor understanding of place value. In their chapter, 'Mathematics learning and its difficulties among Chinese children in Hong Kong', Ho, Wong and Chan state that, from their research, a persistently low level of early place-value understanding appeared to be associated with later low mathematical outcomes. They also note that children appear to go through universal developmental changes in their place-value understanding irrespective of the language of their number system. Difficulties in mathematics are international.

Ho, Wong and Chan's research found that a simple place-value test given half way through first grade identified 95% of the children who were low achievers in second grade. Children in Hong Kong receive early formal education from the age of three at kindergarten and as many as 81% of the kindergartens in Hong Kong teach two-digit addition. In contrast, Ramaa and Gowramma observe that children who are from environmentally deprived populations and are often first generation learners are thus at significant risk of under achievement in mathematics.

Place value is a factor in much of early arithmetic; for example, in their chapter, 'Learning disabilities: mathematics characteristics and instructional exemplars', Bryant, Bryant, Shin and Pfannenstiel advise that, conceptually, students must understand place value for regrouping purposes, otherwise the task of regrouping can be reduced to solution 'tricks' or shortcuts that diminish the conceptual understanding of working with place value. There appear to be many 'tricks' in mathematics; for example, as a secondary pupil I was taught that to divide by a fraction I should 'turn upside down and multiply'.

Zhou and Cheng suggest that mathematical reasoning does not seem to depend on numerosity processing, but rather on semantic knowledge, general reasoning and imagination. Reeve and Gray suggest that work on the role of core number competencies for early mathematics development shows great promise.

As children progress through the grades in school, the demands of mathematics increase in cognitive complexity and in the demand for recall of extensive amounts of knowledge. The developmental nature of mathematics makes any gaps in knowledge and understanding detrimental to progress.

Taking an overview of skills, Geary warns us that determining the skill deficits that define innumeracy is a moving target.

8   What are the key points in time for interventions?
The key time is when the learner is very young, that is, preschool. There are many findings reported in this book to support that claim. But reality tells us that factors such as social deprivation or hearing loss will make that timing unrealistic for many children. Thus identification of the children who are at risk needs to be carried out as early as possible and intervention should follow immediately, which implies that diagnostic teaching should begin as early as possible.

Ashlock's highly influential book on error patterns in computation, first published in 1976 and now in its tenth edition (Ashlock, 2010), on error patterns in computation introduced me to a pragmatic and effective approach to diagnostic teaching.

However, once past the key time, intervention is still critical. The challenges are greater, but it is likely that the mathematics content of any intervention should include work on early concepts as well as the current topics that are creating problems for the child. For example, Reigosa-Crespo and Castro tell us that the behavioural and neuroimaging findings reviewed in their chapter strongly support the importance of training low-level numerical magnitude processing in educational settings in order to enhance mathematical competence in typically developing children and also in children with an atypical development of numerical cognition.

Dowker and Morris note, encouragingly, that children's arithmetical difficulties are highly susceptible to intervention. Further studies are needed as to the duration of these gains. Supporting this optimistic outlook, Gowramma has found that children with hearing impairment can achieve their potential if the (learning) environment, structure and materials are appropriate.

9   How should we teach mathematics?

In her chapter, 'Teacher training: solving the problem', Hornigold, who was based at one of the UK's leading universities for training mathematics teachers, states the problem clearly: 'Mathematics is very susceptible to poor teaching and the pedagogy employed in delivering the mathematics curriculum can have a profound effect on the student. It is the one subject that I feel has been dealt a great disservice by its method of delivery', thus setting the context for answering the question, 'How should we teach mathematics?'

While the combined knowledge of the authors contributing to this handbook might not offer the definitive answer to this question, they offer a great deal of research evidence and experience that builds to provide valuable and pertinent advice.

As stated before, this is an international problem. The learning difficulties are, largely, independent of the language in which mathematics is taught and also largely independent of the perceived intelligence and abilities of the learner. The methods that are efficacious and long lasting are going to be apposite universally. For example, Everatt, Mahfoudhi, Al-Manabri and Elbeheri in their chapter, 'Dyscalculia in Arabic speaking children: assessment and intervention practices', state that the same methods used for teaching in English are applicable to children learning in Arabic. Good teaching practice for children with mathematics learning difficulties is good teaching practice for all children as Murray et al. observe.

Hamak, Astilla and Preclaro's chapter, 'The acquisition of mathematical skills of Filipino children with learning difficulties: issues and challenges', adds further evidence as to the international nature of mathematics learning difficulties. This highly pragmatic chapter brings children's own comments and work to our view. The teaching programme implemented in Wordlab, a specialist school in Manila, is an exemplar of taking research and applying it to effective classroom practice.

In their comprehensive overview of appropriate teaching, Bryant, Bryant, Shin and Pfannenstiel offer the advice: 'Educators will do well to be alert to those mathematics behaviours that are exhibited by struggling students and be prepared to offer intensive interventions that are specifically designed to promote positive mathematics outcomes.'

Clausen-May and Baale describe some creative classroom examples of using materials to teach for understanding, noting that understanding takes time (as opposed to a heavy reliance on rote learning, which gives the illusion of quick learning) and that curricula design has to acknowledge this. For those who feel that manipulatives cannot be used with large classes, Clausen-May and Baale used a practical approach with classes of 80 to 100 students. Their chapter considers, among other aspects of learning, how culture, historical influences and resources can influence learning, sometimes restricting who is taught and how they are taught.

Sharma has long been an advocate of using materials for teaching and, in his chapter, offers detailed practical examples, using materials and visual images, which reflect the research on how children learn. He notes that 'the concurrent thinking of numbers as concrete and abstract is at the core of true number conceptualisation and is a real challenge for many children'.

Further support for the use of a concrete stage in teaching mathematics comes from Bryant, Bryant, Shin and Pfannenstiel who structure learning in three steps: (1) concrete/manipulatives; (2) semi-concrete materials, tallies and pictures; (3) abstract.

McGrath's chapter, 'Mathematical storyteller kings and queens: an alternative pedagogical choice to facilitate mathematical thinking and understand children's mathematical capabilities', describes how the use of story-telling with young children enhances their understanding of the language of mathematics and encourages metacognition. The seminal book, *How People Learn* (Bransford, Brown and Cocking, 2001) identifies three key findings for learning. The third of these key findings concerns the importance of metacognition. Hornigold supports the use of interactions between learners and learners and learners and teachers in her observation that 'constructive dialogue in the classroom is essential for developing mathematical logic and reasoning'. Gowramma found that the performance of children in primary schools with hearing impairments improved significantly when taught through play-way methods.

The mastery model and precision teaching for mathematics (Chinn, 2014) are rarely applicable for students with mathematics disabilities. Ramaa's research showed that, in her testing of children with dyscalculia, there were no 'masters' in many of the criterion measures for multiplication and for all of the criteria for division. The issue of 'catching up' with other learners is highly relevant from many perspectives, including self-esteem. We have to bear in mind that this is a major challenge. Geary states that most children who are behind in learning mathematics will learn number concepts, but they are unlikely to catch up with their peers.

In the chapter from Karagiannakis and Cooreman they describe the application of interventions that focus on each student's strengths. This approach alludes to the critical role of diagnostic teaching (as do other chapters in the handbook).

Whatever methods are employed for teaching, my thirty plus years of experience of teaching and assessing children and young adults with mathematics learning difficulties tells me that the roots of the difficulties often lie way back in the fundamental concepts of mathematics, and that intervention needs to start there. Bryant, Bryant, Shin and Pfannenstiel specify, 'providing a cumulative review of previous concepts' as one of their examples of practices that are designed to provide explicit and systematic instruction. There is much discussion of early learning in this handbook and there has to be optimism that many of the consequent deficits can be addressed effectively, even though there are several findings and comments that suggest that this is a challenging task.

The emerging role of IT in teaching mathematics is discussed in question 16.

10   What is the role of metacognition?

Metacognition has already been mentioned as one of the key components for learning (Bransford et al., 2001), as has the role of discussion and dialogue between learner and teacher (for example, Hornigold and Bryant, Bryant, Shin and Pfannenstiel).

Lee and Johnston-Wilder note that many teachers become convinced that examinations are the measure of success (of both the student and the teacher) and that the best way to enable their pupils to pass these examinations is to adopt a style of teaching that privileges instrumental over relational understanding (Skemp, 1986), an approach that equates to a focus on formulas and algorithms at the expense of understanding. Trott explains that because dyscalculic/MD students make extremely slow progress in their conceptual understanding of mathematics, the pressure of time pushes the style of instruction to a focus on procedural learning.

Insecure learners may well be complicit in this as there is a perceived (erroneously in most cases) security in applying an algorithm, especially when it is sanctioned by a teacher (Chinn et al., 2001). Moreover, this approach by-passes attempts to understand mathematics, and this by-passing might have become, for the learner, a way of preserving self-esteem based on the experience of previous failure. Lee and Johnston-Wilder consider that communication is an important part of developing mathematics resilience and can have a profound effect on the way learners see themselves.

If a learner's long-term memory for mathematics facts and procedures is limited and unreliable, then understanding and cognitive abilities can compensate to a large extent for that deficit. The second key finding from the National Research Council (Bransford et al., 2001) is:

> To develop competence in an area of enquiry, students must: (a) have a deep foundation of factual knowledge [which may not be an easy goal for many learners if addressed predominantly by rote, but parts (b) and (c) identify alternative ways of achieving that 'deep foundation'], (b) understand facts and ideas in the context of a conceptual framework and (c) organise knowledge in ways that facilitate retrieval and application.

The role of strategies and metacognition in helping children with mathematics learning difficulties should not be under estimated.

11 *What is the role of language and vocabulary?*

The key chapters for this question are Donlan's 'Linguistic factors in the development of basic calculation' and McGrath's chapter on story-telling and its value for young children in exploring the role of communication and its subtleties in early mathematics. Hamak, Astilla and Preclaro discuss the critical role of language in learning mathematics, a role that is even more challenging for children learning in a second language.

Language and vocabulary (and symbols) will play a crucial role in mathematics, particularly in children's early experiences of number. Donlan reports on research that suggests that learning the symbol set (Arabic numerals or letters, respectively) and their verbal labels is a critical foundational skill for mathematics and language. However, children with specific language impairments find learning the number word sequence particularly difficult. This problem may, in part, be due to the English language inconsistencies in the number sequence. Unfortunately, there are many other inconsistencies in early mathematics that will create uncertainty. Insecurity in learners and the role of effective communication in addressing the negative impact of those inconsistencies is critical.

Desoete found that expressive language was important for solving simple mathematical operations involving pictures, an observation that is highly pertinent to McGrath's work. Hornigold reports on a successful initiative from Liverpool, UK, 'Talking Mathematics'. This is a ten-week programme that targets speaking and listening skills, skills that are critical for developing mathematical thinking strategies and problem solving.

Because the demands on understanding number increase as mathematics develops, language and vocabulary become increasingly important. Donlan writes about the use of the words 'more' and 'less' as predictors of success with basic calculations, and the role of words such as 'all, few, some' in developing mathematical skills. These simple words can play a key role in developing mathematics proficiency. For example, estimation is not a natural skill for many children and the use of the question, 'Will the answer be bigger or smaller?' encourages basic, non-threatening predictions of results and the appraisal of answers. These words encourage, in a low-stress way, a sense of number as estimation (and of operations, as in selecting the appropriate one and predicting its impact).

12 *Why are word problems difficult?*

There are many reasons why word problems are perceived by students as being 'hard'. It seems that difficulties with word problems appear to be an international problem. The Singapore Model Method (Hong, Mei and Lim, 2009) offers practical solutions based on sound research. Despite such effective interventions, the number of variables that can be built into word problems make this topic very challenging for learners to learn and for teachers to teach. For example, whole-number multiplication problems might not be easy for many learners, but there are limited variations in the challenges that can be constructed for this operation. This means that learners who are instrumental (or inchworm) and have a good memory can be drilled to success in this task without making too many demands on cognitive ability. Word problems are far more unpredictable and variable and thus demand diverse problem-solving skills.

Gowramma notes, however, that an advantage in language and reading skills will not help solve word problems that require analytic and thinking skills.

Bryant, Bryant, Shin and Pfannenstiel make a comment that is pertinent to the Singapore Model Method:

> In a study on the use of diagrams to solve word problems by students with LD, these students created fewer well developed diagrammatic tools and used them in an inefficient manner as compared to their peers. The quality of the diagrams was influenced by insufficient mathematics content knowledge. Thus, in both the elementary and secondary grades, students with MLD struggle to solve mathematics word problems. This is a persistent characteristic behaviour that is sufficiently significant to be a type of MLD for the identification of learning disabilities.

The key chapter on word problems is 'Promoting word problem-solving performance among students with mathematics difficulties: the role of strategy instruction that primes the problem structure' by Jitendra, Dupuis and Lein, based on Jitendra's extensive and comprehensive research into this area of mathematics. The authors note that many of the students who entered a Schema-Based Instruction programme had not mastered the basic computational skills. These are, of course, pre-requisite skills. The situation is another example of the impact of the developmental trajectories in mathematics and the problems that result from gaps in early knowledge and understanding.

13   *Why are fractions and division universally perceived as 'difficult'?*

I have lectured in many countries around the world and often ask teachers the question, 'Which are the topics in mathematics that children find difficult?' 'Fractions and division' is an international answer. ('Word problems' is also a frequent answer internationally.)

Morsanyi and Szücs observations on logical reasoning are apposite for fractions. They state that logical reasoning problems are often designed in such a way that logicality conflicts with the participants' beliefs or intuitions. The observation applies to fractions, for example, children's early experiences of multiplication inculcates a belief that the outcome of multiplication is that the answer is bigger and for division it is smaller. These beliefs are no longer universally applicable in work on fractions. They also comment on the difficulty of reasoning with abstract content. For many children and adults, fractions are perceived as abstract and Trott notes that students in Higher Education with mathematical difficulties often find the task of placing fractions on a number line in sequential order challenging.

The key chapter for learning about why fractions are so difficult and what interventions are appropriate and effective is 'The Center for Improving Learning of

Fractions: a progress report', written by the formidable team of Siegler, Fuchs, Jordan, Gersten and Ochsendorf.

They found that 50 percent of students in eighth grade could not place the fractions 2/7, 1/12 and 5/9 in the correct order of value. They also noted that although fractions do not share most of the properties of whole numbers, they can be located on a number line.

Complementing Morsanyi and Szücs' observation, they note that a major source of difficulty in acquiring a conceptual knowledge of fractions is that children's massive prior experience with integers leads them to a whole-number bias in which the properties of positive integers are incorrectly generalised to fractions. Fractions are a classic example of the apparent inconsistencies of mathematics.

It could be assumed that the children who surmount these obstacles might well progress successfully in future mathematical challenges. Analyses of two large, longitudinal data sets, one from the USA and one from the UK (in which Siegler was involved) indicated that fifth graders' knowledge of fractions uniquely predicted those students' knowledge of algebra and overall mathematics achievement in high school five to six years later.

Division, which plays a key role in understanding fractions, is also notoriously problematic for learners. Chinn (2013) found that, in his UK study, only 44.5 percent of 15 year olds could successfully answer the division question 927 ÷ 9, which dropped to 35 percent for 16–19 year olds, many of whom, at the time of the data collection, were not obliged to take a (basic) mathematics course. Division is often taught as a procedure to follow rather than to understand. The procedure makes many demands on memory and spatial organisation and frequently creates high levels of anxiety. There are many steps in the traditional algorithm and each has to be correct. The chances of a successful outcome for learners with any difficulty, for example, difficulties with spatial organisation or a poor understanding of place value, are extremely small.

14 *Why is algebra hard?*

Children and adults seem to find the replacement of numbers with letters a block to future learning of mathematics. As a 13-year-old girl I assessed said, 'Oh, no! You are bringing letters in'.

Murray, Hillaire, Johnson and Rappolt-Schlichtmann discovered the same reliance on procedure rather than understanding that is found for teaching other topics in mathematics, that is, most programmes focus on describing and calculating, not on the underlying thinking that is essential to truly understanding and applying algebra. They also add that the emphasis on procedural fluency that is common in traditional algebra curricula does not promote understanding or interpretation. As they observe, algebra continues to be a stumbling block for many students, especially those who struggle with mathematics. They outline in more detail the skills and knowledge that algebra demands and discuss the design of computer-based programmes that address those factors, in much the same analytical approach that Siegler, Fuchs, Jordan, Gersten and Ochsendorf use for fractions. Their approaches involve the three interlinked components of learner–mathematics–teacher.

Algebra evolves from an understanding of numbers and operations. It is a prime example of the developmental nature of mathematics. Also, like fractions, algebra comes with a reputation for being incomprehensible and thus is a source of anxiety even before children are taught the topic.

15 *What is the role of anxiety, resilience and the affective domain?*
Unique among school subjects, mathematics is the subject of extensive anxiety. My own informal survey of teachers from around the world, suggests that it becomes a noticeable phenomenon in classrooms for children as young as 7 years old. This problem is pervasive and enduring. Trott's work draws attention to the impact of weak mathematics skills on the everyday lives of students in Higher Education. Anxiety is a feature of mathematics throughout the lives of too many people.

The affective domain is involved in many aspects of learning mathematics and is often linked to cognitive factors, for example, Geary identifies attentional control as a predictor of long-term success in learning formal mathematics, Morsanyi and Szücs discuss the role of inhibition in dealing with belief-inconsistent subject matter, and there is Ashcraft et al.'s (1998) classic work on the influence of anxiety on working memory.

The key chapters on this area of influence on learning are from Lee and Johnston-Wilder, and 'Mathematics anxiety, working memory, and mathematical performance: the triple task effect and the affective drop in performance' from Moore, McAuley, Allred and Ashcraft.

The powerful influence of anxiety is highlighted in the Moore, McAuley, Allred and Ashcraft chapter where they refer to work from Lyons and Beilock (2012): 'the prospect of completing a mathematical task is equivalent to anticipating bodily harm.'

The role of errors in the learning process is crucial. Many learners suffer from a fear of negative evaluation and so the way that teachers deal with errors will be critical to motivation. 'No attempt' errors are one symptom of loss of motivation. Gowramma notes that both her experimental groups, children with hearing impairment and normal hearing children, had high percentages of no attempts for multiplication and division tasks and for word problems.

McGrath observes that oral work for young children reduces the de-motivational influence of errors since, when nothing is committed in writing, there is no permanent record of your failure.

In terms of addressing these very significant influences on learning, Hornigold and Lee and Johnston-Wilder discuss Dweck's (2006) work on mindset, which includes focusing on persistence and learning from mistakes. Children can develop a fixed mindset where they avoid failure and any work perceived of as challenging. Chinn (2012a) has used Seligman's attributional style to develop a resilient classroom ethos. Avoidance and withdrawal are key issues for many learners. If success is not assured then failure will be avoided by 'not trying'. A powerful tool in addressing this problem is to incorporate discussions on error patterns. Ashlock's chapter, 'Deep diagnosis, focused instruction and expanded math horizons', is a master-class in the role of diagnostic teaching and error patterns.

16 How will IT help, now and in the future?

Two chapters look at the exciting potential for this tool. Harskamp's chapter, 'The effects of computer technology on primary school students' mathematics achievement: a meta-analysis', finds that IT effects are stronger for students with low mathematics ability. He speculates that this is probably due to IT providing well-structured programs with individual learning pathways and scaffolded intervention.

The Center for Applied Special Technology has pioneered the application of technology in education for many years. In their current work, Murray, Hillaire, Johnson and Rappolt-Schlichtmann use IT to apply the principles of UDL to the development of teaching programs for algebra. Not surprisingly, with CAST's reputation, they are not producing programs of the type that have been summarised as 'drill and kill', but are specifically addressing reasoning skills. Two further strong elements in the design of these programs is the built-in diagnostic content and a pro-active awareness of perception limit. The capability of well-designed programs to combine visual images, symbols and sound (usually voice) without exceeding the perception limits of the learner makes for powerful learning tools. If they can also be designed not to be age-specific, then many older learners might be able to use this non-judgemental form of intervention.

References

Ashcraft, M., Kirk, E.P. and Hopko, D. (1998). On the cognitive consequences of mathematics anxiety. In C. Donlan (ed.), *The Development of Mathematical Skills*. Hove: The Psychological Corporation.

Ashlock, R. (2010). *Error Patterns in Computation*. 10th edn. Boston: Allyn & Bacon.

Baddeley, A.D. and Hitch, G. (1974). Working memory. In G. Bower (ed.), *The Psychology of Learning and Motivation* (pp. 47–90). New York: Academic Press.

Baddeley, A.D. and Logie, R.H. (1999). Working memory: The multiple component model. In A. Miyake and P. Shah (eds), *Models of Working Memory: Mechanisms of active maintenance and executive control* (pp. 28–61). New York: Cambridge University Press.

Bransford, J.D., Brown, A.L. and Cocking, R.R. (eds). (2001) *How People Learn*. Washington, DC: National Academy Press.

Bronner, A.F. (1917). *The Psychology of Special Abilities and Disabilities*. Boston: Little, Brown and Co.

Buswell, G.T. and Judd, C.H. (1925). Summary of Educational Investigations Relating to Arithmetic. Supplementary Educational Monographs, Chicago, IL: University of Chicago.

Chinn, S. (2012a) *The Trouble with Maths*. 2nd edn. London: Routledge.

Chinn, S. (2012b) *More Trouble with Maths: A complete guide to identifying and diagnosing mathematical difficulties*. London: Routledge.

Chinn, S. (2013) Is the population really woefully bad at maths? *Mathematics Teaching 232*, 25–28.

Chinn, S. (2014) Explainer: what is the mastery model of teaching maths? *The Conversation*. Available from: http://theconversation.com/explainer-what-is-the-mastery-model-of-teaching-maths-25636

Chinn, S. and Ashcroft, J.R. (2007) *Mathematics for Dyslexics, Including Dyscalculia: A teaching handbook*. 3rd edn. Chichester: Wiley.

Chinn, S., McDonagh, D., van Elswijk, R., Harmsen, H., Kay, J., McPhillips, T., *et al.* (2001) Classroom studies into cognitive style in mathematics for pupils with dyslexia in special education in the Netherlands, Ireland and the UK. *British Journal of Special Education* 28(2): 80–85.

Dweck, S. (2006) *Mindset: The new psychology of success*. London: Random House.

Ellis, A.W. (1985) The cognitive neuropsychology of developmental (and acquired) dyslexia: A critical survey. *Cognitive Neuropsychology* 2: 169–205

Gardner, H. (1983) *Learned Optimism*. New York: Pocket Books.

Geary, D.C. (2004) Mathematics and learning disabilities. *Journal of Learning Disabilities* 37(1): 4–15.

Hong, K.T., Mei, Y.S. and Lim, J. (2009) *The Singapore Model Method for learning Mathematics*. Singapore: Ministry of Education.

Lyons, I.M. and Beilock, S.L. (2012) When math hurts: Math anxiety predicts pain network activation in anticipation of doing math. *PLoS ONE* 7(10): e48076. doi:10.1371/journal. pone.0048076.

Rashid, S. and Brooks, G. (2010). *The Levels of Attainment in Literacy and Numeracy of 13- to 19-year-olds in England, 1948–2009*. London: NRDC.

Skemp, R. (1986) *The Psychology of Learning Mathematics*. 2nd edn. Harmondsworth: Penguin.

1

How can cognitive developmental neuroscience constrain our understanding of developmental dyscalculia?

Stephanie Bugden and Daniel Ansari

A developmental cognitive neuroscience approach

Developmental cognitive neuroscience in an advancing field that integrates neuroscience and cognitive science methodology to understand the underlying mechanisms that subserve multiple cognitive processes such as attention, language, and math (for a review see: Munakata, Casey, & Diamond, 2004). Historically, neuroscience and behavioral research were conducted independently from one another. However, in recent years researchers have increasingly been trying to uncover how changes in the brain are related to the emergence of behavioral outcomes. Developmental cognitive neuroscience integrates multiple disciplines of research, such as psychology, neuroscience, cognitive science, genetics and social sciences to track the dynamic relationships between biology, cognition and behavior over the course of development. Non-invasive neuroimaging tools such as magnetic resonance imaging (MRI) and electroencephalography (EEG) afford researchers the ability to investigate these relationships between neurobiology and behavior in both typical and atypical populations. Using developmental cognitive neuroscience methods to investigate typical and atypical developmental trajectories can inform a variety of clinical applications such as diagnosis, intervention and treatment of developmental disorders (e.g. Developmental Dyscalculia (DD)) (Munakata et al., 2004).

The current chapter will explore how developmental cognitive neuroscience research is beginning to inform our understanding of DD. DD has received far less attention than reading disorders such as dyslexia (Gersten, Clarke, & Mazzocco, 2007), despite its similar incidence rates (5–7% of school-aged children) (Shalev, 2004). Although the number of published studies about DD has increased recently, researchers in the field of mathematical cognition are still struggling with the fundamental question of what constitutes the core deficit(s) of DD and how to define them.

Against this background, the chapter will begin with a brief review of the current behavioral evidence supporting multiple different causal theories of DD; followed by an overview of the neural correlates of numerical magnitude processing (numerical magnitude referring to the total number of items in a set) in both typically developing populations, as well as in DD. In subsequent sections, the neural correlates of arithmetic as well as visuospatial working memory will be explored. Additionally, how differences in anatomical brain structures can inform our understanding of the functional organization of numerical and arithmetic processing in children with dyscalculia compared to typically developing controls will be discussed. Finally, the advantages and educational implications of using developmental cognitive neuroscience to further our understanding of DD will be considered.

Developmental Dyscalculia: definition and behavioral evidence

DD is a specific learning disorder that is characterized by impairments in learning basic arithmetic facts, processing numerical magnitude, and performing accurate and fluent calculations (American Psychiatric Association, 2013). These difficulties must be quantifiably below what is expected for the individual's chronological age, and must not be caused by poor educational or daily activities or by intellectual impairments (American Psychiatric Association, 2013). At the behavioral level, children with DD exhibit difficulties retrieving arithmetic facts from memory (Geary, Hoard, & Bailey, 2011) and they commonly rely on immature strategies such as finger counting when their age-matched peers are easily retrieving arithmetic facts from memory. It is generally agreed that children with DD rely on inefficient strategies and have severe difficulties retrieving arithmetic facts. However, despite recent advances in the field by describing the main symptoms of DD, such as arithmetic fact-retrieval difficulties, researchers are struggling with the fundamental question of what constitutes the core deficits of DD and what causes them.

Historically, researchers sought to understand the causes of DD by investigating differences between children with DD and typical controls in domain-general abilities, such as working memory. Some studies have observed deficits in semantic long-term memory and working memory abilities that impair children's ability to convert arithmetic facts into long-term memory (Geary, 1993). Within the behavioral literature, results have been controversial, with some studies finding working memory deficits in children with DD (Geary, Brown, & Samaranayake, 1991; Geary, 2004; McLean & Hitch, 1999), while other studies found no working memory deficits compared to typically developing controls (Landerl et al., 2004). In an attempt to further understand the conflicting findings, Passolunghi and Mammarella (2012) recently investigated the specific role of visuospatial working memory and visual memory processing tasks in children with DD. During the visual memory tasks, children were presented with a set of houses and had to remember and recognize the same houses on a following trial. During the complex visuospatial working memory tasks, participants were given sequences of dot positions in a matrix and were asked to recall the last position or last dot from the sequence, in addition to having to press the space bar every time a specific dot appeared on the screen. They found that only children with persistent and severe difficulties in solving mathematical word problems had impairment in complex visuospatial working memory tasks, where high attentional control was necessary to complete the tasks. But they showed no impairments on visual memory recognition tasks. Additionally, Szücs et al. (2013) found that children with DD showed greater impairments in visuospatial working memory and short-term memory as well as inhibition compared to typical controls. Taken together, children with DD have demonstrated specific impairments in visuospatial working memory (Ashkenazi, Rosenberg-Lee, Metcalfe, Swigart, &Menon, 2013; McLean & Hitch, 1999). From these data, it was suggested that visuospatial working memory provides a work space to hold and manipulate numerical magnitude representations. An impaired visuospatial working memory system in children with DD would negatively impact the development of numerical magnitude representations and basic arithmetic (Ashkenazi et al., 2013).

From these studies, the causal link between a domain-general deficit in visuospatial working memory and domain-specific processes such as numerical magnitude and arithmetic skills in DD remains unclear. Indeed, a recent meta-analysis has provided evidence that children with DD demonstrate numerically specific working memory impairment in comparison to typically developing controls. These deficits are pronounced in working memory tasks that require numerical manipulations, such as backward digit recall; rather than domain-general working memory impairment. Therefore, these findings reflect the domain-specific nature of working memory deficits (Peng & Fuchs, 2014). However, it does not necessarily imply that these domain-general mechanisms cause DD. If that were the case, then it is likely we would see widespread impairments in multiple cognitive domains (Alloway, Gathercole, Kirkwood, & Elliot, 2009; Price & Ansari, 2013).

In contrast to the search for domain-general deficits as proximal causes of DD, recent approaches have focused on low-level, domain-specific numerical abilities as the potential root cause of DD. For example, Butterworth and colleagues (1999, 2005) have proposed that DD is caused by a domain-specific impairment in the core capacity to represent and manipulate numerical information known as the 'defective number module hypothesis' (Butterworth, 1999, 2005; Iuculano et al., 2008). The first evidence supporting this hypothesis came from a study conducted by Landerl and colleagues (2004) who found that children with DD demonstrated difficulties in processing numerical information, such as counting dots, accessing semantic (the numerical magnitude represented by Arabic numerals) and verbal numerical representations and reciting number sequences. However, in contrast to the domain-general account, they found that children with DD were normal or above average on tasks involving phonological working memory and accessing non-numerical verbal information. The defective number module hypothesis assumes a deficit at the level of numerical magnitude representations regardless of the format of presentation. In other words, this hypothesis predicts that children with DD will be equally poor at judging which of two dot arrays is numerically larger (e.g. nonsymbolic discrimination) as they will be at deciding whether the numeral 9 represents a numerical magnitude that is larger or smaller than the numerical magnitude referenced by numeral 7. However, data on the numerical magnitude processing abilities of children with DD have not always been consistent with this hypothesis.

Instead, Rouselle and Noël (2007) argue that the deficit is not with the format-independent representation, but in the connections between number symbols (Arabic digits, i.e. 3, or number words, i.e. three) and their respective meanings. They found that children with DD were slower and less accurate at discriminating between Arabic digits compared to children without DD; however, they failed to exhibit deficits when comparing nonsymbolic quantities (i.e. arrays of dots). Taken together, these findings demonstrate that magnitude representation remains intact in children with DD; however, they have deficits in semantically encoding numerical symbols, also known as the 'access deficit hypothesis' – children with DD have more difficulties than children without DD in accessing the connection between numerical symbols and the quantities they represent (Rousselle & Noël, 2007).

It is evident that current findings in the DD literature are contradictory, and there is no clear conclusion as to what causes DD. Furthermore, there are no universally agreed upon criteria for diagnosing children with DD and, as a result, it is difficult for researchers to make conclusions about what underlying cognitive mechanisms impair DD children's ability to learn basic arithmetic.

As a consequence of the lack of universal classification criteria for DD, studies investigating behavioral and neural correlates of this disorder include samples with varying profiles. Some studies have included samples with milder forms of math deficits (Geary, Hoard, Byrd-Craven, & DeSoto, 2004; Jordan, Hanich, & Kaplan, 2003), while others use more strict criteria, for example Mazzocco and colleagues limited their sample to children below the 10th percentile on math achievement (Mazzocco & Myers, 2003; Mazzocco, Devlin, & McKenney, 2008). Therefore, constraining current theoretical models of DD remains problematic.

Additionally, the heterogeneity of DD contributes to the difficulties of capturing one core deficit (Fias, Menon, & Szücs, 2013) and, therefore, it is probable that various cognitive and neural mechanisms may contribute to different behavioral profiles of DD (Henik, Rubinsten, & Ashkenazi, 2011; Karagiannakis, Baccaglini-Frank, & Papadatos, 2014; Skagerlund & Träff, 2014). Taking a multidisciplinary approach by including both behavioral and cognitive neuroscience methodology is optimal for furthering our conceptual understanding of DD. Exploring the functional and structural composition of the dyscalculic brain will advance our knowledge of the source(s) of cognitive deficits in children who have DD at the neurobiological level.

The following section aims to discuss the cognitive neuroscience evidence that supports or disputes current theoretical explanations for the mechanisms related to poor arithmetic performance in adults as well as children with DD. We first begin with an outline of the current neuroscience evidence of numerical magnitude processing in the typical adult and developing brain. Evidence from typically developing populations provides a framework to inform our understanding of the neurological impairments observed in DD children. Subsequently, the to-date limited neuroscience evidence both from functional and structural studies aiming to better understand the neurobiological correlates of DD will be discussed. Additionally, the neural correlates of arithmetic development in both typically developing children, as well as children with DD will be reviewed. In conclusion, future directions for developmental cognitive neuroscience are considered.

The neural correlates of numerical magnitude processing

Numerical magnitude processing in the typical adult brain

Historically, neuropsychological studies have found associations between brain damage to areas in the parietal lobe (see Figure 1.1(a)) and numerical and calculation impairments (Dehaene & Cohen, 1997; Delazer & Benke, 1997; Lemer, Dehaene, Spelke, & Cohen, 2003; Warrington, 1982). Neuropsychological studies were the first to pinpoint brain regions involved in mathematical and numerical processes and have formed the basis for theoretical frameworks to conceptualize numerical and calculation abilities in the typical adult brain. The most prominent model associating different subcomponents of mathematical cognition with specific brain circuitry (built on the results of neuropsychological studies) is the 'Triple Code Model' (Dehaene & Cohen, 1995). The Triple Code Model of number processing predicts that there are three underlying neurological representational systems that are recruited for different numerical tasks. First, the quantity code, which is associated with the bilateral intraparietal sulcus (IPS), embodies the nonverbal semantic representation of numerical magnitude, and is hypothesized to be analogous to a spatially oriented number line. Second, the visual number code is involved in visually encoding strings of numbers. This system has been proposed to recruit regions belonging to the 'ventral visual pathway' including the bilateral occipito-temporal regions. And last, the verbal code, which is subserved by the left inferior frontal and superior and middle temporal gyri, is not involved in quantity processing, but shows greater activation when verbal coding of numbers is required. For example, a patient with lesions in these areas within the left hemisphere demonstrated severe impairments in solving simple addition problems, such as 2 + 2 (Dehaene & Cohen, 1991), but excelled at comparing approximate quantities, such as discriminating between dot arrays, a process subserved by right hemispheric regions within the quantity code. Furthermore, this same patient successfully identified strings of digits. In view of patterns of performance such as this one, the verbal code is thought to be associated with the verbal storage of arithmetic facts.

More recently, the predictions put forward in the Triple Code Model have been investigated with non-invasive methods, such as functional magnetic resonance imaging (fMRI), to visualize correlates of brain activation. Dehaene and colleagues (1999) were among the first to demonstrate distinct neural circuitry underlying exact

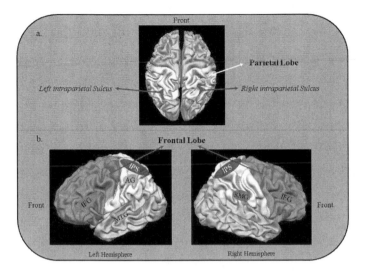

Figure 1.1 (a) An illustration of the parietal lobe, as well as the location of the bilateral IPS. This is a view of the top of the brain. (b) An illustration of the right and left hemispheres demonstrating the location of the frontal lobe as well as the approximate locations of other regions that have consistently demonstrated atypical activation during numerical magnitude processing and/or arithmetic in children with DD.

Note: IFG, inferior frontal gyrus; AG, angular gyrus; SMG, supramarginal gyrus; MTG, middle temporal gyrus.

and approximate calculation, more specifically exact calculation recruited greater activation in left hemispheric regions such as the left inferior frontal lobe, left angular gyrus (AG) and left anterior cingulate, which are associated with language-dependent coding of exact arithmetic facts. In contrast, approximate arithmetic showed greater activation in the bilateral intraparietal sulci in addition to regions within the frontal lobe, suggesting that approximate calculation involves accessing mental representations of quantity (i.e. the quantity code).

Further corroborating Dehaene et al., studies have revealed that the IPS subserves many different numerical processing tasks, including numerical discrimination, and has been referred to as the region that houses the representational system of quantity regardless of notation (e.g. dot arrays, Arabic numerals, e.g. 3, and number words, e.g. three) (e.g. Dehaene, 1999; Pinel, Dehaene, Rivière, & LeBihan, 2001). The numerical discrimination task is commonly used to examine the behavioral and neuronal correlates of numerical magnitude processing (see Figure 1.2(a)). This task is associated with the well-known so-called 'distance effect', which is characterized by slower reaction times and greater errors in trials where the numerical distance is close (e.g. 2 vs. 3) compared to trials where the numerical distance is large (e.g. 2 vs. 9). This effect can be found at the behavioral level, but it is also obtained at the neural level, where brain regions show greater activation during the discrimination of close-distance trials compared to large-distance trials (e.g. 1 vs. 9) (see Figure 1.2(b)). Both behavioral and neural distance effects are used to index the internal representation of numerical magnitudes (Nieder & Dehaene, 2009; Moyer & Landauer, 1967). Evidence supporting an abstract quantity system in the IPS comes from studies using both symbolic (e.g. Arabic numerals and number words) and nonsymbolic (e.g. dot array) numerical discrimination tasks, where bilateral regions of the IPS are modulated by numerical distance between the compared numbers regardless of numerical notation. Therefore, the regions can be said to represent numerical magnitude in an abstract format.

Numerical magnitude processing in the typically developing brain

Comparable to the data from adults, reviewed above, children as young as four years of age have been found to activate the IPS during numerical tasks, but to a lesser degree (Cantlon, Brannon, Carter, & Pelphrey, 2006). More specifically adults demonstrated greater bilateral activity in the IPS, whereas children showed activation in the right IPS. These findings suggest that the IPS is the ontogenetic neuronal origin for processing nonsymbolic numerical magnitudes. In contrast to these findings, Ansari and colleagues have found that elementary school children showed

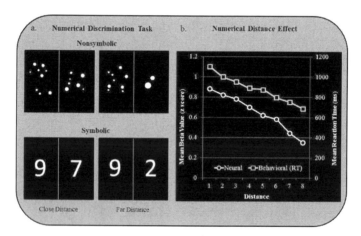

Figure 1.2 (a) An example of symbolic and nonsymbolic trials from the numerical discrimination task. Children or adults are presented with either two dot arrays in the nonsymbolic task, or two Arabic numerals in the symbolic task, and they are asked to choose the numerically larger quantity. The examples of close-distance trials are displayed on the left and examples of far-distance trials are displayed on the right. (b) The figure is hypothetical data demonstrating a typical behavioral and neural distance effect, whereby mean reaction time decreases as the distance between the to-be-compared quantities increases. In the neural distance effect, mean beta values, which represent the amount of activation in a given region, decrease as the distance of the to-be-compared quantities increases.

greater modulation of distance (i.e. the neural distance effect) during symbolic and nonsymbolic numerical discrimination tasks in prefrontal regions (Ansari & Dhital, 2006; Ansari, Garcia, Lucas, Hamon, & Dhital, 2005); however, adults demonstrated greater neural distance effect in the IPS.

The authors interpreted these findings of greater frontal activation in children and more modulation of the IPS in adults in the following way: they argued that children recruit prefrontal regions during numerical discrimination to compensate for imprecise and immature representations of numerical magnitude in the IPS, but as they grow older the IPS becomes functionally specialized to process numerical magnitude (Ansari, 2008). Taken together, these findings are beginning to shed light on the ontogenetic activation differences that support increased automaticity and functional specialization of the parietal cortex for numerical magnitude processing.

It is important to understand the ontogenetic processes underlying numerical abilities in typically developing children to further investigate how the typical developmental trajectory might go awry in children with DD. These findings lead us to question whether the brain system underlying the numerical magnitude representations in the IPS leads to a representational impairment in children with DD. Developmental cognitive neuroscience methods are optimal in elucidating the neural mechanisms that underlie specific numerical abnormalities in children with DD by, for example, exploring the connection pathways between right and left intraparietal regions as well as the functional activation during symbolic and nonsymbolic processing tasks. Such investigations would shed light on the degree to which DD is associated with atypical activation patterns during symbolic and nonsymbolic numerical magnitude processing. More specifically, one would hypothesize atypical brain activation during symbolic processing as well as a disruption in the neural connection pathways that are specific to symbolic number processing if DD was caused by a deficit in accessing the semantic meaning of numerical symbols. In contrast, if DD was caused by a representational (defective number module hypothesis) deficit, it would be hypothesized that children with DD would elicit atypical activation in bilateral regions of the IPS during both symbolic and nonsymbolic numerical processing. To test these hypotheses, developmental cognitive neuroscience methods are required to understand the specific sources of numerical deficits in the brain in children with DD.

Numerical magnitude processing in the dyscalculia brain

To date, only a handful of neuroimaging studies have investigated the functional activation as well as structural brain differences in children with pure DD compared to typically developing children. The following section will discuss what we know about the neural correlates of DD from functional neuroimaging studies. Studies investigating the integrity of numerical representations in children with DD compared to typically developing controls have predominantly used the numerical discrimination task and have found various differences in the neural distance effect.

Using a nonsymbolic discrimination task (children select the numerically larger dot array from two sets of dots), researchers have found that children with DD did not show typical distance-related modulation of activation in the right IPS (Price, Holloway, Räsänen, Vesterinen, & Ansari, 2007). Children with DD showed atypical activation in the right IPS compared to typical controls. More specifically, children with DD demonstrated similar activation in the right IPS during both far- and close-distance trials, suggesting that the representation of quantity in this brain region might be less refined in children with DD, whereas a typical neural distance effect was found in age-matched controls. In addition, the right IPS was recruited to a lesser extent in children with DD. Taken together, these findings demonstrated that a parietal dysfunction might underlie reduced capability to process nonsymbolic numerical magnitudes in children with DD. Atypical activation in the right IPS has also been implicated in processing symbolic numerical magnitudes. Mussolin and colleagues (2009) found that children with DD demonstrated weak modulation of the right IPS and the left superior parietal lobule during a symbolic numerical discrimination task (e.g. the discrimination of Arabic numerals, such as 3 and 5). Additionally, Kaufmann et al. (2009) found atypical activation in bilateral regions of the IPS during nonsymbolic numerical processing in nine-year-old children with DD. However, in contrast to previous findings, differences were driven by stronger activation in the left IPS and less pronounced deactivation in the right IPS. The majority of studies use arrays of dots or objects in a nonsymbolic discrimination task; in Kaufmann et al.'s study, children were instead asked to compare finger patterns. Therefore, it is difficult to interpret the sources of these conflicting findings.

In an attempt to ascertain whether these findings (and others) yield a consistent pattern of data, Kaufmann et al. (2011) conducted a meta-analysis synthesizing the functional neuroimaging data that have investigated the neuronal correlates of both symbolic and nonsymbolic numerical magnitude processing in children with DD. They found that, when considering all available evidence and using meta-analytic analysis tools, children with DD have distinct differences in activation patterns compared to typically developing controls. For example, control children demonstrated greater activation than children with DD in the left precuneus, right inferior parietal lobe, left paracentral frontal lobe, the superior frontal gyrus, the right middle frontal gyrus and the left fusiform gyrus. In contrast, DD participants showed greater activation in the left postcentral gyrus, superior frontal lobe, as well as the bilateral inferior parietal regions, more specifically in the right supramarginal gyrus and the left lateral IPS. These findings, although speaking against reduced activation in the right IPS, demonstrate that children with DD have reduced specialization for processing numerical information in the left IPS in contrast to typically developing controls (Kaufmann, Wood, Rubinsten, & Henik, 2011). It is important to note that the meta-analysis only included three studies that investigated numerical processing abilities merging data from both symbolic and nonsymbolic numerical discrimination in children with DD compared to typical controls. Thus any direct comparisons between the formats are difficult to make.

Taken together, these findings demonstrate atypical recruitment/organization of the IPS, a region known to process semantic representation of numerical magnitude

(Butterworth, 1999, 2005; Dehaene, 1992; Dehaene et al., 2003). To date, no study has investigated both symbolic and nonsymbolic numerical processing abilities in the same sample of DD children and, as a result, there is no cognitive neuroscience evidence to support or refute the representational or access deficits hypotheses as the root mechanism underlying DD.

However, it is important to take note that presently there are very few fMRI studies that have investigated the neural correlates of DD; and these conflicting findings may be explained by differences in methodology. More specifically, the selection criteria for identifying children with DD vary across studies and consequently results cannot be compared across small and heterogeneous samples.

fMRI methodology is advantageous because it measures specific metabolic function from different brain regions with a relatively high spatial resolution. However, the temporal resolution of fMRI is poor. It measures the correlates of neuronal activity on the order of seconds, rather than milliseconds. A vast improvement in terms of temporal resolution is represented by the use of electroencephalography (EEG), which allows for the measurement of electrical currents on the scalp that are produced by synaptic activity – event-related potentials (ERP) – which are a measure of brain response given at specific stimuli onsets and offsets and averaged across a series of trials. Although ERP does not have the spatial resolution of fMRI, it allows researchers to examine differences in brain activity during specific stages before and after the presentation of experimental stimuli. Using ERP, Soltesz et al. (2007) investigated ERP markers of the symbolic numerical distance effect in a group of adolescents with DD. They found that adolescents with DD had a similar distance effect compared to typical controls using reaction time and accuracy measures; furthermore, the topography of early ERP distance effects were found to be similar between the DD and control groups, which were lateralized over the right hemisphere. However, later in the time course typically developing children demonstrated a distance effect over several right hemisphere electrodes, whereas the distance effect was not found in the DD group. The researchers suggest that differences in processing numerical magnitude arose during intentional and controlled processes; however, early automatic processing of single digits remains intact in children with DD.

Neuroimaging studies investigating the cognitive mechanisms that contribute to DD deficits have yielded an inconsistent and hard to interpret pattern of data. Given the early stages of functional MRI and EEG research, it is difficult to interpret from the current set of data what neurobiology underlies cognitive deficits in children with DD. Future studies are required to understand the origins of numerical deficits in the brain, more specifically, developmental cognitive neuroscience methods are necessary to pinpoint neural correlates of symbolic and nonsymbolic processing difficulties. These difficulties cannot be fully explained by behavioral evidence – given that it is unclear whether symbolic processing deficits are caused by underlying magnitude representation deficit or in the decision-level processes that involve accessing the semantic representation leaving the actual representation intact.

Using different neuroimaging analyses and methods, researchers can begin to uncover qualitative differences in the underlying neuronal mechanisms that underpin symbolic and nonsymbolic numerical representations.

For this, multiple analytical approaches are necessary too. Conventional statistical analysis of fMRI uses a univariate statistical method to locate macroscopic brain regions involved in specific numerical tasks. These analyses characterize functional brain regions based on activity as a whole. Recently, there has been growing interest to move beyond investigating total brain activity of particular regions, towards an exploration of activity pattern differences in specific brain regions. Multivariate pattern analysis (MVPA) is an optimal approach to investigate the representation of numeracy in specific brain regions, because it is a more fine-grained measure of patterns of activity within the brain that allows researchers to draw inferences about the representational content (Mur, Bandettini, & Kreigeskorte, 2009).

For example, Boets and colleagues (2013) used MVPA analyses to uncover whether dyslexia is caused by impaired phonological representations or by difficulties accessing an intact representation. They found that despite dyslexic adults demonstrating overall less activity in a network of regions involved in phonetic discrimination, which would be found in traditional univariate analyses, there were no qualitative differences in the patterns of activity compared to typical controls. These findings demonstrate that phonetic neural representations remain intact despite persistent reading difficulties in adults with dyslexia, which could only be uncovered using MVPA analyses. MVPA analysis is a powerful tool that can be used to elucidate the sources of numerical deficits. Similar to Boets et al., it can be used to investigate whether children with DD have impaired numerical representations, as suggested by the 'defective number module hypothesis', or whether children with DD have difficulties accessing the semantic representations from intact numerical representations as suggested by the 'access deficit hypothesis'. Therefore, using novel and fine-grained neuroimaging analyses is advantageous for observing how the neural correlates of magnitude representations evolve over development in children with DD.

In addition to using novel methodological approaches, such as MVPA, to explore the integrity of symbolic and nonsymbolic numerical representations, it is important to explore how numerical representations change throughout development. For instance, symbolic numerals (e.g. Arabic numerals) are cultural inventions that require explicit instruction to learn; therefore, understanding how children map symbolic numerals to their iconic semantic referents can only be explained by taking a developmental approach. Therefore, developmental studies can investigate how symbolic representations emerge in children with DD and whether they are qualitatively different from typical controls at a young age. These studies will further our understanding of the causal relationship between learning symbolic numerals, nonsymbolic representations and later arithmetic difficulties. Moreover, using developmental neuroimaging studies, researchers can investigate compensatory mechanisms and pathways children with DD employ during nonsymbolic and symbolic processing.

The neural correlates of arithmetic

Poor arithmetic abilities are distinct features of DD. Indeed, although researchers vary significantly in how they define a child as presenting with DD, the use of standardized measures of arithmetic processing are used by almost all researchers in their quest to identify groups of children with DD. Evidence suggests that imprecise representation of numerical magnitude or the inability to access such representations from number symbols used to express mathematical problems might be causally related to the development of poor arithmetic skills. In the following section, the neural correlates involved in arithmetic problem solving in typically developing adults as well as children will be discussed, followed by an examination of the functional correlates of arithmetic skills in adults and children with DD.

The neural correlates of arithmetic in the typical adult brain

The triple code theory postulates that parietal circuitry, such as the superior parietal lobule, the AG and the IPS, are involved in the verbal retrieval or calculation of arithmetic facts in typical adults (Dehaene & Cohen, 1997). Although some studies have demonstrated more widespread activation in the prefrontal cortex, in addition to parietal regions (Arsalidou & Taylor, 2011), differences in activation can be attributed to the nature and complexity of basic arithmetic processing. Recruitment of the fronto-parietal network, including the IPS, has been implicated during the solution of larger operands (Grabner et al., 2007) as well as during the solution of problems where adults have reported procedural strategies (Grabner et al., 2009), suggesting that these regions are involved in more effortful calculation strategies to solve arithmetic problems. However, the left AG is involved in the retrieval of verbally stored arithmetic facts (Dehaene et al., 2003). Evidence supporting this notion comes from studies that show greater activation in the left AG during the solution of small number problems (e.g. operands contained single-digit numbers: one operand contained numbers 2–5, and the other operand contained numbers 2–9) (Grabner et al., 2007), as well as during the solution of problems where adults reported using fact-retrieval strategies (Grabner et al., 2009). Additionally, adults with higher mathematical competence demonstrated stronger activation in the left AG while solving multiplication facts, potentially supporting the use of fact-retrieval strategies.

The neural correlates of arithmetic in the typically developing brain

In contrast to adults, children rely to a lesser extent on parietal regions and instead engage prefrontal and medial temporal cortices during arithmetic problem solving (Rivera, Reiss, Eckert, & Menon, 2005). Rivera and colleagues (2005) demonstrated a developmental specialization in the parietal lobe, whereby a positive correlation between age and activation during an arithmetic verification task was found in regions of the lateral occipital temporal cortex, as well as the left supramarginal gyrus, a region adjacent to the AG, and the left anterior IPS with age during arithmetic problem solving. In contrast, a negative correlation between age and activation was found in regions of the prefrontal cortex such as the bilateral superior frontal gyrus, middle and left interior frontal gyrus, as well as cingulate cortex, in addition to regions in the hippocampus and parahippocampal gyrus. Stronger recruitment of the prefrontal cortex during arithmetic performance in children may reflect their greater reliance on attention, working memory and counting processes in order to solve basic arithmetic problems. With increasing arithmetic fluency such functions engaged to a lesser extent and, instead, regions mediating the recall of facts from memory become more strongly associated with simple arithmetic problem solving. This study also supports a role of the hippocampus in arithmetic performance in children, suggesting it is important for the development of retrieval fluency during problem solving (Rivera et al., 2005). These findings were further supported by a study conducted by Cho and colleagues (2012), who demonstrated an influence of the hippocampus and prefrontal regions to the development of arithmetic problem-solving skills in 7–9-year-old children during arithmetic problem solving. These studies emphasize the role of the hippocampus and prefrontal cortex in the acquisition of basic arithmetic in young children, supporting the role of domain-general auxiliary processes to develop specialized and automatic systems for arithmetic problem solving that are associated with the parietal cortex.

The neural correlates of arithmetic in the dyscalculic brain

The neural mechanisms involved in arithmetic problem solving in children with DD are not clearly understood, especially when considering how much we know about the brain mechanisms involved in calculation among typically developing children and adults. In the first study to investigate the neuronal correlates of arithmetic processing in children with and without DD, Kucian et al. (2006) presented DD and TD children with an approximate arithmetic task. Specifically, children with DD were shown a simple single-digit addition problem on the screen followed by two possible incorrect responses. They were asked to estimate the result by selecting the closest number to the correct answer. They found that children with DD, compared to typically developing controls, had weaker activation in the left IPS as well as right inferior frontal gyrus and right medial frontal gyrus in the prefrontal cortex (Kucian et al., 2006). In addition, studies examining children with low math achievement that were not clinically diagnosed with DD found differences during approximate arithmetic were driven by stronger activation in domain-general brain regions, such as clusters within the right prefrontal cortex, left inferior frontal gyrus, right precuneus and the left anterior cingulate that are not typically associated with mathematical processes (Davis et al., 2009).

Furthermore, De Smedt, Holloway and Ansari (2011) found that low math achievers showed greater activation in the right IPS during exact arithmetic solutions with small problem size. Problems were defined as small when the product of the operands was below 25 (e.g. 5 + 2), and as large when the product of operands was above 25. Greater activation in the intraparietal regions during the solving of small problems contrasts with typically developing adults who recruit left AG, a region associated with fact retrieval. Therefore, these findings suggest that low math achievers continue to use quantity-based strategies rather than retrieving simple facts from memory similar to children and adults who have typical math skills. In other words, children with low arithmetic performance do not seem to be able to disengage the use of quantity representation during simple arithmetic and hence exhibit greater activation of their IPS during the processing of such problems.

Similar to De Smedt and colleagues, Ashkenazi et al. (2012) found that 2nd- and 3rd-grade children with DD had atypical activation in the fronto-parietal network while solving more complex arithmetic tasks. More specifically, weaker activation was found in the right IPS, right superior parietal lobule, as well as right supramarginal gyrus located in the dorsal stream. Deficits were also found in the lateral occipital cortex, fusiform gyri and the left medial and inferior temporal gyri located in the ventral visual stream. Additionally, weaker activation was found in the prefrontal cortex, including bilateral dorsolateral prefrontal cortex, suggesting perhaps that children with DD do not sufficiently engage domain-general processes, such as working memory during complex arithmetic problem solving. Not only did children with DD exhibit weaker activation in the dorsal and ventral visual stream, as well as prefrontal cortex during complex problem solving, they demonstrated greater activation in the ventral medial prefrontal cortex and the medial temporal gyrus during simple addition problem solving; evidence that children with DD rely on immature strategies or compensatory mechanisms to perform very basic arithmetic.

These findings are further supported in a recent study conducted by Berteletti, Prado and Booth (2014) who found that brain activation during multiplication of small (e.g. operands < 5) and large problems (e.g. operands > 5 and ≤ 9) differed between 3rd- to 7th-grade children with DD and typically developing children. Specifically, children with DD demonstrated less activation in the left inferior frontal gyrus (IFG), left middle temporal and superior temporal gyri as well as the right superior parietal lobule including the right IPS compared to typically developing children. In comparison to typically developing children, the DD group had greater activation for small problems compared to large problems, suggesting that children rely on counting or calculation procedures for small problems. In the left IFG and the middle temporal and superior temporal gyri, children with DD did not show reliable activations or did not show modulation of problem size suggesting that children with DD did not retrieve solutions verbally for smaller problems. The authors suggest that weak numerical representations in the right IPS in children with DD might impair their ability to use verbally based strategies.

Taken together, these preliminary findings demonstrate that children with low math performance recruit atypical brain regions during arithmetic problem solving and fail to modulate neural activity in response to differences in arithmetic complexity in the same way as participants without DD do. However, these findings are inconsistent and difficult to interpret. The studies discussed above used liberal selection criteria when selecting children with DD and low math achievers meaning that the inclusion of non-dyscalculic children in the DD sample would influence the outcome of results. It remains uncertain from the current studies whether numerical magnitude deficits are causally related to the development of atypical neural networks involved in arithmetic problem solving.

The neural correlates of visuospatial working memory deficits in children with DD

The specific neuronal correlates of arithmetic problem-solving deficits in DD have yet to be uncovered. Like the literature on the neural correlate of basic number-processing deficits in DD, there are only a handful of studies which have yielded a kaleidoscope of conflicting data, against the background of which, unfortunately, no consensus can be articulated.

As is evident from the introduction to this chapter, children with DD often have working memory impairments and it has been hypothesized that such domain-general difficulties might be related to their arithmetic processing difficulties. As discussed above, behavioral studies have found deficiencies in visuospatial working memory, but not verbal working memory in children with DD; however, very few studies have investigated the neural correlates of visuospatial working memory in children with DD.

To explore whether children with and without DD exhibit different neuronal correlates of visuospatial working memory, Rotzer et al. (2009) conducted a functional neuroimaging study to explore brain activation differences during a visuospatial working memory task in 8–11-year-old children with DD compared to typical peers. They found that both groups of children showed activation in brain networks including occipital and parietal regions during visuospatial working memory tasks. However, children with DD elicited weaker activation in the right IPS, right insula and the right inferior frontal gyrus during a visuospatial working memory paradigm adapted from the Corsi Block tapping task (Klingberg et al., 2002). These findings are consistent with the researchers' previous study demonstrating less grey matter density in the right IPS in children with DD (see review of structural imaging data below). These findings, furthermore, give rise to the hypothesis that spatial working memory abilities provide the foundation for building a numerical representational system and, therefore, deficits in the spatial working memory might lead to numeracy (Price et al., 2007) and arithmetic impairments. This hypothesis is further substantiated by a study conducted by Dumontheil and Klingberg (2012), who found that activation in the left IPS during a visuospatial working memory task, relative to the rest of the brain, predicts arithmetic performance two years later in 6–16-year-old participants. These findings are at odds with the suggestion that the IPS is involved in the domain-specific representation of numerical magnitude (the quantity code of the Triple Code Model) and instead suggest that the IPS is associated with individual differences in working memory and that activation differences in these regions among children with DD reflect the impairment of working memory circuitry rather than the domain-specific representation of numerical magnitude. It is possible, of course, that these two accounts of atypical IPS functioning in DD are not mutually exclusive but that there is an interaction of the brain circuits for working memory and numerical magnitude processing within the IPS. Future studies should investigate the neural correlates of both numerical magnitude processing and working memory within the same groups of children with and without DD, to uncover more about the specific nature of the association between atypical activation of the IPS and DD in both working memory and basic number-processing tasks.

The structural organization of the dyscalculic brain

Functional neuroimaging provides a window into the neural activity that supports specific cognitive processes required to perform experimental tasks. However, dyscalculia is very heterogeneous and, for this reason, functional neuroimaging can be challenging in that tasks might not capture the wide spectrum of impairments (Rotzer et al., 2008). Although fMRI augments our ability to understand the functional organization of the brain, and to identify atypical brain functioning, it is task dependent. Therefore, structural neuroimaging approaches, such as Voxel-based Morphometry (VBM) and diffusion tensor imaging (DTI), are complementary techniques to investigate the anatomical structures of the brain that are independent of task demands. Using such structural techniques is advantageous in understanding how differences in brain structure might account for atypical activation during specific mathematical processes. To investigate these relationships, researchers have begun to combine both functional and structural neuroimaging techniques in relation to the behavioral performance of children with DD compared to typically developing age-matched peers.

Voxel-based Morphometry (VBM)

VBM is a statistical technique that allows for investigation of the total volume or density of grey and white matter in the whole brain (see Figure 1.3) or in specific regions of interest. This technique can be used to identify differences in the anatomical structure of both grey and white matter in both adults and children with DD. Investigating differences in the anatomical structure can constrain our understanding of the neural circuitry underlying cognitive processing deficits in children and adults with DD.

Decreased grey matter volume was found in children with DD compared to age-matched typical controls in brain regions within the prefrontal cortex, specifically, the bilateral anterior cingulum, the right and left middle frontal gyrus and the left inferior frontal gyrus, and the right IPS (Rotzer et al., 2008). However, there were no brain regions where children with DD demonstrated increased grey matter integrity compared to their controls. Additionally, children with DD had significantly decreased white matter integrity clusters located in the left frontal lobe and adjacent to the right parahippocampal gyrus.

Grey matter volume differences in the right IPS as well as the frontal regions are consistent with the functional neuroimaging literature that has demonstrated

33

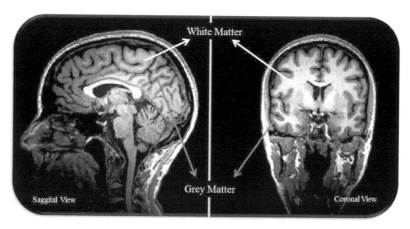

Figure 1.3 A brain image collected from an MRI scanner, where whiter contrasted areas represent white matter and darker contrasted areas represent grey matter in the brain.

atypical activation during numerical magnitude and arithmetic tasks (see review above). Furthermore, impairments in attention and working memory could be a result of less grey matter volume in the frontal lobes, and therefore, negatively impact the development of numerical representation in the IPS, further impairing arithmetic performance. Differences in white matter volume adjacent to the para-hippocampal region might hinder the development of storing arithmetic facts into semantic memories. As a result, the volume of grey and white matter within the whole brain and specific regions that subserve cognitive processes might contribute to functional impairments. However, from this study, it remains unclear how the structural abnormalities found in children with DD underlie differences in neural activity found in fMRI studies. From this study alone, it remains unclear how coarse measures of grey and white matter density are related to specific abnormalities in white matter fiber tracts in children with DD.

Diffusion tensor imaging (DTI)

DTI is a non-invasive imaging tool that utilizes the direction and amount of water diffusion in the brain to infer about the microstructure of white matter. White matter consists of glial cells and myelinated axons that connect and transmit signals between different regions in the brain. Indirect measures of white matter integrity are optimal for investigating the relationship between brain microstructure and cognitive function. Diffusion of water in the brain can either be isotropic, indicating that water flows in all directions, or anisotropic, indicating that water flow is restricted to one major direction. Fractional anisotropy (FA) is a measure taken from a DTI scan that represents the degree of anisotropy in the brain. Diffusion that is isotropic has a value of 0, whereas diffusion that is fully anisotropic has a value of 1. FA is indicative of white matter integrity. A growing body of literature is beginning to uncover the relationships between white matter integrity and arithmetic abilities in both typically and atypically developing samples (Kucian et al., 2013; van Eimeren, Niogi, McCandliss, Holloway, & Ansari, 2008; Tsang, Dougherty, Deutsch, Wandell, & Ben-shachar, 2009; for a review, see also Matejko, 2014).

Research in typically developing children has found associations between FA and mathematical abilities in school-age children. In a study conducted by van Eimeren et al. (2008), FA in the left inferior longitudinal fasciculus (a fiber tract linking occipital and temporal lobes), as well as the left corona radiate, positively correlated with basic arithmetic performance (see Figure 1.4). Similarly, Tsang et al. (2009) found that FA in the left anterior superior longitudinal fasciculus, a fiber tract linking frontal, parietal and temporal lobes, positively correlated with arithmetic approximation skills. These findings are the first to demonstrate a link between white matter tracts within the brain's microstructure and arithmetic development. More specifically, greater FA, which is indicative of greater white matter integrity, is associated with better arithmetic performance. Additionally, they demonstrate that white matter tracts in the left hemisphere play an important role in the development of basic arithmetic skills. Taken together, arithmetic is a complex cognitive process that requires a network of brain regions, and therefore, the construction of intact and effective connections between task-related brain regions is necessary for the successful execution of basic arithmetic. Increased white matter integrity is associated with arithmetic abilities, however, the disruption of white matter tracts might lead to difficulties in

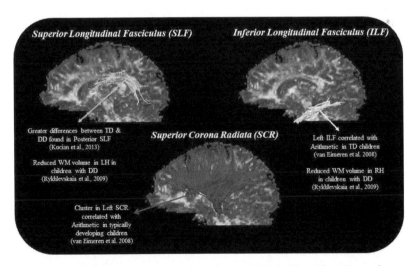

Figure 1.4 White matter tracts consistently associated with arithmetic performance in typically developing children, as well as fractional anisotropy (FA) deficits in children with DD.

Note: TD, typically developing; DD, developmental dyscalculia; WM, white matter; LH, left hemisphere; RH, right hemisphere.

arithmetic found in children with DD. Kucian and colleagues (2013) found lower FA in the left posterior SLF located near the IPS in 8–11-year-old children with DD compared to typically developing age-matched peers (see Figure 1.4). These findings are consistent with Tsang et al. (2009) who identified the SLF as a pertinent tract that connects the parietal lobe to precentral and frontal regions associated with approximate arithmetic among typically developing children. White matter deficiency may be associated with poor myelination (a process whereby white matter tracts become 'insulated' over developmental time allowing for progressively faster transmission of neuronal information) and atypical axonal development in children with DD.

In an effort to merge coarse measures of grey and white matter density and white matter fiber tracts, Rykhlevskaia and colleagues (2009) investigated the relationship between grey and white matter density measures using VBM, and the integrity of white matter tracts using DTI in children with DD compared to well-matched typical controls. The researchers found that several regions showed decreased grey matter volume in children with DD: bilateral parahippocampal gyrus, the left superior parietal lobule, right posterior IPS, in addition, bilateral precuneus, lateral occipital cortex, lingual gyrus and fusiform gyrus. Similar to Rotzer et al. (2008), Rykhlevskaia et al. found grey matter deficits in the right IPS; but, they also observed deficits in the left IPS and superior parietal lobule which has been implicated in the development of number sense and calculation abilities (Ansari, 2008). In contrast to the study conducted by Rotzer et al., white matter volume reductions were found in a large cluster connecting the right temporal-parietal cortices, this region showed overlapping clusters with the right inferior fronto-occipital fasciculus, forceps major of the splenium of the corpus callosum, the inferior longitudinal fasciculus, the corticospinal tract, superior longitudinal fasciculus and anterior thalamic radiation. In addition, white matter volume reductions were found in the left superior longitudinal fasciculus, left forceps major and the left anterior thalamic radiation. No clusters within grey or white matter showed greater volume in DD children compared to typical controls (Rykslevskaia et al., 2009). Using these white matter regions as a region of interest for the DTI analysis, FA was calculated and found to be significantly reduced in children with DD. Furthermore, FA in this region significantly correlated with arithmetic performance, but not mathematical reasoning, word reading or IQ. These findings suggest deficits in the white matter tracts were specific to arithmetic performance rather than general cognitive performance.

Limitations to structural neuroimaging methodology

The structural neuroimaging results in children with DD are limited and inconsistent making it difficult to pinpoint specific white matter tracts and grey matter abnormalities that account for arithmetic deficits in children with DD. Although DTI offers unique and novel approaches to explain the structural white matter connections in the brain, it is important to understand the limitations and challenges this methodology has to offer. First, it is challenging to interpret the direct biological referent of indirect quantitative measures of DTI such as FA (Johansen-Berg & Rushworth,

2009). There are many potential confounding factors, such as crossing fiber tracts, tract length and data quality that influence FA measures. Second, FA is a coarse measure of white matter integrity that does not allow for a fine-grained analysis of the microstructure at the axon or cortical layer. Using current techniques, researchers use indirect measures to hypothesize about the organization of white matter structures and their relation to brain function. Third, FA values are non-directional and, therefore, limit researchers' abilities to examine the direction of information transmission between grey matter regions through white matter tracts. And last, DTI does not explain whether deficits in white matter tracts are the cause of atypical functional activation in parietal regions associated with deficient numerical and arithmetic skills, or a consequence. That being said, DTI is a promising tool that affords researchers the opportunity to investigate further into the atypical neurological impairments found in children with DD, by investigating the integrity of white matter connections in the brain. Although DTI comes with challenges, further research is required to validate and extend the current state of knowledge surrounding the development of atypical brain structures in DD, using coarse measures of white matter and grey matter integrity, as well as activation that underlies cognitive impairments.

Conclusions and future directions

Developmental cognitive neuroscience is a relatively young scientific discipline that aims to better understand human development through the use of both behavioral and brain-imaging tools. Developmental cognitive neuroscience studies have been conducted to try to understand both typical and atypical development across a variety of domains. The aim of a developmental cognitive neuroscience approach is to understand how the brain enables developmental changes in cognitive functions and how such ontogenetic processes might go awry in children who go on to have developmental difficulties. In the present chapter, we review the contributions that developmental cognitive neuroscience research has made to our understanding of DD.

It is well known that there is significantly less research on developmental impairments of math abilities compared to the burgeoning literature on reading impairments (Gersten *et al.*, 2007) such as Developmental Dyslexia. This is true of behavioral studies but is even more striking when reviewing investigations into the neurobiology of DD. As is clear from the review above, the small number of studies that have investigated the neural correlates of DD at both the functional and structural level do not allow for a clear-cut consensus concerning the brain correlates of DD. Thus one of the key take-home messages from this review is that there currently does not exist a sufficient body of research to make definitive/explicit conclusions about the functional and structural neuronal mechanisms underlying DD.

Notwithstanding, the studies of both numerical magnitude processing and arithmetic reviewed above (the two areas within which most of the current cognitive neuroscience research on DD has been concentrated) have revealed that, consistent with predictions from the study of the brain circuitry in children and adults without DD, the parietal cortex shows both structural and functional abnormalities in neuroimaging studies comparing children with and without DD. However, the data reviewed above do not support the notion that DD is associated with the impairment of only one set of brain circuits (i.e. a module), since both structural and functional studies of numerical magnitude processing and arithmetic reveal that many other brain regions have been found to function differently between children with and without DD. The finding of structural and functional differences beyond the parietal lobe suggest that DD may be associated with the atypical development of a network of brain regions, a notion further supported by the findings of abnormalities in the white matter connecting the parietal and frontal areas of the brain.

Furthermore, the above review shows that there is great variability in specifically which brain regions differ between TD and DD children across studies. Such variability might arise from a number of factors, which might not be mutually exclusive, such as (a) the different tasks used by different research groups, (b) their definitions of DD, and (c) the age groups studied.

In order to get a better understanding of the variability across studies and thereby come to an understanding of the common regions, it is necessary to go beyond meta-analyses and conduct studies where children with DD are selected on the basis of strict classification criteria that are aligned with the DSM-V criteria. In addition, multiple different tasks should be used to enable within-subjects comparisons of the neuronal correlates of functions, such as symbolic and nonsymbolic numerical magnitude processing, arithmetic and working memory in order to understand how these are processed differently by the brains of children with DD compared to their TD controls. Moreover, children with DD need to be studied longitudinally using neuroimaging methodologies to better understand how atypical neuronal functions and structures become constructed over developmental time.

It is clear that much more research is needed to better understand how the brains of children with and without DD might differ. The use of cutting-edge neuroimaging methods, such as multivariate analysis tools, will undoubtedly help us to better understand to what extent DD is associated with a deficit in numerical magnitude representation or their access to them, as well as informing our understanding as to which children with DD fail to recruit brain circuits associated with arithmetic fact retrieval.

Beyond constraining our understanding of the causes of DD, a developmental cognitive neuroscience approach to the study of DD can also inform our understanding of diagnosis and remediation of DD. In the field of the study of Developmental Dyslexia, there are many studies that have been conducted to understand the neurobiological consequences of structured remediation programs (Meyler, Keller, Cherkassky, Gabrieli, & Just, 2008; Temple et al., 2003). These studies have revealed that remediations are associated with both normalization of activation as well as the engagement of neuronal circuits not typically associated with reading, which has been interpreted as reflecting the engagement of compensatory mechanisms. Similar studies should be conducted with DD children to understand the extent and limits of neuronal plasticity associated with attempts to remediate the behavioral consequences of DD.

Taken together, developmental cognitive neuroscience investigations of DD are very much in their infancy and few in number. Nevertheless, the above review shows that some interesting patterns are starting to emerge in the data and give us hope that in the near future we will have a more comprehensive understanding of how the brains of children with DD might differ from their typically developing peers. Most importantly, the present literature review has identified areas for future investigations, which should enhance the clarity of our understanding and therefore the constraint that developmental cognitive neuroscience will have on models of DD.

Ladislav Kosc (1970: 192) defined DD as: 'Developmental dyscalculia is a structural disorder of mathematical abilities which has its origin in a genetic or congenital disorder of those parts of the brain that are the direct anatomico-physiological substrate of the maturation of mathematical abilities adequate to age.' Nearly 45 years later we can say that DD is indeed associated with differences in neurophysiology, but that the precise parts of the brain disrupted in DD, how they interact, change over time and are affected by education is a formidable challenge for the next 45 years' of research into DD using a developmental cognitive neuroscience approach.

References

Alloway, T. P., Gathercole, S. E., Kirkwood, H., & Elliott, J. (2009). The cognitive and behavioral characteristics of children with low working memory. *Child Development, 80*(2), 606–21.

American Psychiatric Association. (2013). *Diagnostic and Statistical Manual of Mental Disorders* (5th ed.). Arlington, VA: American Psychiatric Publishing.

Ansari, D. (2008). Effects of development and enculturation on number representation in the brain. *Nature Reviews Neuroscience, 9*(4), 278–91.

Ansari, D., & Dhital, B. (2006). Age-related changes in the activation of the intraparietal sulcus during nonsymbolic magnitude processing: an event-related functional magnetic resonance imaging study. *Journal of Cognitive Neuroscience, 18*(11), 1820–8.

Ansari, D., Garcia, N., Lucas, E., Hamon, K., & Dhital, B. (2005). Neural correlates of symbolic number processing in children and adults. *Neuroreport, 16*(16), 1769–73. Retrieved from http://www.ncbi.nlm.nih.gov/pubmed/16237324

Arsalidou, M., & Taylor, M. J. (2011). Is 2+2=4? Meta-analyses of brain areas needed for numbers and calculations. *NeuroImage, 54*(3), 2382–93.

Ashkenazi, S., Rosenberg-Lee, M., Metcalfe, A. W. S., Swigart, A. G., & Menon, V. (2013). Visuo-spatial working memory is an important source of domain-general vulnerability in the development of arithmetic cognition. *Neuropsychologia, 51*(11), 2305–17.

Ashkenazi, S., Rosenberg-Lee, M., Tenison, C., & Menon, V. (2012). Weak task-related modulation and stimulus representations during arithmetic problem solving in children with developmental dyscalculia. *Developmental Cognitive Neuroscience, 2 Suppl. 1*, S152–66.

Berteletti, I., Prado, J., & Booth, J. R. (2014). Children with mathematical learning disability fail in recruiting verbal and numerical brain regions when solving simple multiplication problems. *Cortex, 57*, 43–55.

Boets, B., Beeck, H. P. Op De, Vandermosten, M., Scott, S. K., Gillebert, C. R., Mantini, D., Sunaert, S. (2013). Intact but less accessible phonetic representations in adults with dyslexia, *1251*.

Butterworth, B. (1999). *The Mathematical Brain*. London: Macmillan.

Butterworth, B. (2005). The development of arithmetical abilities. *Journal of Child Psychology and Psychiatry*, *46*(1), 3–18.

Cantlon, J. F., Brannon, E. M., Carter, E. J., & Pelphrey, K. A. (2006). Functional imaging of numerical processing in adults and 4-y-old children. *PLoS Biology*, *4*(5), e125.

Cho, S., Metcalfe, A. W., Young, C. B., Ryali, S., Geary, D. C., & Menon, V. (2012). Hippocampal-prefrontal engagement and dynamic causal interactions in the maturation of children's fact retrieval. *Journal of Cognitive Neuroscience*, *24*(9), 1849–66.

Davis, N., Cannistraci, C. J., Rogers, B. P., Gatenby, J. C., Fuchs, L. S., Anderson, A. W., & Gore, J. C. (2009). Aberrant functional activation in school age children at-risk for mathematical disability: a functional imaging study of simple arithmetic skill. *Neuropsychologia*, *47*(12), 2470–9.

De Smedt, B., Holloway, I. D., & Ansari, D. (2011). Effects of problem size and arithmetic operation on brain activation during calculation in children with varying levels of arithmetical fluency. *NeuroImage*, *57*(3), 771–81.

Dehaene, S. (1992). Varieties of numerical abilities. *Cognition*, *44*, 1–42.

Dehaene, S., & Cohen, L. (1991). Two mental calculation systems: a case study of severe acalculia with preserved approximation. *Neuropsychologia*, *29*(11), 1045–54. Retrieved from http://www.ncbi.nlm.nih.gov/pubmed/1723179

Dehaene, S., & Cohen, L. (1995). Towards an anatomical and functional model of number processing. *Mathematical Cognition*, *1*, 83–120.

Dehaene, S., & Cohen, L. (1997). Cerebral pathways for calculation: double dissociation between rote verbal quantitative knowledge of arithmetic. *Cortex*, *33*(2), 219–50.

Dehaene, S., Piazza, M., Pinel, P., & Cohen, L. (2003). Three parietal circuits for number processing. *Cognitive Neuropsychology*, *20*(3), 487–506.

Dehaene, D., Spelke, E., Pinel, P., Stanescu, R., & Tsivkin, S. (1999). Sources of mathematical thinking: behavioral and brain-imaging evidence. *Science*, *284*, 970–4.

Delazer, M., Benke, T. (1997). Arithmetic facts without meaning. *Cortex*, *33*(4), 697–710.

Dumontheil, I., & Klingberg, T. (2012). Brain activity during a visuospatial working memory task predicts arithmetical performance 2 years later. *Cerebral Cortex*, *22*(5), 1078–85.

Fias, W., Menon, V., & Szücs, D. (2013). Multiple components of developmental dyscalculia. *Trends in Neuroscience and Education*, *2*(2), 43–7.

Geary, D. C. (1993). Mathematical disabilities: cognitive, neuropsychological, and genetic components. *Psychological Bulletin*, *144*(2), 345–62.

Geary, D. C. (2004). Mathematics and learning disabilities. *Journal of Learning Disabilities*, *37*(1), 4–15.

Geary, D. C., Brown, S. C., & Samaranayake, V. A. (1991). Cognitive addition: a short longitudinal study of strategy choice and speed-of-processing differences in normal and mathematically disabled children. *Developmental Psychology*, *27*(5), 787–97.

Geary, D. C., Hoard, M. K., & Bailey, D. H. (2011). Fact retrieval deficits in low achieving children and children with mathematical learning disability. *Journal of Learning Disabilities*, *45*(4), 291–307.

Geary, D. C., Hoard, M. K., Byrd-Craven, J., & DeSoto, M. C. (2004). Strategy choices in simple and complex addition: contributions of working memory and counting knowledge for children with mathematical disability. *Journal of Experimental Child Psychology*, *88*(2), 121–51.

Gersten, R., Clarke, B., & Mazzocco, M. M. (2007). Historical and contemporary perspectives on mathematical learning disabilities. In D. B. Berch & M. M. M. Mazzocco (Eds.), *Why is Math so Hard for Some Children?*, (pp. 7–28). Grand Rapids, MI: Paul H. Brookes Publishing Co.

Grabner, R. H., Ansari, D., Koschutnig, K., Reishofer, G., Ebner, F., & Neuper, C. (2009). To retrieve or to calculate? Left angular gyrus mediates the retrieval of arithmetic facts during problem solving. *Neuropsychologia, 47*(2), 604–8.

Grabner, R. H., Ansari, D., Reishofer, G., Stern, E., Ebner, F., & Neuper, C. (2007). Individual differences in mathematical competence predict parietal brain activation during mental calculation. *NeuroImage, 38*(2), 346–56.

Henik, A., Rubinsten, O., & Ashkenazi, S. (2011). The 'where' and 'what' in developmental dyscalculia. *The Clinical Neuropsychologist, 25*(6), 989–1008.

Iuculano, T., Tang, J., Hall, C. W. B., & Butterworth, B. (2008). Core information processing deficits in developmental dyscalculia and low numeracy. *Developmental Science, 11*(5), 669–80.

Johansen-Berg, H., & Rushworth, M. F. S. (2009). Using diffusion imaging to study human connectional anatomy. *Annual Review of Neuroscience, 32*, 75–94.

Jordan, N. C., Hanich, L. B., & Kaplan, D. (2003). Arithmetic fact mastery in young children: a longitudinal investigation. *Journal of Experimental Child Psychology, 85*(2), 103–19.

Karagiannakis, G., Baccaglini-Frank, A., & Papadatos, Y. (2014). Mathematical learning difficulties subtypes classification. *Frontiers in Human Neuroscience, 8*(February), 57.

Kaufmann, L., Vogel, S. E., Starke, M., Kremser, C., Schocke, M., & Wood, G. (2009). Developmental dyscalculia: compensatory mechanisms in left intraparietal regions in response to nonsymbolic magnitudes. *Behavioral and Brain Functions : BBF, 5*, 35.

Kaufmann, L., Wood, G., Rubinsten, O., & Henik, A. (2011). Meta-analyses of developmental fMRI studies investigating typical and atypical trajectories of number processing and calculation. *Developmental Neuropsychology, 36*(6), 763–87.

Klingberg, T., Forssberg, H., & Westerberg, H. (2002). Increased brain activity in frontal and parietal cortex underlies the development of visuospatial working memory capacity during childhood. *Journal of Cognitive Neuroscience, 14*(1), 1–10.

Kosc, L. (1970). Psychology and psychopathology of mathematical abilities. *Studia Psychologica, 12*, 159–62.

Kucian, K., Ashkenazi, S. S., Hänggi, J., Rotzer, S., Jäncke, L., Martin, E., & von Aster, M. (2013). Developmental dyscalculia: a dysconnection syndrome? *Brain Structure & Function.*

Kucian, K., Loenneker, T., Dietrich, T., Dosch, M., Martin, E., & von Aster, M. (2006). Impaired neural networks for approximate calculation in dyscalculic children: a functional MRI study. *Behavioral and Brain Functions : BBF, 2*, 31.

Landerl, K., Bevan, A., & Butterworth, B. (2004). Developmental dyscalculia and basic numerical capacities: a study of 8–9-year-old students. *Cognition, 93*(2), 99–125.

Lemer, C., Dehaene, S., Spelke, E., & Cohen, L. (2003) Approximate quantities and exact number words: dissociable systems. *Neuropsychologia, 41*(14), 1942–58.

Matejko, A. (2014). White matter counts: brain connections help us do 2+2. *Frontiers for Young Minds, 2*, 19. Available from: http://kids.frontiersin.org/articles/34/white_matter_counts/

Mazzocco, M. M. M., Devlin, K. T., & McKenney, S. J. (2008). Is it a fact? Timed arithmetic performance of children with mathematical learning disabilities (MLD) varies as a function of how MLD is defined. *Developmental Neuropsychology, 33*(3), 318–44.

Mazzocco, M. M. M., & Myers, G. F. (2003). Complexities in identifying and defining mathematics learning disability in the primary school-age years. *Annals of Dyslexia, 53*(1), 218–53.

McLean, J. F., & Hitch, G. J. (1999). Working memory impairments in children with specific arithmetic learning difficulties, *Journal of Experimental Child Psychology, 74*(3), 240–60.

Meyler, A., Keller, T. A., Cherkassky, V. L., Gabrieli, J. D. E., & Just, M. A. (2008). Modifying the brain activation of poor readers during sentence comprehension with extended remedial instruction: a longitudinal study of neuroplasticity. *Neuropsychologia, 46*, 2580–92.

Moyer, R. S., & Landauer, T. K. (1967). Time required for judgements of numerical inequality. *Nature*, *215*(109), 1519–20.

Munakata, Y., Casey, B. J., & Diamond, A. (2004). Developmental cognitive neuroscience: progress and potential. *Trends in Cognitive Sciences*, *8*(3), 122–8.

Mur, M., Bandettini, P. A., & Kriegeskorte, N. (2009). Revealing representational content with pattern-information fMRI: an introductory guide. *Social Cognitive and Affective Neuroscience*, *4*(1), 101–9.

Mussolin, C., De Volder, A., Gtrandin, C., Schlogel, X., Nassogne, M.C., & Noel, M.P. (2009). Neural correlates of symbolic number comparison in developmental dyscalculia. *Journal of Cognitive Neuroscience*, *22*(5), 860–74.

Nieder, A., & Dehaene, S. (2009). Representation of number in the brain. *Annual Review of Neuroscience*, *32*, 185–208.

Passolunghi, M. C., & Mammarella, I. C. (2012). Selective spatial working memory impairment in a group of children with mathematics learning disabilities and poor problem-solving skills. *Journal of Learning Disabilities*, *45*(4), 341–50.

Peng, P., & Fuchs, D. (2014). A meta-analysis of working memory deficits in children with learning difficulties: is there a difference between verbal domain and numerical domain? *Journal of Learning Disabilities* 1–18.

Pinel, P., Dehaene, S., Rivière, D., & LeBihan, D. (2001). Modulation of parietal activation by semantic distance in a number comparison task. *NeuroImage*, *14*(5), 1013–26.

Price, G. R., & Ansari, D. (2013). *Developmental Dyscalculia. Handbook of clinical neurology* (1st ed., Vol. 111, pp. 241–4). Elsevier B.V.

Price, G. R., Holloway, I., Räsänen, P., Vesterinen, M., & Ansari, D. (2007). Impaired parietal magnitude processing in developmental dyscalculia. *Current Biology: CB*, *17*(24), R1042–3.

Rivera, S. M., Reiss, A. L., Eckert, M. A., & Menon, V. (2005). Developmental changes in mental arithmetic: evidence for increased functional specialization in the left inferior parietal cortex. *Cerebral Cortex*, *15*(11), 1779–90.

Rotzer, S., Kucian, K., Martin, E., von Aster, M., Klaver, P., & Loenneker, T. (2008). Optimized voxel-based morphometry in children with developmental dyscalculia. *NeuroImage*, *39*(1), 417–22.

Rotzer, S., Loenneker, T., Kucian, K., Martin, E., Klaver, P., & von Aster, M. (2009). Dysfunctional neural network of spatial working memory contributes to developmental dyscalculia. *Neuropsychologia*, *47*(13), 2859–65.

Rousselle, L., & Noël, M.-P. (2007). Basic numerical skills in children with mathematics learning disabilities: a comparison of symbolic vs non-symbolic number magnitude processing. *Cognition*, *102*(3), 361–95.

Rykhlevskaia, E., Uddin, L. Q., Kondos, L., & Menon, V. (2009). Neuroanatomical correlates of developmental dyscalculia: combined evidence from morphometry and tractography. *Frontiers in Human Neuroscience*, *3*(November), 51, 1–15.

Shalev, R. S. (2004). Developmental dyscalculia. *Journal of Child Neurology*, *19*, 765–71.

Skagerlund, K., & Träff, U. (2014). Number processing and heterogeneity of developmental dyscalculia: subtypes with different cognitive profiles and deficits. *Journal of Learning Disabilities*, 1–15.

Soltesz, F., Szücs, D., Dekany, J., Markus, A., & Csepe, V. (2007). A combined event-related potential and neuropsychological investigation of developmental dyscalculia. *Neuroscience Letters*, *417*, 181–6.

Szücs, D., Devine, A., Soltesz, F., Nobes, A., & Gabriel, F. (2013). Developmental dyscalculia is related to visuo-spatial memory and inhibition impairment. *Cortex; A Journal Devoted to the Study of the Nervous System and Behavior*, *49*(10), 2674–88.

Temple, E., Deutsch, G. K., Poldrack, R. A., Miller, S. L., Tallal, P., Merzenich, M. M., & Gabrieli, J. D. E. (2003). Neural deficits in children with dyslexia ameliorated by behavioral remediation: evidence from functional MRI. *Proceedings of the National Academy of Sciences of the United States of America*, *100*(5), 2860–5.

Tsang, J. M., Dougherty, R. F., Deutsch, G. K., Wandell, B. A., & Ben-shachar, M. (2009). Frontoparietal white matter diffusion properties predict mental arithmetic skills in children. *Proceedings of the National Academy of Sciences of the United States of America, 106*(52), 22546–51.

Van Eimeren, L., Niogi, S. N., McCandliss, B. D., Holloway, I. D., & Ansari, D. (2008). White matter microstructures underlying mathematical abilities in children. *Neuroreport, 19*(11), 1117–21.

Warrington, E. K. (1982). The fractionation of arithmetic skills. A single study. *Quarterly Journal of Experimental Psychology, 34*, 31–51.

2

Number difficulties in young children
Deficits in core number?

Robert A. Reeve and Sarah Gray

With some exceptions the diagnosis of developmental dyscalculia (DD) depends on computation test performance, which means in practice that a formal diagnosis is delayed until after the beginning of formal education. Moreover, the fact that a diagnosis is often based on an arbitrary cut-point on a standardised test (e.g., below the 10th percentile) is of concern (Butterworth, 2005a). DSM IV suggests DD prevalence rates of 2%; however, recent estimates suggest prevalence rates of 6.5% or above (Butterworth, 2010). Children with DD have difficulty acquiring number concepts, exhibit confusion over maths symbols, lack a grasp of numbers and have problems learning and remembering number facts. Little is known, however, about the origins of DD or its manifestation in infancy or preschool periods. Some claim that its origins lie in core number deficits (i.e., deficits in non-symbolic approximate magnitude and/or small quantity representations). These abilities are of particular interest diagnostically because they do not depend on formal education and can be assessed relatively early in life. We suggest that a defensible account of DD awaits a better understanding of the significance of core number competences in the early years.

In this chapter we review research on young children's core number deficits as a possible account of young children's number difficulties. We begin by describing the core number hypothesis, following which we review contemporary research findings on core number in infancy and preschool children. We then briefly review other neuro-cognitive indices of early number difficulties that might need to be taken into account in the diagnosis of young children with number difficulties.

Core number hypothesis

The abilities to identify, order and compare quantities are considered core aspects of numerical cognition (Berch, 2005; Butterworth, 1999, 2005a, 2005b, 2010; Desoete, Roeyers, & De Clercq, 2004; Gersten, Jordan, & Flojo, 2005; Laski & Siegler, 2007).

Enumerating visual arrays of dots or comparing two quantities/numbers are used to study these abilities. Number/quantity comparison tasks assess the speed and accuracy with which the relative magnitude of two numerical values is identified (e.g., "which quantity/number is larger"). Number/quantities that are closer in magnitude are judged more slowly and less accurately than those that are more distant in magnitude (referred to originally as the symbolic distance effect: Moyer & Landauer, 1967). Performance on number comparison tasks using number symbols (e.g., Arabic digits) or arrays of dots is associated with arithmetic competence (Holloway & Ansari, 2009; Mazzocco, Feigenson & Halberda, 2011). Mazzocco, Feigenson and Halberda (2011), for example, found that accuracy in comparing two arrays of large numbers of dots correlates with measures of school arithmetic in the primary/elementary school years; and Piazza and colleagues (2010) found that children identified as dyscalculics, having a congenital difficulty in learning arithmetic, were significantly less accurate than age-matched controls in comparing magnitudes.

Number comparison abilities have been studied developmentally (Baker et al., 2002; Chard et al., 2005; Clark & Shinn, 2004; Geary, Hoard & Hamson, 1999; Geary, Hamson & Hoard, 2000; Gersten et al., 2005; Jordan, Kaplan, Nabors Olah, & Locuniak, 2006; Locuniak & Jordan, 2008; Mazzocco & Thompson, 2005; Reeve, Reynolds, Humberstone, & Butterworth, 2012; Shalev, Manor, Auerbach, & Gross-Tsur, 1998; Shalev, Manor, & Gross-Tsur, 1997, 2005; Silver, Pennett, Black, Fair, & Balise, 1999). Different number distance effects (different NC slopes) have been observed in children with maths learning deficits (Mussolin, Mejias, & Noël, 2010; Reeve et al., 2012; Rousselle & Noël, 2007), and comorbid visuo-spatial deficits (Bachot, Gevers, Fias, & Roeyers, 2005). Faster and more accurate judgments of numerical magnitudes may thus reflect a growing understanding of cardinal relationships, improvements in transcoding, and automaticity in accessing numerical information (Girelli, Lucangelli, & Butterworth, 2000; Rubinsten, Henik, Berger, & Shahar-Shalev, 2002).

Several groups have found that difficulty in reporting accurately the number of dots in an array is also a marker of dyscalculia in school children (Koontz & Berch, 1996; Landerl, Bevan, & Butterworth, 2004; Reeve et al., 2012). The apparent failure to label the cardinal value of small numerosities without counting (known as subitising) has been implicated in several cognitive disorders and is associated with dyscalculia. Subitising deficits have mostly been associated with right parietal disruptions, particularly the intraparietal sulcus. These disorders include Turner's syndrome (TS) (Bruandet, Molko, Cohen, & Dehaene, 2004), cerebral palsy (CP) (Arp & Fagard, 2005; Arp, Taranne, & Fagard, 2006), Velocardiofacial syndrome (VCFS – also known as Chromosome 22q11.2 Deletion syndrome, or DS22q11.2) (De Smedt et al., 2007; Simon, Bearden, McDonald-McGinn, & Zackai, 2005; Simon et al., 2008), Fragile X syndrome (FXS), and Williams (WS) syndrome (Mazzocco & Hanich, 2010; Paterson, Girelli, Butterworth, & Karmiloff-Smith, 2006). Subitising impairments have also been observed in individuals with acquired Gerstmann's syndrome (Cipolotti, Butterworth, & Denes, 1991; Lemer, Dehaene, Spelke, & Cohen, 2003), who appear to count individual items in arrays of less than four and are poor calculators. Similarly, children who show a constant linear RT increase with no point of discontinuity when enumerating successive numerosities (i.e., who are not subitising small numerosities), are also very poor at arithmetic (Arp & Fagard, 2005; Arp et al., 2006; Koontz & Berch, 1996; Landerl et al., 2004; Reeve et al., 2012).

We suggest that object enumeration and number comparison may be early markers of number disability in young children which are relatively independent of school-based experiences. In what follows, we review what is known about these two core number abilities in the infancy and preschool period.

Core number in infancy

Evidence of numerical processing in preverbal human infants is well documented and provides support for the two core number systems. Infants' ability to discriminate difference between two non-symbolic quantities (i.e., sets of objects) has been found in several paradigms: habituation (Xu & Spelke, 2000), cross-modal discrimination (Izard, Sann, Spelke, & Streri, 2009), numerical change detection (Starr, Libertus, & Brannon, 2013a, 2013b). Infants' discrimination abilities are less precise than those of older children, but their precision increases over the first year of life. For instance, Izard and colleagues showed that newborns (49-hour-old neonates) could discriminate between two numerosities presented in different modalities (i.e., visual and auditory) that differed by a ratio of 3:1; and could discriminate between numerosity ratios of 2:1 at 6 months (Xu & Spelke, 2000), and ratios of 3:2 at 10 months old, (Xu & Arriaga, 2007). Moreover, across-modality discrimination suggests infants possess something akin to an abstract representation of quantity, which contradicts the view that infants rely on perceptual features that correlate with number (e.g., surface area) to discriminate between sets on visual properties (Opfer & Siegler, 2012).

Infants can also represent small numbers of objects precisely, with an upper-bound of three items. For instance, findings from manual search and ordinal choice paradigms suggest that infants can precisely represent and keep track of sets of 1, 2, and 3 objects, but not 4 objects or larger (Feigenson & Carey, 2003, 2005; Feigenson, Carey, & Hauser, 2002). Recently, vanMarle (2013) showed that infants (10–12 months) can discriminate between two small quantities (1 vs 2), or large (4 vs 8), but could not discriminate between a small and large quantity even when the ratio between them was favourable (2 vs 8) (however, see Starr et al., 2013a, 2013b). VanMarle (2013) suggested that infants possess both a precise small-number and an approximate large-number system consistent with the core number hypothesis for two distinct number representation systems.

Neurological research has also shed light on infants' numerical processing. For instance, Hyde and Spelke (2011) found the event related potentials (ERPs) in 6–7.5-month-olds as they viewed large sets of dots evoked ratio-dependent responses in the parietal regions, whereas small numbers evoked occipital-temporal responses. Interestingly, these neurological responses are similar to those observed in adults (Ansari, Dhital, & Siong, 2006; Hyde & Spelke, 2009).

There are clear similarities in the core number abilities of infants and older children, which suggests a developmental continuity between earlier and later number development. Indeed, Starr et al. (2013b) showed that 6-month-olds' numerical discrimination abilities predicted their standardised maths score, number word knowledge, and comparison abilities at 3.5 years of age. This is an important finding since it provides direct evidence that infant quantitative competencies are associated with later core number abilities, as well as providing support for the hypothesis that infant quantitative competencies may be associated with later numerical abilities. Nevertheless, in the Starr et al. study, infants' approximate number acuity accounted for only a small proportion of variance in number abilities at 3.5 years, which suggests that other competencies (e.g., general cognitive competencies, experiences), may also scaffold maths development. As yet though, we know little about the predictive value of infants' precise small-number representations for later number abilities.

Core number abilities in preschoolers

Several studies show that preschoolers' magnitude comparison abilities are related to concurrent (Bonny & Lourenco, 2013; Libertus, Feigenson, & Halberda, 2011) and future (Libertus, Feigenson, & Halberda, 2013a, 2013b; Mazzocco et al., 2011) maths achievement (as assessed by standardised maths tests). Preschoolers' approximate magnitude representations are usually assessed using non-symbolic magnitude comparison tasks, which require them to judge which of two magnitude arrays (e.g., sets of dots, rectangles) is larger. Similar to infants, preschoolers' magnitude comparison abilities show ratio effects, with magnitude discrimination abilities increasing throughout the preschool years: 3-year-olds are able to discriminate 3:4 ratio arrays, while 5-year-olds can discriminate 5:6 ratios (Halberda & Feigenson, 2008).

Several factors caution against drawing strong conclusions about the uniqueness of preschoolers' magnitude comparison abilities as an index of their maths ability (De Smedt, Noël, Gilmore, & Ansari, 2013). Findings vary as a function of a number of factors (e.g., age, IQ, response time, vocabulary, attention, memory, inhibition: see Chu, vanMarle, & Geary, 2013; Fuhs & McNeil, 2013; Libertus et al., 2013b; Mazzocco et al., 2011), suggesting that the relationship between preschoolers' magnitude comparison abilities and maths competence may be only part of the story.

Fuhs and McNeil (2013), for example, found that magnitude comparison abilities no longer explained variance in preschoolers' (44 to 71 months) maths competence when response inhibition was taken into account. Response inhibition, an executive function, has been shown to be related to young children's maths (Clark, Sheffield, Wiebe, & Espy, 2012; Espy et al., 2004), and may influence magnitude comparison abilities because successful performance depends on an ability to ignore competing non-numerical features (e.g., size and surface area of stimuli). Fuhs and McNeil propose that inhibitory control may account for the association between magnitude comparison abilities in several studies that did not assess this particular executive function (Bonny & Lourenco, 2013; Libertus et al., 2011, 2013a, 2013b; Mazzocco et al., 2011). Nevertheless, Fuhs and McNeil's data were obtained with children from low-income homes, who may have few everyday maths activities: indeed, everyday experiences are considered important in facilitating approximate number development (Butterworth, 2010). Nevertheless, the failure to find a relationship between magnitude comparison and maths abilities, after controlling for executive functions, has been found by Chu et al.(2013) with preschoolers at risk of maths learning difficulties, and by Gilmore et al. (2013) with school-aged children (however, see Lonnemann, Linkersdörfer, Hasselhorn, & Lindberg, 2013). While the findings of Fuhs and McNeil (2013), Chu et al. (2013) and of Gilmore et al. (2013) would appear to contradict a unique core number claim (i.e., core number differences uniquely predict number abilities), it is possible that the approximate number system and executive functions jointly support maths development.

Precise small-number representations in preschoolers are most often assessed using dot enumeration tasks. Small sets (typically n ≤ 4) are enumerated accurately and rapidly with a relative flat response time slope (known as the subitising range), while larger sets (n ≥4) are enumerated more slowly, and enumeration is more error-prone and characterised by a steeper RT slope (Chi & Klahr, 1975; Reeve et al., 2012; Schleifer & Landerl, 2011). This pattern of performance is similar for preschoolers, older children, and adults, albeit preschoolers display slower response times on average (Chi & Klahr, 1975; Klahr & Wallace, 1976). Dot enumeration signatures may be based on up to four parameters: the subitising range, the RT slope of the subitising range, the γ-intercept of the subitising RT slope, and the RT slope of the counting range (see Reeve et al., 2012). The development of these performance parameters in the preschool years has not been thoroughly investigated; although it is claimed that preschoolers' subitising range increases from 2–3 dots at 2 years of age to 3–4 dots by age 4 (Starkey & Cooper, 1995).

Similar to research with infants, the relationship between dot enumeration abilities and preschoolers' maths is less studied than their magnitude comparison abilities, which is surprising given the relationships between dot enumeration abilities and maths in kindergarten (Kroesbergen, Van Luit, Van Lieshout, Van Loosbroek, & Van de Rijt, 2009; Yun, Havard, Farran, & Lipsey, 2011) and school children (Desoete & Grégoire, 2006; Fischer, Gebhardt, & Hartnegg, 2008; Fuchs et al., 2010b; Obersteiner, Reiss, & Ufer, 2013; Penner-Wilger et al., 2007; Reeve et al., 2012; Reigosa-Crespo et al., 2012; Träff, 2013). Nevertheless, individual differences in preschoolers' subitising signatures (subitising range and RT slope) (Gray & Reeve, 2014; Starkey & Cooper, 1995) are related to maths abilities. Gray and Reeve (2014), for example, found that a poor subitising profile (smaller range, steeper slope, slower RTs) uniquely predicted poorer non-verbal addition performance in preschoolers (42 to 57 months), after working memory, basic response time, and response inhibition had been taken into account. Gray and Reeve found that inhibition contributed to predicting addition ability and subitising, while working memory contributed to subtraction ability. These findings support the claim that both core (in this case, dot enumeration) and general cognitive abilities play a role in early maths abilities.

Several studies have investigated the significance of symbolic magnitude comparison and precise small-number abilities in school children's computation skills, and have found that both measures predict number abilities (Fuchs et al., 2010a, 2010b; Obersteiner et al., 2013; Reeve et al., 2012; Reigosa-Crespo et al., 2012; Träff,

2013). Moreover, several studies show that precise small-number ability is the better predictor of school computation (addition and subtraction), compared to symbolic magnitude comparison abilities (Fuchs et al., 2010a; Reeve et al., 2012; Reigosa-Crespo et al., 2012). However, it is possible that the two core abilities might be important for different types of computation skills (see Reigosa-Crespo et al., 2012). It also seems likely that the diagnostic significance of the two core abilities changes across development (Reigosa-Crespo et al., 2012). Nevertheless, it remains to be seen how small precise number and magnitude comparison abilities in combination are associated with maths in preschoolers, and how the relative contributions of the two core abilities change across the preschool years and beyond (Gray & Reeve, submitted).

Standardised measures of maths competence (e.g., TEMA-3; Ginsburg & Baroody, 2003) are frequently used to assess preschoolers' maths skills (e.g., Fuhs & McNeil, 2013; Libertus et al., 2011, 2013a, 2013b), which make it difficult to determine the specific maths skills associated with the different core number abilities (De Smedt et al., 2013; Lonnemann et al., 2013; Vanbinst, Ghesquière, & De Smedt, 2012). Standardised tests assess a range of maths skills, some of which are dependent on formal instruction. Aggregating performance measures across a range of different types of problems further makes it difficult to identify specific maths difficulties. Given it is possible that the two core abilities scaffold different maths skills (Reigosa-Crespo et al., 2012), aggregated maths scores may misrepresent the relationship (see Lonnemann et al., 2013). We suggest that a more specific investigation of the associations between magnitude comparison and dot enumeration skills and specific maths skills would provide insight into the role core abilities play in early maths development.

We also need to better understand the diagnostic significance of non-symbolic and symbolic magnitude comparison tasks. It has been suggested that the non-symbolic approximate number/quantity system provides a structure for children to map number symbols onto pre-existing magnitude representations (Opfer & Siegler, 2012). This mapping provides children with an ability to estimate positions of numbers on number lines, estimate quantities, categorise numbers by size, remember numbers, and to estimate and learn answers to arithmetic problems (Opfer & Siegler, 2012). For instance, when learning arithmetic, young children may rely on approximate number representations to grasp the relative magnitudes of addends, and determine the appropriate magnitude of solutions (Lonnemann et al., 2013).

Although many researchers suggest that approximate number representations support symbolic development; others suggest that it might support very early symbolic number learning, but that the non-symbolic system becomes less important once number symbols are acquired (Holloway & Ansari, 2009; Lyons & Beilock, 2011). Indeed, Libertus *et al.* (2013b) showed that preschoolers' non-symbolic magnitude comparison abilities predicted informal maths abilities (including counting, comparing numerals, arithmetic with objects, and cardinality tasks), but not formal maths abilities (numeral literacy, arithmetic fact retrieval and mental and written calculation). Similarly, Chu et al. (2013) found that preschoolers' symbolic number skills (e.g., knowledge of Arabic digits and number words and their cardinal meaning) better predicted maths learning abilities than their non-symbolic magnitude comparison abilities. In general, findings suggest that non-symbolic magnitude comparison abilities are associated with very early number skills, but not with more formal maths abilities.

There are several hypotheses about how precise small-number representations scaffold early maths ability. Several studies have shown that young children can subitise, or accurately name small sets, before they can reliably count (Benoit, Lehalle, & Jouen, 2004; Fuson & Hall, 1983; Starkey & Cooper, 1995), which has been regarded as evidence that subitising has developmental precedence over counting, and may in fact support counting development. Subitising allows children to view the whole and the elements of a set simultaneously, and by labelling and counting these sets, children may begin to acquire the cardinal meanings of number words and the purpose of counting (Benoit, Lehalle, & Jouen, 2004; Carey, 2001; Clements, 1999; Klahr & Wallace, 1976; Starkey & Cooper, 1995; Wynn, 1992). Subitising may also be important for learning addition and subtraction concepts, by allowing children to represent the effect of transformations on small sets (Baroody, Lai, Li, & Baroody, 2009; Carey, 2001; Clements, 1999; Gray & Reeve, 2014; Hunting, 2003; Jung, Hartman, Smith, & Wallace, 2013). It is unclear why the ability to subitise remains a diagnostic predictor of arithmetic skill beyond the small numbers (Piazza, 2010).

Nevertheless, there is evidence that subitising abilities predict maths abilities across the primary/elementary school period, and might well be a better diagnostic measure of maths abilities than magnitude comparison abilities (Reeve et al., 2012). Moreover, Gray and Reeve (submitted) found that dot enumeration ability, and subitising in particular, is a better predictor of preschool children's maths abilities than magnitude comparison abilities. They examined a range of preschool maths abilities, including counting, symbolic number, and arithmetic skills, as well as core number and executive function abilities (working memory and response inhibition) to establish whether different combinations of core number abilities and general cognitive functions contribute to the prediction of different maths abilities. Gray and Reeve show that precise small-number abilities were a strong predictor of most maths abilities assessed, over and above magnitude comparison abilities, and cognitive functions. Their findings also showed that subitising and small-number enumeration efficiency more generally predicted emerging maths abilities. Overall, these findings provide support for the claim that precise small-number abilities are a diagnostic marker of preschoolers' emerging maths competence.

Magnitudes comparison and precise small-number enumeration abilities are claimed to be markers of early maths competence; however, with some exceptions (see Gray & Reeve, submitted) the relative contributions of these abilities for preschool maths have not been examined. It is of diagnostic importance to determine how these abilities are related to each other and to the development of maths abilities in general. Many questions remain unanswered. Is one measure a better predictor of maths than the other? Do they predict the same or different kinds of maths abilities?

What is the relationship between the two core number abilities and other cognitive abilities? We briefly consider some answers to the latter question next.

Cognitive functions

As already noted, some researchers have examined the relative impact of general cognitive functions, over and above contributions of core number abilities, for pre-school children's maths skills. It is probable that general abilities are more important for preschoolers' maths abilities than they are for school-aged children, since maths tasks may be more cognitively demanding for preschoolers (Clark et al., 2012; Fuhs & McNeil, 2013). This claim is supported by neuroimaging evidence which shows that young children rely more heavily on pre-frontal brain regions, associated with executive functioning, when first learning maths; children do not display specialised maths processing regions until later in development, when number knowledge has been acquired (Houdé, Rossi, Lubin, & Joliot, 2010). Several researchers (Fuchs et al., 2010a, 2010b; Östergren & Träff, 2013; Träff, 2013; von Aster & Shalev, 2007) propose that general cognitive abilities (e.g., working memory) support the learning of new maths concepts by facilitating the integration of core number representations with symbolic number systems. While preschoolers might have a core number platform for acquiring number concepts, general cognitive functions may assist by helping children respond to changing task demands, maintain information in memory (working memory), and inhibit distracting inputs (inhibition) (Clark et al., 2012). We should not discount the possibility that different cognitive functions might be important for different maths skills, and their relative contributions may change across preschool and school periods. Furthermore, the relative contributions of relevant abilities might differ depending on a child's unique developmental trajectory: recent evidence suggests the relationships between core number abilities, general abilities and maths is non-linear in preschoolers (Bonny & Lourenco, 2013; Gray & Reeve, 2014). The relationship between patterns of core number and general cognitive abilities in maths development is complex and undoubtedly will be the subject of much future research.

Spatial abilities

A question of some interest is whether core number representation is maths domain specific or part of a more general spatial magnitude representation system (Lourenco, Bonny, Ferdandez, & Rao, 2012; Walsh, 2003). Associations between numerical magnitude representations and space are commonly invoked, with some researchers proposing numerical magnitudes are represented spatially along a mental number line (e.g., Dehaene, Piazza, Pinel, & Cohen, 2003; Opfer & Siegler, 2012). Precise small-number representations have also been proposed to depend on a visual system that allows individuals to track small numbers of objects in space (e.g., Chesney & Haladjian, 2011; Piazza, 2010). Evidence of an association between numbers and space in older children and adults comes from demonstrations of the so-called SNARC effect, in which incongruent spatial cues interfere with numerical processing, and vice versa (see Hubbard, Piazza, Pinel, & Dehaene, 2005). Pinel, Piazza, Le Bihan, and Dehaene (2004) showed that parietal brain regions activated during numerical magnitude comparison overlapped with areas activated when discriminating size and luminance. The joint deficits of space and number commonly observed in patients with Gerstmann's syndrome, have also been suggested as evidence of a shared underlying mechanism (Henik, Rubinsten, & Ashkenazi, 2011). Moreover, evidence shows spatial processing difficulties are associated with maths abilities in children (de Hevia, Vallar, & Girelli, 2008; Opfer, Thompson, & Furlong, 2010; von Aster & Shalev, 2007), and adults (Lourenco et al., 2012). These findings raise the possibility that spatial ability per se might underlie the association between core number and maths abilities.

It is of course possible that the association between number and spatial processes reflects the anatomical proximity of these systems within the IPS (Butterworth, 2005a; Dehaene et al., 2003; Gracia-Bafalluy & Noël, 2008; Hubbard et al., 2005). The IPS has been implicated in cognitive processes besides number and space, including finger-related skills (grasping and pointing) and attention, which have also been shown to be associated with maths (Chinello, Cattani, Bonfiglioli, Dehaene, & Piazza, 2013). Given their anatomical connections, these processes may mature at the same rate and share developmental trajectories (Chinello et al., 2013), while also sharing impairment in the event of parietal lesions (Hubbard et al., 2005).

It is also possible that the associations between number and space are the product of culture-based training aimed at creating links between these domains; such as instruction on the number line, and using fingers and objects to count and solve problems (see Chinello et al., 2013). It is difficult to disentangle the effects of culture-based training given that most research examining number-space relations focuses on formally educated children and adults (e.g., see de Hevia et al., 2008). Recently, Chinello and colleagues (2013) investigated the relationship between magnitude comparison, visuospatial and finger gnosis abilities in adults and preschoolers. Their findings suggest that number, space and finger skills are related (i.e., they share common developmental trajectories) but are functionally distinct (at least partially) prior to formal education, and segregate further throughout development and into adulthood (Chinello et al., 2013). It is possible that the ability to represent one's own fingers and use them in maths tasks facilitates the link between number and space in young children, and might even assist mapping symbols onto pre-existing spatial magnitude representations (Fayol & Seron, 2005; Reeve & Humberstone, 2011). Nevertheless, the precise nature of the links between core number, early maths, space and finger representations requires further elucidation (Butterworth, 1999; Noël, 2005).

Final comments

It is evident that we need to more fully understand the factors that scaffold early maths development prior to formal instruction and ipso facto provide a diagnostic framework for assessing young children's maths abilities. Besides the core number issues discussed herein, other factors likely support symbolic maths development (e.g., the role of language, everyday maths experiences, and general cognitive functions). Moreover, several researchers have emphasised the importance of assessing children's ability to attend to number events in their environment (Butterworth & Reeve, 2012; Gelman, 2000, 2009; Gelman & Williams, 1998; Hannula & Lehtinen, 2005; Hannula, Lepola, & Lehtinen, 2010; Hannula, Rasanen, & Lehtinen, 2007), which requires attention. In conclusion, there is little doubt that recent research assessing the role of core number competencies for early maths development shows great promise, especially as a diagnostic measure of children's maths difficulties. Nevertheless, we must modestly acknowledge that we are at the beginning of a critical research agenda designed to better understand the origins of children's maths difficulties, and much remains to be done.

References

Ansari, D., Dhital, B., & Siong, S. C. (2006). Parametric effects of numerical distance on the intraparietal sulcus during passive viewing of rapid numerosity changes. *Brain Research*, 1067, 181–188.

Arp, S., & Fagard, J. (2005). What impairs subitising in cerebral palsied children? *Developmental Psychobiology*, 47(1), 89–102.

Arp, S., Taranne, P., & Fagard, J. (2006). Global perception of small numerosities (subitising) in cerebral-palsied children. *Journal of Clinical and Experimental Neuropsychology*, 28(3), 405–419.

Bachot, J., Gevers, W., Fias, W., & Roeyers, H. (2005). Number sense in children with visuospatial disabilities: Orientation of the mental number line. *Psychology Science*, 47, 172–183.

Baker, S., Gersten, R., Flojo, J., Katz, R., Chard, D., & Clarke, B. (2002). Preventing mathematics difficulties in young children: Focus on effective screening of early number sense delays (Tech. Rep. No. 0305). Eugene, OR: Pacific Institutes for Research.

Baroody, A. J., Lai, M., Li, X., & Baroody, A. E. (2009). Preschoolers' understanding of subtraction-related principles. *Mathematical Thinking and Learning*, 11(1–2), 41–60.

Benoit, L., Lehalle, H., & Jouen, F. (2004). Do young children acquire number words through subitising or counting? *Cognitive Development*, 19(3), 291–307.

Berch, D. B. (2005). Making sense of number sense: Implications for children with mathematical disabilities. *Journal of Learning Disabilities*, 38(4), 333–339.

Bonny, J. W., & Lourenco, S. F. (2013). The approximate number system and its relation to early math achievement: Evidence from the preschool years. *Journal of Experimental Child Psychology*, 114(3), 375–388.

Bruandet, M., Molko, N., Cohen, L., & Dehaene, S. (2004). A cognitive characterization of dyscalculia in Turner syndrome. *Neuropsychologia*, 42, 288–298.

Butterworth, B. (1999). *The Mathematical Brain*. London: Macmillan.

Butterworth, B. (2005a). Developmental dyscalculia. In J. I. D. Campbell (Ed.), *The Handbook of Mathematical Cognition* (pp. 455–467). Hove: Psychology Press. Retrieved from http://ldx.sagepub.com/content/7/3/164.short

Butterworth, B. (2005b). The development of arithmetical abilities. *Journal of Child Psychology and Psychiatry*, 1, 3–18.

Butterworth, B. (2010). Foundational numerical capacities and the origins of dyscalculia. *Trends in Cognitive Sciences*, 14(12), 534–541.

Butterworth, R., & Reeve, R. A. (2012). Counting words and a principles-after account of the development of number concepts. In M. Siegal & L. Surian (Eds), *Access to Language and Cognitive Development* (pp. 160–175). Oxford: Oxford University Press.

Carey, S. (2001). Cognitive foundations of arithmetic: Evolution and ontogenisis. *Mind and Language*, *16*(1), 37–55.

Chard, D., Clarke, B., Baker, S., Otterstedt, J., Braun, D., & Katz, R. (2005). Using measures of number sense to screen for difficulties in mathematics: Preliminary findings. *Assessment for Effective Intervention*, *30*, 3–14.

Chesney, D. L., & Haladjian, H. H. (2011). Evidence for a shared mechanism used in multiple-object tracking and subitising. *Attention, Perception & Psychophysics*, *73*(8), 2457–2480.

Chi, M. T. H., & Klahr, D. (1975). Span and rate of apprehension in children and adults. *Journal of Experimental Child Psychology*, *19*, 434–439.

Chinello, A., Cattani, V., Bonfiglioli, C., Dehaene, S., & Piazza, M. (2013). Objects, numbers, fingers, space: Clustering of ventral and dorsal functions in young children and adults. *Developmental Science*, *16*(3), 377–393.

Chu, F. W., vanMarle, K., & Geary, D. C. (2013). Quantitative deficits of preschool children at risk for mathematical learning disability. *Frontiers in Psychology*, *4*(May), 1–10.

Cipolotti, L., Butterworth, B., & Denes, G. (1991). A specific deficit for numbers in a case of dense acalculia. *Brain*, *114*, 2619–2637.

Clark, C. A. C., Sheffield, T. D., Wiebe, S. A., & Espy, K. A. (2012). Longitudinal associations between executive control and developing mathematical competence in preschool boys and girls. *Child Development*, *84*(2), 662–677.

Clarke, B., & Shinn, M. (2004). A preliminary investigation into the identification and development of early mathematics curriculum-based measurement. *School Psychology Review*, *33*, 234–248.

Clements, D. H. (1999). Subitising: What is it? Why teach it? *Teaching Children Mathematics*, *5*, 400–405.

De Hevia, M. D., Vallar, G., & Girelli, L. (2008). Visualizing numbers in the mind's eye: The role of visuo-spatial processes in numerical abilities. *Neuroscience and Biobehavioral Reviews*, *32*(8), 1361–1372.

De Smedt, B., Noël, M.-P., Gilmore, C., & Ansari, D. (2013). How do symbolic and non-symbolic numerical magnitude processing skills relate to individual differences in children's mathematical skills? A review of evidence from brain and behavior. *Trends in Neuroscience and Education*, *2*(2), 48–55.

De Smedt, B., Swillen, A., Devriendt, K., Fryns, J. P., Verschaffel, L., & Ghesquiere, P. (2007). Mathematical disabilities in children with velocardio-facial syndrome. *Neuropsychologia*, *45*, 885–895.

Dehaene, S., Piazza, M., Pinel, P., & Cohen, L. (2003). Three parietal circuits for number processing. *Cognitive Neuropsychology*, *20*(3), 487–506.

Desoete, A., & Grégoire, J. (2006). Numerical competence in young children and in children with mathematics learning disabilities. *Learning and Individual Differences*, *16*(4), 351–367.

Desoete, A., Roeyers, H., & De Clercq, A. (2004). Children with mathematics learning disabilities in Belgium. *Journal of Learning Disabilities*, *37*, 50–61.

Espy, K., McDiarmid, M., Kwik, M., Stalets, M., Hamby, A., & Senn, T. (2004). The contribution of executive functions to emergent mathematics skills in preschool children. *Developmental Neuropsychology*, *26*, 465–486.

Fayol, M., and Seron, X. (2005). About numerical representations: Insights from neuropsychological, experimental and developmental studies. In J. I. D. Campbell (Ed.), *Handbook of Mathematical Cognition* (pp. 3–22). New York: Psychology Press.

Feigenson, L., & Carey, S. (2003). Tracking individuals via object files: Evidence from infants' manual search. *Developmental Science*, *5*, 568–584.

Feigenson, L., & Carey, S. (2005). On the limits of infants' quantification of small object arrays. *Cognition*, *97*(1), B13–B23.

Feigenson, L., Carey, S., & Hauser, M. (2002). The representations underlying infants' choice of more: Object files versus analog magnitudes. *Psychological Science*, *13*(2), 150–156.

Fischer, B., Gebhardt, C., & Hartnegg, K. (2008). Subitising and visual counting in children with problems in acquiring basic arithmetic skills. *Optometry & Vision Development*, *39*(1), 24–29.

Fuchs, L. S., Geary, D. C., Compton, D. L., Fuchs, D., Hamlett, C. L., & Bryant, J. D. (2010a). The contributions of numerosity and domain-general abilities to school readiness. *Child Development*, *81*(5), 1520–1533.

Fuchs, L. S., Geary, D. C., Compton, D. L., Fuchs, D., Hamlett, C. L., Seethaler, P. M., Schatschneider, C. (2010b). Do different types of school mathematics development depend on different constellations of numerical versus general cognitive abilities? *Developmental Psychology*, *46*(6), 1731–1746.

Fuhs, M. W., & McNeil, N. M. (2013). ANS acuity and mathematics ability in preschoolers from low-income homes: Contributions of inhibitory control. *Developmental Science*, *16*(1), 136–148.

Fuson, K. C., & Hall, J. W. (1983). The acquisition of early number word meanings: A conceptual analysis and overview. In H. P. Ginsburg (Ed.), *The Development of Mathematical Thinking* (pp. 49–107). New York: Academic Press.

Geary, D. C., Hamson, C. O., & Hoard, M. K. (2000). Numerical and arithmetical cognition: A longitudinal study of process and concept deficits in children with learning disability. *Journal of Experimental Child Psychology*, *77*(3), 236–263.

Geary, D. C., Hoard, M. K., & Hamson, C. O. (1999). Numerical and arithmetical cognition: Patterns of functions and deficits in children at risk for a mathematical disability. *Journal of Experimental Child Psychology*, *74*(3), 213–239.

Gelman, R. (2000). Domain specificity and variability in cognitive development. *Child Development*, *71*(4), 854–856.

Gelman, R. (2009). Learning in core and noncore domains. In L. Tommasi, M. A. Peterson, & L. Nadal (Eds), *Cognitive Biology: Evolutionary and developmental perspectives on mind, brain, and behavior* (pp. 247–260). Cambridge: MIT Press.

Gelman, R., & Williams, E. M. (1998). Enabling constraints for cognitive development and learning: Domain specificity and epigenesis. In W. Damon, D. Kuhn, & R. S. Siegler (Eds), *Handbook of Child Psychology* (5th ed., Vol. 1, pp. 575–630). New York: Wiley.

Gersten, R., Jordan, N. C., & Flojo, J. R. (2005). Early identification and interventions for students with mathematics difficulties. *Journal of Learning Disabilities*, *38*(4), 293–304.

Gilmore, C., Attridge, N., Clayton, S., Cragg, L., Johnson, S., Marlow, N., Inglis, M. (2013). Individual differences in inhibitory control, not non-verbal number acuity, correlate with mathematics achievement. *PloS One*, *8*(6), e67374.

Ginsburg, H. P., & Baroody, A. J. (2003). *Test of Early Mathematics Ability* (3rd ed.). Austin, TX: Pro Ed.

Girelli, L., Lucangeli, D., & Butterworth, B. (2000). The development of automaticity in accessing number magnitude. *Journal of Experimental Child Psychology*, *76*, 104–122.

Gracia-Bafalluy, M., & Noël, M.-P. (2008). Does finger training increase young children's numerical performance? *Cortex*, *44*(4), 368–375.

Gray, S., & Reeve, R. A. (2014). Preschoolers' dot enumeration abilities are markers of their arithmetic competence. *PLoS ONE*, *9*(4), e94428.

Gray, S., & Reeve, R. A. (submitted). 'Cognitive markers of preschoolers' math competence.

Halberda, J., & Feigenson, L. (2008). Developmental change in the acuity of the "Number Sense": The approximate number system in 3-, 4-, 5-, and 6-year-olds and adults. *Developmental Psychology*, *44*(5), 1457–1465.

Hannula, M. M., & Lehtinen, E. (2005). Spontaneous focusing on numerosity and mathematical skills of young children. *Learning and Instruction, 15*(3), 237–256.

Hannula, M. M., Lepola, J., & Lehtinen, E. (2010). Spontaneous focusing on numerosity as a domain-specific predictor of arithmetical skills. *Journal of Experimental Child Psychology, 107*(4), 394–406.

Hannula, M. M., Rasanen, P., & Lehtinen, E. (2007). Development of counting skills: Role of spontaneous focusing on numerosity and subitising-based enumeration. *Mathematical Thinking and Learning, 9*(1), 51–57.

Henik, A., Rubinsten, O., & Ashkenazi, S. (2011). The "where" and "what" in developmental dyscalculia. *The Clinical Neuropsychologist, 25*(6), 989–1008.

Holloway, I. D., & Ansari, D. (2009). Mapping numerical magnitudes onto symbols: The numerical distance effect and individual differences in children's mathematics achievement. *Journal of Experimental Child Psychology, 103*(1), 17–29.

Houdé, O., Rossi, S., Lubin, A., & Joliot, M. (2010). Mapping numerical processing, reading, and executive functions in the developing brain: An fMRI meta-analysis of 52 studies including 842 children. *Developmental Science, 13*(6), 876–885.

Hubbard, E. M., Piazza, M., Pinel, P., & Dehaene, S. (2005). Interactions between number and space in parietal cortex. *Nature Reviews Neuroscience, 6*(6), 435–448.

Hunting, R. P. (2003). Part-whole number knowledge in preschool children. *The Journal of Mathematical Behavior, 22*(3), 217–235.

Hyde, D. C., & Spelke, E. S. (2009). All numbers are not equal: An electrophysiological investigation of small and large number representations. *Journal of Cognitive Neuroscience, 21*(6), 1039–1053.

Hyde, D. C., & Spelke, E. S. (2011). Neural signatures of number processing in human infants: Evidence for two core systems underlying numerical cognition. *Developmental Science, 4*(2), 360–371.

Izard, V., Sann, C., Spelke, E. S., & Streri, A. (2009). Newborn infants perceive abstract numbers. *Proceedings of the National Academy of Sciences of the United States of America, 106*(25), 10382–10385.

Jordan, N. C., Kaplan, D., Nabors Olah, L., & Locuniak, M. (2006). Number sense growth in kindergarten: A longitudinal investigation of children at risk for mathematics difficulties. *Child Development, 77*, 153–175.

Jung, M., Hartman, P., Smith, T., & Wallace, S. (2013). The effectiveness of teaching number relationships in preschool. *International Journal of Instruction, 6*(1), 400–405.

Klahr, D., & Wallace, J. G. (1976). *Cognitive Development: An information-processing view.* Hillsdale, NJ: Erlbaum.

Koontz, K. L., & Berch, D. B. (1996). Identifying simple numerical stimuli: Processing inefficiencies exhibited by arithmetic learning disabled children. *Mathematical Cognition, 2*(1), 1–23.

Kroesbergen, E. H., Van Luit, J. E. H., Van Lieshout, E. C. D. M., Van Loosbroek, E., & Van de Rijt, B. A. M. (2009). Individual differences in early numeracy: The role of executive functions and subitising. *Journal of Psychoeducational Assessment, 27*(3), 226–236.

Landerl, K., Bevan, A., & Butterworth, B. (2004). Developmental dyscalculia and basic numerical capacities: A study of 8–9-year-old students. *Cognition, 93*(2), 99–125.

Laski, E. V., & Siegler, R. S. (2007). Is 27 a big number? Correlational and causal connections among numerical categorization, number line estimation, and numerical magnitude comparison. *Child Development, 78*(6), 1723–1743.

Lemer, C., Dehaene, S., Spelke, E., & Cohen, L. (2003). Approximate quantities and exact number words: Dissociable systems. *Neuropsychologia, 41*, 1942–1958.

Libertus, M. E., Feigenson, L., & Halberda, J. (2011). Preschool acuity of the approximate number system correlates with school math ability. *Developmental Science, 14*(6), 1292–1300.

Number difficulties in young children

Libertus, M. E., Feigenson, L., & Halberda, J. (2013a). Is approximate number precision a stable predictor of math ability? *Learning and Individual Differences, 25*, 126–133.

Libertus, M. E., Feigenson, L., & Halberda, J. (2013b). Numerical approximation abilities correlate with and predict informal but not formal mathematics abilities. *Journal of Experimental Child Psychology, 116*(4), 829–838.

Locuniak, M., & Jordan, N. (2008). Using kindergarten number sense to predict calculation fluency in second grade. *Journal of Learning Disabilities, 41*, 451–459.

Lonnemann, J., Linkersdörfer, J., Hasselhorn, M., & Lindberg, S. (2013). Developmental changes in the association between approximate number representations and addition skills in elementary school children. *Frontiers in Psychology, 4*(October), 783.

Lourenco, S. F., Bonny, J. W., Fernandez, E. P., & Rao, S. (2012). Nonsymbolic number and cumulative area representations contribute shared and unique variance to symbolic math competence. *Proceedings of the National Academy of Sciences of the United States of America, 109*(46), 18737–18742.

Lyons, I. M., & Beilock, S. L. (2011). Numerical ordering ability mediates the relation between number-sense and arithmetic competence. *Cognition, 121*(2), 256–261.

Mazzocco, M. M. M., Feigenson, L., & Halberda, J. (2011). Preschoolers' precision of the approximate number system predicts later school mathematics performance. *PloS One, 6*(9), e23749.

Mazzocco, M. M. M., & Hanich, L. B. (2010). Math achievement, numerical processing, and executive functions in girls with Turner syndrome: Do girls with Turner syndrome have math learning disability? *Learning and Individual Differences, 20*, 70–81.

Mazzocco, M. M. M., & Thompson, R. E. (2005). Kindergarten predictors of math learning disability. *Learning Disabilities Research & Practice, 20*(3), 142–155.

Moyer, R. S., & Landauer, T. K. (1967). Time required for judgments of numerical inequality. *Nature, 215*, 1519–1520.

Mussolin, C., Mejias, S., & Noël, M.-P. (2010). Symbolic and nonsymbolic number comparison in children with and without dyscalculia. *Cognition, 115*(1), 10–25.

Noël, M.-P. (2005). Finger gnosia: A predictor of numerical abilities in children? *Child Neuropsychology, 11*(5), 413–430.

Obersteiner, A., Reiss, K., & Ufer, S. (2013). How training on exact or approximate mental representations of number can enhance first-grade students' basic number processing and arithmetic skills. *Learning and Instruction, 23*, 125–135.

Opfer, J., & Siegler, R. (2012). Development of quantitative thinking. In K. Holyoak & R. Morrison (Eds), *Oxford Handbook of Thinking and Reasoning* (pp. 585–605). Oxford: Oxford University Press.

Opfer, J. E., Thompson, C. A., & Furlong, E. E. (2010). Early development of spatial-numeric associations: Evidence from spatial and quantitative performance of preschoolers. *Developmental Science, 13*(5), 761–771.

Östergren, R., & Träff, U. (2013). Early number knowledge and cognitive ability affect early arithmetic ability. *Journal of Experimental Child Psychology, 115*(3), 405–421.

Paterson, S., Girelli, L., Butterworth, B., & Karmiloff-Smith, A. (2006). Are numerical impairments syndrome specific? Evidence from Williams syndrome and Down's syndrome. *Journal of Child Psychology and Psychiatry, 47*, 190–204.

Penner-Wilger, M., Fast, L., LeFevre, J., Smith-Chant, B. L., Skwarchuk, S., Kamawar, D., & Bisanz, J. (2007). The foundations of numeracy: Subitising, finger gnosia, and fine motor ability. In D. S. McNamara & J. G. Trafton (Eds), *Proceedings of the 29th Annual Conference of the Cognitive Science Society* (pp. 1385–1390). Austin, TX: Cognitive Science Society.

Piazza, M. (2010). Neurocognitive start-up tools for symbolic number representations. *Trends in Cognitive Sciences, 14*(12), 542–551.

Piazza, M., Facoetti, A., Trussardi, A. N., Berteletti, I., Conte, S., Lucangeli, D., Zorzi, M. (2010). Developmental trajectory of number acuity reveals a severe impairment in developmental dyscalculia. *Cognition*, *116*(1), 33–41.

Pinel, P., Piazza, M., Le Bihan, D., & Dehaene, S. (2004). Distributed and overlapping cerebral representations of number, size, and luminance during comparative judgments. *Neuron*, *41*, 983–993.

Reeve, R., & Humberstone, J. (2011). Five- to 7-year-olds' finger gnosia and calculation abilities. *Frontiers in Psychology*, *2*(December), 359.

Reeve, R., Reynolds, F., Humberstone, J., & Butterworth, B. (2012). Stability and change in markers of core numerical competencies. *Journal of Experimental Psychology: General*, *141*(4), 649–666.

Reigosa-Crespo, V., Valdés-Sosa, M., Butterworth, B., Estévez, N., Rodríguez, M., Santos, E., Lage, A. (2012). Basic numerical capacities and prevalence of developmental dyscalculia: The Havana Survey. *Developmental Psychology*, *48*(1), 123–135.

Rousselle, L., & Noël, M.-P. (2007). Basic numerical skills in children with mathematics learning disabilities: A comparison of symbolic vs non-symbolic number magnitude processing. *Cognition*, *102*(3), 361–395.

Rubinsten, O., Henik, A., Berger, A., & Shahar-Shalev, S. (2002). The development of internal representations of magnitude and their association with Arabic numerals. *Journal of Experimental Child Psychology*, *81*, 74–92.

Schleifer, P., & Landerl, K. (2011). Subitising and counting in typical and atypical development. *Developmental Science*, *14*(2), 280–291.

Shalev, R., Manor, O., Auerbach, J., & Gross-Tsur, V. (1998). Persistence of developmental dyscalculia: What counts? Results from a three year prospective follow-up study. *Journal of Pediatrics*, *133*, 358–362.

Shalev, R., Manor, O., & Gross-Tsur, V. (1997). Neuropsychological aspects of developmental dyscalculia. *Mathematical Cognition*, *3*, 105–120.

Shalev, R. S., Manor, O., & Gross-Tsur, V. (2005). Developmental dyscalculia: A prospective six-year follow-up. *Developmental Medicine and Child Neurology*, *47*(2), 121–125. Retrieved from http://www.ncbi.nlm.nih.gov/pubmed/15707235

Silver, C., Pennett, D., Black, J., Fair, G., & Balise, R. (1999). Stability of arithmetic disability subtypes. *Journal of Learning Disabilities*, *32*, 108–119.

Simon, T. J., Bearden, C. E., McDonald-McGinn, D., & Zackai, E. (2005). Visuospatial and numerical cognitive deficits in children with chromosome 22Q11.2 deletion syndrome. *Cortex*, *41*, 145–155.

Simon, T. J., Takarae, Y., DeBoer, T., McDonald-McGinn, D. M., Zackai, E. H., & Ross, J. L. (2008). Overlapping numerical cognition impairments in children with chromosome 22q11.2 deletion or Turner syndromes. *Neuropsychologia*, *46*, 82–94.

Starkey, P., & Cooper, R. G. (1995). The development of subitising in young children. *British Journal of Developmental Psychology*, *13*, 399–420.

Starr, A., Libertus, M. E., & Brannon, E. M. (2013a). Infants show ratio-dependent number discrimination regardless of set size. *Infancy*, *18*(6), 927–941.

Starr, A., Libertus, M. E., & Brannon, E. M. (2013b). Number sense in infancy predicts mathematical abilities in childhood. *Proceedings of the National Academy of Sciences*, 1–5.

Träff, U. (2013). The contribution of general cognitive abilities and number abilities to different aspects of mathematics in children. *Journal of Experimental Child Psychology*, *116*(2), 139–156.

Vanbinst, K., Ghesquière, P., & De Smedt, B. (2012). Numerical magnitude representations and individual differences in children's arithmetic strategy use. *Mind, Brain, and Education*, *6*(3), 129–136.

vanMarle, K. (2013). Infants use different mechanisms to make small and large number ordinal judgments. *Journal of Experimental Child Psychology*, *114*(1), 102–110.

Von Aster, M., & Shalev, R. (2007). Number development and developmental dyscalculia. *Developmental Medicine & Child Neurology*, *49*, 868–873.

Walsh, V. (2003). A theory of magnitude: Common cortical metrics of time, space, and quantity. *Trends in Cognitive Sciences*, *7*, 483–488.

Wynn, K. (1992). Children's acquisition of the number words and the counting system. *Cognitive Psychology*, *251*, 220–251.

Xu, F., & Arriaga, R. I. (2007). Number discrimination in 10-month-old infants. *British Journal of Developmental Psychology*, *25*, 103–108.

Xu, F., & Spelke, E. S. (2000). Large number discrimination in 6-month old infants. *Cognition*, *74*, B1–B11.

Yun, C., Havard, A., Farran, D., & Lipsey, M. (2011). Subitising and mathematics performance in early childhood. In L. Carlson, C. Hoelscher, & T. F. Shipley (Eds), *Proceedings of the 33rd Annual Conference of the Cognitive Science Society* (pp. 680–684). Austin, TX: Cognitive Science Society.

3

Dots and digits

How do children process the numerical magnitude? Evidence from brain and behaviour

Vivian Reigosa-Crespo and Danilka Castro

Introduction

Magnitude is a core dimension of the semantic of numbers. From birth we are continually comparing numerical magnitudes of things in our life. Which one of two boxes has more candies? Is the batting average of the Yankees higher than that of the Mets? Did we receive the correct amount of change in the shopping centre? There are innumerable examples. Numerical magnitude refers to a cardinal aspect of numbers, that is, when they denote the 'numerosity' of a set (e.g., Butterworth, 1999). To grasp the magnitude concept we need to learn the distinction between the transformations that do or do not modify the cardinality of a set (e.g., adding or removing objects in a set modifies the cardinality; spreading or grouping the objects does not). We also need to compare between the numerosity of different sets (e.g., set A could be smaller, larger, or equal to set B). We first learn these principles through our experience with sets of real objects. Later on, we learn with symbols, such as words or Arabic numbers. The nature of magnitude representations in typical and atypical development have been commonly explored with magnitude comparison tasks using non-symbolic (dots) or symbolic (digits) stimuli.

This chapter focuses on a review of the developmental literature about magnitude processing of numbers in non-symbolic and symbolic formats. The first part of the chapter will describe the numerical effects that have been systematically reported in magnitude comparison tasks and, also, will present evidence about the validity and reliability of these effects in typical development. The second part of the chapter will review behavioural data concerning the typical development of non-symbolic and symbolic number processing, as well as the relationship between numerical magnitude processing and mathematical competence. The third part will present evidence of atypical development of magnitude processing and hypotheses about the nature of the deficits. Finally, we will examine neuroimaging data related to number magnitude processing in children with typical and atypical numerical cognition.

Effects in magnitude comparison tasks

Adult and child studies of number magnitude processing have identified several robust effects. In 1967, Moyer and Landauer reported that for adults who were required to compare the relative magnitudes represented by two Arabic numbers the individual's reaction time (RT) was systematically influenced by the linear distance of the values compared (Moyer & Landauer, 1967). In other words, RT decreased with increasing numerical distance between two values (e.g., subjects were faster at 2 versus 9 than 2 versus 3). This effect, named the *numerical distance effect* (NDE), has usually been interpreted as more compression (Dehaene, 1992) or a greater variability (Whalen, Gelman, & Gallistel, 1999) for representing large number magnitudes (see Verguts & Fias, 2004 for a different view). NDE has since been replicated frequently in adults (e.g., Banks, Fujii, & Kayra-Stuart, 1976) and children (e.g., Holloway & Ansari, 2009; De Smedt, Verschaffel, & Ghesquière, 2009; Castro, Estévez, & Pérez, 2009; Castro, Reigosa-Crespo, & González, 2012). Additionally, for equal numerical distance, RTs increase with the size of the numbers (e.g., subjects are faster at 2 versus 3 than 7 versus 8). This *numerical size effect* (NSE) has also been reported many times in adults (e.g., Antell & Keating, 1983; Strauss & Curtis, 1981) and children (e.g., Rouselle & Nöel, 2007; Castro et al., 2009, 2012). On the other hand, the *semantic congruity effect* (first observed by Banks, Fujii, & Kayra-Stuart, 1976) affects RT when subjects make any type of magnitude comparison (e.g. 'which is smaller?'). This effect refers to the finding that small values are more rapidly compared when participants are asked 'Which is smaller?', whereas large values are more rapidly compared when participants are asked 'Which is larger?' In other words, people are faster to compare two numerical values when their overall magnitude is congruent with the semantic of the verbal phrasing of the question. A *spatial congruency effect* (SNARC) has been reported when subjects who answer 'larger' with their left hand are slower than subjects who respond 'larger' with their right hand (Dehaene, Dupoux, & Mehler, 1990). These authors found that the SNARC effect does not reverse in left handed individuals or when participants are asked to respond with their hands crossed.

Finally, a *size congruity effect* has also been observed when number magnitude is processed in tasks for which this dimension is not relevant. This effect is reproduced in a Stroop-like paradigm in which subjects are asked to select the physically larger of two numbers varying along both numerical and physical dimensions (e.g., Besner & Coltheart, 1979). In congruent trials the number that is physically bigger is also the numerically larger (e.g., 2–6); in incongruent trials, the number that is physically smaller is numerically larger (e.g., 2–6). A decrease in latencies (facilitation component) is expected in the congruent condition and an increase in latencies (interference component) is expected in the incongruent condition. The presence of the (numerical) size congruity effect in the physical comparison indicates that the irrelevant magnitude information of number has been automatically processed.

These numerical effects have been replicated in many different languages, cultures and numerical notations. However, currently there exists a lack of systematic investigation into the validity and reliability of the numerical effects across different formats and paradigms in both adults and children.

Validity and reliability of numerical effects

Establishing whether the effects in magnitude comparison tasks are both reliable and valid has important implications for using different variants of these tasks to index the processing of numerical magnitude. This is especially relevant because multiple versions of the comparison tasks produce the same pattern of data (i.e., an NDE), and consequently, the vast majority of researchers implicitly assume that each of these versions index the same stable underlying process. Surprisingly, recent findings challenge this assumption. Holloway and Ansari (2009) presented a group of 6–8-year-old children with symbolic and non-symbolic versions of a number comparison task. In the symbolic variant of the task, Arabic digits were used. In the non-symbolic variant arrays of squares were presented. The authors demonstrated that while symbolic and non-symbolic stimuli elicit an NDE, the individual's NDE on the symbolic version did not correlate with the individual's NDE on the non-symbolic version. Later, this result was replicated in thirty 10–11-year-old children: fifteen children with a poor ability to retrieve arithmetic facts and fifteen children with normal achievement in mathematics (Mussolin, Mejias, & Noël, 2010b). A similar result was obtained in adults (Maloney, Risko, Preston, Ansari, & Fugelsgang, 2010). These authors discussed several alternative explanations for the lack of correlation of symbolic NDE with non-symbolic NDE. Likely, the two variants of comparison tasks index different input-to-representation mapping pathways (Verguts & Fias, 2004), or qualitatively different representations (Cohen Kadosh & Walsh, 2009), or instead reflect different demands on the response-selection component during comparison, which may give rise to a different NDE (Van Opstal, Gevers, De Moor, & Verguts, 2008). These alternative explanations should be explored deeply in future research.

Another important issue is whether or not these measures are reliable. However, this issue has been systematically neglected in cognitive research. One possible cause is the implicit assumption that cognitive processes are inherently reliable because they typically produce robust and replicable empirical phenomena (see Maloney et al., 2010). According to these researchers, the lack of reliability leads to several important limitations. On one hand, it weakens the correlation with other measures. On the other hand, it diminishes the probability for detecting between-group differences even if those differences do exist (Kopriva & Shaw, 1991) and it makes the interpretation of a null result difficult. Thus, assessing whether cognitive measures, such as numerical effects, are reliable has important implications for methodological issues, but also for theoretical explanations and models derived from data obtained with such measures.

Recently, the reliability of various cognitive measures has begun to be investigated using an approach focused on a test–retest assessment correlating the size of a given effect for the first half and second half of the experimental task (e.g., Borgmann, Risko, Stolz, & Besner, 2007; Stolz, Besner, & Carr, 2005). If a measure is reliable, then scores obtained in the first half will be highly predictive of scores obtained in the second half of that test. The studies using this approach have revealed that the implicit assumption that cognitive processes are inherently reliable is not always supported by the data.

In light of this, Maloney et al. (2010), using the test–retest approach, demonstrated that both the symbolic comparison version and the non-symbolic comparison version are reliable. However, the NDE measures elicited by non-symbolic stimuli were far more reliable than measures of the NDE that use symbolic stimuli. Recently, similar results have been obtained in children. Castro and Reigosa-Crespo (unpublished doctoral dissertation, 2013) presented a group of typically developing children (6 to 11 years old) with symbolic and non-symbolic versions of a magnitude comparison task reported in a previous study (Castro et al., 2009). The individual's NDE and also the individual's NSE elicited in each version were obtained. The authors corroborated that both the NDE and the NSE are reliable in the two variants of number comparison tasks. Contrary to Maloney et al. (2010), in this developmental study the numerical effects provoked by non-symbolic stimuli were less reliable than the numerical effects elicited by symbolic stimuli.

To our knowledge, the scarce literature about the validity and reliability of the numerical effects are focused on NDE and NSE and no data about other numerical effects are currently available. In this sense, further attempts are needed, taking into account how critical it is to evaluate the replication, reliability and construct validity of the effects used to gather insights into cognitive processes.

Typical development of non-symbolic representation of number

Using the habituation or the preferential-looking paradigms (Starkey & Cooper, 1980; Antell & Keating, 1983; Strauss & Curtis, 1981; van Loosbroek & Smistman, 1990), several studies have indicated that infants can use the numerosity of visual arrays as a discriminative stimulus (e.g., Starkey & Cooper, 1980). Moreover, infants can select a set of objects and treat them as a single unit (Feigenson & Halberda, 2004; Wynn, 2002). A heterogeneous picture emerges from other studies into early development: infants were able to discriminate large sets presented in a 1:2 ratio (e.g., Xu & Spelke, 2000; Lipton & Spelke, 2003) but failed to do so for small sets such as one versus two (e.g., Feigenson, Carey, & Spelke, 2002; Clearfield & Mix, 1999). Conversely, Xu (2003) reported that 6-month-old infants were successful in discriminating four from eight visual elements but failed to differentiate two from four elements. On the other hand, several studies have shown that the range of subitising (a capacity to discriminate small sets of 1–4 objects 'at a glance' (Mandler & Shebo, 1982)) develops quickly during the first year of life, such that the range at 6 months is limited to a single object, whereas its range reaches a limit of three objects at approximately 12 months (Ross-Sheehy, 2003; Oakes, 2006; Rose, Feldman, & Jankowski, 2001).

Typically developing children also exhibit an increase in the acuity of non-symbolic representations over developmental time. A number of studies have shown that children with more precise representations perform more accurately and faster on dot comparison tasks and that they show smaller effects of ratio or distance (Duncan & McFarland, 1980; Sekuler & Mierkiewicz, 1977). Moreover, accuracy on numerical estimation tasks also increases over developmental time (Petitto, 1990; Booth & Siegler, 2006; Siegler & Booth, 2004; Siegler & Opfer, 2003). Interestingly, changes in estimation reflect a shift in representation from logarithmic in younger children to linear in older children and adults (Booth & Siegler, 2006; Siegler & Booth, 2004; Siegler & Opfer, 2003).

To date, two main views are proposed to explain these developmental findings. According to one view (Feigenson, Dehaene & Spelke, 2004), infants are innately equipped with two core number systems. One system is the 'approximate representations of numerical magnitude' (ANS) which represents numbers in an analogue and compressed mode. Because of these properties, representations within the ANS are noisy and become increasingly imprecise with increasing magnitude. So, two sets can be discriminated only if they differ by a given numerical ratio according to Weber's law. That is, the threshold of discrimination (also referred to as 'smallest noticeable difference') between two stimuli, increases linearly with stimulus intensity. The other is a 'precise representations of distinct individuals' in an 'object-file' system. One of the defining features of this system is that it is limited in capacity to three or four individual objects at a time and it reflects the automatic processing of numerical magnitudes (see Desoete et al. (2009) for a review of this hypothesis).

According to the second view, humans are born with a capacity to quantify over sets. This core capacity derives from a 'number module' (Butterworth, 1999, 2005) and uses an internal 'numerosity code' (Zorzi & Butterworth, 1999; Zorzi, Stoianov & Umiltà, 2005) that represents numerosities exactly – exact 'fiveness', exact 'sixness', and so on (Butterworth, 1999; Butterworth & Reigosa-Crespo, 2007). This would mean that a set can be a type of object that can itself take a property. This property is its numerosity (a subjective form of the logical concept of cardinality) which is not something common to the objects in the set, but it is a property of the set itself. Studies of infant behaviour support the hypothesis that this property can be intermodal and therefore relatively abstract (Jordan & Brannon, 2006; Wynn, 2002).

Typical development of symbolic representation of number

The development of symbolic number processing has been typically investigated using magnitude comparison tasks that involve Arabic digits. Performance on these tasks improves with age (Holloway & Ansari, 2009; Sekuler & Mierkiewicz, 1977) and is also characterised by an effect of distance or ratio. The symbolic NDE decreases over developmental time (Duncan & McFarland, 1980; Sekuler & Mierkiewicz, 1977).

This developmental shift has been explained as reflecting changes in the discriminability of numerical representation; but also as reflecting changes in the response competition (e.g., choose left vs. right side for 'larger'), which increases with increasing distance (Van Opstal et al., 2008; Verguts, Fias, & Stevens, 2005). Supporting the latter explanation, children exhibit the SNARC effect as early as 7 years old when comparing the magnitude of Arabic digits, but at age 9 only when they perform parity (Berch, Foley, Hill, & Ryan, 1999) or detection tasks (van Galen & Reitsma, 2008) in which the number magnitude is less relevant. On the other hand, the *size congruity effect* which is a marker of automatic access to the magnitude of Arabic numerals, is not observed in children until the age of 7–8 (Girelli, Lucangeli, & Butterworth, 2000; Rubinsten, Henik, Berger, & Shahar-Shalev, 2002). According to Ansari (2010), this developmental change reflects an increase in the fluency with which children process the numerical magnitudes associated with numerical symbols.

Performance on symbolic comparison tasks has been interpreted in different ways. Several authors state that numerical effects (e.g. NDE, SNARC effect or *size congruity effect*) elicited by symbolic magnitude processing might be 'traces' of the non-symbolic representation signature (see Piazza, 2010 for a comprehensive review) and, consequently, those effects are reflecting the nature of the non-symbolic representations. Others argue that symbolic magnitudes are acquired through a process of mapping abstract symbols onto those representations that are tapped by non-symbolic stimuli (Rouselle & Nöel, 2007). Alternatively, some authors hypothesise that the numerical effects elicited by symbolic stimuli might reveal the nature of symbolic representations themselves, which are not linked to non-symbolic ones (see Cohen Kadosh & Walsh, 2007 for a discussion of stimulus-dependent, non-abstract representations of numerical magnitude).

Impact of numerical magnitude processing on mathematical competence

Non-symbolic magnitude processing

Recent research has provided mixed evidence concerning the relation of dot comparison tasks and formal mathematical achievement. On the one hand, several longitudinal studies support a significant association in older children who have had years of experience with symbolic mathematics (Halberda, Mazzocco, & Feigenson, 2008) but also, in the first stages of school (Mazzocco, Feigenson, & Halberda, 2011a; see Gilmore et al. (2010) for an alternative correlational analysis using as a variable the comparison ratio obtained in a non-symbolic addition task). However, studies employing similar longitudinal design have failed to find a correlation (Sasanguie, Van den Bussche, & Reynvoet, 2012b; Sasanguie et al., 2013). Mixed evidence is also provided by cross-sectional research that evaluates the relationship concurrently. While a number of studies found a significant association (Mazzocco, Feigenson, & Halberda, 2011b; Mundy & Gilmore, 2009; Inglis et al., 2011; Libertus, Feigenson, & Halberda, 2011), many others have failed to find one (Soltesz, Szücs & Szücs, 2010; Lonnemann, Linkersdörfer, Hasselhorn, & Lindberg, 2011; Fuhs & McNeil, 2013;

Kolkman, Kroesbergen, & Leseman, 2013). These divergent findings could stem from a lack of standardisation of the dot comparison task (e.g., the control of physical features that covariates with the numerical magnitude information, the length of presentation of the stimuli and the performance measures used) (see De Smedt et al. (2013) for a review). Interestingly, a more homogeneous picture emerges from longitudinal studies focused on subitising, a phenomenon that reflects the automatic processing of non-symbolic small quantities (Desoete et al., 2009). LeFevre et al. (2010) found that quantitative skills (subitising latency) measured in preschool and kindergarten, predicted significant unique variability of non-linguistic arithmetic, but also conventional maths measurement of numeration and calculation two years later. More recently, a similar significant relationship was replicated throughout all elementary school years (Reeve, Reynolds, Humberstone, & Butterworth, 2012; Reigosa-Crespo et al., 2013). To our knowledge, no divergent findings concerning the association of subitising and mathematical competence have been reported from longitudinal studies. Furthermore, robust and significant correlations have been systematically found in cross-sectional studies enrolling typically developing children and children with Developmental Dyscalculia (DD) (Koontz and Berch, 1996; Schleifer & Landerl, 2010; Butterworth, 1999; Landerl, Bevan, & Butterworth, 2004)

Symbolic magnitude processing

Children's performance on symbolic comparison tasks has been found to be strongly and significantly associated with concurrent (Holloway & Ansari, 2009; Durand, Hulme, Larkin, & Snowling, 2005; Bugden & Ansari, 2011; Lonnemann et al., 2011; Sasanguie et al., 2012a; Reigosa-Crespo et al., 2012) and prospective mathematics achievement (De Smedt et al., 2009; Sasanguie et al., 2012b, 2013). This relationship seems to be very robust for global RT obtained when numbers are compared. Furthermore, similar associations with performance measures such as accuracy and distance/ratio effects have been observed in the majority, but not all studies (see De Smedt et al. (2013) for a review).

Atypical development of numerical representation

There is now increasing evidence that individuals with DD perform poorly on the simplest tasks requiring the processing of numerical magnitudes. Numerous studies have demonstrated impairments in symbolic number magnitude processing among children with DD (De Smedt & Gilmore, 2011; Landerl & Kölle, 2009; Landerl et al., 2004; Rouselle & Nöel, 2007). However, when dot comparison tasks have been employed, the results are quite divergent. On the one hand, some studies showed a reduced acuity in non-symbolic representations (Mejias, Mussolin, Rousselle, Grégoire,& Noël, 2012; Mazzocco et al., 2011a; Piazza et al., 2010), as well as less accurate performance (Mussolin et al., 2010b) in DD compared to typically achieving children. On the other hand, others failed to observe significant differences between DD and controls in non-symbolic comparison (Iuculano, Tang, Hall, & Butterworth, 2008; Landerl

& Kölle, 2009; De Smedt & Gilmore, 2011; Rousselle & Nöel, 2007), although, in those studies, children with DD showed poorer performance in symbolic magnitude comparison. Interestingly, there is more convincing evidence for a subitising deficit in DD (Koontz & Berch, 1996; Schleifer & Landerl, 2010; Butterworth, 1999; Landerl et al., 2004), but also in populations with dyscalculia associated with genetic diseases: Turner's syndrome (Bruandet, Molko, Cohen, & Dehaene, 2004), children with cerebral palsy (Arp & Fagard, 2005; Arp, Taranne, & Fagard, 2006), velocardiofacial syndrome (De Smedt et al., 2007; Simon et al., 2005, 2008), fragile X syndrome, and Williams syndrome (Mazzocco & Hanich, 2010; Paterson, Girelli, Butterworth, & Karmiloff-Smith, 2006).

An hypothesis for developmental dyscalculia

There are several models that try to explain the mechanisms underlying magnitude processing deficits in children with DD. Some models focus on domain-general cognitive abilities including defective working memory (Bull & Scerif, 2001; Geary, Hoard, Byrd-Craven, Nugent, & Numtee, 2007), spatial abilities (Rourke, 1993), language skills (Donlan, Cowan, Newton, & Lloyd, 2007), retrieval of information from long-term memory (Geary, Hamson, & Hoard, 2000) and executive functions (Passolunghi & Siegel, 2004). However, although there is agreement concerning the contribution of general-domain cognitive processes to the development of numerical competencies, up to now there is no convincing evidence supporting that these cognitive processes are specifically related to DD.

Alternative models are focused on domain-specific capacities assuming that DD is a consequence of an inborn core deficit in 'the number module' (Butterworth, 1999; Butterworth & Reigosa-Crespo, 2007) induced by a highly selective impairment of the capacity to understand and represent numerosities exactly, or in 'number sense' (Dehaene, 2001; Dehaene, Piazza, Pinel, & Cohen, 2003; Wilson & Dehaene, 2007), a term denoting the ability to quickly understand, approximate and manipulate numerical quantities non-verbally on an internal number line. More recently, Rousselle and Nöel (2007) hypothesise that numerical impairments in DD children are a consequence of a deficit in accessing the number representation from the symbolic format, rather than in the internal representation of numbers per se. Impairments in the processing of numerical magnitude information are considered by these researchers as 'low-level' signs consistent with the models proposed.

Brain imaging findings

Neuroimaging studies on the development of numerical cognition are scarce and produce a heterogeneous pattern of results. Moreover, many of these studies are not directly comparable because the authors used different sets of stimuli (non-symbolic: Kaufmann et al., 2008; Kovas et al., 2009; Kucian et al., 2006; Price, Holloway, Räsänen, Vesterinen, & Ansari, 2007, versus symbolic: Kaufmann et al., 2009; Meintjes et al., 2010; Mussolin et al., 2010a), different instructions (active number-related responses: Ansari, Garcia, Lucas, Hamon, & Dhital, 2005; Kaufmann et al., 2006; Ansari & Dhital, 2006, versus passive paradigm without response requirement: Cantlon, Brannon, Carter, & Pelphrey, 2006), different tasks (intentional number comparison: Ansari et al., 2005; Kaufmann et al., 2006; Ansari & Dhital, 2006, versus non-intentional number comparison: Kovas et al., 2009; Kaufmann et al., 2008; Kucian et al., 2006; Meintjes et al., 2010), and also different criteria for subject inclusion (e.g., IQ-maths achievement discrepancy: Kucian et al., 2006; Rotzer et al., 2008, versus arithmetic achievement solely: Price et al., 2007; Rykhlevskaia, Uddin, Kondos, & Menon, 2009).

As an attempt to bypass those limitations, Kaufmann and colleagues (2011) reported a coordinate-based meta-analysis with the aim of identifying brain regions that are commonly activated in functional imaging studies investigating number processing in children. Taken together, convergent findings across these studies revealed that in children symbolic processing produced bilateral parietal activations (including the left posterior superior parietal lobe (PSPL) and the right intraparietal sulcus (IPS)), while non-symbolic processing activated mainly the right parietal lobe (bordering the IPS). Interestingly, intraparietal activation foci in response to symbolic processing were situated near the core of the IPS (similar to data reported in adults by Dehaene et al. (2003)), while neural activation to non-symbolic processing was found adjacent to the anterior IPS and extending to the postcentral gyrus. This pattern of parietal activations elicited by non-symbolic stimuli might reflect a link between fingers and number processing. According to Kaufmann et al. (2011) a potential explanation is that, compared with symbolic Arabic digits, non-symbolic stimuli (e.g., dots) are more likely to elicit finger-based solution strategies (for a similar hypothesis see Kaufmann et al., 2008; Butterworth, 2005 and Gracia-Bafalluy & Noël, 2008). In addition, effects of format were not restricted to parietal regions. For non-symbolic processing, significant activations were found in the inferior and middle frontal gyrus and in striate and extrastriate regions. Also, the cerebellum and subcortical regions were found to respond selectively to symbolic (posterior lobe of cerebellum) and non-symbolic stimuli (claustrum).

Taken together, these findings suggest that in developing brain systems, format modulates the localisation of parietal (and extra-parietal) cerebral activations. Consequently, these findings challenge the notion that numbers are represented in an abstract code and, thus, the IPS is responsible for number processing regardless of format (Dehaene et al., 2003), and provide support for the assumption of initially different representations for symbolic and non-symbolic notation which progressively overlap with the influence of maturation and schooling (Cohen Kadosh & Walsh, 2009; Kucian & Kaufmann, 2009; Kucian et al., 2011).

On the other hand, there is accumulated evidence demonstrating the existence of age-related shifts in functional activity from prefrontal to more parietal areas in response to number magnitude processing. Numerous studies showed that number-related activations in frontal brain regions are stronger in children than in adults (Ansari et al., 2005; Ansari & Dhital, 2006; Holloway & Ansari, 2010; Cantlon et al., 2006; Kaufmann et al., 2006, 2008; Kucian, Von Aster, Loenneker, Dietrich, &

Martin, 2008; Rivera, Reiss, Eckert, & Menon, 2005; but see Wood, Ischebeck, Koppelstaetter, Gotwald, & Kaufmann, 2009). According to Ansari (2010) the differences between children and adults in these studies probably reflect children's greater enrolment of areas involved in attention and working memory in order to successfully process the numerical magnitudes. Such areas are presumably activated to compensate for 'immature' representations of numbers in the parietal cortex. Progressively, children improve their knowledge about numerical magnitude and they need to rely less on these supplementary processes. Unfortunately, to date, the developmental studies have focused on comparing children with adults, but a more precise picture about the neural bases of the numerical development could be obtained from studies contrasting children of different ages (see Ansari (2010) for a deeper analysis).

As a final point, based on the scarce literature to date it can be hypothesised that children with severe impairment in number processing (DD) have a dysfunctional parietal system (Kaufmann et al., 2009; Kovas et al., 2009; Kucian et al., 2006; Mussolin et al., 2010a; Price et al., 2007). According to the meta-analysis from Kaufmann et al. (2011), compared with typically developing children, those with DD tend to have less robust number-related activations in the IPS (deficient bilateral IPS: Kaufmann et al., 2006; Mussolin et al., 2010a; deficient right IPS: Price et al., 2007). Moreover, children with DD seem to recruit either more distributed brain regions (likely reflecting compensatory strategies (e.g., Kaufmann et al., 2008; Kucian et al., 2006; Price et al., 2007)) or alternatively display deficient recruitment of frontal brain regions that – in typically developing children – are found to support domain-general processing (Mussolin et al., 2010a). Considering the rather scarce data these results need to be interpreted with caution.

Summary and conclusions

The nature of magnitude representations in typical and atypical development have been commonly explored with simple magnitude comparison tasks using non-symbolic (dots) or symbolic (digits) stimuli. Adult and children studies of number magnitude comparison have identified several robust effects (e.g. distance/ratio effect, SNARC and *size congruity effect*) that have been replicated in many different languages, cultures and numerical notations. However, there currently exists a lack of systematic investigation into the validity and reliability of the effects across different formats and paradigms in both adults and children. The scarce literature about validity and reliability of the numerical effects is focused on NDE. No correlation of non-symbolic NDE with the NDE generated by symbolic stimuli has been systematically found across the studies. This finding challenges the assumption that the NDE elicited by the two task formats indicates the same underlying process. Several hypotheses try to explain this result including the existence of initially distinct number representations for symbolic and non-symbolic notations that – with maturation and schooling – overlap (Cohen Kadosh & Walsh, 2009). This assumption is recently supported by neuroimaging data (see Kaufmann et al. (2011) for a comprehensive meta-analysis of functional brain imaging in developmental studies). On the other hand, few studies have consistently shown that distance and number magnitude effects are reliable in the two comparison variants. No data about validity and reliability of other numerical effects are currently available.

Studies on the typical development of number magnitude representation reveal that performance on comparison tasks improves with age and is also characterised by several numerical effects (e.g. distance/ratio, SNARC and size congruency). To date, two main views attempt to explain these developmental findings. The 'number module' view (Butterworth, 1999, 2005) and the two 'core systems' view (Feigenson, Dehaene & Spelke, 2004). The most important difference between these two views is that the first assumes an innate capacity to represent sets and their abstract properties (including their numerosity), while in the second, numerical content is related to the capacity to represent approximate magnitudes in an analogue code.

It has been hypothesised that performance on non-symbolic magnitude comparison tasks is related to mathematics achievement, but research has provided mixed evidence concerning the relation of dot comparison tasks and formal mathematical achievement in concurrent and prospective studies. Contrastingly, a more homogeneous picture derived from cross-sectional and longitudinal studies reveals a robust relationship of subitising with mathematical achievement. Such a discrepancy might reflect the difference between dot comparison and subitising paradigms related to their standardisation. On the other hand, children's performance on symbolic comparison tasks has been found to be strongly and significantly associated with concurrent and prospective mathematics achievement. According to Ansari et al. (2010), intervention research focused on non-symbolic processing, symbolic processing or both is necessary in order to determine whether children's symbolic and/or non-symbolic processing skills are causally related to their mathematics achievement. To run these studies across different ages is also important to verify which type of intervention is more appropriate at which age.

There is now increasing evidence that children with DD perform poorly on the simplest tasks requiring processing of numerical magnitudes in both formats, non-symbolic and symbolic. This fact has been explained by models about defective domain-general cognitive abilities. However, to date, there is no convincing evidence to suggest that these cognitive factors are specifically related to DD because they are involved in a variety of non-numerical tasks (see Mussolin & Noël, 2008). Other models are focused on domain-specific capacities assuming that DD is a consequence of an inborn core deficit in the 'number module' (Butterworth, 1999) or in the 'number sense' (Dehaene, 2001; Dehaene et al., 2003; Wilson & Dehaene, 2007). Alternatively, Rousselle & Noël (2007) hypothesised that numerical impairments in DD are a consequence of a deficit in accessing the number representation from the symbolic format, rather than in the internal representation of numbers per se.

Taken together, results of developmental neuroimaging studies on numerical cognition disclose that children's activation patterns are modulated by notation (symbolic vs. non-symbolic) and achievement level (children vs. adults; children with and without DD). Overall, recruitment of anterior intraparietal regions (which in some contrasts extend to postcentral gyrus), (pre)frontal regions, and large portions of striate and extrastriate regions may be interpreted as reflecting effortful number processing. This assumption applies to typically developing children and also to atypically developing children with DD (see Kaufmann et al. (2011) for a meta-analysis).

Finally, as a practical implication, the behavioural and neuroimaging findings reviewed here strongly support the importance of training low-level numerical magnitude processing in educational settings for enhancing mathematical competence in typically developing children and also in children with atypical development of numerical cognition.

References

Ansari, D. 2010. Neurocognitive approaches to developmental disorders of numerical and mathematical cognition: The perils of neglecting the role of development. *Learning and Individual Differences, 20,* 123–129.

Ansari, D. & Dhital, B. 2006. Age-related changes in the activation of the intraparietal sulcus during nonsymbolic magnitude processing: An event-related functional magnetic resonance imaging study. *Journal of Cognitive Neuroscience, 18,* 1820–1828.

Ansari, D., Garcia, N., Lucas, E., Hamon, K. & Dhital, B. 2005. Neural correlates of symbolic number processing in children and adults. *NeuroReport, 16,* 1769–1773.

Ansari, D., Price, G. & Holloway, I. 2010. Typical and atypical development of basic numerical magnitude representations: a review of behavioral and neuroimaging studies. In Ferrari, M. & Vuletic, L. (eds.) *The Developmental Relations among Mind, Brain and Education.* Springer Science+Business Media B.V.

Antell, S. E. & Keating, D. P. 1983. Perception numerical invariance in neonates. *Child Development, 54,* 695–701.

Arp, S. & Fagard, J. 2005. What impairs subitizing in cerebral palsied children? *Developmental Psychobiology, 47,* 89–102.

Arp, S., Taranne, P. & Fagard, J. 2006. Global perception of small numerosities (subitizing) in cerebral-palsied children. *Journal of Clinical and Experimental Neuropsychology, 28,* 405–419.

Banks, W. P., Fujii, M. & Kayra-Stuart, F. 1976. Semantic congruity effects in comparative judgments of magnitudes of digits. *Journal of Experimental Psychology: Human Perception and Performance, 2,* 435–447.

Berch, D. B., Foley, E. J., Hill, R. J. & McDonough, R. P. 1999. Extracting parity and magnitude from Arabic numerals: Developmental changes in number processing and mental representation. *Journal of Experimental Child Psychology, 74,* 286–308.

Besner, D. & Coltheart, M. 1979. Ideographic and alphabetic processing in skilled reading of English. *Neuropsychologia, 17,* 467–472.

Booth, J. L. & Siegler, R. S. 2006. Development and individual differences in pure numerical estimation. *Developmental Psychology, 41,* 189–201.

Borgmann, K. W. U., Risko, E. F., Stolz, J. A. & Besner, D. 2007. Simon says: Reliability and the role of working memory and attentional control in the Simon Task. *Psychonomic Bulletin & Review, 14,* 313–319.

Bruandet, M., Molko, N., Cohen, L. & Dehaene, S. 2004. A cognitive characterization of dyscalculia in Turner syndrome. *Neuropsychologia, 42,* 288–298.

Bugden, S. & Ansari, D. 2011. Individual differences in children's mathematical competence are related to the intentional but not automatic processing of Arabic numerals. *Cognition, 118,* 32–44.

Bull, R. & Scerif, G. 2001. Executive functioning as a predictor of children's mathematics ability: Inhibition, switching, and working memory. *Developmental Neuropsychology, 19,* 273–293.

Butterworth, B. 1999. *The Mathematical Brain.* London, Macmillan.

Butterworth, B. 2005. The development of arithmetical abilities. *Journal of Child Psychology and Psychiatry, 46*(1), 3–18.

Butterworth, B. & Reigosa-Crespo, V. 2007. Information processing deficits in dyscalculia. In Berch, D. B. & Mazzocco, M. M. M. (eds.) *Why is Math so Hard for Some Children? The nature and origins of mathematical learning difficulties and disabilities.* Baltimore, MD: Paul H. Brookes.

Cantlon, J. F., Brannon, E. M., Carter, E. J. & Pelphrey, K. A. 2006. Functional imaging of numerical processing in adults and 4-y-old children. *PLoS Biology, 4,* e125.

Castro, D. 2013. *Nonsymbolic and symbolic magnitude representation: An approximation to the origins of the developmental dyscalculia.* PhD doctoral thesis, Cuban Centre for Neuroscience.

Castro, D., Estévez, N. & Pérez, O. 2009. Typical development of quantity comparison in school-aged children. *The Spanish Journal of Psychology, 14,* 50–61.

Castro, D., Reigosa-Crespo, V. & González, E. 2012. Non-symbolic and symbolic numerical magnitude processing in children with developmental dyscalculia. *The Spanish Journal of Psychology, 15,* 952–966.

Clearfield, M. W. & Mix, K. S. 1999. Number vs. contour length in infants' discrimination of small visual sets. *Psychological Science, 10,* 408–411.

Cohen Kadosh, R. & Walsh, V. 2007. Dyscalculia. *Current Biology, 17,* 946–947.

Cohen Kadosh, R. & Walsh, V. 2009. Numerical representations in the parietal lobes: Abstract or not abstract? *Behavioral and Brain Sciences, 32,* 313–373.

De Smedt, B. & Gilmore, C. K. 2011. Defective number module or impaired access? Numerical magnitude processing in first graders with mathematical difficulties. *Journal of Experimental Child Psychology, 108,* 278–292.

De Smedt, B., Noël, M. P., Gilmore, C. K. & Ansari, D. 2013. How do symbolic and non-symbolic numerical magnitude processing skills relate to individual differences in children's mathematical skills? A review of evidence from brain and behavior. *Trends in Neuroscience and Education, 2,* 48–55.

De Smedt, B., Swillen, A., Devriendt, K., Fryns, J. P., Verschaffel, L. & Ghesquière, P. 2007. Mathematical disabilities in children with velocardiofacial syndrome. *Neuropsychologia, 45,* 885–895.

De Smedt, B., Verschaffel, L. & Ghesquière, P. 2009. The predictive value of numerical magnitude comparison for individual differences in mathematics achievement. *Journal of Experimental Child Psychology, 103,* 469–479.

Dehaene, S. 1992. Varieties of numerical abilities. *Cognition, 44,* 1–42.

Dehaene, S. 2001. Précis of the number sense. *Mind and Language, 16,* 16–36.

Dehaene, S., Dupoux, E. & Mehler, J. 1990. Is numerical comparison digital? Analogical and symbolic effects in two-digit number comparison. *Human Perception and Performance, 16,* 626–641.

Dehaene, S., Piazza, M., Pinel, P. & Cohen, L. 2003. Three parietal circuits for number processing. *Cognitive Neuropsychology, 3,* 487–506.

Desoete, A., Ceulemans, A., Roeyers, H. & Huylebroeck, A. 2009. Subitizing or counting as possible screening variables for learning disabilities in mathematics education or learning. *Educational Research, 4,* 55–66.

Donlan, C., Cowan, R., Newton, E. J. & Lloyd, D. 2007. The role of language in mathematical development: Evidence from children with specific language impairments. *Cognition, 103,* 23–33.

Duncan, E. M. & McFarland, C. E. 1980. Isolating the effects of symbolic distance and semantic congruity in comparative judgments: An additive factors analysis. *Memory and Cognition, 8,* 612–622.

Durand, M., Hulme, C., Larkin, R. & Snowling, M. 2005. The cognitive foundations of reading and arithmetic skills in 7- to 10-year-olds. *Journal of Experimental Child Psychology, 91,* 113–136.

Feigenson, L., Carey, S. & Spelke, E. 2002. Infants' discrimination of number vs. continuous extent. *Cognitive Psychology, 44*, 33–66.

Feigenson, L., Dehaene, S. & Spelke, E. 2004. Core systems of number. *Trends in Cognitive Sciences, 8*, 307–314.

Feigenson, L. & Halberda, J. 2004. Infants chunk object arrays into sets of individuals. *Cognition, 91*, 173–190.

Fuhs, M. W. & McNeil, N. M. 2013. ANS acuity and mathematics ability in preschoolers from low-income homes: Contributions of inhibitory control. *Developmental Science, 16*, 136–148.

Geary, D. C., Hamson, C. O. & Hoard, M. K. 2000. Numerical and arithmetical cognition: A longitudinal study of process and concept deficits in children with learning disability. *Journal of Experimental Child Psychology, 77*, 236–263.

Geary, D. C., Hoard, M. K., Byrd-Craven, J., Nugent, L. & Numtee, C. 2007. Cognitive mechanisms underlying achievement deficits in children with mathematical learning disability. *Child Development, 78*, 1343–1359.

Gilmore, C. K., McCarthy, S. E. & Spelke, E. S. 2010. Non-symbolic arithmetic abilities and mathematics achievement in the first year of formal schooling. *Cognition, 115*, 394–406.

Girelli, L., Lucangeli, D. & Butterworth, B. 2000. The development of automaticity in accessing number magnitude. *Journal of Experimental Child Psychology, 122*, 104–122.

Gracia-Bafalluy, M. & Noël, M. P. 2008. Does finger training increase young children's numerical performance? *Cortex, 44*, 368–375.

Halberda, J., Mazzocco, M. M. M. & Feigenson, L. 2008. Individual differences in nonverbal number acuity predict maths achievement. *Nature, 455*, 665–668.

Holloway, I. D. & Ansari, D. 2009. Mapping numerical magnitudes onto symbols: The numerical distance effect and individual differences in children's mathematics achievement. *Journal of Experimental Child Psychology, 103*, 17–29.

Holloway, I. D. & Ansari, D. 2010. Developmental specialization in the right intraparietal sulcus for the abstract representation of numerical magnitude. *Journal of Cognitive Neuroscience, 22*, 2627–2637.

Inglis, M., Attridge, N., Batchelor, S. & Gilmore, C. K. 2011. Non-verbal number acuity correlates with symbolic mathematics achievement: But only in children. *Psychonomic Bulletin and Review, 18*, 1222–1229.

Iuculano, T., Tang, J., Hall, C. W. B. & Butterworth, B. 2008. Core information processing deficits in developmental dyscalculia and low numeracy. *Developmental Science, 11*, 669–680.

Jordan, K. E. & Brannon, E. M. 2006. A common representational system governed by Weber's law: Nonverbal numerical similarity judgments in 6-year-olds and rhesus macaques. *Journal of Experimental Child Psychology, 95*, 215–229.

Kaufmann, L., Koppelstaetter, F., Siedentopf, C., Haala, I., Haberlandt, E., Zimmerhackl, L. B. & Ischebeck, A. 2006. Neural correlates of a number-size interference task in children. *NeuroReport, 17*, 587–591.

Kaufmann, L., Vogel, S. E., Starke, M., Kremser, C., Schocke, M. & Wood, G. 2009. Developmental dyscalculia: Compensatory mechanisms in left intraparietal regions in response to nonsymbolic magnitudes. *Behavioral and Brain Functions, 5*, 35.

Kaufmann, L., Vogel, S. E., Wood, G., Kremser, C., Schocke, M., Zimmerhackl, L. B. & Koten, J. W. 2008. A developmental fMRI study of nonsymbolic numerical and spatial processing. *Cortex, 44*, 376–385.

Kaufmann, L., Wood, G., Rubinsten, O. & Henik, A. 2011. Meta- analyses of developmental fMRI studies investigating typical and atypical trajectories of number processing and calculation. *Developmental Neuropsychology, 36*, 763–787.

Kolkman, M. E., Kroesbergen, E. H. & Leseman, P. P. M. 2013. Early numerical development and the role of non-symbolic and symbolic skills. *Learning and Instruction, 25*, 95–103.

Koontz, K. L. & Berch, D. B. 1996. Identifying simple numerical stimuli: Processing inefficiencies exhibited by arithmetic learning disabled children. *Mathematical Cognition, 2*, 1–24.

Kopriva, R. J. & Shaw, D. G. 1991. Power estimates: The effect of dependent variable reliability on the power of one-factor anovas. *Educational and Psychological Measurement, 51*, 585–595.

Kovas, Y., Giampietro, V., Viding, E., Ng, V., Brammer, M., Barker, G. J., Plomin, R. 2009. Brain correlates of non-symbolic numerosity estimation in low and high mathematical ability children. *PLoS One, 4*, e4587.

Kucian, K., Grond, U., Rotzer, S., Henzi, B., Schönmann, C., Plangger, F. von Aster, M. 2011. Mental number line training in children with developmental dyscalculia. *NeuroImage, 57*, 782–795.

Kucian, K. & Kaufmann, L. 2009. A developmental model of number representations. A commentary to Cohen Kadosh, R., & Walsh, V. (2009). Numerical representations in the parietal lobes: Abstract or not abstract? *Behavioral and Brain Sciences, 32*, 313–373. *Behavioral and Brain Sciences, 32*, 340–341.

Kucian, K., Loenneker, T., Dietrich, T., Dosch, M., Martin, E. & Von Aster, M. 2006. Impaired neural networks for approximate calculation in dyscalculic children: A functional MRI study. *Behavioral and Brain Functions, 2*, 31.

Kucian, K., Von Aster, M., Loenneker, T., Dietrich, T. & Martin, E. 2008. Development of neural networks for exact and approximate calculation: A fMRI study. *Developmental Neuropsychology, 33*, 447–473.

Landerl, K., Bevan, A. & Butterworth, B. 2004. Developmental dyscalculia and basic numerical capacities: A study of 8–9-year-old students. *Cognition, 93*, 99–125.

Landerl, K. & Kölle, C. 2009. Typical and atypical development of basic numerical skills in elementary school. *Journal of Experimental Child Psychology, 103*, 546–565.

Lefevre, J. A., Skwarchuk, S. L., Smith-Chant, B. L., Bisanz, J., Kamawar, D. & Penner-Wilger, M. 2010. Pathways to mathematics: Longitudinal predictors of performance. *Child Development, 81*, 1753–1767.

Libertus, M. E., Feigenson, L. & Halberda, J. 2011. Preschool acuity of the approximate number system correlates with school math ability. *Developmental Science, 14*, 1292–1300.

Lipton, J. S. & Spelke, E. 2003. Origins of number sense. *Psychological Science, 14*, 396–401.

Lonnemann, J., Linkersdörfer, J., Hasselhorn, M. & Lindberg, S. 2011. Symbolic and non-symbolic distance effects in children and their connection with arithmetic skills. *Journal of Neurolinguistics, 24*, 583–591.

Maloney, E. A., Risko, E. F., Preston, F., Ansari, D. & Fugelsang, J. 2010. Challenging the reliability and validity of cognitive measures: The case of the numerical distance effect. *Acta Psychologica, 134*, 154–161.

Mandler, G. & Shebo, B. J. 1982. Subitizing: An analysis of its component processes. *Journal of Experimental Psychology: General, 111*, 1–21.

Mazzocco, M. M. M., Feigenson, L. & Halberda, J. 2011a. Impaired acuity of the approximate number system underlies mathematical learning disability (dyscalculia). *Child Development, 82*, 1224–1237.

Mazzocco, M. M. M., Feigenson, L. & Halberda, J. 2011b. Preschoolers' precision of the approximate number system predicts later school mathematics performance. *PLoS One, 6*, e23749.

Mazzocco, M. M. M. & Hanich, L. B. 2010. Math achievement, numerical processing, and executive functions in girls with Turner syndrome: Do girls with Turner syndrome have math learning disability? *Learning and Individual Differences, 20*, 70–81.

Meintjes, E. M., Jacobson, S. W., Molteno, C. D., Gatenby, J. C., Warton, C., Cannistraci, C. J. & Jacobson, J. L. 2010. An fMRI study of magnitude comparison and exact addition in children. *Magnetic Resonance Imaging, 28*, 351–362.

Mejias, S., Mussolin, C., Rousselle, L., Grégoire, J. & Noël, M. P. 2012. Numerical and non-numerical estimation in children with and without mathematical learning disabilities. *Child Neuropsychology, 18*, 550–575.

Moyer, R. S. & Landauer, T. K. 1967. Time required for judgements of numerical inequality. *Nature, 215,* 1519–1520.

Mundy, E. & Gilmore, C. K. 2009. Children's mapping between symbolic and nonsymbolic representations of number. *Journal of Experimental Child Psychology, 103,* 490–502.

Mussolin, C., De Volder, A., Grandin, C., Schlögel, X., Nassogne, M. C. & Noël, M. P. 2010a. Neural correlates of symbolic number comparison in developmental dyscalculia. *Journal of Cognitive Neuroscience, 22,* 860–874.

Mussolin, C., Mejias, S. & Noël, M. P. 2010b. Symbolic and nonsymbolic number comparison in children with and without dyscalculia. *Cognition, 115,* 10–25.

Mussolin, C. & Noël, M. P. 2008. Specific retrieval deficit from long-term memory in children with poor arithmetic facts abilities. *The Open Psychology Journal, 1,* 26–34.

Oakes, L. E. A. 2006. Rapid development of feature binding in visual short-term memory. *Psychological Science, 17,* 781–787.

Passolunghi, M. C. & Siegel, L. S. 2004. Working memory and access to numerical information in children with disability in mathematics. *Journal of Experimental Child Psychology, 88,* 348–367.

Paterson, S., Girelli, L., Butterworth, B. & Karmiloff-Smith, A. 2006. Are numerical impairments syndrome specific? Evidence from Williams syndrome and Down's syndrome. *Journal of Child Psychology and Psychiatry, 47,* 190–204.

Petitto, A. L. 1990. Development of number line and measurement concepts. *Cognition and Instruction, 7,* 55–78.

Piazza, M. 2010. Neurocognitive start-up tools for symbolic number representations. *Trends in Cognitive Sciences, 14,* 542–551.

Piazza, M., Facoetti, A., Noemi, A., Berteletti, I., Conte, S., Lucangeli, D., Zorzi, M. 2010. Developmental trajectory of number acuity reveals a severe impairment in developmental dyscalculia. *Cognition, 116,* 33–41.

Price, G. R., Holloway, I., Räsänen, P., Vesterinen, M. & Ansari, D. 2007. Impaired parietal magnitude processing in developmental dyscalculia. *Current Biology, 17,* 1042–1043.

Reeve, R., Reynolds, F., Humberstone, J. & Butterworth, B. 2012. Stability and change in markers of core numerical competencies. *Journal of Experimental Psychology: General, 141,* 649–666.

Reigosa-Crespo, V., González-Alemañy, E., León, T., Torres, R., Mosquera, R. & Valdés-Sosa, M. 2013. Numerical capacities as domain-specific predictors beyond the early mathematics learning: A longitudinal study. *PLoS One,* 8, e79711.

Reigosa-Crespo, V., Valdés-Sosa, M., Butterworth, B., Estévez, N., Rodríguez, M., Santos, E. et al. 2012. Basic numerical capacities and prevalence of developmental dyscalculia: The Havana survey. *Developmental Psychology, 48,* 123–135.

Rivera, S. M., Reiss, A. L., Eckert, M. A. & Menon, V. 2005. Developmental changes in mental arithmetic: Evidence for increased functional specialization in the left inferior parietal cortex. *Cerebral Cortex, 15,* 1779–1790.

Rose, S., Feldman, J. & Jankowski, J. 2001. Visual short-term memory in the first year of life: Capacity and recency effects. *Developmental Psychology, 37,* 539–549.

Ross-Sheehy, S. E. A. 2003. The development of visual short-term memory capacity in infants. *Child Development, 74,* 1807–1822.

Rotzer, S., Kucian, K., Martin, E., Von Aster, M., Klaver, P. & Loenneker, T. 2008. Optimized voxel-based morphometry in children with developmental dyscalculia. *NeuroImage, 39,* 417–422.

Rourke, B. P. 1993. Arithmetic disabilities, specific and otherwise: A neuropsychological perspective. *Journal of Learning Disabilities, 26,* 214–226.

Rousselle, L. & Noël, M. P. 2007. Basic numerical skills in children with mathematics learning disabilities: A comparison of symbolic vs non-symbolic number magnitude processing. *Cognition, 102,* 361–395.

Rubinsten, O., Henik, A., Berger, A. & Shahar-Shalev, S. 2002. The development of internal representations of magnitude and their association with Arabic numerals. *Journal of Experimental Child Psychology, 81*, 74–92.

Rykhlevskaia, E., Uddin, L. Q., Kondos, L. & Menon, V. 2009. Neuroanatomical correlates of developmental dyscalculia: Combined evidence from morphometry and tractography. *Frontiers in Human Neuroscience, 3*, 1–13.

Sasanguie, D., De Smedt, B., Defever, E. & Reynvoet, B. 2012a. Association between basic numerical abilities and mathematics achievement. *British Journal of Developmental Psychology, 30*, 344–357.

Sasanguie, D., Göbel, S. M., Moll, K., Smets, K. & Reynvoet, B. 2013. Approximate number sense, symbolic number processing, or number-space mappings: What underlies mathematics achievement? *Journal of Experimental Child Psychology, 114*, 418–431.

Sasanguie, D., Van Den Bussche, E. & Reynvoet, B. 2012b. Predictors for mathematics achievement? Evidence from a longitudinal study. *Mind, Brain, and Education, 6*, 119–128.

Schleifer, P. & Landerl, K. 2010. Subitizing and counting in typical and atypical development. *Developmental Science, 14*, 1–12.

Sekuler, R. & Mierkiewicz, D. 1977. Children's judgements of numerical inequality. *Child Development, 48*, 630–633.

Siegler, R. S. & Booth, J. L. 2004. Development of numerical estimation in young children. *Child Development, 75*, 428–444.

Siegler, R. S. & Opfer, J. E. 2003. The development of numerical estimation: Evidence for multiple representations of numerical quantity. *Psychological Science, 14*, 237–243.

Simon, T. J., Ding, L., Bish, J. P., McDonald-McGinn, D. M., Zackai, E. H. & Gee, J. 2005. Volumetric, connective, and morphologic changes in the brains of children with chromosome 22q11.2 deletion syndrome: an integrative study. *NeuroImage, 25*, 169–180.

Simon, T. J., Takarae, Y., Deboer, T., McDonald-McGinn, D. M., Zackai, E. H. & Ross, J. L. 2008. Overlapping numerical cognition impairments in children with chromosome 22q11.2 deletion or Turner syndrome. *Neuropsychologia, 46*, 82–94.

Soltesz, F., Szücs, D. & Szücs, L. 2010. Relationships among magnitude representation, counting, and memory in 4- to 7-year-old children: A developmental study. *Behavioral and Brain Functions, 6*, 13.

Starkey, P. & Cooper, R. G. 1980. Perception of numbers by human infants. *Science, 210*, 1033–1035.

Stolz, J. A., Besner, D. & Carr, T. H. 2005. Implications of measures of reliability for theories of priming: Activity in semantic memory is inherently noisy and uncoordinated. *Visual Cognition, 12*, 284–336.

Strauss, M. S. & Curtis, L. E. 1981. Infant perception of numerosity. *Child Development, 52*, 1146–1152.

Van Galen, M. S. & Reitsma, P. 2008. Developing access to number magnitude: A study of the SNARC effect in 7- to 9-year-olds. *Journal of Experimental Child Psychology, 101*, 99–113.

Van Loosbroek, E. & Smitsman, W. 1990. Visual perception of numerosity in infancy. *Developmental Psychology, 26*, 916–922.

Van Opstal, F., Gevers, W., De Moor, W. & Verguts, T. 2008. Dissecting the symbolic distance effect: Comparison and priming effects in numerical and nonnumerical orders. *Psychonomic Bulletin and Review, 15*, 419–425.

Verguts, T. & Fias, W. I. M. 2004. Representation of number in animals and humans: A neural model. *Journal of Cognitive Neuroscience, 16*, 1493–1504.

Verguts, T. O. M., Fias, W. I. M. & Stevens, M. 2005. A model of exact small-number representation. *Psychonomic Bulletin & Review, 12*, 66–80.

Whalen, J., Gelman, R. & Gallistel, C. R. 1999. Non-verbal counting in humans: The psychophysics of number representation. *Psychological Science, 10*, 130–137.

Wilson, A. & Dehaene, S. 2007. Number sense and developmental dyscalculia. In Coch, D., Dawson, G. & Fischer, F. (eds.) *Human Behavior Learning and the Developing Brain: Atypical Development*. New York: Guilford.

Wood, G., Ischebeck, A., Koppelstaetter, F., Gotwald, T. & Kaufmann, L. 2009. Developmental trajectories of magnitude processing and interference control: An fMRI study. *Cerebral Cortex, 19*, 2755–2765.

Wynn, K. E. A. 2002. Enumeration of collective entities by 5-month-old infants. *Cognition, 83*, B55–B62.

Xu, F. 2003. Numerosity discrimination in infants: Evidence for two systems of representations. *Cognition, 89*, B15–B25.

Xu, F. & Spelke, E. S. 2000. Large number discrimination in 6-month-old infants. *Cognition, 74*, B1–B11.

Zorzi, M. & Butterworth, B. 1999. A computational model of number comparison. *Twenty First Annual Meeting of the Cognitive Science Society*.

Zorzi, M., Stoianov, I. & Umiltà, C. 2005. Computational modeling of numerical cognition. In Campbell, J. I. D. (ed.) *Handbook of Mathematical Cognition*. New York: Psychological Press.

4

When and why numerosity processing is associated with developmental dyscalculia

Xinlin Zhou and Dazhi Cheng

Introduction

Developmental dyscalculia (DD) is a problem for children during the acquisition of basic arithmetic skills. Much research has been devoted to investigating the origins of DD. Numerosity processing or approximate number sense (ANS) has been assumed to be an important cognitive origin of DD. However, empirical investigation has shown inconsistent findings. The current investigation, discussed in this chapter, is looking into whether the relationship of numerosity to DD depends on the screening measure for DD, and why a critical relationship has been found through some measures.

Numerosity processing and mathematical performance

Studies have shown that primates and human newborns have the ability to process numerosity (Brannon & Terrace, 1998; Groffman, 1966; Gross et al., 2009; Nieder, Freedman, & Miller, 2002; Xu, Spelke, & Goddard, 2005). In both children and adults, numerosity processing (or ANS or non-verbal number acuity) is significantly correlated with mathematical achievement (Halberda, Mazzocco, & Feigenson, 2008; Libertus, Feigenson, & Halberda, 2011). Gilmore and colleagues found that young children seemed to build on their numerosity ability to learn symbolic mathematics (Gilmore, McCarthy, & Spelke, 2007). Even adults' arithmetic performance was significantly correlated with numerosity ability (Wei, Yuan, Chen, & Zhou, 2012a).

Numerosity processing and developmental dyscalculia

The prevalence of DD is about 5 to 7% (Shalev, 2007; Von Aster & Shalev, 2007). For example, a study of a sample of German children (n = 378) found that the prevalence of dyscalculia was about 6%, 1.8% of which had pure dyscalculia and the others had co-morbid dyslexia (Von Aster & Shalev, 2007). DD can be defined according to computation fluency (Landerl, Bevan, & Butterworth, 2004) or wide-range mathematical achievement (i.e., computation, concepts, and mathematical problem-solving) (McLean & Hitch, 1999).

Studies have found that children with DD have severe impairment in numerosity judgement (Geary, Bailey, & Hoard, 2009; Landerl et al., 2004; Piazza et al., 2010). Some studies have failed, however, to observe a relationship between numerosity and DD (Iuculano, Tang, Hall, & Butterworth, 2008; Rousselle & Noël, 2007).

One cause for the inconsistent findings could be the screening measures. For example, the screening measure based on computational fluency found the relationship (Landerl et al., 2004; Piazza et al., 2010), but the screening measure based on wide-range mathematical achievement did not (de Smedt & Gilmore, 2011). Landerl et al. (2004) used a composite criterion by which children designated as having dyscalculia were either struggling with all three of the arithmetic operations (addition, subtraction, and multiplication), or were having severe difficulties with at least one operation; the arithmetic was timed. On the other hand, De Smedt and Gilmore (2011) found that children with mathematical learning difficulty were different from typically achieving children in symbolic numerical magnitude comparison, but not in non-symbolic numerical magnitude comparison. They used the curriculum-based standardised general mathematics achievement test, Math up to Ten (Dudal, 1999) as a screening measure.

Determinants of a close relationship between numerosity processing and computational fluency

One explanation for the high correlation between numerosity processing and mathematical performance is that they share a common processing of numerical magnitude (Halberda et al., 2008). Few alternative hypotheses, however, have been tested. In this study, we proposed the alternative explanation that low-level visual perceptual processing is the shared mechanism between numerosity processing and mathematical performance. First, visual perceptual processing has been found to be important in another school achievement task – reading (Demb, Boynton, & Heeger, 1998; Eden et al., 1996; Vidyasagar & Pammer, 2010). For example, it has been suggested that developmental dyslexia is due to a deficit in visual perception (e.g., detection of letter-strings, speed discrimination), as well as a deficit in auditory processing of the sounds of language (Bradley & Caldwell, 1978; Demb et al., 1998; Eden et al., 1996; Sperling, Lu, Manis, & Seidenberg, 2005; Valdois et al., 2011). Reading ability has also been closely linked to arithmetic performance (Dehaene, Spelke, Pinel, Stanescu, & Tsivkin, 1999; Wei et al., 2012b). More relevant to the current study, a previous study has shown that numerosity processing is a primary visual task (Burr & Ross, 2008).

The current investigation

The aim of the current study is to explore the relationship between numerosity and DD, and determine whether visual perceptual ability would account for the established relationship between numerosity processing and mathematical performance for DD children (Piazza et al., 2010; Wei et al., 2012a). A figure-matching task was used to assess visual perceptual ability because it has been used by previous studies of the visual system's role in language processing (Demb et al., 1998; Sperling et al., 2005; Valdois et al., 2011). A battery of other cognitive tasks (ranging from attention to intelligence to spatial ability tests) was included as comparison tasks.

Methods

Participants

This study tested 726 third- to fifth-grade children (372 boys and 354 girls, 8.0 to 11.0 years old). They were recruited from 18 classes of four ordinary schools (two urban and two suburban) in Beijing, China. Classes were randomly selected from each school. However, all students in each selected class were asked to participate in the study. There were approximately 30 to 40 children per class. All participants were native Chinese speakers and had normal or corrected-to-normal vision.

The current investigation was approved by the National Key Laboratory of Cognitive Neuroscience and Learning at Beijing Normal University and the Principals of the schools.

Children with DD were defined in terms of standard scores on computational fluency and mathematical achievement, separately. They had scores on computational fluency or mathematical achievement less than the 7th percentile (−1.50 standard deviation), but they had scores on Raven's Progressive Matrices greater than the 25th percentile (−0.67 standard deviation). There were 82 children with DD in terms of computational fluency, and 70 children with DD in terms of mathematical achievement. Children with typical development were also selected from the sample of 726 children. The DD group and typically developing group were matched individually in terms of age, grade, gender, and class (i.e., in same class).

Procedure

The battery of tests was administered in two 45-minute sessions, separated by 7–10 days. The tests were administered to students (one class at a time) in a computer classroom. Each class was monitored by six or seven experimenters (4–6 children per experimenter), as well as the teacher of that class. Instructions were given and a practice session was completed before each formal test. The tasks were administered in the same order for all students. For all but one of the tasks, the children indicated their responses by pressing one of two keys ('P' or 'Q') on a computer keyboard; for the verbal working memory test, they entered a series of digits after hearing them. Students' responses were automatically recorded and sent over the Internet to a server located in our laboratory at Beijing Normal University. All data were collected from December 2011 to June 2013.

The practice session for each task consisted of either four or six trials, which were similar to those used in the formal test. The computer provided the child with feedback on the screen after each practice trial. For all of the tasks, the feedback for correct responses was 'Correct! Can you go faster?' and the feedback for incorrect responses was 'It is wrong. Try again.' Children could ask experimenters any questions that they had during the practice session. After all the children in a class had finished the practice session and had no more questions for the experimenters, the main experimenter said, 'Start,' and the children pressed any key to begin the formal test.

Tasks

In order to study the relationship between numerosity processing, and computational fluency and wide-range mathematical achievement for DD children, we needed to control for potential confounding cognitive processes (Halberda et al., 2008; Wei et al., 2012a).

We included four other cognitive tasks that have been used in previous research on mathematical cognition (Halberda et al., 2008; Wei et al., 2012a). We employed a task to assess visual-tracing ability because poor oculo-motor coordination has been linked to reading disability (Groffman, 1994) and mathematical deficits (Fischer, Gebhardt, & Hartnegg, 2008; Groffman, 2009). A basic reaction time task was used in order to control for the effect of manual response and mental processing speed (cf., Butterworth's (2003) 'Dyscalculia Screener', which included a reaction time task). Raven's Progressive Matrices measured the basic 'intelligence' or reasoning, and scores on this test have been correlated with mathematical performance (Kyttälä & Lehto, 2008; Rohde & Thompson, 2007). Mental rotation tasks were used to control the unique contribution from visuo-spatial ability (Berg, 2008).

A total of seven tasks were used, and they were computerised using Web-based applications in the 'Online Experimental Psychological System (OPES)' (www.dweipsy.com/lattice). In addition, curriculum-based or wide-range mathematical achievement scores were obtained from the schools.

Numerosity comparison

The numerosity-comparison task was adapted from the second edition of the Test of Early Mathematics Ability (Ginsburg & Baroody, 1990). Two sets of dots of varying sizes were presented simultaneously on the screen, and participants were asked to judge which dot array contained more dots, while ignoring the sizes of individual dots (see Figure 4.1). Participants pressed 'Q' if they thought that the array on the left contained more dots, and 'P' if they thought that the array on the right contained more dots. The number of dots in each set varied from 5 to 32. The two dot arrays for each trial were presented for 200 ms. After the participants had responded, there was a one-second blank screen before the next trial. The test consisted of 120 trials. For half of the trials, the total combined area of all dots in each set was controlled to be the same. For the other half of the trials, the average area of all dots in each set was controlled to be the same. The ratios for the two dot arrays ranged from 1.2 to 2.0. The trials were tested in three sessions, with 40 trials for each session. The children were asked to complete all trials.

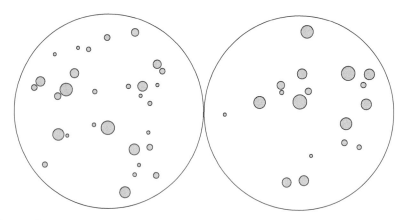

Figure 4.1 Example of stimuli for the numerosity-comparison task. Participants were asked to judge which dot array contained more dots, while ignoring the sizes of the individual dots.

Figure-matching

The figure-matching task was adapted from the identical picture test in the *Manual for the Kit of Factor-Referenced Cognitive Tests* (Ekstrom, French, Harman, & Dermen, 1976). There were 120 trials, each containing one target picture on the left side and three candidate pictures on the right side (see Figure 4.2). The pictures were constructed from 150 abstract line figures. The four pictures were presented simultaneously for 400 ms. Participants were asked to judge whether the picture on the left side also appeared on the right side, by pressing the button 'Q' for yes or 'P' for no. The 120 trials were grouped into three 40-trial sessions. Children were asked to complete all trials.

Computational fluency

The arithmetic task included two parts: simple and complex subtraction. This was a mental arithmetic task; subjects were not allowed to use paper and pencil.

Figure 4.2 Example of stimuli used for the figure-matching task. Participants were asked to judge whether the picture on the left side also appeared among 3 pictures on the right side.

Simple subtraction. For all 92 simple subtraction problems (e.g., 6 − 2, 17 − 8), the minuends were 18 or smaller, and the differences were single-digit numbers. Two candidate answers were presented beneath each problem. Participants were asked to press the 'Q' key to choose the answer on the left and the 'P' key to choose the answer on the right. For this task, each incorrect candidate answer was within the range of the correct answer plus or minus 3 (i.e., ±1, ±2, or ±3). This was a time-limited (2 minute) task.

Complex subtraction. All 96 problems in the complex subtraction task involved two-digit numbers minus two-digit numbers. Most problems required borrowing. Two candidate answers were presented beneath each problem: the correct answer and an incorrect candidate answer (i.e., the correct answer ±1, ±10). The other aspects of the procedure (stimulus presentation, method of responding) were the same as those for the simple subtraction task. This was a time-limited (2 minute) task.

The numbers of correct trials for the two tasks were averaged to yield a total score for computational fluency.

Mathematical achievement test

The local department of education developed and administered a general mathematical achievement test to all students in the county at the end of each semester. This test was curriculum-based and covered computation, mathematical concepts, and applied problem-solving. Students had 90 minutes to complete the test. The current study used the scores of the final examination of the term during which the study was conducted. The scores were provided by the primary schools that participated in the study.

Visual-tracing

The task was adapted from Groffman's visual-tracing test (Groffman, 1966). Several curved lines within a square interweaved with one another starting from the left side of the square and ending on the right side. Participants were asked to track a particular line from the beginning to the end by only using their vision (i.e., they were not allowed to use a finger or the cursor or an object to trace) and then to mark the correct end point. This task became more difficult as the total number of lines increased. There were 12 pictures, each used in three trials. This was a time-limited (4 minute) task.

Raven's Progressive Matrices

A simplified version of Raven's Progressive Matrices test (Raven et al., 1998) was used to assess general intelligence. For this task, participants had to identify the missing segment that would complete a figure's pattern. Two candidate answers were presented side-by-side beneath each problem; participants were instructed to press 'Q' if the missing segment was on the left and 'P' if it was on the right. The test consisted of 80 trials. This was a time-limited (3 minute) test.

Mental rotation

The mental rotation task was adapted from Vandenberg & Kuse (1978). On each trial, one three-dimensional image was presented on the upper part of the screen, and two more were presented on the lower part of the screen. Participants were asked to choose which image from the bottom of the screen matched the image at the top; the matching image could be identified only by mental rotation. The non-matching image was a rotated mirror image of the target. Participants pressed the 'Q' key to choose the image on the left and the 'P' key to choose the image on the right. The mental rotation test consisted of 180 trials. This was a time-limited (3 minute) test. The rotation angles of the matching images ranged from 15° to 345°, in intervals of 15°. On each trial, the stimuli remained on the screen until the participant responded by pressing the 'P' or the 'Q' key.

Choice reaction time

On each trial of the choice reaction time test, a white dot was presented on a black screen, either to the left or to the right of a fixation cross. The position of the dot was within 15° of the visual angle from the cross. Participants were asked to press the 'Q' key if the dot appeared on the left and the 'P' key if it appeared on the right. There were 30 trials in total (15 trials with the dot on the left and 15 trials with the dot on the right). The size of the screen on which the dot appeared varied randomly across trials. Inter-stimulus intervals varied randomly between 1,500 ms and 3,000 ms.

Data analyses

For all but two tasks (i.e., the timed choice reaction time task and mathematical achievement), we calculated scores by subtracting the number of incorrect responses from the number of correct responses in order to control for the effect of guessing (Cirino, 2011; Hedden & Yoon, 2006; Salthouse, 1994; Salthouse & Meinz, 1995). For the choice reaction time task, we calculated each participant's median reaction time and error rate. The gross mean error rate for the reaction time task was 4.2%, and was not further analysed.

Multivariate analysis was conducted to compare the performance on all tasks between the two groups. Figure-matching, as well as other cognitive measures (i.e., Raven's Progressive Matrices, mental rotation, visual-tracing, and choice reaction time) were also treated as covariates to test the difference of numerosity processing between the groups. Additionally, correlation analyses were performed to investigate the relationships between the key measures of the study.

Results

The means and standard deviations of the cognitive tasks and the mathematical achievement for the two groups of children are presented in Table 4.1.

Table 4.1 also shows the results from the multivariate F–test on the differences of task scores between the children with DD and typical development. When DD was diagnosed with computational fluency, the DD children had poorer performance in numerosity processing, figure–matching, and choice reaction time than the children with typical development. They did not show a difference in the Raven's Progressive Matrices. After the scores for the five cognitive tasks (i.e., choice reaction time, mental rotation, figure–matching, visual–tracing, and Raven's Progressive Matrices) were controlled for, the difference of numerosity processing between groups was no longer observed, F (1, 79) = .53, p = .47. When only controlling for the score for figure–matching, the difference also disappeared, F (1, 79) = 2.34, p = .13. When DD was diagnosed with mathematical achievement, the DD children had poorer performance only in the visual–tracing task.

The intercorrelations among task scores are displayed in Table 4.2, separately for each group. As Table 4.2 shows, the correlation between numerosity processing and figure–matching was consistently the highest among all the relationships across all measures. When DD was diagnosed with computational fluency, numerosity processing and figure–matching had the highest correlation with fluency. The high correlation between numerosity processing and computation fluency disappeared after

Table 4.1 Means (standard deviations) of task scores and F-test values on tasks for children with developmental dyscalculia (DD) and typical development (control)

Task	Mean(SD)		
	DD	Control	F-value
DD screened with computational fluency			
Computational fluency	−2.2 (.7)	.3 (.5)	364.91***
Choice reaction time	498 (194)	441 (91)	10.33**
Mental rotation	16.1 (9.4)	19.9 (9.5)	3.26
Raven Progressive Matrices	19.4 (4.9)	19.9 (4.7)	.23
Visual-tracing	14.8 (5.6)	16.2 (5.3)	1.34
Numerosity comparison	45.2 (28.5)	61.0 (19.4)	8.60**
Figure-matching	32.1 (25.3)	50.8 (24.6)	11.42***
DD screened with mathematical achievement			
Mathematical achievement	−2.4 (1.0)	.2 (.5)	189.42***
Choice reaction time	487 (147)	423 (78)	.69
Mental rotation	16.1 (9.1)	20.3 (12.1)	2.70
Raven Progressive Matrices	18.7 (5.1)	20.3 (4.2)	2.06
Visual-tracing	14.4 (5.7)	17.3 (5.3)	4.88*
Numerosity comparison	50.7 (27.3)	60.2 (21.3)	2.63
Figure-matching	39.9 (28.8)	49.6 (22.6)	2.47

Note: *p<.05, **p<.01, ***p<.001

the scores for figure-matching were controlled for, $r(79) = .17$, $p = .13$. However, the relationship was persistent after the scores for choice reaction time, mental rotation, visual-tracing, and Raven's Progressive Matrices were controlled for, $r(79) = .25$, $p = .03$. When DD was diagnosed with mathematical achievement, visual-tracing, other than numerosity processing and figure-matching had the highest correlation with achievement.

Discussion

The current study aimed to investigate when and why numerosity is associated with DD. DD was defined in terms of computational fluency and mathematical achievement, separately. The results showed that, for the computational fluency criterion alone, numerosity processing made a unique contribution to the variance in mathematical performance. The visual processing measured with figure-matching could account for the relationship of DD and numerosity processing. The results suggest that computational fluency, figure-matching, and numerosity processing might share the same mechanism of speed of visual perceptual processing.

The current investigation first replicated the previous finding of a strong relationship between numerosity processing and computational fluency. Further analyses showed that figure-matching accounted for the association between numerosity processing and computational fluency. Our results provide an alternative explanation for the finding of a close association between numerosity processing and computational fluency. That is, the speed of visual perceptual processing as measured by a figure-matching task, rather than the processing of numerical magnitude, might be the mechanism underlying that close relationship. Indeed, one common aspect of the

Table 4.2 Intercorrelations among task scores for children with developmental dyscalculia (DD) and typical development

Test	1	2	3			
DD screened with computational fluency						
Computational fluency	–					
Choice reaction time	.29**	–				
Mental rotation	.19*	−.02	–			
Raven Progressive Matrices	.06	.06	.24*	–		
Visual-tracing	.13	−.02	.23*	.24*	–	
Numerosity comparison	.33***	.25*	.10	−.03	.14	–
Figure-matching	.40***	.09	.06	−.09	.15	.49***
DD screened with mathematical achievement						
Mathematical achievement	–					
Choice reaction time	.03	–				
Mental rotation	.20*	.00	–			
Raven Progressive Matrices	.17	.03	.08	–		
Visual-tracing	.39***	.12	.25*	.19	–	
Numerosity comparison	.23*	.40***	.10	.04	.22*	–
Figure-matching	.27*	.18	.25*	−.04	.34**	.52***

Note: *p<.05, **p<.01, ***p<.001

figure-matching and numerosity-comparison tasks was that both tasks involved brief presentation of the stimuli; rapid visual perception is critical for the tasks. It is not difficult to understand that the two groups showed differences in the choice reaction time task. The speed of visual perception is also important for visual-tracing and mental rotation, especially when there is time pressure. However, both tasks might rely heavily on other cognitive abilities, such as visual attention and visual imagination.

Neither numerosity processing nor figure-matching ability was important for curriculum-based mathematical achievement. The mathematical achievement test included quantitative concepts, computation, applied problems, number series completion, geometry, etc. (Inglis, Attridge, Batchelor, & Gilmore, 2011; Sasanguie, De Smedt, Defever, & Reynvoet, 2012; Sasanguie, Defever, Maertens, & Reynvoet, 2013; Vanbinst, Ghesquière, & De Smedt, 2012). Previous studies found that there was a lack of a strong relationship between numerosity processing and the performance (Inglis et al., 2011). For example, Inglis et al. (2011) found that mathematical reasoning does not seem to depend on numerosity processing. Reasoning would not typically rely on visual perception, but rather on semantic knowledge, general reasoning, and imagination. For example, the processing of mathematical terms is typically supported by general semantic knowledge areas in the brain other than the parietal cortex (Xu et al., 2005; Zhang, Chen, & Zhou, 2012).

In summary, an inability in numerosity processing and figure-matching is associated with DD. The mechanism for this relationship might be the speed of visual perception. Further studies need to be conducted to determine if training on speed of visual perception could help DD children to improve their computation ability.

Acknowledgements

This study was supported by NSFC Projects 31271187, 61105118, and 31221003.

References

Berg, D. H. (2008). Working memory and arithmetic calculation in children: The contributory roles of processing speed, short-term memory, and reading. *Journal of Experimental Child Psychology, 99*(4), 288–308.

Bradley, R. H., & Caldwell, B. M. (1978). Screening the environment. *American Journal of Orthopsychiatry, 48*(1), 114–130.

Brannon, E. M., & Terrace, H. S. (1998). Ordering of the numerosities 1 to 9 by monkeys. *Science, 282*(5389), 746–749.

Burr, D., & Ross, J. (2008). A visual sense of number. *Current Biology, 18*(6), 425–428.

Butterworth, B. (2003). *Dyscalculia Screener*. London: nferNelson Pub.

Cirino, P. T. (2011). The interrelationships of mathematical precursors in kindergarten. *Journal of Experimental Child Psychology, 108*(4), 713–733.

De Smedt, B., & Gilmore, C. K. (2011). Defective number module or impaired access? Numerical magnitude processing in first graders with mathematical difficulties. *Journal of Experimental Child Psychology, 108*(2), 278–292.

Dehaene, S., Spelke, E., Pinel, P., Stanescu, R., & Tsivkin, S. (1999). Sources of mathematical thinking: Behavioral and brain-imaging evidence. *Science, 284*(5416), 970–974.

Demb, J. B., Boynton, G. M., & Heeger, D. J. (1998). Functional magnetic resonance imaging of early visual pathways in dyslexia. *The Journal of Neuroscience, 18*(17), 6939–6951.

Dudal, P. (1999). *Rekenbasis tot 10* [Maths Up to 10]: Torhout, Belgium: PMS Centrum.

Eden, G. F., VanMeter, J. W., Rumsey, J. M., Maisog, J. M., Woods, R. P., & Zeffiro, T. A. (1996). Abnormal processing of visual motion in dyslexia revealed by functional brain imaging. *Nature, 382*(6586), 66–69.

Ekstrom, R. B., French, J. W., Harman, H. H., & Dermen, D. (1976). *Manual for Kit of Factor-referenced Cognitive Tests*. Princeton, NJ: Educational Testing Service.

Fischer, B., Gebhardt, C., & Hartnegg, K. (2008). Subitizing and visual counting in children with problems in acquiring basic arithmetic skills. *Optometry and Vision Development, 39*(1), 24.

Geary, D. C., Bailey, D. H., & Hoard, M. K. (2009). Predicting mathematical achievement and mathematical learning disability with a simple screening tool: The number sets test. *Journal of Psychoeducational Assessment, 27*(3), 265–279.

Gilmore, C. K., McCarthy, S. E., & Spelke, E. S. (2007). Symbolic arithmetic knowledge without instruction. *Nature, 447*(7144), 589–591.

Ginsburg, H. P., & Baroody, A. J. (1990). *Examiners Manual of the Test of Early Mathematics Ability*. Texas: Pro-Ed.

Groffman, S. (1966). Visual tracing. *Journal of American Optometric Association, 37*(2), 139–141.

Groffman, S. (1994). The relationship between visual perception and learning. *Optometric Management of Learning-related Vision Problems*. St. Louis: Mosby-Year Book.

Groffman, S. (2009). Subitizing: Vision therapy for math deficits. *Optometry and Vision Development, 40*(4), 229.

Gross, H. J., Pahl, M., Si, A., Zhu, H., Tautz, J., & Zhang, S. (2009). Number-based visual generalisation in the honeybee. *PLoS One, 4*(1), e4263.

Halberda, J., Mazzocco, M. M. M., & Feigenson, L. (2008). Individual differences in non-verbal number acuity correlate with maths achievement. *Nature, 455*(7213), 665–668.

Hedden, T., & Yoon, C. (2006). Individual differences in executive processing predict susceptibility to interference in verbal working memory. *Neuropsychology, 20*(5), 511.

Inglis, M., Attridge, N., Batchelor, S., & Gilmore, C. (2011). Non-verbal number acuity correlates with symbolic mathematics achievement: But only in children. *Psychonomic Bulletin & Review, 18*(6), 1222–1229.

Iuculano, T., Tang, J., Hall, C. W. B., & Butterworth, B. (2008). Core information processing deficits in developmental dyscalculia and low numeracy. *Developmental Science, 11*(5), 669–680.

Kyttälä, M., & Lehto, J. E. (2008). Some factors underlying mathematical performance: The role of visuospatial working memory and non-verbal intelligence. *European Journal of Psychology of Education, 23*(1), 77–94.

Landerl, K., Bevan, A., & Butterworth, B. (2004). Developmental dyscalculia and basic numerical capacities: A study of 8–9-year-old students. *Cognition, 93*(2), 99–125.

Libertus, M. E., Feigenson, L., & Halberda, J. (2011). Preschool acuity of the approximate number system correlates with school math ability. *Developmental Science, 14*(6), 1292–1300.

McLean, J. F., & Hitch, G. J. (1999). Working memory impairments in children with specific arithmetic learning difficulties. *Journal of Experimental Child Psychology, 74*(3), 240–260.

Nieder, A., Freedman, D. J., & Miller, E. K. (2002). Representation of the quantity of visual items in the primate prefrontal cortex. *Science, 297*(5587), 1708–1711.

Piazza, M., Facoetti, A., Trussardi, A. N., Berteletti, I., Conte, S., Lucangeli, D., Zorzi, M. (2010). Developmental trajectory of number acuity reveals a severe impairment in developmental dyscalculia. *Cognition, 116*(1), 33–41.

Raven, J., Raven, J. C., & Court, J. H. (1998). *Manual for Raven's Progressive Matrices And Vocabulary Scales. Section 5: The Mill Hill Vocabulary Scale*. San Antonio, TX: Harcourt Assessment.

Rohde, T. E., & Thompson, L. A. (2007). Predicting academic achievement with cognitive ability. *Intelligence, 35*(1), 83–92.

Rousselle, L., & Noël, M. (2007). Basic numerical skills in children with mathematics learning disabilities: A comparison of symbolic vs non-symbolic number magnitude processing. *Cognition, 102*(3), 361–395.

Salthouse, T. A. (1994). The nature of the influence of speed on adult age differences in cognition. *Developmental Psychology, 30*(2), 240.

Salthouse, T. A., & Meinz, E. J. (1995). Aging, inhibition, working memory, and speed. *The Journals of Gerontology Series B: Psychological Sciences and Social Sciences, 50*(6), P297–P306.

Sasanguie, D., De Smedt, B., Defever, E., & Reynvoet, B. (2012). Association between basic numerical abilities and mathematics achievement. *British Journal of Developmental Psychology, 30*(2), 344–357.

Sasanguie, D., Defever, E., Maertens, B., & Reynvoet, B. (2014). The approximate number system is not predictive for symbolic number processing in kindergartners. *The Quarterly Journal of Experimental Psychology, 67*(2), 271–280.

Shalev, R. S. (2007). Prevalence of developmental dyscalculia. In D. B. Berch and M. M. M. Mazzocco (Eds.), *Why is Math So Hard for Some Children? The Nature and Origins of Mathematical Learning Difficulties and Disabilities* (pp. 49–60). Baltimore, MD: Paul H. Brookes Publishing Co.

Sperling, A. J., Lu, Z.-L., Manis, F. R., & Seidenberg, M. S. (2005). Deficits in perceptual noise exclusion in developmental dyslexia. *Nature Neuroscience, 8*(7), 862–863.

Valdois, S., Bidet-Ildei, C., Lassus-Sangosse, D., Reilhac, C., N'guyen-Morel, M., Guinet, E., & Orliaguet, J. P. (2011). A visual processing but no phonological disorder in a child with mixed dyslexia. *Cortex, 47*(10), 1197–1218.

Vanbinst, K., Ghesquière, P., & De Smedt, B. (2012). Numerical magnitude representations and individual differences in children's arithmetic strategy use. *Mind, Brain, and Education, 6*(3), 129–136.

Vandenberg, S. G., & Kuse, A. R. (1978). Mental rotations, a group test of three-dimensional spatial visualization. *Perceptual and Motor Skills, 47*(2), 599–604.

Vidyasagar, T. R., & Pammer, K. (2010). Dyslexia: A deficit in visuo-spatial attention, not in phonological processing. *Trends in Cognitive Sciences, 14*(2), 57–63.

Von Aster, M. G., & Shalev, R. S. (2007). Number development and developmental dyscalculia. *Developmental Medicine & Child Neurology, 49*(11), 868–873.

Wei, W., Yuan, H., Chen, C., & Zhou, X. (2012a). Cognitive correlates of performance in advanced mathematics. *British Journal of Educational Psychology, 82*(1), 157–181.

Wei, W., Lu, H., Zhao, H., Chen, C., Dong, Q., & Zhou, X. (2012b). Gender differences in children's arithmetic performance are accounted for by gender differences in language abilities. *Psychological Science, 23*(3), 320–330.

Xu, F., Spelke, E. S., & Goddard, S. (2005). Number sense in human infants. *Developmental Science, 8*(1), 88–101.

Zhang, H., Chen, C., & Zhou, X. (2012). Neural correlates of numbers and mathematical terms. *NeuroImage, 60*(1), 230–240.

5

Predictive indicators for mathematical learning disabilities/dyscalculia in kindergarten children

Annemie Desoete

Introduction

This chapter is devoted to the assessment of children at risk for learning disorders in mathematics (dyscalculia/MLD) and the potential early markers for dyscalculia/MLD in order to prevent children from falling further behind and from developing unrecognized dyscalculia/MLD later on. To provide some background to this, we begin with the definition of learning disorders in mathematics that will be used in this chapter. Next we present findings on logical thinking abilities and counting and their potential as indicators for dyscalculia/MLD in kindergarten. We then document the value of assessing language and number representation as foundations of MLD success. We conclude with findings on the value of including working memory as a learning factor and to enhance our understanding of kindergarten predictors and of dyscalculia/MLD in general.

Learning disorders in mathematics

The term learning disorder in mathematics (dyscalculia/MLD) refers to a significant degree of impairment in the mathematical skills. In addition, children with dyscalculia/MLD do not respond appreciably to regular classroom instruction. This is also referred to as a lack of Responsiveness to Intervention. Finally, the problems of dyscalculia/MLD cannot be totally explained by impairments in general intelligence or external factors that would contribute to scholastic failure (such as significant periods of absence).

Most researchers currently report prevalences of dyscalculia/MLD of 2–14% of children (Barbaresi, Katuskic, Colligan, Weaver, & Jacobsen, 2005; Desoete,

Roeyers, & De Clercq, 2004; Dowker, 2005; Vanmeirhaeghe, 2012). The prevalence of dyscalculia/MLD in siblings ranges from 40 to 64% (Shalev et al., 2001).

However, although the criteria for dyscalculia/MLD seem clear, there are some disagreements on, for example, the criteria used to define the 'degree of impairment'. Mazzocco, Devlin and McKenney (2008) found that children with dyscalculia/MLD (in conjunction with a severe level of general disability) showed qualitatively different profiles in fact-retrieval performances when compared to typically achieving children, whereas the differences between children at the lower end of the continuum (Low Achievers, LA, with a mild form of general disability) and typically achieving children had a quantitative nature. Geary, Hoard, Byrd-Craven, Nugent and Numtee (2007) found that children with MLD (a severe disability) had a severe mathematics cognition deficit and an underlying deficit in working memory and speed of processing. The LA groups (with a mild disability) had more subtle deficits in several math domains.

Logical thinking abilities and counting knowledge as indicators for Dyscalculia/MLD

Piaget and Szeminska (1941) suggested a relationship between 'seriation' (or the logical ability to sort objects based on differences while ignoring similarities) and 'classification' (or the logical ability to sort objects based on similarities, while ignoring differences) and the understanding of number. Although several neo-Piagetian researchers question the causality of seriation and classification for understanding number (e.g., Lourenço & Machado, 1996), recent studies revealed that children adequately solving seriation and classification tasks in kindergarten perform better in mathematical tasks in grades 1 and 2 (Grégoire, 2005; Nunes et al., 2007; Stock, Desoete, & Roeyers, 2010).

Before children start formal schooling, learning about numbers is largely focused on counting (LeFevre et al., 2006). A large body of research has been carried out to explore the conceptual and procedural knowledge in kindergarteners' counting (Dowker, 2005; Duncan et al., 2007; Hannula, Räsänen, & Lehtinen, 2007). 'Procedural knowledge' was defined as children's ability to perform a counting task; for example, a child succeeds in determining that there are five objects in an array (LeFevre et al., 2006). 'Conceptual counting knowledge' reflects a child's understanding of the essential counting principles: the stable order principle, the one-one correspondence principle and the cardinality principle (LeFevre et al., 2006).

A three-year longitudinal study (Stock et al., 2010) on 471 children followed up from kindergarten to grade 2, revealed the percentage of MD children (at age 7 to 8 years) correctly diagnosed in kindergarten by a combination of procedural and conceptual counting knowledge and number representation (assessed with magnitude comparison tasks, see later) was 87.50%. In addition seriation and classification tasks also had some value added in the screening of atypical development.

Moreover, a longitudinal study (Desoete, Stock, Schepens, Baeyens, & Roeyers, 2009) on 158 children followed up at the beginning of elementary school, revealed predictive relationships between children's seriation, classification, procedural counting knowledge and conceptual counting knowledge and their numerical facility and mathematical (calculation) achievement in grades 3, 4 and 5 (see Figure 5.1).

Path analyses revealed a relationship between procedural counting knowledge in grades 1 and 3 and fact-retrieval skills, and between conceptual counting knowledge in grade 1 and mathematical calculation achievement in grades 1 and 2 (see Figure 5.1). In addition, procedural counting knowledge correlated with seriation, and conceptual counting knowledge correlated with classification as well as with seriation in grade 1 (Desoete et al., 2009).

To conclude, seriation and classification (as logical thinking skills) and procedural and conceptual counting knowledge are revealed to be significant predictive indicators for mathematical learning disabilities in kindergarten. However Stock (2008) suggested that it seemed to be easier to screen the children who are not at risk than to detect the at-risk (or dyscalculia/MLD) children based on their kindergarten abilities.

Language abilities as indicators for dyscalculia/MLD

Recently the value of including language as a measure in the prediction of mathematical development has been stressed. However, whether or not a knowledge of number words helps children in kindergarten to solve mathematical problems was discussed by Canobi and Bethune (2008) who demonstrated that children in kindergarten were better problem solvers in the absence of number words. Nevertheless, a larger nominal vocabulary was found helpful for learning number words (Negen & Sarnecka, 2012). In addition, some studies (Negen & Sarnecka, 2012)

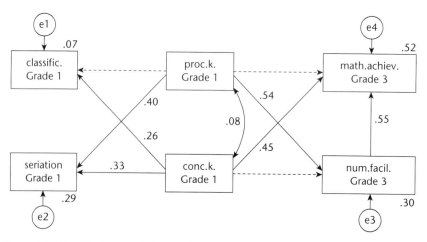

Figure 5.1 Classification, seriation and counting in grade 1 predicting mathematics in grade 3

Note: Values given are standardized path coefficients. classific. = classification. proc.k. = procedural counting knowledge. conc.k. = conceptual counting knowledge. math.achiev. = mathematical achievement. num.facil = numerical facility.

revealed that general measures of language development predict number-word knowledge, although other studies (e.g., Ansari et al., 2003) did not find such a link.

In a recent study (Praet, Titeca, Ceulemans, & Desoete, 2013) the impact of language was studied in a sample of 63 children tested in kindergarten with 23 of them tested again in grade 1. Our findings demonstrated the importance of kindergarten language as a predictor for mathematics, even with logical thinking, counting and intelligence added to the prediction in kindergarten (see Table 5.1).

The results suggest that the core language index of children in kindergarten influences how they understand and solve mathematical problems in kindergarten. Together with the other predictors (see Table 5.1) the variance in mathematical proficiency in kindergarten was predicted for 64.6% ($p < .001$), with especially language, intelligence and procedural counting knowledge as predictive indicators. The regression analysis remained significant in grade 1 ($p < .001$, $R^2 = .742$) but especially so for intelligence (see Table 5.1).

When focusing specifically on which linguistic skills related to children's mathematical performance, expressive language ($p = .003$) was important for solving simple mathematical operations involving pictures (e.g., 'Here you see two red balloons and three blue balloons. How many balloons are there altogether?') in kindergarten, whereas language structure was especially involved in the prediction of how children solve calculations in number-problem (e.g., $16 - 12 = . . .$) or word-problem (e.g., 1 less than 8 is . . . .) format in grade 1 ($p = .018$).

In addition, children with a core language index < 85 in kindergarten did not differ from peers without language problems on procedural ($p = .276$) or conceptual counting knowledge ($p = .937$) or on logical thinking skills ($p = .267$), but they had significantly more problems understanding and solving mathematical problems in

Table 5.1 Predictive indicators for mathematical abilities in kindergarten children

	Unstandardised coefficients	β	t	p
Mathematics in kindergarten				
Constant	−27.5673		−7.030	.000
Logical thinking	−.055	−.026	−.286	.776
Procedural counting knowledge	.815	.201	2.169	.035*
Conceptual counting knowledge	.156	.083	0.908	.368
Intelligence	.192	.492	3.942	.000*
Language	.107	.246	2.202	.032*
Mathematics in grade 1				
Constant	−78.468		−2.034	.058
Logical thinking	2.432	.281		.122
Procedural counting knowledge	−4.801	−.202	−1.442	.167
Conceptual counting knowledge	−1.452	−.099	−.653	.522
Intelligence	1.248	.621	2.924	.009*
Language	.295	.132	0.646	.527

Note: *p ≤ .05

kindergarten (p = .016) and in grade 1 (p = .006) compared to age-matched peers without language problems.

To conclude, the language demands of mathematics should not be overlooked. Different language components might contribute to different mathematical skills, with expressive language and language structure in kindergarten as predictive indicators for mathematical abilities later on.

Number representation as a predictor for dyscalculia/MLD

During the last decades, studies revealed that even preverbal infants process and represent small and large numbers (Ceulemans, Loeys, Warreyn, Hoppenbrouwers, & Desoete, 2012) long before formal education. Accurate number representation was shown to be correlated with mathematics performance (Ashcraft & More, 2012; Geary, 2011; Halberda, Mazzocco, & Feigenson, 2008).

Number representation differences were found in children with dyscalculia/ MLD (e.g., Ceulemans, Titeca, Loeys, & Desoete, 2014; Mussolin, Mejias, & Noël, 2010; Piazza et al., 2010; von Aster & Shalev, 2007) and in siblings of children with dyscalculia/MLD (Desoete, Praet, Titeca, & Ceulemans, 2013).

In addition, a cross-sectional study on 361 children in kindergarten (Stock & Desoete, 2009) revealed that children performing below or at the 10th percentile on the mathematical abilities test in kindergarten also had lower scores on number representation (assessed with a magnitude comparison task) compared to moderate achieving peers (scoring above the 50th percentile on this subtest) (see Table 5.2).

Number representation abilities in kindergarten could add to the prediction of dyscalculia/MLD and serve as powerful early screeners in the detection of children at risk (Stock & Desoete, 2009).

The importance of number representation was confirmed in a longitudinal study (Desoete, Ceulemans, De Weerdt, & Pieters, 2012) following children from kindergarten to grade 2, revealing that children with dyscalculia/MLD had severe problems with number representation (assessed with a magnitude comparison task) in kindergarten. The combination of number representation and symbolic (Arabic numbers and number words) deficits in kindergarten was a predictive indicator for developing dyscalculia/MLD in elementary school.

Furthermore, Praet and colleagues (2013) investigated if number representation assessed with other paradigms revealed the same results, or if the results on number representation deficits depended on the paradigm used. Praet et al. (2013) compared number representation in kindergarten with three paradigms, namely a number line estimation (NLE) task, a quantity comparison task and a quantity naming task. In the NLE task, children were asked to put a single mark on the line to indicate the location of the number. The percentage absolute error (PAE) was calculated as a measure of the estimation accuracy. For example, if a child was asked to estimate 25 on a 0–100 number line and placed the mark at the point on the line corresponding to 40, the PAE would be (40–25)/100 or 15% (Praet & Desoete, 2014). In the quantity comparison task children had to judge (for about 10 minutes) on which side of the screen (the side

Table 5.2 Kindergarten abilities

	≤ pc 10 on arithmetic in kindergartenMD M (**SD**) **N** = 26	> pc 50 on arithmetic in kindergarten M (**SD**) **N** = 167	F (1, 191)	Standard canonical discriminant function coefficients
Procedural counting	43.04 (29.75)	81.53 (21.97)	62.28*	.47
Conceptual counting	49.31 (32.35)	75.33 (22.52)	26.37*	.16
Seriation	55.58 (23.43)	92.51 (17.34)	92.10*	.55
Classification	52.92 (27.14)	78.74 (24.14)	24.88*	.22
Conservation	74.65 (7.21)	84.22 (12.27)	14.96*	.28
Number representation	69.46 (39.79)	94.28 (20.75)	23.82*	.32

Note: * p < .001

with the sun or the side with the moon) they saw more dots. The dot patterns were controlled for perceptual variables using the same procedure as Dehaene, Izard, and Piazza (2005), meaning that on half of the trials dot size was held constant, and on the other half, the size of the total occupied area of the dots was held constant. Children were asked to respond as quickly and accurately as possible. Finally, in the quantity naming task, participants were instructed to estimate aloud the number of squares they saw on the screen. All squares were black on a white background. The individual area, total area, and density of the squares were varied to ensure that participants could not use non-numerical cues to make a correct decision. The results (Table 5.3) suggest significant correlations between the paradigms and a significant relationship between number representation, mathematical skills and intelligence.

These results suggest that number representation can be assessed with different paradigms in kindergarten, with all of them having a significant relationship with mathematical abilities in kindergarten.

To conclude, children with dyscalculia/MLD often already had below average number representation skills in kindergarten independent of the paradigm used.

Working memory as predictor for dyscalculia/MLD

According to Baddeley (1986), working memory has to be seen as an active system that regulates complex cognitive behaviour. In the model, the central executive is an attentional control system, which executes the processing aspects of a task. The central executive strongly interacts with one multi-dimensional and two domain-specific storage systems. The phonological loop is responsible for the storage and maintenance of verbal information; the visuospatial sketchpad has similar responsibilities for visual and spatial information (Baddeley, 1986; 2000; Baddeley, Allen, & Hitch, 2010; Gathercole, Alloway, Willis, & Adams, 2006).

Some studies revealed deficits in all three components of working memory in children with dyscalculia/MLD (e.g., Geary et al., 2007), while others marked only problems in the central executive (e.g., McLean & Hitch, 1999; Passolunghi & Siegel, 2004), the central executive and the phonological loop (e.g., Swanson & Sachse-Lee, 2001), or the central executive and the visuospatial sketchpad (e.g., Gathercole & Pickering, 2000).

Table 5.3 Correlations between number representation paradigms and mathematical skills

	NLE	Q. comparison	Q. naming	TIQ
Mathematics	−.523**	.471**	.542**	.754**
NLE	–	−.413*	−.491*	. −524**
Quantity comparison	–	–	.389*	.445**
Quantity naming	–	–	–	.449**

Notes: * p ≤ .05, ** p≤ .001
Q = quantity, TIQ= Total Intelligence

A recent study (n = 112) confirmed that elementary school children with dyscalculia/MLD differed from peers without learning disabilities on working memory measures, such as (backward) digit recall, (backward) word recall, (backward) block recall, listening span and spatial span. In addition, the central executive component was the most important predictor for dyscalculia/MLD although children with reading disabilities also had deficits in this component confirmed (De Weerdt, Desoete, & Roeyers, 2013).

In addition, a recent longitudinal study followed up 26 children from kindergarten (at age 5 years), until they were 10 years old (grade 5). From this sample, 13 children had no learning disabilities. The other 13 children had been diagnosed with dyscalculia/MLD in grade 2. Analyses indicated that 54% of the children with dyscalculia/MLD (n = 7) in grade 2, still presented with profiles of dyscalculia/MLD at the age of 10 years, but six children no longer did. Spelling and pseudoword reading, measured at the age of 10 years, could classify 76.9% of the children (presenting with profiles of MLD; no longer presenting with MLD/dyscalculia profiles; control children) correctly. Whereas spatial span best predicted children no longer presenting as MLD/dyscalculia, digit recall was the best predictor of children still showing MLD/dyscalculia profiles (De Weerdt, 2012).

To conclude, children with dyscalculia/MLD often have limitations with working memory. In elementary school children the central executive component was the most important predictor for dyscalculia/MLD. In addition digit recall is a predictive indicator for children still presenting with a profile of dyscalculia/MLD.

Conclusion

Based on their kindergarten abilities, 87.50% of children at risk for dyscalculia/MLD can be detected (Stock et al., 2010). However, it seemed to be easier to screen the children who are not at risk than to detect the at-risk (or MLD/dyscalculia) children based on their kindergarten abilities (Stock, 2008). Studies confirmed the value of seriation and classification (logical thinking skills) as well as procedural and conceptual counting knowledge as predictive indicators for dyscalculia/MLD in kindergarten. These indicators were differentially related to children's mathematical skills (Desoete et al., 2009). Procedural counting knowledge and seriation were related to fact-retrieval skills whereas conceptual counting knowledge and classification correlated with mathematical calculation skills in elementary school. In addition, children with very low mathematical skills (Stock & Desoete, 2009), children with dyscalculia/MLD (Desoete et al., 2012) and siblings of children with dyscalculia/MLD (Desoete et al., 2013) frequently had lower scores on number representation tasks in kindergarten. Moreover, language (especially expressive language skills) was related to children's mathematical performance in kindergarten (Praet et al., 2013). Finally, the central executive component of working memory was the most important predictor for dyscalculia/MLD, with dyscalculia/MLD having a dynamic aspect and digit recall revealed as being the best predictor of children not outgrowing dyscalculia/MLD (De Weerdt et al., 2013).

References

Ansari, D., Donlan, C., Thomas, M. S. C., Ewing, S. A., Peen, T. & Karmiloff-Smith, A. (2003). What makes counting count? Verbal and visuo-spatial contributions to typical and atypical counting development. *Journal of Experimental Child Psychology, 85*, 50–62.

Ashcraft, M. H. & Moore, A. M. (2012). Cognitive processes of numerical estimation in children. *Journal of Experimental Child Psychology, 111*, 246–267.

Baddeley, A. (1986). *Working Memory.* Oxford, UK: Clarendon Press.

Baddeley, A. (2000). The episodic buffer: a new component of working memory? *Trends in Cognitive Sciences, 4*, 417–423.

Baddeley, A., Allen, R. J. & Hitch, G. J. (2010). Investigating the episodic buffer. *Psychologica Belgica, 50*, 223–243.

Barbaresi, W. J., Katusic, S. K., Colligan, R. C., Weaver, A. L. & Jacobsen, S. J. (2005). Learning disorder: Incidence in a population-based birth cohort, 1976–82, Rochester, Minn. *Ambulatory Pediatrics, 5*, 281–289.

Canobi, K. H. & Bethune, N. E. (2008). Number words in young children's conceptual and procedural knowledge of addition, subtraction and inversion. *Cognition, 108*, 675–686.

Ceulemans, A., Loeys, T., Warreyn, P., Hoppenbrouwers, K. & Desoete, A.(2012). Small number discrimination in early human development: The case of one versus three. *Education Research International,* vol. 2012, Article ID 964052, 5 pages.

Ceulemans, A., Titeca, D., Loeys, T., & Desoete, A. (2014). Enumeration of small and large numerosities in adolescents with mathematical learning disorders. *Research in developmental disabilities, 36*, 27–35.

Dehaene, S., Izard, V. & Piazza, M. (2005). Control over non-numerical parameters in numerosity experiments. Unpublished manuscript (available at http://www.unicog.org/pm/pmwiki.php/Main/Arithmetics).

Desoete, A., Ceulemans, A., De Weerdt, F. & Pieters, S. (2012). Can we predict mathematical learning disabilities from symbolic and non-symbolic comparison tasks in kindergarten? *British Journal of Educational Psychology, 82*, 64–81.

Desoete, A., Praet, M., Titeca, D. & Ceulemans, A. (2013). Cognitive phenotype of mathematical learning disabilities: What can we learn from siblings? *Research in Developmental Disabilities, 34*, 404–412.

Desoete, A., Roeyers, H. & De Clercq, A. (2004). Children with mathematics learning disabilities in Belgium. *Journal of Learning Disabilities, 37*, 50–61.

Desoete, A., Stock, P., Schepens, A., Baeyens, D. & Roeyers, H. (2009). Classification, seriation, and counting in grades 1, 2, and 3 as two year longitudinal predictors for low achieving in numerical facility and arithmetical achievement. *Journal of Psychoeducational Assessment, 27*, 252–264.

De Weerdt, F. (2012). Working memory, inhibition and naming speed in children with learning disabilities. Unpublished PhD dissertation. Ghent University.

De Weerdt, F., Desoete, A. & Roeyers, H. (2013). Working memory in children with reading and/or mathematical disabilities *Journal of Learning Disabilities, 46*, 461–472.

Dowker, A. D. (2005). *Individual Differences in Arithmetic. Implications for psychology, neuroscience and education.* New York: Psychology Press.

Duncan, G. J., Dowsett, C. J., Claessens, A., Magnuson, K., Huston, A. C., Klebanov, P. Japel, C. (2007). School readiness and later achievement. *Developmental Psychology, 43*, 1428–1446.

Gathercole, S. E., Alloway, T. P., Willis, C. & Adams, A. M. (2006). Working memory in children with reading disabilities. *Journal of Experimental Child Psychology, 93*, 265–281.

Gathercole, S. E. & Pickering, S. J. (2000). Working memory deficits in children with low achievements in the national curriculum at 7 years of age. *British Journal of Educational Psychology, 70*, 177–194.

Geary, D. C. (2011). Cognitive predictors of achievement growth in mathematics: A 5-year longitudinal study. *Developmental Psychology, 47*, 1539–1552.

Geary, D. C., Hoard, M. K., Byrd-Craven, J., Nugent, L. & Numtee, C. (2007). Cognitive mechanisms underlying achievement deficits in children with mathematical learning disability. *Child Development, 78*, 1343 1359.

Grégoire, J. (2005). Développement logique et compétences arithmétiques. Le modèle piagétien est-il toujours actuel? In M. Crahay, L. Verschaffel, E. De Corte & J. Grégoire. *Enseignement et apprentissage des mathématiques*. (pp. 57–77). Brussels: De Boeck.

Halberda, J., Mazzocco, M. M. M. & Feigenson, L. (2008). Individual differences in non-verbal number acuity correlate with maths achievement. *Nature, 455*, 665–U662.

Hannula, M. M., Räsänen, P. & Lehtinen, E. (2007). Development of counting skills: Role of numerosity and subitizing-based enumeration. *Mathematical Thinking, 9*, 51–57.

Le Fevre, J.-A., Smith-Chant, B. L., Fast, L., Skwarchuk, S.-L., Sargla, E., Arnup, J. S. Kamawar, D. (2006). What counts as knowing? The development of conceptual and procedural knowledge of counting from kindergarten through grade 2. *Journal of Experimental Child Psychology, 93*, 285–303.

Lourenço, O. & Machado, A. (1996). In defense of Piaget's theory: A reply to 10 common criticisms. *Psychological Review, 103*, 143–164.

Mazzocco, M. M. M., Devlin, K. T. & McKenney, S. J. (2008). Is it a fact? Timed arithmetic performance of children with mathematical learning disabilities (DYSCALCULIA/MLD) varies as a function of how DYSCALCULIA/MLD is defined. *Developmental Neuropsychology, 33*, 318–344.

McLean, J. F. & Hitch, G. J. (1999). Working memory impairments in children with specific arithmetic learning difficulties. *Journal of Experimental Child Psychology, 74*, 240–260.

Mussolin, C., Mejias, S. & Noël, M. P. (2010). Symbolic and nonsymbolic number comparison in children with and without dyscalculia. *Cognition, 115*, 10–25.

Negen, J. & Sarnecka, B. W. (2012). Number-concept acquisition and general vocabulary development, *Child Development, 83*, 2019–2027.

Nunes, T., Bryant, P., Evans, D., Bell, D., Gardner, A., Gardner, A. & Carraher, J. (2007). The contribution of logical reasoning to the learning of mathematics in primary school. *British Journal of Developmental Psychology, 25*(1), 147–166.

Passolunghi, M. C. & Siegel, L. S. (2004). Working memory and access to numerical information in children with disability in mathematics. *Journal of Experimental Child Psychology, 88*, 348–367.

Piaget, J. & Szeminska, A. (1941). *La genèse du nombre chez l'enfant*. Neuchâtel: Delanchaux et Niestlé.

Piazza, M., Facoetti, A., Trussardi, A. N., Berteletti, I., Conte, S., Lucangeli, D., & Zorzi, M. (2010). Developmental trajectory of number acuity reveals a severe impairment in developmental dyscalculia. *Cognition, 116*, 33–41.

Praet, M., Titeca, D., Ceulemans, D. & Desoete, A. (2013). Language in the prediction of arithmetics in kindergarten and grade 1. *Learning and Individual Differences, 27*, 90–96.

Praet, M. & Desoete, A. (2014). Number line estimation from kindergarten to grade 2: a longitudinal study. *Learning and Instruction, 33*, 19–28.

Shalev, R. S., Manor, O., Kerem, B., Ayali, M., Badichi, N., Friedlander, Y. & Gross-Tsur, V. (2001). Developmental dyscalculia is a familial learning disability. *Journal of Learning Disabilities, 34*, 59–65.

Stock, P. (2008). Prenumeric markers for arithmetic. Unpublished PhD dissertation. Ghent University.

Stock, P. & Desoete, A. (2009). Screening for mathematical disabilities in kindergarten. *Developmental Neurohabilitation, 12*, 389–397.

Stock, P., Desoete, A. & Roeyers, H. (2010). Detecting children with arithmetic disabilities from kindergarten: Evidence from a three year longitudinal study on the role of preparatory arithmetic abilities. *Journal of Learning Disabilities, 43*, 250–268.

Swanson, H. L., & Sachse-Lee, C. (2001). Mathematical problem solving and working memory in children with learning disabilities: Both executive and phonological processes are important. *Journal of Experimental Child Psychology, 79,* 294–321.

Vanmeirhaeghe, B. (2012). *Divided by numbers. Studying with dyscalculia. Documentary:* http://www.studerenmetdyscalculie.be/synopsis. Artevelde University College: Gent, Belgium.

Von Aster, M. G. & Shalev, R. S. (2007). Number development and developmental dyscalculia. *Developmental Medicine and Child Neurology, 49,* 868–873.

6

The link between mathematics and logical reasoning

Implications for research and education

Kinga Morsanyi and Denes Szücs

Are logic and mathematics fundamentally related? There are many reasons to suspect that they are (see, e.g., Ayalon & Even, 2008; Markovits & Lortie-Forgues, 2011; Moshman, 1990; Piaget & Inhelder, 1974). Nevertheless, mathematical and logical reasoning are rarely investigated together, and research into mathematical reasoning is largely dissociated from research into logical reasoning. In the present chapter, we will first give an overview of recent research into the origins of mathematical knowledge. Then we will explain why we expect that there might be a close link between logical and mathematical reasoning. Finally, we will describe one of our recent studies that looked at the relationships between maths and logic in typically developing children with average mathematical skills, mathematically gifted children, and in children with dyscalculia. We will conclude our chapter by discussing the educational implications of this line of research.

The origins of mathematical knowledge

When we think about mathematics, the most obvious thing that comes to mind is numbers. Numbers represent quantities, and the typical question that we answer when we solve mathematical problems is: 'How many?' or 'How much?' It has been suggested that mathematical abilities are rooted in an approximate number system (ANS) or 'number sense', which is shared across many species (Dehaene, 1997; Nieder & Dehaene, 2009). 'Number sense' can be described as the ability to quickly understand, approximate and manipulate non-symbolic numerical quantities.

Some suggest that even babies possess basic mechanisms to process information about quantities in that they might be able to recognize the approximate difference between two quantities (Lipton & Spelke, 2003; Xu & Arriaga, 2007), and solve simple approximate addition and subtraction problems (McCrink & Wynn, 2004). However, it is of note that visual stimulus confounds may distort these results, which is an especially serious problem in babies (see Mix et al., 1997, 2002).

Much research has examined how people handle information about approximate quantities. Nevertheless, it is far from clear how the proposed 'number sense' is related to formal maths skills. Probably the most popular measure of the precision of an individual's magnitude representations (i.e., their ANS) is the (non-symbolic) dot comparison task. In this task participants are presented with two arrays of dots, and their task is to select the more numerous one, disregarding other features of the patterns (such as the size of dots). A number of studies have suggested that there is a link between the ANS and mathematical abilities, as indexed by performance on standardized or curriculum-based mathematics tests (e.g., Desoete, Ceulemans, De Weerdt & Pieters, 2012; Halberda, Mazzocco & Feigenson, 2008; Piazza et al., 2010). Nevertheless, other studies failed to find a relationship between ANS precision and mathematical skills (e.g., Holloway & Ansari, 2009; Iuculano, Tang, Hall & Butterworth, 2008; Vanbinst, Ghesquière & De Smedt, 2012).

Besides the mixed evidence regarding the relationship between the dot comparison task and mathematical skills, recent studies have also challenged the suitability of the dot comparison task as a measure of basic (non-symbolic) magnitude representations. Several studies (Gebuis & Reynvolet; 2011a, 2011b, 2012; Rousselle, Palmers & Noel, 2004; Soltesz, Szücs & Szücs, 2010) demonstrated that performance on the task was unrelated to people's numerical abilities. In fact, childrens' and adults' responses depend simply on the perceptual properties of the stimuli (Gebuis & van der Smagt, 2011; Szücs, Nobes, Devine, Gabriel & Gebuis, 2013b). Additionally, recent studies with adults (Gilmore et al. 2013) and children (Fuhs & McNeil, 2013; Szücs et al., 2013b) have revealed that the task has significant inhibitory control demands, and relationships between the dot comparison task and mathematical skills are explained by this inhibitory component, rather than by the requirement to process magnitudes. Overall, these findings pose a serious challenge to the notion that the ability to process non-symbolic magnitudes would be the key to develop formal mathematical knowledge.

Is mathematics all about quantities?

In the previous section, we suggested that although the meaning of numbers is intimately linked with the magnitudes that they represent, the evidence for a close link between magnitude processing and formal mathematical thinking is controversial. Indeed, mathematics involves much more than just the ability to mentally manipulate magnitude representations. For example, consider the basic arithmetic operations. Addition can be thought of as combining magnitudes, multiplication can be thought of as repeatedly adding the same amount of items, etc. Whereas it is easy to mentally represent these operations in the case of small natural numbers (e.g., $5 + 1$ or 2×3), an exact representation can be difficult, or even impossible in the case of larger numbers (e.g., $274 + 319$) or fractions (e.g., $2/7 \times 1/3$). Note that these are still very simple problems that even primary school children are able to solve. Nevertheless, from these examples it is obvious that even at very basic levels of mathematical thinking, complex cognitive processes might be involved.

One of these cognitive requirements is the ability to process symbolic and abstract representations (i.e., representations without an obvious real-life referent – such as the concept of zero). Further, mathematical reasoning involves the application of rules, and the ability to integrate information and draw conclusions on the basis of given information. Note that all of these are general reasoning processes that we routinely apply in other domains of thinking as well.

Of course, there is nothing new in suggesting that mathematical thinking requires general cognitive resources. There is a wealth of evidence to show that verbal and visual working memory (e.g., Ashcraft & Kirk, 2001; Geary, 2004, 2011; Geary, Hoard & Hamson, 1999; Geary, Hamson & Hoard, 2000; Hitch & McAuley, 1991; Passolunghi & Siegel, 2001, 2004; Passolunghi & Mammarella, 2012; Swanson, Jerman & Zheng, 2008; Szücs, Devine, Soltesz, Nobes & Gabriel, 2013a), inhibitory function (e.g., Blair & Razza, 2007; Bull & Scerif, 2001; Espy et al., 2004), and attentional function (e.g., Ashkenazi, Rubinsten & Henik, 2009; Hannula, Lepola & Lehtinen, 2010; Swanson, 2011) are linked to achievement in mathematics. The same processes have also been identified as being implicated in logical reasoning (see next section). Nevertheless, in the present chapter we will argue that mathematics and logical thinking share more than just the requirement to perform cognitively demanding mental operations. In the following, we will first give a brief introduction into the development of logical thinking skills, before we present evidence for the link between mathematics and logic.

The cognitive determinants of logical thinking

Logical thinking entails the ability to draw conclusions on the basis of given premises. When researchers study logical reasoning skills, participants are typically instructed to ignore the meaning of the premises and the conclusions, and to accept the premises to be true, even if they are not true in real life (e.g., Handley, Capon, Beveridge, Dennis & Evans, 2004; Morsanyi & Handley, 2012). This is important, because logical reasoning problems are often designed in such a way that logicality conflicts with participants' beliefs or intuitions. Further, the concept of logical necessity is defined in the following way. A conclusion is necessary, if it must be true, given that the premises are true (see e.g., Evans, Handley, Neilens & Over, 2007). As an example, consider the following problem:

Elephants have long noses.

Animals with long noses are not heavy.

So, are elephants heavy?

This is an example of a problem where the believability of the conclusion is in conflict with the logical status of the conclusion (i.e., the conclusion is believable, but based on the premises, the logical response is to reject it).

It is well established that logical reasoning is heavily dependent on general cognitive resources, such as working memory, and general and fluid intelligence. This has been demonstrated both in the case of children (e.g., Chiesi, Primi & Morsanyi, 2011; Handley et al., 2004; Kokis, Macpherson, Toplak, West & Stanovich, 2002) and adults (e.g., De Neys, 2006; Gilhooly, 1998; Stanovich & West, 2000). Furthermore, in the case of problems where logicality and beliefs are in conflict, participants have to resist the temptation to base their conclusions on their empirical knowledge. Blocking the intrusion of real-life knowledge requires inhibition processes (e.g., De Neys & Everaerts, 2008; Handley et al., 2004; Simoneau & Markovits, 2003). That is, when we reason about belief-inconsistent materials, we have to actively inhibit the effect of our beliefs, whereas such an inhibition process is not involved in reasoning about belief-consistent content.

Finally, although reasoning on the basis of belief-inconsistent materials is harder than reasoning on the basis of beliefs (e.g., De Neys, 2006; Handley et al., 2004; Simoneau & Markovits, 2003), reasoning with abstract content is even more difficult (e.g., Evans, Handley & Harper, 2001; Markovits & Lortie-Forgues, 2011). Thus, it seems that the extent to which people are able to reason logically depends strongly on the content of reasoning problems.

Developmental studies have provided further evidence of the effect of task content on reasoning processes. Although children around the age of 6 are able to reason logically with familiar, everyday content (e.g., Markovits, 2000), reasoning about empirically false premises is only possible around the age of 11 (e.g., Markovits & Lortie-Forgues, 2011), and even adults' judgements of the validity of conclusions might be strongly affected by their beliefs (e.g., Evans, Newstead, Allen & Pollard, 1994). Finally, some late adolescents and adults are able to reason logically about abstract premises (see Markovits & Lortie-Forgues, 2011), although even educated adults tend to find abstract problems difficult (e.g., Venet & Markovits, 2001).

Potential links between maths and logic

As we described above, both mathematical and logical thinking are cognitively demanding. Specifically, they are heavily dependent on working memory (e.g., Ashcraft & Kirk, 2001; Gilhooly, 1998) and inhibitory processes (e.g., Bull & Scerif, 2001; Simoneau & Markovits, 2003). Mathematics and logical thinking also share the requirement to be able to retrieve and apply normative rules, to draw conclusions on the basis of given premises, and to process abstract or symbolic content. Given these similarities, it can be expected that mathematical abilities should be strongly related to logical reasoning skills, unless logicality is achieved through a domain-specific route in mathematics. Although the research areas of reasoning and mathematical cognition are largely dissociated, there are some studies that have investigated the link between logical and mathematical reasoning.

One study (Handley et al., 2004) involved 10-year-old children, who had to work through a series of logical reasoning problems, some of which included a conflict between logicality and believability. These authors reported a strong correlation ($r(30) = .63$ $p<.001$) between children's logical reasoning ability and their performance on a standardized maths test. Nevertheless, they also found a strong relationship between children's logical reasoning ability and their reading ($r(30) = .60$ $p<.001$) and writing skills ($r(30) = .47$ $p<.01$). Thus, it is possible that these correlations simply reflect a positive relationship between logical reasoning skills and general academic aptitude, rather than a specific link between logic and maths.

Inglis and Simpson (2009) investigated the predictions of the 'theory of formal discipline', the idea that general reasoning skills can be improved by training in a specific discipline (see Nisbett, Fong, Lehman & Cheng, 1987). Specifically, they investigated the link between mathematical and conditional reasoning skills (i.e., the ability to reason on the basis of '*if p then q*'-type statements). An example of this kind of task is the following.

If a card is yellow, then it has a circle on it.

The card is not yellow.

Does it mean that it does not have a circle on it?

This is a Denial of the Antecedent (DA) inference, which is invalid. Nevertheless, a large majority of people believe that the conclusion necessarily follows (e.g., Evans et al., 2007).

Inglis and Simpson (2009) found that mathematics undergraduates outperformed intelligence-matched arts students on an abstract conditional inference task, which included similar problems to the above example. Nevertheless, during their first year of studies, there was no change in mathematics undergraduates' conditional reasoning performance. Inglis and Simpson offered two possible explanations for the initial between-groups difference on entry to university. It is possible that students with better abstract reasoning skills are more likely to study mathematics at university. Another possibility is that mathematics learning improves conditional reasoning skills, but these changes had already occurred at pre-university level. Note that mathematics learning was not compulsory in the UK for students over 16 at the time of that study and thus it is likely that only mathematics undergraduates participated in post-compulsory mathematics education before they entered university.

In a later study, Attridge and Inglis (2013) investigated the changes in the conditional reasoning skills of students studying post-compulsory mathematics, and students studying post-compulsory English literature. The initial reasoning performance of students enrolled in mathematics and literature courses did not differ, and literature students' reasoning performance did not change over the academic year. By contrast, mathematics students' reasoning performance improved. In particular, they were more able to reject invalid conclusions at the end of the academic year, as compared to when they started their courses.

These results suggest that education in mathematics improves general reasoning skills. A potential explanation for this is that mathematics and logical thinking rely on shared inferential processes. If this is the case, the development of mathematical and logical skills might also be related. In the study that we describe below, we investigated the developmental links between mathematics and logic.

Is logical reasoning impaired in developmental dyscalculia, and is it enhanced in mathematically gifted children?

Developmental dyscalculia (DD) is a specific impairment of mathematical ability which affects about 3.5–6.5% of the school-age population (e.g., von Aster & Shalev, 2007). DD is characterized by moderate to extreme difficulties in fluent numerical computations in the absence of sensory difficulties, low IQ or educational deprivation (see Butterworth, 2005). Although the difficulties of individuals with DD are supposed to be restricted to mathematics, recent evidence (Szücs et al., 2013a; Passolunghi & Mammarella, 2012) suggests that individuals with DD also have deficits in visuo-spatial working memory, visuo-spatial short-term memory and inhibition skills. In our study (Morsanyi, Devine, Nobes & Szücs, 2013) we explored the possibility that children with DD might also struggle with logical reasoning. At the same time, we wanted to check whether mathematically gifted children were also outstanding in their logical reasoning skills. These predictions directly follow from the idea that the development of mathematical and logical skills is intimately related. At the same time, the prediction that maths and logic might be linked in DD is in contrast with prevailing theories of DD, which consider it as a domain-specific deficit, restricted to mathematical cognition and to the ability to process and understand magnitude information (e.g., Landerl, Bevan & Butterworth, 2004; Piazza et al., 2010).

The particular form of logical reasoning that we investigated was the ability to make transitive inferences (see Table 6.1). This form of relational reasoning consists of ordering objects along a single dimension according to their relative properties. For example, if A is bigger than B, and C is bigger than A, then it necessarily follows that C is bigger than B. We were interested in this particular aspect of deductive reasoning for the following reasons. First, although transitive inference problems are purely verbal, in order to solve them children need to mentally manipulate the terms included in the problems, adhering to the rules of transitivity. This process is, arguably, very similar to performing transformations in the context of solving equations. Second, by manipulating the content of the conclusions, it is possible to create a conflict between the logical structure of the problems and the believability of the conclusions (i.e., to create valid unbelievable and invalid believable problems) and, thus, to measure children's ability to reason independently of their beliefs.

Drawing logical inferences on the basis of empirically false premises is an intermediate level of abstraction, which constitutes an important step towards developing the ability of abstract logical reasoning. In the present study we included problems with belief-laden conclusions, and problems with belief-neutral conclusions, which were

Table 6.1 Examples of different types of transitive inference problems

	Believable	Neutral	Unbelievable
Valid	Cats are bigger than dogs.	John is stronger than Tom.	Babies are older than children.
	Dogs are bigger than mice.	Adam is stronger than John.	Children are older than adults.
	Are cats bigger than mice?	Is Adam stronger than Tom?	Are babies older than adults?
Invalid	Babies are older than children.	John is stronger than Tom.	Cats are bigger than dogs.
	Children are older than adults.	Adam is stronger than John.	Dogs are bigger than mice.
	Are adults older than babies?	Is Tom stronger than Adam?	Are mice bigger than cats?

neither believable nor unbelievable. Whereas the former problems were intended as measures of reasoning about empirically false content, the latter problems were aimed at measuring abstract reasoning. As we described above, mathematical reasoning relies both on inhibitory processes, and the ability to process abstract and symbolic content. Nevertheless, we also know that these abilities emerge at different points in development. Whereas early adolescents are able to reason about empirically false content, abstract logical reasoning is a developmentally late achievement, which typically emerges around late adolescence (Markovits & Lortie-Forgues, 2011).

The participants in our study were 43 10-year-old children (20 girls). Thirteen children were diagnosed with DD on the basis of their performance on tests of intelligence, verbal working memory, and standardized, curriculum-based tests of mathematical and reading ability. Children were considered to have DD if their intelligence, working memory and reading ability were close to the population mean, whereas their mathematics performance was at least 1SD below the population mean. Population means were established through an initial testing session which involved 1,004 children. The 16 children in the control group were group-matched to the DD children in their intelligence, working memory and reading scores, but their mathematics achievement was very close to the population mean. Finally, 14 children with high mathematical ability were also included in the study. These children typically performed better than the other children on the reading, intelligence and working memory measures as well.

Our findings indicated that the DD group reasoned on the basis of their beliefs with no reliable effect of logicality on their judgements. By contrast, the control and high maths ability groups' judgements were affected by the logicality of conclusions, with a greater effect of logicality in the case of high maths ability participants. At the same time, performance of all groups was similar on belief-neutral problems. Specifically, none of the groups were able to reliably solve these problems on the basis of logicality. Importantly, the difference in logical reasoning about belief-inconsistent problems between the DD and control groups was present, although the groups were well matched, and this difference also remained significant when we controlled for individual differences in several cognitive variables.

Our results have several important implications. First, in contrast with claims that DD is caused by a specific and isolated deficit of 'number sense', our findings show that DD children also performed worse than controls on a purely verbal task, which had no obvious connection with mathematics. More importantly, our thematic problems were designed to measure the ability to draw logical inferences about empirically false content. There is evidence that this ability, which emerges in late childhood, is an important stepping stone towards the development of abstract reasoning (Markovits & Lortie-Forgues, 2011), which, in turn, is essential for high-level mathematical and scientific thinking (e.g., Moshman, 1990). DD children showed a clear disadvantage in the ability to reason logically about imaginary content when compared to children of the same age with similar IQ, working memory, and reading abilities. However, we should point out that although reasoning on the basis of beliefs about empirically false content is less demanding than logic-based reasoning, it is in itself a developmental achievement (e.g., Markovits, 2000; Morsanyi & Handley, 2008). Thus, although DD children clearly show a developmental delay in logical reasoning, this is not to say that they do not have the potential to develop this ability. Nevertheless, our findings indicate that there is a relationship between mathematical abilities and logic, and also between the impairment of these skills and DD.

We would like to briefly discuss the potential reasons why DD children performed so poorly on our measures of logical reasoning, while they did not differ from controls in their IQ, reading ability, and verbal working memory. Probably the most relevant finding here is that DD children not only performed poorly in terms of being able to reason on the basis of logical structure, but they were also more strongly affected by their beliefs than children in the other groups. Thus, one possibility is that they were unable to inhibit the intrusion of their real-life beliefs. Indeed, such an inhibition failure could be a sufficient explanation for the present findings as, although these children also performed poorly on belief-neutral problems, their performance on these tasks was not different from controls. Another possibility is that DD children have problems with using visual imagery and, thus, they were less able to utilize the instructions to rely on their imagination to visualize non-existent possibilities than other children. At this point either (or both) of these explanations seems plausible. Indeed, both of these suggestions are in line with recent findings that children with DD show deficits in visuo-spatial working memory, visuo-spatial short-term memory and inhibition skills (Szücs et al., 2013a; Passolunghi & Mammarella, 2012).

Summary, educational implications and conclusions

In the previous sections we described studies which demonstrated that education in mathematics improves logical reasoning skills (Attridge & Inglis, 2013), and that children with DD show impairments in their ability to reason logically, whereas children with outstanding mathematical abilities excel in logical reasoning (Morsanyi et al., 2013). The studies that we described used two different types of logical reasoning tasks: conditional inferences and transitive reasoning problems. Although so far only a small number of studies have looked at the links between maths and logic, the available results lend strong support to the notion that mathematical and logical reasoning skills are fundamentally linked. Indeed, supporting evidence has been found in the case of young adults (Inglis & Simpson, 2009), late adolescents (Attridge & Inglis, 2013), and both typically developing children and children with DD (Morsanyi et al., 2013).

It is likely that this link is mediated (at least partially) by the general cognitive requirements of logical and mathematical reasoning, including the demand for verbal and visuo-spatial working memory resources, and inhibition. In addition, it also seems plausible that logical reasoning and mathematics share some basic inferential processes – in particular, the ability to draw conclusions on the basis of given premises. Thus, it might be that although having sufficient working memory and inhibitory resources is necessary for maths and logical reasoning, the availability of these resources is not sufficient either for good mathematical or good logical performance. These questions remain to be addressed by future studies. Another question for future studies is whether all types of logical inference are equally important for mathematical skills. Indeed, there are many different types of logical inference. In addition, the cognitive processes involved in a particular logical inference vary to some extent, depending on the content of the problems.

As we described above, when we make transitive inferences, we have to order objects along a single dimension according to their relative properties. It has been influentially suggested that, as part of the development of mathematical knowledge, children organize their mental representations of numbers along a 'mental number line' (Restle, 1970). In this representation, numbers are organized according to their magnitudes: in Western cultures, small numbers appear on the left, and large numbers appear on the right. The precision of such representation of symbolic numbers has been found to be related to mathematical abilities (see De Smedt, Noel, Gilmore & Ansari (2013) for a review). Thus, it is possible that one reason for the link between transitive inferences and mathematical skills is the shared requirement to mentally order items along a single dimension.

Conditional inferences (i.e., the ability to reason on the basis of *if-then* rules) do not require this dimensional representation. Thus, a different explanation for the relationship between conditional reasoning skills and maths skills is required. A very plausible possibility is that the link between conditional reasoning and maths exists because conditional reasoning forms the basis of hypothetical thought (e.g., Evans & Over, 2004), as well as scientific reasoning (Markovits & Lortie-Forgues, 2011; Moshman, 1990). Nevertheless, it is likely that the strongest association between maths and both transitive reasoning and conditional inferences will emerge when the logical reasoning problems involve belief-inconsistent or abstract content, as these problems cannot be solved by simple memory-retrieval processes, but they require people to go beyond their everyday experiences.

Given that existing studies explored the link between conditional inferences and maths in the case of late adolescents and adults (Attridge & Inglis, 2013; Inglis & Simpson, 2009), and transitive inferences in the case of children (Morsanyi et al., 2013), it is also an interesting question for future research whether both types of inferences are equally closely related to mathematical skills at all points of development. Finally, besides conditional inferences and transitive reasoning, the relationship between other types of logical reasoning and maths should also be explored.

With regard to educational interventions, there is evidence that logical reasoning is improved in individuals with a general tendency to consider and generate possibilities (e.g., De Neys & Everaerts, 2008; Janveau-Brennan & Markovits, 1999; Verschueren, Schaeken & d'Ydewalle, 2005) and that logical reasoning can be facilitated by instructing participants to engage in such a generation process (Markovits & Lortie-Forgues, 2011) or simply to use their imagination (e.g., Dias & Harris, 1988, 1990). These interventions could provide new avenues for developing training activities and educational tools for children who struggle with maths.

Another interesting hypothesis is that it might be possible to improve mathematical skills by training children in arranging items along a continuum, and in performing comparisons or transformations across these items. Furthermore, training in simple logical rules might also be useful. With regard to these suggestions, it is important to highlight that these interventions would not have to involve mathematical content, which might be especially useful in the case of children who suffer from mathematical anxiety. Nevertheless, as a limitation of these training methods, it is noteworthy that given that both maths and logical reasoning depend heavily on working memory, attention, and inhibitory processes, the above interventions might be ineffectual in the case of children who suffer from basic deficits in these cognitive abilities.

In summary, although there is evidence for important links between mathematics and logic, research in this area is extremely limited, and there is much work to be done before we can fully understand these links, and exploit them in an educational setting. Having said this, we hope that our chapter has made it clear that this is a potentially very fruitful research area, which would deserve much more attention from the research community.

References

Ashcraft, M.H., & Kirk, E.P. (2001). The relationships among working memory, math anxiety, and performance. *Journal of Experimental Psychology: General, 130*, 224–237.

Ashkenazi, S., Rubinsten, O., & Henik, A. (2009). Attention, automaticity, and developmental dyscalculia. *Neuropsychology, 23*, 535–540.

Attridge, N., & Inglis, M. (2013). Advanced mathematical study and the development of conditional reasoning skills. *PLOS ONE, 8*, e69399.

Ayalon, M., & Even, R. (2008). Deductive reasoning: In the eye of the beholder. *Educational Studies in Mathematics, 69*, 235–247.

Blair, C., & Razza, R.P. (2007). Relating effortful control, executive function, and false belief understanding to emerging math and literacy ability in kindergarten. *Child Development, 78*, 647–663.

Bull, R., & Scerif, G. (2001). Executive functioning as a predictor of children's mathematics ability: Inhibition, switching, and working memory. *Developmental Neuropsychology, 19,* 273–293.

Butterworth, B. (2005). Developmental dyscalculia. In J.I.D. Campbell (Ed.), *The Handbook of Mathematical Cognition* (Vol. 1, pp. 455–468). Hove: Psychology Press

Chiesi, F., Primi, C., & Morsanyi, K. (2011). Developmental changes in probabilistic reasoning: The role of cognitive capacity, instructions, thinking styles and relevant knowledge. *Thinking & Reasoning, 17,* 315–350.

De Neys, W. (2006). Dual processing in reasoning: Two systems but one reasoner. *Psychological Science, 17,* 428–433.

De Neys, W., & Everaerts, D. (2008). Developmental trends in everyday conditional reasoning: The retrieval and inhibition interplay. *Journal of Experimental Child Psychology, 100,* 252–263.

De Smedt, B., Noël, M.P., Gilmore, C., & Ansari, D. (2013). How do symbolic and non-symbolic numerical magnitude processing relate to individual differences in children's mathematical skills? A review of evidence from brain and behavior. *Trends in Neuroscience and Education, 2*(2), 48–55.

Dehaene, S. (1997). *The Number Sense: How the mind creates mathematics.* Oxford: Oxford University Press.

Desoete, A., Ceulemans, A., De Weerdt, F., & Pieters, S. (2012). Can we predict mathematical learning disabilities from symbolic and non-symbolic comparison tasks in kindergarten? Findings from a longitudinal study. *British Journal of Educational Psychology, 82,* 64–81.

Dias, M.G., & Harris, P.L. (1988). The effect of make-believe play on deductive reasoning. *British Journal of Developmental Psychology, 6,* 207–221.

Dias, M.G., & Harris, P.L. (1990). The influence of the imagination on reasoning by young children. *British Journal of Developmental Psychology, 8,* 305–317.

Espy, K.A., McDiarmid, M.M., Cwik, M.F., Stalets, M.M., Hamby, A., & Senn, T.E. (2004). The contribution of executive functions to emergent mathematical skills in preschool children. *Developmental Neuropsychology, 26,* 465–486.

Evans, J.St.B.T., Handley, S.J., & Harper, C. (2001). Necessity, possibility and belief: A study of syllogistic reasoning. *Quarterly Journal of Experimental Psychology, 54A,* 935–958.

Evans, J.St.B.T., Handley, S.J., Neilens, H., & Over, D.E. (2007). Thinking about conditionals: A study of individual differences. *Memory & Cognition, 35,* 1772–1784.

Evans, J.St.B.T., Newstead, S.E., Allen, J.L., & Pollard, P. (1994). Debiasing by instruction: The case of belief bias. *European Journal of Cognitive Psychology, 6,* 263–285.

Evans, J.St.B.T, & Over, D.E. (2004). *If.* Oxford: Oxford University Press.

Fuhs, M.W., & McNeil, N.M. (2013). ANS acuity and mathematics ability in preschoolers from low-income homes: Contributions of inhibitory control. *Developmental Science, 16,* 136–148.

Geary, D.C. (2004). Mathematics and learning disabilities. *Journal of Learning Disabilities, 37,* 4–15.

Geary, D.C. (2011). Cognitive predictors of individual differences in achievement growth in mathematics: A five year longitudinal study. *Developmental Psychology, 47,* 1539–1552.

Geary, D.C., Hamson, C.O., & Hoard, M.K. (2000). Numerical and arithmetical cognition: A longitudinal study of process and concept deficits in children with learning disability. *Journal of Experimental Child Psychology, 77,* 236–263.

Geary, D.C., Hoard, M.K., & Hamson, C.O. (1999). Numerical and arithmetical cognition: Patterns of functions and deficits in children at risk for a mathematical disability. *Journal of Experimental Child Psychology, 74,* 213–239.

Gebuis, T., & Reynvoet, B. (2011a). The interplay between visual cues and non-symbolic number. *Journal of Experimental Psychology: General, 141,* 642–648.

Gebuis, T., & Reynvoet, B. (2011b). Generating non-symbolic number stimuli. *BehaviorResearch Methods, 43,* 981–986.

Gebuis, T., & Reynvoet, B. (2012). The role of visual information in numerosity estimation. *PLOS ONE, 7*(5), e37426.

Gebuis, T., & van der Smagt, M.J. (2011). False approximations of the approximate number system? *PLOS ONE, 6*(10), e25405.

Gilhooly, K.J. (1998). Working memory, strategies, and reasoning tasks. In R.H. Logie & K.J. Gilhooly (Eds.), *Working Memory and Thinking* (pp. 7–22). Hove: Psychology Press.

Gilmore, C., Attridge, N., Clayton, S., Cragg, L., Johnson, S., Marlow, N., Inglis, M. (2013). Individual differences in inhibitory control, not non-verbal number acuity, correlate with mathematics achievement. *PLOS ONE, 8*(6), e67374.

Halberda, J., Mazzocco, M., & Feigenson, L. (2008). Individual differences in non-verbal number acuity correlate with maths achievement. *Nature, 455*, 665–668.

Handley, S., Capon, A., Beveridge, M., Dennis, I., & Evans, J.S.B.T. (2004). Working memory, inhibitory control, and the development of children's reasoning. *Thinking & Reasoning, 10*, 175–195.

Hannula, M.M., Lepola, J., & Lehtinen, E. (2010). Spontaneous focusing on numerosity as a domain-specific predictor of arithmetical skills. *Journal of Experimental Child Psychology, 107*, 394–406.

Hitch, G.J., & McAuley, E. (1991). Working memory in children with specific arithmetical learning difficulties. *British Journal of Psychology, 82*, 375–386.

Holloway, I.D., & Ansari, D. (2009). Mapping numerical magnitudes onto symbols: The distance effect and children's mathematical competence. *Journal of Experimental Child Psychology, 103*, 17–29.

Inglis, M., & Simpson, A. (2009). Conditional inference and advanced mathematical study: Further evidence. *Educational Studies in Mathematics, 72*, 185–198.

Iuculano, T., Tang, J., Hall, C.W., & Butterworth, B. (2008). Core information processing deficits in developmental dyscalculia and low numeracy. *Developmental Science, 11*, 669–680.

Janveau-Brennan, G., & Markovits, H. (1999). The development of reasoning with causal conditionals. *Developmental Psychology, 35*, 904–911.

Kokis, J., Macpherson, R., Toplak, M.E., West, R.F., & Stanovich, K.E. (2002). Heuristic and analytic processing: Age trends and associations with cognitive ability and cognitive styles. *Journal of Experimental Child Psychology, 83*, 26–52.

Landerl, K., Bevan, A., & Butterworth, B. (2004). Developmental dyscalculia and basic numerical capacities: a study of 8–9-year-old students. *Cognition, 93*, 99–125.

Lipton, J.S., & Spelke, E.S. (2003). Origins of number sense: Large number discrimination in human infants. *Psychological Science, 14*, 396–401.

Markovits, H. (2000). A mental model analysis of young children's conditional reasoning with meaningful premises. *Thinking & Reasoning, 6*, 335–347.

Markovits, H., & Lortie-Forgues, H. (2011). Conditional reasoning with false premises facilitates the transition between familiar and abstract reasoning. *Child Development, 82*, 646–660.

McCrink, K., & Wynn, K. (2004). Large-number addition and subtraction by 9-month-old infants. *Psychological Science, 15*, 776–781.

Mix, K., Huttenlocher, J., & Levine, S.C. (2002). Multiple cues for quantification in infancy: Is number one of them? *Psychological Bulletin, 128*, 278–294.

Mix, K., Levine, S.C., & Huttenlocher, J. (1997). Numerical abstraction in infants: Another look. *Developmental Psychology, 33*, 423–428.

Morsanyi, K., Devine, A., Nobes, A., & Szücs, D. (2013). The link between logic, mathematics and imagination: Evidence from children with developmental dyscalculia and mathematically gifted children. *Developmental Science, 16*, 542–553.

Morsanyi, K., & Handley, S.J. (2008). How smart do you need to be to get it wrong? The role of cognitive capacity in the development of heuristic-based judgment. *Journal of Experimental Child Psychology, 99*, 18–36.

Morsanyi, K., & Handley, S.J. (2012). Reasoning on the basis of fantasy content: Two studies with high-functioning autistic adolescents. *Journal of Autism and Developmental Disorders, 42,* 2297–2311.

Moshman, D. (1990). The development of metalogical understanding. In W.F. Overton (Ed.), *Reasoning, Necessity, and Logic: Developmental perspectives* (pp. 205–225). Hillsdale, NJ: Erlbaum.

Nieder, A., & Dehaene, S. (2009). Representation of number in the brain. *Annual Review in Neuroscience, 32,* 185–208.

Nisbett, R.E., Fong, G.T., Lehman, D.R., & Cheng, P.W. (1987). Teaching reasoning. *Science, 238,* 625–630.

Passolunghi, M.C., & Mammarella, I. (2012). Selective spatial working memory impairment in a group of children with mathematics learning disabilities and poor problem-solving skills. *Journal of Learning Disabilities, 45,* 341–350.

Passolunghi, M., & Siegel, L.S. (2001). Short-term memory, working memory, and inhibitory control in children with difficulties in arithmetic problem solving. *Journal of Experimental Child Psychology, 80,* 44–57.

Passolunghi, M.C., & Siegel, L.S. (2004). Working memory and access to numerical information in children with disability in mathematics. *Journal of Experimental Child Psychology, 88,* 348–367.

Piaget, J., & Inhelder, B. (1974). *The Child's Construction of Quantities.* London: Routledge & Kegan Paul.

Piazza, M., Facoetti, A., Trussardi, A.N., Berteletti, I., Conte, S., Lucangeli, D., Zorzi, M. (2010). Developmental trajectory of number acuity reveals a severe impairment in developmental dyscalculia. *Cognition, 116,* 33–41.

Restle, F. (1970). Speed of adding and comparing numbers. *Journal of Experimental Psychology, 91,* 191–205.

Rousselle, L., Palmers, E., & Noël, M.-P. (2004). Magnitude comparison in preschoolers: What counts. Influence of perceptual variables. *Journal of Experimental Child Psychology, 87,* pp. 57–84.

Simoneau, M., & Markovits, H. (2003). Reasoning with premises that are not empirically true: Evidence for the role of inhibition and retrieval. *Developmental Psychology, 39,* 964–975.

Soltesz, F., Szücs, D., & Szücs, L. (2010). Relationships between magnitude representation, counting and memory in 4- to 7-year-old children: A developmental study. *Behavioural and Brain Functions, 6,* 13.

Stanovich, K.E., & West, R.F. (2000). Individual differences in reasoning: Implications for the rationality debate? *Behavioral and Brain Sciences, 23,* 645–665.

Swanson, H.L. (2011). Working memory, attention, and mathematical problem solving: A longitudinal study of elementary school children. *Journal of Educational Psychology, 103,* 821–837.

Swanson, H.L., Jerman, O., & Zheng, X. (2008). Growth in working memory and mathematical problem solving in children at risk and not at risk for serious math difficulties. *Journal of Educational Psychology, 100,* 343–379.

Szücs, D., Devine, A., Soltesz, F., Nobes, A., & Gabriel, F. (2013a). Developmental dyscalculia is related to visuo-spatial memory and inhibition impairment. *Cortex, 49,* 2674–2688.

Szücs, D., Nobes, A., Devine, A., Gabriel, F., & Gebuis, T. (2013b). Visual stimulus parameters seriously compromise the measurement of approximate number system acuity and comparative effects between adults and children. *Frontiers in Psychology, 4,* 444.

Vanbinst, K., Ghesquière, P., & De Smedt, B. (2012). Numerical magnitude representations and individual differences in children's arithmetic strategy use. *Mind, Brain and Education, 6,* 129–136.

Venet, M., & Markovits, H. (2001). Understanding uncertainty with abstract conditional premises. *Merrill-Palmer Quarterly, 47,* 74–99.

Verschueren, N., Schaeken, W., & d'Ydewalle, G. (2005). Everyday conditional reasoning: A working memory-dependent tradeoff between counterexample and likelihood use. *Memory & Cognition, 33*, 107–119.

von Aster, M.G., & Shalev, R.S. (2007). Number development and developmental dyscalculia. *Developmental Medicine and Child Neurology, 49*, 868–873.

Xu, F., & Arriaga, R.I. (2007) Number discrimination in 10-month-old infants. *British Journal of Developmental Psychology, 25*, 103–108.

7

How specific is the specific disorder of arithmetic skills?

Karin Landerl

Dyscalculia refers to a specific developmental disorder which particularly affects the acquisition of arithmetic skills, while other domains of development are intact. However, how specific is developmental dyscalculia? Individuals who experience marked deficits in arithmetic frequently have additional problems such as reading disorder (Barbaresi, Katusic, Colligan, Weaver, & Jacobsen, 2005; Dirks, Spyer, van Lieshout, & de Sonneville, 2008; Landerl & Moll, 2010; Lewis, Hitch, & Walker, 1994), attention deficits (Badian, 1983; Czamara et al., 2013), motoric deficits or problems in visuo-spatial working memory (McLean & Hitch, 1999; Schuchardt, Maehler, & Hasselhorn, 2008; van der Sluis, van der Leij, & de Jong, 2005). All these deficits co-occur significantly more often with problems in arithmetic than would be expected by chance. The important question then arises, whether these deficits are directly and causally related to the problems in arithmetic or whether they constitute instances of comorbidity.

The term comorbidity denotes the frequent co-occurrence of two (or more) disorders. In clinical child psychology and psychiatry, comorbidity of disorders is generally the rule rather than the exception (Angold, Costello, & Erkanli, 1999; Caron & Rutter, 1991). Thus, research on the causes and implications of such comorbidities is essential in order to improve our understanding of developmental disorders like dyscalculia.

Note that understanding the comorbidity of learning disorders requires us not only to explain why two disorders frequently co-occur, but we also need to explain why the same two disorders can dissociate. For example, in a population-based sample of 2600 elementary school children, Landerl and Moll (2010) found that 25.9% of the children who performed more than 1.5 SD below age expectations in mental arithmetic also experienced comparably marked problems in word reading. Thus, among children with dyscalculia, reading problems were about four times as prevalent as in the general population (6.1%). This and other studies (Barbaresi et al., 2005;

Dirks et al., 2008; Lewis et al., 1994) clearly suggest that dyscalculia and dyslexia have certain common risk factors. However, it is highly important to note that more than 60% of the children with dyscalculia had an age-adequate reading level in this epidemiological study.

Comorbidity is similarly well established for dyscalculia and ADHD with clearly higher odds ratios (2.5 to 2.8) for dyscalculia in children with increased and high scores in hyperactivity/inattention (Czamara et al., 2013) compared to the general population. But again, this finding also indicates that the majority of affected children have either dyscalculia or ADHD and do not qualify for both diagnoses. Therefore, any model that aims to explain the frequent co-occurrence (comorbidity) of two learning disorders also needs to explain why the disorders usually occur dissociated from each other.

In the first part of this chapter, general aspects of comorbidity models will be presented. Based on this general background, current empirical evidence on the dominant comorbidities of dyscalculia (dyslexia, ADHD) will be discussed.

Theoretical concepts of comorbidity

Establishing the prevalence rates of the co-occurrence of different disorders is only a very first step in the investigation of comorbidity. A central theoretical challenge is the analysis as to why two or more disorders occur in combination and how these disorders interact with each other during development.

First, we need to differentiate "real" comorbidity from artefactual comorbidity arising for certain methodological reasons although the etiologies of two disorders are in fact independent (Neale & Kendler, 1995; Pennington, 2006). The three most important artefactual explanations are (1) sampling bias, (2) definitional overlap and (3) rater bias.

Sampling bias means that certain characteristics of an investigated sample can induce overrepresentation of comorbidity. This is, for example, typically the case in clinical (compared to epidemiological) samples, as individuals with more complex (comorbid) problems are more likely to seek clinical help than individuals with only one problem affecting a comparatively limited domain of cognitive functioning.

Definitional overlap refers to the fact that certain diagnostic criteria appear in more than one diagnostic category. For example, number reversals (48 − 84) were long thought to be an indication of dyslexia, but transcoding between visual-Arabic and verbal representations of numbers has now been shown to be a specific predictor of arithmetic skills (Moeller, Pixner, Zuber, Kaufmann, & Nuerk, 2011). It is possible that, historically, many children who should have received a dyscalculia diagnosis were assumed to be dyslexic.

Rater bias means that the persons who refer a child for diagnosis may have specific implicit assumptions on symptoms that are of specific relevance for the disorder in question. For example, parents (or teachers) may refer a child for diagnosis for ADHD because they perceive that the inattentiveness of a child causes serious problems in math. However, the causality might be the other way round: Because the child cannot follow the math lessons, he is becoming inattentive. Or the child may require a diagnosis of comorbid ADHD and dyscalculia. Each disorder has a specific neuro-cognitive profile, but in individual cases the differential diagnosis might be difficult.

For non-artefactual, "real" comorbidity, Pennington (2006) proposed a number of theoretical models based on the work of Neale and Kendler (1995). A common feature of all specified theoretical models is the assumption that the liability for a disorder results from the largely independent effects of a variable number of etiologi-cally relevant (genetic and/or environmental) factors. This leads to specific liability profiles for each disorder. Only if a certain threshold is exceeded, does the disorder become manifest.

Based on this assumption, five different models of comorbidity can be specified:

Model 1: Alternate forms. This model refers to two disorders that have largely overlap-ping profiles of liability. Which of the two disorders becomes manifest is then due to environmental risk factors or coincidence. It is also possible that two disorders occur alternately in a single person, as the etiology of the two disorders is identical. We will see that this model does not provide a good explanation for the comorbidities of dyscalculia.

Model 2: Random multiformity model. When disorder A automatically induces an increased risk for disorder B, although there is no increased susceptibility for disorder B, this is referred to as an "epiphenomenon" or a "phenocopy." This model was dis-cussed for the comorbidity of dyslexia and ADHD when early studies (Pennington, Groisser, & Welsh, 1993) suggested that children with both disorders showed the cog-nitive profile of dyslexia (i.e. a phonological deficit), but did not appear to show the typical neurocognitive profile of ADHD (i.e. deficits in executive functions), leading to the assumption that the ADHD symptoms in these children were a consequence of their daily school failure and did not have a second etiology. More recent findings (e.g., Willcutt et al., 2010) suggest that the comorbidity of dyslexia and ADHD has a genetic basis and the assumption of a phenocopy-model is not tenable. Up to date, analogous evidence on the comorbidity of dyscalculia and ADHD is missing.

Model 3: Extreme multiformity model. This model assumes that disorder A increases the liability for disorder B, but disorder B becomes manifest only at the extreme end of the liability of disorder A. In principle, such a model could explain why the arithmetic and reading deficits of children with disorders in both domains are often more severe compared to individuals who appear to have only one learning disorder.

Model 4: Three independent disorders model. This model states that two comorbid dis-orders can constitute a third disorder with an independent clinical nosology and etiology. Note that this model is underlying the current diagnostic categories for developmental disorders of scholastic skills in ICD-10 (http://www.who.int/classifi-cations/icd). In this diagnostic scheme, specific disorders of reading (F.81.0), spelling (F81.1) and arithmetic (F81.2) are diagnosed only if abilities in the other academic domain(s) are intact. Children who have marked problems in arithmetic as well as reading receive the separate diagnosis of a combined disorder of scholastic skills (F81.3). We will see later on, that the assumption of a separate etiology of comorbid dyscalculia and dyslexia is not supported by current empirical evidence.

Model 5: Correlated liabilities. In this model it is postulated that the liabilities of two disorders are correlated. This implies that an increase in the liability for disorder A automatically also increases the liability for disorder B. It does not, however, specify whether the risk factors of the two disorders interact with each other or whether certain risk factors are precursors of other risk factors.

The model of correlated liabilities is applied in contemporary multiple deficit models in which developmental disorders are interpreted as the outcome of complex interactions of so called core deficits that are specific to a particular disorder and other risk factors that are shared between disorders (Bishop, 2008; Pennington, 2006; Rutter, 2006; Snowling, 2012). Such models are particularly attractive for dyscalculia which is characterized by high heterogeneity on the symptom level. This perspective will be explicated in more detail in the next section.

Dyscalculia – a core deficit in numerical processing

Arithmetic is a complex, multi-componential skill depending on various cognitive processes (Dowker, 2005; Hanich, Jordan, Kaplan, & Dick, 2001). Children with good attentional and verbal skills, adequate working memory, and executive control generally show better arithmetic performance than those who have problems in these domains (e.g., Clark, Sheffield, Wiebe, & Espy, 2013; De Smedt, Janssen, Bouwens, Verschaffel, Boets, & Ghesquière, 2009; Donlan, Cowan, Newton, & Lloyd, 2007). However, deficits in these domains are likely to have a strong overall negative impact on children's academic development. It is hard to imagine how such domain-general deficits in cognitive functioning can induce specific problems that are limited to arithmetic development.

In order to identify a core deficit which can be assumed to cause the specific learning disorder of dyscalculia, it is necessary to show that deficiencies in the suspected mechanism are (1) typically associated and therefore characteristic for dyscalculia and (2) specific to dyscalculia and not present in individuals with other developmental disorders who show intact arithmetic performance. Current evidence convincingly suggests that deficiencies in numerical processing constitute such a core deficit (e.g., see Chapters 1, 2 and 4), although the exact specification of this core deficit is as yet under discussion. There is an ongoing debate whether problems in numerical processing identified in dyscalculia reflect underlying deficits in the exact (Butterworth, 2010) or approximate representation of non-symbolic numerosities (Piazza et al., 2010) or whether they constitute problems in accessing analog magnitude representations from numerical symbols (Rousselle & Noël, 2007; see De Smedt, Noël, Gilmore, & Ansari (2013) for a review of the current evidence).

Important evidence for the assumption that a deficit in numerical processing is specific to dyscalculia comes from studies showing that individuals with dyslexia and intact arithmetic skills do not show particular problems with numerical processing tasks (Landerl, Bevan, & Butterworth, 2004; Landerl, Fussenegger, Moll, & Willburger, 2009; Rousselle & Noël, 2007; Rubinsten & Henik, 2006). A second critical finding of these studies is that individuals with comorbid dyslexia and dyscalculia show problems in numerical processing that are similar to those of individuals with dyscalculia only. This evidence clearly suggests that deficits in numerical processing are specifically associated with dyscalculia, irrespective of additional problems, and therefore constitute a core deficit.

Comorbidity with dyslexia

Showing that a core deficit is present in a certain disorder can only be a very first step in establishing a causal model and can lead to inappropriate conclusions. For example, for a long time research on dyslexia strongly dominated the field of learning disorders and it was assumed that comorbid dyscalculia might arise from a phonological deficit which was identified as a core deficit of dyslexia (Geary & Hoard, 2001). Only studies that specifically differentiated between children with arithmetic problems who had comorbid reading problems and those whose reading was unaffected indicated that the two disorders have differential neurocognitive profiles: Problems associated with dyslexia, namely deficits in phonological awareness and rapid automatized naming, are specific to dyslexia (irrespective of additional arithmetic problems) and do not appear in children with dyscalculia only (Landerl et al., 2009; Rousselle & Noël, 2007; Willburger, Fussenegger, Moll, Wood, & Landerl, 2008).

Because of the high rates of comorbidity inherent in developmental disorders, samples selected for poor arithmetic skills are likely to include a certain percentage of individuals who are not only dyscalculic but also have additional problems. The prevalence of these problems will be much lower in a randomly selected control sample so that significant group differences may arise even though the investigated mechanisms might not be directly related to dyscalculia. More specifically, group comparisons of dyscalculia with typically developing children might find significantly impaired phonological skills for the dyscalculic sample simply because this sample includes children with comorbid dyslexia.

Research designs that adequately accounted for this fact could establish that dyslexia and dyscalculia are associated with distinctive cognitive core deficits. Importantly, these studies also showed that the problems of comorbid dyslexia/dyscalculia are additive: Individuals with deficits in arithmetic as well as reading show a combination of the deficits underlying each disorder and do not constitute a separate etiology (Landerl et al., 2004, 2009; Rousselle & Noël, 2007; Rubinsten & Henik, 2006; Willcutt et al., 2013). This is an important finding which indicates that the separate diagnostic category of a mixed disorder of scholastic skills (F81.3) as indicated in ICD-10 (WHO, http://www.who.int/classifications/icd) is obsolete.

Nevertheless, it has to be conceded that the reasons for the comorbidity of dyscalculia and dyslexia are as yet unclear. Preliminary evidence suggests that they might share genetic variance (Knopik, Alarcón, & DeFries, 1997; Kovas, Haworth, Harlaar, Petrill, Dale, & Plomin, 2007). Ludwig et al. (2013) recently identified a genetic risk variant for arithmetic deficits which seemed to be stronger in samples selected for spelling problems than in the general population and might in some way be related to the comorbidity of the two disorders. Plomin and Kovas (2005) proposed that brain processes related to dyslexia and dyscalculia might be genetically correlated. Still, any such genetic and neurophysiological reasons for covariance should be reflected on the cognitive level. As already mentioned, potential explanations of comorbidity need to explain why two disorders are frequently co-occurring, but also, why they can dissociate. Notwithstanding, children with dyslexia frequently experience problems that arise from their verbal and reading deficits, most prominently when they are faced with word problems (Jordan, Hanich, & Kaplan, 2003).

Comorbidity with attention deficits

Attention deficits are also frequently comorbid with dyscalculia (Czamara et al., 2013; Shalev, Auerbach, & Gross-Tsur, 1995; Willcutt et al., 2013). Again, it is difficult to clearly differentiate between cognitive problems that specifically underlie one or the other disorder as problems with arithmetic tasks can easily arise from inattention. Indeed a significant amount of variance in children's arithmetic performance is explained by attentional and executive functions (e.g., Clark et al., 2013). Children with ADHD have been shown to be particularly prone to errors that result from lack of monitoring during written arithmetic (Lindsay, Tomazic, Levine, & Accardo, 1999; Zentall, Smith, Lee, & Wieczorek, 1994). Kaufmann and Nuerk (2008) showed that ADHD may also impact on children's cognitive representation of number. They found an amplified distance effect (increase of errors with decreasing numerical distance) in a number comparison paradigm in children with ADHD (who did not show significant mathematics problems). Kaufmann and Nuerk interpreted this finding as a consequence of larger variability in accessing numerosities due to deficits in attention.

Although this approach has been tremendously helpful to untangle the comorbidity of dyscalculia and dyslexia, studies comparing carefully selected groups of children with dyscalculia only, ADHD only, and comorbid dyscalculia/ADHD are currently lacking. On the contrary, a clinical diagnosis of ADHD is usually an exclusion criterion in dyscalculia samples in order to avoid uncontrolled influences of attentional problems. However, this approach has several problems. First, some children might not yet have received a clinical diagnosis although they fulfill the standard criteria of ADHD. Second and most importantly, developmental disorders constitute categorical classifications for dimensional variables. Many children have below average attentional functions that are not low enough to justify a clinical diagnosis. As a group, individuals with dyscalculia have more such subclinical attentional deficiencies than typically developing children (Landerl & Willburger, 2010). It can be assumed that such subclinical attentional deficiencies are not always identified because (1) many studies do not include measures of attention and executive control and (2) statistical power of relatively small samples is often too low to identify group differences.

Note that attentional deficiencies might also at least partly account for the comorbidity of dyscalculia and dyslexia. Willcutt et al. (2013) recently reported that deficits in set shifting were uniquely associated with poor performance on standardized math tests, while other attentional functions (interference control, inhibition, vigilance, response variability) were equally strongly associated with performance in standardized reading and math tests. More research is needed in order to specify the subcomponents of attention that constitute risk factors that are shared between learning disorders.

Implications for research and practice

Developmental dyscalculia often occurs in association with other developmental disorders such as dyslexia or ADHD and comorbidity of learning disorders seems to be the rule rather than the exception. Multi-deficit model approaches move our perspective from the identification of single cognitive deficits to the investigation of a broad range of risk and protective factors and their interactions. Comorbidity is generally assumed to arise from risk factors that are shared or correlated between disorders.

The multi-deficit perspective has important implications for further research: Instead of applying comorbid disorders as an exclusion criterion, it is seminal to include relevant measures of literacy, attention, working memory and so on in dimensional as well as categorical research designs in order to develop a comprehensive profile of risk (and protective) factors constituting dyscalculia and concomitant problems. More studies that adequately account for comorbidities between developmental disorders will be of seminal importance in order to specify profiles of core deficits and shared risk factors.

The multi-deficit perspective of dyscalculia also has relevant implications for intervention. Based on the finding that problems in numerical processing constitute a core deficit of dyscalculia irrespective of associated problems, any dyscalculia intervention should focus on numerical processing and its relationships with arithmetic. Apart from that, an obvious conclusion is that intervention needs to be specifically tailored towards the profile of risk and protective factors of the individual child. From this it follows that, compared to individuals with dyscalculia only, individuals with comorbid disorders might be less able to use compensatory mechanisms when doing arithmetic due to their co-occurring cognitive deficits and differential treatment effects in math and arithmetic for children with and without comorbid problems are to be expected (e.g., Dowker, 2010; Fuchs, Fuchs, & Compton, 2013; Jordan, 2007).

References

Angold, A., Costello, E.J., & Erkanli, A. (1999). Comorbidity. *Journal of Child Psychology and Psychiatry, 40*, 57–87.

Badian, N.A. (1983). Arithmetic and nonverbal learning. In H.R. Myklebust, (Ed.), *Progress in Learning Disabilities* (pp. 235–264). New York: Stratton.

Barbaresi, W.J., Katusic, S.K., Colligan, R.C., Weaver, A.L., & Jacobsen, S.J. (2005). Math learning disorder: Incidence in a population-based birth cohort, 1976–82, Rochester, Minn. *Ambulatory Pediatrics, 5*, 281–289.

Bishop, D.V.M. (2008). Criteria for evaluating behavioural interventions for neurodevelopmental disorders (Letter). *Journal of Paediatrics and Child Health, 44*, 520–521.

Butterworth, B. (2010). Foundational numerical capacities and the origins of dyscalculia. *Trends in Cognitive Sciences, 14*, 534–541.

Caron, C. & Rutter, M. (1991). Comorbidity in child psychopathology: Concepts, issues and research strategies. *Journal of Child Psychology and Psychiatry, 3*, 1063–1080.

Clark, C.A.C., Sheffield, T.D., Wiebe, S.A., & Espy, K.A. (2013). Longitudinal associations between executive control and developing mathematical competence in preschool boys and girls. *Child Development, 84*, 662–677.

Czamara, D., Tiesler, C.M.T., Kohlböck, G., Berdel, D., Hoffmann, B., Heinrich, J. (2013). Children with ADHD symptoms have a higher risk for reading, spelling and math difficulties in the GINIplus and LISAplus cohort studies. *PLOS ONE, 8*(5), e63859.

De Smedt, B., Janssen, R., Bouwens, K., Verschaffel, L., Boets, B., & Ghesquière, P. (2009). Working memory and individual differences in mathematics achievement: A longitudinal study from first grade to second grade. *Journal of Experimental Child Psychology, 103*, 186–201.

De Smedt, B., Noël, M.-P., Gilmore, C., & Ansari, D. (2013). How do symbolic and non-symbolic numerical magnitude processing skills relate to individual differences in children's mathematical skills? A review of evidence from brain and behavior. *Trends in Neuroscience and Education, 2*, 48–55.

Dirks, E., Spyer, G., van Lieshout, E.C.D.M., & de Sonneville, L. (2008). Prevalence of combined reading and arithmetic disabilities. *Journal of Learning Disabilities, 41*, 460–473.

Donlan, C., Cowan, R., Newton, E.J., & Lloyd, D. (2007). The role of language in mathematical development: Evidence from children with specific language impairments. *Cognition, 103*, 23–33.

Dowker, A. (2005). *Individual Differences in Arithmetic: Implications for psychology, neuroscience and education.* Hove: Psychology Press.

Dowker, A. (2010). Targeted interventions for children with arithmetical difficulties. *British Journal of Educational Psychology Monographs, 11*, 65–81.

Fuchs, L.S., Fuchs, D., & Compton, D.L. (2013). Intervention effects for students with comorbid forms of learning disability: Understanding the needs of nonresponders. *Journal of Learning Disabilities, 46*, 534–548.

Geary, D.C. & Hoard, M.K. (2001). Numerical and arithmetical deficits in learning-disabled children: Relation to dyscalculia and dyslexia. *Aphasiology, 15*, 635–647.

Hanich, L.B., Jordan, N.C., Kaplan, D., & Dick, J. (2001). Performance across different areas of mathematical cognition in children with learning difficulties. *Journal of Educational Psychology, 93*, 615–626.

Jordan, N.C. (2007). Do words count? Connections between mathematics and reading difficulties. In D.B. Berch & M.M. Mazzocco (Eds.), *Why is Math so Hard for Some Children? The nature and origins of mathematical learning difficulties and disabilities* (pp. 107–120). Baltimore, MD: Paul H. Brookes.

Jordan, N.C., Hanich, L.B., & Kaplan, D. (2003). A longitudinal study of mathematical competencies in children with specific mathematics difficulties versus children with comorbid mathematics and reading difficulties. *Child Development, 74*, 834–850.

Kaufmann, L. & Nuerk, H.-C. (2008). Basic number processing deficits in ADHD: A broad examination of elementary and complex number processing skills in 9- to 12-year-old children with ADHD-C. *Developmental Science, 11*, 692–699.

Knopik, V.S., Alarcón, M., & DeFries, J.C. (1997). Comorbidity of mathematics and reading deficits: Evidence for a genetic etiology. *Behavior Genetics, 27*, 447–453.

Kovas, Y., Haworth, C.M.A., Harlaar, N., Petrill, S.A., Dale, P.S., & Plomin, R. (2007). Overlap and specificity of genetic and environmental influences on mathematics and reading disability in 10-year-old twins. *Journal of Child Psychology and Psychiatry, 48*, 914–922.

Landerl, K., Bevan, A., & Butterworth, B. (2004). Developmental dyscalculia and basic numerical capacities: A study of 8–9 year old students. *Cognition, 93*, 99–125.

Landerl, K., Fussenegger, B., Moll, K., & Willburger, E. (2009). Dyslexia and dyscalculia: Two learning disorders with different cognitive profiles. *Journal of Experimental Child Psychology, 103*, 309–324.

Landerl, K. & Moll, K. (2010). Comorbidity of learning disorders: Prevalence and familial transmission. *Journal of Clinical Child Psychology and Psychiatry, 51*, 287–294.

Landerl, K. & Willburger, E. (2010). Temporal processing, attention, and learning disorders. *Learning and Individual Differences, 20*, 393–401.

Lewis, C., Hitch, G.J., & Walker, P. (1994). The prevalence of specific arithmetic difficulties and specific reading difficulties in 9- to 10-year-old boys and girls. *Journal of Child Psychology and Psychiatry, 35*, 283–292.

Lindsay, R.L., Tomazic, T., Levine, M.D., & Accardo, P.J. (1999). Impact of attentional dysfunction in dyscalculia. *Developmental Medicine & Child Neurology, 41*, 639–642.

Ludwig, K.U., Sämann, P., Alexander, M., Becker, J., Bruder, J., & Czamara, D. (2013). A common variant in Myosin-18B contributes to mathematical performance in children with dyslexia and intraparietal sulcus variability in adults. *Translational Psychiatry, 3*, e229.

McLean, J.F. & Hitch, G.J. (1999). Working memory impairments in children with specific arithmetic learning difficulties. *Journal of Experimental Child Psychology, 74*, 240–260.

Moeller, K., Pixner, S., Zuber, J., Kaufmann, L., & Nuerk, H.C. (2011). Early place-value understanding as a precursor for later arithmetic performance: A longitudinal study on numerical development. *Research in Developmental Disabilities, 32*, 1837–1851.

Neale, M.C. & Kendler, K.S. (1995). Models of comorbidity for multifactorial disorders. *American Journal of Human Genetics, 57*, 935–953.

Pennington, B.F. (2006). From single to multiple deficit models of developmental disorders. *Cognition, 101*, 385–413.

Pennington, B.F., Groisser, D., & Welsh, M.C. (1993). Contrasting cognitive deficits in attention deficit hyperactivity disorder versus reading disability. *Developmental Psychology, 29*, 511–523.

Piazza, M., Facoetti, A., Trussardi, A.N., Berteletti, I., Conte, S., Lucangeli, D., Zorzi, M. (2010). Developmental trajectory of number acuity reveals a severe impairment in developmental dyscalculia. *Cognition, 116*, 33–41.

Plomin, R. & Kovas, Y. (2005). Generalist genes and learning disabilities. *Psychological Bulletin, 131*, 592–617.

Rousselle, L. & Noël, M.P. (2007). Basic numerical skills in children with mathematics learning disabilities: A comparison of symbolic vs. non-symbolic number magnitude processing. *Cognition, 102*, 361–395.

Rubinsten, O. & Henik, A. (2006). Double dissociation of functions in developmental dyslexia and dyscalculia. *Journal of Educational Psychology, 98*, 854–867.

Rutter, M. (2006). *Genes and Behavior: Nature–nurture interplay explained.* Oxford: Blackwell.

Schuchardt, K., Maehler, C., & Hasselhorn, M. (2008). Working memory deficits in children with specific learning disorders. *Journal of Learning Disabilities, 41*, 514–523.

Shalev, R.S., Auerbach, J., & Gross-Tsur, V. (1995). Developmental dyscalculia: Attentional and behavioral aspects. *Journal of Child Psychology and Psychiatry, 36*, 1261–1268.

Snowling, M.J. (2012). Editorial: Seeking a new characterisation of learning disorders. *Journal of Child Psychology & Psychiatry, 53*, 1–2.

van der Sluis, S., van der Leij, A., & de Jong, P. (2005). Working memory in Dutch children with reading- and arithmetic-related LD. *Journal of Learning Disabilities, 38*, 207–221.

WHO (World Health Organisation). International Classification of Diseases (ICD-10). Retrieved from http://www.who.int/classifications/icd.

Willburger, E., Fussenegger, B., Moll, K., Wood, G., & Landerl, K. (2008). Naming speed in dyslexia and dyscalculia. *Learning and Individual Differences, 18*, 224–236.

Willcutt, E.G., Betjemann, R.S., McGrath, L.M., Chhabildas, N.A., Olson, R.K., DeFries, J.C., & Pennington, B.F. (2010). Etiology and neuropsychology of comorbidity between RD and ADHD: The case for multiple-deficit models. *Cortex, 46*, 1345–1361.

Willcutt, E.G., Petrill, S.A., Wu, S., Boada, R., DeFries, J.C., Olson, R.K., & Pennington, B.F. (2013). Comorbidity between reading disability and math disability: Concurrent psychopathology, functional impairment, and neuropsychological functioning. *Journal of Learning Disabilities, 46*, 500–516.

Zentall, S.S., Smith, Y.N., Lee, Y.B., & Wieczorek, C. (1994). Mathematical outcomes of attention-deficit hyperactivity disorder. *Journal of Learning Disabilities, 27*, 510–519.

8

Arithmetic difficulties of children with hearing impairment

Gowramma I. P.

Introduction

It has been well documented that hearing impairment in early childhood has an adverse effect on speech and language development. Impairment in the development of speech, language and oral communication skills is known to hinder the educational development of children. Paul and Jackson (1993) reported that differences in language abilities consequent to hearing impairment affects a student's ability to perform in traditional academic areas. The delay in educational achievement of children with hearing impairment (CWHI) compared to their hearing peers has been noted to occur since the educational system is highly language based. Paul and Quigley (1994) reported that students with complete or partial hearing impairment have considerable difficulty succeeding in an educational system that depends primarily on spoken word and written language to transmit knowledge. According to Flexer (1999), irrespective of the degree of impairment, hearing loss if unmanaged can have a negative impact on the development of academic competencies. A decade before this, Greenberg and Kusche (1989) and Martin (1985) had observed that children with mild-to-moderate hearing loss achieve below expectations, based on their performance on a test of cognitive ability.

Literature in the area of mathematics learning of CWHI is rich. A review of literature between 1980 and 2013 indicates that CWHI lag behind their hearing peers in mathematics achievement (Swanwick, Oddy, & Roper, 2005). Disparity in the performance of CWHI and their hearing counterparts was noticed in mathematics achievement on the Stanford Achievement Test. Compared to their reading performance they performed at a higher grade level in mathematics though the performance was below grade level (Stewart & Kluwin, 2001). Paranjape (1998) observed similar results when she compared the performance of CWHI with normally hearing children (NHC) based on achievement tests which showed difference in language performance but not in mathematics. Gowramma (2006) found no significant difference in the performance of CWHI when compared with a matched group of NHC based on the scores of an arithmetic diagnostic test. Wood et al. (1983), based on the performance of standardized tests, concluded that hearing loss is not the direct cause of difficulties in mathematics as 15% of the participants who had profound hearing impairment performed at average and above average levels. Better performance of mainstreamed CWHI is recorded (Kluwin & Moores, 1985; Wood, Wood, Kinsmill, French, & Howarth, 1984) compared to those segregated in special schools. Differences in expectations, exposure, trained teachers, parental involvement and support services were seen as factors bringing in the difference. Meadow (1980) noticed that the learning process is slower among CWHI, though their mathematical reasoning is on par with normal hearing children. Hyde, Zevenbergen and Power (2003), who studied the performance of students with hearing impairment on arithmetic word problems, found them to perform poorly.

Researchers have explored reasons for poor performance of CWHI in mathematics. Limited incidental learning and reinforcement (Gregory, 1998), delay in early access to mathematical conversation (Pau, 1995), limited auditory experience affecting short-term memory (Epstein, Hillegeist, & Grafman, 1994), lack of spoken language which develops inner speech (Hitch, Arnold, & Phillips, 1983) are examples. Stewart and Kluwin (2001) opined that the reasons why mathematics was challenging for CWHI were varied and complex. The reasons ranged from the inability to learn from experiences outside the classroom to utilization of cognitive abilities in the classroom such as the inability to assign meaning and language to mathematical problems. Earlier, Barton (1995) found that the cognitive concepts which involved specific language related to volume, shape, size, comparisons, measurement and reasoning were particularly difficult for CWHI to grasp, which may affect mathematics performance. The above reasons are noted to pose hurdles in information processing and mastering fundamental operations.

Strengths of CWHI in learning mathematical concepts and skills have been researched. It was found that the oral CWHI performed on par with hearing children in number reproduction on the temporal tasks and outperformed in spatial tasks (Zarfaty, Nunes, & Bryant, 2004). Thus, they concluded that the difficulties of CWHI were not consequent to a delay in number representation. A study which compared the performance of CWHI with NHC by Yathiraj et al. (2013) observed that the performance of the two groups did not differ when the tasks were presented visually in a pre-arithmetic school readiness test. Nunes and Moreno (1997) highlight visualization of counting as a factor for learning arithmetic. Vijayalakshmi and Gowramma (2010) confirmed significant improvement in the performance of CWHI when they were taught mathematics through a play-way method which relied on visual and concrete experience.

Nunes and Moreno (1998) reviewed data-based literature and concluded that it does not support a causal link between hearing loss and the difficulties experienced in developing mathematical knowledge and skills. Authors have suggested that hearing impairment should be considered more of a risk factor in learning numerical concepts. Mousley and Kelly (1998) stressed the importance of meta-cognitive skills, repetitive practice, active participation, interactive discussion and evaluative feedback in learning mathematics for CWHI.

Quantitative skills are considered as an important aspect of language development. In addition to basic language concept, vocabulary specific to mathematics is essential in order to learn formal mathematics in school. CWHI, who are usually deficient in these areas, would encounter certain difficulties in learning mathematics. The findings from the literature bring to light that though there are some instances where CWHI exhibited better performance, generally they are found to be performing below their age-appropriate grade levels. Some important conclusions can be drawn based on the review of research. First of all, not all CWHI are weak in mathematics performance. Next, hearing impairment does pose a risk for learning mathematics. Finally, fewer opportunities to learn from the socio-economic context impose a hurdle to learning school mathematics. A review of the literature indicates an encouraging point of view which maintains that CWHI can achieve their potential if the environment, instruction, and materials are appropriate. We need to be able to identify more precisely the areas of specific difficulties and errors in arithmetic of CWHI to plan effective ways to help them acquire the important skills. This study is thus proposed to analyse the difficulties experienced and errors committed in arithmetic by CWHI studying in special schools and compare them with a matched group of NHC.

Participants

Participants were selected from two special schools (coded as SS, N = 47) meant for CWHI. The special schools are residential, run by nongovernmental organizations. This facility is usually availed by children with disabilities from economically weaker sections residing in rural areas where parents either are uneducated or with minimum educational background. The range of hearing loss of the participants was from mild to profound. Only those children who were reported to have no additional disability were selected. To compare their performance NHC from a regular school (coded as RS, N = 18) matching the special schools with respect to economic background and the literacy level of parents were chosen. It was decided to select grades IV and V considering that all the children were exposed to school instruction for at least three years. It was ensured that none of the students had any obvious disability as reported by their teachers. All the schools were located in Mysore city in the State of Karnataka where Kannada, the regional language, is the medium of instruction.

Description of the tool

Arithmetic Diagnostic Test (ADT) for Primary School Children (Ramaa, 1994) diagnoses the specific difficulties encountered by children in primary schools in grade I through IV. The test covers three major areas of arithmetic: namely, number concept, arithmetic operations and reasoning. Since it is a diagnostic test, it includes problems that represent each type and subtype of tasks that fall under each of the major areas. Thus the test is quite comprehensive in identifying the strengths and weaknesses of the individual child.

Due weighting is given to different types of tasks. Each subtype of a task is represented by two items in the case of arithmetic processes and reasoning. This helps in thorough diagnosis of the difficulties faced by the children in dealing with particular subtypes of an arithmetic task. The sub-items and the items are arranged in the order of increasing level of difficulty within the different section of items as well as between the sections.

Selection of items and administration of the test

Some of the items from the test were eliminated based on the opinions of teachers in the participant schools, as they were not covered under the school syllabus. Testing was carried out in small groups within the school premises, using areas that were free from visual and auditory distracters. The rooms selected were located away from sources of noise and had adequate natural lighting. As the test was given at the beginning of the academic year, students studying in grade IV were considered to be performing at grade III level and those studying in grade V were considered to be performing at grade IV level.

Results

Comparison of scores between CWHI and NHC

An independent t-test was performed to check if the difference in scores was statistically significant. The t-test indicated that there was no significant difference between the CWHI and the NHC [$F_{(63)} = 1.64$, $p > 0.05$] for the overall scores. Since the sample size of the two groups was unequal, the result of independent t-test was cross checked with the non-parametric Mann-Whitney U test. Similar results were obtained through both the statistical procedures ($z = 1.36$, $p > 0.05$).

Even though 'z' is not significant, descriptively differences are observed. Table 8.1 depicts the descriptive statistic of the total test scores for the two groups. It can be seen that the mean score of the NHC is higher than that obtained by the CWHI. The standard deviation is high for both the groups suggesting diversity. It is seen that the deviation is greater among CWHI.

Analysis of the specific difficulties experienced in both the groups

For the purpose of analysing the difficulties for each of the criterion measures selected from the diagnostic tool, a score of one was given to a correct item and zero to a wrong or not-attempted item. On the basis of the raw score obtained for each

Table 8.1 Mean and SD of the total test scores of the two groups

Groups	N	*Mean	SD
CWHI	47	93.00	40.45
NHC	18	107.44	35.37

Note: * Maximum possible score = 202

Table 8.2 Number concept – 1

School	Counting			Writing the given numbers in words – up to 2 digits			Writing the given numbers in words – more than 2 digits			Writing the numbers from the words given – up to 2 digits			Writing the numbers from the words given – more than 2 digits		
Criterion measures →	M	PA	NA	M	PA	NA	M	PA	NA	M	PA	NA	M	PA	NA
SS	100	–	–	100	–	–	40	49	11	72	28	–	4	43	53
RS	100	–	–	100	–	–	56	39	6	89	11	–	39	50	11

Table 8.3 Number concept – 2

Criterion measures → School	Sequential representation of numbers in blanks given – less than 2 digits			Sequential representation of numbers in blanks given – more than two digits			Numbers less than and greater than a given number			Arranging the numbers in ascending order – less than 2 digits			Arranging the numbers in ascending order – more than 2 digits		
	M	PA	NA	M	PA	NA	M	PA	NA	M	PA	NA	M	PA	NA
SS	96	4	–	96	4	–	19	47	34	74	9	17	43	15	43
RS	89	–	11	72	6	22	83	–	17	67	17	17	44	22	33

Table 8.4 Addition

School	Addition of single-digit numbers			Addition of 2-digit numbers without carry over			Addition of 2-digit numbers with carry over			Addition of numbers more than 2 digits			Problem solving involving addition based on verbal numerical information			Problem solving involving addition based on verbal numerical information – when more information is given		
	M	PA	NA	M	PA	NA	M	PA	NA	M	PA	NA	M	PA	NA	M	PA	NA
SS	100	–	–	81	15	4	72	9	19	47	42	11	42	26	32	–	–	100
RS	100	–	–	83	17	–	44	22	33	39	61	–	33	39	28	–	–	100

Table 8.5 Subtraction

Criterion measures → / School	Subtracting single digits			Subtracting 2-digit numbers without borrowing			Subtracting 2-digit numbers with borrowing			Subtracting more than 2-digit numbers			Problem solving involving subtraction based on verbal numerical information			Problem solving involving subtraction based on verbal numerical information – involving more than one operation		
	M	PA	NA	M	PA	NA	M	PA	NA	M	PA	NA	M	PA	NA	M	PA	NA
SS	72	13	15	68	11	21	45	6	49	13	45	42	15	25	60	–	–	100
RS	83	6	11	61	28	11	33	28	39	22	56	22	22	39	39	–	–	100

Table 8.6 Multiplication

Criterion measures → / School	Multiplication of 1-digit numbers			Multiplication of 2-digit numbers by 1-digit numbers			Multiplication of more than 2-digit numbers			Problem solving involving multiplication based on verbal numerical information		
	M	PA	NA	M	PA	NA	M	PA	NA	M	PA	NA
SS	60	30	11	23	40	47	4	23	72	–	15	85
RS	89	–	11	44	39	17	17	44	39	–	50	50

Table 8.7 Division

Criterion measures School	Division of less than 2-digit numbers in one step			Division of more than 2-digit numbers with more than one step			Problem solving involving division based on verbal numerical information		
	M	PA	NA	M	PA	NA	M	PA	NA
SS	26	26	49	4	26	70	–	–	100
RS	28	56	11	11	50	33	–	11	89

of the criterion measures, children who scored 75% and above were classified as masters (M), below 75% as partial achievers (PA) and those who scored '0' were grouped under non-achievers (NA). The number of masters, partial achievers and non-achievers were noted for both the groups. The total number of children in each group was converted into a percentage for the purpose of comparison.

Percentage of children who are masters (M), partial achievers (PA) and non-achievers (NA) in the criterion measures of number concept, addition, subtraction, multiplication and division from special schools (SS) and regular school (RS) are given in the Tables 8.2 to 8.7.

Major findings and discussion at the stage of analysis of difficulties

Number concept

As observed in Table 8.2, for the first two criterion measures only, 100% mastery is achieved by both the groups. For the next three criterion measures in Table 8.2, there are more masters and fewer non-achievers among the NHC. However mastery is achieved by a significant number of CWHI also, except for writing the numbers from words for numbers that have more than two digits. It is interesting to note that among CWHI the number of masters is higher for writing the given number in words compared to writing the numbers in digits from the words given. For the latter task more verbal information in sequence has to be decoded compared to the former. Craig and Gordon (1988) observed that verbal sequential skills in cognitive functioning were below average among CWHI. The difficulty might also be due to limited auditory experience effecting short-term memory (Epstein et al., 1994) and lack of spoken language which leads to inner speech (Hitch et al., 1983).

Table 8.3 shows that CWHI have performed better than the NHC in the sequential representation of numbers where there are more masters and no non-achievers. But among the NHC there are still non-achievers. As this relies on visuo-spatial skills CWHI had an advantage over their hearing counterparts (Zarfaty et al., 2004; Craig & Gordon, 1988). In contrast, recalling numbers greater and lesser than the number given was accomplished better by NHC. Cognitive concepts involving language related to volume, size and comparisons are particularly difficult for CWHI (Barton, 1995). This, being a quantitative concept relating to temporal perception requiring the pupil to recall the number coming after and before a given number, meant that CWHI faced difficulty. In addition, the linguistic demand on processing 'lesser than' and 'greater than' might be demanding for CWHI. To arrange the numbers in ascending order, knowledge of sequence and comparison in terms of quantity are both essential. A more or less similar level of difficulty is faced by both the groups for the task.

Fundamental operations

Little difference is observed in the level of difficulty by both the groups for all the criterion measures of addition and subtraction. CWHI might be performing the learnt operation mechanically where they are well practiced. In multiplication and division there are more masters and fewer non-achievers among NHC. This indicates that the difficulty of CWHI increases as the higher order thinking is involved in fundamental operation. The mathematical reasoning of CWHI is on par with hearing children but the learning process is slow (Meadow, 1980).

Arithmetic reasoning

Surprisingly mastery was attained by a slightly higher percentage of CWHI compared to NHC for the statement problems in addition. The difficulty level is almost the same for both the groups with the other operations, especially when the descriptive demand increased. This phenomenon was noticed among CWHI by Kelly and Mousley (2001). Since NHC also experienced significant difficulty in this task, it could be attributed to developmental deficits (Epstein et al., 1994) which is a common factor in both the groups. This clearly signifies the importance of analytical and thinking strategies for solving arithmetic word problems (Hyde et al., 2003). An advantage in language and reading will not help to solve word problems (Kelly, Lang, & Pagliaro, 2003; Mousley & Kelly, 1998; Kelly & Mousley, 2001).

Analysis of errors committed and deficiencies exhibited while attempting the task

The common errors committed and deficiencies exhibited by children from both the groups while doing sums in ADT were analysed qualitatively. The analysis aimed at identifying and classifying the errors and deficiencies. The total number of children in each group was converted into percentages for the purpose of comparing. The results are given in Tables 8.8–8.12 for the two groups, with examples and probable reasons for each type of error/deficiency.

Table 8.8 Number concept

Sl No.	Error/deficiency	Example	% of children		Probable reason
			SS	RS	
1	Writing digit wise while writing in words	214 – Two one four	64	17	Poor understanding of place value and/or poor verbo-sequential processing
2	Delete, add or substitute digits while writing in numbers from words	Three hundred fourteen as 14 Sixty-nine as 699 Four hundred eighteen as 488	53	50	Poor understanding of place value and/or difficulty in coding the verbal information
3	Not attempted as the complexity of the task increases for most of the criterion measures	Did not attempt tasks where more than 2-digit numbers were given	32	28	Poor understanding of place value and/or avoiding as the complexity of the task increases

Table 8.9 Addition

Sl No.	Error/deficiency	Example	% of children		Probable reason
			SS	RS	
1	Forgets to add the carried digit to higher place	85 + 69 ___ 144	30	11	Poor working memory
2	Did not attempt when the numbers exceeded 2 digits and more than two numbers had to be added	429 781 365 ___	28	50	Not learnt the procedure or avoiding the difficult task
3	Added all the numbers given in the statement problem though the numerical information is irrelevant to solve the problem	Krishna had 12 Rupees. He bought 2 books for 5 Rs, 2 pencils for 3 Rs. How much money did he spend? 12+2+5+2+3	87	56	Difficulty in processing verbal numerical information

Table 8.10 Subtraction

| Sl No. | Error/deficiency | Example | % of children | | Probable reason |
			SS	RS	
1	Forgets the number borrowed	73 − 54 —— 29	36	6	Poor working memory
2	Writes '0' as answer when 0 has to be subtracted from a digit	84 − 60 —— 20	53	39	Lack of '0' concept
3	Writes '0' when the corresponding digit in the minuend is greater than the subtrahend	81 − 76 —— 10	6	6	Not learnt operation of borrowing from the higher place
4	Subtracts the smaller number from the larger when the minuend is smaller than its corresponding digit in the subtrahend	92 − 87 —— 15	6	17	Not learnt operation of borrowing from the higher place
5	Added the numbers instead of subtracting in the statement problem	Savithri had Rs 25, she spent Rs 21. How much money does she have left? 25 + 21 = 46	57	39	Not able to process verbal numerical information

Table 8.11 Multiplication

Sl No.	Error/deficiency	Example	% of children		Probable reason
			SS 1	SS 2	
1	Wrote the number as answer when multiplied with 0	6 X 0 = 6	51	11	Lack of '0' concept
2	Adding the numbers instead of multiplying	7 X 2 = 9	11	11	Does not know multiplication, or confusion of symbols + and X
3	Could not perform multiplication involving more than one digit	Did not attempt sums like 21 X 7, 70 X 8, etc.	45	33	Not learnt the skill of multiplying 2-digit numbers
4	Adding all the numbers from the statement problem instead of multiplying	In a class there are 10 rows of chairs. Every row has 6 chairs. How many chairs are there altogether? 10 + 6 = 16	28	33	Not able to apply suitable algorithm depending on the situation. Performing the easier task
5	Not able to solve statement problems	Did not attempt	60	39	Not able to process verbal numerical information

Table 8.12 Division

Sl No.	Error/deficiency	Example	% of children		Probable reason
			SS	RS	
1	Multiplying instead of dividing	$10 \div 5 = 50$	23	17	Does not know division, or does not know the meaning of the symbol
2	Could not perform division when more than one step is required	Did not attempt sums like 95/3, 7007/7	81	83	Not learnt the procedure of division when more than one step is involved
3	Adding all the numbers from the statement problem instead of dividing	There are 59 students in a class. How many groups can be made of 7 boys and how many will be remaining? $59 + 7 = 66$	60	50	Not able to apply suitable algorithm depending on the situation. Performing the easier task
4	Not able to solve statement problems	Did not attempt	70	83	Not able to process verbal numerical information

Major findings and discussion in the error analysis stage

Number concept

The errors in writing digits were observed more among CWHI. As the task requires verbo-sequential processing where CWHI are found to perform below average (Craig & Gordon, 1988), recalling the name of the number in a sequence representing the place of the digit with suitable case markers (in Kannada) between each place might be the reason. Hence, they may simplify it just by writing the digits in words, not processing the number as a whole. This strategy is also adapted by NHC. The rest of the errors are committed by both groups almost equally. This shows that CWHI deal with same conceptual obstacles in understanding numerical concepts as hearing children and they deal with such obstacles in similar ways (Nunes & Moreno, 1998).

Fundamental operations

Forgetting to add the carried number and deduct the borrowed number was committed by a greater number of CWHI compared to NHC. As CWHI are deficient in inner speech (Hitch et al., 1983) or using working memory (Epstein et al., 1994) they may be more likely to commit this error. This suggests that the procedure of carry-over and borrowing is known to them, as the first step in the procedure is attempted correctly. It is also noted while analysing the difficulty, that the percentage of CWHI attaining mastery in these two tasks is greater compared to the NHC. A greater number of CWHI have attempted these items and hence the percentage of children committing the error is higher.

There is not much difference in the percentage of children committing errors/ deficiencies in multiplication and division, indicating similar lines of thought process. Many children did not attempt the multiplication and division items.

Arithmetic reasoning

The error of adding all the digits in the statement problem and adding instead of subtracting and multiplying is due to tackling a problem mechanically without trying to understand it. It is also noticed that a considerable number of children from both the groups did not attempt statement problems, especially under multiplication and division. The negative, disengaged approach to word problem-solving tasks was noted by Kelly and Mousley (2001). The fact that NHC also made this error indicates that the reason is not just language- or reading-based, but a lack of analytical thinking (Hyde et al., 2003).

Conclusion

In the present study, though CWHI had the dual disadvantage of sensory and environmental deprivation, there was no significant difference in their performance when compared with NHC who were drawn from an environmentally deprived population. As the delay was noticed in both the groups, it could be attributed to developmental deficits due to environmental factors rather than hearing impairment. It was observed by Ramaa and Gowramma (2002) that a considerable number of socially disadvantaged children experienced difficulty in performing grade-appropriate mathematical tasks. As noticed by Zarfaty et al. (2004) this could be due to fewer opportunities to learn the culturally transmitted aspects of mathematical knowledge. Schoenfeld (2002) emphasized the importance of environmental factors based on data on disproportionate numbers of poor African-American, Latino, and Native American students dropping out of mathematics and performing below standard on tests of mathematical competency. A comparative study on the arithmetic performance of CWHI from special schools and day schools/inclusive schools from different socio-economic strata would be necessary for a clearer understanding.

For most of the items appropriate for grades I and II, 100% mastery was not achieved by either group. As the students are in grades IV and V, this could be considered as a serious difficulty in learning arithmetic. There is a clear indication that the difficulty level increases as the complexity of the task increases for both the groups in all the areas of arithmetic assessed. This must be viewed seriously as mathematics is a linear subject and this lag could have serious implications for future performance. This can be attributed as Schoenfeld (2002) also noted, to less exposure to mathematical experiences consequent of the environmental deprivation experienced by the economically and educationally disadvantaged families in this sample.

Most of the errors could be due to a poor understanding of the concept of place value. Since it is an abstract concept, all children find it difficult to understand at the primary school stage. The strength areas, like spatial representation (Zarfaty et al., 2004), visualization (Nunes & Moreno, 2002; Yathiraj, Gowramma, Prithi, & Vijetha, 2013), visuo-spatial skill (Craig & Gordon, 1988) and providing concrete experience (Vijayalakshmi & Gowramma, 2010), should be used to develop concepts. Remedial instruction at the right time would decrease the lag in learning and arrest further damage.

Neither of the groups in the present study exhibited errors in number concepts such as the rotation of digits (6 as 9), reversal of numbers (12 as 21) and reproducing the same numbers in the blanks when it was asked to continue the sequence (6, 7, . . ., . . ., as 6, 7, 6, 7), which were noticed by Gowramma (2005) among children with dyscalculia of the same grade level. In addition she noticed errors like adding from the left side, adding all the numbers (21 + 15 as 2 + 1 + 1 + 5) which are due to difficulty in spatial organization and failing to grasp the logic. Most of the items on subtraction and multiplication were not attempted by children with dyscalculia. None of them attempted any item under division. This suggests that the brain and cognitive process disruption stemming from neurobiological deficit leading to difficulty in arithmetic are distinct (Ashkenazi, Black, Abrams, Hoeft, & Menon, 2013). Dyscalculia stems from a core deficit in processing quantity (Butterworth, Varma, & Laurillard, 2011). The difficulties and errors committed by CWHI and those from an environmentally deprived population, as observed in the present study, do not stem from a specific deficit in number processing. It can be compared to the domain-general hypothesis of mathematical disability which posits that working memory (Rotzer et al., 2009; Toll, Van der Ven, Kroesbergen, & Van Luit, 2011) and attention (Ashkenazi & Henik, 2010a, 2010b) cause the deficits in the use of developmentally appropriate arithmetic procedures (Ashkenazi et al., 2013). Ramaa and Gowramma (2004) compared the performance of children with visual impairment, children with dyscalculia and normally developing children in number concept and found that children with visual impairment in primary level had attained mastery in number concept just like their fully sighted age peers, but children with dyscalculia, even at grade IV, had basic difficulties. This further strengthens the fact that sensory impairment per se is not the cause of arithmetic difficulties. Since the core brain areas and functional circuits involved in numerical cognition are unaffected in CWHI and environmentally deprived NHC, unlike children with dyscalculia, age-appropriate mathematical experience will help them learn grade-level arithmetic concepts. Comparative studies on larger samples can direct towards precise behavioral diagnosis for dyscalculia.

Without intervention the difficulties may persist for a longer duration, leading to additional problems. Schoenfeld (2002) cautions on the long-term implications of such deficits as it denies an important pathway to economic and other enfranchisement. In this context, it may be noted that children with dyscalculia were able to show grade-appropriate performance in arithmetic after following systematic remediation based on appropriate principles (Gowramma, 2005). Hence, there is a need to design appropriate remedial strategies suiting the special needs of children. It can be construed from the findings of the present study that CWHI have some areas of strength in addition to having difficulties in learning arithmetic. It was found that the performance of CWHI improved significantly when they were taught through play-way methods in primary school (Vijayalakshmi & Gowramma, 2010). Findings of a study by Mousley and Kelly (1998) demonstrated that problem-solving performance of CWHI can be enhanced through exposure to a number of analytical strategies. Craig and Gordon (1988) suggest using the right hemisphere strengths of visuo-spatial skills to compensate the left hemisphere deficit in verbo-sequential processing. These studies offer a bridge between research and practice and the potential for making effective use of the strengths to surmount the deficiencies and provide the quality of education a student deserves. Matching the educational intervention to the needs of each student implies finding pedagogical methodologies that are effective across the spectrum of abilities. Such a change in the classroom is the need of the hour when the policy is to educate all the children under the same roof, irrespective of their abilities and socio-economic background.

References

Ashkenazi, S., Black, J. M., Abrams, D. A., Hoeft, F., & Menon, V. (2013). Neurobiological underpinnings of math and reading learning disabilities. *Journal of Learning Disabilities, 46*(6), 549–569.

Ashkenazi, S., & Henik, A. (2010a). Attentional networks in developmental dyscalculia. *Behavioral and Brain Functions, 6*(1), 1–12.

Ashkenazi, S., & Henik, A. (2010b). A disassociation between physical and mental number bisection in developmental dyscalculia. *Neuropsychologia, 48*(10), 2861–2868.

Barton, B. (1995). Cultural issues in NZ mathematics education. In J. Neyland (Ed.), *Mathematics Education: A handbook for teacher* (Vol. 2, pp. 150–164). Wellington: Wellington College.

Butterworth, B., Varma, S., & Laurillard, D. (2011). Dyscalculia: From brain to education. *Science, 332*(6033), 1049–1053.

Craig, H. B., & Gordon, H. W. (1988). Specialized cognitive function and reading achievement in hearing-impaired adolescents. *Journal of Speech and Hearing Disorders, 53*, 30–41.

Epstein, K. I., Hillegeist, E. G., & Grafman, J. (1994). Number processing in deaf college students. *American Annals of the Deaf, 139*(3), 336–347.

Flexer, C. (1999). *Facilitating Hearing and Listening in Young Children.* San Diego, CA: Singular Publishing Press.

Gregory, S. (1998). Mathematics and deaf children. In S. Gregory, P. Knight, W. McCracken, S. Powers, & L. Watson (Eds.), *Issues in Deaf Education.* London: Faulton Press.

Gowramma, I. P. (2005). *Development of Remedial Instruction Programme for Children with Dyscalculia in Primary School.* Mysore, India: Chethana Publishers.

Gowramma, I. P. (2006). *Difficulties experienced by children with hearing impairment while doing mathematics.* Unpublished research project report, All India Institute of Speech and Hearing, Mysore, India.

Greenberg, M. T., & Kusche, C. A. (1989). Cognitive, personal and social development of deaf children and adolescents. In M. C. Wang, H. J. Walberg, & M. C. Reynolds (Eds.), *The Handbook of Special Education: Vol. 3 Research and practice* (pp. 95–129). Oxford, England: Pergamon Press.

Hitch, G. J., Arnold, P., & Phillips, L. J. (1983). Counting processes in deaf children's arithmetic. *British Journal of Psychology, 74*(4), 429–437.

Hyde, M., Zevenbergen, R., & Power, D. (2003). Deaf and hard of hearing students' performance on arithmetic word problems. *American Annals of the Deaf, 148*, 56–64.

Kelly, R. R., Lang, H. G., & Pagliaro, C. M. (2003). Mathematics word problem solving for deaf students: A survey of practices in grades 6–12. *Journal of Deaf Studies and Deaf Education, 8*(2), 104–119.

Kelly, R. R., & Mousley, K. (2001). Solving word problems: More than reading issues for deaf students. *American Annals of the Deaf, 146*(3), 253–264.

Kluwin, T., & Moores, D. (1985). The effects of integration on the mathematics achievement of hearing impaired adolescents. *Exceptional Children, 52*, 153–160.

Martin, F. W. (1985). Classroom teachers' knowledge of hearing disorders and attitudes about mainstreaming hard-of-hearing children. *Language, Speech, and Hearing Services in Schools, 19*, 83–95.

Meadow, K. (1980). *Deafness and Child Development.* Berkeley, CA: University of California Press.

Mousley, K., & Kelly, R. (1998). Problem-solving strategies for teaching mathematics to deaf students. *American Annals of the Deaf, 143*, 325–336.

Nunes, T., & Moreno, C. (1997). Solving word problems with different ways of representing the task. *Mathematics and Special Educational Needs, 3*(2), 15–17.

Nunes, T., & Moreno, C. (1998). Is hearing impairment a cause of difficulties in learning mathematics? In C. Donlan (Ed.), *The Development of Mathematical Skills* (pp. 227–254). Hove, UK: Psychology Press.

Nunes, T., & Moreno, C. (2002). An intervention program for promoting deaf pupils' achievement in mathematics. *Journal of Deaf Studies and Deaf Education, 7*(2), 120–133.

Paranjape, S. (1998). Achievement of normal and hearing handicapped pupils at the end of the primary cycle. *Disabilities and Impairments, 10*(2), 73–86.

Pau, C. S. (1995). The deaf child and solving problems of arithmetic: The importance of comprehensive reading. *American Annals of the Deaf, 140*(3), 287–290.

Paul, P. V., & Jackson, D. W. (1993). *Toward a Psychology of Deafness: Theoretical and empirical perspectives.* Boston, MA: Allyn & Bacon.

Paul, P. V., & Quigley, S. P. (1994). *Language and Deafness.* San Diego, CA: Singular Publishing Group, Inc.

Ramaa, S. (1994). *Arithmetic Diagnostic Test for Primary School Children.* Mysore, India: Chetana Publishers.

Ramaa, S., & Gowramma, I. P. (2002). Difficulties in arithmetic problem solving among disadvantaged children of grade V. *Indian Educational Review, 38*(1), 69–86.

Ramaa, S., & Gowramma, I. P. (2004). Analysis of difficulties and errors in number concept among children with dyscalculia, normal achievers and children with visual impairment. Paper presented in the 5th World Congress on Dyslexia, Macedonia, Greece. 23–27 August, 2004.

Rotzer, S., Loenneker, T., Kucian, K., Martin, E., Klaver, P., & von Aster, M. (2009). Dysfunctional neural network of spatial working memory contributes to developmental dyscalculia. *Neuropsychologia, 47*(13), 2859–2865.

Schoenfeld, A. H. (2002). Making mathematics work for all children: Issues of standards, testing, and equity. *Educational Researcher, 31*, 13–25.

Stewart, D., & Kluwin, T. (2001). *Teaching Deaf and Hard-of-Hearing Students: Content, strategies, and curriculum.* Boston, MA: Allyn & Bacon.

Swanwick, R. A., Oddy, A., & Roper, T. (2005). Mathematics and deaf children: An exploration of barriers to success. *Deafness and Education International, 7*(1), 1–21.

Toll, S. W. M., Van der Ven, S. H. G., Kroesbergen, E. H., & Van Luit, J. E. H. (2011). Executive functions as predictors of math learning disabilities. *Journal of Learning Disabilities, 44*(6), 521–532.

Vijayalakshmi, S., & Gowramma, I. P. (2010). Effectiveness of play way method of teaching mathematics to children with hearing impairment. *Student research at AIISH Mysore (articles based on dissertation done at AIISH)* Volume VI: 2007–2008, 66–79.

Wood, D. J., Wood, H. A., & Howarth, S. P. (1983). Mathematical abilities of deaf school-leavers. *British Journal of Developmental Psychology, 1*, 67–73.

Wood, H. A., Wood, D. J., Kinsmill, M. C., French, J. R. W., & Howarth, S. P. (1984). The mathematical achievements of deaf children from different educational environments. *British Journal of Education Psychology, 54*, 254–264.

Yathiraj, A., Gowramma, I. P., Prithi, N., & Vijetha, P. (2013). Pre-arithmetic school readiness test for children with hearing impairment. Unpublished research project report, All India Institute of Speech and Hearing, Mysore, India.

Zarfaty, Y., Nunes, T., & Bryant, P. (2004). The performance of young deaf children in spatial and temporal number tasks. *Journal of Deaf Studies and Deaf Education, 9*(3), 315–326.

9

Arithmetic difficulties among socially disadvantaged children and children with dyscalculia

Ramaa S.

Introduction

Mathematics is the basis for learning other academic subjects and solving daily living problems. Research findings have shown across countries that mathematics is the most difficult subject for the elementary students. Poor performances in mathematics are attributed to inappropriate teaching, behavioural problems, mathematics anxiety, irregularities in attending classes, dyslexia, dyscalculia, cultural and socio-cultural factors. Burr (2008) noted that the problem of underachievement is particularly great for children from economically disadvantaged backgrounds, although underachievement affects pupils from all backgrounds.

The trend reports on research in mathematics education (Miyan, 1991) have identified certain factors responsible for higher rates of failure in mathematics achievement, particularly at secondary level. The major contributing factors are the intelligence and socio-economic background of the students. The reports have stressed the need for continued research in mathematics education, keeping in mind the diversities in Indian schools and for the development of special strategies for teaching first generation learners, children from backward classes (sectors) and children with sensory handicaps and intellectual disabilities as well as children from tribal and hilly areas.

There is a need to understand the specific difficulties faced by different categories of children in order to meet their special needs.

This chapter discusses details of two studies conducted by the author in the Karnataka state of India which attempted to assess the specific difficulties in arithmetic among socially disadvantaged children (SDC) (2001) and children with dyscalculia

(CWD) (1990). These studies were funded by the NCERT, New Delhi, India. The data collected as a part of those studies and a study conducted by the author on the cognitive development of educable mentally retarded children (EMR) were revisited and qualitative meta-analysis and synthesis are attempted. Results are discussed in the light of new developments in the area of dyscalculia and mathematical difficulties.

A study on specific difficulties in arithmetic among socially disadvantaged children

The National Research Council (1989) reported that within the United States, students from low-income families or who are members of linguistic or ethnic minority groups are especially at risk for underachievement in mathematics. This pattern of underachievement is noticed in all levels of schooling (Dorsey et al., 1988; Natriello et al., 1990; Bowman et al., 2001). The cross-cultural and within-cultural differences in mathematical achievement stem from the foundation of the informal mathematical knowledge children develop during their childhood (Starkey and Klein, 2006). Over the past decade or so research on socio-cultural influences on early mathematical development has been rapidly expanded and several studies have revealed the presence of cross-cultural as well as socio-economic status (SES) related differences in informal mathematical knowledge during the preschool years (Starkey and Klein, 2006). These differences are explained in terms of the lack of a stimulating learning environment at home and at preschool. From the findings of these studies it can be hypothesised that SDC who are first generation learners and who did not have preschool education will continue to have serious difficulties in arithmetic at elementary schools.

In India, people who are deprived of basic social rights and security because of poverty, discrimination, or other unfavourable circumstances are called socially disadvantaged. They include the Scheduled Castes (SC), (16% of the Indian population), the Scheduled Tribes (ST) (8.1% of the Indian population), Other Backward Classes (OBC) and the Minorities (linguistic/religious). Among them the most disadvantaged are the SCs and STs, due to social and geographical/cultural exclusions, respectively.

The performance on various indicators related to primary education is consistently poorer among SC children (Jenkins and Barr, 2005). The socially marginalized groups of SC and ST lag behind in attainment levels of Human Development (Sukdeo, 2007). According to the National Sample Survey Organisation (1999), around 40% of SC and ST people live below the poverty line. The proportion of literates is lower among those who belong to SCs and STs. The main reason for this is the deprivation of educational facilities for generations (Sawant and Athawale, 1997). Shukla (1997) noticed severe underachievement among tribal students at primary level. However, studies attempting to identify the specific difficulties in different academic areas, especially in mathematics, among SDC are very limited in India.

The study conducted by the author attempted to identify the specific difficulties in arithmetic among the SDC in Grade V of Elementary Schools and compare their performance with that of CWD.

The study was conducted on Grade V children belonging to the SC and ST categories from low SES families and who were first generation learners. The sample was drawn from four government schools with Kannada Medium Instruction from the Coorg and Mysore districts. On the basis of the teacher's opinion, a list of children who were average and above average in Kannada reading and writing was prepared. The purpose of making this list was to eliminate children who were below average in intelligence, had sensory difficulties, serious emotional and behavioural problems and to include those who had adequate knowledge of Kannada, interest and motivation for academic learning, and regular attendance at school. From among 317 children, 138 (43.53%) were considered to be average in reading and writing by the teachers, of whom 58 (42%) were boys and 80 (58%) were girls.

Description of the tool

In order to identify the difficulties in arithmetic among the subjects of the study, the Arithmetic Diagnostic Test for Primary School Children (Ramaa, 1990, 1994) was administered. The test is diagnostic and criterion referenced in nature and is available both in English and Kannada versions. The Kannada version was used in this study. The test covers three major areas of arithmetic; namely, number concept, arithmetic processes (the fundamental operations – addition, subtraction, multiplication and division) and arithmetic problem solving. In each of these areas a series of basic understandings and skills (criterion measures) expected to be mastered by children of each of these grades are covered.

The subjects of the study were in the beginning stage of Grade V, so it was decided to administer the items meant for Grade IV only. Since the Diagnostic Test is meant for children of Grades I to IV, items which appear to be very simple for Grade IV children were eliminated in order to reduce the time required to administer the tool. Thus the items which assess number concept and arithmetic operations suitable for Grades I to II were not administered. However, all the items assessing arithmetic problem solving skills, multiplication and division were administered. The details of the criterion measures assessed among the subjects are covered in the section relating to analysis of the data.

Data were analysed qualitatively with reference to the attainment of mastery of various criterion measures. On the basis of the raw scores obtained for each of the criterion measures, children were considered to have exhibited different levels of performance, namely, mastery (those who obtained 75% and above of the maximum score), non-mastery (those who obtained '0' for the items or did not attempt the items) or partial achievement (those who were neither masters nor non-masters). The subjects who exhibited these levels of performance were labelled as masters (M), partial-achievers (P-A) and non-masters (N-M), respectively.

The number of children who exhibited different levels of performance was converted into a percentage for the purpose of comparison. Figure 9.1 clearly shows that the SDC of the study had considerable difficulty with all the arithmetic processes, but relatively more so in multiplication and division compared with addition and subtraction.

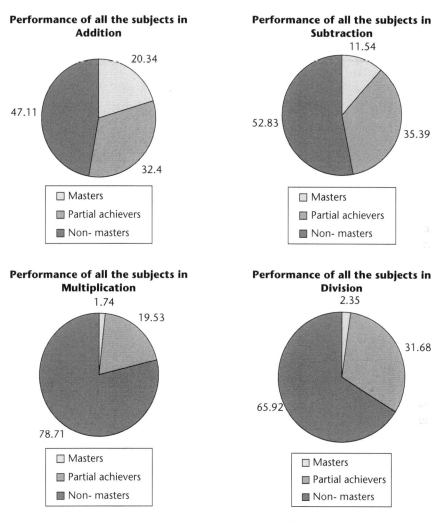

Figure 9.1 Comparison of the performance of SDC in different arithmetic processes

A study on specific difficulties in arithmetic among children with dyscalculia

The concept and nature of dyscalculia have been thoroughly discussed in the literature. There is no need to elaborate the same here as these are discussed in other chapters. In this study children with Arithmetic Disabilities are considered as dyscalculic.

There is a significant overlap between diagnoses of dyslexia and dyscalculia, ranging from 20% to 60% in different studies (Butterworth and Yeo, 2004). However, there is definite evidence that mathematical difficulties are not simply a result of dyslexia, other language difficulties, or generally low IQ, as mathematics and reading difficulties can sometimes dissociate.

Ramaa (1990) and Ramaa and Gowramma (2002a) also noticed that there are dyscalculics without dyslexia or writing difficulties. Dowker (2009) noticed that there is little evidence at present that children with specific mathematical difficulties are fundamentally different, or need to be taught in different ways, from children whose mathematical difficulties are linked more to other problems. This suggests that there is a need to investigate the specific difficulties in arithmetic/mathematics encountered by dyscalculics who either have or are free from reading/writing disabilities and to compare their arithmetic difficulties with other children whose difficulties are due to some other factors. The findings of each one of these might give a different picture of dyscalculics and will have different implications for remedial instruction.

Developmental dyscalculia (DD) has been considered as a cognitive disability in learning about numbers and arithmetic (Ranpura et al., 2013). A review of the research into dyscalculia since 1970 reveals that relatively more studies were aimed at identifying neuropsychological characteristics among dyscalculia compared to other objectives. In dyslexics a core deficiency has been identified as a symbolic processing deficit (Ramaa et al., 1993) and phonological deficit (Goswami, 2013). Along similar lines recently there have been attempts to identify core deficits for DD. The core deficit in DD is now generally agreed to be a disability in processing numerosity, the number of objects in a set (Butterworth and Walsh, 2011; Giedd et al., 2009; Reigosa-Crespo et al., 2012). However, there is a need to find out if there are deficiencies in other areas of development among CWD, so that early identification and intervention are possible.

The study conducted by the author on CWD who were free from dyslexia and writing disabilities aimed at:

- finding the arithmetic difficulties exhibited by each of the subjects;
- comparing the arithmetic difficulties exhibited by CWD with those of SDC;
- finding the deficiencies in certain neuropsychological processes and the components of logico-mathematical structure among CWD;
- comparing CWD with EMR and Normal Children in the components of logico-mathematical structure;
- finding the correlation among different components of logico-mathematical structure and mastery in arithmetic processes among CWD.

The study was conducted on ten CWD from Grade IV who were free from dyslexia and writing disabilities. They were identified from ten primary schools providing instruction in the Kannada medium which are located in Mysore City, Karnataka State, India. The identification procedure involved verification of various exclusionary and inclusionary criteria usually set for dyscalculics. The investigator adopted an elaborate and systematic procedure to identify the subjects. For details, see Ramaa and Gowramma (2002a, 2002b, 2002c).

For the subjects of the study, the Arithmetic Diagnostic Test for Primary School Children (Kannada version) developed by the investigator (1990 and 1994) was administered individually. Unlike the case of SDC, the entire test was administered to CWD. The description of the tool is given in the discussion relating to the study on SDC.

Difficulties Exhibited by CWD in different arithmetic processes

The data collected on the Arithmetic Diagnostic Test for the CWD in the study were analysed using different techniques. Mean, SD and Quartile Deviations were computed for the group. The mean performance of the subjects was considerably below that of maximum scores expected for each component. As a whole, the test was difficult for the CWD in the study. Among the seven criterion measures of number concept, seriating numbers in ascending order was difficult for all the CWD and reading fractions (limited to ¼, ½, ¾) and mixed fractions involving these fractions was difficult for 70% of the CWD. In addition-related problems, addition of fractions and solving problems involving spatial and numerical relations were difficult for 80% and 100% of CWD, respectively. Most of the criterion measures of subtraction, multiplication and division were difficult for them.

In order to find out the specific arithmetic difficulties exhibited by the CWD, the data were analysed qualitatively. The procedure used was the same as that for the analysis of the data for SDC. The subjects were considered as Masters (M), Partial-Achievers (P-A) or Non-Masters (N-M) with reference to each of the criterion measures assessed.

The performances of each child with dyscalculia on different arithmetic processes were analysed in terms of the quartile deviations obtained for the group. Intra-individual differences for the performances in different arithmetic processes were clearly noticed. Each CWD exhibited a unique profile of strengths and weaknesses in different criterion measures.

Table 9.1 shows the criterion measures of arithmetic that were assessed among SDC and CWD. Different groups were compared in terms of their mastery,

Table 9.1 Criterion measures assessed among both CWD and SDC

Arithmetic processes	Sl. No.	Criterion measures
Addition	cm-1	Fundamental operations – adding the numbers
	cm-2	Adding according to place value
	cm-3	Arranging a given set of numbers in ascending order based on their sums
	cm-4	Problem solving involving verbal and numerical relations (V-N-R)
	cm-5	Problem solving involving spatial, verbal and numerical relations(S-V-N-R)

(Continued)

Table 9.1 (Continued)

Arithmetic processes	Sl. No.	Criterion measures
Subtraction	cm-1	Fundamental operations – subtracting the numbers
	cm-2	Subtracting according to place value
	cm-3	Arranging a given set of numbers in descending order based on their differences
	cm-4	Problem solving involving numeral relations only, requiring addition and subtraction
	cm-5	Problem solving involving V-N-R
	cm-6	Problem solving involving S-V-N-R
	cm-7	Problem solving involving N-R only
Multiplication	cm-1	Fundamental operations-multiplying multi-digit numbers
	cm-2	Arranging a given set of numbers in ascending order based on their products
	cm-3	Problem solving – involving numerical relations only, requiring addition, subtraction and multiplication
	cm-4	Problem solving – involving V-N-R
Division	cm-1	Dividing numbers which can be divided by the given divisor without remainder
	cm-2	Dividing where divisor is larger than the first digit (100 or 1000s place) of the dividend
	cm-3	Problem solving involving V-N-R

partial achievement or non-mastery using these criterion measures. Intra-group and inter-group comparisons were also made. The percentages of M, P-A and N-M among CWD were compared with those for SDC on these criterion measures (Figure 9.2).

The comparison revealed that, except for a few, the criterion measures for addition and subtraction were very difficult for the subjects from both of the groups. Those few were mastered by a greater percentage of CWD than SDC. It is very interesting to notice in Figure 9.2(c) and (d) that there were no masters in many of the criterion

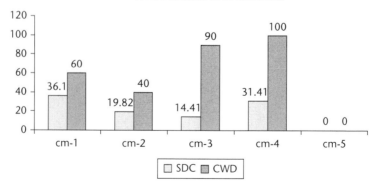

(a) Percentage of Masters among SDC and CWD different Criterion Measures of Addition

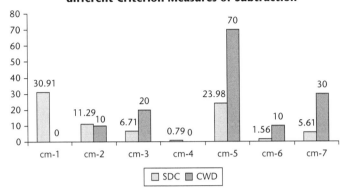

(b) Percentage of Masters among SDC and CWD in different Criterion Measures of Subtraction

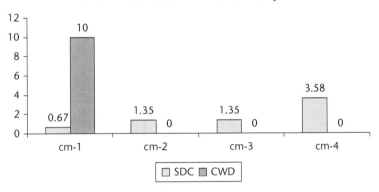

(c) Percentage of Masters among SDC and CWD in different Criterion Measures of Multiplication

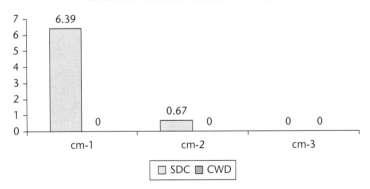

(d) Percentage of Masters among SDC and CWD in different Criterion Measures of Division

Figure 9.2 Specific difficulties in different criterion measures of arithmetic processes assessed among both SDC and CWD

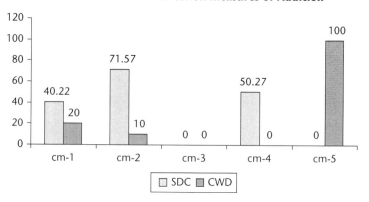

(a) Percentage of partial achievers among SDC and CWD in different criterion measures of Addition

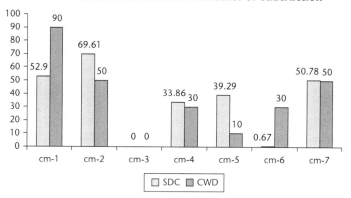

(b) Percentage of Partial achievers among SDC and CWD in different Criterion Measures of Subtraction

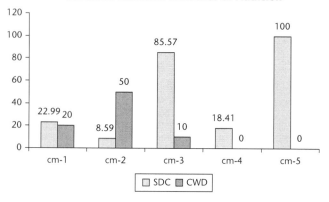

(c) Percentage of Non-masters among SDC and CWD different Criterion Measures of Addition

**(d) Percentage of Non-masters among SDC and CWD in
different Criterion Measures of Subtraction**

Figure 9.3 Comparison of the performance of SDC and CWD in different criterion
measures of addition and subtraction

measures for multiplication or in any of the criterion measures for division among
CWD. Some criterion measures were equally difficult for both the groups.

Figure 9.3 shows that there were no definite patterns of intra-group and inter-
group differences between the percentages of partial-achievers and non-masters in
addition and subtraction.

It can be seen in Figure 9.4 that most of the criterion measures of multiplication
and division were very difficult for both the groups. The percentage of non-masters
was considerably higher in CWD than SDC in these criterion measures.

The responses of the participants in the Arithmetic Diagnostic Test were analysed
for both the groups. There were many procedural errors and application errors in the
problem solving items.

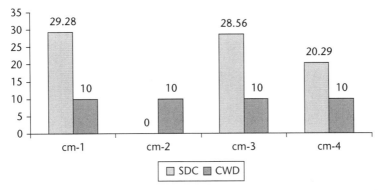

**(a) Percentage of Parital achievers among SDC and CWD in
different Criterion Measures of Multiplication**

(Continued)

(b) Percentage of Partial achievers among SDC and CWD in different Criterion Measures of Division

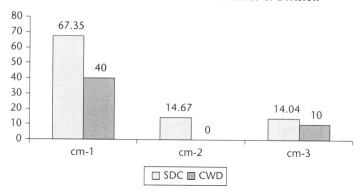

Percentage of Non-masters among SDC and CWD in different Criterion Measures of Multiplication

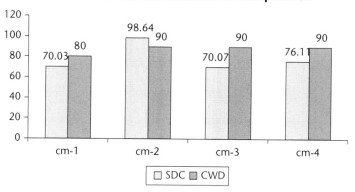

(d) Percentage of Non-masters among SDC and CWD in different Criterion Measures of Division

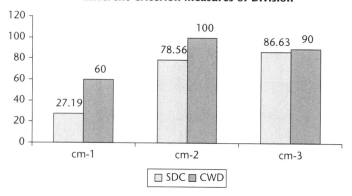

Figure 9.4 Comparison of the performance of SDC and CWD in different criterion measures of multiplication and division

Deficiencies in sequential memory and logico-mathematical thinking among CWD

It was consistently shown in previous studies that dyscalculics have severe deficiency in recalling the items presented through both the modalities, visual and auditory, in a particular sequence (Webster, 1979). It was also noticed that dyscalculics demonstrate a deficient logical-mathematical structure, that is, with conservation, seriation and class (Clarke and Chardwick, 1979; Kingma, 1984; Derr, 1985; Deborah et al., 1986). However, it is not clear in these studies whether the dyscalculics were free from reading and writing disabilities or not. So in this study we attempted to assess these variables and to find out whether they are correlated with mastery of criterion measures of the arithmetic processes assessed in the study.

Assessment instruments

The memory for shapes in sequence and the memory for orally presented digits in sequence were assessed through visual sequential memory (VSM) and auditory sequential memory (ASM) sub-tests of the Illinois Test of Psycholinguistic Abilities (ITPA) (Kirk et al., 1968), respectively. The sub-tests were administered individually.

The logico-mathematic structure among the dyscalculics in the present study was assessed by administration of the Metric relations and Conservation sub-tests of the Mysore Cognitive Development Status Test (MCDST) (Padmini and Nayar, unpublished) and the Classification Test developed by the investigator.

The MCDST is a test of cognitive development status based on a number of cognitive concepts and operations judged appropriate to age group 5 to 7 years. This assesses six areas at the concrete operational stage: Metric relations, Spatial relations, Conservation, Temporal relations, Signs-symbols and Belongingness. However, in this study only two sub-tests, Metric relations and Conservation were used. Each sub-test consists of many tasks. The tests were administered individually to the subjects.

The Classification Test was constructed by the investigator to assess the ability of primary school children Grades I through IV to classify and provide explanation for the classification. The explanation was sought only when the classification was correct. The items were administered and scored as '1' for a correct response and '0' for a wrong response.

The raw scores obtained by administering the sub-tests of VSM and ASM were converted into Psycholinguistic Ages (PA) as per the guidelines given in the Manual of ITPA. The difference between Chronological Age (CA) and PA for VSM of the child, CA of each child and ASM of the child, as well as the difference between the PAs for VSM and ASM were computed for each child. The results showed that PAs for VSM and ASM were very much below that of CA in all the CWD of the study. The difference between CA and PA ranged from 0.5 to 5.1 years for VSM and for ASM ranged from 2.0 to 6.1 years, indicating a greater deficiency in ASM than VSM.

On the basis of the raw scores obtained on the sub-tests of MCDST we attempted to find the percentage of the subjects who had deficiency in different cognitive capabilities. The performance of CWD and that of an age-matched group of EMR children were compared. The data are taken from the study conducted by Ramaa (1980) where the same tool was administered to study cognitive development.

It is interesting to note from Table 9.2 that the Metric relations and Conservation tasks were more difficult for CWD than EMR children except in Volume seriation. In Area seriation both the groups experienced almost the same level of difficulty.

Table 9.3 shows that the performance of CWD in both the Metric relations and Conservation tasks was poorer than Normal Children (standardization sample) and EMR Children. The results relating to the Classification task are given in Table 9.4.

Table 9.2 Percentage of subjects with moderate to high levels of deficiency in different cognitive capabilities

Sub-tests	Test-tasks	Percentage of subjects	
		CWD (N = 10)	EMR (N = 27)
Metric relations (MR)	Length seriation	70	22.20
	Area seriation	10	11.10
	Volume seriation	10	37.00
	Equi-distant points location	90	56.50
	Distance estimation	100	77.70
Conservation (CS)	Judgement of invariance of number	40	0.00
	Judgement of invariance of length	100	3.70
	Judgement of invariance of area	90	14.80
	Judgement of invariance of mass	90	0.00
	Judgement of invariance of liquid	100	14.80

Table 9.3 Comparison between the mean performance among Normal, EMR and CWD

Subjects	Metric relations	Conservation
Normal	15.90	7.50
EMR	14.0	4.54
CWD	12.15	3.6

Table 9.4 Percentage of CWD (N = 10) with a deficiency in Classification and Explanation

Tasks	Classification of numbers according to no. of digits(1–4)		Classification of sets of signs (+) according to odd and even numbers of them		Classification of the series of numbers in terms of ascending and descending orders		Classification of geometric shapes based on the extent of shaded areas – whole, ¼, ½ and ¾ parts	
	C	E	C	E	C	E	C	E
Percentage	0	20	50	10	50	20	30	10

Note: C = Classification; E = Explanation

Spearman's rho was used to determine the correlation among different variables: Seriation (SR), Conservation (CS), Classification (CL), CA-PA for VSM (D-VSM), CA-PA for ASM (D-ASM) and Mastery in all the Criterion Measures of Arithmetic Processes (MAP) taken together. In the Metric relations sub-test only the seriation items were considered for correlation, as earlier studies had involved this variable.

The results showed that the ability to perform the tasks of Seriation and Conservation were significantly and positively correlated with mastery in the criterion measures of the arithmetic processes. Performance in the Conservation tasks was also significantly and positively correlated with Classification tasks and negatively with D-ASM. The correlations between D-VSM and D-ASM were significant and positive but were not related to MAP.

Discussion and conclusion

The SDC in this study had considerable difficulty with all the arithmetic processes. In all the arithmetic processes, there was no observable difference between SC and ST children as both belonged to economically weaker sections of society. The SDC exhibited moderate to severe levels of arithmetic difficulties. However, the difficulties were comparatively greater for multiplication and division.

The prevalence of CWD without dyslexia and writing disabilities was found to be 6% (15/251) in the population studied. The same figure was noticed by Kosc (1968, 1974), Gross (2007), Burr (2008) and Dowker (2009).

The CWD exhibited considerable difficulty in all of the arithmetic processes. However, multiplication and division were most difficult for these children. Similar observations were made by Gowramma (2005).

Each CWD exhibited a unique profile with reference to performance in different arithmetic processes. This was also noticed by Dowker (2009). There were considerable intra-group and intra-individual differences among CWD in the difficulty levels of the criterion measures of arithmetic processes assessed among them. There was no definite pattern in the performance of CWD in the Arithmetic Diagnostic Test. No child with dyscalculia did better in the lower order arithmetic processes such as number concept or addition than the higher order tasks like subtraction, multiplication and division. This finding supports the observation made by Dowker, (2009) that a child may perform well at an apparently difficult task while performing poorly at an apparently easier task, and also the opinion of several investigators such as Denvir and Brown (1986) and Dowker (2009) that it is not possible to establish a strict hierarchy in the different components of arithmetic. This also strengthens the evidence that arithmetic is not a single unitary ability at which people are either 'good' or 'bad' gathered from many converging sources, including experimental, educational and factor-analytic studies of typically developing children and adults (Dowker, 1998, 2005; Ginsburg, 1977; Siegler, 1988); studies of children with mathematical difficulties (Butterworth, 2004; Dowker, 2005; Geary and Hoard, 2005; Russell and Ginsburg, 1984); and functional brain imaging studies (Castelli et al., 2006; Dehaene et al., 1999; Gruber et al., 2001; Rickard et al., 2000). Hence there is a need to plan strategies for intervention by considering the strengths and weaknesses of each CWD as observed through diagnostic testing.

The comparison between SDC and CWD revealed that there were no definite patterns of intra-group and inter-group differences in their performances in addition and subtraction. However, multiplication and division were more difficult for CWD than SDC. There was no appreciable difference in the types of errors committed by both the groups in the items administered to both groups (for a detailed account of errors committed by SDC, see Ramaa and Gowramma (2002a)). As a whole, the differences observed between these two groups were a matter of degree rather than quality. The types of errors committed by dyscalculics are similar to that noticed by many investigators. These findings support the view that there are currently no agreed criteria for diagnosing dyscalculia. Dyscalculia and mathematics difficulties are likely to form part of a continuum of mathematics ability, with a few individuals having severe specific difficulties with arithmetic (Dowker, 2004, 2009) and others with milder difficulties and exhibiting strengths and weaknesses in almost any area of mathematics.

Starkey and Klein (2006) noticed the presence of cross-cultural as well as SES factors related to differences in informal mathematical knowledge during the preschool years and attributed these differences to parental education level and their interest and value for mathematics. Although the study involved SDC studying at elementary schools, the arithmetic difficulties noticed among them may be attributed to the same factors.

The SDC of the present study, though average in reading and writing, demonstrated considerable difficulty in arithmetic. This suggests that performance in arithmetic is more influenced by the socio-economic background of the students (Vygotsky, 1978).

It was noticed in the study that CWD exhibited a deficiency in both the neuropsychological processes of VSM and ASM; however, a greater deficiency was observed in ASM than VSM. Similar observations were noticed in the studies conducted by Webster (1979) and Landerl (2013).

The meta-analysis done by the author revealed that Metric relations and Conservation tasks were more difficult for CWD than age-matched EMR children and younger normally developing children. So in these components of cognitive development the CWD had a considerable deficiency. It is evident from the study that the ability to perform the tasks of Seriation and Conservation were significantly and positively correlated with mastery in the criterion measures of arithmetic processes. These findings strongly support the observations made by other investigators. Clarke and Chadwick (1979) noticed that subjects with arithmetic problems demonstrated a deficient logical-mathematical structure (Conservation, Seriation and Classification). Nishi (1988) also observed that arithmetically disabled children were deficient in conservation tasks even at 9.6 years of age. Childs (1981) noticed that from among the Piagetian tests, the combination of Conservation and Seriation was clearly superior to the intelligence sub-tests in predicting number-language seriation and number line comprehension. He concluded that out of the Piagetian tasks,

Seriation might especially serve as a valuable diagnostic instrument for some aspect of initial arithmetic. Among the CWD of the study conducted by the author, the performance in Conservation tasks was also significantly and positively correlated with the Classification tasks.

In this study, though the correlations between VSM, ASM and Conservation tasks were significant they were not related to mastery in arithmetic processes. Butterworth (2005) concluded that, although various forms of working memory difficulty may well co-occur with mathematics difficulties, there is no convincing evidence implicating any form of working memory as a causal feature in dyscalculia.

The Diagnostic Arithmetic Test developed and used in the study proved to be beneficial in understanding the strengths and weaknesses of individuals with dyscalculia or arithmetic difficulties. However, it did not differentiate between CWD and SDC in the criterion measures assessed among them. So, as suggested by Dowker (2004), tests of attainment must be separated from tests of capacity since attainment can be affected by teaching, attendance and so on. Mathematics 'capacity' implies innate skills that underpin learning and which might be immune to teaching Butterworth (1999).

Most researchers do agree that mathematical difficulties are often, though not always, correlated with problems in other areas and can be linked to language difficulties, spatial difficulties, and/or difficulties with aspects of memory (Chinn, 2004; Dowker, 2004, 2005; Gifford, 2005; Hannell, 2005). In a study conducted by Prema and Ramaa (2003) the ability to read mathematics vocabulary, understanding of mathematical language and performance in mathematics were found to be positively correlated with each other among Grade IV children with Kannada as the medium of instruction. In the opinion of Ramaa (2000b) the diagnosis of underlying factors – neuropsychological processing skills and cognitive developmental deficiencies – helps not only in understanding Indian children but children with LD universally. The majority of the SDC of the study showed serious difficulties in multiplication and division like CWD. This leads to one important question – whether some of them, if not all, were also dyscalculics, or whether their arithmetic difficulties could be attributed to socio-cultural factors alone. There is a definite need to compare SDC and CWD on various neuropsychological processes and Piagetian tasks of logico-mathematical structure in order to understand the differentiating factors between them. It is also necessary to compare dyscalculics with other children with arithmetic difficulties in these measures. Vygotsky's socio-cultural perspective of cognitive development highlights the importance of cultural as well as adult mediators in cognitive development. Since the SC and ST population in India were socially and culturally excluded for generations, their cognitive development might be affected. The deficiency/difficulties in the early mathematical abilities noticed among the economically weaker sections by various investigators may be attributed to a deficient cognitive development. Mohanty (1989) and Ekka (1990) found that the tribal students were not mentally deficient; they were capable of picking up complex knowledge, but their pace of assimilation was slower as their cognitive level was relatively lower due to historical reasons. There is a need to verify these observations in future studies.

There is also a need to compare CWD with SDC in all the criterion measures of arithmetic processes to find out whether any of them differentiate. The findings of the study suggest that a deliberate attempt has to be made to promote cognitive development among dyscalculics. Remedial instruction should take into consideration the strengths and weakness of dyscalculics in neuropsychological processes and cognitive development. If remedial instruction is not given at early stages, the problems may become persistent, with dyscalculics showing serious arithmetic difficulties even at secondary school level (Ramaa and Gowramma, 1999).

There is a need to develop arithmetic/mathematics diagnostic tests in different languages. In countries like India with linguistic diversities, the construction of assessment instruments is a challenging task (Ramaa, 2000a). The teachers have to be trained in diagnosing the specific arithmetic difficulties among children in general and dyscalculics and SDC in particular, as well as in adopting appropriate strategies for teaching arithmetic. There should be provision for SDC children to attend preschools which make a serious attempt to develop arithmetic readiness. In India, many SDC join primary schools without preschool education due to economic reasons.

Mathematics problem solving skills are deficient in CWD and SDC. We cannot assume that problem solving skills develop automatically. There should be deliberate attempts to develop these skills among students.

References

Bowman, B. T., Donovan, M. S., and Burns, M. S. (eds). (2001). *Eager to Learn: Educating our preschoolers*. Washington, DC: National Academy Press.

Burr, T. (2008). *Mathematics Performance in Primary Schools: Getting the best results*. London: National Audit Office/Department for Children, Schools and Families.

Butterworth, B. (1999). *The Mathematical Brain*. London: Macmillan.

Butterworth, B. (2004). *Developmental Dyscalculia*. In J. I. D. Campbell (ed.) *Handbook of Mathematical Cognition* (pp. 455–467). Hove: Psychology Press.

Butterworth, B. (2005). The development of arithmetic abilities. *Journal of Child Psychology and Psychiatry, 46*(1), 3–18.

Butterworth, B. and Yeo, D. (2004). *Dyscalculia Guidance*. London: NFER-Nelson.

Butterworth, B. and Walsh, V. (2011). Neural basis of mathematical cognition. *Current Biology, 21*, R618–621.

Castelli, F., Glaser, D. E. and Butterworth, B. (2006). Discrete and analogue quantity processing in the parietal lobe: a functional MRI study. *Proceedings of the National Academy of Sciences, 103*, 4693–4698.

Childs, R. E. (1981). Developing arithmetic readiness of young EMR children: Piaget applied. *The Pointer* (Fall), *26*(1), 19–21.

Chinn, S. (2004). *The Trouble with Maths: A practical guide to helping learners with numeracy difficulties*. London: Routledge Falmer.

Clarke, N. and Chadwick, M. (1979). Operative and figurative aspects of thinking in children with learning problems in mathematics and reading span. *Revista Latinoamericanade Psicilogia, 11*(2), 261–272.

Deborah, L. S., James, D. M. and Mark, I. A. (1986). Longitudinal development of conservation skills in learning disabled children. *Journal of Learning Disabilities, 19*(5), 305–307.

Dehaene, S., Spelke, E., Pinel, P., Stanescu, R. and Tsivkin, S. (1999). Sources of mathematical thinking: behavioural and brain-imaging evidence. *Science, 284*, 970–974.

Denvir, B. and Brown, M. (1986). Understanding of concepts in low attaining 7–9 year olds: Part 1: Description of descriptive framework and diagnostic instrument. *Educational Studies in Mathematics*, *17*, 15–36.

Derr, A. M. (1985). Conservation and mathematics achievement in the learning disabled child. *Journal of Learning Disabilities*, *18*(6), 333–336.

Dorsey, J. A., Mullis, I. V. S., Lindquist, M. M. and Chambers, D. L. (1988). The mathematics report cards: are we measuring up? NAEP Report No. 17-M-01. Princeton, NJ: Educational Testing Service.

Dowker, A. D. (1998). Individual differences in arithmetical development. In C. Donlan (ed.) *The Development of Mathematical Skills*. London: Taylor & Francis (pp. 275–302).

Dowker, A. D. (2004). *What Works for Children with Mathematical Difficulties?* London: DfES.

Dowker, A. D. (2005). *Individual Differences in Arithmetic: Implications for psychology, neuroscience and education*. Hove: Psychology Press.

Dowker, A. (2009). *What Works for Pupils with Mathematical Difficulties? The effectiveness of intervention schemes*. University of Oxford, Department for Children, Schools and Families. Ref: 00086–2009BKT-EN

Ekka, E. M. (1990). Development of tribal education in Orissa after independence. *Fifth Survey of Educational Research – Trend Reports* (Vol. I). New Delhi: NCERT.

Geary, D. and Hoard, M. (2005). Learning disabilities in arithmetic and mathematics: theoretical and empirical perspectives. In J. I. D. Campbell (ed.) *Handbook of Mathematical Cognition*. Hove: Psychology Press (pp. 253–267).

Giedd, J. N., Lalonde, F. M., Celano, M. J., White, S. L., Wallace, G. L., Lee, N. R. and Lenroot, R. K. (2009). Anatomical brain magnetic resonance imaging of typically developing children and adolescents. *Journal of the American Academy of Child and Adolescent Psychiatry*, *48*(5), 465–470.

Gifford, S. (2005). *Young Children's Difficulties in Learning Mathematics: Review of research in relation to dyscalculia*. London: Qualifications and Curriculum Authority.

Ginsberg, H. P. (1977). *Children's Arithmetic: How they learn it and how you teach it*. New York: Teachers' College Press.

Goswami, U. (2013). Why theories about developmental dyslexia require developmental designs. *Trends in Cognitive Science*, *7*(12), 534.

Gowramma, I. P. (2005). *Development of Remedial Instruction Programme for Children with Dyscalculia in Primary School*. Chethana Book House.

Gross, J. (2007). Supporting children with gaps in their mathematical understanding. *Educational and Child Psychology*, *24*, 146–156.

Gruber, O., Indefrey, P., Steinmetz, H. and Kleinschmidt, A. (2001). Dissociating neural correlates of cognitive components in mental calculation. *Cerebral Cortex*, *11*, 350–369.

Hannell, G. (2005). *Dyscalculia: Action plans for successful learning in mathematics*. London: David Fulton.

Jenkins, R. and Barr, E. (2005). Social exclusion of scheduled caste children from primary education in India. Draft. UNICEF India.

Kingma, J. (1984). Traditional intelligence, Piagetian task and initial arithmetic in kindergarten and primary school grade I. *Journal of General Psychology*, 145(1), 49–60.

Kirk, S. A., McCarthy, J. J. and Kirk, W. D. (1968). *Illinois Test of Psycholinguistic Abilities* (rev. ed.). University of Illinois.

Kosc, L. (1968). Neurological–psychological correlates of dyscalculia (acalculia). *Psychologia a Patopsychologia Dietata*, *2*, 111–135.

Kosc, L. (1974). Developmental dyscalculia. *Journal of Learning Disabilities*, *7*, 165–171.

Landerl, K. (2013). Development of numerical processing in children with typical and dyscalculia arithmetical skills: a longitudinal study. *Frontiers in Psychology*, *4*, 459.

Miyan, M. (1991). Research in mathematics education: a trend report. In *Fourth Survey of Research in Education*. New Delhi: NCERT.

Mohanty, S. L. (1989). Intelligence, perceptual motor and achievement motivation training of tribal and non tribal children. *Fifth Survey of Educational Research – Trend Reports* (Vol. I). New Delhi: NCERT.

National Research Council. (1989). *Everybody Counts: A report to the nation on the future of mathematics education.* Washington, DC: National Academy Press.

Natriello, G., McDill, E. L. and Pallas, A. M. (1990). *Schooling Disadvantaged Children: Racing against catastrophe.* New York: Teachers College Press.

Nishi, M. M. (1988). A study of cognitive development of learning disabled children. Unpublished M.Ed. dissertation, University of Mysore, India.

Padmini, T. and Nayar, P. R. (unpublished) Mysore Cognitive Development Status Test. University of Mysore, India.

Prema, K. S. and Ramaa, S. (2003). Relationship among language–reading–mathematics: an exploratory study. An unpublished report of a project funded by the All India Institute of Speech and Hearing, Mysore, India.

Ramaa, S. (1980). Cognitive development of educable mentally retarded children. Unpublished M.Ed. dissertation, University of Mysore, India.

Ramaa, S. (1990). Study of neuropsychological processes and logico-mathematical structure among dyscalculics. Project Report, NCERT.

Ramaa S. (1994). *Arithmetic Diagnostic Test for Primary School Children.* Mysore: Chethana Book House and Publishing Co.

Ramaa S. (2000a). Two decades of research on learning disabilities in India. *Dyslexia: An International Journal of Research and Practice, 6,* 286–283.

Ramaa S. (2000b). Two views on Dyslexia in India: Dyslexia across the world. *Perspectives, The International Dyslexia Association, 26*(1), 16–17.

Ramaa, S., Miles, T. R. and Lalithamma, M. S.(1993). Dyslexia: symbol processing difficulty in the Kannada language. *Reading and Writing: An Interdisciplinary Journal, 5,* 29–42.

Ramaa, S. and Gowramma, I. P. (1999). Errors committed in mathematics by high school students with learning disabilities. Conference proceedings, National Seminar on Science and Mathematics Education, RIE (NCERT), Bhopal, 12–14 February1999.

Ramaa, S. and Gowramma, I. P. (2002a). Difficulties in arithmetic problem solving among disadvantaged children studying in Grade V. *Indian Education Review,* 38(1), 69–86.

Ramaa, S. and Gowramma I. P (2002b). Analysis of difficulties in arithmetic problem solving among disadvantaged children studying in Grade V, Project Report, NCERT.

Ramaa, S. and Gowramma I.P (2002c) A systematic procedure for identifying and classifying children with dyscalculia among primary school children in India. *Dyslexia, 8,* 67–85.

Ranpura, A., Isaacs, E., Edmonds, C., Rogers, M., Lanigan, A. S., Clayden, J., et al. (2013). Developmental trajectories of grey and white matter in dyscalculia. *Trends in Neuroscience and Education 2*(2), 56–64.

Reigosa-Crespo, V., Valdes-Sosa, M., Butterworth, B., Estevez, N., Rodriguez, M., Santos, E., et al. (2012). Basic numerical capacities and prevalence of developmental dyscalculia: the Havana Survey. *Development Psychology, 48,* 123–135.

Rickard, T. C., Romero, S. G., Basso, G., Wharton, C., Flitman, S. and Grafman, J. (2000). The calculating brain: an fMRI study. *Neuropsychologia, 38,* 325–335.

Russell, R. and Ginsburg, H.P. (1984). Cognitive analysis of children's mathematical difficulties. *Cognition and Instruction, 1,* 217–244.

Sawant, S. B. and Athawale, A. S. (1994). *Population Geography.* Pune: Mehta Publishing House.

Shukla, N. (1997). Education of Scheduled Caste, Scheduled Tribe and Minorities. *Fifth Survey of Educational Research – Trend Reports.* (Vol. I). New Delhi: NCERT.

Siegler, R. S. (1988). Individual differences in strategy choice: good students, not-so-good students and perfectionists. *Child Development, 59,* 833–851.

Starkey, P. and Klein, A. (2006). The early development of mathematical cognition in socio-economic and cultural contexts. Paper presented at the Institute for Education Sciences Research Conference, Washington, DC.

Starkey, P. and Klein, A. (2007). Sociocultural influences on young children's mathematical knowledge. In O. N. Saracho and B. Spodek (eds) *Contemporary Perspectives on Mathematics in Early Childhood Education*. Information Age Publishing (pp. 253–276).

Sukdeo, T. (2007). Human poverty and socially disadvantaged groups in India. Discussion paper Series 18. Human Development Resource Centre, UNDP, India.

Vygotsky, L. S. (1978). *Mind in Society: The development of higher psychological processes*. Cambridge, MA: Harvard University Press.

Webster, R. E. (1979). Short-term memory in mathematics proficient and mathematics disabled students. *Journal of Educational Research*, 72(5), 277–283.

10

Meeting the needs of the 'bottom eighty per cent'

Towards an inclusive mathematics curriculum in Uganda

Tandi Clausen-May and Remegious Baale

Special Needs Education in Uganda

Special Needs Education has a relatively long history in the Ugandan education system. Atim and Okwaput (2003: 174) report that in 1952, ten years before independence, a 'small beginning' was made by the Colonial Government 'focusing on the education of children with disabilities, such as children with visual impairment, hearing impairment, mental retardation and children with motor impairment'. A major step was taken in 1973 when a Department of Special Education was established in the Uganda Ministry of Education to coordinate the increasing activity of non-governmental organisations (NGOs). However, this 'head start in developing special education' was severely disrupted by nearly two decades of civil unrest and instability (Mpofu et al., 2007: 74). It was not until 1991 that the Uganda National Institute of Special Education (UNISE) was established with support from the Danish International Development Agency (DANIDA) to '(train) teachers and others in special needs education' (Kristensen et al., 2003; Kristensen and Omagor-Loican, undated).

Attitudes in Uganda towards disability and disabled people are ambivalent. On the one hand, Kisanji found that in Sub-Saharan Africa 'Community attitudes reflect fairness and equal opportunities for all community members including those with impairments' (Kisanji, 1998: 16). On the other hand, an obvious disability may be regarded as a punishment or the result of a curse (Atim and Okwaput, 2003; Grol, 2000; Mattingly and McInerney, no date). Perhaps for this reason, families and communities might be unwilling to label children as disabled unless this is really unavoidable, for example if they are deaf or blind. In that case the children may be deposited in a residential special school, and left there, even during the holidays (Siima, 2011; Kristensen et al., 2006).

As Siima explains in her discussion of the education of deaf learners in Uganda,

> the parents or the guardians may just not see [the] value in educating these deaf learners. Most homes in Uganda take their children to school as an investment. On completion of schooling and attaining some job, one is expected to provide for the family or support his/her sisters or brothers too; through the same or similar systems. It would be hard for some families to believe that investing in such learners could yield the same or similar dividends.
>
> *(Siima, 2011: 78)*

Thus, schooling is a family and community issue which serves family and community objectives. Education for its own sake, or the sake of the child, may be regarded as a luxury.

Discussions about special education at school or local administration level tend to focus on learners with readily identifiable disabilities, such as hearing, visual or motor impairment. UNISE professional development courses to support inclusive education do target a wider range of learners, including 'Parenting children, street children, children from disadvantaged areas, children living with or affected by HIV/AIDS, children from nomadic tribes, orphans, child soldiers and children who are traumatized and children with chronic health problems' (Atim and Okwaput, 2003: 177). But if a child is not obviously disabled then they are unlikely to be identified as having special educational needs, and there is generally a strong desire to include them in mainstream education. At the family or classroom level learners who struggle with the school curriculum without any obvious physiological 'excuse' are simply seen as stupid, possibly cursed, and, of course, lazy.

This attitude might have its advantages. It has long been argued that a teacher's beliefs about the abilities of a learner can have a strong influence on the probable success of that learner (Rosenthal and Jacobson, 1968). This view has been challenged (for example, Jussim and Harber, 2005), but the wholehearted belief that every learner should be able to succeed has a significant impact in Uganda. Here, as in many places (in fact, if not in theory), success is measured in examination results (Atim and Okwaput, 2003; CGDE, 2011; Clegg et al., 2007; Namirembe Bitamazire, 2005; World Bank, 2008). If a learner is constantly told that they can pass all their examinations if only they try hard enough then at least they are likely to go on trying. Ugandan aspirations for their children – for all their children – are high, and this creates an 'inclusive' outlook of sorts.

However, with the current highly academic curriculum and assessment structure this uncritically inclusive approach leads to a fierce pressure to cram as much knowledge as possible into every learner, in the hopes that they will pass the examinations somehow. In reality, many fail, or only scrape through, particularly in mathematics and science. As Clegg et al. explain, 'The existing curriculum is exclusive; it is a filtration system for excluding all but an academic elite' (Clegg et al., 2007: 10). It was largely inherited from the colonial system (Namirembe Bitamazire, 2005), which 'in its elite form was designed for the top 10% that excelled in primary school'

(Namukasa, 2011: 7). Thus, 'Education in Uganda is highly competitive and the curriculum is tuned in such a way that only those with high academic capability can benefit from the system' (Okech, 1999: 359). For the great majority of learners, in a school population that is expanding rapidly following the successful introduction of a policy of universal primary and secondary education, it is incomprehensible and irrelevant (Baguma and Oketcho, 2010; Clegg et al., 2007; Nakabugo et al., 2008; Namirembe Bitamazire, 2005; Winkler and Sondergaard, 2008; World Bank, 2007).

Barriers to the reformation of school mathematics

The established practice of chalk-and-talk, teacher-dependent pedagogy in Uganda is well documented (CGDE, 2011; Opolot-Okurut et al., 2008; World Bank, 2008). The great pressure to get through the highly academic examination syllabus leads teachers to try to predict which topics will be examined, and to 'spend time working out past paper examination questions for the candidates'. This 'encourages rote memorisation of facts and algorithms or procedures without any deep understanding' (CGDE, 2011: 57). Observers tend to blame teachers for their failure to use 'more active forms of learning', citing 'cultural perceptions of what good teaching is, current inadequate levels of teachers' knowledge and practices, a general misunderstanding of the meaning of learner-centered education, and the shifting roles of teachers'. These issues might be valid, but 'teachers, on the other hand, often forward the lack of physical resources, large classes and an overloaded curriculum as reasons for using teacher dominated classroom strategies' (World Bank, 2008: xiv).

There is evidence that many Ugandan teachers would rather use a more active, learner-centred approach, but they feel they have little choice given the pressure to 'cover' the syllabus with large classes and very limited resources (CGDE, 2011; Kristensen et al., 2003; Sikoyo, 2010; Urwick and Kisa, 2011; World Bank, 2007). Learners normally sit on 'forms' – benches attached to narrow desks – with three or four learners sharing a form (see Figure 10.1). The school may have class sets of text books that the teacher can distribute to learners, but even the process of passing out the books (and getting them all back) is challenging and time consuming in a tightly packed classroom with no room to move between the forms. Furthermore, the ratio of text books provided to learners is one between three or four (GoU, 2010; JICA and IDCJ, 2012; World Bank, 2007). If three (or more often four) learners are sharing one text book then, in reality, at least one of them will not be able to see it. By writing everything on the board for all the learners to copy into their exercise books the teacher is ensuring equality of access, in the most fundamental sense, for all learners (see Figure 10.2). This practice also gives each learner a copy of the material that they can use later for independent study.

However, this teaching approach creates a highly teacher-dependent ethos, with the teacher serving as the fount of all knowledge. It reinforces the abstract, academic nature of the mathematics syllabus as teachers choose textbooks with the requisite 'facts' presented as concisely as possible so that they can be copied onto the board and then into exercise books (Namukasa et al., 2010). Furthermore, it takes an inordinate

Figure 10.1 Crowded forms

Figure 10.2 Ensuring access via the blackboard

amount of time for learners to copy everything down (Hannon, 2009). So, although most of the learners might be able to copy what the teacher writes on the blackboard and learn it off by heart, few are doing mathematics in any meaningful sense.

Changing the way in which mathematics is taught and learnt in the classroom, however, will not be easy. The exclusive, academic syllabus inherited from the colonial

British has become firmly entrenched, even while mathematics pedagogy has moved on elsewhere. As Grol (2000) observes, 'Political leaders are successful products of this system', so they might see no reason to change it. Furthermore,

> applied and vocational mathematics – mathematical literacy – was historically offered to vocational schools for the colonized Africans and not [to] academic schools for the colonizing British. This historical background would make attempts to have less academic mathematics offered to students who are not mathematically gifted a very sensitive matter that needs to be approached with care. Many Ugandans still would like an academic education for their children.
>
> *(Namukasa, 2011: 8)*

In these circumstances, 'inclusion' paradoxically leads to the exclusion of many of the eighty per cent or so of learners for whom the current mathematics curriculum was never intended, but who, with the introduction of universal secondary education, are now being forced through the system.

Inclusion through practical work

It is commonly argued that, in general, what is good for special is good for mainstream education, so 'The best way to improve education for children with disabilities is to improve the education sector as a whole' (Mattingly and McInerney, no date: 3). But the inverse also applies, and with greater force: a problem for mainstream learners is likely to be a more serious problem for those with special needs. The highly abstract mathematics curriculum found in Ugandan schools is not fit for purpose even for the majority of mainstream learners. It is totally unsuitable for those with mathematics learning difficulties.

So in Uganda as elsewhere, 'Inclusion has important benefits for all children as it . . . produces schools that move away from rote learning and place greater emphasis on hands-on, experienced based, active and co-operative learning' (UNESCO, 2005: 23). This pedagogical reformation would help all learners, even the small minority who currently 'obtain high marks by mastering the ritual rather than understanding the subject' (Clegg et al., 2007: 37). For 'the bottom eighty per cent' it is essential. But how is this 'hands-on, experience based, active and co-operative learning' to be achieved, in large, tightly packed classes with very few resources? That is the challenge facing the Ugandan National Curriculum Development Centre (NCDC) as it seeks to reform the mathematics curriculum for the four years of Lower Secondary education which constitute the eighth to eleventh years of uninterrupted formal schooling in Uganda.

Little practical work is done in Ugandan mathematics classrooms at present even though the current Lower Secondary syllabus recommends a practical approach, particularly to some aspects of geometry and measurement. For example, according to the syllabus for Senior 2 (the ninth year of formal schooling), in Topic 16, Nets and Solids, 'The emphasis should be on practical work – construct nets from wires, sticks manilla [*sic*] card using tacking pins, sellotape or adhesives. Properties should be discovered from the practical work' (GoU, 2008). But even such materials as wire and manila card are in scarce supply, particularly in less well-resourced schools. Learners (and even teachers) have little experience of handling three-dimensional shapes, and they often struggle to visualise them. Teachers have difficulty drawing them free-hand on the blackboard, and learners cannot interpret the drawings effectively.

In an effort to enable teachers to relax their current teacher-focused, 'chalk-and-talk' approach to geometry and to increase their use of practical group-based work, the NCDC is seeking alternative readily available, low-cost materials that can be used to make geometric shapes. Bananas are grown in many (although not all) parts of Uganda, and the dried fibre that peels off the thick central stem of the banana plant is often discarded as waste. Banana fibre is already used as a cheap resource for arts and crafts both in schools and for products made for the tourist market. It was found that it could also provide material to make a range of mathematical shapes, whose properties learners could explore and observe for themselves.

This idea was trialled in four mixed-ability Senior 1, 2 and 3 classes in two private and one Government Universal Secondary Education (USE) school, in Wakiso and Mbarara Districts in Uganda. Class sizes varied from about 75 in a private school to 120 in the USE school, and in each class learners worked in groups of between 6 and 8. To create these groups half of the learners rotated their forms through 180° and joined their desks to those of the forms behind (see Figure 10.3). Each group was given a strip of banana fibre, a small bundle of sisal string, two half razor blades, some sticky tape and a set of printed instructions. Razor blades were used as they are the normal cutting tool in Ugandan classrooms (Clausen-May and Baale, 2013).

Figure 10.3 Forms arranged for group work

Figure 10.4 Measuring and cutting banana fibre rectangles

Learners had to be encouraged to read the instructions in order to get started, but once they had done so very little further input was needed from either the teacher or the researchers. In the context of this very practical activity learners in all year groups were able to follow the printed instructions and work largely independently of the teacher.

First they measured and cut rectangles of fibre and lengths of string (see Figure 10.4). Then they rolled a fibre rectangle around a length of string to make a stick with strings hanging out at each end (see Figure 10.5). Then six of these sticks could be tied together to make a tetrahedron (see Figures 10.6 and 10.7).

Figure 10.5 Rolling the fibre to make a stick

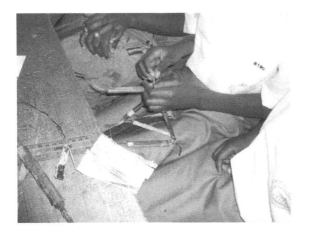

Figures 10.6 and 10.7 Joining six sticks to make a tetrahedron

There was a real sense of excitement as the tetrahedra began to roll off the production line (see Figure 10.8).

Having made their tetrahedron the learners were asked to count its edges, faces and vertices and to observe its properties (see Figure 10.9). Then they recorded their observations. This, too, they were able to do with little assistance (see Figure 10.10).

For all the learners – and all the teachers – involved in these trials, this was their first experience of actually making and handling three-dimensional shapes. It was clear that, at least in these very practical lessons, learners in every year were well able to work in groups, following printed instructions largely independently of the teacher. They made robust and reasonably regular tetrahedra and observed and recorded their properties for themselves. The delight and enthusiasm of 120 learners in a Government USE school, all busily making and discussing tetrahedra, is hard to describe.

Figure 10.8 The first banana fibre tetrahedron

Figure 10.9 Observing the tetrahedron

The work with three-dimensional shapes was taken further with the Senior 3 class to encompass a wider range of polyhedra, as described in Clausen-May and Baale, 2014. For Senior 2, another set of practical activities was developed to give the learners direct, hands-on experience of working with two-dimensional shapes, this time using Tangram tiles (see Figure 10.11). These activities also provided an opportunity for learners to develop, express and record their mathematical reasoning in relation to the areas of these shapes.

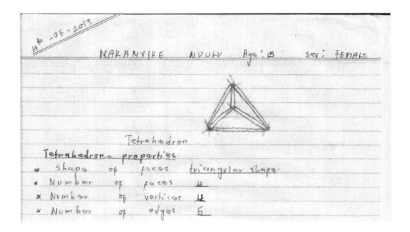

Figure 10.10 Recording the properties of the tetrahedron

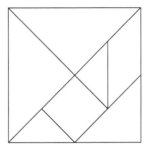

Figure 10.11 Tangram tiles

The Senior 2 Tangram activities were trialled with just 18 mixed-ability learners who were withdrawn from their normal mathematics lesson. Learners worked in pairs, first cutting sets of Tangram tiles out of squares of banana fibre or scrap card. Then they discovered some of the properties of the tiles by using them to solve problems, and finally they explored the concept of 'area' using the tiles.

As with the tetrahedron activity, learners showed some hesitation in getting started, but all nine pairs were able to follow the printed instructions to measure, mark and cut the squares to make a set of tiles with little further assistance (see Figure 10.12).

Once the learners had made a set of tiles they were asked to reconstruct the original full-size square. They all found this a challenge (it is not a trivial task!), but they all succeeded (see Figure 10.13). This straightforward activity gave the learners valuable experience of manipulating their tiles, turning them over and around – carrying out transformations in practice, not just on paper.

The learners went on to use the tiles to solve a series of puzzles – for example, to make a parallelogram with the two small right-angled triangle tiles, or to use

Figure 10.12 Making a set of Tangram tiles

the parallelogram and the two small right-angled triangle tiles to make a rectangle or a bigger parallelogram or right-angled triangle (see Figure 10.14). They visibly struggled with the puzzles, and one or two asked for help, but they responded to encouragement to keep on trying and their eventual success led to exclamations of delight and pride. These learners clearly engaged thoroughly and with great enthusiasm in the problem-solving process, and all solved at least some of the puzzles.

Figure 10.13 Recreating the original Tangram

Figure 10.14 Making a Tangram rectangle

The puzzles served as a preparation for the final activity, when the learners explored the concept (not the 'rules'!) of 'area'. They were told that the area of the individual square Tangram tile was 1 square unit, and they were asked to find the areas of each of the other Tangram tiles (see Clausen-May (2013: 77) for details of this activity). This was particularly challenging because it required learners to overcome their 'rote recall' response to questions about areas and to not think about measurements and formulae. For example, in order to find the area of the small triangle Peter and Eddy, who were identified by their teacher as high-attaining, started by measuring the edge of their square tile and tried to use the formula (see Figure 10.15). This, of course, was not incorrect – but it missed the point that we were working in arbitrary square units this time. However, with prompting they were able to overcome the disadvantage of being 'good' at mathematics. They crossed out their first attempt, and after a bit of discussion substituted an appropriate statement (see Figure 10.16).

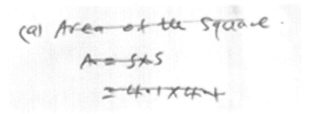

Figure 10.15 Irrelevant formula

(a) Area of one small triangle is half square unit.

Figure 10.16 Area in terms of an arbitrary unit

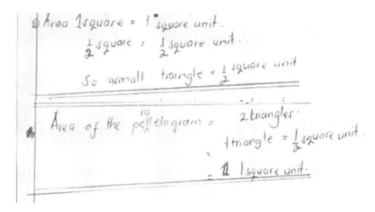

Figure 10.17 Mathematical reasoning in words

Some encouraging demonstrations of mathematical reasoning were observed. For example, Maureen and Prima presented a written justification for the area of the parallelogram, which can be formed out of the two small triangles (see Figure 10.17). Then they went on to find the area of a trapezium made up of a square and two triangles, and to justify this with a sketch (see Figure 10.18).

The girls' use of index notation is unconventional here, but it indicates that they grasped the idea that if the edge of the square is one unit long then its area is 1^2 square units. If this is cut in half then the resulting triangle has an area of 1^2 divided by 2. Thus they formulated their own explanations, the first in words and the second with clear and appropriate diagrams.

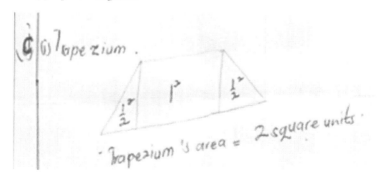

Figure 10.18 Mathematical reasoning in diagrams

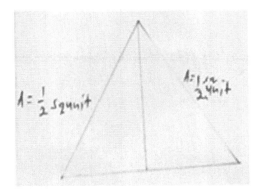

Figure 10.19 Justification for the area of a triangle

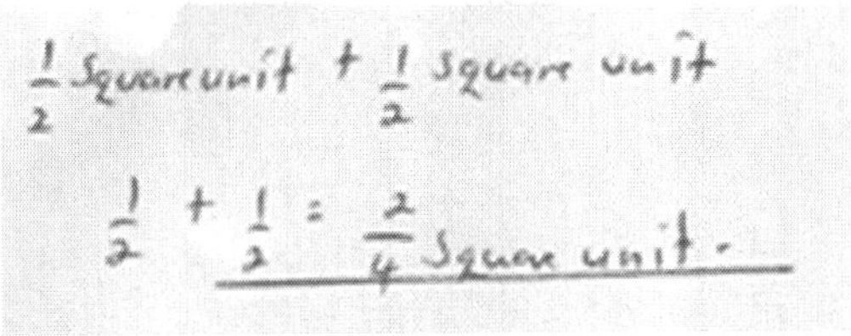

$$\frac{1}{2} \text{Square unit} + \frac{1}{2} \text{Square unit}$$

$$\frac{1}{2} + \frac{1}{2} = \frac{2}{4} \text{Square unit}.$$

Figure 10.20 Meaningless rules

Agnes and Mercy sketched a diagram to show that the larger triangle could be formed out of the two smaller ones (see Figure 10.19). But unfortunately they tried to use half-remembered 'rules' for the addition (or rather multiplication) of fractions when they tried to find its area, and were seduced into arithmetical nonsense (see Figure 10.20). Persuading learners to abandon what they 'know', and encouraging them to use mathematical reasoning instead, will be a significant challenge in the 'move away from rote learning' towards 'hands-on, experienced based, active and co-operative learning' (UNESCO, 2005: 23). But overall, the activities described here demonstrated that Ugandan Lower Secondary learners are very ready to work practically and independently, to make their own observations and to use mathematical reasoning to make their own deductions.

Conclusions

The highly abstract, academic Ugandan Lower Secondary mathematics curriculum serves to exclude, not to include, the majority of learners. Many youngsters leave school feeling that they have 'failed' at mathematics, and they hate and fear the subject for the rest of their lives. There is a strong habit of dependence on the teacher, fostered by a heavy diet of didactic, teacher-focused classroom practice and a lack of independent learner access to text books and resources. Learners have little opportunity to use mathematical reasoning to solve problems independently of the teacher.

However, the lesson trials described here indicate that practical activities such as making and investigating mathematical shapes and models can offer an effective introduction to independent group work. Learners in mixed-ability classes in different year groups in a range of schools engaged enthusiastically with the practical and problem-solving tasks. They were able to access the printed materials largely by themselves, following the written and drawn instructions to make three-dimensional shapes or Tangram tiles. They used sound mathematical reasoning which they were able to express and record in their own words and diagrams. But this change in the learners' behaviour might be easier to introduce in the context of topics and activities that the learners regard as new. Where the mathematics seems familiar, old habits may be more likely to reassert themselves as learners try to use formulae and algorithms that they 'know', but might not understand.

If group work and independent learning are to be encouraged in the mathematics classroom under the new curriculum then practical activities such as those described here could offer a useful strategy. However, this will take up more time in the classroom. It takes much longer to make a tetrahedron and to observe, discuss and record its properties than to copy a list of these from the blackboard and learn them off by heart. The coverage of the reformed curriculum will have to be reduced to allow time for learners to understand, not just to memorise, mathematics.

The impact on effective curriculum reform of good text books that support changes in learning and teaching is well documented (CGDE, 2011; Ward et al., 2006). Ready access to printed materials allows learners to work independently both in and out of the classroom. But where there are only enough copies of a textbook for one between three or four learners it might actually be easier for them to copy written information from the blackboard than to peer across a classmate at a book. If learners are to develop habits of independent learning then they need to be able to access information for themselves, not just via the teacher. Ready access to the textbook would also reduce the amount of time spent copying from the blackboard, and allow more time for learners to actually do mathematics – in all senses of the word 'do'. However, the provision of text books has significant cost implications.

Practical activities such as those described here can often help to take mathematics off the blackboard and put it into the hands of the learners. With practical equipment that they can make themselves out of locally available, low-cost materials, learners at every level can become active mathematicians. They can explore, observe and discuss mathematics, and use mathematical reasoning to draw their own conclusions and solve problems. This can help to change the mathematical experiences of all learners – not just the 'bottom eighty per cent', but academic high-achievers as well. But while banana fibre polygons and polyhedra can go some way to support the process of mathematics curriculum reform in Uganda, this is only a beginning. Much more is needed if they are to have any lasting impact.

References

Atim, S.M. and Okwaput, S. (2003). 'Training special needs education teachers: some experiences from Uganda'. *Proceedings of the International Conference on Inclusive Education*, 16–19 December 2003, Hong Kong Institute of Education, Centre for Special Needs and Studies in Inclusive Education.

Baguma, C. and Oketcho, P. (2010). 'Linking formal and nonformal education: implications for curriculum development and quality assurance in Uganda'. Available: <http://www.academia.edu/1056607/Linking_Formal_and_Nonformal_Education_Implications_for_Curriculum_Development_and_Quality_Assurance_in_Uganda> (accessed 6 November 2013).

CGDE (Centre for Global Development through Education). (2011). 'Teacher effectiveness in the teaching of mathematics and science in secondary schools in Uganda', Limerick: Mary Immaculate College.

Clausen-May, T. (2013). *Teaching Mathematics Visually and Actively*, London: Sage.

Clausen-May, T. and Baale, R. (2013). 'Proving Pythagoras in Uganda', *Mathematics Teaching, 237*, 34–35. Association of Teachers of Mathematics.

Clausen-May, T. and Baale, R. (2014). 'Mathematics curriculum reform in Uganda – what works in the classroom?' Paper presented at the British Congress in Mathematics Education (BCME), Nottingham.

Clegg, A., Bregman, J. and Ottevanger, W. (2007). 'Uganda Secondary Education & Training Curriculum, Assessment & Examination (CURASSE), Roadmap for Reform'. Available: <http://siteresources.worldbank.org/INTAFRREGTOPSEIA/Resources/Uganda_Curasse.pdf> (accessed 6 November 2013).

GoU (Government of Uganda). (2008). 'Ministry of Education and Sports Mathematics Teaching Syllabus, Uganda Certificate of Education'.

GoU (Government of Uganda). (2010). 'Ministry of Education and Sports & Education Development Partners Appraisal Report: Education Sector Strategic Plan'. Available: https://www.globalpartnership.org/download/file/fid/3317 (accessed 9 August 2014).

Grol, C.E.J. (2000). 'The education of pupils with special educational needs in Africa, looked at within the African context'. Paper presented at the International Special Education Congress, University of Manchester, 2000. Available: <http://www.isec2000.org.uk/abstracts/papers_g/grol_1.htm> (accessed 6 November 2013).

Hannon, C. (2009). 'Challenges for teachers in universal secondary education (USE)', University of Notre Dame, School for International Training: Uganda. Available: <http://socialchange.weebly.com/uploads/2/8/1/0/2810785/practicum-isp.doc> (accessed 6 November 2013).

JICA and IDCJ (Japan International Cooperation Agency and International Development Centre Japan). (2012). 'Basic Education sector analysis report – Uganda'. Available: <http://www.opendev.ug/sites/opendataug-01.drupal01.mountbatten.ug/files/basic_education_report.pdf> (accessed 6 November 2013).

Jussim, L. and Harber, K.D. (2005). 'Controversies – teacher expectations and self-fulfilling prophecies: knowns and unknowns, resolved and unresolved', *Personality and Social Psychology Review, 9*, 131.

Kisanji, J. (1998). 'Culture and disability: an analysis of inclusive education based on African folklore'. Paper prepared for the *International Journal of Disability Development and Education*, 1998. Available: <http://www.eenet.org.uk/resources/docs/culture_disability.doc> (accessed 6 November 2013).

Kristensen, K. and Omagor-Loican, M. (undated). 'Towards inclusive education: a case from Uganda'. Available: <http://view.officeapps.live.com/op/view.aspx?src=http%3A%2F%2Fwww.eenet.org.uk%2Fresources%2Fdocs%2FTowards_inclusive_education_Uganda.doc> (accessed 6 November 2013).

Kristensen, K., Omagor-Loican, M. and Onen, N. (2003). 'The inclusion of learners with barriers to learning and development into ordinary school settings: a challenge for Uganda', *British Journal of Special Education, 30*, 194–201.

Kristensen, K., Omagor-Loican, M., Onen, N. and Okot, D. (2006). 'Opportunities for inclusion? The education of learners with special educational needs and disabilities in special schools in Uganda', *British Journal of Special Education*, *33*, 139–147.

Mattingly, J. and McInerney, L. (no date). 'Education for children with disabilities: improving access and quality', DFID practice paper. Department for International Development (DFID). Available: <http://asksource.ids.ac.uk/cf/display/bibliodisplay.cfm?ID=39145&db=keywords&display=full> (accessed 6 November 2013).

Mpofu, E., Oakland, T. and Chimeda, R. (2007). 'Africa, East and Southern, special education in'. In C.R. Reynolds and E. Fletcher-Janzen (eds), *Encyclopedia of Special Education*, Volume 1, pp. 70–78. New York: Wiley.

Nakabugo, M.G., Byamugisha, A. and Bithaghalire, J. (2008). 'The future of schooling in Uganda', *Journal of International Cooperation in Education*, *11*(1), 55–69. CICE, Hiroshima University.

Namirembe Bitamazire, G. (2005). 'Status of education for rural people in Uganda'. Paper presented at the *Uganda Ministerial Seminar on Education for Rural People in Africa: Policy Lessons, Options and Priorities*, Addis Ababa, Ethiopia.

Namukasa, I.K. (2011). 'Critical curriculum renewal: a need in several developing countries'. The University of Western Ontario. Available: <http://www.edu.uwo.ca/centres/documents/CICE_Symposium_discussion_paperApril_5PT_2011.pdf> (accessed 6 November 2013).

Namukasa, I.K., Quinn, M. and Kaahwa, J. (2010). 'School mathematics education in Uganda: its successes and its failures', *Procedia – Social and Behavioral Sciences 2*(2), 3104–3110. Available: <http://libra.msra.cn/Publication/41416200/school-mathematics-education-in-uganda-its-successes-and-its-failures> (accessed 6 November 2013).

Okech, J.B.O. (1999). 'Special needs education in Uganda: a study of implementation of the policy on provision of education for children with 'mental retardation'. Doctoral thesis, Durham University, UK. Available: <http://etheses.dur.ac.uk/1584/> (accessed 6th November 2013).

Opolot-Okurut, C., Opyene-Eluk, P. and Mwanamoiza, M. (2008). 'The current teaching of statistics in schools in Uganda', paper presented at the ICMI Study 18 Conference and IASE 2008 Round Table Conference, ITESM, Monterrey, Mexico Available: <http://www.ugr.es/~icmi/iase_study/Files/Topic5/T5P6_Opolot.pdf> (accessed 6 November 2013).

Rosenthal, R. and Jacobson, L. (1968). *Pygmalion in the Classroom*. New York: Holt, Rinehart & Winston.

Siima, S.B.A. (2011). 'Teaching of Reading and writing to deaf learners in primary schools in Uganda', Master of Philosophy thesis, University of Oslo, Norway. Available: <https://www.duo.uio.no/bitstream/handle/10852/32261/thesis.pdf?sequence=1> (accessed 6 November 2013).

Sikoyo, L. (2010). 'Contextual challenges of implementing learner-centred pedagogy: the case of the problem-solving approach in Uganda', *Cambridge Journal of Education 40*(3), 247–263.

UNESCO (2005). 'Guidelines for inclusion: ensuring access to education for all'. Available: <http://unesdoc.unesco.org/images/0014/001402/140224e.pdf> (accessed 6 November 2013).

Urwick, J. and Kisa, S. (2011). 'Shortages of secondary mathematics and science teachers in Uganda: why they matter and why they occur'. In A. Bwire, Y. Huang, J.O. Masingila and H. Ayot (eds), *Proceedings of the 2nd International Conference on Education* (pp. 295–312). Nairobi, Kenya: Kenyatta University.

Ward, M., Penny, A. and Read, T. (2006). 'Education Reform in Uganda – 1997 to 2004. Reflections on policy, partnership, strategy and implementation', Department for International Development: Educational Papers. Available: <http://r4d.dfid.gov.uk/PDF/Outputs/PolicyStrategy/EducationPaperNo60.pdf> (accessed 6 November 2013).

Winkler, D. and Sondergaard, L. (2008). 'The efficiency of public education in Uganda'. Available: <http://info.worldbank.org/etools/docs/library/244476/day7Uganda%20Efficiency%20Study.pdf> (accessed 6 November 2013).

World Bank (2007). 'Developing science, mathematics, and ICT education in Sub-Saharan Africa: patterns and promising practices'. Working Paper 101, Africa Human Development series.

World Bank (2008). 'Curricula, Examinations and Assessment in Secondary Education in Sub-Saharan Africa'. Working Paper 128, Africa Human Development Series. Available: <http://siteresources.worldbank.org/INTAFRREGTOPSEIA/Resources/No.5Curricula.pdf> (accessed 6 November 2013).

11

Dyscalculia in Arabic speaking children

Assessment and intervention practices

*John Everatt, Abdessatar Mahfoudhi,
Mowafak Al-Manabri and Gad Elbeheri*

Background

The work reported in this chapter was conducted to investigate mathematics learning difficulties, or dyscalculia, in an Arabic language, cultural, educational context. Contrasts with findings reported in the literature primarily derived from work in English language/Western educational traditions will provide evidence for commonalities in the deficits associated with dyscalculia. The work also aimed to contrast dyscalculia with dyslexia in order to determine whether these two learning difficulties could be distinguished within this Arabic context. Such research then can be used to support the development of assessment procedures for Arabic learning contexts – the main practical purpose of the work undertaken. Furthermore, commonalities of findings should enable intervention procedures to be developed that are based on work from around the world.

Definition of dyscalculia

In Kuwait, dyscalculia is considered as a learning disability (LD). The term learning disability is consistent with that used in the USA and, in the case of dyscalculia, would be a child who is struggling to achieve curriculum goals in mathematics despite their IQ being 85 or over (i.e., within the typical range or greater for their age). However, as in many parts of the world (see discussions in Berch & Mazzocco, 2007), work specifically targeted at children with LD-related problems learning mathematics is less common, particularly in comparison with that on literacy learning disability or dyslexia. More informal views about dyscalculia suggest similarities with the rest of the world: i.e., difficulties understanding simple number concepts, poor intuitive grasp of numbers, problems with number fact learning and evidence of performing mathematics problems mechanically and without confidence (see discussions in Everatt, Elbeheri & Brooks, 2013).

This perspective of dyscalculia as an LD provides the potential to distinguish it from poor learning opportunity. Furthermore, given that the underlying problems related to dyscalculia can be identified early in development, screening prior to (or early in) formal learning might be possible (for example, see Mazzocco & Thompson (2005) for evidence of prediction from behavioural measures in kindergarten). Appropriate intervention could then be implemented prior to experiences of failure, potentially reducing negative consequences of low self-esteem, frustration and anxiety. Hence, the current work aimed to look for evidence for similar underlying deficits in Kuwaiti children with mathematics learning weaknesses to those found in children recognised as having dyscalculia elsewhere in the world.

Additionally, for the term to be of value in disability work, it needs to be shown to be specific, in that a child with problems with mathematics related to dyscalculia should be able to perform normally in areas that are not related to the LD (Baroody & Ginsburg, 1991; Jordan & Hanich, 2000). If it is shown always to co-occur with another disability, such as dyslexia, then it might be more parsimonious to include it as an aspect or sub-type of dyslexia rather than a separate condition. Consistent with a potential difficulty with the specificity of the condition, some half of those with dyslexia show evidence of difficulties with mathematics (see Chinn & Ashcroft, 2007; Miles & Miles, 1992). Although research argues for commonalities between dyscalculia and dyslexia, it also suggests that there might be fundamental differences which mean that the two can be dissociated (see Adams, Snowling, Nehhessy & Kind, 1999). In particular, dyslexics have been found to show deficits in phonological skills, whereas efficient number comparisons may be related to mathematics weaknesses (Landerl, Fussenegger, Moll & Willburger, 2009). Similarly, Rubinsten & Henik (2006) have found that tasks in which numeric value versus image size are incongruent can distinguish dyscalculics from dyslexics and controls, and Durand, Hulme, Larkin and Snowling (2005) suggest that the best predictor of arithmetic levels is a factor based around the ability to recognise which digit is numerically larger. Indeed, tasks related to such a conceptual understanding of number might hold the most promise to specify problems underlying dyscalculia from other conditions. The present research, therefore, aimed to investigate evidence for such an underlying deficit within Kuwaiti children that may distinguish those with dyscalculia from those with deficits more associated with dyslexia.

Arabic is an interesting context in which to study the universality of problems related to dyscalculia (though see also, for example, Ramaa & Gowramma (2002)), since as well as differences in language/culture, the way of teaching mathematics in the Arab world often is very different from that used in those countries where much of the work on dyscalculia has taken place. For example, within Kuwait mathematics is taught, typically, in a very rote/drill-based way. Number symbols taught in school are based on the Hindi (sometimes referred to as Eastern Arabic) written form rather than the Arabic (or Western Arabic) form used in schools in the UK and USA. However, the Kuwaiti child will experience both numeric forms in everyday life, since most phone numbers, road signs and car licence plates, as well as many prices on goods, are written in Western Arabic numerals. Hence, the form taught in school might not be the most common form experienced in everyday life. Furthermore, writing proceeds from right to left in Arabic texts and so a child will 'count' and read isolated numbers from right to left. However, ten and above are written as in the West, with the ten symbol to the left of the unit symbol, hence reading such values will also proceed from left to right, making the direction of reading potentially confusing. As an example, this can cause confusions when reading phone numbers since some treat the number as one entity from left to right, whereas others treat the number as comprising separate digits from right to left. Hence, the way numbers are taught and written is different from that found in the West.

Assessment

The present work, therefore, started from the premise of looking for features of poor mathematics learning among Kuwaiti children based on those found in research in other parts of the world. The development of measures involved a detailed search of the literature to identify variables associated with dyscalculia. These measures were then modified for the Arabic context (e.g., the use of Hindi/Eastern Arabic symbols) and in order to ensure that measures were appropriate for Kuwaiti primary school children. Measures were further modified to allow administration via computer – to ensure consistency of presentation and enable a large number of students to be assessed. All measures included instructions with examples that the child completed with the assessor to ensure understanding.

Tests included the assessment of mathematics abilities expected of students in Kuwait across the different grade levels targeted by the research. The Kuwaiti Ministry of Education school curriculum is followed by all public schools in the country and provides a set of guides as to expected abilities of children during different grades. This mapping procedure led to the production of an arithmetic ability test that focused on addition, subtraction, multiplication and division. Each item was presented on the computer screen and the child performed the normal calculation operations as taught to them in their normal classroom learning. These tasks provided a measure of the total number of problems answered correctly. The tasks also provided a measure that assessed addition calculation fluency, determined as the number of addition problems performed correctly per minute. This assessed how fluently the child could perform basic arithmetic procedures. Those with dyscalculia would be expected to show lower efficiency in such basic arithmetic procedures, even if they get them right.

Measures were also designed to assess the underlying ability deficits related to dyscalculia. These deficits have been argued to focus on memory weaknesses and/or a poor understanding of basic concepts in mathematics. Memory weaknesses related to LD, typically, have been assessed by measures of short-term memory and rapid naming (see Bull & Johnston, 1997; though see also Willburger, Fussenegger, Moll, Wood & Landerl, 2008). In the present study, a digit short-term memory task simply required the child to repeat lists of digits presented to them via the computer. The number of digits presented increased by one digit after three correct answers, and the number of items correctly repeated indicated the child's ability to retain digit sequence information for a short period of time. In contrast, the rapid naming task required the child to name individual digits as quickly as possible: i.e., again accessing digit names from memory, but requiring fluency of responding to numeric stimuli. In this task, the assessor pressed a button on the computer which led to the presentation of an array of digits. The child named these digits as quickly as possible, avoiding errors. When the array was completed, the assessor pressed the computer button to stop timing. Although there was only a small number of errors in the pilot data, in order to take these into account non-corrected errors incurred a one second penalty that was added to the time by the assessor.

The ability to apply basic mathematical concepts in task performance was assessed by measures that required the child to determine relationships between items in terms of size or value, as well as to estimate amount. The first conceptual understanding task included mathematic and non-mathematic materials; for example, the child was asked to recognise size differences between small and large circles, or to say whether there were more dots in one display compared to another, or to indicate which has the larger value between '2 or 3'. Consistent with similar measures used in English-language screening tools (see Butterworth, 2003), a measure of fluency was used to determine ability on this task – i.e., the number of tasks completed correctly per minute. Each item was presented on the screen as a two-choice answer, with the child indicating which of the two they considered was the correct answer to the comparison question. The number of correct items per minute was then calculated.

The second conceptual understanding measure comprised of a straight line presented on the computer screen, with 0 at one end of the line and 100 at the other. The task then asked the child to indicate where on the line they considered a particular value would fall. The value 50 was used as an example and was indicated as being expected to fall halfway between 0 and 100. The child was then asked to estimate the position of other values by clicking on the line. A measure of error from correct position was used which ignored whether the error was to the left or right of the correct position: a high score indicated less accuracy in estimation.

In addition to these measures of underlying ability and mathematics learning, a measure of mathematics anxiety was developed. The measure was based on the responses to a questionnaire completed by the child with the assistance of the assessor. Questions asked the child to indicate their feelings when doing mathematics-related tasks both as part of schooling and outside of school; when required to sum money, for example. Responses provided an assessment of how anxious such tasks made the child feel. A total final score was used to assess anxiety level, with a positive score indicating higher anxiety levels, and a negative total indicating less anxiety.

Measures were piloted and standardised in a series of studies assessing test procedures and items, as well as determining reliability coefficients (no measures produced an alpha score below .75), relationships between measures consistent with predicted associations and their ability to discriminate those with reported mathematics weaknesses from those with no reported mathematics problems. In total, over 800 Kuwaiti government primary school children were tested over these various initial pilot stages and standardisation procedures. The current data were then obtained from an additional cohort of 315 children in grades 2, 3 and 4 (approx. 100 per grade) of typical Kuwaiti government primary schools. These children, therefore, had experienced at least one year of formal mathematics education under the normal Kuwaiti curriculum. Participating schools were an opportunity sample, similar to schools across Kuwait. All children available for testing at the time of the work for whom parental/guardian consent could be obtained were tested. Only those who completed all the arithmetic tasks and a single-word reading task were included in the data set.

These 315 children were also assessed on measures of Arabic literacy and literacy-related skills to determine evidence for dyslexia-related difficulties. The primary measure was a single-word reading measure in which the child had to read aloud a series of Arabic words that increased in complexity (based on word length and frequency). The number of words read correctly was used as the measure for this task. The children also completed a reading comprehension (Cloze-based) task in which they were given incomplete sentences (50 in total) and four options with which to complete the sentence. Only one of the four options completed the sentence correctly based on meaning. Therefore, the child had to comprehend the sentences to complete them correctly. The number of sentences completed correctly per minute was used as the measure for this task.

A spelling choice task was also administered in which the child had to select one of four words that was spelt correctly (an English example would be 'wirt word woid worb'); as was a pseudo-word reading task in which the child had to decide if a made-up word sounded like a real word (e.g., 'foks' if sounded-out using English grapheme-phoneme conversion rules would sound like the word 'fox'). These were followed by: a sound deletion task in which the child had to say what would be left if a particular sound was deleted from another word (for example, deleting the /t/ sound from 'cart' would produce 'car'); a non-word repetition task in which the child had to repeat spoken non-words which increased in pronunciation length over the test; and a word chains task where a meaningless sentence was presented in which the spaces between words had been removed and the child's task was to insert the spaces.

The children were divided into four groups based on their performance on the arithmetic problems and the single-word reading measures. For each grade, those children in the bottom 20% of both measures were considered a LowMath+LowRead group (N=31; approximately 10% of the sample), those children in the bottom 20% of the arithmetic measure but not in the bottom 20% of the word reading measures were considered a LowMath+GoodRead group (N=47; approximately 15% of the sample), those children in the bottom 20% of the word reading measure but not in the bottom 20% of the arithmetic measures were considered a GoodMath+LowRead group (N=32; approximately 10% of the sample), and those children not in the bottom 20% of either measure were considered a GoodMath+GoodRead group N=205). These four groups were then compared on the rest of the measures (see Table 11.1 and Figure 11.1).

Table 11.1 Results (means, with standard deviations in brackets) of the four groups on the study measures together with analyses of variance and post-hoc Dunnett results

	LowMath + LowRead (N=31)	LowMath + Good Read (N=47)	GoodMath + LowRead (N=32)	GoodMath + Good Read (N=205)	ANOVA
Arithmetic problems	0.55 (0.96)	0.51 (0.91)	6.19 (5.13)	8.12 (5.99)	
Single-word reading	1.55 (1.61)	12.74 (11.25)	1.25 (1.27)	17.88 (11.53)	
Addition fluency	0.18*** (0.38)	0.11*** (0.24)	1.30 (0.92)	1.37 (1.00)	$F_{(3,311)}=38.35$ p<.001
Comparison fluency	6.89*** (2.59)	6.46*** (2.12)	8.71 (0.92)	8.79 (1.00)	$F_{(3,311)}=31.47$ p<.001
Line estimation	204.58*** (86.98)	206.89*** (87.48)	161.97* (1.78)	119.12 (1.41)	$F_{(3,311)}=19.10$ p<.001
Memory span	4.23*** (2.79)	5.51** (3.60)	6.72 (109.28)	7.47 (83.45)	$F_{(3,311)}=8.76$ p<.001
Rapid naming	71.68*** (39.28)	65.49*** (33.09)	58.78* (3.75)	43.86 (3.95)	$F_{(3,311)}=16.03$ p<.001
Maths anxiety	-0.58 (7.98)	1.95** (9.80)	-1.31 (42.43)	-3.38 (19.43)	$F_{(3,311)}=4.17$ p=.006
Reading comprehension	5.90* (3.62)	8.04 (5.14)	7.19 (12.50)	8.73 (9.57)	$F_{(3,311)}=2.67$ p=.05
Spelling decision	8.03*** (3.14)	10.45 (4.43)	9.44** (4.44)	11.76 (6.15)	$F_{(3,311)}=12.05$ p<.001
Non-word reading	2.42*** (4.59)	5.83 (6.94)	1.74*** (2.86)	7.85 (3.64)	$F_{(3,309)}=13.09$ p<.001
Sound deletion	2.26*** (2.53)	5.94** (5.23)	3.78*** (2.10)	8.79 (6.90)	$F_{(3,310)}=22.27$ p<.001
Non-word repetition	6.84*** (4.31)	9.02 (4.55)	8.38* (4.40)	10.73 (5.42)	$F_{(3,310)}=8.56$ p<.001
Word Chains	2.03*** (1.59)	3.30 (2.76)	2.06*** (5.04)	4.27 (4.55)	$F_{(3,306)}=11.32$ p<.001

Notes: * Differs from good math and reading group by p<.05
** Differs from good math and reading group by p<.01
*** Differs from good math and reading group by p<.001

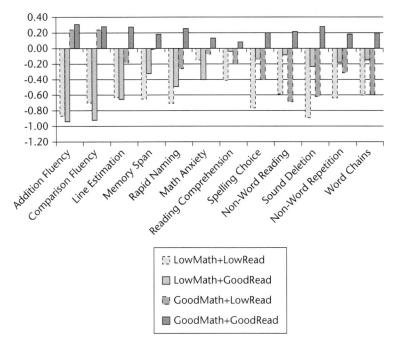

Figure 11.1 Comparisons of the four groups on the study measures in terms of z-scores

For each measure, the four groups were compared using an analysis of variance (presented in the final column of Table 11.1), with post-hoc analyses (Dunnett tests) contrasting each low-performing group against those children with reasonable-to-good levels of mathematics and reading (the GoodMath+GoodRead group). The GoodMath+GoodRead group, therefore, were considered representative of expected levels of performance, with the low-performing groups contrasted against these (the level of significance of the Dunnett tests is represented by asterisks in the table). These analyses indicated that the two groups with poor arithmetic scores differed from expected in measures of addition fluency and the two measures of mathematical concepts. This can be most clearly seen in Figure 11.1: those with poor arithmetic scores are represented by the lighter shaded blocks – those with poor word reading levels are represented by blocks with dashed outlines. Specific mathematics deficits can be contrasted with the evidence for specific weaknesses associated with dyslexia. Consistent with the literature on dyslexia, the poor word reading groups showed significant weaknesses in spelling, non-word reading and recognising word boundaries (the word chains task); though reading comprehension deficits seemed to be more specific to those with weaknesses in both reading and mathematics – and the sound deletion task seemed to be somewhat of a problem for those with poor arithmetic scores as well as those with reading weaknesses.

In addition to the specific effects of mathematical concepts, there was also evidence for poor scores in short-term recall of digits (memory span) being a problem for those with weak arithmetic; though this was smaller for those with good reading levels and might suggest an additive effect of both dyscalculia and dyslexia (see Figure 11.1). If memory were to form part of an assessment procedure, these data argue for deficits to be more easily identified when using items related to the potential area of problem: digits for those with dyscalculia, novel word-like items for those with phonological weaknesses associated with dyslexia. Along with the poor arithmetic groups, those with poor word reading levels were also likely to show evidence of poor scores in the rapid digit naming task, suggesting that this might not be a specific area of weakness for the child with dyscalculia, but rather another common area of deficit with dyslexia. Interestingly, it was only the children with poor mathematics and good reading that showed evidence of significant mathematics anxiety levels – potentially, only those with mixed skills levels will show evidence of negative affect, at least among these relatively young learners.

Overall, these data were consistent with the view that an understanding of number (or amount/value) is a fundamental specific aspect of dyscalculia. Arab children with problems with learning mathematics show deficits in conceptual tasks similar to evidence reported in the literature for children from other language and educational backgrounds. Furthermore, the data argue that children with specific problems in number concepts can be distinguished from those with problems with literacy learning, consistent with an underlying dissociation between dyslexia and dyscalculia.

Intervention practices

Given that an assessment based on the above developmental work identifies the problems associated with dyscalculia, recommendations for intervention or support should follow. Although the current work in Kuwait is still in the early stages of developing intervention strategies, the data argue that similar methods found to be effective for those with dyscalculia in other educational contexts should provide a useful basis on which to develop intervention techniques in the current context. Many of the techniques used for children with difficulties can be useful with non-LD learners: clearly, good pedagogy is good for all (see Gersten et al., 2009). However, for those who are struggling, and in contexts where inclusive teaching methods are relatively novel (as in many parts of the Arab world), specific LD-related intervention procedures could be useful. The present project, therefore, is developing teaching methods in Arabic consistent with those proposed in the literature for children with dyscalculia (as in: Bird, 2009; Butterworth & Yeo, 2004; Chinn & Ashcroft, 2007). In addition, methods are focusing on the development of training tools to support children in the acquisition of an understanding of the basic concepts related to number (Wilson, Revkin, Cohen, Cohen and Dehaene (2006), provide an example of these types of techniques). These latter tools aim to reduce the underlying problems associated with dyscalculia as early as possible in formal education.

Conclusions

The findings reported in this chapter argue for the existence of dyscalculia in an Arabic language, cultural context in which numerical symbols and teaching methods differ from those where much of the research on dyscalculia has been conducted. The data indicate that problems with arithmetic computations are associated with poor fluency of performing basic mathematical calculations, as well as poor understanding of mathematical concepts, weaknesses in memory for numbers and anxiety when required to perform mathematical tasks. Consistent with the literature on dyscalculia, problems with the concept of number, and relationships between numbers, provide the most compelling evidence for an underlying dysfunction that is specific to dyscalculia. This specific characteristic of dyscalculia differs from that related to dyslexia, providing further evidence that these two conditions can be distinguished with appropriate assessment procedures. Such assessment procedures should inform educational intervention practices, and the current work argues that the same basic method found to be supportive of children with dyscalculia in other learning contexts should be useful for Arab learners.

References

Adams, J.W., Snowling, M.J., Nehhessy, S.M. & Kind, P. (1999). Problems of behaviour, reading and arithemetic. *British Journal of Educational Psychology, 69*, 571–585.

Baroody, A.J. & Ginsburg, H.P. (1991). A cognitive approach to assessing the mathematical difficulties of children labelled 'learning disabled'. In J.W. Learner (Ed.), *Learning Disabilities: Theories, diagnosis and teaching strategies*. Boston, MA: Houghton Mifflin.

Berch, D.B. & Mazzocco, M.M.M. (Eds.). (2007). *Why is Math so Hard for Some Children? The nature and origins of mathematical learning difficulties and disabilities*. Baltimore, MD: Paul H. Brookes Publishing.

Bird, R. (2009). *Overcoming Difficulties with Number: Supporting dyscalculia and students who struggle with maths*. London: Sage.

Bull, R. & Johnston, R.S. (1997). Children's arithmetical difficulties: Contributions from processing speed, item identification, and short-term memory. *Journal of Experimental Child Psychology, 65*, 1–24.

Butterworth, B. (2003). *Dyscalculia Screener*. London: NFER-Nelson.

Butterworth, B. & Yeo, D. (2004). *Dyscalculia Guidance: Helping pupils with specific learning difficulties in math*. London: NFER-Nelson.

Chinn, S.J. & Ashcroft, J.R. (2007). *Mathematics for Dyslexia Including Dyscalculia, 3rd edition*. London: Wiley.

Durand, M., Hulme, C., Larkin, R. & Snowling, M. (2005). The cognitive foundations of reading and arithmetic skills in 7- to 10-year-olds. *Journal of Experimental Child Psychology, 91*, 113–136.

Everatt, J., Elbeheri, G. & Brooks, P. (2013). Dyscalculia: Research and practice on identification and intervention across languages. In A.J. Holliman (Ed.), *The Routledge International Companion to Educational Psychology*. Abingdon: Routledge (pp. 317–326).

Gersten, R., Chard, D.J., Jayanthi, M., Baker, S.K., Morphy, P. & Flojo, J. (2009). Mathematics instruction for students with learning disabilities: A meta-analysis of instructional components. *Review of Educational Research, 79*, 1202–1242.

Jordan, C.N. & Hanich, B. (2000). Mathematical thinking in second grade children with different forms of LD. *Journal of Learning Disabilities, 33*, 567–578.

Landerl, K., Fussenegger, B., Moll, K. & Willburger, E. (2009). Dyslexia and dyscalculia: Two learning disorders with different cognitive profiles. *Journal of Experimental Child Psychology, 103*, 309–324.

Mazzocco, M.M.M. & Thompson, R.E. (2005). Kindergarten predictors of math learning disability. *Learning Disabilities Research & Practice, 20*, 142–155.

Miles, T.R. & Miles, E. (1992). *Dyslexia and Mathematics*. London: Routledge.

Ramaa, S. & Gowramma, I.P. (2002). A systematic procedure for identifying and classifying children with dyscalculia among primary school children in India. *Dyslexia, 8*, 67–85.

Rubinsten, O. & Henik, A. (2006). Double dissociation of functions in developmental dyslexia and dyscalculia. *Journal of Educational Psychology, 98*, 854–867.

Willburger, E., Fussenegger, B., Moll, K., Wood, G. & Landerl, K. (2008). Naming speed in dyslexia and dyscalculia. *Learning and Individual Differences, 18*, 224–236.

Wilson, A.J., Revkin, S.K., Cohen, D., Cohen, L. & Dehaene, S. (2006). An open trial assessment of 'The Number Race', an adaptive computer game for remediation of dyscalculia. *Behavioral and Brain Function, 30*, 2–20.

12

Mathematics learning and its difficulties among Chinese children in Hong Kong

Connie Suk-Han Ho, Terry Tin-Yau Wong,
and Winnie Wai Lan Chan

As in many of the Asian cultures, academic achievement is highly valued in Hong Kong (e.g., Biggs & Watkins, 1996; Chan & Chan, 2003). Mathematic skills, being one of the important academic skills, receive much of teachers' and parents' attention. Children in Hong Kong receive early formal education from the age of three at kindergarten. A local study has reported that as many as 81% of the kindergartens in Hong Kong teach kindergartners two-digit addition, and 42% teach two-digit addition with carry-over (Cheng, Chan, Li, Ng, & Woo, 2001). This is in great contrast with the teaching practice in Western cultures, which include very little, if any, formal instructions of arithmetic before primary school (Aunio, Ee, Lim, Hautamäki, & Van Luit, 2004; Gonzales & Paik, 2011). This great emphasis on early numeracy education, together with the linguistic characteristics of the Chinese number system (e.g., short pronunciation of numbers in Chinese, and regular number naming structure; see Ng and Rao (2010) for a review), might explain why Chinese children often perform relatively better in terms of both pre-numeracy skills (e.g., Ho & Fuson, 1998; Aunio et al., 2004; Siegler & Mu, 2008) as well as mathematics achievement (e.g., Mullis, Martin, Foy, & Arora, 2012) than children in Western countries. Given the relative advancement in mathematical skills among Chinese children, do they process numbers in similar or different manners compared with their Western counterparts?

Past research studies have identified a number of cognitive skills that are important for learning arithmetic. Some of these skills are domain-general and may be used in many types of learning tasks. Working memory (e.g., Fuchs et al., 2010; Meyer, Salimpoor, Wu, Geary, & Menon, 2011) and processing speed (e.g., Fuchs et al.,

2006) are two typical examples of these domain-general skills. Some other skills are specifically related to number processing. These domain-specific skills include number sense (e.g., Jordan, Kaplan, Locuniak, & Ramineni, 2007; Halberda, Mazzocco, & Feigenson, 2008), estimation skills (e.g., Booth & Siegler, 2006), place-value concepts (e.g., Miura & Okamoto, 1989), counting skills (e.g., Passolunghi, Vercelloni, & Schadee, 2007), fact retrieval (e.g., Jordan, Hanich, & Kaplan, 2003), and arithmetic procedural skills (e.g., Geary, Hamson, & Hoard, 2000). The relationships between these number processing skills and children's mathematics achievement have also been examined in some studies with Chinese children. Examining how Chinese children learn mathematics might help us address whether the numerical skills are universally important for learning mathematics in diverse language groups. We will review in the next section some of the core numerical skills for learning mathematics among Chinese children.

Core numerical skills for learning mathematics in Chinese children

Several numerical skills have been found to be fundamental for learning mathematics among Chinese children. Two of these relatively important skills, namely number sense and place-value understanding, will be examined in detail in the following sections.

Number sense

Number sense is among the most frequently investigated subjects in recent research literature. However, the term "number sense" is rather broad and may include a lot of different capabilities and skills. Berch (2005), for example, has listed 30 components of number sense, ranging from understanding the meaning of numbers to developing strategies for solving complex maths problems. Yet, within the broad term of "number sense", a particular component, known as the Approximate Number System (ANS), has become increasingly popular in the research literature of mathematical cognition. We will first discuss research findings on ANS and next findings on the more general conception of "number sense".

According to Dehaene (2001), the ANS, which represented numerosity in an approximate, analog manner, was the basis for our numerical cognition. Humans are innately equipped with this representation. The ability to discriminate numerosities has been found in both infants (e.g., Xu & Spelke, 2000) and people in indigenous cultures (e.g., Pica, Lemer, Izard, & Dehaene, 2004). However, this representation is rather noisy. In order for two numerosities to be distinguished, they should differ by a certain ratio. This ratio, reflecting the preciseness of representation of numerosities in the human brain, is called the number acuity (w). The number acuity of humans is found to improve with age (Piazza et al., 2010) and it is related to people's mathematics achievement (Halberda et al., 2008). ANS appears to be a promising model to explain the importance of number sense in mathematics learning. Could ANS adequately account for mathematics learning among Chinese children?

Two recent studies were conducted with Chinese children in Hong Kong to investigate the relationship between children's number acuity and their arithmetic performance. In the first study (Tang, 2012), a group of 86 Chinese children were first assessed in Grade 1 before they learned about multiplication and the second time in Grade 2 after they have learned multiplication in school. The children's number acuity was assessed using three tasks, including approximate comparison, approximate addition, and approximate multiplication. After controlling for the effect of age and IQ, it was found that most of the ANS scores on the approximate tasks correlated significantly with arithmetic performance and the ANS scores accounted for 10.4% of the variance in arithmetic performance. On the other hand, the ANS score on multiplication was also predictive of children's performance in multiplication problems half a year later. The results replicated a link between ANS and general arithmetic achievement among Chinese children. The novel finding of this study was that the contribution of ANS may go beyond addition to more advanced skills such as multiplication.

In another longitudinal study (Wong, Ho, & Tang, under review), 156 Chinese kindergarteners were assessed on their number acuity, number–numerosity mapping skills (i.e., the association between number symbols and the underlying numerosity representation), and arithmetic performance. Using structural equation modeling analyses, it was found that kindergarteners' number acuity associated significantly with their arithmetic performance, both cross-sectionally and longitudinally. Furthermore, this linkage was mediated by the children's number–numerosity mapping skills. The cross-sectional model explained 44.1% of the variance in arithmetic, while the longitudinal model explained 45.8%. Findings of these two studies have enriched our understanding about why ANS and arithmetic skills could be related. It appears that some number–numerosity mapping skills, like counting and estimation skills, might reflect how well children associate the number symbols with their numerosity representation, which is an important step for doing arithmetic well.

Apart from number acuity, other studies have examined number sense in a broader way. In Chan and Ho's study (2010), 168 Chinese elementary school children were tested with a comprehensive number sense task which included items on comparison of number magnitudes, number sequencing, estimation, and number sense application in practical situations. The number sense score was found to correlate strongly with children's performance on a standardized mathematics achievement test (r=.50). The domain-specific numerical skills (number sense, fact retrieval, and place-value understanding) accounted for 18% of the variance in children's mathematics achievement, after controlling for the effect of age, IQ, working memory, and processing speed. Findings in all the studies reviewed above suggest that the link between number sense and mathematics achievement is significant in various cultural-linguistic groups.

Place-value understanding

Apart from number sense, place-value understanding (i.e., understanding the structure of the number system) is another core numerical skill for learning mathematics. In the Hindu-Arabic base-ten number system, each digit in a number carries a value of power of ten depending on its position, i.e., the place value. In a multi-digit (whole) number, the rightmost digit is in the ones place, the digit to its left is in the tens place, etc. Hence, in the number 24, for example, the digit 4 in the ones place carries a value of 4 (4 × 1); the digit 2 in the tens place carries a value of 20 (2 × 10).

Western studies have shown that place-value understanding is crucial to comprehension and production of numbers (McCloskey, 1992), mathematical problem-solving (Collet, 2003; Dehaene & Cohen, 1997; Fuson et al., 1997b), and early mathematical achievement (Miura & Okamoto, 1989). Consistently, accumulating evidence has also suggested the importance of such understanding among Chinese children in simple computation (Ho & Cheng, 1997) and early mathematical outcome (Chan, Au, & Tang, 2014).

In a recent study with Chinese children (Chan et al., 2014), 72 kindergarteners and 60 first graders were assessed for their place-value understanding through their counting strategies on a novel task – a strategic counting task. They also completed a battery of numerical tasks on simple counting (i.e., counting objects and reciting the number sequence), number representation (i.e., reading aloud numbers and writing them in words), and arithmetic calculation (i.e., symbolic and nonsymbolic additions). Results suggested that children with weaker place-value understanding were generally outperformed by their peers in the numerical tasks, pointing to a close relationship between place-value understanding and various numerical skills. In two follow-up studies (Chan et al., 2014), it was found that the first graders' place-value understanding in the first semester was the strongest predictor of their mathematical achievement at the end of the first and second grade, among other numerical skills.

Children's counting strategies offered a window onto their conception of number, or essentially their place-value concept (Fuson et al., 1997a, 1997b). In the strategic counting task (Chan et al., 2014), Chinese children were shown outline diagrams of base-ten blocks (ones squares, tens bars, and/or hundreds large squares) and asked to count the number of ones squares in each diagram. By clustering their counting strategies, a development trend was found going from count-all strategy (counting by ones; e.g., 1, 2, 3 . . . 24), through sequence strategy (counting by tens; e.g., 10, 20, 21, 22 . . . 24), to separate strategy (counting by the places; e.g., 2 tens and 4 ones yield 24). This suggested that children developed from perceiving number as an undivided entity to seeing it as a collection of independent groups of powers of ten – a trend of increasing place-value understanding. A similar trend has also been found with Western children (Fuson et al., 1997a, 1997b). Hence, children appear to go through universal developmental changes in their place-value understanding, irrespective of the language of their number systems (Chan et al., 2014). On top of that, the relationship between place-value understanding and mathematics achievement also seems to be universal.

Cognitive profiles of Chinese children with mathematics learning difficulties

Children who are deficient in the above core numerical skills may encounter difficulties in learning mathematics. Studies examining the cognitive profiles of Chinese children with mathematics learning difficulties (MLD) tend to confirm this expectation. For example, in Tang's (2012) study mentioned above, children with MLD were identified using the Learning Achievement Measurement Kit (LAMK), a locally normed, standardized mathematics achievement test developed by the Hong Kong Education Bureau. Children with MLD had normal intelligence (i.e., IQ≥80), but their scores in LAMK were below the 20th percentile. This group of children performed more poorly in all the approximate tasks measuring number acuity, compared to a group of age- and IQ-matched controls. On the other hand, while the control group improved significantly in the approximate multiplication task after a period of half a year, the children with MLD did not show any improvement in this task. The results suggested that children with MLD were impaired in terms of number acuity.

Other than the specific deficits in number acuity, children with MLD might also have deficits in other aspects of number sense and understanding of place-value concepts. In another study mentioned above (Chan & Ho, 2010), a group of Chinese children, who had been diagnosed by pediatricians or clinical psychologists to have MLD, were compared with a group of age-, IQ-, and SES-matched controls. The children with MLD had normal intelligence (i.e., IQ≥85), and their scores in the standardized Hong Kong Attainment Test (HKAT) were below the bottom 25th percentile. A comparison of the two groups suggested that children with MLD were worse than the controls in all the measures in the study, including both domain-specific skills (i.e., general number sense, place-value understanding, fact-retrieval skills, arithmetic procedural skills) and domain-general skills (i.e., working memory and processing speed). The effect sizes of the comparisons were stronger among domain-specific skills (partial η^2 ranging from .15 to .24) than among the domain-general skills (partial η^2 ranging from .05 to .13). The study suggested that children with MLD were worse than their peers in both domain-general and domain-specific skills, and their deficits in domain-specific skills were more severe.

Another study in Hong Kong echoed the results from the above study in terms of the deficits on place-value understanding that children with MLD showed. Chan and her colleagues (2014) recruited 193 Chinese first graders and they were divided into three groups based on their performance on a standardized mathematics achievement test – high, at or above the 75th percentile; average, between the 25th and 75th percentiles; low, at or below the 25th percentile. The children were traced for their place-value understanding over four time points from the fall semester of first grade to the spring semester of second grade using growth curve modeling. Results suggested that children who ended up with different mathematical achievement at the end of second grade had followed diverse paths in developing place-value understanding. In general, children in the high maths group in second grade had already shown the best understanding of the place-value concept in early first grade. Children with average mathematical achievement at the end of second grade, although they had started off with a lower level of place-value understanding than the high maths group, managed to catch up with their peers by the end of second grade. Children who ended up as the bottom 25% maths performers, however, had been lagging behind their counterparts in place-value understanding all along since early first grade. Although the children of the low maths group showed improvement in their place-value understanding over the four time points, they failed to catch up with their peers at the end of second grade and could only attain a level of understanding comparable to that achieved by the high maths group 18 months earlier. Hence, a persistently low level of early place-value understanding appeared to be associated with later low mathematical outcome.

These numerical skills were also found to be significant predictors of MLD status. For instance, Chan & Ho (2010) have showed that place-value understanding and fact-retrieval skills were significant predictors of the MLD status across age groups (i.e., 7–8 years old and 9–10 years old). For the younger group, arithmetic procedural errors were also a significant predictor of the disability status. The model correctly identified 77.5% children into the corresponding group membership among the younger group, while the correct classification rate was 77.3% for the older group. On the other hand, in Chan et al.'s (2014) study, the authors attempted to make use of the brief version of their strategic counting task – a test of place-value understanding – to screen for potential low mathematics achievers. Receiver operating characteristic (ROC) curve analysis indicated that a score of less than or equal to one (out of a total of 5 marks) as the cutoff at the end of the fall semester of first grade could correctly identify 95% of children who turned out to be low maths achievers (bottom 25% in mathematical achievement) in second grade (i.e., sensitivity = 95%), and 59% of children who ended up as on-track in maths (top 75% in mathematical achievement) in second grade (i.e., specificity = 59%), with the overall correct classification rate being 68%. Follow-up screening with the same test at the end of the spring semester of first grade provided a more accurate classification: a score of two or below as the cutoff would yield a reasonably good sensitivity of 87% and an acceptable specificity of 66% for the screening of later low mathematics status; the correct overall classification rate was 71%. In both studies, place-value understanding was identified as a significant predictor of children's potential difficulties in learning mathematics, while the first study also highlighted fact-retrieval and arithmetic procedural skills as potential predictors of MLD.

Identification of MLD among Chinese children in Hong Kong

The learning needs of children with MLD have received increasing attention in Hong Kong's research and practical fields in recent years. The urge for developing a local standardized screening/assessment tool for MLD is growing among the psycho-educational professionals. Although there is still a long way to go for the development of such a tool in Hong Kong, recent efforts in devising some home-grown screening tools have marked the first steps forward.

As an informal reference, some clinical and educational practitioners in Hong Kong may adopt the assessment tools from Western countries (e.g., KeyMaths) to get a sense of a child's ability level in various numerical domains and relative strengths and weaknesses in particular maths areas. This method offers a rough sketch of the child's maths profile. An alternative method is curriculum-based assessment, which sets an arbitrary cutoff (e.g., two standard deviations below average) based on a child's school mathematics performance for deciding whether further learning support is warranted. These two methods are non-standardized informal ways for practitioners to gain an idea about children's mathematical abilities.

The Hong Kong Education Bureau has developed a standardized teacher observation checklist for the screening of first graders with difficulties in basic number skills. A total of 27 maths items cover four numerical domains, namely preschool concepts (e.g., a general concept of "more", "larger", etc.), counting (e.g., knowledge of the number list from 1 to 20), concept of quantity (e.g., ability to compare two quantities), and place-value concept (e.g., knowledge of the place value of a digit in a two-digit number). By filling in the 27-item checklist for the first graders at the end of the fall semester, teachers can correctly identify 59% of children with difficulties in basic number skills (i.e., sensitivity = 59%) and 74% of children without such difficulties (i.e., specificity = 74%). An electronic version is under development for handy scoring.

An attempt to develop a Hong Kong standardized web-based test battery is also under way (Tang, 2010). The battery is modeled after the Dyscalculia Screener developed in the UK (Butterworth, 2003) for the screening of children with dyscalculia. As with the Screener, the test battery consists of: (1) two simple reaction time tasks for controlling the general response time; (2) a capacity subscale that includes a number comparison task and a dot–number matching task; and (3) an achievement subscale based on an addition task. Currently efforts are being made to establish a local norm for the test.

Intervention strategies for children with MLD in Hong Kong

A resource package for teaching basic maths topics (Education Bureau, 2010) is available for local primary schools. It consists of four chapters on (1) graded baseline assessment (first to third grade level), (2) counting, place-value concept, addition and subtraction, (3) multiplication and division, and (4) word problems and time reading. Handy teaching plans and materials, and exercises for the children are included. In general, each topic starts with an illustration of the essential concept with interactive slides on computer, followed by activities with concrete manipulatives (e.g., base-ten blocks and number cards), and take-home exercises. Teachers are recommended to administer the grade-appropriate baseline assessment to children with potential maths difficulties. Based on the children's areas of weakness, teachers may flexibly select suitable topics in the package to teach. The materials of the package can also be used for group intervention, peer tutoring, and parent workshops.

Another resource package for strengthening children's basic number concepts, particularly the place-value concept, is under development (Hong Kong Education Bureau, in preparation). It is designed for group intervention in the spring semester for those first graders who were suggested to be weak in basic number skills following the screening by the teacher observation checklist on numeracy at the end of the previous fall semester. The package contains six learning sessions covering the topics on (1) ones place and number bonds, (2) tens place, (3) hundreds place, (4) one-digit additions, (5) one-digit plus two-digit additions, and (6) two-digit additions. Each topic is instructed through interactive slides on computer and games with concrete materials. A learning session starts with a quick revision of the previous topic and ends with a short assessment test on the topic of that session. A warm-up session on basic counting principles goes before the first learning session, and a game day is set after the last learning session for revision through fun games. To evaluate the program's effectiveness and a child's learning progress, a 20-item maths test on counting, number reading, place-value concept, and arithmetic addition is administered twice – before the warm-up session and after the game day. In a pilot study, 134 Chinese first graders from 11 local primary schools, who were suggested to be weak in basic number skills, participated in the program conducted by their maths teachers at their schools. The preliminary results showed that all participating children achieved improvement on the 20-item maths test after joining the program. A larger scaled and more systematic pilot study is under way to provide further evidence for the efficacy of the intervention program.

Conclusions and future directions

Number sense and place-value understanding are found to be core numerical skills for Chinese children learning early mathematics. Deficiencies in these two numerical skills, together with problems in fact-retrieval and procedural skills could predict Chinese children having difficulties learning mathematics in the first few school years. Understanding the profile of those with MLD helps to develop effective identification and intervention procedures. Although the level of mathematical attainment might be different, the importance of the core numerical skills for mathematics learning appears to be universal across different language groups.

Research of mathematics learning and its difficulties among Chinese populations is still in its infancy. More large-scale and comprehensive studies are needed in the future. Since a considerable number of children with MLD may have other disabilities, such as dyslexia and dyspraxia, at the same time, future directions might investigate the profiles of children with comorbid or multiple conditions of learning disabilities. Knowledge of this will help educators to develop appropriate intervention strategies for children with diverse and complex learning needs. Longitudinal studies that examine children and adolescents with MLD beyond the early schooling years are also recommended. As for now, we have limited knowledge about what learning problems these individuals might encounter when they have to master complicated mathematical problems of a different nature beyond simple arithmetic. Would children's early number sense and place-value understanding still predict their later mathematical performance in senior grades? This awaits further validation by future research.

References

Aunio, P., Ee, J., Lim, S. E. A., Hautamäki, J., & Van Luit, J. (2004). Young children's number sense in Finland, Hong Kong and Singapore. *International Journal of Early Years Education, 12*, 195–216.

Berch, D. B. (2005). Making sense of number sense: Implications for children with mathematical disabilities. *Journal of Learning Disabilities, 38*, 333–339.

Biggs, J. B., & Watkins, D. A. (1996). The Chinese learner in retrospect. In D. A. Watkins & J. B. Biggs (Eds.), *The Chinese Learner: Cultural, psychological and contextual influences* (pp. 269–285). Hong Kong/Melbourne: Comparative Education Research Centre, The University of Hong Kong/Australian Council for Educational Research.

Booth, J., & Siegler, R. (2006). Developmental and individual differences in pure numerical estimation. *Developmental Psychology, 42*, 189–201.

Butterworth, B. (1999). *The Mathematical Brain*. London: Macmillan.

Butterworth, B. (2003). *Dyscalculia Screener*. London: nferNelson Publishing Company Ltd.

Chan, B. M.-Y., & Ho, C. S.-H. (2010). The cognitive profile of Chinese children with mathematics difficulties. *Journal of Experimental Child Psychology, 107*, 260–279.

Chan, L. K. S., & Chan, L. (2003). Early childhood education in Hong Kong and its challenges. *Early Child Development and Care, 173*, 7–17.

Chan, W. W. L., Au, T. K., & Tang, J. (2014). Strategic counting: A novel assessment of place-value understanding. *Learning and Instruction, 29*, 78–94.

Cheng, P. K. J. (2010). Exploring the identification of children with specific mathematical difficulties. Unpublished Master's dissertation. The University of Hong Kong, Hong Kong.

Cheng, Z., & Chan, L. K. S. (2005). Chinese number-naming advantages? Analyses of Chinese pre-schoolers' computational strategies and errors. *Interventional Journal of Early Years Education, 13*, 179–192.

Cheng, Z. J., Chan, K. S., Li, Y. L., Ng, S. N., & Woo, Y. S. (2001). Preschool children's actual computational ability, *Educational Journal, 29*, 121–135 (in Chinese).

Collet, M. (2003). *Diagnostic assessment of the understanding of the base-ten-system*. Paper presented at the Symposium Current Issues in Assessment of Learning Disabilities of the Congress of the European Federation of Psychologists Associations (EFPA), Vienna.

Dehaene, S. (2001). Précis of the number sense. *Mind & Language, 16*, 16–36.

Dehaene, S., & Cohen, L. (1997). Cerebral pathways for calculation: Double dissociation between rote verbal and quantitative knowledge of arithmetic. *Cortex, 33*, 219–250.

Education Bureau. (2010). 數之樂：小學生數學輔助教材. Hong Kong SAR Government.

Education Bureau. (in prep). 輕鬆學數學輔導教材. Hong Kong SAR Government.

Fuchs, L. S., Fuchs, D., Compton, D. L., Powell, S. R., Seethaler, P. M., Capizzi, A. M., & Schatschneider, C. (2006). The cognitive correlates of third-grade skill in arithmetic, algorithmic computation, and arithmetic word problems. *Journal of Educational Psychology, 98*, 29–43.

Fuchs, L. S., Geary, D. C., Compton, D. L., Fuchs, D., Hamlett, C. L., Seethaler, P. M., Schatschneider, C. (2010). Do different types of school mathematics development depend on different constellations of numerical versus general cognitive abilities? *Developmental Psychology, 46*, 1731–1746.

Fuson, K. C., Smith, S. T., & Lo Cicero, A. M. (1997a). Supporting Latino first graders' ten-structured thinking in urban classrooms. *Journal for Research in Mathematics Education, 28*, 738–766.

Fuson, K. C., Wearne, D., Hiebert, J., Murray, H. G., Human, P. G., Olivier, A. I., Fennema, E. (1997b). Children's conceptual structures for multidigit numbers and methods of multidigit addition and subtraction. *Journal of Research in Mathematics Education, 28*, 130–162.

Geary, D. C., Hamson, C. O., & Hoard, M. K. (2000). Numerical and arithmetical cognition: A longitudinal study of process and concept deficits in children with learning disability. *Journal of Experimental Child Psychology, 77*, 236–263.

Gonzales, M. M., & Paik, J. H. (2011). Cross-cultural differences in general preschool teaching styles and maths instruction. *International Journal of Learning, 17*, 251–263.

Halberda, J., Mazzocco, M. M. M., & Feigenson, L. (2008). Individual differences in non-verbal number acuity correlate with maths achievement. *Nature, 455*, 665–668.

Ho, C. S. H., & Cheng, F. S. F. (1997). Training in place-value concepts improves children's addition skills. *Contemporary Educational Psychology, 22*, 495–506.

Ho, C. S. H., & Fuson, K. C. (1998). Children's knowledge of teen quantities as tens and ones: Comparisons of Chinese, British, and American kindergarteners. *Journal of Educational Psychology, 90*, 536–544.

Jordan, N. C., Hanich, L. B., & Kaplan, D. (2003). Arithmetic fact mastery in young children: A longitudinal investigation. *Journal of Experimental Child Psychology, 85*, 103–119.

Jordan, N. C., Kaplan, D., Locuniak, M. N., & Ramineni, C. (2007). Predicting first-grade maths achievement from developmental number sense trajectories. *Learning Disabilities Research & Practice, 22*, 36–46.

McCloskey, M. (1992). Cognitive mechanisms in numerical processing: Evidence from acquired dyscalculia. *Cognition, 44*, 107–157.

Meyer, M. L., Salimpoor, V. W., Wu, S. S., Geary, D. C., & Menon, V. (2011). Differential contribution of specific working memory components to mathematics achievement in 2nd and 3rd graders. *Learning and Individual Differences, 20*, 101–109.

Miura, I. T., & Okamoto, Y. (1989). Comparisons of U.S. and Japanese first graders' cognitive representation of number and understanding of place value. *Journal of Educational Psychology, 81*, 109–113.

Mullis, I. V. S., Martin, M. O., Foy, P., & Arora, A. (2012). *TIMSS 2011 International Results in Mathematics.* Chestnut Hill, MA: TIMSS & PIRLS International Study Center, Boston College.

Ng, S. S. N., & Rao, N. (2010). Chinese number words, culture, and mathematics learning. *Review of Educational Research, 80*, 180–206.

Passolunghi, M. C., Vercelloni, B., & Schadee, H. (2007). The precursors of mathematics learning: Working memory, phonological ability and numerical competence. *Cognitive Development, 22*, 165–184.

Piazza, M., Facoetti, A., Trussardi, A. N., Berteletti, I., Conte, S., Lucangeli, D., Zorzi, M. (2010). Developmental trajectory of number acuity reveals a severe impairment in developmental dyscalculia. *Cognition, 116*, 33–41.

Pica, P., Lemer, C., Izard, W., & Dehaene, S. (2004). Exact and approximate arithmetic in an Amazonian indigene group. *Science, 306*, 499–503.

Siegler, R. S., & Mu, Y. (2008). Chinese children excel on novel mathematics problems even before elementary school. *Psychological Science, 19*, 759–763.

Tang, J. (2010). Developing a web-based testing platform for the identification of developmental dyscalculia. *Chinese Medical Journal, 123*, 283.

Tang, W. Y. (2012). Nonsymbolic numerical magnitude processing and arithmetic performance: An investigation on first-grade children with and without mathematics difficulties. Unpublished Master's dissertation. The University of Hong Kong, Hong Kong.

Wong, T. T. Y., Ho, C. S. H., & Tang, J. (under review). The relationship between ANS and arithmetic achievement: The mediating role of number-numerosity mappings. Manuscript submitted for publication.

Xu, F., & Spelke, E. S. (2000). Large number discrimination in 6-month-old infants. *Cognition, 74*, B1–B11.

13

The acquisition of mathematics skills of Filipino children with learning difficulties

Issues and challenges

Sherlynmay Hamak, Jai Astilla and Hazelle R. Preclaro

Introduction

Wordlab School Inc. started in 1995 as a multi-grade classroom to provide basic education at the primary and intermediate levels for children with learning and behavioural needs. It has since added a secondary programme and continues to provide not only classroom instruction but specialised intervention for reading and mathematics. Students from Metro Manila and neighbouring provinces have been referred to Wordlab for reading and mathematics assessments in order to address observed difficulties in these areas. This chapter focuses on the issues and challenges in the acquisition of mathematics skills of Filipino children who have been diagnosed with learning disabilities and accompanying conditions such as Attention Deficit/ Hyperactivity Disorder (AD/HD) who have attended the school since its inception. An analysis of archive records which include mathematics assessments, intervention programmes, lesson plans, student work and summary reports yielded a pattern of errors on three components of mathematics: (1) number operations, (2) mathematics language and (3) word problems. An awareness of these key focus areas may help to determine the kind of intervention in mathematics that might benefit these children.

The Philippine context

In the Philippines, the Filipino child's right to education is protected by the 1987 Constitution (Section 2, Article 14) which states that learners, however diverse, must receive education that is relevant and of high quality. Recent educational reforms on curriculum and policy have an impact on how basic education is taught. The Republic Act 10533 or the Enhanced Basic Education Act of 2013 aims to protect the rights of all learners by providing 12 years of education instead of 10 years. In the new basic education programme, the mathematics curriculum strongly emphasises critical thinking and problem solving. It covers five content areas, Number and Number Sense, Measurement, Geometry, Patterns and Algebra, and Probability and Statistics. The new curriculum allows students to learn by asking relevant questions and discovering new ideas. The ability to communicate these queries and ideas is given importance in the new curriculum. It recognises the different contexts of Filipino learners, which is an essential tool in influencing their study and use of mathematics. Another important reform is the institutionalisation of Mother Tongue-Based Multilingual Education (MTB-MLE) through the Department of Education Order No. 74, Series 2009. It states that instruction on basic literacy and numeracy skills should be taught using the vernacular. However, the transition from a bilingual education policy to mother tongue-based instruction is a difficult one. Several challenges are faced by mathematics teachers, from translating textbooks and instructional materials to relearning concepts previously taught in English in the varied mother tongues. An added challenge for mathematics teachers who work with children who have been diagnosed with learning disabilities is learning how to design instruction so that mathematics-related tasks are relevant, manageable and mastered.

Mathematics instruction for children with learning disabilities: the Wordlab experience

Number operations

One major challenge encountered in performing number operations is retrieving mathematics facts from memory. Research supports the finding that retrieval deficits for these types of learners are persistent (Geary, 1993). When unable to solve problems involving number facts they resort to more rudimentary methods which subsequently result in difficulties performing tasks involving multi-digit numbers. As shown in Figure 13.1 Sample 1, the student was unable to use his knowledge of the multiplications tables (4, 6 and 7) to solve a single-digit equation. The student instead resorted to concretely representing each of the sets by drawing x marks. In Figure 13.1 Sample 2,

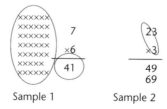

Sample 1   Sample 2

Figure 13.1 Sample work showing difficulties in retrieving mathematics facts

the student was unable to automatically retrieve the product of 2 and 3 which is 6. Research has shown that people with dyslexia usually experience at least some difficulty in learning number facts such as multiplication tables (Dowker, 2004).

Difficulties in solving multi-digit equations include following through a computational process till its completion. When carrying out operations such as multiplication, difficulties arise when the equation has a double- rather than single-digit multiplier. As shown in Figure 13.2 Sample 1, the student has not mastered the process of multiplying a multiplicand with a 2-digit multiplier. Instead, problems were solved by columns. And due to the fact that learning mathematics is interrelated, sequential and reflective (Chinn & Ashcroft, 2007) difficulties experienced in solving simpler equations would naturally negatively influence the solving of multi-digit equations. When multiplying a 3-digit multiplicand with a 2-digit multiplier, the steps involved in solving this equation include: Step 1: working out the product of the multiplicand and the multiplier (ones place); Step 2: getting the product of the multiplicand and multiplier (tens place); Step 3: aligning and adding up the answers to Steps 1 and 2 correctly to get the final product. In Figure 13.2 Sample 1, the student did not have difficulty with the first step but took the result of that process as the final product so that Steps 2 and 3 were no longer executed, rendering the answer incorrect. In Figure 13.2 Sample 2, the added process of regrouping proved to be even more challenging.

Aside from the aforementioned difficulties, because working with 2–3-digit equations is a multi-step process, there is an increased likelihood that students may skip or miss a step. Research by Bryant, Bryant and Hammill (2000) found one of the most common problems experienced by children with mathematical weakness was *carrying out multi-step arithmetic*. In Figure 13.3 Sample 1, although the student was able to multiply the multiplier with the multiplicand, problems arose with adding up the numbers to generate the final product. In Figure 13.3 Samples 1, 2 and 3, the student's errors in computation also stemmed from a difficulty in managing space (e.g. where to put the answers, which numbers should be grouped together and added up).

Difficulties also arise when students are unable to sustain attention long enough to note subtle changes in signs, shift mental sets to transfer from one operation to another and perform mathematics operations mentally. This finding is consistent with research conducted by Geary et al. (1999) that identified specific difficulties with the central executive component of working memory, specifically, the control of attentional resources.

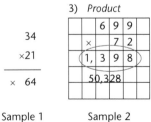

Sample 1   Sample 2

Figure 13.2 Sample work showing difficulties in following computational processes

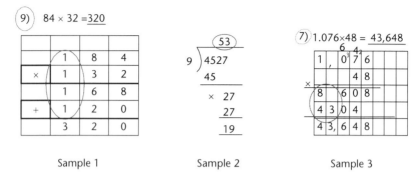

Sample 1   Sample 2   Sample 3

Figure 13.3 Sample work showing difficulties in managing computational space

Students that have been observed to be inattentive might not notice subtle changes in signs that indicate the use of a specific operation (i.e. +, −, ×, ÷), especially so when answering a test that presents a variety of equations. In Figure 13.4 Samples 1 and 2, the student added the numbers instead of subtracting them, while in Sample 3, the student subtracted the numbers instead of adding them.

Sometimes the difficulty lies in shifting from one operation to another, most especially when answering test items with 2–3-digit numbers. In Figure 13.5, the task involves subtracting 17 from 33. However, instead of subtracting the numbers, the student begins his computation by first adding the right-hand column and then proceeds to subtract for the left-hand column. While there is an attempt at shifting from the use of one operation to another, the fact that the task was done incorrectly lends evidence that this is a task where the student found it difficult to keep track. Difficulties in shifting operations may persist later on when attempting multiplication and division tasks.

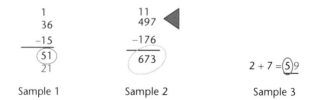

Sample 1   Sample 2   Sample 3

Figure 13.4 Sample work of difficulties in sustaining attention to signs

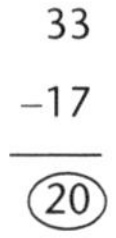

$$
\begin{array}{r}
33 \\
-17 \\
\hline
\boxed{20}
\end{array}
$$

Figure 13.5 Sample work showing difficulty in shifting mental sets

As students are given more examples that require regrouping, the ability to retrieve number facts and perform calculations mentally will be an advantage. In the following examples, the students exhibit an awareness of how to perform computational tasks but display a weakness in doing mental calculations. In Figure 13.6 Samples 1 and 2, the students had a difficult time mentally adding and subtracting numbers that have been regrouped.

Mathematics language

In the Philippines, the challenges for developing mathematics language are primarily curricular and instructional. Curricular challenges include how the development of mathematics language is often overlooked or not given enough emphasis. Its use is limited to labelling parts of a number sentence or a mathematics figure and evaluated through matching specific mathematics terms to their corresponding definitions. Mathematics instruction has focused mainly on providing drills, basic computation tasks and solving word problems. In addition to this, the language of mathematics in books and teacher resources is not in the *vernacular*, thus a large amount of information is likely not to be properly translated for and by teachers. An added challenge is the varying abilities of students in the classroom, most especially those with learning difficulties. Identified difficulties in mathematics language include limitations in English language proficiency, retention of terminology, discerning multiple meanings and its practical application.

One of the factors that seems to affect student performance in mathematics is their level of English language proficiency. Students who are primarily Filipino speakers show limitations in understanding what is taught and in expressing ideas. They tend to formulate their thoughts in the vernacular then translate it to English, making communication awkward and ineffective. Sometimes they offer phrases, and at other times explanations tend to be circuitous in their effort to arrive at the answer.

Because mathematics is often taught in English the retention of foreign (English) terminology and its application remains quite challenging. The students tend to confuse terms with similar roots such as *multiplicand* and *multiplier* as well as contextually related terms such as *area* and *perimeter*. It was noted that two trimesters or a year after learning new mathematics terms, the students had forgotten them.

There were also difficulties noted in discerning multiple meanings of words and related terms from one another. The terms *one, ten, hundred* and *thousand* are taught and mastered as number concepts. Moving on to regarding these terms by their

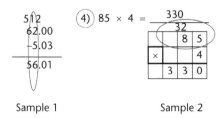

Sample 1   Sample 2

Figure 13.6 Sample work showing difficulties with mental mathematics

equivalent amounts, the students had similar difficulties adjusting their understanding (in this case number concept) and accommodating a new representation (the topic of place value). Another example includes the word *difference*, which in mathematics language no longer means *dissimilar* but, rather, refers to the remaining amount after one number has been subtracted from another.

Students also exhibited difficulty identifying the appropriate operations despite having been given similarly worded descriptions. To illustrate, a third grade student who could subtract numbers was not able to answer items that required her to *find the difference*. The equation $4 + 3 = 7$ is only stated as '*four plus three equals seven*' and is not translated to '*3 added to 4 makes 7*' or even '*3 and 4 make seven*'. Similarly, when reading fractions the symbol ¾ is labelled as '*three-fourths*' but not readily associated with the concept that it represents, which could be visualised as three out of four shaded quadrants in a circle.

Word problems

Answering word problems requires an integration of several mathematics skills and different levels of memory. First, the children need to read the problem and hold relevant details in their working memory while reading more sentences. Second, they need to retrieve those details and utilise them to demonstrate the solution. As they demonstrate the solution, more is required from them in utilising working memory as well as long-term memory systems. Dysfunctions in these areas will consequently lead to failure in performing the task. The language used in word problems also adds to the complexity of the task.

Several challenges were noted when attempting word problem tasks. Since the students included in this study are predominantly Filipino speakers, their lack of facility with the English language hampered their ability to understand mathematics situations independently. The language used become a barrier in their understanding of word problems. Several studies (e.g. Jan & Rodrigues, 2012) have shown that students' failures on word problem tasks are often due to linguistic knowledge. A comparison of the students' comprehension skills in stories and word problems was done to specifically identify the areas where the breakdown occurs in their performance. A group of these students showed ample literal comprehension skills in both stories and word problems. These students were able to answer simple and direct word problems utilising familiar English words.

Lapses in their comprehension for the task were also noted when mathematics-specific terms were utilised. The students' performances showed limitations in their recall of the meaning of these relevant words.

However, since most of the students have reading difficulties, one major challenge is the accurate decoding of word problems. An analysis of several word problems presented at the primary grades involve words or phrases such as *altogether, all in all, total* and *change*. These are relevant words that are not always within the students' reading level. Inaccuracies in reading these relevant words greatly affected their ability to comprehend mathematics word problems.

Aside from concerns on the mechanical aspect of reading and limitations in understanding both English and mathematics language, students also showed difficulty processing and managing details. The cognitive processes involved in comprehending texts are also necessary in mathematics problems (Lucangeli & Cabrele, 2006). Several of the students showed difficulty in isolating relevant explicit details as well as recognising implied information. They also showed difficulty in recognising two-step word problems. They tended to grab numbers from the problem statement and translate these into a numerical format.

At the higher levels in the curriculum, word problems with implied information and multiple steps are introduced. The students' performances showed that they are able to identify relevant explicit details presented in word problems. Aside from their difficulties in managing details, they also exhibited difficulties in planning an organised approach to solving the problems. Students who showed poor memory for mathematics concepts struggled on word problems that required them to integrate several concepts. The group of students who struggled in comprehending stories in their English classes also showed difficulties in processing story situations in mathematics. Most of these children were diagnosed with mixed receptive-expressive language disorder. Even at the literal level these students were often provided with scaffolds to isolate relevant explicit details as well as assistance in processing these efficiently. The structure used in word problems made the processing task more tedious for them.

Intervention strategies

Wordlab School employs systematic and strategic instruction for teaching mathematics in order to address the students' learning needs. At the beginning of a term, individual goals are set for each student, which are based on their assessment or diagnostic test results. When teachers create lesson plans, these goals are considered and incorporated into the class activities. Subsequent lessons are designed according to the students' responses.

A mathematics class starts with an introductory or warm-up activity to activate the students' schema and prepare them for the day's lesson. Quick drills are then done to review basic skills such as mathematics facts and mental computation strategies, in preparation for the computations that will be done later on. This is followed by a review of the previous lesson to facilitate the transition to the new lesson. After the new lesson is introduced and discussed, guided and independent practice activities are done. Evaluation is done afterwards, before the class ends with a wrap-up activity.

Engaging the students in the mathematics lesson is crucial so that their attention is sustained and to achieve better retention of the lesson. To achieve this, the teaching of mathematics facts involves the use of various games/drills and the provision of manipulative objects to help concretise abstract concepts. The principles of multisensory instruction and Concrete-Representational-Abstract (CRA) progression are deemed beneficial in addressing students' concerns in mathematics learning.

Addressing difficulties with number operations

Strategies for retrieving number facts

BREAKING DOWN BIGGER QUANTITIES INTO MANAGEABLE CHUNKS

In the primary levels, students' knowledge for number bonds was established using concrete materials. These materials developed their ability to visualise numbers, which consequently helped them in breaking quantities down as well as in carrying out mental mathematics activities. Figure 13.7 shows an example of the visualisation of numbers using concrete materials. When this skill has been established, students are able to utilise this knowledge to break down quantities into manageable values.

Breaking quantities down into manageable values was deemed effective for students who struggled in retrieving mathematics facts from memory. As shown in Figure 13.8 Sample 1, the number 7 was broken down into 5 and 2. These broken down values are familiar skip-counting patterns which make the retrieval of facts manageable for the student. To answer the given number problem, the student multiplies 5 by 6 as well as 2 by 6. The products of these are then added to get the

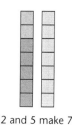

2 and 5 make 7

Figure 13.7 Use of concrete materials in developing number bonds and mental mathematics abilities

$7 \times 6 =$ ___	$9 + 8 =$ ___
5 2	1 7
$5 \times 6 = 30$	$9 + 1 = 10$
+	$10 + 7 = 17$
$2 \times 6 = 12$	
42	
Sample 1	Sample 2

Figure 13.8 Breaking down quantities to facilitate the retrieval of mathematics facts

final answer. Familiar number bonds could also be used to develop quick retrieval for addition facts. In Figure 13.8 Sample 2, the number 8 was broken down into 1 and 7. The students applied their knowledge of the bonds for 10, to more easily answer the number problem 9 + 8. They added 9 and 1 to make 10 and then added the remaining quantity. Adding a number to 10 is a number problem that most students easily answer.

DEVELOPING PATTERN RECOGNITION

Pattern recognition is a skill that is beneficial for children with deficits in their memory systems. This helps them to retrieve mathematics facts strategically both in isolated drills and in computational tasks. The table of multiplication facts for 9 (Figure 13.9) shows an interesting pattern that children quickly recognise. It shows that the digits in the ones place increase while the digits in the tens place decrease. Utilising pattern recognition can lessen the struggles of children with working memory problems when carrying out solving tasks.

Strategies for following through computational processes

VERBALISATION AND VISUALISATION

Understanding mathematics operations and computational steps is necessary in developing students' accuracy in performing and solving tasks. Concretising these using manipulative materials is an essential tool in developing their comprehension for this. It is even more effective when these tools are accompanied by verbalisation exercises. Verbalisation of steps and processes using a simplified and consistent sentence structure was noted to benefit students who showed difficulty in recalling and applying multi-step computational tasks. Talking through the process helped them monitor their performance and correct the errors they had made during the solving activities. Since most of the students were noted to be visual learners, a checklist of the steps (Figure 13.10) was considered as an effective tool in addressing any limitations in their recall for multi-step processes.

$$
\begin{aligned}
9 \times 1 &= 9 \\
9 \times 2 &= 18 \\
9 \times 3 &= 27 \\
9 \times 4 &= 36 \\
9 \times 5 &= 45 \\
9 \times 6 &= 54 \\
9 \times 7 &= 63 \\
9 \times 8 &= 72 \\
9 \times 9 &= 81 \\
9 \times 10 &= 90
\end{aligned}
$$

Figure 13.9 Using patterns in retrieving mathematics facts

LONG DIVISION

☐   D – Divide

☐   M – Multiply

☐   S – Subtract

☐   B – Bring Down

☐   R – Repeat Process

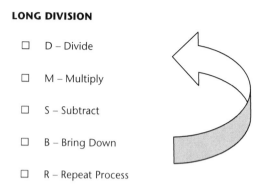

Figure 13.10 Using a checklist in recalling computational processes

Strategies for managing computational space and signs

Structured activities and worksheets (Figure 13.11) were beneficial in developing students' organisational skills for documenting their solutions as well as mapping efficient ways of retaining concepts and skills. Organising their thinking was done through the use of guide questions utilising a consistent sequence and structure. The consistency in the sequence and structure of these questions enables them to efficiently rehearse these as they independently perform mathematics tasks. Organising information using a systematic approach enables children with long-term memory problems to efficiently retrieve lessons. An organised storing and filing system helps them access information easily.

Strategies for encouraging mental mathematics

Number bonds are foundation numeracy concepts that can be used to develop mental mathematics abilities. The number bonds for 5 and 10 are usually used when developing

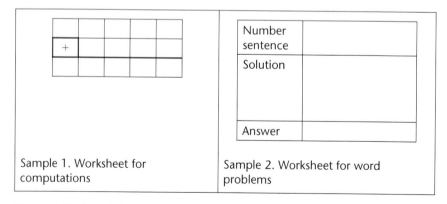

Figure 13.11 Sample format of structured worksheets

| 5 + 3 + 8 + 7 + 9 + 2 + 5 = _____ | 5 + 5 + 3 + 7 + 8 + 2 + 9 |
| | 10 + 10 + 10 + 9 |

Figure 13.12 Sample strategy for encouraging mental mathematics

| 25 + 33 + 17 + 15 + 28 | 25 + 15 + 33 + 17 + 28 |
| | 40 + 50 + 28 |

Figure 13.13 Sample strategy for encouraging mental mathematics involving 2-digit numbers

this skill. For instance, when given a series of numbers to add, children tend to solve these in a linear manner. Having them group quantities that build to 5 or 10 makes the mental solving task more manageable for them. Figure 13.12 shows how this is done. This knowledge can be extended as they work on 2-digit numbers. Figure 13.13 demonstrates this. Initially, these activities are presented using manipulative cards or tiles. These tools help students understand the commutative properties of addition and multiplication, which is useful knowledge to apply when carrying out mental mathematics activities.

Addressing difficulties with mathematics language

The active incorporation of mathematics language development activities in mathematics classes helps to increase students' ability to learn mathematics concepts. This involves teaching vocabulary and word-attack skills, the use of language in mathematics contexts and the use of mathematics language in oral and written expression. The inclusion of this component in mathematics lessons proved beneficial for the students with different learning concerns, and was especially helpful for bilingual students.

Direct instruction of mathematics terminology

A basic component incorporated into lessons is the direct instruction of vocabulary terms. This includes common words that have specific meanings in the mathematics context (even, pound, table) and content words (radius, perimeter, tetrahedron). The manner of delivery of the lessons was also important. Providing direct instruction using concise statements was necessary to get straight to the point and avoid confusion. This was helpful for students with directional confusion and language concerns.

Word-analysis strategies

Word-analysis strategies are also taught to increase understanding and lower the demands on memory. An example of word analysis includes finding the affixes that have been added to a word, for example:

- *Identifying prefixes (that denote quantity):* centi – hundred (century, centipede, centimetre).
- *Identifying suffixes:* a word with 'or' at its end may indicate the doer of the action (e.g. inventor is one who invents, generator is one that generates, hence divisor – the one that divides).

Use of illustrations

Since these strategies may be limited to select terms only, concrete examples and visual illustrations of concepts were used to promote understanding and retention of concepts. The use of task cards with pictures or illustrations also helped the retention of concept terms and their definitions. Simplified flowcharts were found to be beneficial in helping them to retain processes, especially for students at the higher levels who are learning complex procedures.

Using mathematics language in context

In addition to defining terms, it was also important for the students to be exposed to using the terms in context. While they might understand individual words, their contextual meanings may be changed according to their function or order in a statement. Subtraction phrases such as 'how many more' or 'how much longer' proved to be confusing and had to be unlocked, for example. Thus, in addition to learning the keywords that signify the operation needed to solve a word problem, studying word problem phrases was also helpful in promoting their skills in this area.

Developing metacognitive skills

Providing children who have learning difficulties and language disorders with opportunities to verbalise and explain the methods that they use helps to promote their ability to give descriptions of what they are doing. The provision of sentence structures helps them organise their thoughts and express ideas in a more elaborate and detailed manner. This is also an effective way for modelling the language and the habit of verbalisation. These skills are essential in promoting oral and written expression. In addition to being able to assign words to their thoughts, practice

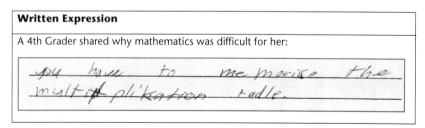

| **Written Expression** |
| A 4th Grader shared why mathematics was difficult for her: |
| *[handwritten] ...pu have to memorise the multiplication tadle.* |

Figure 13.14 Journal writing activity for mathematics class

in using mathematics terms is also accomplished. Journal writing activities are occasionally included to provide an outlet for students to also express themselves (Figure 13.14). A sentence structure or a visual organiser helps students express their ideas.

Addressing difficulties with word problems

The cognitive processes involved in the comprehension of texts are also necessary in mathematics problems (Lucangeli & Cabrele, 2006). Both decoding and linguistic comprehension abilities are necessary for students to carry out word problem tasks correctly. Since most of the students showed limited facility in both skills, several scaffolds were necessary in accomplishing these tasks. Given their limited facility with the English language as well as their poor retention for mathematics-specific terms, vocabulary exercises and translations were necessary to develop their understanding for key terms and story situations. To better facilitate both their retention and understanding for mathematics terms, visuals and word association techniques were utilised. Students were asked to create key cards for the terms introduced. Icons or visual associations were used to represent the meaning of these terms. This allowed them to efficiently file these key terms in their long-term memory system which consequently enabled them to retrieve these quickly.

The use of task analysis

In Wordlab, the development of word problem solving skills starts from a discussion of the concepts. In this phase, keywords and the phrases used in word problems later on are indirectly introduced through their use in discussions. The students start with single-step problems containing quantities according to their respective grade levels. The information given is explicit at first. Students are also taught to detect the keywords that are associated with each of the operations to help them determine the right procedure to employ. This progresses to finding context clues, which helps students infer the situation shown in the problem.

Providing translations

Students who encountered difficulties in visualising problem situations were given translations. They were also assisted in using tools to help them imagine, such as drawing, role-playing, and restating the problem as a story.

Use of prior knowledge/sociocultural context

The student's background knowledge for the contexts used in word problems was essential in their understanding of these story situations. Hence, it was imperative that the contexts used in the different mathematics word problems were within the child's schema. Unfamiliar concepts and situations were unlocked to facilitate better understanding.

215

The guided processing technique/scaffolding

Aside from limitations in their vocabulary for both English words and mathematics-specific terms, their limited grasp of the structure of the English language was also a factor that hindered their ability to comprehend word problem tasks. Guided processing techniques were employed to simplify questions and sentences. The guide questions given were sequenced in a way that helped them note relevant details and organise these in an efficient way.

Word problem reading routine

Problems with working memory affect students' ability to recall and manage details in mathematics word problems. To address this, a reading routine was carried out to aid them in recognising and isolating relevant details. Students were asked to underline the question and box the relevant information. These details were translated into pictorial representations and diagrams to graphically represent their understanding. This tool was deemed effective for visual learners.

Conclusion

Students enrolled in Wordlab who have been diagnosed as having learning difficulties and attentional challenges have exhibited problems in *retrieving mathematics facts*, *using mathematics language* and *solving word problems*. Providing direct, strategic and multisensory mathematics instruction addresses these key focus areas. However, proficiency in the language of instruction is key. A review of current practices on the use of *mother tongue* in mathematics instruction and the creation of instructional materials that acknowledge the students' sociocultural context using the target medium should take priority.

References

Bryant, D.P., Bryant, B.R. & Hammill, D.D. (2000). Characteristic behaviours of students with learning disabilities who have teacher-defined mathematics weaknesses. *Journal of Learning Disabilities, 33*, 168–179.

Chinn, S. & Ashcroft, R. (2007). *Mathematics for Dyslexics, 3rd ed.* Chichester: J. Wiley & Sons.

Dowker, A. (2004). *What works for children with mathematical difficulties?* Research Report No. 554: University of Oxford.

Geary, D.C. (1993). Mathematics disabilities: cognitive, neuropsychological, and genetic components. *Psychological Bulletin, 114*, 345–362.

Geary, D.C., Hoard, M.K. & Hamson, C.O. (1999). Numerical and arithmetical cognition: Patterns of functions and deficits in children at risk for a mathematics disability. *Journal of Experimental Child Psychology, 74*, 213–239.

Jan, S., & Rodrigues, D.S. (2012). Students' difficulties in comprehending mathematics word problems in English language learning contexts. *International Researchers, 1*(3), 151–160.

Lucangeli, D. & Cabrele, S. (2006). Mathematics difficulties and ADHD. *Exceptionality, 14*, 53–62.

14

The enigma of dyscalculia

Jane Emerson

Developmental dyscalculia has been written about since the 1970s but it has remained something of an enigma because many different writers have attempted to define it, with widely differing criteria. It depends on the definition applied and the definitions vary enormously. Dyscalculia is also frequently misdiagnosed when other co-occurring conditions are either causing or contributing to complex presenting issues. The often co-occurring conditions of dyslexia and dyspraxia, as well as other factors including attention deficits and maths anxiety, complicate the presenting evidence under the overall umbrella term of 'mathematical difficulties'.

What is dyscalculia?

Ladislav Kosc defined developmental dyscalculia as

> a structural disorder of mathematical abilities which has its origin in a genetic or congenital disorder in those parts of the brain that are the anatomical-physiological substrate of the maturation of the mathematical abilities adequate to age, without a simultaneous disorder of general mental functions.
>
> *(Kosc, 1974)*

In the twenty-first century the definition in the UK that stands out to support Kosc is the DfES (2001) definition.

> Developmental Dyscalculia is a condition that affects the ability to acquire arithmetical skills. Dyscalculic learners may have difficulty understanding simple number concepts, lack an intuitive grasp of numbers and have problems learning number facts and procedures. Even if they produce a correct answer or use a correct method, they may do so mechanically and without confidence.

More recently dyscalculia has been called a 'Specific Disorder of Arithmetical Skills' which

> involves a specific impairment in arithmetical skills that is not solely explicable on the basis of general mental retardation or of inadequate schooling. The deficit concerns mastery of basic computational skills of addition, subtraction, multiplication and division rather than of the more abstract mathematical skills involved in algebra, trigonometry, geometry or calculus.
>
> *(World Health Organization, 2010)*

Sharma (2003) highlighted the effects of spatial deficits and stated that 'dyscalculia can be quantitative, which is a difficulty in counting and calculating; or qualitative, which is a difficulty in the conceptualizing of mathematics processes and spatial sense; or mixed, which is the inability to integrate quantity and space'. Muter (2013) commented that 'spatial and perceptual difficulties can impact on the child's ability to understand visual concepts in maths, e.g. geometry and symmetry, fractions etc.' Others have defined different subtypes of dyscalculia and this has led to considerable confusion in this emerging field. Geary and Hoard (2005) proposed subtypes related to aspects of working memory affecting verbal or spatial representations of number, or attentional control of procedures and error checking.

In 2013, Kaufmann et al. proposed a preliminary new definition:

> Primary Developmental Dyscalculia is a heterogeneous disorder resulting from individual defects at behavioural, cognitive, neuro-psychological and neuronal levels. The term Secondary Developmental Dyscalculia should be used if numerical/arithmetic dysfunctions are caused by non-numerical impairments such as attention disorders.

Numeracy skills are important in life, making the impact of dyscalculia significant and serious. For example, National Numeracy (2013) stated that 'Numeracy is a life skill. Being numerate goes beyond simply doing sums; it means having the confidence and competence to use numbers and think mathematically in everyday life. Being numerate is about appreciating number relationships and interpreting answers and not just about doing calculations'. In other words, it is important not only to be able to perform calculations, but to do so with understanding and to solve real problems in life that involve numbers. Anghileri (2006) wrote: 'The basis of numeracy is number sense: understanding what numbers represent and how they can be used to solve problems. Underlying all calculations are the basic facts and most importantly, the connections that people continue to establish about the way numbers relate to each other.'

What is the problem with the different definitions?

Since there are so many different definitions of developmental dyscalculia, it makes diagnosis and thus appropriate intervention, very difficult. The range of definitions was discussed by Gifford and Rockliffe (2008) in their paper 'In search of dyscalculia'.

Is it useful to consider more closely domain-specific and domain-general approaches to investigation?

Many researchers have investigated a single deficit model of learning disorders such as dyscalculia as well as dyslexia and dyspraxia. This is based on the model of innate modules in specified brain regions that process certain kinds of information (e.g., Butterworth, 1999). However, the single deficit model does not explain why learning difficulties tend to co-occur. Pennington (2009) suggested that co-occurrence can be explained by genes and cognitive risks being shared across different learning disorders.

Domain-specific definitions

The number module has been described by Butterworth et al. (2011) with research that has focused on the role of the parietal lobe in number processing. In the field of cognitive and developmental neuroscience, this approach has emphasised a core deficit of understanding groups or sets and their numerosity. Understanding numerosity means knowing that collections of things have a certain number of items in their set. The sets can be changed by combining them, or by removing or adding sub-collections to them so that a set can be the same size as another or bigger or smaller in numerosity than another. These collections can be abstract collections of say, wishes, as well as concrete items that can be touched.

Domain-general definitions

Other researchers have investigated multiple deficit models that might explain individual variations in how these disorders are expressed in any one pupil. The manifestations in individual pupils might differ widely depending on other factors. Gifford and Rockliffe (2012) suggested that long-term monitoring of a variety of key number aspects 'might be the most effective way of identifying, remedying, and preventing mathematical difficulties'. Muter (2013) suggests that 'cognitive functioning seems to depend on the connections and interactions that a specific brain region has with other brain regions'. This supports domain-general explanations of mathematical difficulties.

Co-occurrence with other conditions

Dyscalculia can occur with other conditions such as dyslexia and dyspraxia (developmental coordination disorder, DCD). These might be accompanied by weaknesses in attention referred to as attention deficit disorder with or without hyperactivity (ADD/ADHD).

It is crucial for investigators and assessors, as well as those devising interventions, to consider these other conditions because they could impact on the successful development of mathematical abilities and affect the results of interventions.

Co-occurrence with dyslexia

Dyslexia was often thought to affect mainly the development of literacy. Chinn and Ashcroft (1993) and Yeo (2003) have written extensively about the cognitive features associated with dyslexia that can affect maths. The majority of dyslexic pupils have long-term memory weaknesses in memorising facts as verbal associations, as in times tables and in memorising step-by-step procedures, such as in following maths 'recipes' in long multiplication and division. They commonly have auditory and/or visual working memory difficulties so that holding items in mind, either in words or in images, while they process material, may be a weakness. They might also have sequencing difficulties which could affect learning the counting sequence, as well as vulnerabilities with some aspects of language, such as naming items rapidly and the language of maths. Auditory memory weaknesses will make performing mental maths calculations difficult.

Co-occurrence with dyspraxia

Dyscalculia frequently overlaps with dyspraxia (Yeo, 2003) which involves coordination weaknesses and left/right orientation weaknesses. Poor visualising in dyspraxia can affect maths learning in very significant ways since good mathematicians visualise many aspects of mathematical concepts. Some poor visualisers might be unable to visualise number lines to support their thinking during calculation tasks, for example. These pupils will need to create their own number lines to support their thinking.

Further research is needed in order to understand if weaknesses in the non-motor aspects of visuo-spatial processing are part of a dyspraxic profile or commonly associated with aspects of dyslexia and/or dyscalculia. The motor difficulties associated with dyspraxia can cause difficulties with developing cardinality and ordinal number knowledge when counting real items. This can be difficult if the motor aspects of one-to-one correspondence have not been established from an early stage in the development of number sense. Persistent miscounting can delay the development of a stable sense of quantity.

Co-occurrence with anxiety

Feeling anxious about numeracy has come to be recognised as a condition of 'maths anxiety'. This can affect memory and so consequently have a deleterious effect on maths performance. Chinn (2012b) has written extensively about maths anxiety and produced a questionnaire on the subject.

What to look for in assessment

It is possible to conduct a maths assessment in isolation in order to form an opinion for the purposes of a differential diagnosis between dyslexia, dyspraxia and dyscalculia or, indeed, low numeracy caused by other factors.

The *Dyscalculia Screener* (Butterworth, 2003) is very useful for screening a population of pupils aged 6 to 14 in order to select those who should be put forward for further investigation of their mathematical development.

It is our experience (Emerson and Babtie, 2013) that the primary deficit in dyscalculia can be taken to be poor number sense that affects the acquisition of the four basic operations – addition, subtraction, multiplication and division – and the application of these operations to solving word problems. If non-verbal deficits such as spatial perception are affecting acquisition, then this is understood to be part of possible non-motor dyspraxic effects on the interpretation of visually presented material. These motor and non-motor effects can be investigated using the Beery Tests of Motor and Non-Motor Skills (2010). A study by Tsai, Wilson and Wu (2008) supported the stance that 'we should consider the heterogeneous characteristics of children with developmental coordination disorder . . . when developing educational interventions'.

Further to this, the non-motor visual perceptual difficulties are analysed and intervention is designed to address the pupils' perception of visually presented material .These difficulties which affect mathematical development, can be seen as being part of a dyspraxic profile rather than a dyscalculic one. They have been identified in the absence of a dyscalculic profile which is based on deficits in quantitative reasoning related to lack of number sense and are treated differently, sometimes with the help of an occupational therapist.

Further investigation can be conducted informally using *The Dyscalculia Assessment* (Emerson and Babtie, 2013) to find out if the pupil shows evidence of number sense and any ability to calculate, rather than counting in ones to solve number problems.

Number sense consists of having a 'feel' for numbers which involves understanding that a number represents a specific quantity or value which is part of a sequence and can be compared with other numbers in terms of magnitude. Early number sense could be demonstrated by the use of counting to solve 'one more' and 'one less' problems. Understanding that 2 + 3 is just one more than 2 + 2 shows the beginnings of more sophisticated number sense when learners are moving out of 'the counting trap'.

A formal assessment of achievement level and error patterns is provided by a 15-minute maths test by Chinn (2012b) where a standardised score is obtained. Careful scrutiny of the nature of errors in any testing gives diagnostically important information to the assessor and leads to more targeted intervention.

Best practice would indicate that it is desirable to have access to a report which has been conducted by a chartered educational psychologist to give more general information about an individual's intellectual functioning. In the UK the Wechsler Intelligence Scale for Children (WISC-IV; Wechsler, 2004) is most commonly used. The information obtained gives four Index Scores which provide a summary of the pupil's verbal and non-verbal (perceptual reasoning) abilities as well as information concerning working memory status and speed of processing. With this information, the practitioner can assess the strengths and weaknesses of an individual learner and the impact these can have on their maths learning. In particular, the sub-scores within each index provide valuable insights into the possible presence of dyslexic or dyspraxic traits from the scores concerning auditory and visual memory as well as spatial and constructional skills.

The same report may also contain information about the individual's educational attainments. This can provide valuable information from the Wechsler Individual Achievement Tests (WIAT-II; Wechsler, 2005) about literacy levels, including single-word reading and reading comprehension scores as well as spelling levels, which can be compared to levels of arithmetic from the numerical operations (NO) and the mathematical reasoning (MR) tests. Typically, pupils with poor mathematical understanding but stronger rote knowledge of formal procedures, tend to score higher on the NO subtest than on the MR subtest which contains more items concerned with understanding concepts. Analysis of these scores can reveal information that might provide pointers to aid differential diagnosis between dyslexia, dyspraxia and dyscalculia. Further research is needed in this area.

Other diagnostic information, for example, from the Comprehensive Test of Phonological Processing (Rashotte et al., 1999) could indicate a dyslexic profile. Information obtained using the Beery Test of Visual Perception (Beery et al., 2010) could point towards a dyspraxic profile.

Why is the differential diagnosis of these conditions important? It is important because both dyslexia and dyspraxia can affect the development of mathematical skills. Dyslexia can affect both auditory and visual memory and dyspraxia can affect both motor and non-motor skills.

Lack of information about the presence or absence of these other conditions will influence the diagnosis of dyscalculia by the assessor. Dyscalculia is a serious condition that is not fully recognised yet by funding authorities in the UK and, as such, a diagnosis should not be given without comprehensive evidence of its existence.

In an initial informal assessment, it is very important to consider the oral language skills of an individual, which would include both their understanding and expressive abilities. This can be achieved in a short amount of time by asking the individual to create a story sequence from four pictures and then to retell it in their own words using the past tense. If any significant difficulties are detected, such as persisting difficulties with irregular past tense forms, then a referral to a speech and language therapist would be indicated for further investigation. Adequate oral language skills are considered to be important for pupils who will benefit from a language-based reasoning approach to maths intervention.

The Dyscalculia Assessment (Emerson and Babtie, 2013) can be used to conduct a formative assessment of pupils in order to provide evidence on which to plan teaching, based on error analysis. An ability to apply calculation strategies, rather than to count in ones, is carefully noted throughout. Those pupils who remain in the 'counting trap' described by Gray and Tall (1994), are showing evidence of possible dyscalculia. They described how 'the maths that low achievers are learning is a more difficult maths' because they 'continued to count in more and more complex situations'.

A pupil's number sense can be assessed by investigating their ability to estimate quantities and subitise small numbers of items without counting. Subitising is the ability to take in the numerosity of a random array of items at a glance and without counting.

The ability to count forwards and backwards from roughly age-appropriate points in the counting sequence can be investigated to assess flexibility of counting. Flexible counting means that this skill can be used as an early calculation skill.

Awareness of number relationships can be looked at through the use of comparative vocabulary of 'more than' and 'less than'. An individual's knowledge and understanding of number bonds can be checked to find if they have a unitary approach to numbers, seeing 5 as 'just 5' or just a pile of ones, or if they show evidence of understanding that each number apart from one, can be broken into other components such as $5 = 3 + 2 = 4 + 1$, for example.

The four numerical operations are investigated to check conceptual understanding. Many pupils with mathematical weaknesses may know that $3 \times 2 = 6$ but are unable to explain in words or with objects that the equation means 3 groups of 2 and how that differs from 2×3 even though the answer 6 is the same in both cases.

Pupils' knowledge of place value can be checked to find out if they can write numbers involving units, tens and hundreds of thousands as well as those containing zeros. Many vulnerable pupils have weaknesses in their understanding of the place value of the digits. Some believe that since zero means 'nothing' it can be ignored or omitted. Word problem solving should also be assessed to check if pupils are able to apply their knowledge and understanding to realistic situations involving number.

At the present time, most informal and formal assessments suggest whether evidence of dyscalculia has been found rather than giving a firm diagnosis. Rotzer et al. (2008) found in brain images reduced grey matter brain density in the right parietal numerosity-processing area in dyscalculic children. It is possible that, in the future, further brain imaging studies will shed light on brain differences linked to activation levels of specific areas while performing certain number tasks.

A programme of intervention

A multi-sensory approach to arithmetic is recommended for pupils with poor number sense, who apply 'ones-based' counting strategies to problem solving and who exhibit very few alternative calculation strategies. It is essential to use concrete manipulatives that pupils can look at, touch, move and can talk about what they see. At first, discrete materials are used, including counters, glass nuggets, and bead strings. A Slavonic abacus can be used so that pupils can use the colour changes to identify different quantities of beads without just counting in ones.

Three dimensional items can be represented in two dimensional forms on cards and drawn by pupils once they have had plenty of experience with real objects. Later, continuous materials can be used, such as Cuisenaire rods where numbers are represented by the length of the rods representing the numbers 1–10.

A reasoning-based approach is used. For example, pupils are encouraged to talk about what they see as they count objects in lines of 10 to emphasise the tens-based nature of the number system. Items are then arranged in lines of tens on number tracks so that a firm image of the items in tens becomes familiar.

Pupils work with the canonical dice patterns to 6, and later construct distinctive dot patterns for 7, 8, 9 and 10, based on the dice patterns. The dot patterns represent the doubles and near doubles numbers to 10. By working with the patterns, building them and talking about what they see, pupils become familiar with the patterns and learn to recognise them and order them according to the counting sequence, as well as developing their quantitative awareness of the numbers in relation to each other.

These patterns for each number can be used to work on the components of each number, at first learning the bonds that can be seen when looking at the dot pattern, for example 7 could be described as being made of 4 and 3 and then as 3 and 4, thus introducing the commutative property of addition at an early stage. The inverse relationship between addition and subtraction is inherent in these patterns, but might still need explanation. Pupils move on to expressing as equations what they have worked with concretely. At all times the mathematical language must be introduced carefully and systematically. Oral word problems are used at every stage to ensure that pupils start solving realistic problems from the start. Gifford and Rockliffe (2012) discussed this approach in their article, 'Mathematics difficulties: does one approach fit all?' They noted that 'the use of recognising and subitizing dot patterns is distinctive and may be significant, since this is such a key difficulty'. It was felt then that this approach could make a significant and positive difference if included in intervention.

Pupils are trained to record their thinking through drawing and using number lines that are partially empty to avoid counting in ones. Cuisenaire rods are used to represent partitioned numbers. For example, six plus eight could be regrouped into ten and four. In this way pupils are shown how to represent and regroup to form 'tens and some left over' as a prelude to learning to calculate by bridging tens. This is an important strategy when ten, or a tens number, is used as a stepping stone towards adding two numbers where the answer will be more than 10. For example, $5 + 8$ is regrouped to form $(5 + 5) + 3$ to make $10 + 3$ to make 13. Bridging back involves using ten or a multiple of 10 when subtracting a number. For example, $23 - 5 = (23 - 3) - 2 = 20 - 2 = 18$. Complementary addition can be used as an alternative strategy for pupils who find working with numbers descending difficult. In this method, the difference between two numbers is found by working forwards from a small number to a larger one (counting on). For some pupils, finding the difference is easier than subtraction methods. Many pupils with dyscalculic traits find counting and working backwards along a number line harder than thinking forwards in the number sequence.

Base 10 materials, designed by Zoltan Dienes, can be used to study the place value system. This work is carried out on place value mats so that it is clear how the hundreds, tens and units (HTU) designations are repeated within larger numbers. In this way pupils can be encouraged to visualise large numbers, such as billions, as three groups of three places rather than nine, for example. This approach reduces the load on memory and the structure can be more easily visualised even when the blocks are not present.

Pupils should be taught to partition numbers of increasing size into their component parts so that 36 can be understood as $30 + 6$ or three tens and six units.

Flexible partitioning is also taught so that 36 can also be partitioned into 26 and 10, for example.

Once pupils are working confidently with addition and subtraction equations and can record their thinking on number lines, as well as solving word problems, they can progress to working on multiplication and division concepts. Just as addition and subtraction are inverse operations, so multiplication is linked to division in an inverse relationship.

Multiplication is first taught concretely following the equal repeated group model. Equal sized groups can be built on grids and step counting for the lower and easier tables is practised. The tables for twos, fives and tens are studied, at first using real objects to build the groups in dot pattern formation and later using cards to represent the dot pattern groupings. In due course a reasoning-based multiplication tables strategy is taught. The key facts for each table are learnt as $10n$, $5n$ as well as n and $2n$. Pupils are guided to see that $5n$ represents half of $10n$. For example if $10 \times 2 = 20$ then 5×2 is half of 20 so $5 \times 2 = 10$. Flexible partitioning is used to calculate half of the 'odd' tens numbers such as 30, which can be partitioned into 20 and 10 so that half of 20 and 10 can be seen to be $10 + 5 = 15$, especially when demonstrated with Cuisenaire rods. In this way, pupils who are unable to retain their tables by rote can use an understanding-based method to derive unknown facts from known facts. For those with co-occurring dyslexia, with the commonly associated verbal memory weaknesses, rote methods might have failed in the past. This strategy supports a 'return to first principles' way of reasoning for deriving multiplication and division facts from known key facts (Chinn, 2012a). Pupils work on understanding the connections between multiplication and division using Cuisenaire rods. They can discover and show that if $3 \times 5 = 15$ then $15 \div 3 = 5$ and $15 \div 5 = 3$ so that they can later visualise the number relationships.

It is important that pupils learn to apply the same basic facts and strategies as they progress up through the higher decades. Many pupils showing evidence of dyscalculia do not understand that fundamental number relationships such as $2 + 2 = 4$ can be extended right up to understanding that two million plus two million makes four million and beyond.

Word problems should be embedded throughout teaching and provide an essential way of revising previous knowledge and understanding. Askew (2009) in his *Word Problems* books, describes how pupils progress from being novice problem solvers who treat each problem as a completely new one. More experienced problem solvers get an overall feel for what the problem is about and seek out the parts that will help in a solution. He stresses that it is important that pupils do not rely just on key words to guess what operation is needed to solve a word problem; 'the problem solver has to bring meaning to the wording of the problem'. Boaler (2009) describes how some students 'are taught only to follow rules and not to engage in sense-making reasoning or thought, acts that are critical to an effective use of mathematics' and 'most mathematics problems can be tackled through the understanding of concepts and active problem solving'. This underlines the importance of embedding word problems in every lesson.

The teaching approach outlined above features detailed assessment and teaching content targeted through careful error analysis. The approach finds starting points based at the proximal level of development of each pupil so that teaching starts at a point where the pupil can succeed at the edge of their competence before moving on in small steps. Teaching must be cumulative and move steadily forwards from that point. Progression should be carefully monitored from work on early number and counting, to more abstract concepts supported by the use of concrete materials used in a multi-sensory way (Emerson and Babtie, 2014).

Other forms of intervention that show promise are digital ones. At the London Knowledge Lab activities have been developed using manipulatives presented digitally that enable pupils to practise activities to develop number sense and number bonds. They are an adjunct to, not a replacement for, concrete materials, allowing pupils to work independently after they have worked with a teacher and in this way receive more practice on essential activities (www.number-sense.co.uk).

In conclusion, the field of dyscalculia remains full of challenges, challenges that will ultimately lead to a fuller understanding of the nature of this enigmatic condition. A new think tank, Learnus (www.learnus.co.uk), is promoting further collaboration between cognitive and educational neuroscientists who continue to work closely with educators to investigate the connections between these cognitive processes to find out how they influence individual learning.

References

Anghileri, J. (2006). *Teaching Number Sense*. 2nd edition. London: Continuum.

Askew, M. (2009). *Word Problems*. London: BEAM.

Beery, K.E., Beery, N.A. and Buktenica, N.A. (2010). *Beery Test of Visual Perception*. 6th edition. London: Pearson.

Boaler, J. (2009). *The Elephant in the Classroom*. London: Souvenir Press.

Butterworth, B. (1999). *The Mathematical Brain*. London: Macmillan.

Butterworth, B. (2003). *Dyscalculia Screener*. London: nferNelson.

Butterworth, B., Varma, S. and Laurillard, D. (2011). Dyscalculia: from brain to education. *Science, 332*(6033), 1049–1053.

Chinn, S. (2012a). *The Trouble with Maths*. 2nd edition. London: Routledge.

Chinn, S. (2012b). *More Trouble with Maths*. London: Routledge.

Chinn, S. and Ashcroft, J.R. (1993). *Mathematics for Dyslexics*. London: Whurr.

DfES (2001). *The National Numeracy Strategy. Guidance to Support Learners with Dyslexia and Dyscalculia*. London. DfES.

Emerson, J. and Babtie, P. (2013). *The Dyscalculia Assessment*. 2nd edition. London: Bloomsbury.

Emerson, J. and Babtie, P. (2014). *The Dyscalculia Solution*. London: Bloomsbury.

Geary, D.C. and Hoard, M.K. (2005). Learning disabilities in arithmetic and mathematics: Theoretical and empirical perspectives. In J.I.D. Campbell (ed.), *Handbook of Mathematical Cognition* (pp. 253–267). Hove: Psychology Press.

Gifford, S. and Rockliffe, F. (2008). In search of dyscalculia. *Proceedings of the British Society for Research into Learning Mathematics, 28*(1), 21–27.

Gifford, S. and Rockliffe, F. (2012). Mathematics difficulties: does one approach fit all? *Research in Mathematics Education, 14*(1), 1–15.

Gray, E. & Tall, D. (1994). Duality, ambiguity, and flexibility: a 'proceptual' view of simple arithmetic. *Journal for Research in Mathematical Education, 25*(2), 116–140.

Kaufmann, L., Mazzocco, M.M., Dowker, A., von Aster, M., Göbel, S.M., Grabner, R.H. et al. (2013). Dyscalculia from a developmental and differential perspective. *Frontiers in Psychology, 4,* 516.

Kosc, L. (1974). Developmental dyscalculia. *Journal of Learning Disabilities, 7*(3), 164–177.

Muter, V. (2013). Dyslexia: Why more than one difficulty? How multiple deficit models influence assessment and intervention. Patoss Bulletin. Summer 2013.

National Numeracy (2013). www.nationalnumeracy.org.

Pennington, B. (2009). *Diagnosing Learning Disorders.* New York: Guilford.

Rashotte, C., Torgensen, J. and Wagner, R. (1999). *Comprehensive Test of Phonological Processing (CTOPP).* London: Pearson.

Rotzer, S., Kucian, K., Martin, E., von Aster, M., Klaver, P. and Loenneker, T. (2008). Optimized voxel-based morphometry in children with developmental dyscalculia. *NeuroImage, 39*(1), 417–422.

Sharma, M. (2003). *What is dyscalculia?* BBC Skillswise. Available from www.brainhe.com/staff/types/dyscalculiatext.html (accessed 17 August 2014).

Tsai, C.L., Wilson, P.H. and Wu, S.K. (2008). Role of visual perceptual skills (non motor) in children with developmental co-ordination disorder. *Human Movement Science, 27*(4), 649–664.

Wechsler, D. (2004). *The Wechsler Intelligence Scale for Children Fourth UK Edition (WISC-IV).* London: Harcourt Assessment.

Wechsler, D. (2005). *The Wechsler Individual Achievement Test 2nd Edition (WIAT-II).* London: The Psychological Association.

World Health Organization. (2010). F81.2 Specific disorder of arithmetical skills. In *The ICD-10: Classification of Mental and Behavioural Disorders.* Available from: http://www.who.int/classifications/icd/en/bluebook.pdf (accessed 30 October 2013).

Yeo, D. (2003). *Dyslexia, Dyspraxia and Mathematics.* London: Whurr.

15

Deep diagnosis, focused instruction, and expanded math horizons

Robert B. Ashlock

We often use tests, interviews, and other forms of assessment as tools to determine, among other things, areas of strength and weakness for individual learners. Diagnosing deeply can lead to truly focused intervention; then students can make connections and their math horizons expand.

Diagnosis that digs deeply

Whenever your diagnostic procedure is well-defined (possibly a test or a script) you will survey areas of knowledge or skill. This helps you identify particular areas where you need to focus further, with deeper diagnosis. Ultimately, you need to dig deeply to discover very specific misconceptions and error patterns.

Day by day as you guide the learning of your students, you stop to collect data about what particular students have or have not learned so far. You do this in order to refocus the teaching-learning process. Effective instruction is actually cyclical, rotating between instruction and diagnosis; you are able to intervene as needed during instruction because you have diagnosed. But there are times when you truly need to *focus* on diagnosis and dig deeply – apart from instruction.

Distinguish between diagnosis and instruction

Whenever you focus on diagnosis, be careful not to intervene with instruction; merely look and listen. Think about *what* the student knows and is doing – and think about *why* the student learned it. Try to understand the student's thinking. At such times, your goal is to learn what the student understands to be true and what the student can and cannot do.

While you are digging deeply, be careful how you respond to whatever the student says or does; do *not* say "very good" or "that is correct." (Remember, your goal is to collect information from the student – data that will help you to plan needed instruction.) Instead, respond to student expressions by being supportive and saying something like, "That is helpful," or asking a question like, "How do you know that is true?" Be very accepting of student responses *whether correct or not*. You might even want to tell the student that you are not testing, but you are collecting information you need to know in order to plan lessons that will be helpful.

Identify what students know and can do

You need to know where your students are in the learning process before you plan further instruction. You need to identify what *each* student knows and can do already. That includes big ideas – major concepts and understandings – as well as more specific concepts and skills.

Big ideas are foundational and your students will be able to build upon them, connecting them with more specific concepts. Examples of big ideas include number, equivalence, various properties of operations, and principles of compensation and distribution. A student might suddenly discover a pattern, such as the pattern of place values within a system of numeration, or a pattern suggesting a compensation principle such as, "In a subtraction situation, when the same number is added to the sum (minuend) and to the known addend, the difference is unchanged."

You also need to know which *specific* concepts a particular student understands and can apply, and which specific skills the student can demonstrate. For example, does the student understand that the operation of subtraction, given a sum (minuend) and one of the addends (subtrahend) can produce the number that is the missing addend (difference)? In other words, does the student know *when to use* the operation of subtraction (by calculator or algorithm)? Specific skills can include simple or complex algorithms; but you need to know if a particular student can or cannot do them.

Typically, the ability to recall missing sums and products from the basic facts of arithmetic needs to be diagnosed. A set of flash cards usually includes subtraction facts and division facts, as well as addition facts and multiplication facts; but the author does not believe that subtraction and division facts need diagnosis and instruction as such. Rather, it is the ability to *use* addition facts in subtraction situations and the ability to *use* multiplication facts in division situations that requires diagnosis and instruction.

Identify missing content

As you dig deeply you will learn that a particular student does *not* understand certain big ideas; and specific concepts that are needed will be missing. You will also find that certain skills are not present. Make a list of those big ideas and specific concepts the student does not understand; include skills the student cannot do. Eventually you will need to teach the student those particular big ideas, concepts and skills; and when you do teach them make sure the student builds on big ideas, specific concepts and skills s/he *already* understands and can do. Help students understand how what they already know and can do is connected with new material you are teaching.

Learn how students are thinking

Consider a particular student. What is the student thinking? Interview the student and encourage responses that have as much detail as possible. Present alternatives and ask why a particular choice was made; then have the student comment on her or his thought process. Whenever a student explains something listen carefully to how words are used; some words might be used to mean something different from what you mean when you use the word.

When you ask students to comment on their thoughts, differentiate between *introspection* and *retrospection*; both kinds of responses are needed. Call for introspection when you ask a student to "think out loud" *while* solving a problem or using an algorithm. Call for retrospection when you ask for a student to comment *after* s/he has solved the problem or completed the algorithm (Ashlock, 2002, pp. 26–28).

Listen for overgeneralizations and overspecializations. During instruction a student might over*generalize* and "jump to a conclusion" before considering adequate data. For example, as you teach you might have good reasons to present $4 + 2 = 6$ and $6 - 2 = 4$ together, but later a student who learned that in $4 + 2 = 6$ the 6 is the sum, might conclude that the 6 in the first equation and the 4 in the second are both sums. That student has overgeneralized and thinks of both numbers at the right as "the result." Clearly, the student does not understand equality or what a sum is. Consider another example of overgeneralization. Students who know that fractions must have like denominators in order to be added or subtracted sometimes conclude that fractions must also have like denominators to be multiplied or divided.

Students may also over*specialize*. When observing examples of a concept or procedure these students conclude that the concept or procedure is limited to characteristics of examples they have seen. For example, students learning to round a two-digit number to a multiple of ten may conclude that the procedure consists of replacing the units digit with zero (this seemed to happen in some of the examples they observed). Or, students learning about a right triangle might conclude that a right triangle always has a right angle along the base of the triangle – because it did in the examples they observed. (Graeber, 1992).

Clearly, teachers need to use a rich *variety* of examples when teaching concepts and procedures. Teachers might also need to contrast examples with non-examples if their students are to avoid overgeneralizing and overspecializing.

Look and listen

As you examine written work, *look* for patterns. Look for patterns in whatever a student writes, whether a computational procedure or an explanation. Look for evidence of correct thinking. Even though a procedure or answer is correct, you can ask the student how s/he knows it is correct, or why the procedure provides correct answers. Also look for error patterns. Sometimes the answer is incorrect part of the time but correct part of the time – even when the student uses an erroneous procedure. The student might have inferred an erroneous procedure that produces the correct answer part of the time. You could suggest an example for the student to solve using his or her procedure – an example you know will produce an incorrect answer. Let the student discover that something is wrong. You might want to ask, "Do you know why you use that procedure?"

If you want to learn *why* a student learned the particular misconceptions and error patterns you identified, take a personal interest in that student. Learn more about the student's life outside of school. Are there reasons for his or her difficulties? Students with limited experiences outside of school might not perceive mathematics as anything they can use. Frequent absences or a recent transfer could be relevant (Sherman, Richardson, and Yard, 2009, pp. 5–6).

Instruction that is focused

If you diagnose deeply, you will be enabled increasingly to provide instruction that is focused. You will learn which big ideas, specific concepts, and skills the child is ready to learn; and you can focus instruction where needed. Consider the illustrations that follow.

For the student who said the 7 in 37 is in the tens column (she explained "because 7 is the biggest") you can reintroduce whole number numeration, being careful to have her record each digit as a record of what she is observing while she counts and groups objects. For the student who adds numerators and *also* adds like denominators when adding with fractions, you can focus on the difference between addition with fractions and multiplication with fractions; have the student use fractional parts to show addition with fractions (you might also want to use drawings to show multiplication with fractions). Carefully record step-by-step what you do with fractional parts when adding; your record should be an example of the addition procedure.

Consider the student who believes a triangle has only one altitude – a line between the angle opposite a horizontal base, and perpendicular to that base. You can have the student cut out three congruent triangles, then place them on a table in three different orientations illustrating three different base lines. Then have the student draw an altitude in each cut-out triangle and explore questions like: How many altitudes does this particular triangle have? Do all triangles have the same number of altitudes? Why? What *is* an altitude of a triangle? (Ashlock, 2010, p. 120).

While you are teaching, watch the way you use words. Teachers interpret mathematical expressions in different ways; this often confuses our students. For example, something as simple as 3 + 4 can be interpreted in these ways:

- three and four
- three plus four
- three and four more.

Students might not understand that the expressions actually say the same thing; they are equivalent. Furthermore, teachers sometimes say things that are more linguistically complex than they need to be, and what those teachers say confuses students (Ashlock, 2010, pp. 159).

When you plan problem-solving tasks for individuals and for groups of students, plan for students to reflect. Make sure each student can connect more specific concepts to big ideas and to related specific concepts. Consider these examples:

- Individual basic facts of arithmetic can be connected to one another and to big ideas. In both $7 + 8 = 15$ and $15 - 8 = 7$ the 15 is the sum or total amount, and the eight and seven are both addends because the operations of addition and subtraction with whole numbers are related (we sometimes say with young students that subtraction "undoes" addition). Students can use a basic addition fact to answer a subtraction question like $14 - 8 = . . .$, because $6 + 8 = 14$. An open number sentence (often an equation) asks a question; for example, a question using subtraction can be changed into the same question using addition.
- These same ideas can help a student who confuses signs of numbers and signs of operations while adding and subtracting integers. Even with signed numbers, a subtraction question can be changed to an addition question. In the following illustration a number line might be needed to help the student picture the addition situation.

$$^-9 - 4 = \square \qquad \rightarrow \qquad \square + 4 = {}^-9$$

(Ashlock, 2010, p. 139)

- While students are learning to describe polygons and three-dimensional shapes, individual polygons can be connected to (related to) one another and to other polygons and to three-dimensional shapes. A square is also a rectangle and a rhombus, but not every rectangle or rhombus is a square because of conditions specified by specific definitions. Circles can be connected to (observed in) cylinders. Truly, specific two-dimensional shapes are often part of the definition of a three-dimensional shape. Have students identify models of three-dimensional shapes and tell why their name for the model is correct; have them point to or trace the edges of two-dimensional shapes they name as they explain.
- While students are learning about relatively prime numbers, ask questions like, "How many natural numbers less than 100 are relatively prime to 15"? After each student finds an answer (probably by making a drawing), have students reflect on their answers and the various ways students found their answers (Bair and Mooney, 2012).

In order to provide truly focused instruction when teaching procedures such as algorithms, have students explain *why* particular procedures do or do not provide correct answers. Ask questions like, "Does this procedure *always* give the correct answer or result? How do you know?" For simple procedures, encourage younger students to use manipulatives or drawings as they explain why the procedure provides a correct answer; encourage older students to use what they know about numeration and particular operations as they explain. When working with a group of students, ask other students in the group if they agree with the explanation – even when everything is correct.

Student math horizons

Our instruction must eventually go beyond specific examples – even examples of specific big ideas. Instruction must focus on helping students make connections and see patterns among the big ideas, specific concepts, and procedures they learn. We see the fruit of focused diagnosis and instruction whenever we observe our students expanding their math horizons.

Students at a particular grade level can make connections and see patterns in what they are studying at that grade level; this may be a rather linear development of concepts and skills. Examples with young children can be as simple as connecting the set of counting numbers with adding one, and connecting the set of even numbers to adding two. At a different grade level, a procedure for subtracting whole numbers may be incorporated into a procedure for dividing whole numbers; or two-dimensional shapes may be connected to (observed in) three-dimensional shapes. Complex names for the number one may be incorporated into algorithms with fractions.

You also need to make sure your students observe connections *across* grade levels. Can your students explain how what they learned in a previous year is related to what they are learning at present? Likewise, you need to help your students understand how what they are learning now is connected to what they will be learning during succeeding years. Enable your students to continue deepening their understanding of fraction equivalence as they learn about fractions as parts and wholes (using drawings or manipulatives), learn about ratios, and relate those experiences to their study of measurements.

Students make connections as they observe and extend patterns. For example, place values can be expressed as powers of 10, and these values can be extended to both greater and lesser values, the latter introducing decimal place values.

...	10^3	10^2	10^1	10^0	10^{-1}	10^{-2}	...
...	1,000	100	10	1	0.1	0.01	...

A number can be multiplied by the same factor repeatedly to produce what is sometimes called multiplicative reasoning.

$$1 \times 2 = 2 \rightarrow 2 \times 2 = 4 \rightarrow 4 \times 2 = 8 \rightarrow 8 \times 2 = 16 \ldots$$

Moving beyond additive thinking to multiplicative thinking (a challenge for many students) is an example of expanding horizons. Tasks involving similarity can be given to enable students to contrast the results of additive and multiplicative reasoning (Cox and Edwards, 2012).

By making connections, your students learn that mathematics makes sense; they learn how concepts are related and they see patterns and structures among the concepts they are learning and extending. The procedures they learn are also connected as more complex procedures are learned.

Conclusion

Diagnosing is not using a procedure like a machine; a machine is a poor analogy for diagnosis. Instead, diagnosing should be refreshing – like getting water from a deep well – because it permits us to help each student move ahead successfully. Diagnosing can be *deep* like a well; we have to probe deeply to find what the difficulties are.

When you find a pattern that suggests misunderstanding of a concept or a procedure, dig down to find out *why* the student learned the erroneous concept or procedure; then you can provide instruction that focuses on the needs of particular students. In time those students come to understand more big ideas, and connect them to other big ideas and to an increasing number of specific concepts and procedures; mathematical horizons expand greatly. Students go from struggling to soaring.

References

Ashlock, R. B. (2002). *Error Patterns in Computation: Using Error Patterns to Improve Instruction.* 8th edition. Upper Saddle River, NJ: Prentice Hall.

Ashlock, R. B. (2010). *Error Patterns in Computation: Using Error Patterns to Help Each Student Learn.* 10th edition. Boston, MA: Allyn & Bacon.

Bair, S. L. and Mooney, E. S. (2012). "Relatively Speaking," *Mathematics Teaching in the Middle School, 18*, 202–205.

Cox, D. C. and Edwards, M. T. (2012). "Sizing Up the Grinch's Heart," *Mathematics Teaching in the Middle School, 18*, 228–235.

Graeber, A. O. (1992). *Methods and Materials for Preservice Teacher Education in Diagnostic and Prescriptive Teaching of Secondary Mathematics: Project final report* (pp. 4–49). (NSF funded grant). College Park, MD: University of Maryland.

Sherman, H. J., Richardson, L. I. and Yard, G. J. (2009). *Teaching Learners Who Struggle with Mathematics: Systematic Intervention and Remediation.* Upper Saddle River, NJ: Pearson.

16

Preschool children's quantitative knowledge and long-term risk for functional innumeracy

David C. Geary

It has now been well established that children's quantitative competencies when they enter formal schooling predict their relative mathematics achievement throughout schooling (Duncan et al., 2007; Ritchie & Bates, 2013), and their mathematical competencies when they leave school predict their employability and wages throughout adulthood (Bynner, 1997; Rivera-Batiz, 1992). The consequences of poor school-entry quantitative knowledge can thus be life-long. As a result, identifying the school-entry quantitative knowledge that is the foundation for later mathematics learning and the factors that facilitate their acquisition are necessary first steps in the development of interventions to reduce these long-term risks. Fortunately, there has been recent interest in this issue and a spate of studies that have focused on the early quantitative competencies that predict mathematics achievement at school entry or earlier (Jordan, Kaplan, Ramineni, & Locuniak, 2009; Libertus, Halberda, & Feigenson, 2011; Mazzocco, Feigenson, & Halberda, 2011; Star, Libertus, & Brannon, 2013; vanMarle, Chu, & Geary, 2014). I review the results of these studies, but first discuss who is at risk for functional innumeracy in adulthood and consider domain-general contributions to mathematics learning.

Who is at risk?

From a long-term, practical perspective the individuals most at risk are those adults who do not have the quantitative competencies needed to remain gainfully employed in occupations that will pay a living wage. These adults have difficulty solving simple word problems that require whole number arithmetic, fractions, simple algebra, and measurement, and can be considered functionally innumerate (Bynner, 1997; Parsons

& Bynner, 1997; Rivera-Batiz, 1992). Determining the skill deficits that define innumeracy is a moving target, because of recent historical increases in the quantitative skills needed to function well in most white-collar and many blue-collar jobs and to understand many now routine day-to-day tasks (for example, following a medication regiment; Reyna, Nelson, Han, & Dieckmann, 2009). At this time, the best estimate for countries like the United States (U.S.) and the United Kingdom (U.K.) are that 20% to 25% of adults are functionally innumerate (Baer, Kutner, Sabatini, & White, 2009; Hudson, Price, & Gross, 2009). Adolescents in the U.S. and U.K. score about average on international tests that are good measures of numeracy, such as the Programme for International Student Assessment (PISA; http://www.oecd.org/pisa/aboutpisa). It is likely that there are lower proportions of functionally innumerate adults in countries with above average mathematics scores on the PISA and related tests (for example, China, Finland), and a higher proportion in countries with below average scores (for example, Peru).

Regardless of the proportion, children who start school with a poor understanding of Arabic numerals, the magnitudes they represent and the relations among them (for example, $7 = (6 + 1) = (5 + 2) = (4+3)$) score poorly on functional numeracy tests as adolescents (Geary, Hoard, Nugent, & Bailey, 2013). In this six-year longitudinal study, Geary et al. assessed children's understanding of Arabic numerals at the beginning of first grade and their functional numeracy in seventh grade. Based on the above noted findings, risk of innumeracy was defined as scoring below the 25th percentile on a composite numeracy measure. First graders who were 1 standard deviation below average in their understanding of numerals were four times more likely to be functionally innumerate adolescents than were children with average numeral knowledge, controlling for intelligence, working memory, in-class attentive behavior and demographic factors. From second to fifth grade, the at-risk children's numerical abilities improved at the same rate as those of other children, but the initial school-entry gap remained. In other words, children in the bottom quartile in their understanding of basic numerical concepts are at elevated risk for innumeracy as adults, but most of these children readily learn these concepts once they start school but do not catch up. The early identification and remediation of the skills deficits of these at-risk children before they begin formal schooling thus has the potential to yield substantial individual and societal benefits.

Domain-general abilities

Children's learning of formal mathematics is influenced by both domain-general abilities, such as attentional control and intelligence, as well as by specific numerical and arithmetical competencies (Fuchs, Geary, Compton, Fuchs, & Hamlett, 2014; Fuchs, Geary, Compton, Fuchs, Hamlett, & Bryant, 2010; Siegler et al., 2012). With respect to the former, it has been well established that young children's ability to focus and control their attention predicts their long-term success in learning formal mathematics (Blair & Razza, 2007; Bull, Espy, & Wiebe, 2008; Clark, Pritchard, & Woodward, 2010), above and beyond the influence of specific quantitative competencies (for example, Geary, 2011). Attentional control includes the ability to keep irrelevant information from intruding into conscious awareness while processing goal-relevant information, as well as the ability to ignore external distractions (for example, another child) and stay focused and organized in classroom settings. Surprisingly, for school-age children attentional control as measured by standard working memory tests and as rated by classroom teachers make independent contributions to mathematics learning (Fuchs et al., 2006; Geary, Hoard, Nugent, & Bailey, 2012), indicating control of internal distractions (as assessed by working memory tests) and external distractions in classroom settings are to some extent different skills.

General fluid intelligence is particularly important for ease of learning evolution-arily novel symbol systems that are dependent on logical problem solving (Geary, 2005) and thus it is not surprising that intelligence is a strong predictor of mathematics achievement and learning (Deary, Strand, Smith, & Fernandes, 2007). The impor-tance of attentional control and logical problem solving does not mean that children disadvantaged in these areas cannot learn mathematics. However, it does suggest that explicit, direct instruction of core numerical relations may be particularly important for these children, and fortunately these interventions are now available (see Clements et al., 2011; Fuchs et al., 2013; Gersten et al., 2008; Jordan & Dyson, 2014).

What are the core early quantitative skills?

One necessary step toward reducing risk for long-term innumeracy is to identify the kindergarten and preschool precursors of school-entry numeral knowledge. There is, in fact, a long history of psychological research on infants' and young children's early quantitative development (Geary, 1994), but until recently very little of this work was directly tied to individual differences in children's later mathematics achieve-ment. These foundational skills include the learning of number words and Arabic numerals and their cardinal value (for example, that '4' = '••••') and relative magni-tudes (for example, '4' < '5'). It is debated at this time whether children's inherent approximate number system provides the early foundation for learning these core symbolic skills, or whether this inherent system is no longer relevant once children know these foundational skills (De Smedt, Noël, Gilmore, & Ansari, 2013; Geary, 2013; Nieder, 2009; Noël, 2009).

Human infants and, in fact, individuals of many other species are sensitive to relative quantity, that is, they can discriminate smaller from larger collections of items (Feigenson, Dehaene, & Spelke, 2004). This sensitivity is supported by the approxi-mate number system (ANS) that is situated in part of the parietal cortex called the intraparietal sulcus (Dehaene, Piazza, Pinel, & Cohen, 2003). The ANS provides a sense of the approximate quantity of items, or a 'number sense'. These approxima-tions are accurate for smaller quantities and become less precise as quantities increase; another inherent system (object tracking system) can represent the exact quantity of three or four items and may be activated instead of the ANS in some contexts (for a review see Mou & vanMarle, 2014). To get a sense of quantity, children have to attend to the collection of items but because this is a built in, evolved system attention is automatically allocated to numerosity (for example, '•••') and thus effortful controlled attention as described above is not necessary. Figure 16.1 illustrates how this is assessed in young children. These types of items are presented for about two seconds (to prevent counting) and the child determines if there were more circles or boxes in this example (based on Halberda, Mazzocco, & Feigenson, 2008).

The sensitivity of the ANS increases with development and with experience. Generally, the ease of discriminating smaller from larger quantities varies with their ratio. Infants can reliably discriminate sets that differ by a ratio of 2 to 1 (8 vs. 16; Xu & Spelke, 2000), and adults a ratio of 10 to 11 (Halberda & Feigenson, 2008). It has been proposed that developmental delays or deficits in the fidelity of the ANS can result in mathematical learning disabilities or dyscalculia and contribute to individual differences in mathematics achievement more generally (Mazzocco et al., 2011; Piazza et al., 2010). One consequence is that at an age when typically achieving children easily discriminate a set of 5 from a set of 6, for instance, same-age children with an ANS deficit cannot make this discrimination without counting, which in turn could slow their learning of number words and Arabic numerals.

In support of the deficit hypothesis, Piazza et al. (2010) found that the ANS fidelity of 10-year-old children with dyscalculia was about the same as that of typically achieving 5-year-olds matched on intelligence. Starr et al. (2013) found that six-month-olds' ANS sensitivity predicted their ANS sensitivity three years later, indicating some degree of continuity in number sense from infancy to the preschool years. They also found six-month-olds' ANS sensitivity predicted their mathematics achievement three years later, controlling for intelligence. Several other studies have also found a direct relation between fidelity of the ANS and concurrent mathematics achievement (Bonny & Lourenco, 2013; Libertus et al., 2011), but other studies have not found a consistent relation (De Smedt et al., 2013; Iuculano, Tang, Hall, & Butterworth, 2008; Rousselle & Noël, 2007).

As noted, one possibility is that children with a sensitive ANS learn number words, Arabic numerals, and cardinal value more easily than other children, but once they know and understand these basic formal mathematical symbols, the ANS is no longer

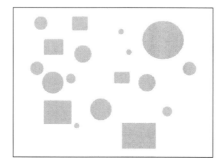

Figure 16.1 An example of the type of task used to assess the sensitivity of the approximate number system for determining relative quantity

important. VanMarle et al. (2014) tested this hypothesis with children in their first of two years of preschool (average age 3 years, 10 months), that is, three years before starting first grade. The children were administered the ANS task along with a set of tasks that assessed their understanding of early mathematical symbols, including number words and Arabic numerals. Children with strong ANS acuity knew more number words, Arabic numerals, and had a better understanding of their cardinal value than did children with poor ANS acuity, controlling for age, sex, parental education, preliteracy skills (alphabet knowledge), attentional control, and intelligence. Performance on the ANS task was also correlated with mathematics achievement at the end of the school year. However, once children's understanding of number words, Arabic numbers, and cardinality was controlled, the ANS no longer predicted mathematics achievement. In other words, having a strong intuitive sense of number appears to help young children learn core early mathematical symbols, but once they know and understand these symbols the ANS is not important, at least for preschool children.

The most critical symbolic knowledge identified in the vanMarle et al. (2014) study was cardinal knowledge. Children's performance on this task (give-a-number; Wynn, 1990) predicted 50% of the variation in mathematics achievement at the end of one year of preschool, and an understanding of cardinality was almost certainly a prerequisite to skilled performance on the number knowledge tasks administered in the Geary et al. (2013) functional numeracy study. Preschool children's understanding of cardinal value, in turn, was related to the acuity of the ANS, as mentioned, as well as intelligence, attentional control, and their alphabet knowledge. The latter suggests that parents who taught their children the alphabet before starting preschool also taught them numbers, which in turn provided these children with a head start in learning cardinality; we do not know exactly what these parents were teaching their children, but it almost certainly included number words and recognition of Arabic numerals.

Overall, children with a strong inherent number sense appear to learn the foundational symbols of mathematics – number words and Arabic numerals – more readily than other children, but once they understand these basics the inherent systems no longer seem to be important (De Smedt et al., 2013; vanMarle et al., 2014). Even though it is inherent, recent studies indicate that the ANS is malleable and becomes more sensitive to quantify with repeated engagement in tasks that require comparison of collections of items and even with formal schooling in mathematics (Halberda, Ly, Wilmer, Naiman, & Germine, 2012; Park & Brannon, 2013), indicating that early interventions may be beneficial even if the ANS is not important for long-term mathematics achievement.

Conclusions

The quantitative competencies that adolescents bring into adulthood will influence their employability and wages, as well as their ability to manage the now routine quantitative activities of daily life (Bynner, 1997; Reyna et al., 2009). Setting the foundation for student learning of employment-related numeracy has to begin before formal schooling, because students who start school behind in basic quantitative skills (for example, understanding of numerals) are at high risk of staying behind throughout schooling and thus into adulthood (Duncan et al., 2007; Geary et al., 2013). A better understanding of the factors that facilitate children's early quantitative learning will be critical to the development of interventions that put at-risk children on the path to numeracy. These mechanisms include both the domain-general abilities of effortful attentional control and intelligence, as well as domain-specific competencies. At this time it appears that one of the most critical, if not the most critical of the latter competencies is cardinality, that is, children's learning of the exact quantities associated with number words and Arabic numerals (Wynn, 1990).

Multiple factors contribute to young children's emerging understanding of cardinality, which provides multiple avenues for early intervention. Before children enter preschool, exposure to number words and Arabic numerals at home is important, and having parents focus children's attention on the numerical features of routine activities is likely to be helpful too (Hannula, Lepola, & Lehtinen, 2010). These could involve asking children "how many toys" for example during their play. On the basis of children's early sensitivity to quantities, keeping these questions to collections of three or fewer items is preferable (Mou & vanMarle, 2014). These types of activities may also improve the acuity of the ANS, as can practice at discriminating larger from smaller collections (Halberda et al., 2012; Park & Brannon, 2013) and this, in turn, may make young children's learning of core mathematical symbols and concepts easier for them. The importance of intelligence and attentional control for children's emerging understanding of cardinality suggests structured, adult-directed activities that explicitly link number word and Arabic numerals to the corresponding collections of items will be helpful for many children.

Acknowledgement

During preparation of this chapter, Geary was supported by grants R37HD045914 from the Eunice Kennedy Shriver National Institute of Child Health & Human Development (NICHD), and DRL-1250359 from the National Science Foundation.

References

Baer, J., Kutner, M., Sabatini, J., & White, S. (2009). *Basic reading skills and the literacy of America's least literate adults: Results from the 2003 National Assessment of Adult Literacy (NAAL) supplemental studies*. Washington, DC: U.S. Department of Education.

Blair, C., & Razza, R. P. (2007). Relating effortful control, executive function, and false belief understanding to emerging math and literacy ability in kindergarten. *Child Development, 78*, 647–663.

Bonny, J. W., & Lourenco, S. F. (2013). The approximate number system and its relation to early math achievement: Evidence from the preschool years. *Journal of Experimental Child Psychology, 114*, 375–388.

Bull, R., Espy, K. A., & Wiebe, S. A. (2008). Short-term memory, working memory, and executive functions in preschoolers: Longitudinal predictors of mathematical achievement at age 7 years. *Developmental Neuropsychology, 33*, 205–228.

Bynner, J. (1997). Basic skills in adolescents' occupational preparation. *Career Development Quarterly, 45*, 305–321.

Clark, C. A. C., Pritchard, V. E., & Woodward, L. J. (2010). Preschool executive functioning abilities predict early mathematics achievement. *Developmental Psychology, 46*, 1176–1191.

Clements, D. H., Sarama, J., Spitler, M. E., Lange, A. A., & Wolfe, C. B. (2011). Mathematics learned by young children in an intervention based on learning trajectories: A large-scale cluster randomized trial. *Journal for Research in Mathematics Education, 42*, 127–166.

De Smedt, B., Noël, M. P., Gilmore, C., & Ansari, D. (2013). How do symbolic and non-symbolic numerical magnitude processing skills relate to individual differences in children's mathematical skills? A review of evidence from brain and behavior. *Trends in Neuroscience and Education, 2*, 48–55.

Deary, I. J., Strand, S., Smith, P., & Fernandes, C. (2007). Intelligence and educational achievement. *Intelligence, 35*, 13–21.

Dehaene, S., Piazza, M., Pinel, P., & Cohen, L. (2003). Three parietal circuits for number processing. *Cognitive Neuropsychology, 20*, 487–506.

Duncan, G. J., Dowsett, C. J., Claessens, A., Magnuson, K., Huston, A. C., Klebanov, P. et al. (2007). School readiness and later achievement. *Developmental Psychology, 43*, 1428–1446.

Feigenson, L., Dehaene, S., & Spelke, E. (2004). Core systems of number. *Trends in Cognitive Sciences, 8*, 307–314.

Fuchs, L. S., Fuchs, D., Compton, D. L., Powell, S. R., Seethaler, P. M., Capizzi, A. M., et al. (2006). The cognitive correlates of third-grade skill in arithmetic, algorithmic computation, and arithmetic word problems. *Journal of Educational Psychology, 98*, 29–43.

Fuchs, L. S., Geary, D. C., Compton, D. L., Fuchs, D., &. Hamlett, C. L. (2014). Sources of individual differences in emerging competence with numeration understanding versus multidigit calculation skill. *Journal of Educational Psychology, 106*, 482–498.

Fuchs, L. S., Geary, D. C., Compton, D. L., Fuchs, D., Hamlett, C. L., & Bryant, J. D. (2010). The contributions of numerosity and domain-general abilities for school readiness. *Child Development, 81*, 1520–1533.

Fuchs, L. S., Geary, D. C., Compton, D. L., Fuchs, D., Schatschneider, C., Hamlett, C. L., et al. (2013). Understanding and promoting at-risk learners' mathematics development in first grade: A randomized control trial. *Journal of Educational Psychology, 105*, 58–77.

Geary, D. C. (1994). *Children's Mathematical Development: Research and practical applications.* Washington, DC: American Psychological Association.

Geary, D. C. (2005). *The Origin of Mind: Evolution of brain, cognition, and general intelligence.* Washington, DC: American Psychological Association.

Geary, D. C. (2011). Cognitive predictors of individual differences in achievement growth in mathematics: A five year longitudinal study. *Developmental Psychology, 47*, 1539–1552.

Geary, D. C. (2013). Early foundations for mathematics learning and their relations to learning disabilities. *Current Directions in Psychological Science, 22*, 23–27.

Geary, D. C., Hoard, M. K., Nugent, L., & Bailey, D. H. (2012). Mathematical cognition deficits in children with learning disabilities and persistent low achievement: A five year prospective study. *Journal of Educational Psychology, 104*, 206–223.

Geary, D.C., Hoard, M. K., Nugent, L., & Bailey, H. D. (2013). Adolescents' functional numeracy is predicted by their school entry number system knowledge. *PLoS ONE, 8*(1), e54651.

Gersten, R., Ferrini-Mundy, J., Benbow, D., Clements, D. H., Loveless, T., Williams, V., et al. (2008). Report of the task group on instructional practices. In National Mathematics Advisory Panel, *Reports of the Task Groups and Subcommittees* (pp. 6-i–6–224). Washington, DC: United States Department of Education.

Halberda, J., & Feigenson, L. (2008). *Developmental change in the acuity of the "number sense": The approximate number system in 3-, 4-, 5-, and 6-year-olds and adults. Developmental Psychology, 44*, 1457–1465.

Halberda, J., Ly, R., Wilmer, J. B., Naiman, D. Q., & Germine, L. (2012). Number sense across the lifespan as revealed by a massive Internet-based sample. *Proceedings of the National Academy of Sciences, 109*, 11116–11120.

Halberda, J., Mazzocco, M., & Feigenson, L. (2008). Individual differences in nonverbal number acuity correlate with maths achievement. *Nature, 455*, 665–669.

Hannula, M. M., Lepola, J., & Lehtinen, E. (2010). Spontaneous focusing on numerosity as a domain-specific predictor of arithmetical skills. *Journal of Experimental Child Psychology, 107*, 394–406.

Hudson, C., Price, D., & Gross, J. (2009). *The Long-term Costs of Numeracy Difficulties*. London, UK: Every Child a Chance Trust.

Iuculano, T., Tang, J., Hall, C. W. B., & Butterworth, B. (2008). Core information processing deficits in developmental dyscalculia and low numeracy. *Developmental Science, 11*, 669–680.

Jordan, N. C., & Dyson, N. (2014). *Number Sense Interventions*. Baltimore, MD: Brookes Publishing.

Jordan, N. C., Kaplan, D., Ramineni, C., & Locuniak, M. N. (2009). Early math matters: Kindergarten number competence and later mathematics outcomes. *Developmental Psychology, 45*, 850–867.

Libertus, M.E., Halberda, J., & Feigenson, L. (2011). Preschool acuity of the Approximate Number System correlates with math abilities. *Developmental Science, 14*, 1292–1300.

Mazzocco, M., Feigenson, L., & Halberda, J. (2011). Preschoolers' precision of the approximate number system predicts later school mathematics performance. *PLoS ONE, 6*(9), e23749.

Mou, Y., & vanMarle, K. (2014). Two core systems of numerical representation in infants. *Developmental Review, 34*, 1–25.

Nieder, A. (2009). Prefrontal cortex and the evolution of symbolic reference. *Current Opinion in Neurobiology, 19*, 99–108.

Noël, M.-P. (2009). Counting on working memory when learning to count and add: A preschool study. *Developmental Psychology, 45*, 1630–1643.

Park, J., & Brannon, E. M. (2013). Training the approximate number system improves math proficiency. *Psychological Science, 24*, 2013–2019.

Parsons, S., & Bynner, J. (1997). Numeracy and employment. *Education and Training, 39*, 43–51.

Piazza, M., Facoetti, A., Trussardi, A. N., Berteletti, I., Conte, S., Lucangeli, D., et al. (2010). Developmental trajectory of number acuity reveals a severe impairment in developmental dyscalculia. *Cognition, 116*, 33–41.

Reyna, V. F., Nelson, W. L., Han, P. K., & Dieckmann, N. F. (2009). How numeracy influences risk comprehension and medical decision making. *Psychological Bulletin, 135*, 943–973.

Ritchie, S. J., & Bates, T. C. (2013). Enduring links from childhood mathematics and reading achievement to adult socioeconomic status. *Psychological Science, 24*, 1301–1308.

Rivera-Batiz, F. (1992). Quantitative literacy and the likelihood of employment among young adults in the United States. *Journal of Human Resources, 27*, 313–328.

Rousselle, L., & Noël, M.-P. (2007). Basic numerical skills in children with mathematical learning disabilities: A comparison of symbolic vs non-symbolic number magnitude processing. *Cognition, 102*, 361–395.

Siegler, R. S., Duncan, G. J., Davis-Kean, P. E., Duckworth, K., Claessens, A., Engel, M., et al. (2012). Early predictors of high school mathematics achievement. *Psychological Science, 23*, 691–697.

Starr, A., Libertus, M. E., & Brannon, E. M. (2013). Number sense in infancy predicts mathematical abilities in childhood. *Proceedings of the National Academy of Sciences USA*.

VanMarle, K., Chu, K., Li, Y., & Geary, D. C. (2014). Acuity of the approximate number system and preschoolers' quantitative development. *Developmental Science, 17*, 492–505.

Wynn, K. (1990). Children's understanding of counting. *Cognition, 36*, 155–193.

Xu, F., & Spelke, E. S. (2000). Large number discrimination in 6-month-old infants. *Cognition, 74*, B1–B11.

Learning disabilities

Mathematics characteristics and instructional exemplars

Diane Pedrotty Bryant, Brian R. Bryant, Mikyung Shin, and Kathleen Hughes Pfannenstiel

Introduction

Increasingly, more attention is focusing on students who demonstrate challenges learning mathematics concepts and skills, which are taught across the grade levels (Bryant et al., 2011; L. Fuchs et al., 2005; Jordan, Kaplan, Ramineni, and Locuniak, 2009). Beginning as early as preschool, parents, educators, and researchers are recognizing that some students seem perplexed when learning simple mathematics ideas that many take for granted. For example, some young children have difficulty learning number names, counting, and recognizing how many items are in a group. For some of these students, their mathematics difficulties persist and are pervasive as they proceed through the school years and into their post-secondary education and adulthood. These mathematics difficulties can be manifested in problems with learning increasingly complex mathematics concepts and procedures in domain areas such as number and operations, fractions, algebraic thinking, measurement and data, geometry, ratios and proportional relationships, expressions and equations, algebra, functions, and statistics and probability, to name a few (Common Core State Standards for Mathematics [CCSSM]; Council of Chief State School Officers and National Governors' Association [CCSSO and NGA], 2010). In fact, a group of students is eventually diagnosed as having a learning disability (LD) with a disorder in mathematics, or mathematics learning disabilities (MLD) due in part to the persistent, chronic nature of their learning difficulties.

An MLD is characterized by an unexpected learning problem after a classroom teacher or other trained professional (e.g., mathematics specialist) has provided the student with scientifically or evidence-based instruction as part of the core curriculum and more intensive intervention for a period of time (i.e., often 10–12 weeks or an academic year) (see http://www2.ed.gov/nclb for more information about scientifically based research) and a battery of psychological and achievement measures have been administered to document the presence of the LD with a disorder in mathematics. Evidence-based instruction refers to practices that are supported by sound research and that are implemented with adherence to the intended procedures as designated by the authors of the practices. The time period refers to the duration of time that is needed to help the student learn the concepts and procedures, which have been identified as problematic. Typically, students with an MLD have made insufficient school progress in mathematics comparable to their peer group despite the implementation of evidence-based instructional practices over time. Unfortunately, the gap between the mathematics performance of students with an MLD compared to their peer group continues to widen as students fall further behind, lacking mastery of earlier important foundational and conceptual knowledge and understanding (Aunola, Leskinen, Lerkkanen, and Nurmi, 2004; National Mathematics Advisory Panel [NMAP], 2008).

Prevalence studies have shown that about 7% of the school-aged population has MLD (Barbaresi, Katusic, Colligan, Weave, and Jacobsen, 2005; Geary, 2011; Shalev, Manor, and Gross-Tsur, 2005); further, about 5% to 10% of the school-aged population may be classified as having persistent low achievement in mathematics (Berch and Mazzocco, 2007; Geary, 2011; Geary, Hoard, Byrd-Craven, Nugent, and Numtee, 2007). Taken together, a significant number of children and adolescents demonstrate poor mathematics achievement (Swanson, 2006) that is persistent and pervasive with potentially long-term consequences in mathematic performance (B. Bryant et al., 2008; Geary, 2004; Murphy, Mazzocco, Hanich, and Early, 2007), eligibility for more advanced college-readiness mathematics courses, and competitive employment in the workforce (D. Bryant, Pfannenstiel, Bryant, Hunt, and Shin, 2014; Jordan, Glutting, and Ramineni, 2009). Moreover, with changed expectations relative to the implementation of the CCSSM (CCSSO and NGA, 2010), it is likely that even more students will struggle to meet the demands of increased rigour, which has implications for stakeholders, such as practitioners and policymakers and, more importantly, students (EPE Research Center, 2013). It is important to better understand the nature of mathematics instruction and MLD in order for researchers to develop and test interventions that can address the struggles exhibited in learning the mathematics curriculum. Thus, the purpose of this chapter is to (a) describe briefly mathematical domains for instruction, (b) provide an overview of the mathematics behaviors that are characteristic of students with MLD, (c) discuss predictors of mathematics achievement in later grades, and (d) describe exemplars of interventions that can be implemented to improve the mathematics performance of students with MLD.

Mathematical domains

The purpose of this section is to provide an overview of the attention that has been devoted to studying the mathematics performance of students with MLD or mathematics difficulties on the mathematical domains identified in the CCSSM (2010).

Research on the mathematics performance of students with MLD in the CCSSM domains (e.g., number and operations in base ten, operations and algebraic thinking, measurement and data, geometry, fractions, ratios and proportional relationships, the number system, expressions and equations, statistics and probability, functions, algebra) has largely been limited in both the specific domains and across age groups. For example, findings from a synthesis of middle school mathematics intervention studies (2000–2008) showed that the majority of studies have focused on problem solving involving computation and fractions (Kim et al., 2009). Additionally, elementary grades students who are not identified as having an MLD but, rather, are having mathematics difficulties in the areas of number and operations, have been the focus of studies that sought to examine the effects of mathematics interventions on their mathematics performance (e.g., D. Bryant et al., 2008a; D. Bryant et al., 2011; Doabler et al., in press; Fuchs et al., 2005).

Other domains such as number and operations-fractions (Hecht, Vagi, and Torgesen, 2007; Mazzocco and Devlin, 2008) and algebra involving older students with MLD have been the focus of fewer studies. Moreover, studies on the effects of word problem-solving interventions have been implemented not only with elementary (e.g., Jitendra et al., 2009; Swanson, Jerman, and Zheng, 2008) but also with secondary level students (van Garderen, Scheuermann, and Jackson, 2012). Overall findings have shown that students with MLD perform less well than age- or grade-matched students who do not have difficulties on mathematical calculation (e.g., number facts) and arithmetic strategies, word problem-solving, and number sense activities (D. Bryant, Bryant, and Hammill, 2000; D. Bryant, Smith, and Bryant, 2008b; Mazzocco and Devlin, 2008; Shin and Bryant, 2013).

Mathematical learning characteristics

In this section, a brief review of findings from several studies is presented on the mathematical learning characteristics of students with MLD. Bryant, Bryant, and Hammill (2000) examined the mathematics characteristic behaviors of students who ranged in age from 8 years 0 months to 18 years 11 months (M = 11 years 10 months) who were diagnosed by their school districts as having LD. Their teachers were identified from a commercial mailing list of 56,258 individuals who worked with students with LD nationwide; through random selection an initial sample of 15,000 was identified with 391 professionals (n = 361 special education teachers, n = 8 general education teachers, and n = 22 other) agreeing to participate in the study. Of the 1,724 students who were identified for the study, their teachers rated 870 (50%) as having mathematics weaknesses (MW; MLD); 854 students were viewed as not having mathematics weaknesses (MN). The teachers rated these students on a scale comprised of a variety of mathematics behaviors, which were gleaned from the theoretical and research literature in LD and neuropsychology with a focus on the mathematics characteristic behaviors and LD in mathematics. Sources included research articles, rating inventories, diagnostic tests, and theoretical papers. The scale was comprised of 33 items, which were the result of a review of an expert panel of

36 professionals who held various roles (e.g., professor, diagnosticians) in the field of LD. These professionals rated the initial pool of items as minimally, somewhat, or considerably suggestive of an LD in mathematics. Findings from empirical studies confirmed the validity of the characteristic mathematics behaviors and the scale's reliability. Then, teachers were asked to rate for each of their identified students the degree to which the characteristic mathematics behaviors were exhibited (ratings of 1–3 = frequently; 4–6 = sometimes, 7–9 = rarely) by students with MW and MN. Table 17.1 contains the means and standard deviations of the ratings for each of the mathematics characteristic behaviors in order of frequency of occurrence for students with MW and MN, the mean difference between the two groups, and the *t* value ($p < .05$).

Table 17.1 shows that on the word problems item, the teachers rated the MW group in the low range of performance (mean = 2.3) meaning the students frequently exhibited difficulties with this area; whereas, the rating for the MN fell in the "sometimes" category (mean = 4.1). Shin and Bryant 2013) found similar findings in their synthesis of the mathematical performance of students with MLD, that is, these students had significantly poorer problem-solving abilities compared to their age- or grade-matched peers with MN. At the elementary level, the poor performance results occurred on both complex story problems and real-world problems compared to students with NLD-grade (L. Fuchs and Fuchs, 2003). At the secondary level, students with NLD-grade significantly outperformed students with MLD on applying the use of a cognitive strategy for solving word problems (Montague, Enders, and Dietz, 2011). More recently, in a study on the use of diagrams to solve word problems by students with LD, gifted students, and typically achieving students (N = 95 for all three groups) in fourth through seventh grades, van Garderen, Scheuermann, and Jackson (2012) found that students with LD created fewer well-developed diagrammatic tools and used them in an inefficient manner as compared to their peers. Van Garderen et al. indicated that the quality of the diagrams was influenced by insufficient mathematics content knowledge. Thus, in both the elementary and secondary grades, students with MLD struggle with solving mathematics word problems; this is a persistent characteristic behavior that is sufficiently significant to be a type of MLD for the identification of learning disabilities (Mathematics Problem Solving; Individuals with Disabilities Education Improvement Act [IDEA], 2004).

IDEA (2004) also includes mathematics calculations as another type of MLD. The findings from D. Bryant et al. (2000) supported mathematics calculations as a problem area for students with MW. The mathematics characteristic behaviors, "has difficulty with multi-step problems" and "cannot recall number facts automatically," revealed mean ratings of 2.6 and 3.9, respectively, which fell in the "frequently" category, compared to students with MN whose ratings were a mean of 5.0 and 6.3, respectively. Shin and Bryant's (2013) synthesis findings showed that for mathematical calculations, students with MLD performed comparable to younger students with no learning disabilities (NLD) (Keeler and Swanson, 2001; Swanson, 1993). Additionally, when compared to same-age or same-grade NLD, at the elementary and secondary levels, students with MLD scored significantly

Table 11.1 Behavior comparisons across groups

Behavior	MW		MN		M diff	df	t_1
	M	SD	M	SD			
Has difficulty with word problems	2.3	1.6	4.1	2.5	1.7	1, 1266	17.0
Has difficulty with multi-step problems	2.6	1.8	5.0	2.5	2.4	1, 1346	22.6
Has difficulty with the language of math	3.1	2.0	5.2	2.4	1.9	1, 1448	18.8
Fails to verify answers and settles for first answer	3.2	2.1	5.3	2.6	2.1	1, 1472	17.9
Cannot recall number facts automatically (i.e., unable to perform simple calculations)	3.9	2.4	6.3	2.3	2.4	1, 1583	20.0
Takes a long time to complete calculations	4.0	2.3	6.3	2.3	2.3	1, 1575	19.4
Makes "borrowing" (i.e., regrouping, renaming) errors	4.1	2.2	6.7	2.1	2.6	1, 1574	22.8
Counts on fingers	4.2	2.6	6.4	2.4	2.2	1, 1584	17.4
Reaches "unreasonable" answers	4.3	2.1	6.5	2.0	2.2	1, 1576	21.3
Misspells number words (writes 13 as threeteen, 20 as twoty)	4.5	2.7	5.3	2.8	0.8	1, 1531	6.1
Calculates poorly when the order of digit presentation is altered	4.6	2.3	6.8	2.0	2.2	1, 1579	20.4
Orders and spaces numbers inaccurately in multiplication and division	4.6	2.4	6.8	2.1	2.2	1, 1556	19.8
Misaligns vertical numbers in columns	4.6	2.2	6.5	2.1	1.9	1, 1578	17.5
Disregards decimals	4.7	2.4	6.8	2.1	2.1	1, 1548	19.3
Fails to carry (i.e., regroup) numbers when appropriate	4.7	2.3	6.9	2.0	2.2	1, 1579	19.5
Fails to read accurately the correct value of multidigit numbers because of their order and spacing	4.8	2.4	7.0	2.0	2.2	1, 1579	19.5
Jumps impulsively into arithmetic operations	4.9	2.5	6.5	2.2	1.6	1, 1583	13.6
Misplaces digits in multidigit numbers	4.9	2.4	6.9	2.1	2.0	1, 1572	18.4
Misaligns horizontal numbers in large numbers	4.9	2.5	6.9	2.1	2.0	1, 1568	17.4
Skips rows or columns when calculating (i.e., loses his or her place)	5.0	2.4	6.9	2.0	1.9	1, 1575	17.2
Makes errors when reading Arabic numbers aloud	5.1	2.4	6.7	2.2	1.6	1, 1560	14.2
Experiences difficulties in the spatial arrangement of numbers	5.2	2.3	6.9	2.0	1.7	1, 1571	16.0
Does not follow spatial commands or directions (e.g., "place the triangle above the cross")	5.4	2.3	6.9	2.0	1.5	1, 1574	14.0
Misreads computational signs (e.g., reads + as −)	5.4	2.3	7.2	1.9	1.8	1, 1552	16.3
Reverses numbers in problems	5.4	2.4	6.9	2.0	1.5	1, 1571	13.7
Has difficulty learning to tell time	5.6	2.6	7.2	2.1	1.6	1, 1550	13.5
Does not remember number words or digits	5.7	2.4	7.1	2.0	1.4	1, 1557	12.4
Writes numbers illegibly	5.8	2.5	6.8	2.3	1.0	1, 1583	7.4
Starts the calculation from the wrong place	5.9	2.4	7.6	1.6	1.7	1, 1461	16.8
Cannot copy numbers accurately	6.0	2.3	7.2	1.9	1.2	1, 1568	11.0
Exhibits left–right disorientation of numbers	6.1	2.4	7.5	1.7	1.4	1, 1508	13.0
Omits digits on left or right side of a number	6.2	2.4	7.7	1.6	1.5	1, 1433	14.2
Does not recognize operator signs (e.g., +, −)	6.8	2.3	7.8	1.6	1.0	1, 1486	10.8

Note: Behaviors are ranked in order of frequency of occurrence for the MW group. MW = Math weakness. MN = Math nonweakness. M diff = mean difference between groups. $t_1 = t$ value ($p < .05$); all values met Bonferroni adjustment criterion ($p < .0015$).
Diane Pedrotty Bryant, Brian R. Bryant, and Donald D. Hammill, Characteristics behaviors of students with LD who have teacher-identified math weaknesses, p. 173,
Copyright 2000 Hammill Institute on Disabilities
Reprinted by permission of SAGE publications.

lower than their peers without LD on standardized mathematics tests (e.g., *Wechsler Individual Achievement Test-Second Edition-Abbreviated* Numerical Operations; *Woodcock-Johnson Psycho-Educational Battery-Revised* Calculations); thus, the poorer performance on calculations, which were evident in the elementary grades persisted into the middle grades. These findings are consistent with those of Swanson and Jerman (2006) who concluded that MLD are persistent across ages; these findings are disturbing because of the need to be fluent with foundation skills, such as calculations, in preparation for more advanced mathematics coursework such as algebra.

Prediction of MLD

In addition to identifying weaknesses in mathematics behaviors exhibited by students with MLD, researchers are interested in identifying the predictive variables of persistent mathematics difficulties, which often times result in the identification of MLD (L. Fuchs et al., 2005; Jordan, Hanich, and Kaplan, 2003). Overall, findings provide strong evidence for early number competence, that is, understanding number operations and relationships, solving word problems, and using efficient counting and calculation strategies to solve arithmetic combinations (i.e., number facts) (Jordan, Kaplan, Ramineni, and Locuniak, 2009) as a significant predictor of later mathematics outcomes. For example, Roberts and Bryant (2011) found in their work on early mathematics achievement trajectories for English-language learners and native English speakers, that mathematics school readiness is a significant factor in explaining future achievement differences across the range of mathematics skills. This finding is supported in the longitudinal work of Geary et al. (2009) with kindergarten then first-grade students, confirming the significance of early number sense for mathematics achievement. Moreover, in yet another longitudinal study, Jordan, Glutting, and Ramineni (2009) found for students in kindergarten (n = 378) to third grade (n = 196), a strong relationship between number competence and mathematics achievement, leading the authors to conclude that number sense is a powerful predictor of mathematics outcomes in later years.

Finally, Bryant et al. (2000) sought to determine those items that best predicted the inclusion in the MW group in their study on mathematics characteristics behaviors. A forward inclusion stepwise regression procedure was employed (see Bryant et al. (2000) for an explanation of procedures) resulting in nine mathematics behaviors that were the strongest predictors of MW. Table 17.2 shows a summary of these findings; interestingly, a little less than 31% of the variance was accounted for with two behaviors: "has difficulty with multi-step problems" and " makes 'borrowing' [regrouping] errors." In thinking about these results, both behaviors at first glance could be viewed as indicative of difficulties with the procedural knowledge that is necessary to perform the steps to solve problems. Rittle-Johnson, Siegler, and Alibali (2001) described procedural knowledge as "the ability to execute action sequences to solve problems" (p. 346). Relatedly, Shin and Bryant (2013) in their synthesis work revealed studies that showed students with MLD exhibiting computational errors, basic fact errors, use of faulty operation, difficulties with borrowing, and algorithmic errors of following steps to solve the problems.

Additionally, the two mathematics behaviors that were the most predictive of inclusion in the MW group should also be examined in terms of conceptual knowledge, which refers to "implicit or explicit understanding of the principles that govern a domain and of the interrelations between units of knowledge in a domain" (Rittle-Johnson et al., 2001, pp. 346–347).

Because mathematics involves the use of both procedural and conceptual knowledge in an iterative manner for solving problems, indicators of MLD/MW should be examined from both perspectives. Thus, for example, conceptually, students must understand place value for regrouping purposes; otherwise, the task of regrouping can be reduced to solution "tricks" or shortcuts that diminish the conceptual understanding of working with place value. Also, difficulties with multi-step problems could interfere with a number of mathematical domains such as solving algebraic equations, simplifying fractions, and computing ratios.

Together, these findings corroborate the Bryant et al. (2000) results (i.e., difficulties with solving multi-step problems and conducting arithmetic calculations with regrouping), suggesting issues related to procedural and conceptual knowledge should be strongly considered along with those mathematics behaviors that teachers rated as occurring "frequently" (i.e., solving word problems and retrieving number facts) when examining the mathematics performance of students who are struggling. Additionally, utilizing evidence-based practices for addressing these prominent mathematics characteristic behaviors should be a focus for educators and researchers, alike. Fortunately, there is a solid body of evidence regarding instructional design and delivery for students with LD that can be utilized to increase the likelihood of improved mathematics performance.

Table 17.2 Summary of stepwise regression procedure

Variable entered	Multiple r	r^2	Increase in r^2
Has difficulty with multi-step problems	.508	.258	.258
Makes "borrowing" (i.e., regrouping, renaming) errors	.555	.308	.050
Cannot recall number facts automatically (i.e., unable to perform simple calculations)	.564	.318	.010
Misspells number words (writes 13 as threeteen, 20 as twoty)	.575	.330	.012
Reaches "unreasonable" answers	.581	.337	.007
Calculates poorly when the order of digit presentation is altered	.584	.341	.004
Cannot copy numbers accurately	.589	.346	.005
Orders and spaces numbers inaccurately in multiplication and division	.592	.350	.004
Does not remember number words or digits	.595	.354	.004

Note: Diane Pedrotty Bryant, Brian R. Bryant, and Donald D. Hammill, Characteristics behaviors of students with LD who have teacher-identified math weaknesses, p. 174, Copyright 2000 Hammill Institute on Disabilities
Reprinted by permission of SAGE publications.

Instructional exemplars

In this section, we describe exemplars of evidence-based mathematics practices (Milgram, 2007; National Council of Teachers of Mathematics [NCTM] 2006; NMAP, 2008; Wu, 2006) and instructional procedures that are necessary for teaching struggling students (Swanson, Hoskyn, and Lee, 1999). These practices should be incorporated into intervention instruction to address the mathematics difficulties exhibited by students with MLD or MW. Additionally, the What Works Clearinghouse (WWC) offers practice guides that include the evidence for specific practices and recommendations for effective instruction on topics such as mathematical problem solving, fractions, and response to intervention and teaching mathematics at the elementary and secondary levels (http://ies.ed.gov/ncee/wwc/publications).

We know that students with MLD exhibit difficulties because of an inadequate development of the foundational knowledge and understanding of whole and rational numbers, relationships among the four operations, arithmetic calculations, and problem-solving strategies (D. Bryant et al., 2011; Geary et al., 2009; Jordan, Kaplan, Ramineni, and Locuniak, 2009; NMAP, 2008). We also know that difficulties exhibited in mathematics are persistent and pervasive, affecting mathematics achievement in advanced mathematics (Cawley and Parmar, 1992; Deshler et al., 2004); thus, teachers should make the connection of instructional concepts to more advanced mathematics within and across grades to help students understand why they are learning specific concepts in each grade (Milgram, 2007; NMAP, 2008; Wu, 2006). Evidence-based instructional exemplars should be incorporated into mathematics interventions for students with MLD to follow.

Explicit, systematic mathematics practices

Evidence-based mathematics interventions are comprised of best practices that embrace both the special and mathematic education fields. These practices ensure that explicit, systematic instruction is coupled with mathematically precise practices that are intended to promote the development of conceptual and procedural knowledge.

The use of explicit, systematic instruction is well documented for teaching mathematical concepts and skills (Butler, Miller, Crehan, Babbitt, and Pierce, 2003; Gersten et al., 2009) and problem solving (Jitendra et al., 2009; Montague et al., 2011), and research studies have shown strong evidence for the use of these procedures for mathematics interventions (D. Bryant et al., 2011; Fuchs et al., 2005; Gersten et al., 2009; Swanson et al., 1999). Examples of practices that provide explicit and systematic instruction include:

- Providing cumulative review of previous concepts.
- Modeling or demonstrating how to solve problems.
- "Thinking aloud" the procedures for solving problems or using cognitive strategies.

- Engaging students in guided practice with sufficient opportunities to practice new skills and concepts.
- Providing error correction procedures to correct mistakes and mathematical misunderstandings.

Equally important are mathematics practices that are crucial for all students as well as those students with MLD. For example, intervention materials should include opportunities for students to work with multiple representations (e.g., manipulatives, number lines, arrays, models) to help students develop and build conceptual knowledge of concepts, operations, and properties (e.g., commutative property). Results from studies confirm the use of multiple representations to help students better understand mathematical concepts (Clements and Sarama, 2009; Gersten et al., 2009). Other mathematics practices for teachers to incorporate include:

- Using the precise mathematical definitions for the content being taught; definitions should be developmentally appropriate while retaining the intended meaning of the concepts (Milgram, 2005; Wu, 2005, 2006).
- Providing a mathematical rationale that underlies algorithms, explaining why some algorithms are not generalizable, and applying logical reasoning to solve problems (Askey, 1999; Wu, 2006).
- Translating between verbal and symbolic statements (Wu, 2005).
- Applying information to real-world problem sets (Askey, 1999).

Concrete–semi-concrete–abstract (CSA) teaching sequence

CSA is another evidence-based exemplar for the delivering of instruction in a mathematics intervention (Miller and Mercer, 1993) and fractions (Butler et al., 2003) to students with mathematics difficulties. The teaching sequence includes three steps: Step 1 is the Concrete Representation, which involves the use of manipulatives to represent concepts. Step 2 is the Semi-concrete Representation, where tally marks or pictures are used to show the concept. Finally, Step 3 is the Abstract Representation, which involves the use of symbols. Certainly, the types of representations can be used in the same lessons to model the mathematics.

Progress monitoring

Typically, intervention begins after students have been given a test to determine (a) their current level of functioning, and (b) whether they qualify for the intervention. Once the decision is made that students qualify for an intervention, another decision is made: How well does the student have to perform on a similar test during or at the end of the intervention to determine whether they can then exit the intervention? Most often, that exit point is called a "benchmark," and is set at a score achieved by typical students who did not qualify for the intervention. Often the benchmark is a score that corresponds to the low end of average, the

25th percentile, for example. Note: Many experts agree that the normal range of performance is between the 25th and 75th percentiles, thus, the 25th percentile would be considered the low end of average.

Consider Sean, as an example. Sean and all his classmates were given a 40-item math test at the beginning of the year. The cutoff, or the benchmark score for qualifying for the intervention, was set at a raw score (that is, the number of items answered correctly) of 17, which, in this scenario, corresponds to the 25th percentile. Sean got 12 items correct, so he scored below the cutoff score of 17 and qualified for the intervention. In the winter, a similar test was given again to all students. Because most students score higher as the year progresses, the 25th percentile corresponded to 26 points, so Sean would have to answer 26 items correctly to reach the benchmark. Once he reaches the benchmark he qualifies for exiting the intervention. Progress monitoring of student's mathematics performance is critical to determine the level of responding to intensive interventions and the resulting data inform further instructional decision-making.

Conclusions

As discussed in this chapter, research findings have identified specific mathematics characteristic behaviors of students with MLD (MW). These behaviors or difficulties are persistent and pervasive throughout the school years and into adulthood. Researchers have also identified difficulties manifested in the primary grades that are reliably predictive of later mathematics problems including MLD. Students with MLD must receive intensive interventions that are grounded in evidence-based practices from both special and mathematics education fields to ensure appropriately mathematically structured interventions. Educators will do well to be alert to those mathematics behaviors that are exhibited by struggling students and be prepared to offer intensive interventions that are specifically designed to promote positive mathematics outcomes.

References

Askey, R. (Fall, 1999). Knowing and teaching elementary mathematics. *American Educator/ American Federation of Teachers*, 1–8.

Aunola, K., Leskinen, E., Lerkkanen, M.-K. and Nurmi, J.E. (2004). Developmental dynamics of math performance from preschool to grade 2. *Journal of Educational Psychology, 96*(4), 699–713.

Barbaresi, W. J., Katusic, S. K., Colligan, R. C., Weaver, A. L. and Jacobsen, S. J. (2005). Math learning disorder: Incidence in a population-based birth cohort, 1976–82. *Ambulatory Pediatrics, 5*(5), 281–289.

Berch, D. B. and Mazzocco, M. M. M. (Eds.) (2007). *Why is Math so Hard for Some Children? The nature and origins of mathematical learning difficulties and disabilities*. Baltimore, MD: Paul H. Brookes Publishing Co.

Bryant, B. R., Bryant, D. P., Kethley, C., Kim, S., Pool, C. and Seo, Y. (2008). Preventing mathematics difficulties in the primary grades: The critical features of instruction in textbooks as part of the equation. Special series, *Learning Disability Quarterly, 31*(1), 21–35.

Bryant, D. P., Bryant, B. R., Gersten, R., Scammacca, N., Funk, C., Winter, A., Shih, M. and Pool, C. (2008a). The effects of Tier 2 intervention on first-grade mathematics performance. *Learning Disability Quarterly, 31*(2), 47–63.

Bryant, D. P., Bryant, B. R. and Hammill, D. D. (2000). Characteristic behaviours of students with learning disabilities who have teacher-identified math weaknesses. *Journal of Learning Disabilities, 33*(2), 168–177, 199.

Bryant, D. P., Bryant, B. R., Roberts, G., Vaughn, S., Hughes, K., Porterfield, J. and Gersten, R. (2011). Effects of an early numeracy intervention on the performance of first-grade students with mathematics difficulties. *Exceptional Children, 78*(1), 7–23.

Bryant, D. P., Pfannenstiel, K. H., Bryant, B. R., Hunt, J. and Shin, M. (2014). Tailoring interventions for students with mathematics difficulties. In J. T. Mascolo, D. P. Flanagan and V. C. Alfonso (Eds.), *Essentials of Planning, Selecting, and Tailoring Interventions for the Unique Learner* (pp. 178–203). Hoboken, NJ: Wiley.

Bryant, D. P., Smith, D. D. and Bryant, B. R. (2008b). *Teaching Students with Special Needs in Inclusive Classrooms*. Boston, MA: Allyn and Bacon.

Butler, F. M., Miller, S. P., Crehan, K., Babbitt, B. and Pierce, T. (2003). Fraction instruction for students with mathematics disabilities: Comparing two teaching sequences. *Learning Disabilities Research and Practice, 18*(2), 99–111.

Cawley, J. F. and Parmar, R. S. (1992). Arithmetic programming for students with disabilities: An alternative. *Remedial and Special Education, 13*(3), 6–18.

Clements, D.H. and Sarama, J. (2009). *Learning and Teaching Early Math: The learning trajectories approach*. New York: Routledge.

Council of Chief State School Officers and National Governors' Association. (June, 2010). *Common Core State Standards for Mathematics*. Common Core State Standards Initiative. Retrieved from http://www.corestandards.org/assets/CCSSI_Math%20Standards.pdf.

Deshler, D. D., Lenz, B. K., Bulgren, J., Schumaker, J. B., Davis, B., Grossen, B. and Marquis, J. (2004). Adolescents with disabilities in high school settings: Student characteristics and setting dynamics. *Learning Disabilities Contemporary Journal, 1*(2), 30–48.

Doabler, C., Clarke, B., Fien, H., Baker, S., Kosty, D., and Strand Cary, M. (2014). The science behind curriculum development and evaluation: Taking a design science approach in the production of a Tier 2 mathematics curriculum. *Learning Disability Quarterly, 38*(1), 1–15.

EPE Research Center. (2013). *Findings From a National Survey of Teacher Perspectives on the Common Core*. Bethesda, MD: Editorial Projects in Education.

Fuchs, L. S., Compton, D. L., Fuchs, D., Paulsen, K., Bryant, J. D. and Hamlett, C. L. (2005). The prevention, identification, and cognitive determinants of math difficulty. *Journal of Educational Psychology, 97*, 493–513.

Fuchs, L. S. and Fuchs, D. (2003). Enhancing the mathematical problem solving of students with mathematics disabilities. In H. L. Swanson, K. R. Harris and S. E. Graham (Eds.), *Handbook on Learning Disabilities* (pp. 306–322). New York: Guilford.

Geary, D. C. (2004). Mathematics and learning disabilities. *Journal of Learning Disabilities, 37*, 4–15.

Geary, D. C. (2011). Consequences, characteristics, and causes of mathematical learning disabilities and persistent low achievement in mathematics. *Journal of Developmental and Behavioural Pediatrics, 33*(30), 250–263.

Geary, D. C., Bailey, D. H., Littlefield, A., Wood, P., Hoard, M. K. and Nugent, L. (2009). First-grade predictors of mathematical learning disability: A latent class trajectory analysis. *Cognitive Development, 24*, 411–429.

Geary, D. C., Hoard, M. K., Byrd-Craven, J., Nugent, L. and Numtee, C. (2007). Cognitive mechanisms underlying achievement deficits in children with mathematical learning disability. *Child Development, 78*, 1343–1359.

Gersten, R., Beckmann, S., Clarke, B., Foegen, A., Marsh, L., Star, J. R. and Witzel, B. (2009). *Assisting students struggling with mathematics: Response to Intervention (RtI) for elementary and middle schools* (NCEE 2009–4060). Washington, DC: National Center for Education Evaluation and Regional Assistance, Institute of Education Sciences, U.S. Department of Education. Retrieved from http://ies.ed.gov/ncee/wwc/publications/practiceguides.

Hecht, S., Vagi, K. J. and Torgesen, J. K. (2007). Fraction skills and proportional reasoning. In D. B. Berch and M. M. M. Mazzocco (Eds.), *Why is Math So Hard for Some Children?* (pp. 121–132). Baltimore, MD: Paul H. Brookes Publishing Co.

Individuals with Disabilities Education Improvement Act (IDEA) of 2004, PL 108–446, 20 U.S.C. 1400 *et seq.*

Jitendra, A. K., Star, J., Starosta, K., Leh, J., Sood, S., Caskie, G., et al. (2009). Improving students' learning of ratio and proportion problem solving: The role of schema-based instruction. *Contemporary Educational Psychology, 34*(9), 250–264.

Jordan, N. C., Glutting, J. and Ramineni, C. (2009). The importance of number sense to mathematics achievement in first and third grades. *Learning and Individual Differences*. Online first.

Jordan, N. C., Hanich, L. B. and Kaplan, D. (2003). Arithmetic fact mastery in young children: A longitudinal investigation. *Journal of Experimental Child Psychology, 85*, 103–119.

Jordan, N. C., Kaplan, D., Ramineni, C. and Locuniak, M. N. (2009). Early math matters: Kindergarten number competence and later mathematics outcomes. *Developmental Psychology, 45*(3), 850–867.

Keeler, M. L. and Swanson, H. L. (2001). Does strategy knowledge influence working memory in children with mathematical disabilities? *Journal of Learning Disabilities, 34*(5), 418–434.

Kim, S. A., Hughes, K., Porterfield, J., Bryant, D. P. and Bryant, B. R. (2009, February). *A synthesis of middle school mathematics intervention research for students with learning disabilities*. Poster session presented at the annual meeting of the Pacific Coast Research Conference, Coronado, CA.

Mazzocco, M. M. and Devlin, K. T. (2008). Parts and "holes": Gaps in rational number sense among children with vs. without mathematical learning disabilities. *Developmental Science, 11*(5), 681–691.

Milgram, R. J. (2005). What is math proficiency? Retrieved September 10, 2012 from ftp://171.64.38.20/pub/papers/milgram/milgram-msri.pdf.

Milgram, R. J. (2007). What is mathematical proficiency? In A. H. Schoenfeld (Ed.), *Assessing Mathematical Proficiency* (pp. 31–58). Cambridge, UK: Cambridge.

Miller, S. P. and Mercer, C. D. (1993). Mnemonics: Enhancing the math performance of students with learning difficulties. *Intervention in School and Clinic, 29*, 78–82.

Montague, M., Enders, C. and Dietz, S. (2011). Effects of cognitive strategy instruction on math problem solving of middle school students with learning disabilities. *Learning Disability Quarterly, 34*(4), 262–272.

Murphy, M. M., Mazzocco, M. M. M., Hanich, L. B. and Early, M. C. (2007). Cognitive characteristics of children with mathematics learning disability (MLD) vary as a function of the cutoff criterion used to define MLD. *Journal of Learning Disabilities, 40*, 458–478.

National Council of Teachers of Mathematics (2006). *Curriculum Focal Points for Prekindergarten through Grade 8 Mathematics: A quest for coherence*. Reston, VA: Author.

National Governors Association Center for Best Practices, Council of Chief State School Officers. (2010). Common *Core State Standards* for Mathematics. Washington, DC: National Governors Association Center for Best Practices, Council of Chief State School Officers. Retrieved from http://www.corestandards.org/assets/CCSSI_Math%20Standards.pdf

National Mathematics Advisory Panel. (2008). *Foundations for Success: The final report of the National Mathematics Advisory Panel*. Washington, DC: U.S. Department of Education.

Rittle-Johnson, B., Siegler, R. S. and Alibali, M. W. (2001). Developing conceptual understanding and procedural skill in mathematics: An iterative process. *Journal of Educational Psychology, 93*(2), 346–362.

Roberts, G. and Bryant, D. P. (2011). Early mathematics achievement trajectories: English-language learner and native English-speaker estimates using the Early Childhood Longitudinal Survey. *Developmental Psychology, 47*(4), 916–930.

Shalev, R., Manor, O. and Gros-Tsur, V. (2005). Developmental dyscalculia: A prospective six-year follow-up. *Developmental Medicine and Child Neurology, 47,* 121–125.

Shin, M. and Bryant, D. P. (2013). A synthesis of mathematical and cognitive performances of students with mathematics learning disabilities. *Journal of Learning Disabilities.* Published Online First, 23 October 2013. doi:10.1177/0022219413508324

Swanson, H. L. (1993). Working memory in learning disability subgroups. *Journal of Experimental Child Psychology, 56*(1), 87–114.

Swanson, H. L. (2006). Cognitive processes that underlie mathematical precociousness in young children. *Journal of Experimental Child Psychology, 93,* 239–264.

Swanson, H. L., Hoskyn, M. and Lee, C. (1999). *Interventions for Students with Learning Disabilities. A meta-analysis of treatment outcomes.* New York: Guilford Press.

Swanson, H. L. and Jerman, O. (2006). Math disabilities: A selective meta-analysis of the literature. *Review of Educational Research, 76*(2), 249–274.

Swanson, H. L., Jerman, O. and Zheng, X. (2008). The role of WM growth on growth in word problem solving in children at risk for math difficulties. *Journal of Educational Psychology, 100,* 343–379.

van Garderen, D., Scheuermann, A. and Jackson, C. (2012). Examining how students with diverse abilities use diagrams to solve mathematics word problems. *Learning Disability Quarterly, 36*(3), 145–160.

Wu, H. (2005, September). *Key mathematical ideas in grades 5–8.* Retrieved September 10, 2012 from http://math.berkeley.edu/~wu/NCTM2005a.pdf.

Wu, H. (2006, October). *Professional development: The hard work of learning mathematics.* Presentation at the fall southeastern section meeting of the American Mathematical Society, Johnson City, TN.

18

Targeted interventions for children with difficulties in learning mathematics

Ann Dowker and Peter Morris

Difficulty with arithmetic is a common problem (Butterworth, Varma & Laurillard, 2011; Reigosa-Crespo et al., 2012). For example, in the UK, over 20 per cent of the population have severe numeracy difficulties that have a serious impact on their occupational and social chances. This is at least four times as high as the proportion that have equivalent difficulties in literacy (Bynner & Parsons, 1997; Parsons & Bynner, 2005). A recent survey indicates that nearly half of working-age adults in the UK have only the level of numeracy that one would expect at the end of primary school (BIS, 2011). There are significant international differences in numeracy performance; but even generally high-achieving countries include people who have serious problems with numeracy; e.g. in Finland (Räsänen et al., 2009) and in the Pacific Rim countries (Chan & Ho, 2010; Lee, Chang, & Lee, 2001). There has been increasing recent interest in developing interventions to help children with such difficulties (Butterworth et al., 2011; Clements & Sarama, 2011; Cohen Kadosh, Dowker, Heine, Kaufmann & Kucian, 2013; Dowker, 2009; Gersten, Jordan & Flojo, 2005).

Interventions must take into account that mathematical difficulties are not unitary. Studies of both atypical and typical mathematical development (Cowan et al., 2011; Desoete, Roeyers & DeClerq, 2004; Dowker, 2005; Gifford & Rockcliffe, 2012; Jordan, Mulhern & Wylie, 2009; Russell & Ginsburg, 1984), studies of adults with acquired dyscalculia (Cappelletti, Butterworth & Kopelman, 2012; Delazer, 2003; Warrington, 1982) and behavioural and brain imaging studies of adult mathematical cognition (Stanescu-Cosson et al., 2000; Van Eimeren et al., 2010) have provided increasing and converging evidence that arithmetical cognition is made up of multiple components, and that it is quite possible for children and adults to show strong discrepancies, in either direction, between the components. In other words, although the components often correlate with one another, people can show weaknesses in virtually any component.

Such findings have suggested the desirability of developing interventions that assess and target children's weaknesses in specific components of numeracy, rather than taking a 'one size fits all' approach.

History of targeted interventions

Individualized, component-based techniques of assessing and remediating mathematical difficulties have surprisingly early origins (Dowker, 2005). People have been developing such interventions, perhaps especially in the United States, at least since the 1920s (Brownell, 1929; Buswell & John, 1926; Tilton, 1947; Williams & Whitaker, 1937).

Long before most of the evidence was obtained that confirmed this view empirically, Weaver (1954, pp. 300–301) proposed some of the most important principles of targeted intervention:

> Arithmetic competence is not a unitary thing but a composite of several types of quantitative ability: e.g. computational ability, problem-solving ability, etc. . . . [T]hese abilities overlap to varying degrees, but most are sufficiently independent to warrant separate evaluations . . . Children exhibit considerable variation in their profiles or patterns of ability in the various patterns of arithmetic instruction . . . [E]xcept for extreme cases of disability, which demand the aid of clinicians and special services, remedial teaching is basically good teaching, differentiated to meet specific instructional needs.

If componential theories of arithmetical ability, and their applications to differentiated instruction and remediation in arithmetic have been advocated for many decades, the question arises of why they had, until very recently, comparatively little impact on theory and practice. There are probably two main reasons. One is practical. For much of the last century, classes tended to be large (even as recently as the 1960s, classes of over 40 were common) and under-resourced. In overcrowded and under-resourced classes, it is difficult to provide individualized instruction. The other reason is that, in the past, there was often relatively little communication of ideas and findings between different countries, or between researchers, policymakers and teachers. The Internet has probably played a crucial role in facilitating such communications. In addition to these factors, it must be admitted that at least until very recently, numeracy and mathematical difficulties were rarely given the same emphasis as, for example, literacy difficulties. For example, a National Numeracy organization was only established in the United Kingdom in 2012, about 20 years after the establishment of the National Literacy Trust.

Recent increases in individualized interventions

At least in the UK, there has been an increased focus on individualized interventions since the beginning of the twenty first century (Dowker, 2004; Gross, 2007) and especially since the Williams Review of primary mathematics education (Williams, 2008) recommended such interventions. Dowker (2009) reported a significant increase in the use of interventions for mathematical difficulties in British primary schools. It is likely that economic recession and spending cuts have resulted in some reduction in their use since that report; but there is still far more focus on such interventions than at an earlier time.

Intensive interventions

Highly intensive interventions have been devised mainly for use with children who have severe mathematical difficulties (typically those scoring in the lowest 5%). One of the best-known interventions is Mathematics Recovery, originally developed in Australia (Wright, Cowper, Stafford, Stanger & Stewart, 1994; Wright, Martland & Stafford, 2006; also see Willey, Holliday & Martland, 2007). This programme involves thorough initial diagnostic assessment followed by half an hour of individualized intervention per day, and must be delivered by people who have received 60 hours of training. It involves a wide variety of components of arithmetic; but places particular emphasis on methods of counting and number representation.

Numbers Count was developed in the UK toward the end of the first decade of the twenty first century (Dunn, Matthews & Dowrick, 2010; Torgerson et al., 2011). Like Mathematics Recovery, it involves thorough initial diagnostic assessment, followed by half an hour of individualized intervention per day. It is delivered by teachers who have received Master's level training. Studies so far indicate that it results in considerable improvement at least in the short term; to the point that children who have been very low attainers in mathematics may catch up with their typically developing peers.

Interventions of this level of intensiveness are unlikely to be possible from a practical or economic point of view for the majority of children who experience milder mathematical difficulties; and, even if they could be implemented, might take up too much time from such children's other educational activities. Yet, as the findings mentioned in the first paragraph of this chapter indicate, there are many children who, though they are not among the lowest attainers, still struggle with mathematics and are at risk of persistent numeracy difficulties in adulthood. Lighter-touch interventions are needed for such children.

Catch Up Numeracy[1]

We now report such a lighter-touch targeted intervention for children with mathematical difficulties. This intervention is Catch Up Numeracy, which was developed through a collaboration between the first author and Catch Up, a not-for-profit British educational charity (Dowker & Sigley, 2010; Holmes & Dowker, 2013).

The programme is based on Dowker's (2001) 'Numeracy Recovery' scheme originally piloted in six schools in Oxford, and has been extensively adapted and developed, in particular to include a system of training teachers and teaching assistants to make the programme widely applicable. The target pupils for the Catch Up

Numeracy intervention are pupils in Years 2 to 6 who have numeracy difficulties. Over 45,000 children in England and Wales are estimated to have taken part in this intervention since its development in 2007.

The intervention begins by assessing the children on ten components of early numeracy. Each child is assessed individually by a trained teacher/teaching assistant using 'Catch Up Numeracy formative assessments' which the member of staff then uses to complete the 'Catch Up Numeracy learner profile'. This personalised profile is used to determine the entry level for each of the ten Catch Up Numeracy components and the appropriate focus for numeracy teaching (based on the profile and the individual learner's needs). Children are provided with mathematical games and activities targeted to their specific levels in specific activities.

Teachers and teaching assistants receive three days' formal training from the Catch Up organization in delivering the programme. The children receive weekly intervention (two 15-minute sessions per week for approximately one school term, focusing on components with which they have difficulty.

Each 15-minute teaching session includes (a) a review and introduction to remind the child of what was achieved in the previous session and to outline the focus of the current session; (b) a numeracy activity; and (c) a linked recording activity where the child records the results of the activity, in oral, written and/or concrete fashion, and where the child receives focused teaching related to their performance in the activity and any observed errors.

The ten components are as follows:

1   Counting verbally (subcomponents: counting verbally from 0 or 1; counting on from a given number; counting back from a given number).
2   Counting objects (subcomponents: counting objects; order irrelevance; repeated addition of objects; repeated subtraction of objects).
3   Reading and writing numbers (subcomponents: reading numerals; reading number words; writing numerals).
4   Hundreds, tens and units (subcomponents: number comparison; adding tens and units; subtracting tens and units).
5   Ordinal numbers. The ordinal task involves showing children pictures of bead strings and telling them that the bead with the dot in the middle is the first (or in some pictures tenth) bead. One bead in each picture is shaded, and the children are asked to say which bead it is (e.g. second, fourth, ninth, etc.).
6   Word problems.
7   Translation between different formats (subcomponents: translating from objects to numerals; translating from numerals to objects; translating from number words to numerals; translating from number words to objects).
8   Derived fact strategies (the use of known facts, combined with arithmetical principles such as commutativity, to derive new facts; e.g. if $44 + 23 = 67$, $23 + 44$ must also be 67).
9   Estimation of quantities and of answers to arithmetic problems.
10 Remembered number facts.

It should be noted that these are not intended to be a universal, all-encompassing set of components, either from a psychological or a mathematical point of view. Rather, they were selected because initial discussions with teachers suggested that these are seen as important educationally, and because earlier research (Dowker, 1998, 2005) suggested that there are extensive individual differences in these components in children of primary school age.

Evaluation

The main evaluation study so far (Dowker & Sigley, 2010; Holmes & Dowker, 2013) included 440 children between the ages of 6 and 10, approximately equally divided between males and females from a range of local authorities in England and Wales. Of these children, 348 received the Catch Up intervention programme; 50 were given the same amount of time for non-targeted individualized mathematics work, and 42 children received no intervention, except for the usual school instruction. The children were given the Hodder Basic Number Screening Test (Gillham & Hesse, 2001) before and after intervention, and their Number Age was recorded.

The mean starting chronological ages of the groups were 103.85 months (s.d. 14.5) for the Catch Up intervention group; 106.45 months (s.d. 13.4) for the matched-time group; and 105.78 months (s.d. 12.79) for the no-intervention group. The mean starting Number Ages on the Hodder Number Screening Test were 96.75 months (s.d. 14.5) for the Catch Up intervention group; 94.39 months (s.d. 14.11) for the matched-time group; and 97.39 (s.d. 15.96) for the no-intervention group. Analyses of variance showed no significant differences between the groups with regard to either initial chronological age or initial Mathematics Age.

Ratio gain (gain in Number Age divided by amount of time between first and second testing) was computed for all children. Children who received Catch Up Numeracy showed a mean ratio gain of 2.51 (standard deviation 1.9). Those who received matched-time intervention showed a mean ratio gain of 1.47 (s.d. 1.78). Those who received no intervention showed a mean ratio gain of 1.25 (standard deviation 1.8). An analysis of variance showed very significant group differences ($F(2, 437)$ = 8.92, $p < .001$). Post hoc tests showed that the children who received Catch Up Numeracy improved significantly more than either of the other two groups, who did not differ significantly from each other.

Thus, the findings support the view that individualized interventions in arithmetic, especially those that focus on the particular components with which an individual child has difficulty, can be highly effective. The children who received Catch Up Numeracy intervention, achieved average Number Age gains of more than twice that expected of typically achieving learners over the same amount of time, and very significantly more than achieved by children receiving other mathematics support. Moreover, the amount of time given to such individualized work does not, in many cases, need to be very large to be effective. Thus, children's arithmetical difficulties are highly susceptible to intervention. It cannot be said that large numbers of children are simply 'bad at maths' and not capable of significant improvement.

Further questions

There are still many questions that need answering. In particular, more research is needed to determine whether the most crucial factor in the success of Catch Up Numeracy is indeed its targeted nature, or whether some other factor is involved. It is unlikely that the mere fact that Catch Up Numeracy involves one-to-one attention is the sole reason for the progress made by the children, because children who experienced matched time, but less targeted, intervention, did not make the same level of progress. However, there is still the question of whether the important aspect is the targeting; the particular components used in the intervention; and/or some other feature of the intervention, such as the frequency or length of the interventions.

In particular, an important question is whether these ten specific components are the crucial ones on which an intervention should focus, or whether almost any set of components could be appropriate, so long as they are related to the mathematics curriculum and are addressed in a targeted fashion.

A related important question is that of when intervention should ideally begin, and the extent to which different approaches might be appropriate to different ages. So far, our research with primary school children does not indicate that the age of starting the numeracy interventions has a great influence on the children's progress. However, we do not know whether there would be an age where intervention becomes less likely to be successful: perhaps when children reach secondary school, especially as attitudes to mathematics tend to become more negative, and anxiety stronger, with age. On the other hand, it might be necessary and desirable to provide new types of interventions for some secondary school pupils, as they begin to deal with topics that are commonly found more difficult than basic arithmetic.

At the other end of the scale, the question arises of whether mathematical difficulties could be predicted at the time of school entry, or even earlier, and whether targeted interventions might prevent or ameliorate such difficulties before they arise. There is already much evidence that numerical abilities at the time of school entrance do predict later mathematical ability (e.g. De Smedt, Verschaffel & Ghesquière, 2009; Tymms, 1999). What is less clear is whether specific aspects of early numerical ability predict specific aspects of later mathematical ability and, if so, whether it would ever be possible to diagnose and target these aspects at or before the time of school entrance.

Finally, one of the most important questions is, of course, how long the effects of interventions last. Are the effects permanent, or are children likely eventually to fall behind again, despite initial improvement? Are there any factors in interventions, or in the children's subsequent environment and teaching, that are crucial in influencing the long-term maintenance of gains? Extensive longitudinal follow-up studies will be vital in answering such questions.

Acknowledgements

We are grateful to the staff and pupils at the schools involved in the research. We are grateful for all the help and collaboration of the Catch Up organization, including

Graham Sigley and Julie Lawes. We thank the Esmee Fairbairn Charitable Trust and the Caxton Trust for financial support. We thank Wayne Holmes of the Department of Education, Oxford University for his collaboration. Chongying Wang helped to collect data.

Note

1 Catch Up is a not-for-profit UK registered charity (1072425). Catch Up Ltd is an endorsed charitable institute ABN- 62154644498. Catch Up is a registered trademark.

References

BIS (2011). *BIS Research Paper 57: Skills for Life Survey headline findings.* London: Department of Business, Innovation and Skills.

Brownell, W. (1929). Remedial cases in arithmetic. *Peabody Journal of Education, 7*, 100–107.

Buswell, G.T. & John, L. (1926). Diagnostic studies in arithmetic. *Supplementary Educational Monographs, 30.* Chicago: University of Chicago Presa.

Butterworth, B., Varma, S. & Laurillard, D. (2011). Dyscalculia: from brain to education, *Science, 332*, 1049–1053.

Bynner, J. & Parsons, S. (1997). *Does Numeracy Matter?* London: Basic Skills Agency.

Cappelletti, M., Butterworth, B. & Kopelman, M. (2012). Numeracy skills in patients with degenerative disorders and focal brain lesions: a neuropsychological investigation. *Neuropsychology, 26*, 1–19.

Chan, B.M.Y., & Ho, C.S.H. (2010). The cognitive profile of Chinese children with mathematics difficulties. *Journal of Experimental Child Psychology, 107*, 260–279.

Clements, D.H. & Sarama, J. (2011). Early childhood mathematics intervention. *Science, 333*, 968–970.

Cohen Kadosh, R., Dowker, A., Heine, A., Kaufmann, L. & Kucian, K. (2013). Interventions for improving numerical abilities: present and future. *Trends in Neuroscience and Education, 2*, 85–93.

Cowan, R., Donlan, C., Shepherd, D.L., Cole-Fletcher, R., Saxton, M., & Hurry, J. (2011). Basic calculation proficiency and mathematics achievement in elementary school children. *Journal of Educational Psychology, 103*, 786–803.

De Smedt, B., Verschaffel, L. & Ghesquière, P. (2009). The predictive value of magnitude comparison for individual differences in mathematics achievement. *Journal of Experimental Child Psychology, 103*, 469–479.

Delazer, M. (2003). Neuropsychological findings on conceptual knowledge of arithmetic. In A. Baroody and A. Dowker (eds.) *The Development of Arithmetical Concepts and Skills* (pp. 385–407). Mahwah, NJ: Erlbaum.

Desoete, A., Roeyers, H. & De Clercq, A. (2004). Children with mathematics learning disabilities in Belgium. *Journal of Learning Disabilities, 37*, 32–41.

Dowker, A. (1998). Individual differences in arithmetical development. In C. Donlan (ed.) *The Development of Mathematical Skills* (pp. 275–302). London: Taylor & Francis.

Dowker, A.D. (2001). Numeracy Recovery: a pilot scheme for early intervention with young children with numeracy difficulties. *Support for Learning, 16*, 6–10.

Dowker, A.D. (2004). *What Works for Children with Mathematical Difficulties?* London: DfES.

Dowker, A.D. (2005). *Individual Differences in Arithmetic: Implications for psychology, neuroscience and education* (Chapter 10). Hove: Psychology Press.

Dowker, A.D. (2009). *What Works for Children with Mathematical Difficulties? The effectiveness of intervention schemes.* London: DCSF.

Dowker, A. & Sigley, G. (2010). Targeted interventions for children with arithmetical difficulties. *British Journal of Educational Psychology, II(7)*, 65–81.

Dunn, S., Matthews, L. & Dowrick, N. (2010). Numbers Count: developing a national approach to intervention. In I. Thompson (ed.) *Issues in Teaching Numeracy in Primary Schools* (pp. 224–234). Maidenhead: Open University Press.

Gersten, R., Jordan, N. & Flojo, J.R. (2005). Early identification and interventions for students with mathematics difficulties. *Journal of Learning Disabilities, 38*, 293–324.

Gifford, S., & Rockliffe, F. (2012). Mathematics difficulties: does one approach fit all? *Research in Mathematics Education, 14*, 1–16.

Gillham, B. & Hesse, K. (2001). *Basic Number Screening Test: National Numeracy Strategy Edition: Forms A & B, for Ages 7 to 12 Years.* 3rd edition. London: Hodder Education.

Gross, J. (2007). Supporting children with gaps in their mathematical understanding. *Educational and Child Psychology, 24*, 146–156.

Holmes, W. & Dowker, A.D. (2013). Catch Up Numeracy: a targeted intervention for children who are low attaining in mathematics. *Research in Mathematics Education, 15*, 249–265.

Jordan, J.A., Mulhern, G. & Wylie, J. (2009). Individual differences in trajectories of arithmetical development in typically achieving 5–7-year-olds. *Journal of Experimental Child Psychology, 103*, 455–468.

Lee, N.H., Chang, S.C.A. & Lee, P.Y. (2001). The role of metacognition in the learning of mathematics among the low-achieving students. *Teaching and Learning, 22*, 18–30.

Parsons, S. & Bynner, J. (2005). *Does Numeracy Matter More?* London: NRDC.

Räsänen, O., Salminen, J., Wilson, A., Aunio, P., & Dehaene, S. (2009). Computer-assisted intervention for children with low numeracy skills. *Cognitive Development, 24*, 450–472.

Reigosa-Crespo, V., Valdes-Sosa, M., Butterworth, B., Estevez, N., Rodriguez, M., Santos, E., Lage, A. (2012). Basic numerical abilities and prevalence of developmental dyscalculia: the Havana Survey. *Developmental Psychology, 48*, 123–135.

Russell, R. & Ginsburg, H.P. (1984). Cognitive analysis of children's mathematical difficulties. *Cognition and Instruction, 1*, 217–244.

Stanescu-Cosson, R., Pinel, P., Van de Moortele, P.F., Le Bihan, D., Cohen, L. and Dehaene, S. (2000). Understanding dissociations in dyscalculia: a brain-imaging study of the impact of number size on the cerebral networks for exact and approximate calculation. *Brain, 123*, 2240–2255.

Tilton, J.W. (1947). Individualized and meaningful instruction in arithmetic. *Journal of Educational Psychology, 38*, 83–88.

Torgerson, C.J., Wiggins, A., Torgerson, D.J., Ainsworth, H., Barmby, P., Hewitt, C., Tymms, P. (2011). *Every Child Counts: The Independent Evaluation Executive Summary.* London: Department for Education (DfE).

Tymms, P. (1999). Baseline assessment, value-added and the prediction of reading. *Journal of Research in Reading, 22*, 27–36.

Van Eimeren, L., Grabner, R.H., Koschutnig, K., Reishofer, G., Ebner, F. & Ansari, D. (2010) Structure-function relationships underlying calculation: a combined diffusion tensor imaging and fMRI study. *Neuroimage, 52*, 358–363.

Warrington, E.K. (1982). The fractionation of arithmetical skills: a single case study. *Quarterly Journal of Experimental Psychology, 34A*, 31–51.

Weaver, J. (1954). Differentiated instruction in arithmetic: an overview and a promising trend. *Education, 74*, 300–305.

Willey, R., Holliday, A. & Martland, J. (2007). Achieving new heights in Cumbria: raising standards through Mathematics Recovery. *Educational and Child Psychology, 24*, 108–118.

Williams, C. & Whitaker, R.L. (1937). Diagnosis of arithmetical difficulties. *Elementary School Journal, 37*, 592–600.

Williams, P. (2008). *Independent Review of Mathematics Teaching in Early Years Settings and Primary Schools.* London: Department for Children, Schools and Families.

Wright, R.J., Cowper, J., Stafford, A., Stanger, G. & Stewart, R. (1994). The mathematics recovery project: a progress report. Specialist teachers working with low-attaining first-graders. *Proceedings of the 17th Annual Conference of the Mathematics Education Group of Australia*. 2: 709–716.

Wright, R.J., Martland, J. & Stafford, A. (2006). *Early Numeracy: assessment for teaching and intervention*. 2nd edition. London: Paul Chapman.

19

Focused MLD intervention based on the classification of MLD subtypes

Giannis N. Karagiannakis and Anny Cooreman

Introduction

The difficulties that a student might face with mathematics could be attributed to a number of factors. The inherent difficulties and the high demands that stem from the nature of the subject itself, as well as the failures that might have added up in the years following beginner's classes, often cause mathematics anxiety. Additionally, inadequate teaching strategies, as well as traditional approaches to the teaching of mathematics, that aim simply at the spreading of information rather than the deeper understanding of concepts, might result in additional difficulties. If the above factors are controlled for and excluded, but difficulties remain, then these difficulties might be attributed to Mathematical Learning Difficulties (MLD). Understanding the cognitive nature of MLD has fascinated researchers from different fields: from mathematics education to developmental and cognitive psychology and neuroscience. Concerning the question of a definition, operational criteria, and prevalence of MLD, there is still disagreement (Mazzocco, 2008; Lanfranchi et al., 2008).

Dealing with numbers and with mathematics in general, requires the utilization of a multitude of skills. More specifically, skills that are deemed necessary include: *number sense* (for subitizing and approximate estimation), *verbal skills* (for processing number-words, decoding the terminology of mathematics, as well as reading and understanding verbal tasks), *memory* (for the memorization of basic arithmetic facts, procedures, rules, forms, symbols), *spatiotemporal perception*, *mathematical logic*, as well as the *meta-cognitive skills*. Students with difficulties in any of these abilities or in their coordination, may experience MLD. Within the field of mathematics education, many frameworks and theories have been developed to analyze teaching and learning processes and difficulties involved in mathematics (Freudenthal, 1991; Schoenfeld, 1992, 2011; Bharath & English, 2010). Recently, the field has shown interest in perspectives from cognitive neuroscience. For example a special issue of the ZDM has been dedicated to "promises and potential pitfalls of a 'cognitive neuroscience of mathematics learning'," focusing especially on the relevance of subject populations, methodological limitations of current neuroimaging methods and theoretical questions concerning the relationship between the well-studied neural correlates of numerical magnitude processing and the less-investigated neural processes underlying higher level mathematical skills, such as algebraic reasoning (Grabner & Ansari, 2010).

As mathematics educators in primary and secondary education, we believe that reaching a model that combines existing hypotheses on MLD, based on known cognitive processes and mechanisms, could be used to provide a *mathematical profile* for every student. Such profiles could be used by educators to ameliorate their teaching both in the classroom and in one-on-one settings, by strengthening, on the one hand, students' weaker processes and building, on the other hand, their strong cognitive processes to compensate the weaker processes and foster their development of overall better mathematical skills and concepts. Our aims with this contribution are to: (1) propose a classification model for MLD describing four basic domains based on the "triple-code" number processing model, the most relevant MLD hypotheses in the present literature as well as our clinical experience; (2) discuss possible profiles of MLD students based on the aforementioned model, proposing intervention strategies for each domain.

Number processing models

The most widely discussed models of number processing are those of McCloskey, Caramazza and Basili (1985), the "encoding complex theory" of Campbell and Clark (1988) and the "triple-code model" of Dehaene (1992). We support the "triple-code model" of Dehaene which proposes that numbers are represented in three codes that serve different functions, have distinct neuroarchitectures, and are related to performance on specific tasks:

1   The *analog form* of numbers is used in activities like: subitizing (1 to 4 items), placing numbers on number lines, magnitude estimation as well as comparison.
2   The *auditory-verbal form* of numbers is exploited in arithmetic skills, such as counting, applying mathematic rules and retrieval of number facts.
3   The *Arabic symbol form* is necessary to solve an equation or to make mental calculations with two-digit or multi-digit numbers.

Hypotheses and classifications of MLD

According to the literature, the processing of numbers is of primary importance among the hypotheses for MLD. To be more specific, there are two preverbal or non-symbolic systems for processing quantities: the object tracking system (OTS) and the approximate number system (ANS). The main MLD hypotheses based on deficits in these systems and other mechanisms specific to numerical processing are: (1) *defective ANS*; (2) *defective OTS*; (3) *defective numerosity-coding*; (4) *access deficit*;

(5) *multiple deficit* (for review see: Andersson & Östergren, 2012). Therefore, the core systems of number seem to be quite important in understanding the nature of the development of numerical cognition, but these are not the only systems upon which success in mathematics lies.

There also exists a hypothesis of a *domain general cognitive deficit* underlying MLD (Geary, 2004; Geary & Hoard, 2005), which emanates from converging evidence showing that several cognitive functions are involved in mathematical performance in both adults and children (Andersson, 2007; 2008; Fuchs et al., 2005; Swanson et al., 2008). According to this hypothesis, deficits may reside in: (a) *working memory* (phonological and visual-spatial WM) in storing and processing simultaneously information; (b) *long-term memory* (semantic memory) in learning and storing knowledge mathematical concepts and procedures, in storing and retrieving arithmetic facts (for example, times tables); (c) *executive functions*: processing speed, inhibition of irrelevant associations from entering WM, updating relevant information, shifting from one operation-strategy to another, attention, updating and strategic planning; (d) *fact retrieval* and, by extension, *calculation and fluency*.

Doing mathematics involves a wide range of skills: even if we limit ourselves to think about arithmetic, such knowledge cannot be interpreted as a general cognitive competence per se; rather, it depends on competencies such as arithmetic calculation, number processing, problem solving, computation, conceptual and procedural knowledge. Moreover, such a complex cognitive system depends on the awareness of many different interrelated subcomponents such as quantity, numbers, procedures, and use of strategies (Lanfranchi et al., 2008). The wide range of skills involved implies a spectrum of potential disabilities based on failure in one or more of these cognitive skills (Desoete, 2007).

Many researchers have attempted to describe subtypes in MLD (Fuchs & Fuchs, 2002; Geary, 2004; Geary & Hoard, 2005). Geary was one of the first who tried to connect "Mathematics Disorder" with neuropsychological deficits (Geary, 1994). He posited three key subtypes of deficits (confirmed in Geary & Hoard, 2005): (a) *procedural*, in which children present a delay in acquiring simple arithmetic strategies; (b) *semantic memory*, in which children show deficits in retrieval of facts because of a long-term memory deficit; (c) *spatial*, in which children show deficits in the spatial representation of number.

In general, Geary's classification and the others proposed in the literature (for a review see: Desoete, 2002, 2007; Stock et al., 2006) lead to the identification of the three subtypes listed, as well as one based on a *number knowledge* deficit. However, such classifications are not completely satisfactory because, in general, the profiles of the children met in practice do not appear to belong to any subtype, but instead are constituted of several characteristics pertaining to different subtypes (Desoete, 2007).

Classification model of mathematical learning difficulties

Taking into account the "triple-code model," recent research in cognitive psychology and neuroscience as well as our clinical observations, we propose a classification model for MLD consists of four basic domains: the Core Number; Visual-Spatial; Memory; and the Logical. We list for each domain mathematical difficulties that might manifest as well as possible involved cognitive systems and relevant MLD hypotheses.

Core Number

This domain is manifested through difficulties in: the basic sense of numerosity (Butterworth, 2005), and estimating accurately a small number of objects e.g., 4–5 (subitizing) (Butterworth, 2010; Piazza, 2010), estimating approximate quantities (Piazza et al., 2010), placing numbers on number lines (Menon et al., 2000; Zorzi et al., 2005), managing Arabic symbols (Rousselle & Noël, 2007; Ansari et al., 2006), transcoding a number from one representation to another (analog–Arabic–verbal) (Wilson & Dehaene, 2007), grasping the basic counting principles (Gallistel & Gelman, 1992; Geary & Hoard, 2005), capturing the meaning of place value (including in decimal notation) (Geary, 1990; Russell & Ginsburg, 1984); capturing the meaning of the basic arithmetic operation symbols ($+$, $-$, $\{x\}$, $\div$). The ANS, OTS, Numerosity-Coding and Access deficit hypotheses seem involved in the particular domain.

Visual-Spatial

This domain is manifested through difficulties in: interpreting and using spatial organization of representations of mathematical objects (for example, numbers in decimal positional notation, exponents, or geometrical figures), placing numbers on a number line (Cooper, 1984; Dehaene & Cohen, 2000), recognizing Arabic numerals and other mathematics symbols (confusion in similar symbols), written calculation, especially where position is important (e.g., borrowing/carrying) (Heathcote, 1994; Mammarella et al., 2010), controlling irrelevant visuo-spatial information (Mammarella & Cornoldi, 2005), visualizing and analyzing geometric figures (or subparts of them), interpreting graphs, understanding and interpreting when the math information is organized visual-spatially (tables), remembering and managing formulas. The visuo-spatial working memory and visuo-spatial reasoning/perception may be related to this domain.

Memory

This domain is manifested through difficulties in: retrieving numerical facts (Geary, 1993, 2004; von Aster, 2000; Woodward & Montague, 2002), decoding – confusing terminology (numerator, denominator, isosceles, equilateral, . . .) (Geary, 1993; Hecht et al., 2001), transcoding verbal rules or orally presented tasks (Rourke & Finlayson, 1978; Rourke, 1993; Brysbaert et al., 1998; Dehaene & Cohen, 2000; Andersson, 2007; Swanson et al., 2008), performing mental calculation accurately (Andersson & Östergren, 2012; Ashcraft, 1992; Campbell,

1987a, 1987b, 1991), remembering and carrying out procedures as well as rules and formulas (Gerber et al., 1994; Pellegrino & Goldman, 1987); digit span performance (Torgesen & Houck, 1980; Geary et al., 1996), (arithmetic) problem solving (keeping track of steps) (Jitendra & Xin, 1997; Fuchs & Fuchs, 2002, 2005; Andersson, 2007; Swanson et al., 2008). The working memory (in particular the phonological), inhibition of irrelevant associations from entering working memory and the semantic memory are engaged in this domain.

Reasoning

This domain is manifested through difficulties in: grasping mathematical concepts, ideas and relations (Geary, 1993; Schoenfeld, 1992), understanding multiple steps in complex procedures/algorithms (Bryant et al., 2000; Geary, 2004; Russell & Ginsburg, 1984), grasping basic logical principles (conditionality – "if . . . then . . ." statements – commutativity, inversion, . . .) (Núñez & Lakoff, 2005); problem solving (decision making) (Desoete & Roeyers, 2006; Schoenfeld, 1992). In this domain the concepts of entailment, inhibition, updating relevant information, shifting from one operation-strategy to another, updating and strategic planning, as well as decision making are also involved.

An analysis of a student's performance on a set of well-designed tasks can lead to singling out specific areas of difficulty (and strength if the proposed classification model is being used to identify the mathematical abilities), by comparing the specific systems and difficulties implied in each incorrect (or correct) answer to the tasks. The student's profile will then be described as a single domain or as a combination of domains in which types of mathematical tasks and possible deficits to specific systems are highlighted.

Intervention

A well and clearly structured teaching method plays a key role in the academic progress of every student and, particularly, of MLD students. This teaching approach aims at providing clear objectives, explicit steps and varied exercises that refer to basic background knowledge. Based on our 30 years of experience in teaching, we can confidently say that MLD students show greatest progress when provided with direct, explicit, and multisensory instructions adapted to their individual learning profile, strengths and weaknesses. Considering the multidisciplinary domains of the model introduced in this chapter, we will discuss the variations within the diagnostic profiles of MLD students and introduce targeted intervention strategies that deal with each domain deficit.

We aim to provide an individually tailored intervention program that focuses on the strengths of the students as a way of compensating for the deficiencies that exist. The following interventions and examples are derived from our extensive experience in diagnosis and intervention programs targeted for (M)LD students. Our experience has taught us the importance of ecological intervention. Our inclusive approach is designed to benefit MLD students as well as students who do not have MLD.

Core Number

Children with severe weaknesses in the Core Number domain show a significant lack of progress during the early months of their arithmetic education. Math activities that focus on emphasizing the connection between numbers and math symbols in everyday life activities prove helpful. This can be done using simple and familiar material such as fingers, playing cards, rulers or number cards. Guided instructions combined with practical exercises and frequent self-verbalization usually give promising results. The style is to encourage the thinking process and metacognition rather than focusing on final answers.

Following the above, these students often have difficulties retrieving facts, not necessarily due to a memory deficit, but because of their weak ability to mentally visualize and associate the Arabic symbols with the relevant quantity and number-word representation of the same number. A way to help a student strengthen this ability is to help him practice combining the different number representations. For example, a child can hold a playing card showing 5 and be encouraged to show the same number (5) on his fingers, step up to the fifth step of a stairway and collect 5€ or 5c.

Attention should be paid to the meaning of the math symbols. For instance, a child can understand the meaning of '=' by placing money in both his hands and investigating the concept of equality (5 = 2 + . . .). In the example given here the pupil holds 5€ in one hand and 2€ in the other hand. The aim is to achieve an equal amount of money in both left and right hands. Going up and down the stairs can help the child make the distinction between the symbols '+' and '−'.

Verbalization ('Add 2 to 5') should be followed by an action (start at step 5 of a staircase and go up two steps and/or add a 2c coin to a 5c coin) and symbolic visual representation (5 + 2). Students can become anxious and confused when confronted with numbers and math symbols. It is therefore recommended to combine math symbols, words and meanings within the same exercise as much as possible.

Through time students need frequent repetition of the meaning of the mathematical symbolic language and its application in exercises. Students should persistently be encouraged to use and refer to their individual charts which include number facts, math vocabulary and math symbols, with or without visual clues or examples. It is useful to check final answers using a calculator.

Children with severe difficulties in this domain are often referred to as pure dyscalculics. Anxiety and the negative emotions that arise as a consequence of frequent failure need to be addressed by the teacher. Some of these students show strengths in the Reasoning domain. They are capable of understanding and applying procedures, as well as making logical decisions. Many of these children are also capable of obtaining average results in the Visual-Spatial domain, where no numbers are used. It is therefore possible to develop a student's Reasoning and Visual-Spatial abilities and support him to move on and acquire higher math concepts and operations. In our experience some of these children have been able to be successful in higher level algebra. Allowing students to solve exercises by using compensating strategies to overcome the primary numerosity problem stimulates a student's confidence in maths. It is important to set and work towards long-term goals. For example, an educator might choose to develop addition operations to a high level and use compensatory tools, such as a calculator, to do subtractions. This method aids in developing the mental logical math operations and symbolic or abstract math concepts. Finally, it stimulates the use of compensating strategies in deficit areas.

Visual-Spatial

A deficit in the Visual-Spatial domain is not always identified pre-emptively. Students with a visual-spatial deficit do not always show early or obvious maths difficulties. The teacher should be particularly aware of the visual component when analyzing wrong answers. Reading and manipulating large numbers is often visually challenging. Students should be supported in structuring the visual information. Playing cards grouped by triads (for example, 456 375 675) and verbalizing the numbers while pointing at the cards helps students learn how to read large numbers.

Topics where visual positioning is required such as number lines, shapes, rotations, reflections, translations and graphs often remain fairly challenging. Reading graphs and tables can be difficult due to the fact that students need to locate a position on the crossing of vertical and horizontal lines. In this case appropriate visual support, such as L-shape cardboard or rulers to follow the lines, is required. When using instruments, such as protractor, compass, or ruler, where hand-eye coordination is involved, these students need support. In lower level math, this type of deficit has a negative influence on solving exercises that involve drawing and measuring angles, drawing parallel or perpendicular lines and geometric figures.

Enough practice using real objects and clear explanations of the relationship between the object and its corresponding two-dimensional image on paper are necessary. The use of motor and verbal clues to analyze the visual representation is also helpful. For example, the definition of a cube can be learned using a real cube and drawing attention to exercises that involve a cube. Just like dealing with any other deficit, simultaneous self-verbalization should be encouraged. In geometry, students often struggle to understand what elements of a shape they should be focusing on, therefore explicit instructions are required. In exercises where students are required to detect figures in a complex visual background (e.g. congruency in triangles), the use of colours and markers is incredibly useful.

Students experiencing weaknesses in the Visual-Spatial domain benefit the most from a verbal approach. Prior to the interventions that need to be implemented it is important to have a discussion with the student about the impact of his impairment. This will help the student himself to recognize the areas where the visual aspect of a topic might be causing difficulties. This will boost the student's confidence and enable him to seek help when needed. This group of students needs special support in acquiring strategies for solving exercises that require visual information, visual representation and creative visual imagination. Detailed and straightforward verbal decision-making models should be introduced when exploring visual information. Only look for visual clues after determining exactly what it is that the student wants to know when solving an exercise.

Students affected by deficiencies in the Visual-Spatial domain often become confused when visual and verbal information are introduced at the same time. They tend to pay little attention to, or even ignore, the visual information. It is therefore essential to invent appropriate strategies with the student, to assist them with understanding the verbal clues. Using these strategies, the student will then be able to gradually start integrating the visual clues. It is recommended that educators combine verbal support with concrete material and emphasize the link between the exercises and everyday life situations. Students show greater understanding and motivation when able to make links between visual information found in their math books and real life.

Memory

Pupils with a memory related deficiency tend to puzzle teachers and experts. On the one hand, they appear unable to automatically retrieve calculations such as 5 + 8 or 7 {x} 6, while on the other hand they show no difficulties with higher level math topics that do not require the retrieval of memory information. Teachers often refer to these students as students who make "silly mistakes," students who have attention deficit or just lack of capability. Feeling stupid acts as a restraint on the students' further development in math. As soon as they overcome their memory problem, with the use of compensating materials, they can begin to show real interest in mathematical procedures.

These students benefit from using diagrams and structured algorithms as well as decision and formula charts. These tools are later used spontaneously. An educator should be careful to avoid memory overload through long verbal explanations. The focus when practicing should be on memorizing "how" something is solved instead of "what" needs to be done to reach the solution. Repeated practice of the same complex model exercise until the student can successfully complete it, within the appropriate time, has also proven to be very effective in learning.

Dyslexic students often struggle with deficits in the memory domain. It is therefore easier for them to turn to reasoning connections and associative qualitative strategies rather than memorizing facts. Compensating, using the calculator, a multiplication table square or division tables can be taught at a very early stage. This can keep the pupil from experiencing negative frustration with written arithmetic or fractions. Explicit feedback about their strengths and weaknesses in the different domains stimulates and motivates these students.

Reasoning

Students with a deficit in the Reasoning domain begin to struggle when strategies, rules and algorithms need to be applied without an example to refer back to. They tend to use memory-based strategies to retrieve rules, formulas and algorithms or seek help on how to apply operations. In the case of rules and algorithms a memory-based intervention proves beneficial, however this is not the case with all maths topics. Showing the association of maths procedures and everyday life situations is very important when working with this group of students. Materials used in everyday life, such as money, help children grasp the meaning of mathematical logic in missing operand exercises like $8 - \_ = 6$ or $6 + \_ = 8$. Another possible intervention, involving small groups of pupils, could include role-play where children are encouraged to play the teacher's role and discuss their solutions with peers. The focus should always be on the "why" and "how" rather than on the final answers.

The memory domain (if these students are motivated and hard working) of these students is strong enough often to compensate for their reasoning deficit. This is the case when exercises are not solely logic based and similar ones have been practiced in the past. For example, where subtypes of equations are involved, this group of students do not need to understand the meaning of the equation. Instead, they can learn to recognize specific cues that would direct them to the appropriate equation subtype. These students are good at lower level math because that is when good memory offers many benefits. When faced with more abstract subjects, such as remarkable identities or statistics which necessitate decision making, students usually experience failure. They tend to look for details and lose track of the whole picture. They like using qualitative strategies, applying the rules step by step.

Decision-making charts that direct pupils to the key clues needed in the decision-making process while solving an exercise, have proven extremely beneficial. Again, consistent encouragement for the student to self-verbalize while working on the solution strategy, as a way of activating the thinking process, is crucial. Significantly more solid and long-term effects are experienced when the above teaching method is implemented before the age of 10.

Conclusion

Considering all of the above, we conclude by highlighting the innovative value of the etiological model presented above. First, its *multidimensional* nature proposes a transition from the existing one-dimensional "Dyscalculia" to the multidimensional "Mathematical Learning Difficulties,"[1] bringing into the picture new mathematical domains. In addition to the above, the model allows for the early identification of the mathematical profiles of MLD students. These profiles can prove valuable when designing effective and comprehensive intervention programs, by allowing educators to focus on the students' strengths in order to compensate for the weaknesses. This has further benefits on a student's confidence and motivation that often entrap students into a vicious circle of anxiety towards math.

Note

1 This is in line with the choice of the diagnostic term "Specific Learning Disorder" in the *DSM-5* (APA, 2013), that combines diagnoses of reading disorder, mathematics disorder, disorder of written expression, and learning disorder not otherwise specified.

References

American Psychiatric Association. (2013). *Diagnostic and Statistical Manual of Mental Disorders. Fifth Edition. DSM-5*. American Psychiatric Publishing, Inc.

Andersson, U. (2007). The contribution of working memory to children's mathematical word problem solving. *Applied Cognitive Psychology, 21*, 1201–1216.

Andersson, U. (2008). Working memory as a predictor of written arithmetical skills in children: The importance of central executive functions. *The British Journal of Educational Psychology, 78*, 181–203.

Andersson, U., & Östergren, R. (2012). Number magnitude processing and basic cognitive functions in children with mathematical learning disabilities. *Learning and Individual Differences, 22*, 701–714.

Ansari, D., Dhital, B., & Siong, S. C. (2006). Parametric effects of numerical distance on the intraparietal sulcus during passive viewing of rapid numerosity changes. *Brain Research, 1067*, 181–188.

Ashcraft, M. H. (1992). Cognitive arithmetic: A review of data and theory. *Cognition, 44*, 75–106.

Bharath, S., & English, L.D. (2010). *Theories of Mathematics Education: Seeking new frontiers*. New York: Springer.

Bryant, D. P., Bryant, B. R., & Hammill, D. D. (2000). Characteristic behaviors of students with LD who have teacher-identified math weaknesses. *Journal of Learning Disabilities, 33*, 168–177.

Brysbaert, M., Fias, W., & Noel, M. P. (1998). The worfian hypothesis and numerical cognition: Is "twenty-four" processed the same way as "four and twenty"? *Cognition, 66*, 51–77.

Butterworth, B. (2005). The development of arithmetical abilities. *Journal of Child Psychology and Psychiatry, 46*, 3–18.

Butterworth, B. (2010). Foundational numerical capacities and the origins of dyscalculia. *Trends in Cognitive Sciences, 14*, 534–541.

Campbell, J. I. D. (1987a). Network interference and mental multiplication. *Journal of Experimental Psychology: Learning, Memory, and Cognition, 13*, 109–123.

Campbell, J. I. D. (1987b). Production, verification, and priming of multiplication facts. *Memory & Cognition, 15*, 349–364.

Campbell, J. I. D. (1991). Conditions of error priming in number-fact retrieval. *Memory & Cognition, 19*, 197–209.

Campbell, J. I. D., & Clark, J. M. (1988). An encoding complex view of cognitive number processing: Comment on McCloskey, Sokol, and Goodman (1986). *Journal of Experimental Psychology: General, 117*, 204–214.

Cooper, R. G. (1984). Early number development: Discovering number space with addition and subtraction. In C. Sophian (Ed.), *Origins of Cognitive Skills* (pp. 157–192). Hillsdale, NJ. Erlbaum.

Dehaene, S. (1992). Varieties of numerical abilities. *Cognition, 44*, 1–42.

Dehaene, S., & Cohen, L. (2000). Un modél anatomique et fonctionnel de l'aritmétique mentale. In M. Presenti & X. Seron (Eds.), *Neuropsychologie des troubles du calcul et du traitement des nombres*. Marseille: Solal.

Desoete, A. (2002). Dyscalculie: stand van zaken. *Tijdschrift voor Logopedie & Audiologie,32*(2), 57–74.

Desoete, A. (2007). Students with mathematical disabilities in Belgium: from definition, classification and assessment to STICORDI devices. *Advances in Learning and Behavioral Disabilities, 20*, 121–221.

Desoete, A., & Roeyers, H. (2006). Metacognitive macroevaluations in mathematical problem solving. *Learning and Instruction, 16*, 12–25.

Freudenthal, H. (1991). *Revisiting Mathematics Education: China lectures*. Kluwer Academic Publishers.

Fuchs, L. S., Compton, D. L., Fuchs, D., Paulsen, K., Bryant, J. D., & Hamlett, C. L. (2005). The prevention, identification, and cognitive determinants of math difficulty. *Journal of Educational Psychology, 97*, 493–513.

Fuchs, L. S., & Fuchs, D. (2002). Mathematical problem-solving profiles of students with mathematics disabilities with and without comorbid reading disabilities. *Journal of Learning Disabilities, 35*, 563–57.

Fuchs, L.S., & Fuchs, D. (2005). Enhancing mathematical problem solving for students with disabilities. *The Journal of Special Education, 39*(1), 45–57.

Gallistel, C., & Gelman, R. (1992). Preverbal and verbal counting and computation. *Cognition, 44*, 43–74.

Geary, D. C. (1990). A componential analysis of an early learning deficit in mathematics. *Journal of Experimental Child Psychology, 49*, 363–383.

Geary, D. C. (1993). Mathematical disabilities: Cognitive, neuropsychological, and genetic components. *Psychological Bulletin, 114*, 345–362.

Geary, D. C. (1994). *Children's Mathematical Development*. Washington, DC: American Psychological Association.

Geary, D. C. (2004). Mathematics and learning disabilities. *Journal of Learning Disabilities, 37*, 4–15.

Geary, D. C., Bow-Thomas, C. C., Liu, F., & Siegler, R. S. (1996). Development of arithmetical competencies in Chinese and American children: Influence of age, language, and schooling. *Child Development, 67*, 2022–2044.

Geary, D., & Hoard, M. (2005). Learning disabilities in arithmetic and mathematics: Theoretical and empirical perspectives. In J. I. D. Campbell (Ed.), *Handbook of Mathematical Cognition* (pp. 253–267). New York: Psychology Press.

Gerber, M., Semmel, D., & Semmel, M. (1994). Computer-based dynamic assessment of multidigit multiplication. *Exceptional Children, 61*, 114–125.

Grabner, R. H., & Ansari, D. (2010). Promises and potential pitfalls of a "cognitive neuroscience of mathematics learning". *ZDM Mathematics Education, 42*, 655–660.

Heathcote, D. (1994). The role of visuospatial working memory in the mental addition of multi-digit addends. *Current Psychology of Cognition, 13*, 207–245.

Hecht, S. A., Torgesen, J. K., Wagner, R., & Rashotte, C. (2001). The relationship between phonological processing abilities and emerging individual differences in mathematical computation skills: A longitudinal study of second to fifth grades. *Journal of Experimental Child Psychology, 79*, 192–227.

Jitendra, A. K., & Xin, Y. (1997). Mathematical word-problem-solving instruction for students with mild disabilities and students at risk for math failure: A research synthesis. *The Journal of Special Education, 30*(4), 412–438.

Lanfranchi, S., Lucangeli, D., Jerman, O., & Swanson, H. L. (2008). Math disabilities: Italian and US perspectives. *Advances in Learning and Behavioral Disabilities, 21*, 277–308.

Mammarella, I. C., & Cornoldi, C. (2005). Difficulties in the control of irrelevant visuospatial information in children with visuospatial learning disabilities. *Acta Psychologica, 118*, 211–228.

Mammarella, I. C., Lucangeli, D., & Cornoldi, C. (2010). Spatial working memory and arithmetic deficits in children with nonverbal learning difficulties. *Journal of Learning Disabilities, 43*(5), 455–468.

Mazzocco, M. M. (2008). Defining and differentiating mathematical learning disabilities and difficulties. In D. B. Berch & M. M. Mazzocco (Eds.), *Why is Math So Hard for Some Children? The nature and origins of mathematical learning difficulties and disabilities*. Baltimore, MD: Brookes Publishing Company.

McCloskey, M., Caramazza, A., & Basili, A. (1985). Cognitive mechanisms in number processing and calculation: Evidence from dyscalculia. *Brain and Cognition, 4*, 171–196.

Menon, V., Rivera, S. M., White, C. D., Glover, G. H., & Reiss, A. L. (2000). Dissociating prefrontal and parietal cortex activation during arithmetic processing. *Neuroimage, 12*, 357–365.

Núñez, R., & Lakoff, G. (2005). The cognitive foundations of mathematics: The role of conceptual metaphor. In J. I. D. Campbell (Ed.), *Handbook of Mathematical Cognition* (pp. 109–125). New York: Psychology Press.

Pellegrino, J. W., & Goldman, S. J. (1987). Information processing and elementary mathematics. *Journal of Learning Disabilities, 20*, 23–32.

Piazza, M. (2010). Neurocognitive start-up tools for symbolic number representations. *Trends in Cognitive Sciences, 14*, 542–551.

Piazza, M., Facoetti, A., Trussardi, A. N., Berteletti, I., Conte, S., Lucangeli, D., et al. (2010). Developmental trajectory of number acuity reveals a severe impairment in developmental dyscalculia. *Cognition, 116*, 33–41.

Rourke, B. P. (1993). Arithmetic disabilities, specific and otherwise: A neuropsychological perspective. *Journal of Learning Disabilities, 26*(4), 214–226.

Rourke, B. P., & Finlayson, M. A. I. (1978). Neuropsychological significance of variations in patterns of academic performance: Verbal and visualspatial abilities. *Journal of Abnormal Child Psychology, 6*, 121–133.

Rousselle, L., & Noël, M. P. (2007). Basic numerical skills in children with mathematics learning disabilities: A comparison of symbolic vs non-symbolic number magnitude processing. *Cognition, 102*, 361–395.

Russell, R. L., & Ginsburg, H. P. (1984). Cognitive analysis of children's mathematical difficulties. *Cognition and Instruction, 1*, 217–244.

Schoenfeld, A. (1992). Learning to think mathematically: Problem solving, metacognition, and sense making in mathematics. In D. A. Grouws & the NCTM (Eds.), *Handbook of Research on Mathematics Teaching and Learning* (pp. 334–370). New York: Maxwell Macmillan International.

Schoenfeld, A. (2011). *How We Think: A theory of goal-oriented decision making and its educational applications*. New York: Routledge.

Stock, P., Desoete, A., & Roeyers, H. (2006). Focussing on mathematical disabilities: A search for definition, classification and assessment. In Soren V. Randall (Ed.), *Learning Disabilities New Research*. Nova Science Publishers.

Swanson, H. L., Jerman, O., & Zheng, X. (2008). Growth in working memory and mathematical problem solving in children at risk and not at risk for serious math difficulties. *Journal of Educational Psychology, 100*, 343–379.

Torgesen, J. K., & Houck, D. G. (1980). Processing deficiencies of learning-disabled children who perform poorly on the digit span test. *Journal of Educational Psychology, 72*(2), 141–160.

von Aster, M. (2000). Developmental cognitive neuropsychology of number processing and calculation: Varieties of developmental dyscalculia. *European Child & Adolescent Psychiatry, 9*, II/41–II/57.

Wilson, A. J., & Dehaene, S. (2007). Number sense and developmental dyscalculia. In D. Coch, G. Dawson, & K. W. Fischer (Eds.), *Human Behavior, Learning and the Developing Brain*. 2nd edition. New York: Guilford Press.

Woodward, J., & Montague, M. (2002). Meeting the challenge of mathematics reform for students with LD. *The Journal of Special Education, 36*(2), 89–101.

Zorzi, M., Stoianov, I., & Umiltà, C. (2005). Computational modeling of numerical cognition. In J. I. D. Campbell (Ed.), *Handbook of Mathematical Cognition* (pp. 67–84). New York: Psychology Press.

20

Numbersense

A window into dyscalculia and other mathematics difficulties

Mahesh C. Sharma

Acquiring the *number concept* or *numberness* – understanding number, its representation, and its applications, is a fundamental skill. It is like acquiring the alphabet of the mathematics language with arithmetic facts as its words.

Much of the research (Geary, 1993; Robinson et al., 2002) has focused on developing a theoretical understanding of mathematics learning difficulties. This chapter looks at the role of number concept and numbersense in mathematics learning difficulties and implications for instruction and interventions. Children's understanding and level of mastery of number concept and numbersense provide a window into their arithmetic difficulties, particularly dyscalculia (Dehaene et al., 1998, 1999; Gersten & Chard, 1999).

Numbersense deals with number concept, number combinations – arithmetic facts, computing and place value. Numbersense is a cluster of integrative skills: number concept, making meaning and ways of representing and establishing relationships among numbers, visualizing the relative magnitude of collections, estimating numerical outcomes and mastering arithmetic facts and proficiency in their usage (Dehaene et al., 1999; Fleischner et al., 1982). Numbersense is the flexible use of number relationships and making sense of numerical information in various contexts. Students with numbersense can represent and use a number in multiple ways depending on the context and purpose. In computations and operations, they can decompose and recompose numbers with ease and fluency. This proficiency and fluency in numbersense helps children acquire *numeracy*.

Numeracy is the ability to execute standard whole-number operations/algorithms correctly, consistently and fluently with understanding and estimate, calculate accurately and efficiently, both mentally and on paper using a range of calculation strategies and means. Numeracy is the gateway to higher mathematics, beginning with the study of algebra and geometry.

Many individuals encounter difficulties in mastering numeracy. Some have difficulties because of environmental factors – lack of appropriate number experiences, ineffective instruction and a fragmented curriculum, inefficient conceptual models and strategies, lack of appropriate skill development, and low expectations, and others because of individual capacities and learning disabilities. For example, teaching arithmetic facts by sequential counting ("counting up" for addition, "counting down" for subtraction, "skip counting" on a number line for multiplication and division), as advocated by many researchers and educators, is not an efficient strategy for many children including dyscalculics (Gelman & Gallistel, 1978; Gelman & Meek, 1983; Gelman et al., 1986).

Among those who exhibit learning problems in mathematics, some experience difficulty in specific aspects of mathematics – difficulty only in procedures, in conceptual processes, or in both. Some have difficulty in arithmetic, algebra or geometry. Some may have general learning disabilities in mathematics while others display symptoms only of dyscalculia.

Learning disability may manifest as deficits in the development of prerequisite skills: following sequential directions, spatial orientation/space organization, pattern recognition and extension, visualization and visual perception and deductive and inductive thinking. These deficits may affect learning ability in different aspects of mathematics, for example, a few isolated skills in one concept/procedure or several areas of arithmetic/mathematics. Some learning problems fall in the intersection of quantity, language and spatial thinking.

Because of the range of mathematics disabilities, we cannot clearly identify a cause or effect; no single explanation adequately addresses the nature of learning problems in mathematics. Most mathematics problems and difficulties, such as carryover problems, dyscalculia, or mathematics anxiety are manifested as lack of quantitative thinking. In this chapter, we are interested in one area of mathematics disabilities, the problems related to numeracy due to dyscalculia or acquired dyscalculia.

Nature of number-related learning problems: dyscalculia

Difficulties associated with numberness, numbersense, and numeracy are known as *dyscalculia*. Dyscalculia has the same prevalence as dyslexia (about 6–8% of children) although it is far less widely recognized by parents and educators (Ardilla & Roselli, 2002).

Dyscalculia is manifested as poor number concept, difficulty in estimating the size and magnitude of numbers, lack of understanding and fluency in number relationships, and inefficiency of numerical operations. Dyscalculics depend on immature and inefficient strategies such as sequential counting to solve problems that most children know by heart. At the same time, they find it hard to learn and remember arithmetic facts by sequential methods. Like dyslexics, they need special academic support. When taught with appropriate methods and efficient models, children respond favorably (Cohn, 1968; Dunlap & Brennen, 1982; Shalev et al., 2005).

A characteristic many dyslexics share with dyscalculics (Light & DeFries, 1995) is limited lexical entries for number and number relationships, and thus they face problems with automatic labeling of the outcome of number relationships – instant recall of arithmetic facts (e.g., multiplication tables). They do not have "sight facts" in their minds for numbers. Sight facts are like sight vocabulary, for example, knowing that 7 is 6 and 1; 5 and 2; and 4 and 3. Sight facts are instrumental in achieving automatization, the fluency to produce, for example, the fact $8 + 7 = 15$ in two seconds or less orally and three seconds in writing and understanding (using a non-counting strategy, e.g., $8 + 7$ is one more than $7 + 7$, therefore, $8 + 7 = 15$, or $8 + 2$ is 10 and then 5 more is 15). This lack of automatization, in most cases, is an artifact of poor instruction rather than a real difficulty or disability.

Problems that most dyscalculics face in arithmetic are due to poor number conceptualization and numbersense (Dehaene, 1997). Without exposure to efficient and effective methods of learning, children do not acquire proper number concepts, arithmetic facts, and standard procedures, and risk not gaining proficiency in mathematics by the end of first grade. Lack of success in the development of number becomes the main reason for a child's difficulty in learning mathematics and dyscalculia (Jordan et al. as cited in Gersten et al., 2005).

Just as it is possible to build lexical entries for words, letters and word-parts, it is also possible to acquire strategies to develop lexical entries for numbers, number facts, symbols, formulas and even equations. Although mathematical symbols themselves are not phonetic, each symbol represents a lexical entry whose meaning and interpretation can be understood (Ball & Blanchman, 1991).

Literacy and numeracy

There are many parallels in the development of literacy and numeracy, which we need to explore. Young children develop literacy through literacy practices (e.g., being read to at bedtime). Similarly, early exposure to the language and symbols of quantity and space creates lexical entries for quantity (number words) and the role of number (size/quantity) – what and how to quantify, what and how to measure, and how to represent and use quantities (Adams, 1990).

The complex process of mastering reading involves a variety of brain components and systems – both localized and global – that perform and integrate tasks such as recognizing and organizing symbols – visual and aural, discerning and analyzing sound patterns, perceiving spatial arrangements – source of speech or location of the symbol, and verbal and non-verbal clues. Some of the same mechanisms are called upon in acquiring numeracy and are related to language, visuo-spatial skills, sequencing, and working memory. A breakdown and deficits in any of these areas can affect learning letters and numbers alike. Many dyslexics, therefore, show symptoms of dyscalculia (Light & DeFries, 1995).

While there are important similarities in learning to read and conceptualizing number, there are also important differences. Some unique abilities and systems are needed to learn number and its applications. For this reason, there are people who can read and have poor numeracy skills, but there are very few numerates who cannot learn to read. Keeping in mind these unique differences, we need to design activities for making numeracy accessible to all children.

279

Phonemic awareness, numberness, and numbersense

Fluent reading and fluency in numberness are analogous. Research (Williams, 1995) in reading shows that phonemic awareness – the insight that words are composed of sounds and the ability to connect fluently grapheme to phoneme, and phonological sensitivity – the ability to break words into meaningful "chunks" and then "blend" them fluently – are predictors of early reading performance (better than IQ tests, readiness scores, or socioeconomic level) and essential for reading acquisition. Processes of numberness – one-to-one correspondence, sequencing, visual clustering, and decomposition/recomposition, representation of number orally and graphically – are similar. The ability to associate a number to a cluster is like phonemic awareness and the ability to instantly recognize that a number is made of smaller numbers (decomposition/recomposition) is equivalent to chunking and blending. Numberness is a predictor for future proficiency and fluency in arithmetic.

Understanding of phonemic awareness has revolutionized the teaching of beginning reading. Numberness and numbersense carry similar implications for instruction for children with or without learning difficulties. The proper definition and development of numberness and numbersense is the key to planning remediation for dyscalculics and preventing acquired dyscalculia. However, educators and psychologists have taken a narrow view of number concept – for example, the ability to count forward and backward (Gelman & Gallistel, 1978; Klein et al., 2002; McCloskey & Mancuso, 1995; Moomaw & Hieronymous, 1995).

In reading one needs to focus on the phonemes in a word; in math one needs to see clusters of objects in the mind's eye. Most children have difficulty forming visual clusters in their minds and sight facts by one-to-one counting. Decoding letters in a word does not lead to reading; similarly, counting individual objects/numbers (concretely or sub-vocally) does not lead to numberness. In fact, one-to-one counting turns most children into counters – that is all. To conceptualize number, one needs to see clusters (decomposition) in a collection and integrate smaller clusters into larger clusters (recomposition). Associating a number name to the collection and relating this number to smaller clusters (numbers) is forming sight facts. Recognizing clusters (sight facts) is like recognizing phonemes and sight words. With the help of sight facts, children can move beyond counting and learn arithmetic facts at an automatized level. Many LD children have difficulty forming visual clusters in their minds and sight facts by one-to-one counting (Schaeffer et al., 1974).

The mastery of numberness and proficiency in arithmetic and phonemic awareness and the ability to read with understanding are parallel activities; nevertheless, it is also important to recognize the differences between the two processes. Phonemic awareness involves a focus on auditory processes and phonological decoding associates grapheme and phoneme, whereas visual perceptual integration – recognizing clusters, estimating by observation, and decomposition/recomposition of clusters – is fundamental to the development of numberness.

Parallels: letter recognition and number concept – numberness

A child knows the alphabet when he can:

- Identify the letter (shown M, he recognizes it instantly),
- Recognize the letter in its variant forms (e.g., *MS*, ms, *MS*, ms, *MS*, ms, *MS*, ms, *MS*, etc.),
- Recognize letters among other symbols (e.g., M in CALM, MILK, WARMER, M569A, etc.),
- Write the letter and describe the various strokes in the proper order, and
- Associate a sound to the letter (e.g., M as in monkey).

This should be true for all letters of the alphabet. Mastery of number is similar and is more than just reciting and writing the numbers. A child has number concept when he:

- Possesses lexical entries for number (knows number names and the difference between number words and non-number words) (Fuson, 1980; Fuson et al., 1982),
- Can meaningfully count (one-to-one correspondence + sequencing) (Fuson et al., 1982; Piaget, 1968; Pufall et al., 1973; Saxe, 1979),
- Can recognize and assign a number to a collection/cluster (organized in a pattern up to ten objects) without counting (Resnick, 1993),
- Can represent a collection – a *visual cluster* of seven objects *graphical representation*, e.g., 7,
- Can write the number when heard (hears *s-e-v-e-n* and writes 7), and
- Can decompose and recompose a cluster into two sub-clusters (i.e., a number, up to 10, as sum of two numbers and vice-versa).

Images of visual clusters in the mind's eye provide a child a base of "sight facts." For example, when one sees the visual cluster of seven objects, one recognizes the sight facts: $7 = 1 + 6 = 2 + 5 = 3 + 4$ without counting. These sight facts, with strategies of addition and subtraction based on decomposition/recomposition, provide a strong base for arithmetic facts mastery beyond 10. *Numberness*, thus, is the integration of:

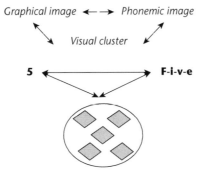

Mastery of number concept/numberness, arithmetic facts (arrived at by using decomposition/recomposition) and place value is called *numbersense*. Lack of proper instruction in numberness and numbersense poses conditions of failure in early mathematics. Instruction in strategies for deriving arithmetic facts and procedures are much more productive when number concept is intact (Geary, 1994; Gelman, 1977).

Language and number

Early number conceptualization begins with concrete experiences – counting objects in context. Many children become and remain counters because of this early emphasis on counting. Appropriate concrete experiences accompanied with rich language, on the other hand, help abstract the experience into concepts with labels. Neither concrete experiences alone, nor purely language-based teaching develop the concept of number for all children. For abstraction of concrete experiences into numberness, language is essential. Children must transcend the concrete models in order to learn to solve problems and communicate through mathematical symbols. This concurrent thinking of numbers as concrete and abstract is at the core of true number conceptualization and is a real challenge for many children (Baroody, 1992; Brainerd, 1992; Copeland, 1974).

Mathematics language and native language

In the child's native language, numbers function as predicators and qualifiers: five dishes, many books, fewer children, etc. They function like adjectives in a sentence. Most children are quite fluent in this before they enter kindergarten (Carruthers & Worthington, 2005).

Later, numbers function not only as predicators but also as real, concrete objects: six hundred is a big number, an even number, or much smaller than the number six hundred thousand. Thus, in the language of mathematics, numbers are qualifiers as well as "real" abstract objects. Mathematical operations can be performed on numbers when we treat them as real, concrete entities (Williams, 1977).

Conceptualizing number requires a child to perform two simultaneous abstractions: to *translate sensory, concrete representations of quantity into symbolic entities* (5 represents any collection of five objects) and to *transform a number as a predicate in the native language to its conception as objects in the language of mathematics* (Wynn, 1996, 1998). For some children, particularly LD children, these transitions are not easy and need to be facilitated carefully using *appropriate language*, an *enabling questioning process*, and *efficient instructional models*.

Mastering the concept of number

Lexical entries and egocentric counting to the cardinality of the set

Children develop lexical entries for number by hearing others count and copying this process. Number words are essential but not sufficient for fluent number conceptualization and usage. Consider the number work of a five-year-old.

Teacher: How many cubes are there? (Points to the collection.)

□ □ □ □ □ □ □

Child: (Counts by touching each cube) Seven.
Teacher: What number came just before seven?
Child: One? Three? Five? I don't know.
Teacher: Can you give me six cubes?
Child: Do I have enough? Maybe I do. (She counts six cubes and gives them to the teacher.)
Teacher: That is right.
(Teacher rearranges them.)
Teacher: How many cubes are there now?
Child: (She counts them) Seven.
Teacher: Yes!

Most children can count objects in a rote manner. For many of them, even at age 6, the cardinality of the set is the outcome of their counting process, not a property of the collection. Number is the product of *egocentric* counting ("These are six blocks. I just counted them") rather than the property of the collection ("These are six cubes"). This is a key step in number conceptualization. Consider number work with another kindergartener.

Teacher: How many cubes are there? (Points to the collection.)
Child: (Counts them) Seven.

□ □ □ □ □ □ □

Teacher: Yes! You counted them from left to right (points to the direction). Do you think you will have the same number if you counted them from right to left? (Points to the direction.)
Child: I do not know. Let me try.
Child: (Counts them) Seven.
Teacher: That is right.
Child: (Counts them again) Seven. It is always seven.

The child associates a number to the collection as the property of the collection. Scaffolding questions resulted in converting a child's concrete experiences and egocentric counting into the cardinal number.

Development of visual clusters

For number conceptualization, the child must transcend counting (Turner, 2003; Sophian & Kalihiwa, 1998). Young children spontaneously use the ability to recognize and discriminate small numbers of objects. This is called subitizing (Clements, 1999; Klein & Starkey, 1988). Subitizing is instantly seeing how many are in a small collection of objects. But some young children cannot immediately name the number of objects in a collection. It is important for number conceptualizing. Work with dominos, dice, and playing cards helps in the process (Clements & Callahan, 1986). However, for efficient number concept, subitizing must be extended to numbers up to ten. We term that process as forming visual clusters in the mind. Visual Cluster Cards™ (VCC), with modified arrangements of clusters, are especially effective for developing visual clustering and then number concept.

A VCC deck (60 cards) consists of cards with 1 to 10 pips in four suits (heart, diamond, club, and spade); two cards with no pips represent zero; and 2 jokers (can be assigned any value). Numbers 3, 8, 9, and 10 have two representations in each suit. For example, number 3 is represented as:

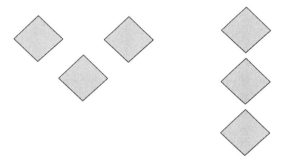

The pips on higher number cards are organized so that the sub-clusters of smaller numbers can be instantaneously recognized. For example, on the 7-card, one can see clusters of 4 and 3; 5 and 2; and 6 and 1. No number names are displayed on the cards.

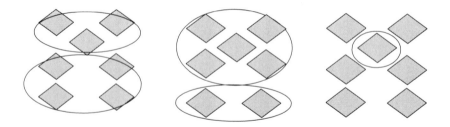

Creating images of visual clusters and developing the decomposition/recomposition process of numbers are at the heart of number conceptualization and arithmetic facts. Many children might achieve the decomposition/recomposition skill through counting; however, many children, particularly those with special needs, have difficulty achieving this with counting. Robinson et al. (2002) proposed that interventions for students with poor mastery of arithmetic combinations should include two aspects: (a) interventions to help build more rapid retrieval of information and (b) concerted instruction in any areas of numbersense that are underdeveloped in a child. VC cards help achieve both.

The teacher introduces the VC cards for 1, 2 and 3. She identifies the cards by counting the pips. The card with two pips is identified as 2; 1 and 1; or two ones. Children learn that each visual cluster card is made of sub-clusters. For example, the teacher displays the card with three pips.

Teacher: Look at the card. How many diamonds are on the card?
Child One: Three.
Teacher: What three numbers make 3?
Child Two: 1 + 1 + 1.
Teacher: Look at the card with a circle around the diamonds. How many diamonds are circled?

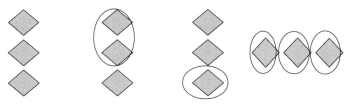

Children: Two.
Teacher: How many are not circled?
Children: One.
Teacher: What two numbers make 3?
Child One: 2 and 1.
Child Two: 1 and 2.
Teacher: Right! 2 + 1 makes 3 (traces the two circled diamonds and the one diamond); 1 + 2 also makes 3 (traces the one individual circled diamond and then the two diamonds); 1 + 1 + 1 also makes 3 (traces the three individual circled diamonds).

Once children have created the image of number 3 in the standard form, they do the same with the three objects organized in another form. For example:

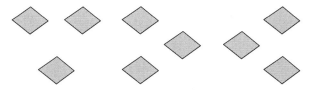

The same process is used for developing the cluster images for higher numbers. For example, the teacher introduces the card representing number 5.

Teacher:	How many diamonds are there?
Children (count the diamonds on the card and say):	Five.
Teacher:	We will call this the 5-card. How many diamonds are there in the first column of the card? (She traces the first column.)
Children:	2.
Teacher:	Yes. It represents the number 2.
Teacher:	Now, how many diamonds are there in the last column? (She traces the last column.)
Children:	2.
Teacher:	Good! It also represents number 2.
Teacher:	Look at the middle column. How many diamonds are in the middle column?
Children:	One!
Teacher:	What if the middle diamond was not there, what number will the card represent?
Children:	4.
Teacher:	Very good! (If a child is unable to answer, the teacher displays the card by covering the middle pip or shows the 4-card again.) What if the first column was not there, what number will the rest of the card represent?
Children:	3.
Teacher:	Very good! What if the last column was not there, what number will the rest of the card represent?
Children:	3.

The teacher continues till children have created the image of the cluster of number 5 in their minds. Every child should be able to identify the card in less than two seconds (without counting). They also know that the cluster of 5 has component sub-clusters of 2 and 3; 4 and 1; or 2, 2, and 1.

Teacher:	Remember the card we have been looking at? I am going to show the card, but a portion of the card will be hidden. You need to tell me the missing number. (She hides the first column.) How many are visible?
Children:	3.
Teacher:	How many are hidden?
Children:	2.
Teacher:	What two numbers make 5?
Children:	2 and 3.
Teacher:	Great! (She uncovers the hidden part of the card and shows the 5-card). Yes, 2 and 3 make 5.

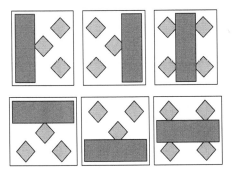

Finally, each child has formed images of the number 5 as a visual cluster and its relationship with other numbers (decomposition/recomposition) as 4 + 1; 3 + 2; 2 + 2 + 1; and 1 + 1 + 1 + 1 + 1. Then she asks them to write these relationships.

Thus, knowing a number means having the ability to write the number, use it as a count, recognize the visual cluster, and understand that it is made up of smaller numbers. This is true for all ten numbers:

2 = 1 + 1

3 = 2 + 1 = 1 + 2

4 = 3 + 1 = 1 + 3 = 2 + 2

. . .

10 = 9 + 1 = 1 + 9 = 8 + 2 = 2 + 8 = 3 + 7 = 7 + 3 = 6 + 4 = 4 + 6 = 5 + 5

Without the idealized image of these numbers and the decomposition/recomposition process, children have difficulty in developing fluency in number relationships. Most dyscalculics and many underachievers in mathematics have not learned number concept properly.

Cuisenaire rods are another efficient tool for developing and extending the decomposition/recomposition of numbers achieved through visual cluster cards. For example, the number 10 can be shown as the combination of two numbers as follows (the same process is used for other numbers):

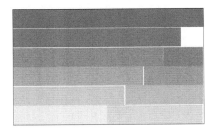

$$10 = 9 + 1 = 1 + 9$$

$$10 = 8 + 2 = 2 + 8$$

$$10 = 7 + 3 = 3 + 7$$

$$10 = 4 + 6 = 6 + 4$$

$$10 = 5 + 5$$

Both Visual Cluster Cards and Cuisenaire rods help children to create and learn these decompositions.

Concept of addition

Early mathematics interventions should focus on building fluency and proficiency with basic arithmetic facts as well as more accurate and efficient use of addition strategies (Gersten et al., 2005; Siegler, 1991, 1988). When children achieve fluency and efficiency in arithmetic combinations, teachers can assume that they are able to follow explanations of concepts or procedures.

Once children conceptualize idealized images of the ten numbers in the 'mind's eye', they form sight facts and then easily learn addition facts. For example:

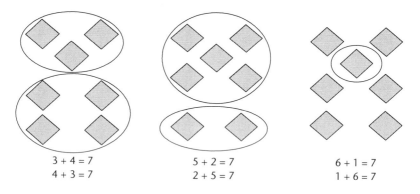

| $3 + 4 = 7$ | $5 + 2 = 7$ | $6 + 1 = 7$ |
| $4 + 3 = 7$ | $2 + 5 = 7$ | $1 + 6 = 7$ |

7 is made up of 4 and 3; 5 and 2; and 6 and 1.

Addition of numbers is facilitated through strategies of decomposition and recomposition of numbers. For example, to add 8 and 6 it is much easier to take two from 6 and give it to 8 so that the number combination can easily be seen as: $8 + 6 = 8 + (2 + 4) = (8 + 2) + 4 = 10 + 4$ equals 14. Decomposition (the breaking of 6 as $2 + 4$ and thinking of 10 as $8 + 2$) and recomposition (thinking of $10 + 4$ as 14) are key strategies for learning addition and subtraction facts.

When children do not automatize facts, they are unable to apply their knowledge to newer situations. To find the answer to a number problem, they digress from the main problem to generate the facts needed for solving problems. Because of the use of inefficient strategies, such as counting, their working memory space is filled in the process of constructing these facts, then it is not available to pay attention to instruction, observe patterns, or focus on concepts, nuances, relationships, and subtleties involved in the concepts.

A child's struggles with arithmetic facts in kindergarten and first grade reflect a difficulty in transitioning from concrete to abstract number relationships and should trigger an intense intervention program in numberness and numbersense that focuses on visual clustering and decomposition/recomposition skills (Van Engen & Steffe, 1970). The use of tools such as Visual Cluster Cards and Cuisenaire rods can achieve that goal, prevent the development of acquired dyscalculia, and mitigate the effects of dyscalculia.

References

Adams, M. J. (1990). *Beginning to read: Thinking and learning about print.* Cambridge, MA: MIT Press.

Ardilla, A., & Rosselli, M. (2002). Acalculia and dyscalculia. *Neuropsychology Review, 12*(4), 179–231.

Ball, E. W., & Blanchman, B. A. (1991). Does phoneme awareness training in kindergarten make a difference in early word recognition and developmental spelling? *Reading Research Quarterly, 26,* 49–99.

Baroody, A. J. (1992). Remedying common counting difficulties. In J. Bideaud, J. P. Fischer, C. Greenbaum, & C. Meljac (Eds.), *Pathways to number: Children's developing numerical abilities* (pp. 307–324). Hillsdale, NJ: Erlbaum.

Brainerd, C. J. (1992). *The origins of the number concept.* New York: Praeger.

Carruthers, E., & Worthington, M. (2005). *Children's mathematics: Making marks, making meaning.* London, UK: Sage.

Clements, D. H. (1999). Subitizing: What is it? Why teach it? *Teaching children mathematics* (December), Reston, VA: NCTM.

Clements, D. H., & Callahan, L. G. (1986). Cards: A good deal to offer. *Arithmetic Teacher, 34,* 14–17.

Cohn, R. (1968). Developmental dyscalculia. *Pediatric Clinics of North America, 75*(3), 651–668.

Copeland, R. (1974). *How children learn mathematics: Teaching implications of Piaget's research.* New York: Macmillan.

Dehaene, S. (1997). *The number sense: How the mind creates mathematics.* New York: Oxford University Press.

Dehaene, S., Dehaene-Lambertz, G., & Cohen, L. (1998). Abstract representations of numbers in the animal and human brain. *Trends in Neuroscience, 21,* 355–361.

Dehaene, S., Spelke, E., Pinel, P., Stanescu, R., & Tsivkin, S. (1999). Sources of mathematical thinking: Behavioral and brain-imaging evidence. *Science, 284*(5416), 970–973.

Dunlap, W., & Brennen, A. (1982). Blueprint for the diagnosis of difficulties with cardinality. *Journal of Learning Disabilities, 14*(1), 12–14.

Fleischner, F., Garnett, K., & Shepard, M. (1982). Proficiency in arithmetic basic fact computation by learning disabled and nondisabled children. *Focus on Learning Problems in Mathematics, 4*(2), 47–55.

Fuson, K. (1980). The counting word sequence as a representation tool. In R. Karplus (Ed.), *Proceedings of the Fourth International Conference for the Psychology of Mathematics Education.* Berkeley, CA: University of California.

Fuson, K., Richards, J., & Briars, D. (1982). The acquisition and elaboration of the number word sequence. In C. Brainerd (Ed.), *Children's logical and mathematical cognition.* New York: Springer Verlag.

Geary, D. (1993). Mathematical disabilities: Cognitive, neuropsychological, and genetic components. *Psychological Bulletin, 114,* 345–362.

Geary, D. (1994). *Children's mathematical development.* Washington, DC: American Psychological Association.

Gelman, R. (1977). How young children reason about small numbers. In N. J. Castellan, D. B. Pisoni, & G. R. Potts (Eds.), *Cognitive Theory, 2,* 219–238. Hillsdale, NJ: Erlbaum.

Gelman, R., & Gallistel, C. R. (1978). *The child's understanding of number.* Cambridge, MA: Harvard University Press.

Gelman, R., & Meek, E. (1983). Preschooler's counting: Principles before skills. *Cognition, 13,* 343–360.

Gelman, R., Meek, E., & Merkin, S. (1986). Young children's numerical competence. *Cognitive Development, 1,* 1–30.

Gersten, R., & Chard, D. (1999). Number sense: Rethinking arithmetic instruction for students with mathematical disabilities. *The Journal of Special Education, 33*(1), 18–28.

Gersten, R., Jordan, N. C., & Flojo, J. R. (2005). Early identification and interventions for students with mathematics difficulties. *Journal of Learning Disabilities, 38*(4), 293–304.

Klein, A., Starkey, P., & Ramirez, A. B. (2002). *Pre-K mathematics curriculum.* Boston, MA: Scott-Foresman.

Light, J., & DeFries, J. (1995). Comorbidity of reading and mathematics disabilities: Genetic and environmental etiologies. *Journal of Learning Disabilities, 28*(2), 96–106.

McCloskey, M., & Mancuso, P. (1990). Representing and using numerical information. *American Psychologist, 50,* 351–363.

Moomaw, S., & Hieronymus, B. (1995). *More than counting: Whole mathematics for preschool and kindergarten.* St. Paul, MN: Redleaf Press.

Piaget, J. (1968). Quantification, conservation, and nativism. *Science, 162,* 976–979.

Pufall, P., Shaw, R., & Syrdal-Lasky, A. (1973). Development of number conservation: An examination of some predictions from Piaget's stage analysis and equilibration model. *Child Development, 44*(1), 21–27.

Resnick, L. (1993). A developmental theory of number understanding. In H. Ginsberg (Ed.), *The development of mathematical thinking* (pp. 109–151). New York: Academic Press.

Robinson, C., Menchetti, B., & Torgesen, J. (2002). Toward a two-factor theory of one type of mathematics disabilities. *Learning Disabilities Research & Practice, 17,* 81–89.

Saxe, G. (1979). A developmental analysis of notational counting. *Child Development, 48,* 1512–1520.

Schaeffer, B., Eggleston, V., & Scott, J. (1974). Number development in young children. *Cognitive Psychology, 6,* 357–379.

Shalev, R. S., Manor, O., & Gross-Tsur, V. (2005). Developmental dyscalculia: A prospective six-year follow-up. *Developmental Medicine and Child Neurology, 47*(2), 121–125.

Siegler, R. (1988). Individual differences in strategy choices: Good students, not-so good students, and perfectionists. *Child Development, 59,* 833–851.

Siegler, R. (1991). In young children's counting, procedures precede principles. *Educational Psychology Review, 3,* 127–135.

Sophian, C., & Kailihiwa, C. (1998). Units of counting: Developmental changes. *Cognitive Development, 13,* 561–585.

Turner, M. (2003). *Tally marks: How to visualize and develop first skills in mental maths* (report). Essex, UK: SEN and Psychological Services.

Van Engen, H., & Steffe, L. (1970). First-grade children's concept of addition of natural numbers. In R. Ashlock & W. L. Herman (Eds.), *Current research in elementary school mathematics.* New York: Macmillan.

Williams, J. (1995). Phonemic awareness. In T. Harris & R. Hodges (Eds.), *The literacy dictionary* (pp. 185–186), Newark, DE: International Reading Association.

Williams, R. (1977). Ordination and cardination in counting and Piaget's number concept task. *Perceptual and Motor Skills, 45,* 386.

Wynn, K. (1996). Origins of numerical knowledge. In B. Butterworth (Ed.), *Mathematical cognition* (vol. 1) (pp. 35–60). London, UK: Erlbaum, Taylor & Francis Ltd.

Wynn, K. (1998). Numerical competence in infants. In C. Donlan (Ed.), *The development of mathematical skills* (pp. 2–25). Hove, UK: Psychology Press.

Suggested reading

Chomsky, N. (2006). *Language and mind*. Cambridge, UK: Cambridge University Press.

Sharma, M. (2008). *How to master arithmetic facts easily and effectively*. Framingham, MA: CT/LM.

Sharma, M. (2008). *Mathematics number games*. Framingham, MA: CT/LM.

Sharma, M. (1981). Prerequisite and support skills for mathematics learning. *The Math Notebook, 2*(1).

Sharma, M. (1981). Visual clustering and number conceptualization. *The Math Notebook, 2*(10).

Sharma, M., & Loveless, E. (Eds.) (1986). Developmental dyscalculia. *Focus on Learning Problems in Mathematics, 8*(3 & 4).

Shipley, E., & Shepperson, B. (1990). Countable entities: Developmental changes. *Cognition, 34*, 109–136.

Skemp, R. (1971). *Psychology of learning mathematics*. Harmondsworth, UK: Pelican.

Vygostky, L. (1962). *Thought and language*. Cambridge, MA: MIT Press.

21

The Center for Improving Learning of Fractions

A progress report

Robert Siegler, Lynn Fuchs, Nancy Jordan,
Russell Gersten, and Rob Ochsendorf

This chapter has two interrelated purposes. The first, and primary, goal is to report findings from our Center regarding the development of understanding of fractions and the effectiveness of interventions based on those findings. The second goal is to describe how research centers that bring together investigators with complementary skills and knowledge can pursue objectives of scholarly and public importance that none of the investigators could reach individually.

History of the project

In the last ten years, knowledge on the cognitive underpinnings of learning difficulties in mathematics has increased substantially (e.g., Berch & Mazzocco, 2007; Geary, 2010). These advances have been achieved in large part through the application of cognitive theory and experimental methods to understanding cognitive processing in individuals with such difficulties. For example, sophisticated experimental paradigms have revealed that children with mathematics difficulties often have limited working memory resources relative to peers without such difficulties (e.g., Geary, Hoard, Byrd-Craven, Nugent, & Numtee, 2007; Swanson & Jerman, 2006).

Despite these advances in our understanding of cognitive processes underlying mathematics difficulties, relatively little work has been done to capitalize on this research and develop innovative strategies for improving instruction for students who struggle to learn mathematics – in particular, for students with learning disabilities in mathematics or those who are at-risk for developing learning disabilities in mathematics.

To complement its existing research programs in mathematics education, in 2010 the National Center for Special Education Research (NCSER) at the Institute of Education Sciences (IES) held a competition for a research and development center on improving mathematics instruction for students with mathematics difficulties. The

Request for Applications stipulated that the center would conduct a focused program of research utilizing cognitive science to develop innovative approaches to improving instruction for students with learning difficulties in mathematics. The focused program of research was intended to extend scientific knowledge of the underlying cognitive processes that contribute to learning difficulties in mathematics in order to identify new approaches for intervening and providing more effective instruction for these students. IES has demonstrated a strong commitment to funding research projects that make use of cognitive science principles to help tackle the challenges inherent in formal education. It was the Institute's hope that such an interdisciplinary approach would lead to effective innovations in mathematics instruction for students with disabilities.

As a result of this competition, in 2010 IES announced a five-year, $10 million cooperative agreement with the University of Delaware to launch the Center for Improving Learning of Fractions. Fractions seemed a particularly important focus for this Center, because fractions are so difficult for so many children. For example, despite children in the U.S. receiving substantial fractions instruction *beginning in third or fourth grade* (NCTM, 2006), the 2004 National Assessment of Educational Progress (NAEP) revealed that 50% of *eighth graders* could not correctly order three fractions (2/7, 1/12, and 5/9) from least to greatest. The difficulty continues in high school and college; for example, on another NAEP item, fewer than 30% of 11th graders translated 0.029 into the correct fraction (Kloosterman, 2010). Community college students also struggle with fractions; a sample of such adults could identify the larger of two fractions on only 70% of trials, despite chance yielding 50% correct performance (Schneider & Siegler, 2010).

The Center's core activities involve three simultaneous strands of research: (1) small-scale experimental studies examining the cognitive processes underlying magnitude representations of fractions, (2) a longitudinal study to identify key predictors of learning difficulties with fractions, (3) development and testing of an intervention focused on improving understanding of fraction magnitudes. Different co-PI's on the grant had expertise in each of these three areas – Siegler in small experimental studies and the theoretical analyses they are designed to test, Jordan in large-scale longitudinal studies, and Fuchs in randomized controlled trial intervention studies. In addition, Russell Gersten has expertise in all of these areas, as well as in dissemination of research. The remainder of this chapter will focus on the considerable progress that we have made in each of these strands.

Theoretical analysis and small-scale experimental tests

Underlying the research in all three strands of our project is the integrated theory of numerical development (Siegler, Thompson, & Schneider, 2011). Within this theory, fractions are viewed as crucial not only because they express values that cannot be expressed with whole numbers but also because they provide most children's first opportunity to expand their understanding of numbers beyond the properties of whole numbers. All whole numbers can be represented by a single numeral, have unique successors, never decrease with multiplication, never increase with division, and so on. Many children naturally assume that these are properties of all numbers, because all of their numerical experience has been with whole numbers. However, none of these properties is true of fractions or of numbers in general. Instead, the only property that all real numbers have in common is that they have magnitudes that can be located and ordered on number lines. Thus, understanding fractions contributes to the process of numerical development both by indicating that many properties that are true of all whole numbers are not true of numbers in general and by indicating that one quality unites all types of real numbers – that they possess magnitudes and can be ordered on number lines.

Understanding fractions requires both conceptual and procedural knowledge. Conceptual knowledge of fractions involves knowing what fractions are: that they are numbers that stretch from negative to positive infinity; that between any two fractions are an infinite number of other fractions; that the numerator-denominator relation, rather than either number alone, determines fraction magnitudes; that fraction magnitudes increase with numerator size and decrease with denominator size; that fractions can be represented as points on number lines; and so on.

A particularly important type of conceptual understanding of fractions is knowledge of their magnitudes. Several measures of fraction magnitude knowledge, including number line estimation, magnitude comparison, and ordering of several fractions, correlate highly with proficiency at fraction arithmetic and overall mathematics achievement among people 10 years and older (Bailey, Hoard, Nugent, & Geary, 2012; Booth & Newton, 2012; Jordan, et al., 2013; Mazzocco & Devlin, 2008; Siegler & Pyke, 2013; Siegler et al., 2011, 2012). The relation between fraction magnitude knowledge and overall mathematics achievement remains strongly present even when procedural knowledge (fraction arithmetic competence) is statistically controlled.

Acquiring conceptual knowledge of fractions poses several challenges. A major source of difficulty acquiring conceptual knowledge of fractions is that children's massive prior experience with integers leads to a whole-number bias, in which properties of positive integers are incorrectly generalized to fractions (Ni & Zhou, 2005). For example, based on their knowledge of whole numbers, even high school students often claim that there are no numbers between fractions such as 5/7 and 6/7 (as there are no integers between 5 and 6), and that multiplication cannot yield products smaller than both multiplicands (Vamvakoussi & Vosniadou, 2004, 2010). A related difficulty comes in understanding how the relation between numerator and denominator, rather than either alone, determines fraction magnitude – for example, that 2/3 > 5/9, even though both the numerator and denominator of 2/3 are smaller (Fazio, Bailey, Thompson, & Siegler, 2014).

Procedural knowledge of fractions – knowledge of fraction arithmetic – is also difficult. One reason is that fraction arithmetic violates several patterns that children observe with whole numbers. Learning that multiplication can produce answers smaller than either multiplicand (e.g., 1/2 ⋆ 1/4 = 1/8) is difficult to grasp for children who conclude from their experience or teacher statements that multiplication cannot have this effect. Another source of difficulty is that fraction arithmetic procedures overlap in complex ways that underlie several widespread types of errors. For example, maintaining the same denominator is appropriate when adding or subtracting fractions (e.g., $3/5 - 1/5 = 2/5$), but it is inappropriate when multiplying or dividing them (e.g., $3/5 \star 1/5 \neq 3/5$). Children often become confused regarding the operations that require equal denominators and what to do on problems that have equal denominators when the operation does not require them (as in $3/5 \star 1/5$). Similarly, performing the same operation on numerators and denominators independently leads to correct multiplication answers (e.g., $1/2 \star 1/3 = (1\star1)/(2 \star 3) = 1/6$), but operating independently on numerator and denominators leads to incorrect addition and subtraction answers (e.g., $1/2 + 1/3 \neq 2/5$). Conceptual understanding of why some fraction arithmetic procedures are appropriate and others inappropriate would almost certainly reduce or eliminate such errors, but few U.S. teachers have such understanding themselves (unlike East Asian teachers, who typically do possess this conceptual understanding of fraction arithmetic procedures; see Ma (1999) and Moseley, Okamoto & Ishida (2007)).

Consistent with the central role accorded to fractions in the integrated theory of numerical development, failure to master fractions has large consequences. It impedes acquisition of more advanced mathematics (National Mathematics Advisory Panel, 2008); indicative of this phenomenon, a nationally representative sample of 1,000 U.S. Algebra 1 teachers rated fractions as one of the two largest weaknesses in students' preparation for their course (NORC, 2008). Failure to master fractions also precludes participation in many remunerative and satisfying occupations (McCloskey, 2007).

Consistent with these informed opinions, a variety of studies have found that fraction knowledge is closely related to overall mathematics achievement, both when the two are measured at the same age and when earlier knowledge of fractions is related to later mathematics achievement (Bailey et al., 2012; Booth & Newton, 2012; Mazzocco & Devlin, 2008; Siegler & Pyke, 2013; Siegler et al., 2011). For example, analyses of two large, longitudinal data sets, one from the U.S. and one from the U.K., indicated that fifth graders' knowledge of fractions uniquely predicted those students' knowledge of algebra and overall mathematics achievement in high school 5–6 years later, even after statistically controlling for other mathematical knowledge, verbal and nonverbal IQ, reading comprehension, working memory, and family income and education (Siegler et al., 2012).

Children with difficulties learning mathematics in general tend to have particular problems learning fractions. One example of this phenomenon was evident in a study of sixth and eighth graders' knowledge of fractions (Siegler & Pyke, 2013). Typically achieving sixth graders (those in the top two-thirds of their age group on mathematics achievement test scores) were already more advanced in their knowledge of fraction arithmetic than low-achieving peers, and the typically achieving students' fraction arithmetic knowledge increased substantially between sixth and eighth grade, from 49% to 73% correct. In contrast, low-achieving children, those in the bottom one-third of their age group on the same achievement test, were already behind in sixth grade and only increased from 32% to 40% correct from sixth to eighth grade. This much slower rate of progress occurred despite all of the children being in the same classrooms and having the same teachers and textbooks. Thus, at least in the U.S., children generally have difficulty acquiring conceptual and procedural knowledge of fractions, and children with math learning difficulties have particular difficulty.

Longitudinal tests of theoretical predictions

The Delaware longitudinal study is examining the development of fraction concepts and procedures from third through sixth grade. The goal is to identify key component processes and skills that predict or underlie fraction learning. Tests were presented to 481 children in the winter of their third grade year (2010–2011). Drawn from two school districts in Delaware (U.S.A.), the children represented a diverse range of ethnicities, SES status, and ability levels. Because we were especially interested in children at-risk for learning difficulties or disabilities in mathematics, we oversampled in schools located in low-income communities (i.e., about 60% of children in our sample were identified as low-income based on their participation in free or reduced lunch programs).

Based on the integrated theory of numerical development, we hypothesized that accurate representations of numerical magnitudes would be uniquely important for acquisition of fraction knowledge. To test this premise, we examined the degree to which domain-general cognitive processes and number-specific knowledge in third grade predicted fraction outcomes at the end of fourth grade, after children had finished their first year of formal instruction on rational numbers (Jordan et al., 2013). General predictors included attentive behavior in the classroom, working memory, language, reading fluency, and nonverbal reasoning; number-specific predictors were number line estimation of whole numbers (0 to 1000), approximate number system acuity (e.g., rapid distinction between sets of items without counting), and calculation fluency. Fraction outcomes included measures of fraction concepts (e.g., magnitude comparisons and equivalence judgments) and fraction procedures (i.e., computation with fractions).

Confirming our main hypothesis, ability to estimate placement of whole numbers on a number line was the most important contributor to both aspects of fraction knowledge. For fraction concepts, the full set of predictors accounted for 56% of the variance, with number line estimation, calculation fluency, language, nonverbal reasoning, and attentive behavior each making significant unique contributions. For fraction procedures, the set of predictors accounted for only 30% of the variance in performance, with number line estimation, working memory, attentive behavior, and calculation fluency each making unique contributions.

Why is facility on a number line estimation task that involves whole numbers an important predictor of knowledge of fractions, over and above general calculation skill? Both whole numbers and fractions have magnitudes that can be located on number lines (Siegler et al., 2011). Insights with whole numbers give children an advantage in learning fraction concepts as well. Moreover, proportional reasoning, which underpins fraction understanding, may be involved in the whole-number line estimation task (Barth & Paladino, 2011).

In a follow-up study, one year later (end of fifth grade), we examined whether ability to estimate whole-number magnitudes on a number line continues to predict fraction outcomes, or whether other fraction-relevant processes supersede whole-number understanding (Hansen et al., under review). We re-administered the number line estimation task with whole numbers to the same group of children early in fifth grade, along with tasks assessing the ability to estimate fractions on a number line (ranging from 0 to 1, 0 to 2, and 0 to 5) and to judge proportional equivalence of visually depicted proportions (Boyer & Levine, 2012). Estimating on a fraction number line task requires more strategic analysis than on a whole-number line. To locate 2/3 on a 0–2 number line, for example, students must understand that 2/3 is less than one, in an absolute sense. They might divide the line in half to find the location of 1, then divide one into thirds, and then place their mark at 2/3. The proportional reasoning task draws on spatial processes specifically related to scale relations and multiplicative reasoning, which are important for understanding the concept of fraction equivalence (e.g., 1/3 is the same as 3/9; Boyer & Levine, 2012; Gunderson, Ramirez, Beilock, & Levine, 2012).

Multiple regression analyses revealed that whole-number magnitudes, fraction magnitudes, and proportional reasoning all made unique contributions to fraction concepts (once again controlling for general cognitive processes). However, only fraction magnitudes contributed independently to fraction arithmetic procedures. These findings suggest that whole-number magnitude knowledge contributes to acquisition of fraction magnitude knowledge, which in turn contributes to learning of fraction arithmetic.

The importance of both whole-number and fraction magnitude knowledge to fraction achievement has implications for intervention research and instructional practice. It supports a measurement approach to teaching rational numbers. Students who develop an understanding that all real numbers, including fractions, are assigned to their own location on the number line have an advantage in learning not only fractions but also algebraic concepts (Booth, Newton, & Twiss-Garrity, 2014; Siegler et al., 2011). Relations among proportional reasoning, multiplicative reasoning, and fraction equivalence also should be considered in intervention programs.

An intervention based on the theoretical analysis and empirical findings

The integrated theory of numerical development, the results of experimental studies, and the results of longitudinal studies converge on the conclusion that understanding of fraction magnitudes is crucial for both conceptual and procedural knowledge of fractions and for subsequent mathematics learning. Therefore, in a series of three randomized control trials, we have assessed the efficacy of an intervention, *Fraction Face Off*, which focuses heavily on inculcating understanding of fraction magnitudes. In each study, we contrasted the effects of this core program against a business-as-usual control condition that largely addressed the part-whole interpretation of fractions – the dominant representation of fractions in the U.S. mathematics curriculum.

In Study 1 (Fuchs, Schumacher, Long, et al., 2013), students were randomly assigned to two conditions, the core fraction intervention and a business-as-usual control condition. In Study 2, Fuchs, Schumacher, Sterba, et al. (2014) contrasted two variants of the core intervention program against the business-as-usual condition. One variant included activities aimed at building fluency with four measurement interpretation topics; the other variant included activities designed to consolidate understanding (rather than build fluency) with the same four topics. In the third study (Fuchs, Schumacher, Long, et al., 2013), we again randomly assigned students to three conditions: two variants of the core program and a business-as-usual control group. This time, one variant incorporated a word-problem intervention designed to encourage multiplicative thinking, while the other included a word-problem intervention requiring additive thinking.

In this brief overview, we focus on the overall effect of the core program versus the business-as-usual control group, as illustrated in the Year 1 study. (For additional information on the core *Fraction Face Off* program, and also for information on strategies to extend the core program using findings from Studies 2 and 3, consult the cited research reports.)

The three studies shared six key design features. First, students were at-risk fourth graders, with risk operationalized as performance on whole-number calculations below the 35th percentile at the start of fourth grade. To ensure the full distribution of risk status, we sampled students so that half of the sample in each study was below the 15th percentile, and the other half was between the 16th and 34th percentiles.

Second, we randomly assigned students to conditions, while stratifying by risk status and classroom. Third, interventions occurred in small groups, with three 30-minute sessions per week for 12 weeks. Fourth, we pre- and post-tested students on the measurement interpretation of fractions (using the fraction number line task, as described earlier in this chapter), calculation skill (adding and subtracting fractions), and released fraction items from the NAEP (easy, medium, and hard fourth-grade items as well as easy eighth-grade items). In Study 3, we also measured performance on fraction word problems that tapped multiplicative and arithmetic reasoning. Fifth, we evaluated the fidelity with which the intervention was conducted by audiotaping every session; randomly sampling tapes to comparably represent tutors, students, conditions, and sessions; and coding the accuracy with which key intervention components were implemented. In each study, fidelity was strong. Finally, we indexed the pre- and post-test performance of low-risk classmates (>34th percentile at the start of the study) to gain insight into how the intervention affected the achievement gap for at-risk versus low-risk students on fractions.

The major focus of the core fraction intervention program, as mentioned, is the measurement interpretation of fractions, which focuses primarily on representing, comparing, ordering, and placing fractions on number lines. This focus is supplemented by attention to the part-whole interpretation (e.g., showing objects with shaded regions and enumerating them relative to the total number of regions) and "fair shares" representations to build on prior knowledge and classroom instruction. Number lines, fraction tiles, and fraction circles are used to explain concepts throughout the 36 lessons, with a greater emphasis on these visuals at the start of the program. We start with proper fractions and fractions equal to one and midway through, we introduce improper fractions >1 and <2. We teach students to convert between improper fractions and mixed numbers, to place fractions on a 0–2 number line, and to order, compare, add, and subtract improper fractions and mixed numbers. We also focus on adding and subtracting fractions, but approximately 85% of content is allocated to understanding fractions rather than fraction arithmetic.

Each 30-minute lesson comprises four activities, with activity names reflecting the *Fraction Face Off* sports theme. In "Training," tutors introduce concepts, skills, problem-solving strategies, and procedures, relying on manipulatives and visual representations. "The Relay" involves group work on concepts and strategies taught during that day's Training. Students take turns completing problems while explaining their work to the group. All students simultaneously show work for each problem on their own papers. The third activity, "Sprint," provides supplementary activities designed to promote fluency with four key measurement topics. In the final activity, "The Individual Contest," students independently complete paper-pencil problems on content representing that day's and previous Training topics.

In each study, on each outcome, results favored students in the core fraction intervention program over those in the business-as-usual control group. For example, in Study 1, on comparing fraction magnitudes, the effect size (ES) favoring the intervention was 1.82 *SD*s; on the fraction number line task, it was 1.09. On comparing fractions, intervention students initially performed 0.12 *SD*s behind low-risk classmates, but completed the intervention 1.04 *SD*s ahead. By contrast, the achievement gap for control students increased from .05 to 0.42 *SD*s. (We did not collect fraction number line data on low-risk classmates, but post-test performance of intervention students was at the 75th percentile for a normative sample of sixth-grade students, as per Siegler & Pyke (2013).) NAEP effects were also significant and strong. The ES favoring intervention over control children was 0.92 *SD*s. The achievement gap between high- and low-risk children in the control condition remained large (1.09 at pre-test; 0.96 at post), while the gap for intervention students decreased substantially (from 1.07 to 0.08).

On calculations, effects again favored the intervention over the control condition. Here the ES was 2.50; the achievement gap between intervention students and low-risk classmates narrowed, while the gap for control students increased; and intervention students' post-test fraction arithmetic performance exceeded that of low-risk classmates. Given that classroom instruction allocated substantially more time to fraction arithmetic calculations than did the intervention, this suggests that understanding of the measurement interpretation transfers to procedural skill, at least for adding and subtracting fractions (e.g., Hecht, Close, & Santisi, 2003; Mazzocco & Devlin, 2008; Rittle-Johnson, Siegler, & Alibali, 2001; Siegler et al., 2011). This finding has practical significance and is supported by instructional theory (Siegler et al., 2011).

Importantly, analyses revealed that improvement in the measurement interpretation of fractions (but not improvement in the part-whole interpretation of fractions) mediated the effects of the intervention. This supports the hypothesis that the measurement interpretation is important to the development of students' fraction knowledge and suggests the need to reorient fraction instruction in the U.S. to include a dominant focus on the measurement interpretation of fractions.

Conclusions

Two hypotheses have guided the research described in this chapter. The first was a belief that knowledge of fractions is critical for success in more advanced mathematics, especially for success in algebra. The second was the critical importance of teaching students the measurement interpretation of fractions (i.e., that fractions can be represented as points on a number line). Results from the first several years of research have supported both these positions.

Knowledge of fractions is critical for success in algebra

The National Mathematics Advisory Panel (2008), on which two of the authors of this chapter served, reached this conclusion based on input from mathematicians, cognitive psychologists, mathematics education researchers, and mathematics teachers. The reasoning was that the level of abstraction required to truly understand fractions is essential before students can grasp the even more abstract notions of functions that is the core of algebra.

At that time, however, there was no empirical support for this assertion. However, since then, as noted earlier in this chapter, a host of longitudinal research has supported the critical role that knowledge of fractions at the end of elementary school and beginning of middle school plays in subsequent success in algebra and more advanced mathematics. Thus, the focus on improving the teaching of fractions and providing effective interventions for students who are in the "at-risk" category in the critical years for fractions instruction (grades 4, 5, and 6) seems well supported. The three intervention studies discussed in the previous section indicate that effective curricula can be developed for this population that focus heavily on building students' facility to understand and work with the measurement interpretation of fractions.

Importance of the measurement interpretation of fractions

The three strands of research at the Center all concentrate heavily on the importance of developing a linear representation of fraction magnitudes, that is, one in which a child's subjective representation of fractions' magnitudes increases linearly with the objective size of the fractions' magnitudes. This knowledge is often referred to as the *measurement interpretation* of fractions. Until recently, this emphasis was rare in American mathematics curricula in the elementary grades, but commonplace in many Asian curricula.

Case and colleagues (e.g. Okamoto & Case, 1996) hypothesized that development of increasingly sophisticated mental number lines was a key milestone in the development of number sense. The research described in this chapter strongly supports that insight. The longitudinal research conducted by both Siegler and Jordan and their colleagues demonstrates consistently strong predictive validity for measures involving placing fractions accurately on a number line, above and beyond general cognitive abilities and proficiency with computation.

A few issues come to mind from these lines of research. The first issue is whether there are other ways to measure understanding of fractions, above and beyond the measures of number line estimation and magnitude comparison used in this line of research. Our longitudinal research raises several other fascinating issues. The first is the important role that number line estimation (as assessed in third grade) plays in predicting fifth-grade performance in all aspects of fractions. Fluency and precision with the number line appears to be linked, as Jordan suggests, to the beginning of proportional reasoning. Proportional reasoning is, of course, integral to understanding what fractions mean, and how to interpret and use them accurately and precisely. Another interesting issue raised by Jordan and colleagues' research is that third graders' mathematics knowledge predicts fourth graders' understanding of fractions far better than it predicts their procedural competence (56% vs. 30% of explained variance). This leads one to wonder whether conventional instruction does a better job teaching students algorithms for addition and subtraction of fractions than in building the essential understanding of fractions necessary for future success in mathematics. The intervention research conducted by Fuchs and colleagues demonstrates that, at least for at-risk students, facility with the number line and accurate locations of fractions on a number line can be taught if instruction is well designed, very systematic, and very extensive in the amount of practice it provides in use of the number line. This issue is critical information to share as schools begin to implement what, to many, will be a much more challenging mode of mathematics instruction than teaching whole numbers.

The research of the Center demonstrates how a team of researchers can center a wide array of different type of research designs upon a central topic. In this case, a major focus– though hardly the entire focus– of the three strands of research has been the importance of the measurement interpretation of fractions (i.e. understanding of how to place fractions accurately on a number line). Mathematicians and mathematics educators deem competence in this area critical and thus it seemed an appropriate focal point for the research. Each strand approached the issue from a different lens. The small-scale experimental research indicated that understanding fraction magnitudes is a particularly important part of conceptual understanding of fractions, one that contributes substantially to both fraction arithmetic and to overall mathematics achievement. It also showed that children with mathematics difficulties progress remarkably slowly in acquiring fraction understanding. The longitudinal research indicated how number line estimation ability predicts future success in learning fractions above and beyond other measures of mathematics proficiency and general cognitive abilities, and that fraction knowledge more generally predicts algebra proficiency and overall mathematics achievement years later. Finally, the measurement interpretation served as a major instructional target in the series of three intervention studies (all RCTs) conducted in the intervention strand. The interventions unambiguously demonstrated that at-risk students could benefit from instruction that is explicit and systematic and targets this difficult but critical part of fraction knowledge.

Taken together, research conducted under the auspices of the Center has provided empirical support for significant shifts in the teaching of fractions, especially for students in the at-risk category. It also shows promise for improving screening and assessment in mathematics for students in the upper elementary grades. More generally, the strategy of funding centers that combine the efforts of researchers with different types of expertise to pursue specific, educationally significant goals seems likely to be fruitful in many different areas, not just this one.

References

Bailey, D. H., Hoard, M. K., Nugent, L., & Geary, D. C. (2012). Competence with fractions predicts gains in mathematics achievement. *Journal of Experimental Child Psychology, 113*(3), 447–455.

Barth, H. C., & Paladino, A. M. (2011). The development of numerical estimation: evidence against a representational shift. *Developmental Science, 14*(1), 125–135.

Berch, D., & Mazzocco, M. M. M. (Eds.). (2007). *Why is math hard for some children?: The nature and origins of mathematics learning difficulties and disabilities.* Baltimore, MD: Brookes Publishers.

Booth, J. L., & Newton, K. J. (2012). Fractions: Could they really be the gatekeeper's doorman? *Contemporary Educational Psychology, 37*(4), 247–253.

Booth, J. L., Newton, K. J., & Twiss-Garrity, L. K. (2014). The impact of fraction magnitude knowledge on algebra performance and learning. *Journal of Experimental Child Psychology, 118*, 110–118.

Boyer, T. W., & Levine, S. C. (2012). Child proportional scaling: Is 1/3=2/6=3/9=4/12? *Journal of Experimental Child Psychology, 111*(3), 516–533. doi:10.1016/j.jecp.2011.11.001

Fazio, L. K., Bailey, D. H., Thompson, C. A., & Siegler, R. S. (2014). Relations of different types of numerical magnitude representations to each other and to mathematics achievement. *Journal of Experimental Child Psychology, 123*, 53–72.

Fuchs, L. S., Schumacher, R. F., Long, J., Namkung, J., Hamlett, C. L., Cirino, P. T., Changas, P. (2013). Improving at-risk learners' understanding of fractions. *Journal of Educational Psychology, 105*(3), 683–700.

Fuchs, L. S., Schumacher, R. F., Sterba, S. K., Long, J., Namkung, J., Malone, A., Changas, P. (2014). Does working memory moderate the effects of fraction intervention? An aptitude-treatment interaction. *Journal of Educational Psychology, 106*, 499–514.

Geary, D. C. (2010). Missouri longitudinal study of mathematical development and disability. *British Journal of Educational Psychology Monograph Series II, 7*, 31–49.

Geary, D. C., Hoard, M. K., Byrd-Craven, J., Nugent, L., & Numtee, C. (2007). Cognitive mechanisms underlying achievement deficits in children with mathematical learning disability. *Child Development, 78*(4), 1343–1359.

Gunderson, E. A., Ramirez, G., Beilock, S. L., & Levine, S. C. (2012). The relation between spatial skill and early number knowledge: The role of the linear number line. *Developmental Psychology, 48*(5), 1229–1241.

Hansen. N., Jordan, N. C., Fernandez, E., Siegler, R., Fuchs, L., Gersten, R., & Micklos, D. (under review). General and math-specific predictors of sixth-graders' knowledge of fractions.

Hecht, S. A., Close, L., & Santisi, M. (2003). Sources of individual differences in fraction skills. *Journal of Experimental Child Psychology, 86*(4), 277–302.

Jordan, N. C., Hansen, N., Fuchs, L. S., Siegler, R. S., Gersten, R., & Micklos, D. (2013). Developmental predictors of fraction concepts and procedures. *Journal of Experimental Child Psychology, 116*(1), 45–58.

Kloosterman, P. (2010). Mathematics skills of 17-year-old students in the United States: 1978–2004. *Journal for Research in Mathematics Education, 41*(1), 20–51.

Ma, L. (1999). *Knowing and teaching elementary mathematics: Teachers' understanding of fundamental mathematics in China and the United States.* Mahwah, NJ: Erlbaum.

Mazzocco, M. M. M., & Devlin, K. T. (2008). Parts and "holes": Gaps in rational number sense among children with vs. without mathematical learning disabilities. *Developmental Science, 11*(5), 681–691.

McCloskey, M. (2007). Quantitative literacy and developmental dyscalculias. In D. B. Berch & M. M. M. Mazzocco (Eds.), *Why is math so hard for some children? The nature and origins of mathematical learning difficulties and disabilities* (pp. 415–429). Baltimore, MD: Paul H. Brookes Publishing.

Moseley, B. J., Okamoto, Y., & Ishida, J. (2007). Comparing U.S. and Japanese elementary school teachers' facility for linking rational number representations. *International Journal of Science and Mathematics Education, 5*(1), 165–185.

National Council of Teachers of Mathematics (NCTM). (2006). Curriculum focal points for pre-kindergarten through grade 8 mathematics. Washington, DC: National Council of Teachers of Mathematics. Pdf available at http://www.nctm.org/focalpoints/down-loads.asp.

National Mathematics Advisory Panel (NMAP) (2008). *Foundations for success: The final report of the National Mathematics Advisory Panel.* Washington, DC: U.S. Department of Education.

Ni, Y. J., & Zhou, Y. D. (2005). Teaching and learning fraction and rational numbers: The origins and implications of whole number bias. *Educational Psychologist, 40*(1), 27–52.

NORC (2008). *National Survey of Algebra Teachers*, OMB No. 1875–0243. Prepared for the National Mathematics Advisory Panel.

Okamoto, Y., & Case, R. (1996). Exploring the microstructure of children's central conceptual structures in the domain of number. *Monographs of the Society for Research in Child Development, 61*(1–2), 27–58.

Rittle-Johnson, B., Siegler, R. S., & Alibali, M. W. (2001). Developing conceptual understanding and procedural skill in mathematics: An iterative process. *Journal of Educational Psychology, 93*(2), 346–362.

Schneider, M., & Siegler, R. S. (2010). Representations of the magnitudes of fractions. *Journal of Experimental Psychology: Human Perception and Performance, 36*(5), 1227–1238.

Siegler, R. S., Duncan, G. J., Davis-Kean, P. E., Duckworth, K., Claessens, A., Engel, M., Chen, M. (2012). Early predictors of high school mathematics achievement. *Psychological Science, 23*(7), 691–697.

Siegler, R. S., & Pyke, A. A. (2013). Developmental and individual differences in understanding fractions. *Developmental Psychology, 49*(10), 1994–2004.

Siegler, R. S., Thompson, C. A., & Schneider, M. (2011). An integrated theory of whole number and fractions development. *Cognitive Psychology, 62*(4), 273–296.

Swanson, H. L., & Jerman, O. (2006). Math disabilities: A selective meta-analysis of the literature. *Review of Educational Research, 76*(2), 249–274.

Vamvakoussi, X., & Vosniadou, S. (2004). Understanding the structure of the set of rational numbers: A conceptual change approach. *Learning and Instruction, 14*(5), 453–467.

Vamvakoussi, X., & Vosniadou, S. (2010). How many decimals are there between two fractions? Aspects of secondary school students' understanding of rational numbers and their notation. *Cognition and Instruction, 28*(2), 181–209.

22

Lights and shadows of mental arithmetic

Analysis of cognitive processes in typical and atypical development

Sara Caviola and Daniela Lucangeli

Arithmetical learning is not only a fundamental part of children's education but it is also central in several daily activities.

The focus of this chapter is to analyse how children at different ages use limited mental resources to manage complex mental calculation from a developmental perspective. Moreover, some sections will deal with the processes in children's minds when they are solving arithmetic problems, paying particular attention to the strategies applied.

Recent research revealed that problem features (such as problem size, operation, presentation format) have large effects on arithmetic performance. At the same time, calculation ability also depends on strategy use and on individual difference variables, such as cognitive measures.

Several cognitive processes are involved in the solution of mental calculation tasks. A great deal of research has confirmed the involvement of working memory as an essential aspect of numerical cognition (for a recent review see Raghubar, Barnes and Hecht, 2010; but see also DeStefano and LeFevre, 2004; LeFevre, DeStefano, Coleman and Shanahan, 2005; Noël, Seron and Trovarelli, 2004), thus making the relationship between numerical cognition and working memory a leading area of research for understanding the architecture of arithmetical processing.

An understanding of the basic four algorithms (i.e., being able to solve simple addition, multiplication, subtraction, and division problems) is an inescapable component of everyday life, providing the essential means for dealing with a diverse variety of problem-solving situations. Basic arithmetic also provides the foundation for the higher mathematical skills that are central to more advanced scientific subjects. Consequently, understanding this fundamental academic skill is an important goal for cognitive and educational sciences.

The foundations of arithmetic emerge well before school begins, and pre-school children often display striking knowledge of arithmetic facts, procedures and concepts prior to entering school. Indeed, pre-school children can show an understanding of the directional effects of addition and subtraction problems in situations that do not require exact computation (Brush, 1978; Villette, 2002). Young children also show some skill in exact computations, but their levels of success vary greatly with age and depend on the characteristics of the problem and how the problems are presented (Hughes, 1981; Huttenlocher, Jordan and Levine, 1994; Starkey, 1992). Moreover, beyond this age and throughout school, children learn to write and read number words and acquire formal computational procedures, as well as learning arithmetical facts and more proficient strategies.

In formal curricula, multiplication, division and fractions typically follow addition and subtraction, because they are explained in terms of repeated addition and repeated subtraction and partitions of sets, thus building on concepts of sets and numerosities. For example, the mathematics curriculum in Italy begins in kindergarten (4–5 yrs) with the pre-mathematical concepts. In Grade 1 (5–6 yrs) children consolidate their counting skills and start learning adding and subtracting principles. In Grade 2 they are taught the procedures for solving complex addition and subtraction (Cornoldi and Lucangeli, 2004). Children are trained in the table facts and the concept of multiplication in Grades 2–3. Fractions are introduced in Grade 4, and division, as the complement of multiplication is introduced in Grades 4–5. The studies presented in this chapter will focus principally on addition problems as the most frequently studied algorithms.

Especially in recent years, several psychological studies have been developed in order to delineate the general cognitive mechanisms that underlie mathematics abilities. Among the most common candidates for underlying cognitive mechanisms is working memory, which is in charge of holding information in short-term memory, using this information to guide actions, keeping track of the order of steps in solving a problem or carrying out an activity and keeping track of the results of each/the last of these steps while carrying out the next. Actually, multi-digit arithmetic problems involve more than one single step and require several resources from working memory, not only because of demands on place value concepts, but because it is necessary to process several steps while keeping track of partial results.

A great deal of research has confirmed the involvement of working memory as an essential aspect of numerical cognition (for a recent review see Raghubar et al., 2010; but see also Ashcraft, 1995; DeStefano and LeFevre, 2004; Fürst and Hitch, 2000; Heathcote, 1994; LeFevre et al., 2005; Noël, Désert, Aubrun and Seron, 2001), thus making this relationship area a key aspect of research not only to further understand the architecture of arithmetical processing but also, and above all, to develop effective interventions for children who struggle with this subject.

The main aim of this chapter is to look more deeply into the role of working memory in children arithmetic's performance, trying to understand how, when children solve mental calculation, they allocate working memory resources differently according to both the complexity of the task and the features of the problem. How does this process take place? Which variables affect the relationship between working memory and arithmetic calculations?

Working memory and mental calculation

Mathematical abilities involve a variety of complex mental activities such as identification of quantities, encoding and transcribing those quantities into an internal representation, application of procedural knowledge (e.g. borrowing in subtraction), keeping track of partial results while carrying out the next step, and so forth. In recent years much research has been done on understanding the working memory system and its influence on mental arithmetic. Working memory is likely to be involved both in the early stages of mental arithmetic, where information is encoded verbally or visually and in the maintenance of information in further calculation processes (Bull, Epsy and Wiebe, 2008; De Smedt et al., 2009; Fuchs et al., 2010; Passolunghi and Lanfranchi, 2012).

In the literature different theoretical perspectives of the construct of working memory have been provided and all these prominent models vary in a number of aspects (Miyake and Shah, 1999). Nevertheless, the commonality among these models is that they describe how information is encoded into the working memory system and how the system temporarily maintains this information. As noted by DeStefano and LeFevre (2004), the vast majority of empirical work on working memory and mental arithmetic has been conducted by applying the multi-componential model of working memory developed by Baddeley and Hitch (1974) and Baddeley (1986, 2007). This multi-modal system of working memory states that storage is functionally independent from processing and consists of limited-capacity slave systems: the phonological loop and visuo-spatial sketchpad, responsible for the temporary storage and rehearsal of verbal and visuo-spatial material, respectively. A domain free processor, the central executive, coordinates the activity within the two slave systems. The central executive is responsible for a range of distinct processes including planning, switching, inhibition, monitoring, response selection and the activation of representations within long-term memory (Baddeley, 1986; Miyake et al., 2000). This executive component is a modality free, limited-capacity system that coordinates and integrates information incoming and outgoing to the two slave systems. According to a recent review (Raghubar et al., 2010), each component of the original working memory model is thought to play a role in mathematical cognition, thereby supporting a range of discrete steps in calculation such as encoding or manipulation of numerical information. Since, in the analysis of the relation between arithmetic and working memory, a great number of variables (and theoretical frameworks) come into play, the findings are even more conflicting than those concerning the relationships between other cognitive competencies. Actually, an increasing number of recent studies have investigated these relationships, and even if the issue of central executive involvement in the execution of mental calculation seems clear and widely studied (Ashcraft, Donley, Halas and Vakali, 1992; De Rammelaere, Stuyven and Vandierendonck, 1999, 2001; De Rammelaere and Vandierendonck, 2001; Lemaire,

Abdi and Fayol, 1996), the involvement of the working memory sub-components in mental calculation is still sparsely studied and is not clear (DeStefano and LeFevre, 2004; Heathcote, 1994; Imbo and LeFevre, 2010; Logie, Gilhooly and Wynn, 1994; Seitz and Schumann-Hengsteler, 2002; Trbovich and LeFevre, 2003).

It is indubitably true that arithmetic tends to be impaired by (and to impair) the concurrent performance of any cognitive task that competes to achieve attention and planning resources, and that some features of arithmetic problems, such as the presence of carrying procedures, the complexity of the operands, are more difficult than others to combine with such tasks (Fürst and Hitch, 2000). In this perspective, a selective interference paradigm, also called dual task paradigm, has been widely used and employed to investigate dealings between working memory and arithmetic performance. In this paradigm, the participants perform a primary task (a mental calculation problem) in combination with a secondary task that selectively involves one working memory component. The paradigm assumes that if both the primary and secondary tasks use overlapping cognitive resources, then performance on the primary task will worsen as the secondary task becomes more demanding.

This next section reports on the results of recent research that specifically analysed the role of the two working memory sub-components during the solution of a specific algorithm in children with typical and atypical development. In particular, by means a dual-task paradigm, the role of verbal and visuo-spatial working memory components has been investigated during the execution of complex addition problems, controlling for different problem features, such as type of required calculation (exact versus approximate calculation), complexity (carrying versus no carrying procedure) and presentation format (horizontal versus vertical format). This approach has been widely used with typically achieving adults but only rarely extended to children (McKenzie, Bull and Gray, 2003; Imbo and Vandierendonck, 2007). Thus, based on Kalaman and LeFevre's (2007) results and Trbovich and LeFevre's (2003) research on adults, a series of dual-task experiments have been carried out to examine the performance on exact and approximate calculations of simple and complex addition problems in typically developing children attending Grades 3 and 4 of primary school (Caviola, Mammarella, Lucangeli and Cornoldi, 2012). Moreover, in a subsequent study, the same experimental methodology, but only considering exact complex addition problems, has been applied to different samples of children with specific profiles of learning disabilities (Mammarella, Caviola, Cornoldi and Lucangeli 2013, Caviola et al., in preparation).

Typical development

Caviola et al. (2012) carried out three experiments, which tested the involvement of both verbal and visuo-spatial working memory loads in multi-digit mental addition problems, with and without carrying, in different groups of children attending Grades 3 and 4 of primary school. Children were asked to solve either exact or approximate mental calculations, either of which was presented either horizontally or vertically. The age-range was selected in relation to the national curriculum. Children at these ages are at a sensitive moment in their development of mental calculation skills because while they might have complete mastery of written calculation they usually do not possess completely automatised mental calculation skills and, in particular, they might be unfamiliar with approximate calculation (estimation).

Results showed that, as already observed in adults, working memory is also involved for children solving mental addition problems, and that different working memory components are involved according to task constraints. With regards to the specific feature problems, the analysis of the percentages of correct responses showed that mental additions presented in a horizontal format were generally more impaired than those in a vertical format by verbal working memory load and, vice versa, the vertical format was more affected than the horizontal one by visuo-spatial working memory load. Nevertheless, these findings emerged only when additions with carrying were considered. Therefore, the carrying procedure has been assumed to be crucial in determining the specific involvement of different working memory components during the solution process. Moreover, this interaction was stronger for approximate than for exact calculation.

Thus, with regards to the type of computation, the results showed that children generally found approximate calculation more difficult than exact calculation. While in the adult population the main difference between the two forms of mental calculation is that exact calculation involves more computations and makes greater requirements for the maintenance of intermediate sums than approximate calculation (Duverne, Lemaire and Michel, 2003; Lemaire and Lecacheur, 2011; Lemaire, Lecacheur and Farioli, 2000). This is not the case in children. These results are consistent with the observations (LeFevre, Greenham and Waheed, 1993) that the ability of computational estimation is poor in children and increases with age and that the most important hurdle is to achieve the conceptual knowledge used to perform the task. Indeed, only from Grade 6 do children seem to understand and use the different kinds of rounding strategies in estimation processes (see also Dowker, 2003, 2005).

Atypical development

In order to better understand the specific weakness of children with different profiles of mathematical difficulties, the authors extended the dual task paradigm to children diagnosed with developmental dyscalculia (DD) and with non-verbal learning disability (NLD). In particular, children with DD and with NLD were administered a dual-task paradigm in which they were asked to perform a primary task (i.e., addition problems with carrying) in combination with a secondary task (that is, recall of either verbal or visuo-spatial material; Imbo and LeFevre, 2010; Trbovich and LeFevre, 2003) in order to analyse the impact of verbal and visuo-spatial secondary tasks according to the presentation format.

The decision to focus only on these particular two clinical samples has been driven by their common impairments in calculation skills and their weakness in WM tasks (DD: Passolunghi and Cornoldi, 2008; Passolunghi and Mammarella, 2012; Schuchardt, Maehler and Hasselhorn, 2008. NLD: Bloom and Heath, 2010; Galway and Metsala, 2011; Mammarella, Lucangeli and Cornoldi, 2010).

Findings revealed that the selective interference paradigm applied to children with learning disabilities leads to results not completely overlapping those observed in previous research with typically developing children. In particular, DD children's performance was mostly damaged/depressed by horizontal problems presented in association with verbal information, revealing that verbal weaknesses are critical in the majority of children with DD. Moreover this outcome was replicated in a subsequent analysis, in which the sample was split into children with DD plus dyslexia and children with DD only (Mammarella et al., 2013). This further analysis simply confirmed that children with just DD outperformed children with combined mathematics and reading disorders (Rubinsten and Henik, 2009).

Conversely, NLD children's performance on exact calculations were found to be more in line with those registered on approximate calculations in typically developing children. Actually, NLD children's performance was selectively impaired in relation to the presentation format and type of domain associated, revealing that the presence of carrying procedures makes the calculation process sufficiently highly demanding on working memory resources to produce selective interference.

Educational and clinical implications

There is an increasing body of evidence supporting the concept that mathematical deficits could be dependent on poor working memory abilities. For example, poor computational abilities are often associated with low working memory scores (Bull and Scerif, 2001; D'Amico and Guarnera, 2005; Gathercole and Pickering, 2001; Geary, Hoard, Byrd-Craven, Nugent and Numtee, 2007; McLean and Hitch, 1999; Passolunghi and Siegel, 2001; Swanson and Sachse-Lee, 2001; Wilson and Swanson, 2001). Thus the importance of adequate and specific educative training is evident not only for calculation but, above all, not just for children with learning disabilities, but also for typically developing children. Common failures in scholastic achievement might depend on a working memory weakness, which implies forgetting lengthy instructions, place-keeping errors (for example, missing out numbers in dictation tasks) and problems coping with simultaneous processing and storage demands. Other complex tasks, in turn, amplify the working memory demands, leading to memory overload (see Gathercole, Lamont and Alloway, 2006).

Educational and clinical implications can easily be seen in our results, showing that children's difficulties in solving mental calculations are related to limited resources in working memory. Thus, particular attention should be devoted to supporting children, especially when mental computation increases in complexity by requiring great working memory resources.

In order to cope with working memory loads effectively during classroom activities, it is important that the teacher is aware of the typical memory capacities for that specific age group. In the same way, the learning progression through Grade content can be improved dramatically by reducing working memory demands during lessons. For example, in many circumstances, children simply forget what they are doing, leading to them missing the mark in several learning activities. A worthwhile expedient to facilitate children's memory for instructions is to use concise and clear instructions and, when possible, these instructions should be broken down into single steps. Another solution is to frequently repeat the crucial information contained in the original instructions, especially for tasks that take place over an extended period of time. Moreover, it is important to use a simple vocabulary and an easy syntax.

Further recommendations might refer to the complex activity itself. Perhaps that complexity can be reduced by breaking it down into simpler tasks and by providing external memory supports.

External memory aids, such as notebooks with squared paper are widely used in classrooms in Italy, even if children and teachers are not aware of their purpose (to position digits correctly). Last, but no less important, children with a weak working memory capacity often rely on less functional strategies (for example, using a simple counting strategy) even when they have to execute complex tasks, resulting in a depression of performance efficiency (Alloway, 2006). Hence, teachers should help children in "building" more efficient strategies, such as derived-fact strategies, which involve knowledge and reasoning about arithmetical properties (such as commutativity), which lead to working out arithmetical facts not stored in the memory. In general, developing a metacognitive strategic behaviour for dealing with complex cognitive activities helps to improve learning successes. This strategic behaviour includes encouraging the pupil to ask for forgotten information where necessary, training in the correct use of memory aids, and encouragement to continue with complex tasks rather than abandoning them even if some of the steps are not completed due to memory failure.

By the same token, namely by reducing the demands on working memory systems, several educational implications can be applied also to the clinical field. The outcomes of the research in learning disability may provide valuable feedback (obviously restricted to these particular clinical profiles only) that can be transformed in simple suggestions applicable both during a specific intervention program and during daily activity in the classroom. A comprehensive example could be addressed considering written calculation: a recommendation for NLD children is to present complex operations already displayed in columns, in order to avoid possible errors due to the transcription process from a horizontal presentation. Conversely, DD children would find it helpful not to overload their WM with too many verbal requests, for example, verbally summarise the steps of the procedure while they are executing a computation.

Although the investigation of the involvement of working memory in arithmetic abilities is noteworthy as well as highly motivating for several implications in the practical field, the issue still leaves open several other aspects that may be addressed in further research.

Since arithmetical content is composed of different aspects, it is possible to find several dissociations among them. To provide some examples, multiplication and division tend to be more challenging than addition or subtraction and many children find particular difficulty in dealing with fractions and decimals. Thus, future research might use the selective interference paradigm to investigate the role of working memory components in solving each different algorithm, as well as the processing of decimal numbers and symbolic fractions.

Another important aspect of arithmetic abilities is written arithmetic. Written calculations might also be dependent on working memory, for the accurate recognition and processing of written symbols. Actually, it requires the correct sequential organisation of material and procedures, the maintenance and elaboration of numerical information displayed in space, as well as a correct visual analysis of the graphic symbols. For these reasons, it could be interesting to the tangled puzzle of working memory and written calculations.

Another important aspect that is worth addressing are the discrepancies between mental and written calculation (Thompson, 1997). This may be reflected by different cognitive styles. Mental calculation might be more dependent on cognitive resources (e.g., working memory), whereas written calculation might be more dependent on knowledge of procedures (e.g., accurate recognition of place value, processing written symbols, correct application of procedures). The difference in these two types of arithmetic may also reflect teaching methods and aspects of life experience. At different times and in different countries, schools give varying degrees of emphasis to mental and written calculation. For example, Italian educational policies have, in the last few years, placed a greatly increased emphasis on mental calculation in the primary school, whereas written calculation received much more emphasis in the past. It emerges that children are often more mindful of concepts, and more inclined to reason, when carrying out mental arithmetic; and more inclined to execute procedures strictly as recipes when carrying out written arithmetic. This is one reason why some countries have chosen to begin by teaching mental arithmetic before proceeding to written arithmetic.

To conclude, there is space for even more research in the combined domain of arithmetic content and working memory resources. As is often the case in scientific research, this chapter not only tried to answer relevant (albeit few) questions, but it also raised numerous new ones.

References

Alloway, T. P. (2006). How does working memory work in the classroom? *Educational Research and Reviews, 1*(4), 134–139.

Ashcraft, M. H. (1995). Cognitive psychology and simple arithmetic: A review and summary of new directions. *Mathematical Cognition, 1*, 3–34.

Ashcraft, M. H., Donley, R. D., Halas, M. A., and Vakali, M. (1992). Working memory, automaticity, and problem difficulty. In J. I. D. Campbell (Ed.), *The nature and origins of mathematical skills* (pp. 301–329). Amsterdam: Elsevier.

Baddeley, A. D. (1986). *Working memory*. New York: Clarendon Press/Oxford University Press.

Baddeley, A. D. (2007). *Working memory, thought and action*. Oxford: Oxford University Press.

Baddeley, A. D., and Hitch, G. J. (1974). Working memory. In G. H. Bower (Ed.), *The psychology of learning and motivation* (pp. 47–90). New York: Academic Press.

Bloom, E., and Heath, N. (2010). Recognition, expression, and understanding facial expression of emotion in adolescents with nonverbal and general learning disabilities. *Journal of Learning Disabilities, 43*, 180–192.

Brush, L. R. (1978). Preschool children's knowledge of addition and subtraction. *Journal for Research in Mathematics Education, 9*, 44–54.

Bull, R., Espy, K. A., and Wiebe, S. A. (2008). Short-term memory, working memory, and executive functioning in preschoolers: Longitudinal predictors of mathematical achievement at age 7 years. *Developmental Neuropsychology, 33*, 205–228.

Bull, R., and Scerif, G. (2001). Executive functioning as a predictor of children's mathematics ability: Inhibition, switching, and working memory. *Developmental Neuropsychology, 19*, 273–293.

Caviola, S., Mammarella, I. C., Lucangeli, D. and Cornoldi, C. (2012). The involvement of working memory in children's exact and approximate mental additions. *Journal of Experimental Child Psychology, 112*(2), 141–160.

Cornoldi, C. and Lucangeli, D. (2004). Arithmetic education and learning disabilities in Italy. *Journal of Learning Disabilities, 37*, 42–49.

D'Amico, A., and Guarnera, M. (2005). Exploring working memory in children with low arithmetical achievement. *Learning and Individual Differences, 15*, 189–202.

De Rammelaere, S., Stuyven, E., and Vandierendonck, A. (1999). The contribution of working memory resources in the verification of simple mental arithmetic sums. *Psychological Research, 62*, 72–77.

De Rammelaere, S., Stuyven, E., and Vandierendonck, A. (2001). Verifying simple arithmetic sums and products: Are the phonological loop and the central executive involved? *Memory and Cognition, 29*, 267–273.

De Rammelaere, S., and Vandierendonck, A. (2001). Are executive processes used to solve simple mental arithmetic production tasks? *Current Psychology Letters: Behaviour, Brain and Cognition, 5*, 79–89.

De Smedt, B., Janssen, R., Bouwens, K., Verschaffel, L., Boets, B., and Ghesquière, P. (2009).Working memory and individual differences in mathematics achievement: A longitudinal study from first grade to second grade. *Journal of Experimental Child Psychology, 103*, 186–201.

DeStefano, D., and LeFevre, J.-A. (2004). The role of working memory in mental arithmetic. *European Journal of Cognitive Psychology, 16*, 353–386.

Dowker, A. (2003). Young children's estimates for addition: The zone of partial knowledge and understanding. In A. J. Baroody and A. Dowker (Eds.), *The development of arithmetic concepts and skills: Constructing adaptive expertise* (pp. 243–265). Hove, UK: Lawrence Erlbaum Associates Ltd.

Dowker, A. (2005). *Individual differences in arithmetic: Implications for psychology, neuroscience and education.* Hove, UK: Psychology Press.

Duverne, S., Lemaire, P., and Michel, B. F. (2003). Alzheimer's disease disrupts arithmetic fact retrieval processes but not arithmetic strategy selection. *Brain and Cognition, 52*, 302–318.

Fuchs, L. S., Geary, D. C., Compton, D. L., Fuchs, D., Hamlett, C. L., Seethaler, P. M., Bryant, J. D., Schatschneider, C. (2010). Do different types of school mathematics development depend on different constellations of numerical and general cognitive abilities? *Developmental Psychology, 46*, 1731–1746.

Fürst, A. J., and Hitch, G. J. (2000). Separate roles for executive and phonological components of working memory in mental arithmetic. *Memory and Cognition, 28*, 774–782.

Galway. T. M., and Metsala, J. L. (2011). Social cognition and its relation to psychosocial adjustment in children with nonverbal learning disabilities. *Journal of Learning Disabilities, 44*, 33–49.

Gathercole, S. E., Alloway, T. P., Willis, C., and Adams, A.-M. (2005). Working memory in children with reading disabilities. *Journal of Experimental Child Psychology, 93*, 265–281.

Gathercole, S. E., Lamont, E., and Alloway, T. P. (2006). Working memory in the classroom. In S. Pickering (Ed.), *Working memory and education* (pp. 219–240). Elsevier Press.

Gathercole, S. E., and Pickering, S. J. (2001). Working memory deficits in children with special educational needs. *British Journal of Special Education, 28*, 89–97.

Geary, D. C., Hoard, M. K., Byrd-Craven, J., Nugent, L., and Numtee, C. (2007). Cognitive mechanisms underlying achievement deficits in children with mathematical learning disability. *Child Development, 78*, 1343–59.

Heathcote, D. (1994). The role of visuo-spatial working memory in the mental addition of multi-digit addends. *Cahiers de Psychologie Cognitive, 13*, 207–245.

Hughes, M. (1981). Can preschool children add and subtract? *Educational Psychology, 1*, 207–219.

Huttenlocher, J., Jordan, N., and Levine, S. (1994). A mental model for early arithmetic. *Journal of Experimental Psychology: General, 123*(3), 284–296.

Imbo, I., and LeFevre, J.A. (2010). The role of phonological and visual working memory in complex arithmetic for Chinese- and Canadian-educated adults. *Memory and Cognition, 38*(2), 176–185.

Imbo, I., and Vandierendonck, A. (2007). The development of strategy use in elementary school children: Working memory and individual differences. *Journal Experimental Child Psychology, 96*, 284–309.

Kalaman, D., and LeFevre, J.-A. (2007). Working memory demands of exact and approximate addition. *European Journal of Cognitive Psychology, 19*, 187–212.

LeFevre, J.A., DeStefano, D., Coleman, B., and Shanahan, T. (2005). Mathematical cognition and working memory. In J. I. D. Campbell (Ed.), *Handbook of mathematical cognition* (pp. 361–377). New York: Psychology Press.

LeFevre, J.A., Greenham, S. L., and Waheed, N. (1993). The development of procedural and conceptual knowledge in computational estimation. *Cognition and Instruction, 11*, 95–132.

Lemaire, P., Abdi, H., and Fayol, M. (1996). The role of working memory resources in simple cognitive arithmetic. *European Journal of Cognitive Psychology, 8*, 73–104.

Lemaire, P., and Lecacheur, M. (2011). Age-related changes in children's executive functions and strategy selection: A study in computational estimation. *Cognitive Development, 26*, 282–294.

Lemaire, P., Lecacheur, M., and Farioli, F. (2000). Children's strategy use in computational estimation. *Canadian Journal of Experimental Psychology, 54*, 141–148.

Logie, R. H., Gilhooly, K. J., and Wynn, V. (1994). Counting on working memory in arithmetic problem solving. *Memory and Cognition, 22*(4), 395–410. Psychonomic Society.

Mammarella, I. C., Caviola, S., Cornoldi, C., and Lucangeli, D. (2013). Mental additions and verbal-domain interference in children with Developmental Dyscalculia (DD). *Research in Developmental Disabilities, 34*(9), 2845–2855.

Mammarella, I. C., Lucangeli, D., and Cornoldi, C. (2010). Spatial working memory and arithmetic deficits in children with nonverbal learning difficulties (NLD). *Journal of Learning Disabilities, 43*, 455–468.

McKenzie, B., Bull, R., and Gray, C. (2003). The effects of phonological and visual-spatial interference on children's arithmetical performance. *Educational and Child Psychology, 20*, 93–108.

McLean, J. F., and Hitch, G. J. (1999). Working memory impairments in children with specific arithmetic learning difficulties. *Journal of Experimental Child Psychology, 74*, 240–260.

Miyake, A., and Shah, P. (1999). *Models of working memory. Mechanisms of active maintenance and executive control*. Cambridge, UK: Cambridge University Press.

Miyake, A., Friedman, N. P., Emerson, M. J., Witzki, A. H., Howerter, A., and Wager, T. D. (2000). The unity and diversity of executive functions and their contributions to complex tasks: A latent variable analysis. *Cognitive Psychology, 41*, 49–100.

Noël, M.-P., Désert, M., Aubrun, A., and Seron, X. (2001). Involvement of short-term memory in complex mental calculation. *Memory and Cognition, 29*, 34–42.

Noël, M.-P., Seron, X., and Trovarelli, F. (2004). Working memory as a predictor of addition skills and addition strategies in children. *Current Psychology of Cognition, 22*, 3–25.

Passolunghi, M. C., and Cornoldi, C. (2008). Working memory failures in children with arithmetical difficulties. *Child Neuropsychology, 14*, 387–400.

Passolunghi, M., and Lanfranchi, S. (2012). Domain specific and domain general precursors of mathematical achievement: A longitudinal study from kindergarten to first grade. *British Journal of Educational Psychology, 82*, 42–63.

Passolunghi, M. C., and Mammarella, I. C. (2012). Selective spatial working memory impairment in a group of children with mathematics learning disabilities and poor problem-solving skills. *Journal of Learning Disabilities, 45*, 341–350.

Passolunghi, M. C., and Siegel, L. S. (2001). Short-term memory, working memory, and inhibitory control in children with difficulties in arithmetic problem solving. *Journal of Experimental Child Psychology, 80*, 44–57.

Raghubar, K. P., Barnes, M. A., and Hecht, S. A. (2010). Working memory and mathematics: A review of developmental, individual difference, and cognitive approaches. *Learning and Individual Differences, 20*, 110–122.

Rubinsten, O., and Henik, A. (2009). Developmental dyscalculia: Heterogeneity might not mean different mechanisms. *Trends in Cognitive Sciences, 13*(2), 92–99.

Schuchardt, K., Maehler, C., and Hasselhorn, M. (2008). Working memory deficits in children with specific learning disorders. *Journal of Learning Disabilities, 41*, 514–523.

Seitz, K., and Schumann-Hengsteler, R. (2002). Phonological loop and central executive processes in mental addition and multiplication. *Psychologische Beiträge, 44*, 275–302.

Starkey, P. (1992). The early development of numerical reasoning. *Cognition, 43*, 93–126.

Swanson, H. L., and Sachse-Lee, C. (2001). Mathematical problem solving and working memory in children with learning disabilities: Both executive and phonological processes are important. *Journal of Experimental Child Psychology, 79*, 294–321.

Thompson, I. (1997). Mental and written algorithms: Can the gap be breached? In I. Thompson (Ed.), *Teaching and learning early number*. Buckingham: Open University Press.

Trbovich, P. L., and LeFevre, J.-A. (2003). Phonological and visual working memory in mental addition. *Memory and Cognition, 31*, 738–745.

Vilette, B. (2002). Do young children grasp the inverse relationship between addition and subtraction? Evidence against early arithmetic. *Cognitive Development, 17*, 1365–1383.

Wilson, K. M., and Swanson, H. L. (2001). Are mathematics disabilities due to a domain-general or a domain-specific working memory deficit? *Journal of Learning Disabilities, 34*, 237–248.

23

Teacher training
Solving the problem

Judy Hornigold

Mathematics is universally accepted as one of the key subjects in education. Yet, it is a subject that can cause great anxiety and stress in both pupils and teachers alike. Mathematics has the unique and unenviable status of being a subject that many are happy to admit being bad at. Whereas one would not dream of saying 'I can't do English', it is socially acceptable and in some cases seen as a badge of honour to be bad at mathematics. Mathematics is perceived as a difficult subject and Chinn (2012a) has noted that it is a subject that students as young as seven are being switched off from. Since mathematics is a compulsory subject in the UK up to the age of 18 years old, we do not have the option of accepting that some people will be bad at mathematics. Being numerate is a life skill that we all need and for people with dyscalculia the effects can be devastating. Butterworth and Yeo (2004) found that people with poor numeracy skills are more likely to be unemployed, depressed or ill. Parsons and Bynner (2005) noted that around 20% of the UK population have difficulties with mathematics which cause significant practical, educational or functional difficulties.

The implications are not only social; Gross et al. (2009) reported that innumeracy in adults costs the UK exchequer as much as £2.4 billion every year.

So how have we got mathematics teaching so wrong and what can we do to rectify this situation?

Mathematics is very susceptible to poor teaching and the pedagogy employed in delivering the mathematics curriculum can have a profound effect on the student. It is the one subject that I feel has been dealt a great disservice by its method of delivery.

The teaching of mathematics is all too often focused around using the tools of the trade rather than investigating what these tools can be used for. You can teach someone how to use a hammer, nails and wood and they can happily hammer away for hours on end, but the whole endeavour will be pointless unless you show them the wonderful things that they can make.

Du Sautoy (2008) eloquently sums this up: 'Being a good speller does not make you a good writer, being a good calculator does not make you a good mathematician.'

Mathematics teaching has become too compartmentalised. Topics are taught discretely and students are encouraged to become proficient in using procedures at speed, regardless of whether they understand the mathematical concepts that underlie them. The results orientated focus in UK schools today, driven by the need to prove success to Ofsted (Government) inspectors is not conducive to embracing a problem-solving, concept-led approach to the teaching of mathematics. Teachers are forced to follow a curriculum that rewards speed and accuracy above all else and does not allow for creativity, collaboration or curiosity. For students with dyscalculia this only serves to make the world of mathematics even more abstract and meaningless.

Boaler (2009) has called the mathematics that is taught in schools 'fake mathematics', and claims that there is a huge gap between this and 'real mathematics'; a gap which we urgently need to bridge.

It seems that there is a significant mismatch between the way that we teach mathematics and the way that students learn mathematics. Rawson (1984) offered this advice on the teaching of mathematics: 'Teach the subject as it is to the student as he is.'

It seems that this mismatch is based on a fundamental misunderstanding of what mathematics actually is. Devlin (2000) states:

> Mathematics is not about numbers, but about life. It is about the world in which we live. It is about ideas. And far from being dull and sterile, as it is so often portrayed, it is full of creativity.

Chinn (2012b) reiterated this mismatch between teaching and learning by suggesting that

> there is a need to take an approach to teaching mathematics that is more cognisant of how pupils learn partly by using our knowledge of why children with special needs do not learn to inform how we teach all of our children.

There is too much focus on being correct and too little focus on being prepared to conjecture and to make mistakes. Children's anxiety around mathematics is only heightened by this obsession with accuracy. Conversely, we should be developing a culture in mathematics that embraces, and learns from, mistakes. Such a culture would enable the dyscalculic learner to explore the subject in a way that is meaningful to them.

So what is wrong with mathematics teaching?

To ascertain how students view their mathematics lessons a simple question was posed to a class of 14 to 15 year olds in a secondary school in the South of England, chosen for being a demographically typical UK school.

The students were asked what they would change in their mathematics lessons to make them more enjoyable and some of their responses are detailed below.

'Make it harder to be honest. My maths lesson is pretty easy. Less sheet work and more interactive.'

'There could be more time to have discussions with your friends about it because sometimes they can explain it better and then I understand it.'

'She will ask if anyone doesn't understand and to put up your hand but no-one does because it's embarrassing.'

'My lessons seem to fit more to the people who know what they're doing. They'll start off explaining something on the board and those people who understand it are those who are answering the questions and then we're given a worksheet and are expected to answer it.'

These comments were representative of the group and highlight some interesting points. The students want to be challenged. If they are able to tackle something harder, then they will have a greater sense of achievement when they are successful in meeting that challenge.

Universally the students wanted the lessons to be more interactive and to give them the opportunity to discuss their ideas with their peers. In essence they were asking for a more collaborative approach to mathematics with the opportunity to ask questions without the fear of ridicule.

Schifter (2007) in her article 'What's right about looking at what's wrong?' asserted that: 'Both students and teachers gain new mathematical understanding by examining the reasoning behind a student's incorrect answer.' Knowing that a student has an incorrect answer tells us nothing. The valuable information comes from exploring how the student arrived at that answer.

Schifter goes on to state:

Mathematics should not be treated as a set of facts and procedures to be learned, with a goal of 100% correct answers. It is much more organic than this and should be treated as a subject to be explored and investigated set against a background where mistakes are positive learning experiences.

However, this approach to mathematics requires a deep level of understanding on the part of the teacher and the confidence to teach mathematics in a more conceptual way. Many teachers themselves were taught mathematics as a set of discrete procedures and definitions to be memorised, so there is a significant challenge in enabling them to implement a more collaborative and inquisitive approach to mathematics teaching.

The Williams Independent Review of Mathematics Teaching (2008), produced by the Department for Education in the UK, highlighted two key issues. First, the eed for an increased focus on the 'use and application' of mathematics, and second, the vital importance of classroom discussion of mathematics. The review highlighted that 'constructive dialogue in the classroom was essential for fully developing mathematical logic and reasoning'.

Another area of concern in the pedagogy of mathematics is that too many lessons focus on answering questions. It may be more meaningful to turn this idea on its head and view the essence of mathematics as inherently being able to come up with questions rather than answers. Such an approach would make mathematics lessons much more creative and would also make them more inclusive for the student with dyscalculia.

Boaler (2009) states that students need to be given the opportunity to ask their own questions in order to 'bring mathematics back to life'. There is a need to move away from the notion that all the mathematics in the world has previously been discovered and all that children need to do is to learn it. Duckworth (1996) makes the point that the most valuable learning experiences come from your own thoughts and ideas. We need to encourage this in mathematics as much, if not more, than in any other subject and let the children discover the mathematics for themselves.

Clearly, students also need to have the tools of the trade in order to be able to explore and discover mathematics for themselves. They will need to be competent in the basic skills of arithmetic. The issue that we have is how these skills are taught. These skills do not come easily to the dyscalculic learner and we need to ensure that our teaching strategies meet their specific needs.

What works for learners with dyscalculia?

Sharma (2009) identified three components of a mathematical idea: procedure, concept and language. He asserted that the goal of the mathematics curriculum and instruction should be to help students acquire a mathematical way of thinking so that they can recognise and appreciate the applications and beauty of mathematics. He emphasised the importance of mathematical language by identifying the need to have a 'language container for the mathematical concept'. Without this we cannot receive, comprehend or communicate a mathematical concept. He goes on to explain that each concept passes through six levels of knowing: intuitive, concrete, pictorial, abstract, application and communication.

In the work that I have done with children with dyscalculia, I have found this to be a very successful model to follow. It helps the child to make sense of the abstract and to make links between one area of mathematics and another. Furthermore if this model is embedded in a culture of questioning, then the understanding can be developed to a much greater level and the fear of being wrong disappears as the child is so used to asking questions that it becomes second nature. They begin to realise that all questions are useful and will help to further their understanding.

Sharma breaks down the process behind this type of Socratic questioning to illustrate its strengths and value. He explains that:

Questions instigate language; language instigates models, models instigate thinking, thinking instigates understanding, understanding produces skills, knowledge, and mastery, mastery produces competent performance, competent performance produces long lasting self-esteem and self-esteem is the basis of motivation necessary for all learning.

Gilderdale (2007) offers a different model, focusing on the characteristics that good mathematicians have rather than the characteristics of mathematics itself. He identified three key characteristics of students who were high achievers in mathematics. These students worked systematically, could generalise and conjecture, and they were able to offer proofs and explanations. He offers a framework for lessons that enables students to develop their mathematical thinking. This framework consists of:

1   *Promoting a conjecturing atmosphere.* This can be achieved by encouraging risk taking, accepting 'messy' work, promoting discussion and giving plenty of thinking time. He, like Sharma, also emphasises the value of Socratic questioning. Boaler (2013) takes this idea of questioning a step further by encouraging children to defend their solutions to a mathematical problem by convincing a friend that their argument is correct and then furthermore by convincing an enemy. Thus they have to rigorously defend their mathematical thought processes and this will inevitably lead to deeper understanding.
2   *Low threshold, high ceiling tasks.* This involves using problems that are accessible to everyone regardless of ability, but which also offer opportunities for working at a higher level. These types of task are particularly valuable to students with dyscalculia as they are inclusive and can help to reduce fear and anxiety.
3   *Modelling behaviour.* Ideally students should be taught by a teacher who is curious about mathematics and who has a positive attitude towards it.
4   *Whole-class discussion.* Gilderdale goes on to suggest that whole-class discussion should happen at three different stages in the lesson:

    o   early on, to share and to explore opening thoughts and ideas,
    o   half way through, to share possible findings, to highlight useful strategies and to answer new questions, and finally,
    o   towards the end, to share conclusions, explanations and proofs.

He also advocates 'HOTS not MOTS', which stands for 'Higher Order Thinking Skills' not 'More Of The Same'. This is an area that I feel needs to be addressed in much of our mathematics teaching. All too often students who fail are given 'more of the same' in the hope that practice will make perfect and sadly this is rarely the case for the student with dyscalculia.

So one way that we can help is to follow Sharma's model and Gilderdale's approach when planning an intervention to support someone with dyscalculia or Mathematics Learning Difficulties.

Dowker (2009) in her report 'What works for children with mathematical difficulties', asserts that it is vital when planning an intervention that it is specifically targeted. Keogh et al. (1980) concluded that:

> Interventions that focus on the particular components with which an individual student has difficulty are likely to be more effective than those which assume that all children's arithmetical difficulties are similar.

Some areas that most commonly cause difficulty for children are memory for arithmetical facts, word problem solving and place value.

Dowker and Sigley (2010) found that:

> Individualized interventions in arithmetic, especially those that focus on the particular components with which an individual student has difficulty, can be highly effective. Moreover, the amount of time given to such individualized work does not, in many cases, need to be very large to be effective. Thus, children's arithmetical difficulties are highly susceptible to intervention.

The Williams Review (2008) went on to recommend a number of intervention programmes. Talking Mathematics (Education Works, 2011) is one such intervention, which was developed by the Liverpool Local Authority (UK) to address the issue of mathematical language. It is a short-term, ten-week intervention programme that targets speaking and listening skills, which are crucial skills for mathematical thinking strategies and problem solving. It supports children in using mathematical vocabulary and terminology and also supports teachers on how to model good mathematical language and questioning. Furthermore, it develops children's abilities to reason, generalise, predict and recognise patterns and relationships.

Gilmore and Hawkins (2003) looked at how collaboration and creativity are key elements when teaching mathematical concepts. They explored this through 'the lesson study approach'. By using a lesson study approach, teachers can deepen their own content knowledge, adopt effective teaching strategies, and become more reflective about their instruction. It aims to achieve the following outcomes:

- To deepen teachers' mathematics content understanding,
- To investigate the conceptual basis of mathematics as a tool for inquiry as well as a process for problem solving,
- To model effective instruction and assessment practices to create meaningful learning opportunities for all students.

Fuchs et al. (2008) proposed seven principles of intensive intervention designed to address 'serious mathematics deficits' in children aged 8–9 years old. The intervention was focused on the two areas of number combinations and story problems.

- Number combinations involved problems with single-digit operations. These could be solved by counting or by committing the solution to long-term memory. The resource used was called Math Flash.
- Story problems involved linguistic information and problem solving using a resource called Pirate Math.

Both approaches were found to be very effective, with effect sizes in comparison to the control group of 0.85 standard deviations for Math Flash and 0.72 standard deviations for Pirate Math. The seven principles that they proposed are detailed below.

The first principle is *instructional explicitness*. Students with dyscalculia need an explicit didactic approach, where the teacher makes clear exactly what the student needs to learn. As is often the case with students with specific learning differences, we cannot assume that they will 'pick up information' the way that other students might.

The second principle is *instructional design to minimise the learning challenge*. There are common mathematical concepts that many students find hard to grasp, such as place value and fractions. The idea here is to pre-empt the difficulty and use precise explanations to avoid these misunderstandings before they happen.

The third principle is that instruction should provide a *strong conceptual basis* for the procedures that are taught. If students are taught the procedure without understanding the underlying concept then mathematics becomes a list of abstract algorithms to remember and the process is meaningless and very demotivating for many students. This reiterates Sharma's view of mathematical learning.

The fourth principle is already present in most mathematics teaching and that is *drill and practice*. There is certainly a place for drill and practice, to develop automaticity, but only when the underlying concept has been explicitly explained by the teacher and understood by the student. Mathematics is very cumulative in its nature and, as such, each building block needs to be thoroughly mastered before moving on in order to avoid confusion and gaps in learning.

Cumulative review is the fifth principle of effective intensive mathematics intervention which ensures that concepts are revisited and are fully understood. It also provides the opportunity for teachers to address any areas of weakness or confusion. This is one of the areas where the current UK curriculum fails students as there is little time for review and revision. This can have a catastrophic effect on students, particularly those who have missed school through illness. There is simply no opportunity for them to catch up and consequently they fall further and further behind.

The sixth principle is that the intervention needs to be *motivating*. Students who have found mathematics challenging can be very frustrated by their lack of progress and they need to be given the opportunity to enjoy the subject once more.

The final and most important principle of intensive intervention is *ongoing progress monitoring*. This will determine the effectiveness or otherwise of an intervention programme for a given student. This links back to Dowker's (2009) findings that the intervention should be individualised and specifically targeted in order to be most effective.

The UK publication, the *Times Educational Supplement* published an article in March 2010, entitled 'Must trig harder: how can we make mathematics count in primaries?' It elicited the views of several experts to reveal where they think the problems lie, and what their solutions would be. Extracts from the article are summarised below:

Richard Dunne, the creator of 'Mathematics Makes Sense', advocated a move away from real-life problem solving, which he viewed as intrinsically confusing for children. He supports an approach that embraces the 'wonderful clarity of its logical symbolic language'. His multisensory mathematics approach aims to help prevent misconceptions in mathematics and make abstract ideas more accessible.

Margaret Brown, Professor of mathematics education, King's College, London criticises the UK National Numeracy strategy for going 'too far too fast'. She also looks at problem solving but sees the issue here that the children are being presented with the wrong type of problem. She states:

> We need to get more genuine problem solving into the primary curriculum, and not just little word problems, such as: 'You have five rows of chairs in four rows, how many chairs are there?' This is not a problem. It is just deciding what operation to use. A problem is something like: 'You are having a class party, how much food do you need?'

Boaler (2009) has identified from her extensive research three main areas that she felt were implicated in the problems that young children have in acquiring mathematical competence.

First, she feels that children have a much too narrow experience of mathematics, with too much emphasis on reproducing methods that have been demonstrated by the teacher. This is demotivating for the children and can lead to mathematics anxiety. Since they do not have a grasp of the underlying concepts, they have no option but to rely on just remembering procedures. Second, in agreement with Brown, she feels the children are presented with 'too much too early'. Children are introduced to too many methods, too soon. Her final point is that ability grouping in mathematics can lead to children believing that they are 'no good at mathematics' from a very early age.

Boaler advocates mixed-ability groups, and also supports Gilderdale's advice on giving higher order tasks that are accessible on different levels as a good way forward in advancing mathematical understanding. She also advocates the promotion of a 'growth mindset' in mathematics. This follows on from the work of Dweck (2006) which focused on how differing attitudes affect the way that people view both themselves and their interactions with others. She argues that there are two fundamental mindsets that people use: the fixed mindset and the growth mindset.

Boaler (2013) relates the concept of a growth mindset to the teaching of mathematics. She suggests that these two opposing beliefs have huge implications for learning. Those people with a growth mindset are persistent, they learn from mistakes and they are encouraged by other people's success. Those with a fixed mindset hate to fail because they believe that this tells them that they are bad at mathematics and consequently they avoid challenging work at all costs.

This has implications for the dyscalculic learner, as adopting a growth mindset will encourage them to persist and will give them the belief that they can develop their mathematical ability.

Case study

One school that has adopted an effective approach to teaching mathematics is Frederick Bird Primary School in Coventry. This school was chosen because of its impressive results in mathematics teaching. In 2012, 88% of children in the school made two levels of progress in mathematics, this is above national targets and all the more remarkable considering the challenging demographics of the school population.

Frederick Bird does not follow a particular numeracy scheme as they take a bespoke tailored approach which means that creativity is encouraged and not stifled by adherence to the structure of any one scheme. The school has specially trained numeracy teachers (as recommended by the 2008 Williams Review) from the MaST (Mathematics Specialist Teacher) programme delivered at Edge Hill University (UK). There is also a specialist dyscalculia teacher on the staff.

The approach to mathematics teaching has a strong emphasis on mathematical reasoning and problem solving. The mathematics department has had specific training on problem solving using Bloom's taxonomy. Metacognition skills are specifically taught, to give the children a wider toolkit of strategies and the flexibility to move away from basic calculation strategy. Constructive feedback is given verbally and in writing using the star and a wish technique with green pen questions[1] for the children to complete at the beginning of the next session. Hattie (2009) in his meta-analysis of educational research found that 'The highest effects accrued when teachers provided feedback data or recommendations to students.'

The children are taught to self-regulate and to transfer skills, by communicating their mathematics through strategies such as 'Talking Mathematics' (Education Works, 2011) and 'Talk it, Solve it' (Pennant and Thomson, 2005). The 'Every Child Counts' programme (Edge Hill, 2011) is used for children aged 6 to 7 years old. 'Every Child Counts' is designed to promote an internal locus of control in the student. It makes the student aware of their own strengths and of the strategies they used to solve a problem successfully. It develops metacognition so that children are thinking about their thinking and encourages teachers to stand back and let the children solve the problems on their own or collaboratively in groups with their peers. It also encourages children to teach what they know to others as an effective way of consolidating their understanding. Planning is flexible and done on a day-to-day basis and this is shared between year teams so that the school can draw on the skills and strengths of all members of staff.

Many of the pedagogical methodologies explored in this chapter are addressed in this flexible and creative approach and the results are, indeed, impressive. By taking a more organic approach to teaching and by moving away from the constraints of maths schemes and worksheets, the learning experience can be much more enjoyable and rewarding for the children. Frederick Bird has gone a long way to bridging the gap between 'fake maths and real maths'.

Conclusion

We need to take a step back and critically examine the way that mathematics is taught. It is clear that dyscalculic students should be explicitly taught the arithmetical skills needed to be competent mathematicians, but they also need to be given the opportunity to explore the inherent beauty and creativity of mathematics. They need time to develop their understanding and to work in an environment where they feel able to make mistakes and to learn from these mistakes. They need to be able to work collaboratively with their peers and to put forward their own thoughts and conjectures.

The British Dyslexia Association is currently campaigning for specialist dyslexia training to be an integral part of the initial teacher training programme in the UK and it would be highly desirable if dyscalculia could also be specifically addressed in teacher training establishments. We owe it to our young students to teach mathematics in the way that they learn it so that they can enter adulthood as numerate adults, with an appreciation and enjoyment of this rich and fascinating subject.

Note

1 Green pen questions are target questions for the child to address before they start their next piece of work.

References

Boaler, J. (2009). *The Elephant in the Classroom*. London: Souvenir Press.

Boaler, J. (2013). *How to Learn Math*. Available at https://class.stanford.edu (accessed 23 October 2013).

Butterworth, B. and Yeo, D. (2004). *Dyscalculia Guidance: Helping pupils with specific learning difficulties in maths*. London: NFER-Nelson.

Chinn, S. (2012a). Beliefs, anxiety, and avoiding failure in mathematics. *Child Development Research*, Vol. 2012.

Chinn, S. (2012b). Keynote speech at the First International Dyscalculia Conference. London.

Devlin, K. (2000). *The Math Gene: How mathematical thinking evolved and why numbers are like gossip* (p. 7). New York: Basic Books.

Dowker, A. and Sigley, G. (2010). Targeted interventions for children with arithmetical difficulties. *Understanding Number Development and Difficulties, 65–81 BJEP Monograph Series II*, 7. The British Psychological Society.

Dowker, A. (2009). *What works for children with mathematical difficulties*. Department for Education.

du Sautoy, M. (2008). *'I'm not very fast at my times tables'*. Available from http://www.guardian.co.uk/science/2008/nov/03/marcus-dusautoy (accessed 10 October 2013).

Duckworth, E. (1996). *'The Having of Wonderful Ideas' and Other Essays on Teaching and Learning*. New York: Teacher's College Press.

Dweck, S. (2006). *Mindset: The new psychology of success*. London: Random House.

Edge Hill University. (2011). *1st Class@number*. Available from https://everychildcounts.edgehill. ac.uk/ecc-for-schools/what-is-1stclassnumber (accessed 23 October 2013).

Edge Hill University. (2011). *Every Child Counts*. Available from https://everychildcounts. edgehill.ac.uk/ (accessed 23 October 2013).

Education Works. (2011). *Talking Mathematics*. Available from http://www.educationworks. org.uk/what-we-do/mathematics.html (accessed 23 October 2013).

Fuchs, L., Fuchs, D., Powell, S., Seethaler, P., Cirino, P. and Fletcher, J. (2008). Intensive intervention for students with mathematics disabilities: seven principles of effective practice. *Learning Disability Quarterly, 31*(2), 79–92.

Gilderdale, C. (2007). *Addressing Core Issues and Concerns in Science and Mathematics*. Council of Boards of School Education in India Conference in Rishikesh, India in April 2007.

Gilmore, J. and Hawkins, A. (2003). The lesson study approach: collaboration and creativity are key to teaching mathematics concepts. *SEDL Letter, XV*(1), December 2003, Improving Achievement in Mathematics and Science.

Gross, J., Hudson, C., and Price, D. (2009). *The Long Term Costs of Numeracy Difficulties*. Every Child a Chance Trust and KPMG.

Hattie, J. (2009). *Visible Learning: A synthesis of over 800 meta-analyses relating to achievement*. London: Routledge.

Keogh, B. K., Major, S. M., Omari, H., Gandara, P. and Reid, H. P. (1980). Proposal for markers in learning disabilities research. *Journal of Abnormal Student Psychology, 8*, 21–31.

Parsons, S. and Bynner, J. (2005). *Does numeracy matter more?* National Research and Development Centre for Adult Literacy and Numeracy, Institute of Education, London.

Pennant, J. and Thomson, J. (2005). *Talk it, Solve It: Reasoning skills in mathematics Yrs 5 & 6*. BEAM Education.

Rawson, M. (1984). Margaret Byrd Rawson Institute. http://mbri.org (accessed 23 October 2013).

Schifter, D. (2007). What's right about looking at what's wrong? *Making Math Count, 65*(3), 22–27.

Sharma, M. (2009). *Mathematics Curriculum Core Concepts, Skills and Procedures*. Available from www.info@mathematicsforall.org (accessed 15 October 2013).

Times Educational Supplement. (2010). Must trig harder: how can we make maths count in primaries? Published 26 March, 2010. Available from http://www.tes.co.uk/article. aspx?storycode=6039830 (accessed 23 October 2013).

Williams, P. (2008). *The Independent Review of Mathematics Teaching in Early Years Settings and Primary Schools*. London: DFES.

24

Mathematics anxiety, working memory, and mathematical performance

The triple-task effect and the affective drop in performance

Alex M. Moore, Amy J. McAuley, Gabriel A. Allred, and Mark H. Ashcraft

In reference to the development of modern computing as we know it today, Alan Turing, the esteemed mathematician and pioneer of computer science, wrote, "The idea behind digital computers may be explained by saying that these machines are intended to carry out any operations which could be done by a human computer" (Turing, 1950, pp. 436). This quote is not to be taken as hyperbole; note that much of Turing's efforts were aimed at designing computer programs and software that would mimic person-to-person interactions so well that the human observer would be unable to determine if their counterpart in a conversation was a sentient being or a machine. This drive has since inspired the annual Turing Test competition, where individuals attempt to create sophisticated programs designed to outsmart people into believing that they are having a person-to-person conversation over a computer interface. In light of these advancements in computer science, we find it slightly humorous to think that such an innovator of science, the man we can thank for our smart phones and laptops, would strive to design the perfect proxy for the "human computer."

A quick look into the chronicle of calculation devices that litter the history of mathematics would suggest that Turing was not unique in his drive to represent human thought in machine form. The abacus, counting boards, analog calculators, and Leibniz's calculation machine are just a few of the many devices created to relieve the individual of relying on mental processing. Do these examples reveal the lazy nature of scientists? It would appear that the great scientific scholars spent as much time developing machines that would do their work for them as they did advancing the theory that left indelible legacies in their respective fields.

This reasoning is certainly flawed; however, we begin our chapter in this way because, as we see it, the chronicle of calculation devices underscores one crucial aspect of mathematical thought. That is, regardless of the complexity of the math surrounding these devices, the drive for their development can be traced to the idea that the "human computer," as Turing referred to it, is not nearly as efficient or predictable as we would like it to be. As we will describe in the present chapter, these realities of the mind apply even when an individual is not engaged in cutting edge mathematical proofs, and even the mental mechanisms held responsible for simple arithmetic are vulnerable to the weaknesses of the human computer. Further, the field is quite clear that an affective condition specific to math, mathematics anxiety, threatens to undermine even basic success with mathematical processing. To follow are overviews of a critical cognitive system employed during mathematical thought, and ways in which the literature suggests mathematics anxiety interferes with its normal function.

Working memory

Generally speaking, working memory refers to the system of mental mechanisms responsible for the integration, manipulation, and temporary storage of information that is relevant to an individual's focus of attention (see Miyake & Shah, 1999). The processes engaged by this system have been implicated in the function of a wide array of cognitive mechanisms contributing to reasoning and even general intelligence (e.g. Engle, 2002; Engle, Tuholski, Laughlin, & Conway,1999). Additionally, the contribution of this system to mathematical processing has been a steadily growing focus of the field, and the results of these investigations have revealed just how pervasive its role is in mathematical thought, particularly in mental calculation (for full reviews, see DeStefano & Lefevre, 2004; Raghubar, Barnes, & Hecht, 2010).

Most researchers in math cognition have utilized the dual-task paradigm as the primary approach of examining the function and contribution of the separate subcomponents of Baddeley and colleagues' multicomponent model of working memory (Baddeley, 1996, 2000; Baddeley & Logie, 1999). Briefly, this model posits that information is handled differently based on the intended use and nature of the relevant information. That is, the most developed form of this model specifies the separate roles and functions of three components: the phonological loop, the visuospatial sketchpad, and the central executive. The phonological loop and visuospatial sketchpad are collectively known as the "slave systems" of working memory, as their primary responsibility is thought to be to store verbal or visual information in coordination with the central executive, or the governing command center of the working memory system.

Seyler, Kirk, and Ashcraft (2003) illustrated how the dual-task paradigm can be used to test the three components. The goal of the study was to test the role of the phonological loop in simple subtraction calculation by loading the component with information that was irrelevant to the subtraction problems. The design increased processing load through the use of a letter recall secondary task (remembering sequences of either two, four, or six letters in length for later recall) to see if consuming the phonological loop's resources would impair the participants' ability to effectively complete the task demands of the subtraction primary task. This design follows the reasoning that, if the two unrelated tasks are reliant on the resources of the same working memory component, then deficits in the primary or secondary task should be present, as the mutually relied upon resources would be overburdened and the component would be unable to maintain both kinds of information proficiently. Conversely, if the primary and secondary tasks did not rely on the same resources, then processing deficits would not be observed.

The results of this study demonstrated such a deficit in letter recall performance, indicating that completing the two tasks relied on the same pool of limited resources, and that participants allocated those resources in a way to maximize accuracy on the subtraction problem solution. Further, Seyler et al. tested each participant on an independent measure of working memory capacity, and, not surprisingly, the results confirmed that diminished resource availability was associated with the letter recall deficit. Participants with lower overall working memory capacity were the ones to show the worse letter recall, especially in conditions involving the borrow procedure and heavy letter load – the conditions most demanding of working memory resources. Thus, these results demonstrate that even simple subtraction is reliant on working memory, and that phonological resources contribute to the problems' successful completion.

Using similar methods to those in Seyler et al., the field has shown that taxing the function of three subcomponents results in processing impairments during the completion of tasks ranging from simple counting procedures in arithmetic to more complex problem solving such as multi-digit arithmetic across all of the operations, and in the maintenance of intermediate totals (e.g. DeRammelaere, Stuyven, & Vandierendonck, 1999, 2001; Fürst & Hitch, 2000; Heathcote, 1994; Hecht, 2002; Imbo & Vandierendonck, 2007; Lemaire, Abdi, & Fayol, 1996; Logie, Gilhooly, & Wynn, 1994; Seitz & Schumann-Hengsteler, 2000; Trbovich & LeFevre, 2003).

Given these results, the field has also examined the system's role in developmental samples. Indeed, performance on central executive measures predicts the use of more sophisticated addition problem solving (e.g. min strategy, counting up by the smaller addend), and students exhibiting superior working memory function utilize direct retrieval during problem solving more frequently than do peers who showed poorer executive function (Barrouillet & Lépine, 2005; Geary, Hoard, & Nugent, 2012). Likewise, the literature shows that processing related to working memory (e.g. inhibition, task switching, central executive function) is associated with children's concurrent mathematical understanding and future math fluency (LeFevre et al., 2013), and that measures testing first grade working memory predict later math performance to the same degree as early mathematical achievement assessments (Toll, Van der Ven, Kroesbergen, & Van Luit, 2011). The growing consensus from these lines of research is that providing working memory assessments early in schooling might be an effective measure for identifying children who are at risk for poor mathematical achievement in subsequent years (e.g. Toll et al., 2011).

The studies reviewed in this section clearly illustrate two important points. First, they demonstrate that, across development, working memory is crucial for proficient mathematical performance in a wide range of tasks. The second point is that, at least in adult samples, the field has clearly shown that the dual-task paradigm is a powerful tool for understanding the nature of working memory's contribution to mathematical problem solving. More generally, the research demonstrates that the intrusion of additional mental processing, even if irrelevant to the primary task, can significantly impair task performance. Importantly, the extant literature provides evidence that an individual difference factor, mathematics anxiety, is associated with many of the performance deficits elicited in dual-task manipulations, even when cognitive load is not directly manipulated.

Mathematics anxiety

Briefly, math anxiety is a negative and potentially impairing emotional reaction to mathematics, affecting those with the condition in common day-to-day and academic situations involving mathematics (Richardson & Suinn, 1972). Interestingly, the presence of the condition is related to concurrent and long-term outcome measures in both children and adults. For example, two meta-analyses on the topic describe that high math anxious individuals tend to pursue math-related courses, degrees, and careers less often than those with low math anxiety. Further, the presence of math anxiety is also related to worse grades in both high school and college (Hembree, 1990; Ma, 1999).

Given these negative associations, coupled with research indicating that difficulties in mathematical understanding can lead to long-term detriments to career opportunities and earning (Bynner & Parsons, 1997) potential, the field has been increasingly examining math anxiety in behavioral, neurophysiological, and developmental investigations in an attempt to better understand the complex mechanisms driving its influence. In this section, we outline three major characteristics of math anxiety, describe the initial work bringing these components to light, and describe how the field has advanced our understanding of these characteristics. More specifically, the literature has expanded upon the link between math anxiety and the working memory system, concurrent and long-term avoidance behaviors related to the domain, and characteristics of its presence in early childhood.

Impairment of working memory

Early work in math anxiety sought to confirm the suspicion that the condition was related to online task performance deficits. Briefly, across the four operations of arithmetic (Ashcraft & Faust, 1994; Faust, 1988; Faust, Ashcraft, & Fleck, 1996), we found that, indeed, high math anxious individuals were often slower to calculate the answers of the problems, and tended to respond with less accuracy than their low math anxious peers. Importantly, the discrepancy between the high and low math anxious performance appeared to vary as a function of the size of the problems solved, leading us to suspect a relationship between the observed deficits and the working memory system. Further, the results were in strong agreement with Eysenck and colleagues' processing efficiency theory, which described that by-products of general anxiety (negative ruminations, intrusive thoughts) were thought to consume working memory resources (Eysenck & Calvo, 1992; Eysenck, Derakshan, Santos, & Calvo, 2007). Given the moderate relationship between the two anxiety constructs (Hembree, 1990), it seemed plausible that high math anxious individuals would be less able than low math anxious individuals to maintain, integrate, and manipulate mathematical information in a dual-task setting. Ashcraft and Kirk (2001) confirmed these hypotheses; worse performance was observed for both levels of math anxiety in conditions with large problem size and high secondary task load, but the difficulty specific to the high math anxious was exacerbated. Thus, it seemed clear to us that one of the associated effects of math anxiety was a compromised working memory system.

In strong support of this conclusion is a more recent paper that reports on the association of the neurophysiological marker of stress, cortisol, during problem solving (Mattarella-Micke, Mateo, Kozak, Foster, & Beilock, 2011). Importantly, heightened levels of the hormone in an individual are believed to be related to impaired working memory functioning in humans (e.g. Elzinga & Roelofs, 2005) and the animal equivalent hormone, corticosterone, is likewise believed to impair performance in animal models of working memory function (Roozendaal, McReynolds, & McGaugh, 2004).

Interestingly, in a pre- versus post-test measurement of cortisol levels, Mattarella-Micke et al. found that both the low and high math anxious individuals exhibited greater levels of cortisol in the post-test measurement; however, this increased concentration was related to worse performance in the task for the high math anxious, while the low math anxious actually improved in task performance as the hormone's concentration increased. Furthermore, these effects were specific to large problem solution; no relationships between cortisol concentrations and task performance were found for small problems. These results suggest that it is the interpretation of arousal during problem solving, not the mere presence of arousal itself, that is negatively impacting the performance of high math anxious individuals.

Importantly, evidence supporting the link between math anxiety and the working memory system will be echoed throughout this chapter. As such, we end our focused discussion on the topic here. From these results, it seems clear that individuals with math anxiety must complete task demands in the presence of additional processing that is not directly related to task completion. Thus, the high math anxious participant seems to undertake processing in a triple-task setting, whereby task demands, irrelevant distractors, and affect must be juggled simultaneously, resulting in an "affective drop" in performance (Ashcraft & Moore, 2009; Moore & Ashcraft, 2013).

Avoidance characteristics

Another compelling aspect of mathematics anxiety is that it is strongly predictive of long-term and concurrent avoidance of the mathematics domain. In terms of the long-term behaviors, the two meta-analyses already described provide evidence detailing a lack of motivation in excelling in the domain (–.64), lower levels of enjoyment (–.75 pre-college; –.47 for college enjoyment), and intent to pursue additional math courses (–.32). Furthermore, behavioral data in our early studies revealed that high math anxious individuals were more likely to exhibit performance indicative of a speed/accuracy trade-off; the high math anxious individuals would tend to respond with latencies that rivaled those provided by the low math anxious participants, but with much higher error rates.

Given our review of the important role working memory plays in mathematics, and how this system appears to be compromised in individuals with high math anxiety, it appeared to us that the high anxious were merely attempting to terminate their participation in the experiment quickly without expending the necessary mental effort to ensure that their solutions were correct. It is quite compelling that high math anxious individuals display such a wide spread aversion to the *entire* domain throughout their academic lives and into adulthood. So, the pressing question is, "What would drive students to evade this area of study so strongly?"

The cortisol assay just described provides an important clue that the interpretation of physiological arousal is possibly a factor corresponding to the performance exhibited in a math task. Additional neuroimaging evidence supports this claim. Lyons and Beilock (2012a) set out to examine patterns of brain activity in high and low math anxious individuals during the preparation for and completion of a mathematical task. Before completing either a task that contained mathematical or lexical information, a cue was presented to the participant indicating which task to prepare for. Brain scans were recorded during cue presentation and task completion. Briefly, the post-cue behavioral results mirror those already discussed; the high math anxious performed more poorly in difficult problem types as compared to the low math anxious. Importantly, performance between the groups did not differ on a difficulty-matched word task, supporting the idea that math anxiety is a domain-specific condition.

The neurological evidence, however, indicated that brain activity during cue presentation in frontoparietal areas (bilateral inferior frontal junction, bilateral inferior parietal lobe, and left inferior frontal gyrus) was related to the deficits observed in the completion of the math task by the high math anxious. More specifically, they found that as the activation of these areas increased, the deficit exhibited decreased. Furthermore, the high math anxious individuals' activation recorded during task completion (right caudate and left hippocampus) was found to mediate the relationship between cue activity and the performance deficit observed. These results indicate that the emotional regulation described is engaged even before calculation begins, and that *some* high math anxious individuals might be able to mentally prepare for the upcoming math task and reduce the extent of the affective drop (see Bishop, 2007).

Lyons and Beilock (2012b) sought to explore these patterns further, and found evidence supporting a compelling neurological reason for the high anxious to avoid math; the prospect of completing a mathematical task is equivalent to anticipating bodily harm. The data were collected in the cueing paradigm just described, however the authors were interested in examining the possibility that the math-related cue would serve to increase the high math anxious participants' emotional awareness (interoception; Craig, 2003), which is the result in cases of increased general anxiety (Domschke, Stevens, Pfleiderer, & Gerlach, 2010). Furthermore, this increase in awareness has been shown to result in heightened sensitivity to pain (e.g. Esteve & Camacho, 2008). Essentially, the authors were expecting to find neural activation patterns suggesting the anticipation of physical harm in relation to the math anxiety reported. Their results showed just that; those with high math anxiety were found to have increased activation in dorso-posterior insular and mid-cingulate cortex regions during the math cue, but not the reading task cue. These activations were not found in the low math anxious individuals. Importantly, these regions are believed to be responsible for pain perception (Lenz et al., 1993), and their activation during the math cue suggests that knowledge of an upcoming math problem is neurologically equivalent to anticipating a physically painful event.

The results described thus far allow for the interpretation that one of the avenues through which math anxiety operates is the re-routing of working memory resources away from the task completed and toward emotion regulation centers in the brain. Further, it appears that the emotions encountered include the fear of pending physical harm, and almost undoubtedly include years of experience with failure in the domain and the fear of appearing incompetent if performance is being observed by peers or researchers (see Moore & Ashcraft (2013) for a review of the relations between math anxiety and belief states). One important caveat to this interpretation, however, is that the emotional burden experienced by math anxious individuals does not necessitate years of negative performance or exposure to the domain. Instead, it appears that even children in the first grade deal with the negative aspects of the condition, and recent work has uncovered potential sources for developing such a negative reaction to the domain.

Developmental Evidence

Work investigating the development of math anxiety is a most recent focus for the field; however, evidence is quickly accumulating and is bringing to light important details about the condition in its early stages. For example, in accordance with the adult results already discussed, two recent studies suggest that working memory function is associated with the presence of math anxiety in the first few years of primary school (Ramirez, Gunderson, Levine, & Beilock, 2013; Vukovic, Kieffer, Bailey, & Harari, 2013). This aspect of math anxiety is to be expected in childhood, given its prevalent role in the associated deficits of adult performance; however, the novel component of the developmental evidence is that it was those with *superior* working memory function that suffered from the condition. That is, these regression studies found that the interaction term comprised of math anxiety and working memory scores of children in the first and second grades was associated with performance on measures of applied mathematics, such as word problems and data interpretation from tables, concurrently (Ramirez et al., 2013), and longitudinally (Vukovic et al., 2013). Although the exact reason for this interesting effect is not known, the broader uncertainty of the cause for math anxiety so young in childhood is gaining focus in the field.

In the first fMRI study to examine math anxiety in children, Young, Wu, and Menon (2012) found brain activations in 7 to 9 year olds that tell a similar story to that found in adult samples. That is, Young et al. found that high math anxious children exhibited stronger activation in the basolateral nucleus of the left amygdala, a site previously tied to the learned fear response in adults (Phelps & LeDoux, 2005). Additionally, the authors report that the functional connectivity between this area and the ventromedial prefrontal cortex was stronger in the high math anxious children, suggesting that, indeed, even children exhibit patterns of emotional regulation if high levels of math anxiety are experienced (e.g. Phelps, Delgado, Nearing & LeDoux, 2004). Importantly, activation in parietal areas was reduced in high math anxious children (areas believed to engage during mathematical thought; Dehaene, Spelke, Pinel, Stanescu, & Tsivkin, 1999). Thus, as with adult math anxiety, it appears that children also suffer from the re-routing of working memory resources from calculation to regulating emotions. Given the surprising finding that children with superior working memory function demonstrate worse longitudinal growth than low working memory children with high math anxiety, the exact nature of the emotional regulation described here deserves thorough investigation.

The developmental work in math anxiety has begun to unravel the influence of the condition in children, but we are still unsure about the triggers for its onset in children. One likely source for developing negative attitudes about the domain, at least, could simply come from cultural, family, and peer influences (e.g. Moore & Ashcraft, 2013). Interestingly, another potential source for acquiring the affective reaction might come from more formal figures in the child's life, namely their own teachers.

Beilock, Gunderson, Ramirez, and Levine (2010) investigated the potential role that elementary school teachers play in the development of the condition, specifically because of the disproportionate number of female teachers at this level who also report high levels of math anxiety (Hembree, 1990). Their study tracked performance of first grade students from the beginning to the end of the school year, measuring math anxiety and achievement. Also, given the tendency for children to adopt same-gender stereotypes at this age (Bussey & Bandura, 1984; Perry & Bussey, 1979), they also collected measures of gender-role beliefs (e.g. "math is for boys, reading is for girls"). They found that, although no differences were reported at the beginning of the school year, the girls in the class showed worse math achievement at the end-of-year testing. Further, this effect was dependent on the math anxiety of the teacher as well as the gender beliefs of the girls; the stronger math anxiety was in teachers, and the stronger gender beliefs adopted by the girls, the worse math achievement was at the end of the year. Boys' achievement scores were unrelated to these attitudes. This study serves to highlight the variety of sources through which mathematics anxiety can be a learned reaction to the domain.

Our review has characterized math anxiety as a condition that is thought to consume working memory resources during calculation and influence individuals to avoid situations in which mathematical thought is a component. Importantly, these characteristics persist across the lifespan of the individual with high levels of the condition. Research on the causal factors of math anxiety is still in its infancy, although promising directions have already begun to emerge (see Maloney, Ansari, & Fugelsang, 2011; Maloney, Risko, Ansari, & Fugelsang, 2010). As we gain greater knowledge about math anxiety and its consequences, we will surely gain greater insight into effective strategies for reducing (e.g. Ramirez & Beilock, 2011) or preventing this unnecessary impediment.

References

Ashcraft, M. H., & Faust, M. W. (1994). Mathematics anxiety and mental arithmetic performance: An exploratory investigation. *Cognition and Emotion, 8*, 97–125.

Ashcraft, M. H., & Kirk, E. P. (2001). The relationships among working memory, math anxiety, and performance. *Journal of Experimental Psychology: General, 130*, 224–237.

Ashcraft, M. H., & Moore, A. M. (2009). Mathematics anxiety and the affective drop in performance. *Journal of Psychoeducational Assessment, 27*, 197–205.

Baddeley, A. D. (1996). Exploring the central executive. *Quarterly Journal of Experimental Psychology: Human Experimental Psychology, 49A*, 5–28.

Baddeley, A. D. (2000). The episodic buffer: A new component of working memory? *Trends in Cognitive Sciences, 4*, 417–423.

Baddeley, A. D., & Logie, R. H. (1999). Working memory: The multiple-component model. In A. Miyake & P. Shah (Eds.), *Models of working memory: Mechanisms of active maintenance and executive control* (pp. 28–61). Cambridge: Cambridge University Press.

Barrouillet, P., & Lépine, R. (2005). Working memory and children's use of retrieval to solve addition problems. *Journal of Experimental Child Psychology, 91*, 183–204.

Beilock, S. L., Gunderson, E. A., Ramirez, G., & Levine, S. C. (2010). Female teachers' math anxiety affects girls' math achievement. *Proceedings of the National Academy of Sciences, 107*, 1860–1863.

Bishop, S. J. (2007). Neurocognitive mechanisms of anxiety: An integrative account. *Trends in Cognitive Sciences, 11*, 307–316.

Bussey, K., & Bandura, A. (1984). Influence of gender constancy and social power on sex-linked modeling. *Journal of Personality and Social Psychology, 47*, 1292–1302.

Bynner, J. & Parsons, S. *Does numeracy matter? Evidence from the national child development study on the impact of poor numeracy on adult life*. London: The Basic Skills Agency.

Craig, A. D. (2003). Interoception: The sense of the physiological condition of the body. *Current Opinion in Neurobiology, 13*, 500–505.

Dehaene, S., Spelke, E., Pinel, P., Stanescu, R., & Tsivkin, S. (1999). Sources of mathematical thinking; Behavioral and brain-imaging evidence. *Science, 284*, 970–974.

DeRammelaere, S., Stuyven, E., & Vandierendonck, A. (1999). The contribution of working memory resources in the verification of simple mental arithmetic sums. *Psychological Research, 62*, 72–77.

DeRammelaere, S., Stuyven, E., & Vandierendonck, A. (2001). Verifying simple arithmetic sums and products: Are the phonological loop and the central executive involved? *Memory & Cognition, 29*, 267–273.

DeStefano, D., & LeFevre, J. (2004). The role of working memory in mental arithmetic. *European Journal of Cognitive Psychology, 16*, 353–386.

Domschke, K., Stevens, S., Pfleiderer, B., & Gerlach, A. L. (2010). Interoceptive sensitivity in anxiety and anxiety disorders: An overview and integration of neurobiological findings. *Clinical Psychology Review, 30*, 1–11.

Elzinga, B. M., & Roelofs, K. (2005). Cortisol-induced impairments of working memory require acute sympathetic activation. *Behavioral Neuroscience, 119*, 98–103.

Engle, R. W. (2002). Working memory capacity as executive attention. *Current Directions in Psychological Science, 11*, 19–23.

Engle, R. W., Tuholski, S. W., Laughlin, J. E., & Conway, A. R. A. (1999). Working memory, short-term memory and general fluid intelligence: A latent variable approach. *Journal of Experimental Psychology: General, 128*, 309–331.

Esteve, M. R., & Camacho, L. (2008). Anxiety sensitivity, body vigilance and fear of pain. *Behaviour Research and Therapy, 46*, 715–727.

Eysenck, M. W., & Calvo, M. G. (1992). Anxiety and performance: The processing efficiency theory. *Cognition and Emotion, 6*, 409–434.

Eysenck, M. W., Derakshan, N., Santos, R., & Calvo, M. G. (2007). Anxiety and cognitive performance: Attentional control theory. *Emotion, 7*, 336–353.

Faust, M. W. (1988). Arithmetic performance as a function of mathematics anxiety: An in-depth analysis of simple and complex addition problems. Unpublished M.A. thesis, Cleveland State University, Cleveland, Ohio.

Faust, M. W., Ashcraft, M. H., & Fleck, D. E. (1996). Mathematics anxiety effects in simple and complex addition. *Mathematical Cognition, 2*, 25–62.

Fürst, A. J., & Hitch, G. J. (2000). Separate roles for executive and phonological components of working memory in mental arithmetic. *Memory and Cognition, 28*, 774–782.

Geary, D. C., Hoard, M. K., & Nugent, L. (2012). Independent contributions of the central executive, intelligence, and in-class attentive behavior to developmental change in the strategies used to solve addition problems. *Journal of Experimental Child Psychology, 113*, 49–65.

Heathcote, D. (1994). The role of visuo-spatial working memory in the mental addition of multi-digit addends. *Current Psychology of Cognition, 13*, 207–245.

Hecht, S. A. (2002). Counting on working memory in simple arithmetic when counting is used for problem solving. *Memory and Cognition, 30*, 447–455.

Hembree, R. (1990). The nature, effects, and relief of mathematics anxiety. *Journal for Research in Mathematics Education, 21*, 33–46.

Imbo, I., & Vandierendonck, A. (2007). The role of phonological and executive working memory resources in simple arithmetic strategies. *European Journal of Cognitive Psychology, 19*, 910–933.

LeFevre, J. A., Berrigan, L., Vendetti, C., Kamawar, D., Bisanz, J., Skwarchuk, S. L., & Smith-Chant, B. L. (2013). The role of executive attention in the acquisition of mathematical skills for children in Grades 2 through 4. *Journal of Experimental Child Psychology, 114*, 243–261.

Lemaire, P., Abdi, H., & Fayol, M. (1996). The role of working memory resources in simple cognitive arithmetic. *European Journal of Cognitive Psychology, 8*, 73–103.

Lenz, F. A., Seike, M., Richardson, R. T., Lin, Y. C., Baker, F. H., Khoja, I., Gracely, R. H. (1993). Thermal and pain sensations evoked by microstimulation in the area of human ventrocaudal nucleus. *Journal of Neurophysiology, 70*, 200–212.

Logie, R. H., Gilhooly, K. J., & Wynn, V. (1994). Counting on working memory in mental arithmetic. *Memory & Cognition, 22*, 395–410.

Lyons, I. M., & Beilock, S. L. (2012a). Mathematics anxiety: Separating the math from the anxiety. *Cerebral Cortex, 22*, 2102–2110.

Lyons, I. M., & Beilock, S. L. (2012b). When math hurts: math anxiety predicts pain network activation in anticipation of doing math. *PLoS ONE, 7*(10), e48076.

Ma, X. (1999). A meta-analysis of the relationship between anxiety toward mathematics and achievement in mathematics. *Journal for Research in Mathematics Education, 30*, 520–541.

Maloney, E. A., Ansari, D., & Fugelsang, J. A. (2011). The effect of mathematics anxiety on the processing of numerical magnitude. *Quarterly Journal of Experimental Psychology, 64*, 10–16.

Maloney, E. A., Risko, E. F., Ansari, D., & Fugelsang, J. (2010). Mathematics anxiety affects counting but not subitizing during visual enumeration. *Cognition, 114*, 293–297.

Mattarella-Micke, A., Mateo, J., Kozak, M. N., Foster, K., & Beilock, S. L. (2011). Choke or thrive? The relation between salivary cortisol and math performance depends on individual differences in working memory and math-anxiety. *Emotion, 11*, 1000–1005.

Miyake, A., & Shah, P. (1999). *Models of working memory: Mechanisms of active maintenance and executive control.* Cambridge, UK: Cambridge University Press.

Moore, A. M., & Ashcraft, M. H. (2013). Emotionality in mathematical problem solving. In C. Mohiyeddini, M. Eysenck, & S. Bauer (Eds.), *The psychology of emotions: Recent theoretical perspectives and novel empirical findings* (pp. 115–141). New York: Nova Science Publishers, Inc.

Perry, D. G., & Bussey, K. (1979). The social learning theory of sex differences: Imitation is alive and well. *Journal of Personality and Social Psychology, 37*, 1699–1712.

Phelps, E. A., Delgado, M. R., Nearing, K. I., LeDoux, J. E. (2004). Extinction learning in humans: Role of the amygdala and vmPFC. *Neuron, 43*, 897–905.

Phelps, E. A., & LeDoux, J. E. (2005). Contributions of the amygdala to emotion processing: From animal models to human behavior. *Neuron, 48*, 175–187.

Raghubar, K. P., Barnes, M. A., & Hecht, S. A. (2010). Working memory and mathematics: A review of developmental, individual difference, and cognitive approaches. *Learning and Individual Differences, 20*, 110–122.

Ramirez, G., & Beilock, S. L. (2011). Writing about testing worries boosts exam performance in the classroom. *Science, 331*, 211–213.

Ramirez, G., Gunderson, E. A., Levine, S. C., & Beilock, S. L. (2013). Math anxiety, working memory, and math achievement in early elementary school. *Journal of Cognition and Development, 14*, 187–202.

Richardson, F. C., & Suinn, R. M. (1972). The mathematics anxiety rating scale: Psychometric data. *Journal of Counseling Psychology, 19*, 551–554.

Roozendaal, B., McReynolds, J. R., & McGaugh, J. L. (2004). The basolateral amygdala interacts with the medial prefrontal cortex in regulating glucocorticoid effects on working memory impairment. *The Journal of Neuroscience, 24*, 1385–1392.

Seitz, K., & Schumann-Hengsteler, R. (2000). Mental multiplication and working memory. *European Journal of Cognitive Psychology, 12*, 552–570.

Seyler, D. J., Kirk, E. P., & Ashcraft, M. H. (2003). Elementary subtraction. *Journal of Experimental Psychology. Learning, Memory, and Cognition, 29*, 1339–1352.

Toll, S. W., Van der Ven, S. H., Kroesbergen, E. H., & Van Luit, J. E. (2011). Executive functions as predictors of math learning disabilities. *Journal of Learning Disabilities, 44*, 521–532.

Trbovich, P. L., & LeFevre, J. (2003). Phonological and visual working memory in mental addition. *Memory & Cognition, 31*, 738–745.

Turing, A. M. (1950). Computing machinery and intelligence. *Mind: A Quarterly Review of Psychology and Philosophy, 59*, 433–460.

Vukovic, R. K., Kieffer, M. J., Bailey, S. P., & Harari, R. R. (2013). Mathematics anxiety in young children: Concurrent and longitudinal associations with mathematical performance. *Contemporary Educational Psychology, 38*, 1–10.

Young, C. B., Wu, S. S., & Menon, V. (2012). The neurodevelopmental basis of math anxiety. *Psychological Science, 23*, 492–501.

25

Mathematical resilience

What is it and why is it important?

Clare Lee and Sue Johnston-Wilder

Many people have difficulties learning mathematics for many different reasons. However, many people, otherwise good learners, find mathematical tasks difficult, to the point that they steer clear of any engagement with mathematics. Such people may exhibit a high degree of phobia or anxiety, but many of them simply avoid any situation that might involve mathematical reasoning; we would say too many. This chapter is about what might be done to stop young learners from developing a need to disengage from mathematics.

Working explicitly to develop *mathematical resilience* (Johnston-Wilder & Lee 2010) seems to offer a way of recognising the issues that many people encounter when learning mathematics and enabling them to succeed despite those issues. The construct mathematical resilience indicates a positive approach to mathematics that allows people to overcome affective barriers presented when learning mathematics. Mathematical resilience can be developed by anyone; there are clear indicators from literature and from our research about how this can be done. Learners who display mathematical resilience will continue despite feeling 'stuck'; they will persevere by recruiting resources to help them. These resources might be their peer group or possibly on-line resources or an adult who will listen or even their textbook. Above all, they will not accept the state of 'being stuck' as a permanent position. They will have a growth or incremental theory of learning (Dweck 2000) and therefore know that they can learn more mathematics, provided they find the support they need.

What is mathematical resilience?

Mathematical resilience (Johnston-Wilder & Lee 2010) is a pragmatic, mathematised understanding of the well-established concept resilience. It has been shown (e.g. Kooken et al. 2013) that in order to be resilient mathematically a student must understand the need to struggle mathematically, hold a growth theory of learning and have resources available to them to support their learning. Therefore, mathematical resilience describes that quality by which some learners approach mathematics with agency, persistence and a willingness to discuss, reflect and research.

Far too many students, particularly in the US and UK, leave compulsory education without effective numeracy. Although reasons for this are complex, a major contributory factor is the quality of mathematics teaching (e.g. Nardi & Steward 2003; Ofsted 2008). We use 'teaching' here and not 'teachers' deliberately; all teachers we have talked with want the best for their students. However, many teachers become convinced (Harlen 2005), with some justification, that examinations are the measure of success and that the best way to enable their pupils to pass these examinations is to adopt a style of teaching that privileges instrumental over relational understanding (Skemp 1972) and which equates to a focus on formulas and algorithms (Stigler & Hiebert 2009). Thus memorising is valued over depth of understanding, and 'teaching to the test' over enabling pupils to see the power and connectivity of mathematics.

Stigler and Hiebert (2009) showed that mathematics teachers see their role as path-smoothing (Wigley 1992), instead of allowing students to develop strategies to overcome any obstacles they encounter when learning mathematics. Teachers tend to feel they have failed if their students get 'stuck' and seek to provide help promptly. As a consequence, students develop 'learned helplessness' and assume that inability to immediately see the way forward with a mathematics problem indicates they 'cannot do mathematics'. Many mathematics lessons use a *restricted practice* of teacher exposition of a single isolated technique followed by pupil completion of exercises practising the technique, the exercises being aimed at helping pupils remember how and when to use that technique (Nardi & Steward 2003; Ofsted 2008). Teachers feel they must adopt an algorithmic approach, taking their students step-wise through a process that leads to a solution. 'Remember this!' they say, 'And you will not get stuck.' Now the path is smooth but there are huge demands on memory and limited scope to adapt ideas. Students do not positively experience the state of 'being stuck' which Mason (1988) regards as a precursor to real learning.

Narratives from people who exhibit mathematics phobia (e.g. Ashcraft 2002; Newman 2004; Hoffman 2010) clarify that the way mathematics is often taught in mathematics classrooms could be termed an unwitting form of cognitive abuse. Boaler (2009), Jain & Dowson (2009) and Baloglu & Koçak (2006) all indicate that certain common ways of working in mathematics classrooms cause anxiety, sometimes extreme, among learners. Instances given include asking learners to perform tasks that require rapid feats of memory, requiring pupils to memorise formulas without understanding, and divorcing mathematical ideas from the reality they model so powerfully. In this sense, mathematical resilience is a positive adaptation to enable success (Newman 2004). If learners are to engage willingly with mathematics, they must learn that they can struggle through problems, deal with barriers and misunderstandings and think through mathematical ideas; thus, they need mathematical resilience.

All learning requires resilience; we contend that the resilience required for learning mathematics is a particular construct because of various factors, including: the type of teaching often used when teaching mathematics, the nature of mathematics itself, and pervasive beliefs about mathematical ability being 'fixed'. The idea of 'mathematical resilience' offers a positive construct that can help those who are supporting learners of mathematics have a vision of what they are seeking to develop in students and thus to make positive pedagogical choices about the way that they help learners. We understand supporters of those who are learning mathematics to include teachers but also parents or workplace colleagues, anyone who undertakes to be alongside someone seeking to learn mathematics.

The quest for a definition of the construct *mathematical resilience* (Johnston-Wilder & Lee 2010) is no simplistic task. There is extensive literature concerning psychological resilience, and how young people 'at risk' of educational failure succeed despite overwhelming trauma or disadvantage. Resilience is *'ordinary magic . . . made up of ordinary rather than extraordinary processes'* (Masten 2001, p. 227). Studies in educational settings in the latter half of the twentieth century focused on students who, despite being classified as 'at risk', succeeded academically. This led to the development of the term 'resilience' to describe this invulnerability (Garmezy 1985). The emphasis in these enquiries was on the circumstances that prevented some students succumbing to the risks that appeared to encompass them. This, in turn, resulted in ideas for helping children to become resilient. Resilience is not a once and for all attribute. 'Children may be more or less resilient at different points in their lives depending on the interaction and accumulation of individual and environmental factors' (Howard & Johnson 1999, p. 310). Benard (1991) believes that schools could foster resilience by paying attention to social competence, problem-solving skills, critical consciousness, autonomy and a sense of purpose in students. Carr and Claxton (2002) view resilience as a key learning disposition and define it as 'the inclination to take on (at least some) learning challenges where the outcome is uncertain, to persist with learning despite temporary confusion or frustration and to recover from setbacks or failures and rededicate oneself to the learning task' (Carr & Caxton 2002, p. 12).

Working to develop resilience must involve changes to mindsets (Yeager & Dweck 2012). Many common occurrences in the learning of mathematics foster an entity theory of learning. Such things as the common practice of 'setting' or 'streaming' assume that 'ability' can be accurately measured and changes very little. Although students are sometimes moved between sets or streams, this system assumes that students' ability is both measureable and fixed. In addition, a prevalent marking system which gives students a mark out of ten, proves to those with an entity theory of learning that they can or cannot 'do' mathematics. When advice on improving is given this indicates an expectation that everyone can improve. The on-going work of Dweck and her colleagues shows how holding an incremental or growth view of learning allows students to engage with pedagogies that enable deep learning in mathematics, allowing students to understand mathematics and also increase their scores in mathematics:

> [I]f students can be redirected to see intellectual ability as something that can be developed over time with effort, good strategies, and help from others, then

they are more resilient when they encounter the rigorous learning opportunities presented to them.

(Yeager & Dweck 2012, p. 306)

Best practice comes back to the ideas that other work has identified as constituting effective teaching (e.g. educational psychology, educational counselling, teacher professional development). Thus, achievement in school is higher when: teachers teach for mastery; curricula are relevant to students' present and future needs; authentic assessment practices are used; democratic classrooms are created where students contribute to the rule-making and governance; rational, humane and consistent behaviour management techniques are adopted; teachers are warm, approachable, fair and supportive; and a range of ways of being successful are made available to students (Porter & Brophy 1988; Nuthall & Alton-Lee 1990).

Furthermore, speaking or otherwise communicating is an important part of developing mathematical resilience; becoming able to articulate mathematical ideas, concepts and reasoning has a profound effect on the way that learners see themselves (e.g. Lee 2006, Mercer & Littleton 2007, Vygotsky 1981). An individual takes on the identity of a mathematician (Holland et al. 1998) by learning how to talk like a mathematician. Giving learners the opportunity to 'talk like a mathematician' means that they become someone who 'knows and can do mathematics'; that is, they begin to see themselves as mathematically resilient. Supporters of learners of mathematics seeking to build mathematical resilience will encourage collaborative working where learners support one another in learning, enabling pupils to both understand and articulate their own knowledge and needs in the process of learning, and to support others.

Developing mathematical resilience

There are many ways that mathematical resilience can be developed. There are changes that can be made to pedagogy in schools that are known to make a difference to young people. However, if mathematical resilience was not developed in school, it can be developed later. We have shown that three groups of people can use ideas about mathematical resilience to improve learners' attitudes to mathematics and thus increase the likelihood that they will learn and use mathematical ideas.

Teaching for mathematical resilience

Currently mathematical resilience is not developed purposively; it seems to occur by happenstance where it is developed at all. The term 'mathematical resilience' is useful in drawing teachers' attention to the harm that can be perpetrated and towards using pedagogies that can mitigate any harm that has already been done. As students study mathematics for longer in many countries, teaching in ways that result in young people avoiding mathematics is increasingly untenable. It is not hard to find ideas for developing mathematical resilience; journals aimed at mathematics teachers provide many such ideas. Many mathematics teachers work hard in their classrooms to enable their pupils to enjoy and succeed in mathematics in ways that are known to develop resilience. They encourage their pupils to work collaboratively and to explore, articulate and make connections between areas of mathematics and how it is used in the world outside school. They see understanding as important, rather than speed of recall. Teachers who help their students develop resilience do not pretend that mathematics is easy, or attempt to remove the challenges that mathematics presents. They acknowledge that students will need to struggle to overcome the barriers that most people find when learning mathematics. They help their students find their own ways to overcome these barriers, because they believe that every person can improve their understanding of mathematics given the right support from resources such as the teacher themselves, other students, the internet and so on.

Teachers must be reassured that teaching for understanding and using mathematics lessons to discuss and collaborate in working for deep learning of mathematical ideas will not harm examination results and has the added advantage that their students will be more resilient, i.e. prepared and able to learn and to use mathematical ideas beyond school.

Coaching for mathematical resilience

Many schools have a shortage of well-qualified mathematics teachers and are judged on their pupils' examination results. This has often resulted in unsustainable stress placed on teachers who remain in post. Thus, many mathematics learners do not receive high-quality teaching designed to enable them to persist with their mathematical learning. One place where such difficulties need to be modified urgently is the workplace, particularly where apprentices are being trained. Any adult in the workplace can be called upon to coach another in using mathematics, and the more they encourage explicitly the development of mathematical resilience the more likely they are to truly enable mathematical thinking in those that they coach.

We offered, through the auspices of Asdan, working with the Progression Trust, a training course for people whose role was to help apprentices develop mathematical ideas in the workplace. The role of a coach for mathematical resilience is to help learners to stay longer in what we termed their learning 'growth zone'. The coaches were themselves coached in: using language in such a way that the students could recognise and articulate the degree of challenge they are facing; encouraging increasing independence and agency; modelling resilient approaches to mathematics; being part of a community of practice and knowing how to access help (Johnston-Wilder et al. 2013).

Many of the course participants suffered mathematics anxiety themselves; the initial meetings were dedicated to helping them understand that they could bring the resilience that they used in many areas of their life to bear on mathematical learning. They had to begin to explore resilient behaviours before they could feel safe enough to begin to think mathematically. The differing roles of the two tutors on the course were important. One was a mathematics education specialist and the other a coaching specialist; their collaboration ensured the participants were supported as they overcame their own difficulties in approaching mathematics. Time is needed to develop a community of practice; by week three, the group was beginning to function effectively. An effective coach knows and understands mathematical resilience because they have worked through their own anxieties and developed a more positive stance towards mathematics in a safe and collaborative environment. Once this process has been worked through they can coach learners to develop a resilient attitude towards mathematics. Participants should be exposed to mathematical ideas, despite the fact that this is likely to cause discomfort. Only in these circumstances will they learn to manage their own reactions and thereby reflect on how to help someone else.

Parenting for mathematical resilience

Many parents have developed an anxiety which has made them feel helpless in the face of their own children's difficulties for all the reasons discussed above. Left unrecognised, this anxiety is likely to be passed onto their children. Heather, a young mother, experienced many negative events while at school. Here is one of Heather's descriptions:

> We were doing maths. We were working on long division, I got a red cross on some of my work when I checked on the calculator the answer was correct, (mmm) this puzzled me so when I questioned my teacher she said it was because my working out was wrong and made me feel stupid in front of my peers when I explained (translated) my methods.

Heather had demonstrated mathematical resilience as a child; she was willing to 'have a go', and puzzled by the teacher's marking. The teacher's response in this situation undermined Heather; she experienced loss of social esteem, became unwilling to ask questions in the future and thus lost much of her innate mathematical resilience. This is her description of the result when she tried to help her daughter.

> Throughout the years when I've worked with my daughter on maths homework it's been a combination of falling out, shouting, tears, avoidance, feeling stupid on both parts, her putting herself down, me trying to restore her confidence but both of us to[o] tense and stressed for it to make any difference.

Heather had resources from her daughter's school, she had the expectation that 'she should be able to help' as she did with other subjects; but her own self-image was of total failure in relation to mathematics. Heather sought help from us; she was offered a resource, in the form of a mathematics dictionary. We encouraged her to be aware of her own everyday use of mathematics, and to focus her attention on her role as 'curious, supportive, listening mother' rather than inadequate mathematics 'expert'. With no extra mathematical knowledge, the change was dramatic.

> One day after she came home from school she curiously asked me for the text book they had been working from that day in school, she confidently flicked

the page open to an angles section where there was a page full of lines in all directions, and said 'We were doing this today but I don't get it' so I said well let's have a look then, with a few minutes she understood, it turned out that all that really confused her was the layout of the page as it was full of lines set up in twos connecting at one point and were heading in all sorts of directions.

Heather's response is one of supportive curiosity and listening, of modelling resilient behaviours, of talking things through and using resources available, encouraging persistence in thinking with a dash of curiosity and support, along with an expectation that given time a plan of action could be put in place. Thus the home situation is no longer stressful and becomes one of growth in small steps. Instant recognition and answers were no longer expected, greater benefit could be obtained by applying mathematically resilient behaviours.

Developing a culture that promotes mathematical resilience

Learners of mathematics often expect to be T.I.R.E.D. (Nardi & Stewart 2003); where expectations are raised and students are challenged and supported appropriately (Lee & Johnston-Wilder 2013, Watson & DeGeest 2005), they meet, often exceed, the challenges set. Mathematically resilient students succeed despite barriers: they are adaptive; able to cope with ambiguity; expect problems and challenges and expect to meet them successfully. They solve problems logically and flexibly; look for creative solutions to challenges; are curious and learn from experience; have an internal locus of control; are aware of their feelings; have a strong social network and are able to ask for help. Mathematically resilient role-models will not respond 'Oh I can't do maths', but 'that is an interesting question – how shall we find out?' A learning culture that emphasises inclusion, group work, a growth theory of learning, struggle, persistence and curiosity fosters mathematical resilience and therefore a willingness to take part in mathematical learning. It is also a culture where the learners are doing the work and experiencing the positive emotions of challenges met, peers supported, being listened to, being part of a purposeful community and learning.

Conclusion

Mathematically resilient learners have the following four characteristics:

- belief that brain capability can be grown – that intelligence is not fixed but that with support and effort everyone can get smarter at mathematics;
- understanding of the personal value of mathematics – that it is worth making the effort;
- understanding of how to work at mathematics – that it requires perseverance, curiosity and struggle;
- awareness that support is available from peers, other adults, ICT, internet, etc.

A resilient stance towards mathematics can be developed in learners through a strategic and explicit focus on the culture of learning mathematics, within both formal and informal learning settings.

Part of the solution lies in developing mathematical resilience outside the mathematics classroom in all adults and children. If learners are surrounded by adults who find mathematics is something to be anxious about, is different and that normal ways of learning cannot be used for mathematics, then it is unsurprising that learners also develop negative attitudes to mathematics. We have shown that small changes make a difference. Instead of the supporting person taking the stance of the one who must show the 'correct' way to the answer, a supporter can model resilient behaviour by being the one who asks pertinent questions or encourages articulation and listens to explanations, who suggests resources that might help or who simply struggles alongside. Instead of modelling avoidance and fear, the resilience that many people demonstrate in areas of their lives can be brought to mathematical learning, emotions can be managed and difficulties can be overcome, and the development of mathematical resilience and skills can be shared.

References

Ashcraft, M. 2002. Math anxiety: personal, educational, and cognitive consequences. *Current Directions, Psychological Science, 11*(5), 181–185.

Baloglu, M. & Koçak, R. 2006. A multivariate investigation of the differences in mathematics anxiety. *Personality & Individual Differences, 40*(7), 1325–1335.

Benard, B. 1991. *Fostering Resiliency in Kids: Protective Factors in the Family, School, and Community*. San Francisco: Far West Laboratory for Educational Research and Development. ED 335 781.

Boaler, J. 2009. *The Elephant in the Classroom: Helping Children Learn and Love Maths*. London: Souvenir Press Ltd.

Carr, M. & Claxton, G. 2002. Tracking the development of learning dispositions. *Assessment in Education, 9*, 9–37.

Dweck, C. 2000. *Self Theories: Their Role in Motivation, Personality and Development*. Lillington, NC: Psychology Press, Taylor & Francis.

Garmezy, N. 1985. Stress-resistant children: the search for protective factors. In: J. E. Stevenson (ed.) *Recent research in developmental psychopathology, Journal of Child Psychology and Psychiatry Book Supplement, 4*, (213–233). Oxford: Pergamon Press.

Harlen, W. 2005. Teachers' summative practices and assessment for learning: tensions and synergies. *The Curriculum Journal, 16*(2), 207–223.

Hoffman, B. 2010, 'I think I can, but I'm afraid to try': the role of self-efficacy beliefs and mathematics anxiety in mathematics problem-solving efficiency. *Learning and Individual Differences, 20*(3), 276–283.

Holland, D., Skinner, D., Lachicotte, W. & Cain, C. 1998. *Identity and agency in cultural worlds*. Cambridge, MA: Harvard University Press.

Howard, S. & Johnson, B. 1999. Tracking student resilience. *Children Australia, 24*(3), 14–23.

Jain, S. & Dowson, M. 2009. Mathematics anxiety as a function of multidimensional self-regulation. *Contemporary Educational Psychology, 34*, 240–249.

Johnston-Wilder, S. & Lee, C. 2010. Mathematical resilience. *Mathematics Teaching, 218*, 38–41.

Johnston-Wilder, S., Lee, C., Garton, E., Goodlad, S. & Brindley, J. 2013. *Developing Coaches for Mathematical Resilience*, Proceedings of ICERI Seville.

Kooken, J., Welsh, M., Mccoach, B., Johnston-Wilder, S. & Lee, C. 2013. *Measuring Mathematical Resilience: An Application of the Construct of Resilience to the Study of Mathematics.* In: AERA 2013, San Francisco, California, 27 Apr–1 May 2013.

Lee, C. 2006. *Language for Learning Mathematics: Assessment for Learning in Practice.* Buckingham: Open University Press.

Lee, C. & Johnston-Wilder, S. 2013. Learning mathematics: letting the pupils have their say. *Educational Studies in Mathematics, 83*(2), 163–180.

Mason, J. 1988. *Learning and Doing Mathematics.* London: Macmillan.

Masten, A. 2001. Ordinary magic resilience processes in development. *American Psychologist, 56*(3), 227–238.

Mercer, N. & Littleton, K. 2007. *Dialogue and the Development of Children's Thinking: A Sociocultural Approach.* London: Routledge.

Nardi, E. & Steward, S. 2003. Is mathematics T.I.R.E.D.? A profile of quiet disaffection in the secondary mathematics classroom. *British Educational Research Journal, 29*(3), 345–366.

Newman, T. 2004. *What Works in Building Resilience?* London: Barnardo's.

Nuthall, G. & Alton-Lee, A. 1990. Research on teaching and learning: thirty years of change. *Elementary School Journal, 90*(5), 547–570.

Ofsted 2008. *Understanding the Score.* London: Ofsted.

Porter, A. & Brophy, J. 1988. Synthesis of research on good teaching: insights from the work of the Institute for Research on Teaching. *Educational Leadership, 45*(8), 74–85.

Skemp, R. 1972. *The Psychology of Learning Mathematics.* London: Penguin.

Stigler, J. & Hiebert, J. 2009. *The Teaching Gap.* New York: Free Press.

Vygotsky, L. S. 1981. The genesis of higher mental functions. In: J. V. Wertsch (ed.) *The Concept of Activity in Soviet Psychology.* Armonk, NY: Sharpe.

Watson, A. & De Geest, E. 2005. Principled teaching for deep progress: improving mathematical learning beyond methods and materials. *Educational Studies in Mathematics, 58*(2), 209–234.

Wigley, A. 1992. Models for teaching mathematics. *Mathematics Teaching, 141*, 4–7.

Yeager, D. & Dweck, C. 2012. Mindsets that promote resilience: when students believe that personal characteristics can be developed. *Educational Psychologist, 47*, 302–314.

26

Linguistic factors in the development of basic calculation

Chris Donlan

Number words in early childhood

Driving in the country. Three year old Leo (in the back of the car) calls to his mum (who is driving).

L: Hey, Mum, I seen some cows

M: Did you . . . some cows?

L: Yeah. Thee* many

M: What? How many?

L: Thee many . . . Mum, thee many

M: *(Looks round to see Leo holding up the (four) fingers of one hand against the palm of the other)*

L: Thee many. Is it four, Mum, is it five?

(* perhaps Leo means 'This many')

Non-verbal foundations of number

There is strong evidence that infants in the first year of life can discriminate between large sets of items where the proportionate numerical difference is sufficiently great, such as eight items versus 16 items (Brannon, Abbott & Lutz, 2004; Xu & Spelke, 2000), and are sensitive to changes in the numbers of items in small sets, where the set size is below four (e.g., Feigenson & Carey, 2005; Wynn, 1992). An influential formulation of this research by Feigenson, Dehaene and Spelke (2004) proposes two core systems of number, one for representing large, approximate numeri-cal magnitudes, and a second for the precise representation of small numbers of individual objects; these core systems may form the foundation of later numerical concepts. There is some debate concerning the complex relation between infants' representation of number and their representation of associated non-numeric variables such as area, size and arrangement of items (Brannon et al., 2004; Clearfield & Mix, 2001). However, it is widely accepted that these early number-related behaviours of infants are not influenced by verbal systems of thought. Gelman and Butterworth (2005) cite a wide range of evidence, including studies of brain function, to support a modular position within which language and mathematical systems develop and operate independently. An important extension of the core systems approach is articulated by Butterworth, Varma and Laurillard (2011), proposing that specific mathematical learning difficulties are traceable to a neurological deficit at the core systems level.

The integration of number-word knowledge with non-verbal number systems

In contrast to the position outlined in the previous section, Carey (2004) suggests that linguistic factors play a 'bootstrapping' role in number development (i.e., they combine with earlier non-verbal representations of number to produce a new, dynamic and comprehensive learning system). Carey suggests that children learn to identify sets of one, two, and three objects partly through their experience of number-relevant language (e.g., plural marking, use of 'some' versus 'a', etc.). The child's initial representation of the number-word sequence is as a simple string of words without numerical meaning, but with ordinal properties. This ordinal knowledge is then enriched through linkage with corresponding representations of small sets of items. The resulting combination provides the basis for a comprehensive system of symbolic representation of number.

An important critique of the logical basis of Carey's position is provided by Rips, Asmuth and Bloomfield (2008), suggesting that a sequence of words per se is insufficient to support conceptual development. Only at a much later stage, dubbed by Rips et al. (2008) 'advanced counting', does the learner become able to construct the next term from any given point in the sequence, based on the correspondence between the structure of the number-word sequence and the properties of natural numbers: for example, a young child might be able to recite the number-word sequence just as they would sing a song or recite a poem, without awareness of the fact that successive words represent specific increases in value or magnitude. Work by Sarnecka and Carey (2008) goes some way to supporting the position outlined by Rips et al. (2008). They examined in detail the number concepts of pre-schoolers (aged 2.10–4.3 years). Almost all these children were able to produce the number-word sequence to 10. However, conceptual understanding was very varied; 40% of the children showed no evidence of understanding that going forward in the number-word sequence corresponds to adding items and going backwards corresponds to subtracting.

These studies suggest that simply learning the sequence of number words to 10 does not produce understanding of number concepts, but that a minimum requirement for such understanding is repeated experience of using the number-word sequence in active counting of sets of items.

Natural language supports children's understanding of number

An intriguing study by Hodent, Bryant and Houde (2005) was based on the contrast between quantifiers (words expressing number and quantity) in French and English. In French, but not in English, the same word, 'un', is used as the indefinite article ('a' in English) and as the first element in the number-word sequence ('un, deux, trois . . .'). Thus, in English, asked if you have any pets, you might say 'I've got a cat'; on the other hand, if you were asked 'How many pets have you got?' you might say, 'I've got one cat'. In French the two statements would be identical ('J'ai un chat'). The experimental task used by Hodent et al. (2005) made no explicit use of these quantifiers, but required that children watch a series of events on a small stage. Puppets entered, were concealed and revealed in such a way that simple arithmetic facts were represented (e.g., 1 + 1 = 2); the 'show' was set up so that some 'impossible' events occurred (e.g., 1 puppet was joined behind a screen by 2 more puppets, then the screen was removed to reveal 4 puppets). French, but not English, two-year-olds were happy to accept this series of events (1 + 2 = 4). The authors had predicted this particular outcome, arguing that the ways in which 2-year-olds represent number could be strongly influenced by the natural language environment. Where there is possible confusion between, for example, the meanings 'one car' and 'a car', the child might be less likely to represent specific numerical values. Hodent et al. (2005) acknowledge that cultural (as opposed to linguistic) differences between their samples are uncontrolled; nonetheless, these findings alert us to the possible importance of language in shaping early number concepts.

Recent work by Almoammer et al. (2013) provides further insight into the role of language. The study was motivated by the contrasting ways in which different languages use noun morphology (variations in the form of the noun) to mark number. English uses singular/plural marking ('car' vs. 'cars'). Some other languages (including Saudi-Arabic and Slovenian) make a further distinction for sets of two items. These languages have singular/dual/plural marking ('car' vs. 'car-dual' vs. 'cars'). Almoammer et al. (2013) compared number-word knowledge in 2–4-year-olds in Saudi Arabia, Slovenia and the United States. They found that children whose language uses dual markers are much more likely to be able to respond accurately to the instruction 'Give me two' than those whose language marks just singular and plural. These findings are particularly striking given the different cultural contexts within which Saudi-Arabic and Slovenian children are learning. They emphasise the importance of children's experience of number within the grammar of natural language, beyond the rote-counting routine that we often prioritise. Thus we may understand the broad framework of natural language interaction as a primary vehicle for the development of number knowledge, and an important means by which children learn to use the number-word sequence as a tool for purposeful counting, and a base for the elaboration of number concepts.

Elaboration of number knowledge

Extended knowledge of the count-word sequence plays an important role in the development of number concepts

It has been observed above that the ability to produce the number-word sequence 1–10 does not entail understanding of number-word meanings. Children at the age of three may be able to recite the sequence without fully understanding its relation to quantity. However, it appears that extended knowledge of the sequence beyond 10 is closely associated with extended conceptual understanding. Lipton and Spelke (2005) categorised five-year-olds into skilled versus unskilled counters, depending on their ability to produce the spoken sequence accurately across decade boundaries 50 to 100. Skilled counters were able to provide approximate matches between number words and sets of items across the range 20–120. Unskilled counters were able to perform this mapping only within their count range (20–50). Thus it appears that learning the spoken sequence beyond 10 affords understanding of the approximate magnitudes represented, and that the upper bound of the count range constrains the linkage to approximate magnitudes.

In their next study, Lipton and Spelke (2006) presented a further test of understanding to another group of five-year-olds, similarly classified as skilled vs. unskilled counters. Correctly informed that there were N objects in a jar (values up to 120), children were then asked 'Are there N objects?' after each of four manipulations: (a)stirring the objects, but not removing or adding to the set, (b) removing one object, (c) removing about half the objects, (d) returning these objects to restore the original set. In contrast to the findings of the previous study, children were able to respond accurately whether or not the target number fell within their count range. All these five-year-olds showed evidence of logical reasoning. It seems, therefore, that children at this stage are able to exploit the number sequence as a tool for understanding principles that can be applied even outside the number range with which they are familiar. The process of extending from 'procedures' (e.g., simple counting) to 'concepts' (grasping the underlying principles), is an important characteristic of learning throughout the preschool years and beyond. It appears that the child's developing knowledge of the spoken number sequence makes a substantial contribution to this learning process.

Integration of spoken number knowledge and Hindu-Arabic notation

Understanding and use of Hindu-Arabic notation is critical to success in school mathematics. The place-value principle has long been seen as a significant and often persistent learning challenge (Fuson, 1990; Moeller et al., 2011). An important part of this challenge concerns the structural relation between the spoken number sequence and the Hindu-Arabic system. For example, the transparent mapping of decade representation from Asian languages to the Hindu-Arabic system, compared to the complex mapping from English (with its '-teen' versus '-ty' construction) has been understood to provide advantaged access to place-value knowledge for

Asian-language learners, and restricted access for English-language learners (Miura & Okamoto, 1989). Responses to this challenge to English learners have typically entailed a third level of representation, the use of concrete 'manipulatives', e.g. blocks that can be used to represent place value through active grouping and decomposition of sets of ten (Saxton & Towse, 1998; Fuson & Briars, 1990).

Recent work by Mix, Prather, Smith and Stockton (2014) offers a different perspective. The study used simple forced-choice questions and focused on the child's grasp of basic principles of the Hindu-Arabic system: *the same digit represents more when it is to the left than to when it is to the right in a string of digits* (which is more: 123 versus 321?); *numbers are read left to right* (which is two hundred and sixty-seven? 267 versus 627?); *the number of digits is related to both magnitude* (which is more: 101 versus 99?) *and identity* (which is four hundred and two: 402 versus 42?). Surprisingly, many preschool children showed good understanding of these principles. Furthermore, children were better able to map from spoken numeral inputs to written numerals (symbol to symbol) than to blocks or dot arrays (symbol to concrete object). The researchers also conducted a small-scale intervention study which indicated that training based on symbols (spoken and written forms) was more effective than training based on blocks. Mix and her colleagues interpret these important findings within the broader context of language learning. The preschoolers in their study had not been explicitly taught to use multi-digit numerals, but their exposure to such numerals in everyday life is extensive. In the same way that young children typically extract grammatical rules from regularities in the natural language environment without explicit training (Aslin & Newport, 2012), they may also learn the basic correspondence between spoken and written numerals and the basic principles of number notation. Thus we may understand the learning of number notation as based initially on linguistic forms, their structures and regularities, and their accessibility to the learner. As we shall see below (in the section 'Implications for educators'), addressing the learning challenge from a linguistic perspective could provide a useful first stage in supporting children with learning difficulties.

Knowledge of number notation predicts the development of arithmetic skill

We have examined the spoken language basis of children's number knowledge, and the linkage between spoken and written number symbols. However, while these are clearly important aspects of numeracy, are they fundamental to the development of arithmetic skills? Butterworth et al. (2011) propose that non-verbal 'core systems' underlie arithmetic development and specific arithmetic learning difficulties. Recently, particular attention has been given to one of the proposed core systems, the approximate number system (ANS), as indicated by the ability to distinguish between sets of concrete objects or shapes on the basis of number. This aspect of the ANS is non-symbolic, but is seen by some researchers to underlie the development of symbolic arithmetic skills. Mazzocco, Feigenson & Halberda (2011) and Libertus, Feigenson & Halberda (2013) found that ANS tasks of this sort were predictive of children's later arithmetic skill, but the sample sizes of these studies and the breadth of assessments were limited. A large-scale longitudinal study by Goebel, Watson, Lervag and Hulme (2014) addresses the issue more comprehensively, by comparing measures of ANS with measures of number notation (spoken to written numeral mapping) and testing their utility as predictors of arithmetic skill. The growth in arithmetic skills at a critical period of development (6 years 3 months to 7 years 2 months) was powerfully predicted by notation (numeral mapping, as described in the previous section), with no additional contribution from ANS. The effect of numeral mapping is therefore decisive, and is explained by the authors as follows:

> Such an effect might be seen as directly analogous to the role of early letter knowledge as a critical longitudinal predictor of reading development. In short, for both arithmetic and reading development, we suggest that learning the symbol set (Arabic numerals or letters, respectively) and their verbal labels is a critical foundational skill.
>
> *(Goebel et al., 2014, p. 14)*

Evidence from children with specific language impairments

Effects of SLI on counting, notation and arithmetic development

Around 7% of five- to six-year-old children have specific language impairments (SLI), that is, they have significant deficits in one or more areas of language despite scoring within or above the average range on tests of non-verbal ability (Bishop, 1997; Tomblin, Smith & Zhang, 1997). While there are substantial individual differences in mathematical development within this group (Koponen, Mononen, Rasanen & Ahonen, 2006), most children with SLI find production of the number-word sequence particularly difficult. Fazio (1994) found that five-year-olds with SLI could recite the sequence up to six or so, while their typically developing peers were accurate to 20 and beyond. Based on the research described above one might expect that this deficit in counting procedure would entail a commensurate deficit in conceptual understanding. However, Fazio found that her SLI group showed a relatively strong grasp of logical principles in object counting, in particular the principle that the final count word indicates the value of the set (cardinality). A larger study by Donlan, Cowan, Newton and Lloyd (2007) extended these findings. Forty per cent of seven-year-olds with SLI were unable to produce the sequence to 20 accurately. Only 4% of typically developing five- to six-year-olds had problems within this range. Most of the children with SLI also showed significant deficits in basic calculation. However, in order to test understanding of arithmetic principles independent of notation and counting skills, Donlan et al. (2007) introduced a scenario in which participants were introduced to unfamiliar numerals and asked to 'mark' simple addition and subtraction problems. The scenario allowed evaluation of children's understanding of logical principles, for example the principle that the order of addends in addition can be reversed (2 + 3 = 3 + 2), though the same principle (commutativity) does not apply to subtraction. This test of arithmetic principles was the only task on which the performance of children with SLI approximated that of typically developing peers.

A common pattern of conceptual strength and procedural weakness emerges from Fazio's (1994) study of five-year-olds with SLI and from Donlan and colleagues' (2007) study of seven-year-olds. Further confirmation of the procedural deficit came from follow-up studies (Fazio, 1996, 1999), in which Fazio's original sample subsequently observed at two-year intervals showed particular deficits in procedural aspects of basic calculation. It is notable that the relative strength of conceptual understanding identified by Fazio (1994) and by Donlan et al. (2007) was found in tasks that required no knowledge of Hindu-Arabic notation. Where notational knowledge was tested, deficits were usually found. Even using a non-verbal judgement task, in which participants simply choose the greater of two Hindu-Arabic numerals, Donlan et al. (2007) found that children with SLI were significantly less able than age-matched peers to select the greater of two double- or multi-digit numbers. Although this was a purely non-verbal task, performance was strongly correlated with participants' ability to produce the spoken number sequence, and both tasks were strong correlates of basic calculation. In this way studies of children with SLI confirm the general pattern as observed in typically developing children. Mastery of the spoken number sequence provides a foundation for the development of notational understanding, and thereby establishes the necessary foundation for the development of arithmetic skills.

Language of comparison and its association with arithmetic skills

A further task included in the study by Donlan et al. (2007) and reported more recently (Newton, Donlan, Cowan & Lloyd, 2010) tested children's ability to extract meaning from sentences containing the words 'more' and 'less'. The task was relatively complex. Given a sentence such as 'the red bowl has more ice cream than the yellow bowl', the child had to select the correct illustration from four which included: (a) red = yellow (small amount of ice cream in each); (b) red = yellow (large amount of ice cream in each); (c) yellow > red; (d) red > yellow (correct). Comprehension of 'more' and 'less' was tested using this demanding format over a series of six trials. Performance on this task proved to be of particular importance in explaining variation in arithmetic skills. In a comprehensive analysis of the data from 55 seven-year-olds with SLI it emerged that comprehension of 'more' and 'less' was a stronger predictor of basic calculation than general language comprehension, non-verbal ability and production of the number sequence combined. Furthermore, similar analyses applied to the performance of typically developing five-year-olds produced strikingly similar results. How should we interpret these novel findings? Perhaps they simply represent the importance of the language of comparative quantity in arithmetic instruction. If children fail to interpret this aspect of teachers' language, then a major learning pathway is obstructed. An alternative explanation could be offered based on the specific task used, and the demand it makes on the child. This goes beyond the simple understanding of 'more' as 'increase' (e.g. 'more food please!'), and requires understanding of the direction of the quantitative relation, red > yellow rather than yellow > red. This ability to represent the quantitative relation could operate as a conceptual basis for learning to do arithmetic. Current research is addressing this issue.

Pragmatic factors

Much of the research we have reviewed above points to the importance of natural language. If we give consideration to the ways in which number-word meanings operate in everyday communication then we must necessarily broaden our view and look outside the constraints of rigidly controlled experimental tasks, and examine linguistic interaction in a more naturalistic setting, taking account of pragmatics (the way context contributes to meaning). Musolino (2004) provides a powerful demonstration of the role of context in modifying the intended meaning of a simple phrase like 'two hoops'; given the right context, intended meanings 'at least two' or 'at most two' may be readily accepted. If you need to get two hoops to win a game, then the meaning 'at least two' applies. On the other hand, if the rules of a game require that not more than two hoops be dropped, then the meaning 'at most two' applies. Musolino showed that five-year-olds show implicit understanding of these subtle differences, though their formal number skills are as yet relatively limited. Research in this area is in its infancy. As yet, we know little about the learning mechanisms involved, and the linkage between 'natural' pragmatic understanding and formal number learning. However, it seems clear that children's understanding of quantifiers (a linguistic category which includes specific number words as well as 'all', 'some', 'few', 'more' and 'less') is of great importance in the development of mathematical concepts. As our knowledge in this area expands, we might find new ways in which mathematical learning may be enhanced.

Conclusion: Implications for Education

Teacher: What would you do if I asked you to do four add two? What would you do?

Child A: Add a one.

Teacher: Would you?

Child B: Add a two.

Teacher: What would you use to help you?

Child A: Plus.

Teacher: You'd use plus? What does plus mean?

Child C: Equals.

Teacher: Does it? Really?

Child A: It's a plus.

Teacher: Plus means putting things together . . . putting numbers together. If I put numbers together do I get more, or less?

Child D: Yes. Yes. Yes.
Child A: More!

(Mills, personal communication, 2012)

We have examined linguistic influences on the development of basic calculation. First, we saw the importance of the spoken number sequence in early numeracy, and the ways in which the procedures of counting (using the spoken sequence) interact with concept development. At the same time, we considered evidence of the influence of natural language interaction in the early stages of number learning. These foundational elements can be poorly established for some children for a range of different reasons (e.g. atypical development of language caused by genetic factors, or poverty of the linguistic environment (Knowland & Donlan, 2014)). Some children entering formal schooling may, for example, be unable to use the spoken number sequence to count purposefully (Habermann, Mills & Donlan, in preparation). The educational challenge in such a case is considerable: setting up a learning context in which the child can participate in number-based communication is a necessary start point. This requires resources to support small group teaching and very considerable expertise on the part of the teacher, whose responsibility it is to nurture and develop the child's spoken number knowledge in action, and to provide the natural language context which might have been lacking (Habermann, Mills & Donlan, in preparation).

We have examined in some detail the importance of the elaboration of the spoken number sequence and its relation to Hindu-Arabic notation. It is clear that deficits in number sequence knowledge are very common among children with SLI, and that these children are at risk for mathematical difficulties. It is also clear that these pathways to learning also present obstacles to typical learners. Overcoming these obstacles requires a keen understanding of the linguistic challenge (i.e. the particular characteristics of the spoken number sequence in the child's language). Teachers working with children with SLI have offered guidance here (Donlan & Hutt, 1991; Grauberg, 1998). The phonological similarities of the English '-teen' and '-ty' words are challenging, and the inconsistency between the spoken order elements in the '-teens' and the written order of digits in the corresponding Hindu-Arabic numerals sets up a further potential barrier. The decade boundaries of the spoken sequence are particularly challenging, likely to be traceable to concurrent demands on memory (producing the base set 1–9 while tracking the successive decades. Formal assessment of children's levels of number knowledge (spoken and written) is an important first step here, and the methods sections of research papers (Donlan et al. 2007; Goebel et al. 2014; Mix et al., 2014) provide all the necessary information to carry out an initial screen (note that Goebel et al. used group assessments, which are both efficient and economic).

In the final section we looked briefly at the role of pragmatics in communication about number communication. More needs to be learned about the role of pragmatics in arithmetic instruction, and there is strong motivation to bring together academic and educational research in this area. The short excerpt from a small group teaching session (Mills, Personal Communication, 2012), shown above, gives us an indication of what is possible. Some experienced and gifted teachers have what appears to be a natural ability to engage in 'number talk'. They can provide a conversational setting in which children have the confidence to test their use of number-related language, and enhance their understanding. The excerpt shown is part of a longitudinal study in which the development of children's grasp of basic calculation, supported by language-based intervention, was recorded, and successful outcomes observed (Habermann, Mills & Donlan, in preparation). Our hope is to expand this work so that those of us to whom these skills do not come naturally may be able to learn them.

References

Almoammer, A., Sullivan, J., Donlan, C., Marusic, F., Zaucer, R., O'Donnell, T., & Barner, D. (2013). Grammatical morphology as a source of early number word meanings. *Proceedings of the National Academy of Sciences of the United States of America*.

Aslin, R. N., & Newport, E. L. (2012). Statistical learning: from acquiring specific items to forming general rules. *Current Directions in Psychological Science, 21*, 170–176.

Bishop, D. M. V. (1997). *Uncommon understanding: development and disorders of language comprehension in children.* Hove, East Sussex, England: Psychology Press.

Brannon, E. M., Abbott, S., & Lutz, D. J. (2004). Number bias for the discrimination of large visual sets in infancy. *Cognition, 93*, B59–B68.

Butterworth, B., Varma, S., & Laurillard, D. (2011). Dyscalculia: from brain to education. *Science, 332*, 1049–1053.

Carey, S. (2004). Bootstrapping and the origins of concepts. *Daedalus, 133*, 59–68.

Clearfield, M. W., & Mix, K. S. (2001). Amount versus number: infants' use of area and contour length to discriminate small sets. *Journal of Cognition and Development, 2*, 243–260.

Donlan, C., Cowan, R., Newton, E. J., & Lloyd, D. (2007). The role of language in mathematical development: evidence from children with specific language impairments. *Cognition, 103*, 23–33.

Donlan, C., & Hutt, E. (1991). Teaching maths to young children with language disorders. In K. Durkin & B. Shire (eds) *Language in mathematical education.* Milton Keynes: Open University Press.

Fazio, B. B. (1994). The counting abilities of children with specific language impairment: a comparison of oral and gestural tasks. *Journal of Speech and Hearing Research, 37*, 358.

Fazio, B. B. (1996). Mathematical abilities of children with specific language impairment: a 2-year follow-up. *Journal of Speech and Hearing Science, 39*, 839–849.

Fazio, B. B. (1999). Arithmetic calculation, short-term memory, and language performance in children with specific language impairment: a 5-year follow-up. *Journal of Speech, Language and Hearing Research, 42*, 420–431.

Feigenson, L., & Carey, S. (2005). On the limits of infants' quantification of small object arrays. *Cognition, 97*, 295–313.

Feigenson, L., Dehaene, S., & Spelke, E. (2004). Core systems of number. *Trends in Cognitive Sciences, 8*, 307–314.

Fuson, K. (1990). Issues in place value learning and multi digit addition and subtraction learning and teaching. *Journal for Research in Mathematics Education, 21*, 273–280.

Fuson, K., & Briars, D. (1990). Using a base-10 blocks learning and teaching approach for 1st grade and 2nd grade place-value and multidigit addition and subtraction. *Journal for Research in Mathematics Education, 21*, 180–206.

Gelman, R., & Butterworth, B. (2005). Number and language: how are they related? *Trends in Cognitive Sciences, 9*, 6–10.

Goebel, S., Watson, S., Lervag, A., & Hulme, C. (2014). Children's arithmetic development: it is number knowledge, not the approximate number sense that counts. *Psychological Science, 25*(3), 789–798.

Grauberg, E. (1998). Elementary mathematics and language difficulties: a book for teachers, therapists and parents. London: Whurr Publishers Limited.

Habermann, S., Mills, K., & Donlan, C. (in preparation). Exploring the relation between language and early arithmetic skills.

Hodent, C., Bryant, P., & Houde, O. (2005). Language-specific effects on number computation in toddlers. *Developmental Science, 8*, 420–423.

Knowland, V., & Donlan, C. (2014). Language development. In M. Mareschal, B. Butterworth & A. Tolmie (eds), *Educational neuroscience*. Chichester, UK: Wiley-Blackwell.

Koponen, T., Mononen, R., Rasanen, P., & Ahonen, T. (2006). Basic numeracy in children with specific language impairment: heterogeneity and connections to language. *Journal of Speech Language and Hearing Research, 49*, 58–73.

Libertus, M. E., Feigenson, L., & Halberda, J. (2013). Is approximate number precision a stable predictor of math ability? *Learning and Individual Differences, 25*, 126–133.

Lipton, J. S., & Spelke, E. S. (2005). Preschool children's mapping of number words to nonsymbolic numerosities. *Child Development, 76*, 978–988.

Lipton, J. S., & Spelke, E. S. (2006). Preschool children master the logic of number word meanings. *Cognition, 98*, B57–B66.

Mazzocco, M. M., Feigenson, L., & Halberda, J. (2011). Preschoolers' precision of the approximate number system predicts later school mathematics performance. *PLoS ONE, 6*(9), e23749.

Miura, I., & Okamoto, Y. (1989). Comparisons of United States and Japanese 1st graders' cognitive presentations of number and understanding of place value. *Journal of Educational Psychology, 81*, 109–113.

Mix, K., Prather, R., Smith, L. B., Stockton, J. (2014). Young children's interpretation of multidigit number names: from emerging competence to mastery. *Child Development, 85*(3), 1306–1319.

Moeller, K., Pixner, S., Zuber, J.. Kaufmann, L., & Nuerk, H.-C. (2011) Early place-value understanding as a precursor for later arithmetic performance: a longitudinal study on numerical development. *Research in Developmental Disabilities, 32*, 1837–1851.

Musolino, J. (2004). The semantics and acquisition of number words: integrating linguistic and developmental perspectives. *Cognition, 93*, 1–41.

Newton E., Donlan, C., Cowan, E., & Lloyd, D. (2010). *Linguistic correlates of children's emergent skill in formal arithmetic; typical and atypical patterns.* Poster presented at Festschrift for Brian Butterworth, Institute of Cognitive Neuroscience, University College London.

Rips, L. J., Asmuth, J., & Bloomfield, A. (2008). Do children learn the integers by induction? *Cognition, 106*, 940–951.

Sarnecka, B. W., & Carey, S. (2008). How counting represents number: what children must learn and when they learn it. *Cognition, 108*, 662–674.

Saxton, M., & Towse, J. (1988). Linguistic relativity: the case of place value in multi-digit numbers. *Journal of Experimental Child Psychology, 69*(1), 66–79.

Tomblin, J. B., Smith, E., & Zhang, X. (1997). Epidemiology of specific language impairment: prenatal and perinatal risk factors. *Journal of Communication Disorders, 30*, 325–344.

Wynn, K. (1992). Addition and subtraction by human infants (Erratum). *Nature, 360*, 768.

Xu, F., & Spelke, E. S. (2000). Large number discrimination in 6-month-old infants. *Cognition, 74*, B1–B11.

27

Promoting word problem solving performance among students with mathematics difficulties

The role of strategy instruction that primes the problem structure

Asha K. Jitendra, Danielle N. Dupuis and Amy E. Lein

The purpose of this chapter is to describe research on word problem solving interventions for improving the mathematics learning of students with mathematics difficulties (MD). Word problems represent "the most common form of problem solving" (Jonassen, 2003, p. 267) in school mathematics curricula. According to Depaepe, De Corte, and Verschaffel (2010), word problems are "typically composed of a mathematics structure embedded in a more or less realistic context" (p. 152). Solving word problems involves understanding the language and factual information to define the problem situation, constructing an adequate representation of the problem situation using the relevant elements and relations among quantities, planning how to solve the problem, executing the plan, and interpreting the appropriateness and reasonableness of the outcome in relation to the original problem situation (Depaepe et al., 2010; Mayer & Hegarty, 1996). Word problems are considerably more challenging to solve than no-context problems for many students with MD who not only have difficulties with the abstract formal structures of mathematics, but also have difficulties with the language of mathematics (Andersson, 2008; Fuchs et al., 2010).

Students with MD have persistent difficulties solving word problems (Cawley, Parmar, Foley, Salmon, & Roy, 2001; Fuchs & Fuchs, 2005; Gersten et al., 2009). For example, they have difficulties in representing the problem situation, identifying the correct operation (Montague & Applegate, 1993), computing the solution (Cirino, Ewing-Cobbs, Barnes, Fuchs, & Fletcher, 2007), and reasoning (Maccini &

Ruhl, 2001). Therefore, several researchers have developed interventions to enhance the word problem solving performance of students with MD (e.g., Fuchs et al., 2008; Jitendra, 2007; Montague, 2003). Given the importance of priming the underlying problem structure that is supported by research reports (see Gersten et al., 2009), several interventions have focused on the common underlying problem structure. This chapter begins with a discussion of strategy instruction for solving word problems that primes the underlying problem structure. Next, the nature and results of specific intervention approaches are described to understand the instructional conditions that need to be in place to promote the word problem solving performance of students with MD. Finally, the chapter concludes with lessons learned, limitations and recommendations for future research.

Strategy instruction that primes the problem structure

A growing body of evidence suggests that students with MD can benefit from word problem solving instruction that makes explicit the common underlying problem structures (Gersten et al., 2009). Arithmetic word problems consist of additive or multiplicative problem structures. According to Christou and Philippou (1999), "A problem belongs to the additive field when the solution operation is either addition or subtraction, and it belongs to the multiplicative field when the solution operation is either multiplication or division" (p. 269). Strategy instruction that primes the problem structure should improve understanding when it teaches students to move beyond the superficial features of a problem (e.g., format, vocabulary, irrelevant information) "to identify problems of a given type by focusing on the problem structure" (Gersten et al., 2009, p. 26). Instruction that focuses on the "underlying structural connections between familiar and unfamiliar problems" enables students to understand the problem to "apply meaningfully learned procedures flexibly and creatively" (Hatano, 2003, p. xi) to solve unfamiliar, novel problems that are in the same class of problem types as the familiar problem. According to Gersten et al. (2009), "problem types are groups of problems with similar mathematical structure" (p. 27). Strategy instruction that primes the problem structure often works to make visible the underlying problem structure (e.g., part-part-whole, rate/ratio) by explicitly and systematically teaching students to model problems using representations (e.g., diagrams).

Research and evidence of effectiveness of intervention approaches that prime the problem structure

In this section, the focus is on studies examining the effectiveness of word problem solving strategy instruction that primes the problem structure, and studies are organized in terms of grade level. Due to space limitations and relevance, only group design studies with a comparison group are included. Additionally, the studies had to include mathematical tasks that involved additive (e.g., change, group, compare) or multiplicative (e.g., multiplicative compare, proportion) problem structures described in the mathematics education literature, to allow for a direct comparison of related studies.

The next section describes each study in terms of the nature and effectiveness of the intervention. Students' response to intervention is discussed in terms of the strength of the effect of the intervention on word problem solving outcomes. Although this chapter focuses on students with mathematics and/or reading difficulties (e.g., scoring low on mathematics and/or reading tests), the effects of the intervention for students with and without mathematics and/or reading difficulties were reported when authors provided the information. One reason for including the effectiveness of the intervention for all students is that it provides a normative comparison sample to inform the design of interventions to better address the needs of students with mathematics and/or reading difficulties.

Elementary grades

Seven studies conducted by three teams of researchers using different intervention approaches are examined. Of these, six studies addressed addition and subtraction problems involving *change*, *group/total*, and *compare/difference* problem types; one study focused on *multiplicative compare* and *equal groups* problem types.

Schema-based instruction

In a series of studies with elementary aged students with and without MD, Jitendra and colleagues documented the benefits of schema-based instruction (SBI) using single subject (e.g., Jitendra & Hoff, 1996) and group design studies (Jitendra et al., 1998, 2007, 2013, in press). SBI is grounded in schema theories of cognitive psychology, research on expert problem solvers, and research regarding effective instructional practices (e.g., explicit instruction, corrective feedback, cumulative review) for students at-risk for MD. One of the earliest attempts to teach word problem solving using SBI to students with MD was a small study conducted by Jitendra et al. (1998), in which students with mild disabilities and students with MD were blocked on pre-test scores and randomly assigned to SBI or a comparison tutoring condition (i.e., general strategy instruction (GSI), typical textbook word problem solving instruction). SBI involved explicit instruction in priming the problem structure using schematic diagrams. Instruction occurred in two phases. Phase 1 (problem representation) provided students with story situations with no unknowns and instruction focused on identifying the three problem types (i.e., *change*, *group*, and *compare*) based on the relevant elements and relations between quantities and representing the problem situation using a schema diagram. Phase 2 (problem solution) presented one-step word problems and required students to not only identify the problem type and represent it using a schema diagram, but also to solve the problem by determining whether to add or subtract based on the part-whole concept by examining the problem situation (e.g., add when the whole is unknown and subtract when one of the parts is unknown). Students in the GSI condition engaged in several math activities (e.g., logical reasoning, discovering patterns, number puzzles, number relationships, money, place value) during Phase 1 of instruction and in Phase 2 were taught a five-step heuristic to solve the same set of word problems as those in the SBI condition. The heuristic consisted of the following five steps: (a) understand the question by focusing on the question, (b) find the needed data given in the problem, (c) plan what to do (e.g., add or subtract) by guessing and checking, (c) find the answer, and (d) check back by rereading the problem to decide whether the answer is reasonable.

Student learning was assessed using a measure of word problem solving administered at pre-test, post-test, and delayed post-test (1 to 2 weeks following the end of the intervention). Results indicated moderate, positive effects favoring SBI at post-test and large positive effects favoring SBI on the delayed post-test. In addition, results revealed a large positive effect size favoring SBI on a transfer measure of novel problems derived from curricula not used in the treatment.

In the next study, Jitendra et al. (2007) tested the effectiveness of SBI with third-grade students from one of the lowest achieving schools in an urban school district. Students were randomly assigned to either the SBI or comparison condition (i.e., GSI). Teachers provided all instruction in a whole-class arrangement. In addition to the components of SBI found in Jitendra et al. (1998), students were also given problem-solving checklists (FOPS – Find the problem type, Organize information in the problem using the diagram, Plan to solve the problem, and Solve the problem). The checklists not only provided elaborated and specific prompts to guide problem solving, but also helped students to monitor and reflect on the problem-solving process. Students in the GSI condition were taught a four-step general heuristic to (a) understand the problem, (b) plan to solve the problem, (c) solve the problem, and (d) look back or check. Problem-solving strategies such as using objects, acting out the problem or drawing a diagram, choosing an operation – writing a number sentence, and using data from a graph or table were incorporated in the planning step of the problem-solving heuristic.

Students were assessed on a measure of word problem solving administered at pre-test, post-test, and delayed post-test (6 weeks following the end of the intervention). In addition, data were collected on a state-administered test of mathematics achievement. Results indicated a statistically significant effect favoring not at-risk SBI students compared to not at-risk GSI students on the immediate post-test and delayed post-test. For students at-risk for MD, no statistically significant effect was found at immediate post-test. On the delayed post-test, a statistically significant effect was found favoring the SBI group. On the state-administered test of mathematics achievement, results revealed a statistically significant effect, favoring not at-risk SBI students on the immediate post-test compared to not at-risk GSI students. For students at-risk, although the effect was not statistically significant, the effect size was practically significant ($g = 0.80$) favoring SBI.

While the above studies contrasted SBI with traditional textbook problem-solving practices, Jitendra et al. (2013) investigated the efficacy of SBI for improving the word problem solving performance of students with MD when compared to standards-based instruction. Although SBI and standards-based curricula are similar in their theoretical underpinnings (i.e., emphasize meaningful learning to develop conceptual understanding), they differ in terms of their instructional practices. SBI incorporates an explicit, teacher-mediated approach, whereas standards-based instruction is characterized by an inquiry-based, student-directed approach. Third-grade students with MD in a large urban school district were randomly assigned to one of two conditions: SBI or comparison tutoring (standards-based textbook instruction). Twenty tutors, recruited from the community (e.g., parents, instructional assistants, undergraduate students), were randomly assigned to the two conditions and provided all instruction. SBI materials and instructional procedures were the same as in Jitendra et al. (2007). SBI students received tutoring in solving one-step and two-step word problems; the control group received small-group tutoring in whole-number concepts and procedures, including word problem solving using the school-provided standards-based practice.

On the immediate post-test measure of word problem solving, results indicated a statistically significant effect, but practically non-significant effect size ($g = 0.02$). On the retention test (six weeks following the end of the intervention), the effect for condition was not statistically significant. Interaction effects on the immediate and retention post-tests showed that SBI students with higher incoming (pre-test) scores outperformed comparison students with higher pre-test scores, whereas comparison students with lower pre-test scores outperformed SBI students with lower pre-test scores. Results revealed statistically non-significant effects on the mathematics and reading subtests of a district-administered achievement test. Jitendra et al. speculated that many students who entered the study without mastering the basic computational skills did not benefit from SBI word problem solving tutoring alone.

The next study (Jitendra et al., in press) extended the focus of SBI beyond word problem solving instruction to also include instruction in foundational concepts (e.g., understanding addition and subtraction as inverse operations) essential to successful problem solving. The methods and procedures were the same as in Jitendra et al. (2013). Students and 18 tutors were randomly assigned to one of two conditions: SBI or comparison tutoring (standards-based textbook instruction). Results indicated statistically significant differences, with students in the SBI group outperforming students in the control group on a word problem solving post-test. However, there were no statistically significant effects on the word problem solving retention test (eight weeks later). On a district-administered mathematics achievement test, SBI students scored significantly higher than control students.

Schema-broadening instruction

Several early studies by Fuchs and colleagues' provide strong support for schema-broadening instruction, an instructional approach that not only emphasizes categorizing problem types into groups that require similar solutions, but also explicitly addresses transfer in its instructional design (e.g., Fuchs, Fuchs, Hamlett, & Appleton, 2002; Fuchs et al., 2003). Transfer occurs when the learner recognizes that novel problems, even though different in certain features (e.g., irrelevant information), are related to previously solved problems. The early work on schema-broadening instruction involved word problem solving tasks that were complex and involved all four operations. More recently, the authors have focused on commonly defined classes of problem types (e.g., *change, total, difference*) involving the additive structure, which is the emphasis of this chapter.

In the first small study, Fuchs et al. (2008) randomly assigned students with mathematics and reading difficulties (MDRD) to one of two conditions: schema-broadening instruction tutoring or no-tutoring control (i.e., school-designed classroom math program). Tutoring instruction included an introductory unit on teaching foundational skills (e.g., adding and subtracting numbers using a number line, solving problems with and without regrouping) followed by instruction on solving the three problem types (i.e., *change, total, difference*) using schema-broadening instruction. Schema-broadening instruction included (a) using concrete materials and role-playing to teach the underlying problem structure, (b) explicitly teaching for transfer using problems with unexpected features (irrelevant information, unknown information in different positions, two-digit operands, format) within the taught problem type, and (c) a sorting activity to review the three problem types.

Student learning was assessed using both experimental (Jordan's story problems, Peabody Word Problem Test) and standardized measures (KeyMath – Revised Problem Solving, Iowa Test of Basic Skills [ITBS]: Problem Solving and Data Interpretation). Results indicated that schema-broadening instruction students out-performed the control group on the experimental measures, while there were no statistically significant differences between groups on the standardized tests.

In the next study, Fuchs et al. (2009) examined the efficacy of schema-broadening instruction for students with MD only or MDRD. Students were randomly assigned to one of three conditions: schema-broadening word problem solving tutoring, number combinations (NC) tutoring, or control with no tutoring. NC tutoring comprised computerized practice and instruction on addition and subtraction number combinations. Schema-broadening instruction materials and instructional procedures were the same as in Fuchs et al. (2008).

Student learning was assessed using both experimental (Vanderbilt Story Problem Test) and standardized measures (KeyMath – Revised Problem Solving, ITBS: Problem Solving and Data Interpretation). Results indicated that schema-broadening word problem solving group outperformed both the control and NC groups on the experimental measure. Results indicated statistically significant differences between groups on the KeyMath Problem Solving, with schema-broadening word problem solving group scoring higher than the control group; the NC tutoring group did not differ from the control or schema-broadening word problem solving group. On the ITBS, there were no statistically significant effects for treatment.

Conceptual model-based problem solving

This method is based on contemporary approaches to word problem solving that emphasize mathematical modeling. According to Xin et al. (2011), conceptual model-based problem solving (COMPS) "requires expression of mathematics relations in a generalizable conceptual model (e.g., factor-factor-product)" (p. 383). Following two single subject design studies (Xin, 2008; Xin, Wiles, & Lin, 2008) that provided preliminary evidence of the effectiveness of COMPS on the word problem solving performance of students with learning problems, Xin et al. extended that work by investigating the efficacy of COMPS when compared to a general heuristic instructional approach (GHI) using a small group design study. Xin et al. randomly assigned students to one of two conditions: COMPS or GHI. COMPS instruction, implemented by researchers and special education teachers, occurred in three phases: (a) an introductory session on understanding the concept of equal groups, (b) instruction on *equal groups* (EG) and *multiplicative compare* (MC) problems using the COMPS approach, and (c) mixed review of EG and MC problems. Intervention materials included conceptual model diagrams, problem-solving checklist, and word problem story grammar prompt cards to guide problem representation. Students in the GHI condition received the typical school-based intervention of word problem solving using a five-step heuristic, SOLVE: "(a) search for the question, (b) organize the information, (c) look for a strategy, and (d) visualize and then work the problem (e.g., draw a picture, make a table, write an equation), and (e) evaluate the answer.

To assess student learning, a measure of word problem solving was administered at pre-test, post-test, and delayed post-test (one to two weeks following the end of the intervention). In addition, data were collected on a standardized test of problem solving. On the measure of word problem solving, results revealed large, statistically significant effects favoring COMPS at post-test and delayed post-test. On the standardized problem-solving test, results revealed a statistically non-significant effect.

In summary, a review of elementary school studies revealed that the three intervention approaches (SBI, schema-broadening instruction, COMPS) are effective in enhancing the word problem solving performance of students with mathematics and/or reading difficulties. With regard to SBI, results suggest that it is effective for all students, including students with MD. However, SBI appears to be most beneficial when students possess some threshold level of computational skills or are provided with word problem solving instruction in conjunction with basic skills instruction. Findings for schema-broadening instruction indicate that researcher-taught individual supplemental word problem solving tutoring that incorporates instruction in basic skills benefits students with MD and is more effective than no tutoring or NC tutoring. Additionally, COMPS is effective for teaching students to solve word problems involving multiplication and division relative to textbook problem-solving practice.

Middle school

Schema-based instruction

Three studies investigated the effectiveness of SBI for middle school students with and without MD. In the first small study, Xin, Jitendra, and Deatline-Buchman (2005) randomly assigned students with MD to either the SBI or GSI condition. Similar to the previously discussed SBI studies, students received instruction in two phases: problem representation and problem solution instruction. Two researchers and two special education teachers provided all instruction. Students in the SBI group scored significantly higher than students instructed in GSI at immediate post-test and on the retention test. On an experimental measure of novel word problems a statistically significant transfer effect was found favoring SBI students.

The next two pilot studies were conducted in typical seventh-grade math classrooms, with math teachers providing all instruction during the regularly scheduled mathematics instructional period. In the first study (Jitendra et al., 2009), the mathematical tasks focused on the topics of ratio and proportion and instruction occurred in early January; the second study (Jitendra & Star, 2012) focused on the topic of percent and was conducted in May of the same year. Jitendra and colleagues reviewed the district-adopted mathematics textbook to identify problem-solving skills related to the target topics as well as the underlying concepts (e.g., ratio/rate, percent) and designed SBI units on ratio/proportion and percent that included more tasks than in Xin et al. (2005). SBI was designed to include four critical elements: (a) priming the underlying problem structure, (b) using schematic diagrams to represent the mathematical situation, (c) explicitly teaching problem solving and metacognitive strategy use, and (d) emphasizing procedural flexibility (when to use cross multiplication, unit rate, and equivalent fractions based on the number in the problem).

Jitendra et al. (2009) investigated the effectiveness of SBI for students from eight seventh-grade mathematics classrooms. Blocking by classroom ability level (i.e., high, average, and low), classrooms were randomly assigned to either SBI or a "business as usual" control condition. To assess learning, data were collected at pre-test, post-test, and delayed post-test (four months later) on a measure of problem solving and a state-administered test of mathematics achievement. On the test of problem solving, results indicated moderate to large effects sizes for both high- and average-achieving students, favoring SBI on the immediate and delayed post-tests. On the test of mathematics achievement, results revealed a moderate effect favoring SBI for high-achieving students and no effect for average-achieving students. Findings for low-achieving students were mixed, with no effect for SBI at post-test and a small effect favoring SBI at delayed post-test on the measure of problem solving. Interestingly, a small effect favored the low-achieving control students on the test of mathematics achievement. Jitendra et al. (2009) explained these unexpected findings to suggest "the value of integrating metacognitive strategy knowledge as an instructional feature in schema-based instruction, particularly using schematic diagrams to represent information, may not have been realized in the short-term (10-day) intervention for low-ability students" (p. 260). It could be that not only the metacognitive component of SBI, but also low-achieving students' reported difficulty in mastering the two conceptually based strategies (unit rate, equivalent fractions) may explain their inconsistent performance. Perhaps, these students need more practice, time, and scaffolding of instruction to be able to benefit from SBI.

The next study focused on percent, which is a challenging topic for many middle school students (see Parker & Leinhardt, 1995). Jitendra and Star (2012) collected data from four (two high-ability and two low-ability classrooms) of the eight classrooms in the Jitendra et al. (2009) study. On a measure of percent problem solving, high-achieving students in the SBI condition statistically outperformed high-achieving students in the control condition. For low-achieving students, no statistically significant differences were found; however, a small to medium effect size favored control students. Results for the transfer test indicated no statistically significant differences for either high- or low-achieving students. Unlike previous SBI studies that were implemented for 12 weeks on average, low-achieving students did not benefit from SBI, possibly due to the short duration (i.e., 9 days) of the study. Jitendra and Star (2012) explained the findings for low-achieving students by noting that they might have needed more time and support to recognize the underlying problem structure to "show gains in flexible knowledge of procedures for solving a wide range of problems" (p. 157).

Together, these results provide evidence of the efficacy of SBI for students with MD taught in small groups when compared to students who received a contrasting word problem solving instruction for the same amount of time. When implemented by teachers in real classrooms for the same amount of time typically scheduled by schools to teach a more extended set of topics than in Xin et al. (2005), SBI seems to work for average and high-achieving students; however, the benefits for students with MD are less clear based on the two low intensity studies (Jitendra et al., 2009; Jitendra & Star, 2012). Jitendra and colleagues have since conducted two rigorous randomized controlled studies to address the limitations of the prior work, by increasing the number of classrooms and participants, the length of professional development training, and time allocated to teaching the topics of ratio, proportion, and percent. Results of these two studies provide strong support for SBI in improving the learning of students without mathematics and/or reading difficulties. Additionally, results separated by MD status indicate the same general pattern of findings favoring SBI for students with MD (Jitendra, Star, Bauer, & Dupuis, 2012).

Lessons learned, limitations, and implications for future research

The studies reviewed suggest that strategy instruction that primes the problem structure could promote understanding and lead to improved problem-solving performance of students with MD. An important finding across the studies reviewed is that differences in responsiveness to interventions for students with MD appeared to be associated with variations in the content, intensity of the instructional programs, and the nature of the control condition. At the elementary grades, with the exception of one study (Jitendra et al., 2013), moderate to large effect sizes favored the three different intervention approaches. One possible explanation for studies with strong effects could be related to the intensity and consistency of instruction. The interventions in these studies ranged in duration from 540 to 1,800 minutes. However, the studies varied in terms of instructional grouping, with the majority of studies implementing instruction in small groups (2–6 students), one study providing students with one-on-one instruction, another study conducting whole-class instruction, and two studies that did not report the instructional grouping. In addition, the consistency with which these interventions were implemented was relatively high (range = 86% to 100%).

Of the seven elementary grade studies, only one study (i.e., Xin et al., 2011) focused on word problems involving the multiplicative structure and yielded a large effect size when compared to a control condition that also taught word problem solving using typical school practice (GHI). The remaining studies addressed the additive structure and varied in the nature of the control conditions employed. Interestingly, except for the Xin et al. (2011) study, treatment effects were larger when there was less overlap with the control condition both in terms of problem-solving content and instructional time. At the same time, whether or not the treatment is contrasted with a true control condition that is realistic (i.e., typical classroom instruction) and controls for history and maturation is an important consideration to meaningfully interpret the results.

With regard to the three middle school studies, which addressed more complex content (e.g., ratio, proportion, percent), although strategy instruction that primes the problem structure (i.e., SBI) benefitted average and high-achieving students, the effects were mixed for students with MD. In terms of intensity and consistency of instruction, we would expect lower intensity and consistency to be related to poorer student outcomes. Interestingly, this pattern of results was only evident when the students in the sample were identified as low achieving (LA). Specifically, in Jitendra and Star (2012) and Jitendra et al. (2009), the fact that there were fewer minutes of instruction (400 and 360, respectively), undifferentiated whole-class instruction, and lower percentages of implementation fidelity (80 and 76, respectively) resulted in poorer effect sizes on the immediate post-test for the LA students (0.006 and −0.39, respectively) but not the typically achieving students. The practically non-significant effects for students with MD in the studies by Jitendra et al. (2009) and Jitendra and Star (2012) relative to the large effects found in Xin et al. (2005) could possibly be due to differences in content and intensity of instruction. Xin et al. addressed a relatively limited set of mathematical topics and also invested more time (720 minutes) and provided small-group instruction (4–7 students) in teaching word problems involving the targeted topics (i.e., EG and MC) than the studies by Jitendra et al.

While the research base described above provides important evidence about the effectiveness of strategy instruction that primes the problem structure in improving the problem-solving performance of students with MD, several limitations of the current research suggest important avenues for future research. First, few studies investigated the effectiveness of instructional approaches for students with comorbid math and reading difficulties (e.g., Fuchs et al., 2008). Furthermore, the criteria and measures for identifying mathematics and/or reading difficulties varied across the studies. In fact, the criterion for word problem solving difficulties (i.e., scores < 70% correct on an experimental problem-solving measure) in some studies seemed high and could have included a sample of students without MD (e.g., Xin et al., 2005, 2011). These studies also yielded the largest effects sizes in the sample of studies. More research is warranted that not only identifies students with MD using commonly agreed cutoff scores, but also investigates the comorbid effects of sample (i.e., mathematics and reading problems vs. mathematics problems only) as a potential moderator in treatment outcomes. Second, the majority of studies examined elementary school student populations and content, with only three studies conducted in middle schools. Furthermore, little is known about how best to support the development of advanced mathematics (e.g., algebra, geometry) for students with MD not only in secondary schools, but also in late elementary grades. Another limitation is related to the intensity of instruction. Studies about the dosage and frequency of instruction to address the needs of students with severe MD are not available.

References

Andersson, U. (2008). Mathematical competencies in children with different types of learning difficulties. *Journal of Educational Psychology, 100*, 48–66.

Cawley, J. F., Parmar, R. S., Foley, T., Salmon, S., & Roy, S. (2001). Arithmetic performance of students with mild disabilities and general education students on selected arithmetic tasks: Implications for standards and programming. *Exceptional Children, 67*, 311–328.

Christou, C., & Philippou, G. (1999). Role of schemas in one-step word problems. *Educational Research and Evaluation (An International Journal on Theory and Practice), 5*(3), 269–289.

Cirino, P. T., Ewing-Cobbs, L., Barnes, M., Fuchs, L. S., & Fletcher, J. M. (2007). Cognitive arithmetic differences in learning disability groups and the role of behavioral inattention. *Learning Disabilities Research and Practice, 22*, 25–35.

Depaepe, F., De Corte, E., & Verschaffel, L. (2010). Teachers' approaches towards word problem solving: Elaborating or restricting the problem context. *Teaching and Teacher Education: An International Journal of Research and Studies, 26*, 152–160.

Fuchs, L. S., & Fuchs, D. (2005). Enhancing mathematical problem solving for students with disabilities. *Journal of Special Education, 39*, 45–57.

Fuchs, L. S., Fuchs, D., Hamlett, C. L., & Appleton, A. C. (2002). Explicitly teaching for transfer: Effects on the mathematical problem-solving performance of students with mathematics disabilities. *Learning Disabilities Research & Practice, 17*, 90–106.

Fuchs, L. S., Fuchs, D., Prentice, K., Burch, M., Hamlett, C. L., Owen, R., Jancek, D. (2003). Explicitly teaching for transfer: Effects on third-grade students' mathematical problem solving. *Journal of Educational Psychology, 95*, 293–305.

Fuchs, L., Powell, S., Seethaler, P., Cirino, P., Fletcher, J., Fuchs, D., Zumeta, R. (2009). Remediating number combination and word problem deficits among students with mathematics difficulties: A randomized control trial. *Journal of Educational Psychology, 101*, 561–576.

Fuchs, L. S., Seethaler, P. M., Powell, S. R., Fuchs, D., Hamlett, C. L., & Fletcher, J. M. (2008). Effects of preventative tutoring on the mathematical problem solving of third-grade students with math and reading difficulties. *Exceptional Children, 74*, 155–173.

Fuchs, L. S., Zumeta, R. O., Schumacher, R. F., Powell, S. R., Seethaler, P. M., Hamlett, C. L, Fuchs, D. (2010). The effects of schema-broadening instruction on second graders' word-problem performance and their ability to represent word problems with algebraic equations: A randomized control study. *The Elementary School Journal, 110*, 440–463.

Gersten, R., Beckmann, S., Clarke, B., Foegen, A., Marsh, L., Star, J. R., Witzel, B. (2009). *Assisting students struggling with mathematics: Response to Intervention (RtI) for elementary and middle schools* (NCEE 2009–4060). Washington, DC: National Center for Education Evaluation and Regional Assistance, Institute of Education Sciences, U.S. Department of Education. Retrieved from http://ies.ed.gov/ncee/wwc/publications/practiceguides.

Hatano, G. (2003). Foreword. In A. J. Baroody & A. Dowker (Eds.), *The development of arithmetic concepts and skills* (pp. xi–xiii). Mahwah, NJ: Lawrence Erlbaum.

Jitendra, A. K. (2007). *Solving math word problems: Teaching students with learning disabilities using schema-based instruction.* Austin, TX: Pro-Ed.

Jitendra, A. K., Dupuis, D. N., Rodriguez, M., Zaslofsky, A. F., Slater, S., Cozine-Corroy, K., & Church, C. (2013). A randomized controlled trial of the impact of schema-based instruction on mathematical outcomes for third grade students with mathematics difficulties. *The Elementary School Journal, 114*, 252–276.

Jitendra, A. K., Griffin, C. C., Haria, P., Leh, J., Adams, A., & Kaduvettoor, A. (2007). A comparison of single and multiple strategy instruction on third-grade students' mathematical problem solving. *Journal of Educational Psychology, 99*, 115–127.

Jitendra, A. K., Griffin, C. C., McGoey, K., Gardill, M. C., Bhat, P., & Riley, T. (1998). Effects of mathematical word problem solving by students at risk or with mild disabilities. *The Journal of Educational Research, 91*, 345–355.

Jitendra, A. K., & Hoff, K. (1996). The effects of schema-based instruction on mathematical word problem solving performance of students with learning disabilities. *Journal of Learning Disabilities, 29*(4), 422–431.

Jitendra, A. K., Rodriguez, M., Kanive, R. G., Huang, J.-P., Church, C., Corroy, K. C., Zaslofsky, A. F. (2013). The impact of small-group tutoring interventions on the mathematical problem solving and achievement of third grade students with mathematics difficulties. *Learning Disability Quarterly, 36*, 21–35.

Jitendra, A. K., & Star, J. R. (2012). An exploratory study contrasting high- and low-achieving students' percent word problem solving. *Learning and Individual Differences, 22*, 151–158.

Jitendra, A. K., Star, J. R., Bauer, C., & Dupuis, D. N. (2012, April). *The effectiveness of schema-based instruction as a Tier 1 intervention on the proportional reasoning of students with different types of learning difficulties.* Paper presented at the American Educational Research Association (AERA) annual convention, Vancouver, Canada.

Jitendra, A. K., Star, J. R., Starosta, K., Leh, J. M., Sood, S., Caskie, G., Mack, T. R. (2009). Improving seventh grade students' learning of ratio and proportion: The role of schema-based instruction. *Contemporary Educational Psychology, 34*, 250–264.

Jonassen, D. H. (2003). Designing research-based instruction for story problems. *Educational Psychology Review, 15*, 267–296.

Maccini, P., & Ruhl, K. L. (2001). Effects of a graduated instructional sequence on the algebraic subtraction of integers by secondary students with learning disabilities. *Education and Treatment of Children, 23*, 465–489.

Mayer, R. E., & Hegarty, M. (1996). The process of understanding mathematics problems. In R. J. Sternberg & T. Ben-Zeev (Eds.), *The nature of mathematical thinking* (pp. 29–53). Mahwah, NJ: Lawrence Erlbaum Associates.

Montague, M. (2003). *Solve It! A practical approach to teaching mathematical problem-solving skills.* Reston, VA: Exceptional Innovations, Inc.

Montague, M., & Applegate, B. (1993). Mathematical problem-solving characteristics of middle school students with learning disabilities. *The Journal of Special Education, 27*, 175–201.

Parker, M., & Leinhardt, G. (1995). Percent: A privileged proportion. *Review of Educational Research, 65*, 421–481.

Xin, Y. P. (2008). The effect of schema-based instruction in solving mathematics word problems: An emphasis on prealgebraic conceptualization of multiplicative relations. *Journal for Research in Mathematics Education, 39*, 526–551.

Xin, Y. P., Jitendra, A. K., Deatline-Buchman, A. (2005). Effects of mathematical word problem-solving instruction on middle school students with learning problems. *The Journal of Special Education, 39*, 181–192.

Xin, Y. P., Wiles, B., & Lin, Y. Y. (2008). Teaching conceptual model-based word problem story grammar to enhance mathematics problem solving. *The Journal of Special Education, 42*, 163–178.

Xin, Y. P., Zhang, D., Park, J. Y., Tom, K., Whipple, A., & Si, L. (2011). A comparison of two mathematics problem-solving strategies: Facilitate algebra-readiness. *The Journal of Educational Research, 104*, 381–395.

28

Mathematical storyteller kings and queens

An alternative pedagogical choice to facilitate mathematical thinking and understand children's mathematical capabilities

Caroline McGrath

'Penguin' (retold by Freya, age 5 years and 11 months)

Once upon a time there was a duck

And this duck said to a seal 'My Mum wants you to go and get some fish from the pond, the magical pond which shines and glistens.'

So he went to the pond and he jumped into the pond

And he caught two yellow fish

– And he caught two yellow fish

Two yellow fish, and three pink fish, and four orange fish and one blue fish

So he counted them one, two, three, four, five, six, seven, eight, nine, ten

He had ten altogether

And then he picked them up

And he went back home to Goose

Here's your ten lovely fish

'But I'm still hungry' said Goose

So he went back to the pond

And he caught one pink fish and four blue fish and he caught three yellow fish and he caught two orange fish

And he counted them one, two, three, four, five, six, seven, eight, nine, ten

And he picked them up counting them in his head

And he took them back to Goose

'But I'm still hungry' said Goose

So he went back to the glistening and shining pond

And he caught two orange fish and took them back and counted them and took them back to Goose

'I'm still hungry'

So he went back to the pond

And he went back to Goose

And she said 'I want eleven fish this time'

So he went back to the glistening and shining pond

And he caught five orange fish and four yellow fish . . .

And five yellow fish and one blue fish

[Freya puts down five orange fish then four yellow, then one yellow then one blue fish]

So he counted them one, two, three, four, five, six, seven, eight, nine, ten, eleven

And he picked them up counting them

And he took them back to Goose

And they had a big meal

Then when Goose was full after they all had those fish

She thought 'I'm too full up. Maybe I should have said I wanted two more fish.'

The End.

Introduction

Freya imitates an oral mathematical story based on number complements using different coloured fish to make the number ten, told by her Reception class teacher. She creates two possibilities for ten: $2 + 3 + 4 + 1 = 10$; $1 + 4 + 3 + 2 = 10$ before moving on to apply the idea to eleven: $5 + 5 + 1 = 11$. This chapter tells the story of how children respond to an alternative creative pedagogical approach to facilitating mathematical thinking. The project, based in a British State Infant School, includes work with children aged between four and six years, class teachers, teaching assistants,

Figure 28.1 Freya tells a story about 'Penguin' using coloured fish to represent her mathematical ideas

and parents. Class teachers accept the challenge of telling mathematical stories to thirty and then smaller groups of children, where it is notable how adults move from looking down on to sitting alongside the children. A unique feature of the project is that the researcher contributes oral mathematical stories, allowing teachers and teaching assistants to observe children's responses. Video and audio recordings of teachers and teaching assistants telling oral mathematical stories copied onto DVDs facilitate reflective comments from the children, educators, and parents. A semicircle of six to eight cushions contributes to a storytelling culture, where children ask to be storytellers, telling imaginative mathematical stories with remarkable skill.

School mathematics requires that children translate between representations, and this ability to translate may be a cause of difficulty for some children. Story offers meaningful, memorable context, which motivates children's mathematical thinking. Story-related props assist movement between abstract and concrete representations of mathematical ideas. In mathematics, story, and play, the question 'What if?' prompts possibility thinking. This question fits well with a playful approach to oral mathematical storytelling: children change stories in ways that pose imaginative mathematical possibilities.

Children watch and listen as adults construct mathematical stories using materials to make ideas explicit and then imitate these demonstrations, in ways that reveal surprises about their mathematical capabilities. Qualitative data derived from audio recordings, video and digital photography, inform assessments about mathematical learning which are shared with children, colleagues and parents. Oral mathematical story as a pedagogical choice complements other teaching approaches and opens out possibilities for inventive mathematical thinking.

Mathematics

Mathematics is about problem posing, problem solving and making connections between ideas. Polya (1945) advises that to be a problem solver is not enough, advocating that children become skilled at problem posing. Hersh (1998, p.6) proposes that questions drive mathematics and that 'mathematics is a vast network of interconnected problems and solutions'. Our aim is to build coherent connections in the mind of the child (Haylock and Cockburn 2013) through story. A child's disposition to learning in a problem posing way is framed by the question 'What if?' Watson and Mason (1998, cited by Casey 2011) propose that this question provokes children into awareness of mathematical possibilities. Sheffield (1999, cited by Casey 2011) suggests applying the question, 'What if I change one or more parts of the problem?' which, with mathematical stories, potentially disturbs relationships between story and mathematical ideas. If we change something about the story we change the mathematical idea, or if we change the mathematical idea we change the story. Jake tells a story, which we come to later, where it is noticeable how it is his manipulation of representational ladybird spots that prompts construction of his story. When children play, it is often their physical action with story related materials that can pose the possibility question 'What if?'

Play is implicitly, and can be explicitly, mathematical

Play is implicitly mathematical as children test things out, adjust and readjust, pose problems and find new solutions. Children are natural problem posers and solvers in play (McGrath 2012; Pound 2008; Pound and Lee 2011). Sometimes play following a mathematical story is explicitly mathematical. Children listen to a Russian tale based on *Knock, Knock, Teremok!* (Arnold 1994), a story similar to, 'Who Lived in the Skull?' (Ransome 2003) about animals fitting into a small hut (or skull), with the storyteller emphasising positional language and capacity, and then they play with vegetable boxes and soft toy animals:

'Oh! He fits in there, if you squeeze him in. Maybe,' says Corey.

'Little animals go underneath and big animals go on top,' says Olivia. 'The little ones go underneath, the little ones go underneath, and the big ones go on top.'

'She's asking if she can fit in?' says Corey with a mooing cow in his hand.

'Only the little one can come in,' confirms Olivia.

In this play scenario children carry forward mathematical ideas of capacity and positional language of the story in explicit ways.

Playing with plot

After the Russian tale, Toby takes the role of storyteller and changes the idea. Instead of bringing animals to the box one by one, he brings two rabbits and then four dogs, changing the rate at which the box fills. A story about 'The Greedy Triangle' (Burns 1994) where a dissatisfied triangle changes to become a square, a pentagon, a hexagon, prompts children to ask about the possibility of the triangle becoming a circle. Stories and play are proven to be important and effective ways of enhancing young children's enjoyment of mathematical concepts (Haylock and Cockburn 2013, p. 86). Oral mathematical stories allow playful problem posing with the story and related materials in ways that support enjoyable thinking about mathematical possibilities.

Mathematical difficulties

There is an irony in that children can be natural problem solvers in play and yet fail in school situations which call upon problem-solving skills. Hughes identifies that it can be difficult for children to translate between their own concrete knowledge and the abstract or 'context-free' nature of arithmetic statements (1986, p.45). When Hughes (1986, p. 45) asks a four-year-old boy, 'How many is three and one more?' the boy asks 'One more what?' not applying his concrete knowledge to this abstract question but, as Hughes points out, this boy's response ' . . . is unusual in that he is explicitly prepared to translate the abstract question into concrete form' by trying to locate the context. Translating is an important way of children thinking about mathematics, and an inability to translate fluently between different modes of mathematical representation can be misleading about true capabilities (Hughes 1986; Nunes and Bryant 1986). Hughes suggests that translation can be supported by devices such as Turtle Graphics devised by Papert, which allows links to be made between the concrete world of the Turtle and the formal language of mathematics (1986, p.165). Hughes states that 'In Papert's terms, the Turtle is a transitional device which helps children link the formal and the concrete' (italics in original, 1986, p.172): oral story represents a 'transitional device' which allows children to connect abstract story related mathematical ideas to concrete representations through story related props, so that the mathematical ideas become 'context-bound'. Story and related language support this translation and provide meaningful, memorable, metaphorical contexts which help children think about and articulate mathematical ideas. Children in the project listen to and tell stories, translating between abstract and concrete or concrete and abstract, through physical manipulation of props, such as the different coloured fish for 'Penguin'.

Mathematical errors

Mathematical errors are worth noting as these provide future learning or teaching opportunities. Marshall (1992, cited in Carr 2001, p. xiii) expresses the view that errors are a source of new learning. In some storytelling instances children were noted correcting errors by checking, recounting accurately with one-to-one correspondence, or asking others to check. Jake (whose story we come to later) makes an error, saying nine spots where he means eight (12 − 4 = 8) but this does not present a problem and goes unnoticed as he corrects this mistake when replacing four spots. In a small group telling of 'Blue Egg Dinosaur' where 'Jack-o-Saurus' disturbs two nests of eggs, children are coaxed to check an error, taking eggs out and lining them up, rather than counting a cluster, to establish possible ways of making eight between two nests. Errors can be seen as learning opportunities tackled through story context.

Story related materials

Story related materials allowed children to translate abstract story and mathematical ideas into concrete representations: cut out coloured fish supported Freya's telling of Penguin; two nests and eight blue dinosaur eggs allowed children to find different number complements for the number eight; and a three dimensional lady bird with Velcro spots served a dual function as story character and as a way of visualising an addition and subtraction pattern. It was remarkable how children created mathematical problems through their story constructions using the supporting material. For some storytellings the story construct drove children's physical action (Goose wants eleven fish and Freya arranges a combination of coloured fish to make eleven); for others, children constructed story as a result of their physical manipulation of props. Together, story context and related materials stimulated intuitive and meaningful mathematical expression. Before considering possible relationships between the story Little *Lumpty* (lmai 1994) and mathematical ideas in more detail, it is appropriate to define what story and oral mathematical story mean.

Story and oral mathematical story

A story is a series of events, located in time and place, involving a character who is posed a problem and told from a particular point of view. The character often has a consciousness about the problem and it is the connecting of the problem, the character and their consciousness which shapes the story (Bruner 1986). The story events will be sequenced into a beginning, middle and end. Referring to picture books, author and illustrator Eileen Browne (2013) describes stories 'as inadvertently having mathematical threads running through them'. If 'story' is considered as a sequence of events, 'oral' as a form of discourse (McQuillan 2000, p. 317), 'narrative' as a mode of knowledge (Lyotard 1984, cited in McQuillan 2000, p. 323) then 'oral narrative story' can be extended to 'oral mathematical narrative story' or contracted to 'mathematical narrative', a phrase used by Pound and Lee (2011). Oral mathematical story is a sequence of events bound by plot with connections between story and mathematical ideas.

Oral story

Oral storytelling brings a unique experience to educator and child, and Grugeon and Gardner (2000, p. 2) explain the difference between reading and telling a story. Reading is interpreting text in a shared way, but telling a story is a personal performance. When educators read a prescribed story they can remain separate (Schiro 2004). When educators create oral story, a more intimate relationship with both the story and the audience develops. Schiro (2004) compares educators employing children's storybooks to engaging in oral storytelling and describes how: the storyteller is free from text; needs to be spontaneous; has a closer connection with their audience; has a personal consciousness; advising that educators explore the instructional power of story. Playfulness with oral storytelling requires that adults get under the skin of both story and mathematical ideas, which can be achieved by thinking through these relationships, devising story maps (Corbett 2006, 2007) and mathematical maps (McGrath 2014).

Relationship between story and mathematics in *Little Lumpty*

Humpty Dumpty, a traditional nursery rhyme, inspires Little Lumpty, a character in a picture book (Imai 1994), to climb the wall that Humpty Dumpty climbed. This picture book, adapted for oral storytelling, accommodates the idea of Lumpty succeeding to ascend and descend the wall without adult knowledge or help. Mathematical ideas of counting forwards and backwards in multiples of a number are achieved by attaching importance to the choice of a twelve-rung ladder, the gap between the rungs of the ladder equating with a number of bricks in the wall: the rungs could be equal to two bricks of the wall so that going up the ladder allows counting in twos to twenty-four. The story *Little Lumpty* is shared with a class of five and six year olds, motivated to help Lumpty steady his nerves by counting in multiples of two to the twelfth multiple: 2, 4, 6, 8, 10, 12, 14, 16, 18, 20, 22, 24 forwards and backwards, so that he arrives safely back on the ground, without breaking (as Humpty Dumpty did) or needing to shout for help (as Lumpty does in the picture book). Before telling the story, I write up and share the mathematical intention 'counting in multiples of two' which serves to set the aim and scaffold mathematical language. During the telling the class teacher notes 'one hundred percent concentration' as children are 'fixated' on the story. After the story, a child categorised as lower ability explains perceptively: 'when you counted in twos you missed one out, so it's like a pattern' (McGrath 2013). A boy with autistic characteristics takes the mathematical idea to a drawing and describes Lumpty counting in twos to forty-eight. Children acquiring English as a Second Language join in with actions and repetitive phrases. This oral mathematical story experience elicits surprising results about how children respond and disturbs the culture of ability grouping (Boaler 2002, 2009) in this infant classroom.

Mathematical capabilities

Children imitate adults as oral mathematical storytellers and this imitative activity reveals something of their mathematical capabilities. Vygotsky places value on children learning from adults and more capable peers when he proposes the concept of the Zone of Proximal Development (ZPD): 'It is the distance between the actual developmental level as determined by independent problem solving and the level of potential development as determined through problem solving under adult guidance or in collaboration with more capable peers' (Vygotsky 1978, p. 86). Vygotsky develops this idea, positioning learning ahead of development, valuing children imitating adults to achieve a zone of proximal capability. He explains how demonstrating influences how a child might solve problems independently. He advocates that child development can more accurately be determined by considering actual and proximal development, arguing that diagnostic tests of development should include assessment of imitative activity in order to be conclusive. Adult intervention by demonstrating oral mathematical storytelling leads to imitative activity where children take the role of storyteller, and in this way the ZPD is supported mathematically.

Children's imitative activity offers rich insight into their mathematical capabilities. In the case of *Little Lumpty* the relationship between the ladder and the bricks in the wall can be played with, so that the gaps in the ladder rungs equal three or five bricks and a count in multiples of three or five to the twelfth multiple creates different number patterns. Mya (5 years 9 months) makes a mathematical intention explicit by writing 'counting in fives' on a white board. Mya retells *Little Lumpty* using the character prop and a wooden ladder counting '5, 10, 15, 30, 35, 40, 45, 50, 55, 60, 65' (note her error as there is a break in the sequence for 20 and 25). Mya sends Lumpty up another wall and expresses a connection with the height of the wall as '70 bricks high', before moving the ladder prop to another wall to find 'the highest wall in town'. Anna (5 years 1 month) counts forwards in ones, twos and 'zoomy numbers', deciding against counting in multiples of higher numbers. In a different context, a six year old tells the story of Lumpty counting in multiples of three forwards but not backwards. Children decide on the scope of the mathematical idea they will manage. Imaginative mathematical ideas arise from children thinking creatively about stories and such playfulness tells something of children's mathematical creative capabilities.

Figure 28.2 Anna using Little Lumpty and a wooden ladder to count in multiples of a number

Mathematical storyteller: kings and queens

Contemporary China's early childhood education mirrors a national goal to connect creativity and mathematics which Tobin et al. (2011) explain is driven by a need to create a new generation of creative citizens who will lead China to compete globally. An older emphasis on mastery, performance and competition is evident in an account of 'The Storytelling King' activity (Tobin et al. 2011, p. 156). Children listening to adult storytelling request to be storytellers and one child who tells a story to his peers is voted as 'Storytelling King' but is encouraged to reflect on constructive comments from those who do *not* vote him as king. This 'Storytelling King' activity represents a hybrid pedagogy which combines Chinese and Western pedagogical notions: direct instruction where adults model storytelling; child initiated storytelling; and mastery of storytelling skills based on reflection (Tobin et al. 2011, p. 157). Oral mathematical story experiences represent a hybrid of pedagogical approaches in that it is a traditional idea combined with modern practice, opening out opportunities for children to demonstrate mastery of mathematics and storytelling which can be reflected upon by sharing audio or video recordings with children, parents and colleagues.

The most interesting outcome from the research findings is not how children play in mathematical ways, but how children use story-related materials in playful ways to create stories with mathematical ideas of their own choice, going beyond those demonstrated by the adult, and how through story children challenge themselves mathematically.

Jake: Mathematical storyteller King

Jake (4 years and 5 months) plays with story-related materials after listening to 'Ladybird on a Leaf'. A ladybird, too proud to share a secret that her spots are artificial and need to be stuck on each morning, is under pressure to get ready as a friend, who always arrives early, will call so that they can go on a trip to ladybird London. Just before the doorbell rings, a rain cloud washes some spots off and an ant, who watches from a higher leaf, replaces them.

The mathematical idea of this story is that a number, say 'N', will always remain unchanged if a number added to it and then subtracted from it is the same, or if a number subtracted from it and then added to it is the same. Haylock and Cockburn offer a specific example from which a generalisation can be made: 'if you add 6 to a number and then subtract 6 from the answer you always get back to the number you started with' (2013, p. 297). The story idea of the rain and the ant connects with this mathematical idea which can be mapped generally as: $N + n - n = N$ and $N - n + n = N$.

Jake carefully arranges twelve spots as a six and a six on each wing and starts his story.

Italics indicate words spoken by Jake. Square brackets contain observational notes about Jake's actions.

> [Jake counts out twelve spots placing six spots on each wing of the sugar paper ladybird.]
>
> *The sneaky rain took four away.*
>
> *And soon the sun came along, the sun came along and put four back.*

[Jake removes and then replaces two spots on each wing.]

The ladybird thanks the sun for making the spots come back.

But this time the sneaky rain took more than four away. She, the sneaky rain takes two away.

She decided to take more than two, more than four.

She decided to take three more than four. Three more makes . . . Hey, how many does it makes? One, two, three, four, five, six, seven.

She took seven away. The rain took seven away. She only had five spots left.

Soon she called for her friend the little ant [Jake starts replacing spots] *she puts on one, two, three* [Jake places three spots on one wing], *four ,five, six, seven* [he places four spots on the other wing].

[The spot arrangement is restored to six on each wing.]

Where did my other ones go? [Jake asks looking around].

There is only one, two, three, four, five, six, seven, eight, nine, ten, eleven, and twelve . . . there is twelve actually'.

[Jake touches each spot saying the corresponding number name.]

The ladybird thanked her friend the little ant.

The ant went away to have some tea and cake [Jake shows motion of ant walking off with fingers. Using both hands he brushes off six spots from each wing.]

She says [difficult to hear but something about 'I have no spots'. He holds the ladybird shape up vertically.]

Soon she called 'help' and the ant says 'what now?'

And she said 'all my spots are washed away'

And soon the ant put one, two, three, four, five, six seven, eight, nine, ten, eleven, twelve. She putted twelve more on.

[He pushes the spots further up the ladybird figure.]

And then soon she thanked the ant. And soon . . . the rain washed this many away.

[He starts to count the spots on the carpet.]

One, two, three, four, five, six, seven, eight, nine . . . nine away

And then soon the ant came along and the ant was quite cross and soon the ant said 'I was just about to have my tea and cake.'

And soon the sun sawed the naughty rain trying to get the spots away and soon the sun was so cross and said 'Go away naughty rain, go away'.

[Jake replaces six spots on each wing, restoring the twelve spots to how he started.]

Jake represents the pattern $N - n + n = N$ through four number relationship patterns:

$12 - 4 + 4 = 12$

$12 - 7 + 7 = 12$

$12 - 12 + 12 = 12$

$12 - 10 + 10 = 12$

Jake uses story language to support expression of mathematical ideas: the sneaky rain takes spots away and the ant adds spots back on, articulating mathematical ideas in imaginative ways. Jake chooses a larger number (12) than that of the story he hears (10) and constructs his own number relationships (e.g. $12 - 7 = 5$) as he plays with story-related materials. Jake's physical action of removing spots poses the question 'What if?' He has to work out the outcome of his action. Jake expresses ideas of the original story heard, that is, you start with a number N, then subtract a number n, then replace the same number n, to arrive back to the original number 'N'. Jake uses the ladybird body and spots to support an abstract idea in visual, physical and verbal ways. Copies of audio, video and digital photographs are shared with Jake and his mother. Jake's mother, Li writes: 'It seems that this creative approach of using ladybird spots really has got Jake interested and has made him think mathematically in relation to the story.'

Freya: Mathematical storyteller queen

Whereas Jake plays with props, after hearing the story Freya asks to be the storyteller. Freya's story 'Penguin' is rich in mathematical thinking and told with remarkable precision and imagination. Freya (5 years and 11 months) extends the story heard to find number complements for eleven rather than ten. Freya works through number relationships, using coloured fish to support articulation of these number relationships. She counts the fish accurately, with one-to-one correspondence. She uses mathematical thinking to combine 5 orange, 5 yellow and 1 blue to make eleven fish. Other children listen with Suzanne her class teacher, who later comments on how Freya is quiet in whole-class teaching situations.

Oral mathematical storytelling challenges children

As adults we need to be careful with our expectations of children as mathematical storytellers. Similar to play, oral mathematical storytelling is unpredictable. Play is more a narrative stream, whereas story is bound by sequence and plot. Children choose, but are challenged by their choice to create an oral mathematical story, possibly because as authors of stories they manage relationships between story and mathematics, represent mathematical ideas by manipulating materials, connect actions to words. After hearing the Russian tale Toby sits on the storyteller cushion and says 'This is hard'. Freya retells 'Penguin' on another occasion but it lacks the quality of the first telling. Children as mathematical storytellers can appear at ease, uninhibited, playful, but as is the case for adults, there is the risky challenge of creativity.

Jake and Freya are examples of children who tell stories rich in mathematics, consolidating what they know and linking unfamiliar ideas with existing knowledge, translating between abstract and concrete representations of mathematical ideas (Hughes 1986), using story-related materials to support mathematical thinking. There is scope to capture mathematical thinking as qualitative data in an observational learning story (Carr 2001) and capitalise on the value Paley (1981; 1999) associates with audio recordings, and to encourage children to reflect on their skills as mathematical storytellers (see McGrath 2014 for further detail). A culture of taking creative risks and assessing mathematics in qualitative ways tells interesting stories about children's capabilities.

Conclusion

Mathematics involves posing, solving and creating problems. Hughes (1986) identifies how children have difficulty translating between representations of mathematical ideas, compounded for young children when ideas are 'context-free'. Oral mathematical stories provide contexts that children find purposeful: ideas that are 'context-bound'. Children translate between stories and concrete representation of mathematical ideas using story-related props, with remarkable precision and imagination.

Freya and Jake extend mathematical ideas beyond stories told by educators, applying their mathematical knowledge to solving and posing practical problems through story context using props, words and actions. In some cases physical actions pose mathematical questions: Jake removes spots from the ladybird, posing mathematical challenges which he works through using story context to explain his actions, in his case translating outcomes of his physical actions into story context. Jake preserves the pattern $N - n + n = N$ of the story, working through four specific relationships for the number twelve.

Children's 'imitative activity' (Vygotsky 1978) as oral mathematical storytellers reveals surprises about their mathematical capabilities. Vygotsky (1978) cautions that both actual and proximal levels of development should be considered: where the child is at independently, and what the child can potentially achieve after adult demonstration, illuminate children's capabilities. Vygotsky attributes value to the role of imitation: children given opportunities to imitate adult mathematical stories tell us about their *capabilities* as mathematicians and as storytellers. Older traditions of oral storytelling combined with modern methods of recording allow oral mathematical stories to be documented and contribute to qualitative assessment of children's learning (Carr 2001). Digital photographs, audio and visual recordings, along with narrative accounts, can be shared with children, parents and educators.

A child considered as 'lower ability' describes a story idea about counting in multiples of two with mathematical perception, surprising her class teacher and, in doing so, challenges the practice of ability grouping. Children with autistic characteristics, acquiring English as a Second Language, or those considered quiet, and others, respond favourably to this alternative pedagogical approach to teaching mathematics. A classroom culture of democracy where children develop the ritual of sitting, listening, and becoming mathematical storytellers is quickly established. Storyteller kings and queens bring childlike inventiveness to mathematical monarchies, and will enrich the lands of countries which encourage and capture creative mathematical thinking of these future rulers.

References

Arnold, K. (1994). *Knock, Knock, Teremok!* New York: North-South Books.

Boaler, J. (2002). *Experiencing School Mathematics: Revised and Expanded Edition.* Mahwah, NJ: Lawrence Erlbaum Associates.

Boaler, J. (2009). *The Elephant in the Classroom: Helping Children Learn and Love Maths.* London: Souvenir Press Ltd.

Browne, E. (2013). E-mail to Caroline McGrath, 26 July.

Bruner, J. (1986). *Actual Minds, Possible Worlds.* Cambridge, MA: Harvard University Press.

Burns, M. (1994). *The Greedy Triangle.* London: Scholastic.

Carr, M. (2001). *Assessment in Early Childhood Settings: Learning Stories.* London: SAGE Publications Ltd.

Casey, R. (2011). 'Teaching mathematically promising children', in Koshy, V. and Murray, J. (eds) *Unlocking Mathematics Teaching* (2nd edn). Oxford: Routledge, pp. 124–150.

Corbett, P. (2006). *The Bumper Book of Storytelling into Writing Key Stage 1.* Wiltshire: Clown Publishing.

Corbett, P. (2007). Developing Creative Writing Skills Available at: http://www.learning-works.org.uk/index.php?id=566 (accessed: 15 November 2013).

Grugeon, E. and Gardner, P. (2000). *The Art of Storytelling for Teachers and Pupils: Using Stories to Develop Literacy in Primary Classrooms.* London: David Fulton.

Haylock, D. and Cockburn, A. (2013). *Understanding Mathematics for Young Children* (4th edn). London: SAGE.

Hersh, R. (1998). *What is Mathematics Really?* London: Vintage.

Hughes, M. (1986). *Children and Number: Difficulties in Learning Mathematics.* Oxford: Blackwell Publishers Ltd.

Imai, M. (1994). *Little Lumpty.* London: Walker Books.

McGrath, C. (2014). *Teaching Mathematics through Story: A Creative Approach for the Early Years.* Abingdon: Routledge.

McGrath, C. (2013). Private notes. Unpublished PhD research thesis. Plymouth University.

McGrath, C. (2012). 'From posing to solving', *Early Years Educator,* 14(4), pp. 24–26.

McQuillan, M. (ed.). (2000). *The Narrative Reader.* London: Routledge.

Nunes, T. and Bryant, P. (1986). *Children Doing Mathematics.* Oxford: Blackwell.

Paley, V. G. (1981). *Wally's Stories: Conversations in the Kindergarten.* London: Harvard University Press.

Paley, V. (1999). *The Kindness of Children.* London: Harvard University Press.

Polya, G. (1945). *How to Solve it: A new aspect of mathematical method* (2nd edition). Princeton, NJ: Princeton University Press.

Pound, L. (2008). *Thinking and Learning about Mathematics in the Early Years.* Abingdon: Routledge.

Pound, L. and Lee, T. (2011). *Teaching Mathematics Creatively.* Abingdon: Routledge.

Ransome, A. (2003). *Old Peter's Russian Tales*. London: Jane Nissen Books.

Schiro, M. (2004). *Oral Storytelling and Teaching Mathematics: Pedagogical and Multicultural Perspectives*. California: SAGE.

Tobin, J., Hayashi, A. and Zhang, J. (2011). 'Approaches to promoting creativity in Chinese, Japanese and US preschools', in Sefton-Green, J., Thomson, P., Jones, K. and Bresler, L. (eds) *The Routledge International Handbook of Creative Learning*. Oxon: Routledge, pp. 150–158.

Vygotsky, L. (1978). *Mind in Society: The Development of Higher Psychological Processes*. Translated by Cole, M. and edited by Cole, M., John-Steiner, V., Scribner, S. and Souberman, E. London: The MIT Press, 1986.

29

The effects of computer technology on primary school students' mathematics achievement

A meta-analysis

Egbert Harskamp

Introduction

Students with difficulties in learning mathematics can be found in almost every classroom. About 5% to 10% of the students in primary education have difficulties with mathematics (Kroesbergen and Van Luit, 2003). The potential causes of these difficulties are numerous and can partly be explained by such child characteristics as intellectual functioning, motivation, memory skills or lack of metacognitive strategies. Another important cause of mathematics difficulties might be a poor fit between the learning characteristics of the individual students and the instruction they receive (Räsänen, Salminen, Wilson, Aunio and Dehaene, 2009). Students with poor mathematics ability often lag behind in their group and have special educational needs.

Next to instruction by the teacher, computer-assisted instruction can provide extra instruction and training for these students. The National Council of Teachers of Mathematics (NCTM, 2000) emphasized the importance of the use of technology in mathematics education especially for students with mild disabilities. Learning mathematics concepts and procedures can be a challenge for these students (Miller, Brown and Robinson, 2002). In both the initial stages of concept instruction and in subsequent practice sessions, computer programs can be effective, motivating, and adaptive to the student's level of skill (Main and O'Rourke, 2011).

At the beginning of the 1980s Burns and Bozeman (1981) examined 40 primary studies on computer-assisted instruction in mathematics education. In computer-assisted instruction students receive direct instruction, practice and feedback adapted to their level of mastery of a skill. Research has consistently shown direct instruction to be very effective for students with mathematics learning difficulties to attain both automaticity and problem-solving skills (Kroesbergen, Van Luit and Maas, 2004). Burns and Bozeman (1981) concluded that computer-assisted instruction raised student achievement by .4 standard deviations in comparison to regular whole-class teaching. For students scoring below the average of their class the effects are even greater. Reviews conducted by Kulik and Kulik (1991) and Christmann and Badgett (2003) indicate that in the 1980s and 1990s similar results were found. Recently, Li and Ma (2010) focused on the impact of computer technology on mathematics education by examining primary studies conducted after 1990. Based on a total of 85 independent findings extracted from 46 primary studies involving 26,793 learners, they found a moderate but significantly positive effect (standard deviation of .28). The effect of computer programs on mathematics achievement was greater for students with lower mathematics ability. They concluded that the effect of computer-assisted instruction is not as strong as in previous decades.

In this study the term computer software refers to programs that help students to learn new mathematics knowledge or practise existing knowledge. In past decades, different types of software have been developed and applied in an attempt to enhance mathematics teaching and learning. We classify software into two main categories: (a) tutorials as part of computer-assisted instruction, and (b) exploratory environments (Lou, Abrami and d'Apollonia, 2001). We leave out tools such as calculators and simple drill programs or communication tools.

Tutorials are programs that assist the teacher. These programs practise or re-teach mathematics by providing students with demonstrations and explanations and guided practice. Practice can be taken in games with help and instruction on demand or software that systematically teaches and guides students through content to be learned.

Figure 29.1 shows an example of a tutorial. It helps students to practise dividing numbers up to ten. The program has 24 levels and is aimed at students in kindergarten through grade two. Students first receive instruction from a pedagogical agent (blue bear) showing a worked example. During practice the student can ask the agent for help. Students receive informative feedback after both a correct and incorrect answer, which allows them to work independently.

Exploratory environments seek to encourage active learning through discovery and exploration. Hypermedia-based learning, simulations, and LOGO are examples of this category. Figure 29.2 is an example of an exploratory environment for student in grade 6.

The programme has assignments. The student will first learn to explore angles of a polygon by programming the path the turtle has to walk. Then the students have to find out how to make basic polygons (triangle, rectangle, hexagon, etc.). They use the buttons in the interface to make the turtle draw lines. The programme has different levels and the student can ask for help.

Tutorial programs offer structured learning paths and they are better suited to practising students' knowledge and skills. Exploratory environments are helpful in

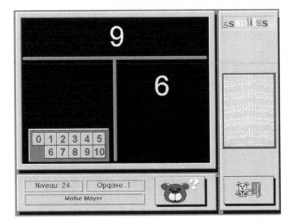

Figure 29.1 Example of a tutorial program

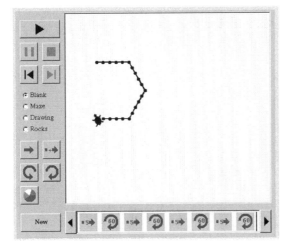

Figure 29.2 Example of an exploratory environment program

developing students' problem-solving skills. Hence, various learning outcomes can be attained with these types of programs.

Research question

This meta-analysis focuses on the use of computers for different groups of students in primary education and contains recent studies. It discusses sub-domains of mathematics, which the study from Li and Ma does not distinguish. The research question is as follows:

What are effective computer technologies for different sub-domains of mathematics for low and high ability groups of students in primary education?

Method

A search procedure was undertaken to find as many studies as possible that reported empirical evidence on the effectiveness of computer technology in mathematics education for primary school students. The studies had to use mathematics achievement as the outcome. Mathematics achievement refers to performance scores on solving mathematical problems that are measured by mathematics tests. These tests concern both standardized tests and teacher-made/researcher-made tests.

In this meta-analysis, only educational studies from 2000 onwards have been included in order to give a current overview. The following search procedure was used to find relevant studies. First, an electronic search was conducted in the Educational Resources Information Center (ERIC). The search descriptors included: math(ematics), arithmetic, addition, subtraction, multiplication, division, number sense, geometry, measurement, technology, computer, ICT, software, primary (education), and achievement. Second, a manual search was conducted of journals related to this study. The inclusion of only published journal articles may have weakened the external validity of the present meta-analysis, because of a tendency to only publish studies with significant positive effects. When interpreting the results, this should be kept in mind.

In order to be included in the meta-analysis, a study had to meet the following criteria:

- The study was published in 2000 or later (with no restriction on geographical area or language).
- The study employed an experimental or quasi-experimental design. In a true experiment, researchers randomly assign participants to treatment groups and control groups. Random assignment is not used in a quasi-experiment.
- The study reported quantitative data that generated sufficient detail for the calculation of an intervention effect size (i.e. number of subjects, means, and standard deviations for both the pre-test and post-test).
- The study used mathematics achievement as outcome measure.

The applications of the above-mentioned selection criteria yielded a total of 16 studies for inclusion in the meta-analysis.

As a measure of effect size, Cohen's *d* was calculated as the standardized mean difference using the means, standard deviations, and sample sizes of both the treatment and control groups. The sample sizes were used to calculate weighted mean effect sizes for each sub-domain of mathematics and for the overall effect size.

A random-effects model was adopted for data analysis. Under the random-effects model, the true effect can vary from study to study (Borenstein, Hedges, Higgins and Rothstein, 2009).

Results

In total, 19 effect sizes were extracted from 16 studies to examine the effects of computer technology for different sub-domains of mathematics in primary education. The studies included a total of 2,599 students from 34 schools.

The average weighted Cohen's *d* for the effect of computer software versus traditional teaching in this study was .48 SD. Hattie (2009) suggests $d = .2$ for small, $d = .4$ for medium, and $d = .8$ for large effect sizes when judging educational outcomes. Thus, this meta-analysis indicated an overall medium positive effect of computer technology on mathematics achievement in primary education. There was an overall extra effect for 'type of student'. For low achieving students the overall effect of computer programs versus traditional teaching was slightly greater (.59 SD) than for the higher achieving students.

Results for different sub-domains

Four sub-domains were distinguished: number sense, number operations, geometry/measurement, and word problems.

Number sense

Table 29.1 indicates that two large and significant effect sizes were found, as well as one small and non-significant effect size. In general, the three studies suggest a medium significant effect of computer technology on number sense. The mean effect size is .53 SD.

Clements and Sarama (2007) evaluated the efficacy of a pre-school mathematics program in which software and print curriculum were combined: *Building Blocks*. The objects in the computer tasks were creating, duplicating, combining, separating, counting, moving, and labelling objects and numbers. For example, children worked on a software program in which they saw three toppings on a pizza, then, after the top of the box closes, one more was being placed on the pizza. Children had to put the same number of toppings on another pizza. The effect of this program was compared to regular early childhood mathematics programs and the program turned out to be more effective. Lan et al. (2010) report on an experiment where fourth graders were randomly assigned to two groups. All students received problem-based estimation instruction from a teacher. The students had to learn to round off numbers and make rapid estimations. For example: I have 450 dollars. Is this enough to pay

Table 29.1 Effect sizes for the domain number sense

Study	Computer technology	Effect size	p-value
Clements and Sarama (2007)	Tutorial	.76	.001
Clements and Sarama (2008)	Tutorial	.70	.000
Lan, Sung, Tan, Lin, and Chang (2010)	Exploratory environment	.18	.627
	Mean effect size:	.53	.000

Table 29.2 Effect sizes for the domain number operations

Study	Computer technology	Effect size	p-value
Clements and Sarama (2007)	Tutorial	.66	.001
Clements and Sarama (2008)	Tutorial	.60	.000
Fuchs et al. (2006): addition	Tutorial	.48	.176
Fuchs et al. (2006): subtraction	Tutorial	.02	.949
Shin, Norris, and Soloway (2010)	Tutorial	.31	.344
Rutherford et al. (2010): grade 2	Tutorial	.03	.931
Rutherford et al. (2010): grade 3	Tutorial	−.29	.397
Rutherford et al. (2010): grade 4	Tutorial	.65	.036
Rutherford et al. (2010): grade 5	Tutorial	.72	.041
Schoppek and Tulis (2010): experiment 1	Tutorial	.70	.000
Schoppek and Tulis (2010): experiment 2	Tutorial	.61	.005
Main and O'Rourke (2011)	Tutorial	.40	.145
	Mean effect size:	*.42*	*.000*

for goods of 39, 23, 151, 48, 62, and 82 dollars? After instruction, the experimental group used collaborative learning software to work on problems in small group discussions. The control group worked face to face in small groups on the problems. The results demonstrate that students in the experimental group did not improve their estimation skills more than students in the control group.

Number operations

Table 29.2 demonstrates eight studies that addressed operations. Six substantive significant effects were found, and six small but non-significant effects.

Overall, the studies suggest a medium effect of computer technology on number operations. The mean effect size is .42 SD.

In the Schoppek and Tulis (2010) study, basic arithmetic operations were trained by means of adaptive training software called Merlin's Math Mill. The animated character Merlin accompanies the student through the program and provides feedback. Each problem can be tried twice. If the students solve more than half of the problems of a set correctly, they can open a door in a cabinet with 40 doors. This triggers a short video clip or a joke that the students can watch or read.

Geometry/measurement

Four studies in this meta-analysis explored the effects of computer technology on geometry/measurement. Table 29.3 indicates that all effects are significant, and that mainly large effect sizes were found. Only the study by Campuzano, Dynarski, Agodini and Rall (2009) reports a negative effect. In general, the four studies suggest a medium significant effect of computer technology on geometry/measurement. The mean effect size is .59 SD.

Steen, Brooks and Lyon (2006) investigated the impact of virtual manipulatives on students. Virtual manipulatives are interactive, web-based visual representations of a dynamic object that presents opportunities for constructing mathematical knowledge.

Table 29.3 Effect sizes concerning geometry/measurement

Study	Computer technology	Effect size	p-value
Clements and Sarama (2007)	Tutorial	.88	.000
Clements and Sarama (2008)	Tutorial	.80	.000
Steen, Brooks and Lyon (2006)	Exploratory environment	.79	.035
Olkun, Altun and Smith (2005)	Tutorial	.73	.001
Campuzano, Dynarski, Agodini and Rall (2009)	Tutorial	−.23	.003
	Mean effect size:	*.59*	*.045*

They typically include additional features or options that expand on what a physical manipulative can offer. In this study, textbooks were used for instructional purposes, but students used virtual manipulatives for practice. Virtual manipulatives are especially effective for students with low mathematics ability.

Word problems

Finally, Table 29.4 demonstrates the effect sizes of five studies concerning word problems. All effects are positive and three studies report significant effect sizes. Overall, the studies report a large significant effect of computer technology on word problems. The mean effect size is .57.

Since both statistically significant effective studies have already been described above, the studies of Jacobse and Harskamp (2010) and Kajamies et al. (2010) will be utilized as examples of the use of computer programs for word problems.

Jacobse and Harskamp assessed the effect of metacognitive hints in a computer environment by replacing the mathematics content of a computer program known from previous research with word problems. In addition, metacognitive hints were added to the cognitive content of the word problems. The metacognitive hints were based on the so-called 'Task stairs procedure'. In this procedure, a picture of a staircase is shown with the steps 'I read carefully' (orientation), 'I make a plan' (planning), 'I check my answer' (evaluation), and 'What did I learn?' (reflection). Students were free to choose the hints in any order they liked. Systematic help in problem solving is especially effective for students with low academic ability.

Table 29.4 Effect sizes concerning word problems

Study	Computer technology	Effect size	p-value
Clements and Sarama (2007)	Tutorial	.56	.001
Clements and Sarama (2008)	Tutorial	.70	.000
Schoppek and Tulis (2010): experiment 1	Tutorial	.70	.000
Schoppek and Tulis (2010): experiment 2	Tutorial	.61	.005
Kajamies, Vauras and Kinnunen (2010)	Tutorial	.51	.168
Jacobse and Harskamp (2010)	Exploratory environment	.50	.089
	Mean effect size:	*.57*	*.000*

The Kajamies et al. study describes the effects of an intervention designed to develop the mathematical word problem solving of low-achievers. In the intervention, a pilot version of the computer-supported adventure game called *The Quest of the Silver Owl* was used. The adventure goal in the game is to find the Silver Owl, which allows the two adventurers to save the Realm of Secret Numbers. The owl can be found after the adventurers have acquired enough points by solving word problems that reflect the spirit of the game.

Discussion

The purpose of the current study was to determine effective computer technology for different sub-domains of mathematics in primary education. The studies in this meta-analysis that addressed number sense reported a mean effect size of .53 SD. For operations, the mean effect size was .42 SD. The mean effect size for geometry/measurement was .59 SD. Finally, the mean effect size for word problems was .57 SD. Thus, it can be concluded that computer technology had an effect in these sub-domains. There is no difference in effect.

Overall, the findings suggested a medium positive effect (.48 SD) of computer technology on mathematics achievement in primary education. Low mathematics ability students especially profit from the use of computer programs as compared to whole-class teaching. This result is more positive compared to the result of Li and Ma (2010), who found an overall effect size of .28 SD. An explanation could be that the use of ICT has a more positive effect on mathematics achievement in primary education than in secondary education. Furthermore, the current meta-analysis did not include many studies in which no effect or a negative effect were found. This might indicate some publication bias in favour of experiments with positive outcomes.

Our study indicates that the most frequently utilized ICT in primary education are tutorials and that exploratory environments are utilized far less. Examples of effective ICT for different sub-domains of mathematics are: Building Blocks, Merlin's Math Mill, Spatial-Temporal maths software games, and virtual manipulatives. It should be kept in mind, however, that these types of ICT proved effective in the experimental studies. More research is needed to draw firm conclusions concerning the effectiveness of these examples of ICT in school practice.

Instruction should obviously take the particular difficulties of children with low mathematics ability into account. Kroesbergen, Van Luit and Maas (2004) suggest that teaching step-by-step from concrete to abstract, working with materials to mental representations and providing task-relevant examples can certainly help. These students need directed and detailed instruction, explicit task analysis, and explicit instruction for automatization of mathematics knowledge and generalization. Our analysis shows that tutorials (with direct instruction and individualized feedback) might lead to better results than regular whole-class teaching. The tutor programs are generally built up following the same pattern. In the opening phase, the students' attention is gained, prior knowledge is reviewed and the goals of the learning unit are stated. In the main part of the unit the program demonstrates how a particular task can be solved and then the students can work on the task, when necessary, with the help that the program has to offer. When the student appears to have sufficient understanding of the task (giving many correct answers), they are given problems on a somewhat higher level to practise. The teacher monitors the student's results (log files) in the program and provides feedback on completed tasks. If a student fails to succeed in the program the teacher needs to step in and guide the student in effective use of the program. As Slavin and Lake (2008) state: computer technology can be used effectively in classrooms. But, teachers should keep in mind that computer programs are effective if they are used regularly (more than 30 minutes a week during a longer period of time). Teachers need to choose programs that are in line with the mathematics curriculum the students follow and teachers should integrate the instruction for the programs into their regular classroom instruction. When these requirements are met computer programs will be effective for students with low mathematics abilities.

References

References marked with an asterisk indicate studies included in the meta-analysis.

Borenstein, M., Hedges, L.V., Higgins, J.P., and Rothstein, H.R. (2009). *Introduction to Meta-Analysis*. Chichester, UK: John Wiley and Sons Ltd.

Burns, P.K., and Bozeman, W.C. (1981). Computer-assisted instruction and mathematics achievement: Is there a relationship? *Educational Technology, 21*(10), 32–39.

*Campuzano, L., Dynarski, M., Agodini, R., and Rall, K. (2009). *Effectiveness of reading and mathematics software products*. National Center for Education Evaluation and Regional Assistance.

Christmann, E.P., and Badgett, J.L. (2003). A meta-analytic comparison of the effects of computer-assisted instruction on elementary students' academic achievement. *Information Technology in Childhood Education Annual,* (1), 91–104.

*Clements, D.H., and Sarama, J. (2007). Effects of a preschool mathematics curriculum: Summative research on the building blocks project. *Journal for Research in Mathematics Education, 38*, 136–163.

*Clements, D.H., and Sarama, J. (2008). Experimental evaluation of the effects of a research-based preschool mathematics curriculum. *American Education Research Journal, 45*, 443–494.

*Fuchs, L.S., Fuchs, D., Hamlet, C.L., Powell, S.R., Capizzi, A.M., and Seethaler, P.M. (2006). The effects of computer-assisted instruction on number combination skill in at-risk first graders. *Journal of Learning Disabilities, 39*, 467–475.

Hattie, J. (2009). *Visible Learning. A synthesis of over 800 meta-analyses relating to achievement*. London and New York: Routledge.

*Jacobse, A.E., and Harskamp, E.G. (2010). Student-controlled metacognitive training for solving word problems in primary school mathematics. *Educational Research and Evaluation, 15*, 447–463.

*Kajamies, A., Vauras, M., and Kinnunen, R. (2010). Instructing low-achievers in mathematical word problem solving. *Scandinavian Journal of Educational Research, 54*, 335–355.

Kroesbergen, E.H., and Van Luit, J.E.H. (2003). Mathematics interventions for children with special educational needs: A meta-analysis. *Remedial and Special Education, 24*, 97–114.

Kroesbergen, E.H., Van Luit, J.E.H., and Maas, C.M. (2004). Effectiveness of explicit and constructivist mathematics instruction for low-achieving students in The Netherlands, *Elementary School Journal, 104*, 233–251.

Kulik, C., and Kulik, J. (1991). Effectiveness of computer-based instruction: An updated analysis. *Computers in Human Behavior, 7*, 75–94.

*Lan, Y., Sung, Y., Tan, N., Lin, C., and Chang, K. (2010). Mobile-device supported problem-based computational estimation instruction for elementary school students. *Educational Technology and Society, 13*, 55–69.

Li, Q., and Ma, X. (2010). A meta-analysis of the effects of computer technology on school students' mathematics learning. *Educational Psychology Review, 22*, 215–243.

Lou, Y., Abrami, P.C., and d'Apollonia, S. (2001). Small group and individual learning with technology: A meta-analysis. *Review of Educational Research, 3*, 449–521.

*Main, S., and O'Rourke, J. (2011). 'New directions for traditional lessons': Can handheld game consoles enhance mental mathematics skills? *Australian Journal of Teacher Education, 36*(2).

Miller, D., Brown, A., and Robinson, L. (2002). Widgets on the web. Using computer-based learning tools. *Teaching Exceptional Children, 35*, 24–28.

National Council of Teachers of Mathematics (NCTM). (2000). *Principles and Standards for School Mathematics*. Reston, VA: NCTM.

*Olkun, S., Altun, A., and Smith, G. (2005). Computers and 2D geometric learning of Turkish fourth and fifth graders. *British Journal of Educational Technology, 36*, 317–326.

Räsänen, P., Salminen, J., Wilson, A.J., Aunio, P., and Dehaene, S. (2009). Computer-assisted intervention for children with low numeracy skills. *Cognitive Development, 24*, 450–472.

*Rutherford, T., Kibrick, M., Burchinal, M., Richland, L., Conley, A., Osborne, K., Martinez, M. E. (2010). *Spatial temporal mathematics at scale: an innovative and fully developed paradigm to boost math achievement among all learners*. Paper presented at the Annual Meeting of the American Educational Research Association.

*Schoppek, W., and Tulis, M. (2010). Enhancing arithmetic and word-problem solving skills efficiently by individualized computer-assisted practice. *The Journal of Educational Research, 103*, 239–252.

*Shin, N., Norris, C., and Soloway, E. (2010). *Effects of handheld games on students' learning in mathematics*. International Conference on Learning Sciences.

Slavin, R.E., and Lake, C. (2008). Effective programs in elementary mathematics: A best evidence synthesis. *Review of Educational Research, 78*(3), 427–455.

*Steen, K., Brooks, D., and Lyon, T. (2006). The impact of virtual manipulatives on first grade geometry instruction and learning. *Journal of Computers in Mathematics and Science Teaching, 35*, 373–391.

30

Representing, acting, and engaging

UDL and mathematics

Elizabeth Murray, Garron Hillaire, Mindy Johnson and
Gabrielle Rappolt-Schlichtmann

Over the last decade algebra has taken on an increasingly important role in secondary education. Influential education organizations have considered it the gateway to success in the twenty first century because it is a prerequisite for the higher mathematics needed for postsecondary education, as well as a skill needed by many professionals who do not attend college. Yet algebra continues to be a stumbling block for many students, particularly those who struggle with mathematics. Even students who previously have been successful in mathematics can find algebra to be a stumbling block as it is often the first course that requires abstract reasoning. We wondered why algebra should be such a good predictor of success and why so many students continue to struggle with it. We discovered that most programs focus on describing and calculating, not on the underlying thinking that is essential to truly understanding and applying algebra. The emphasis on procedural fluency that is common in algebra curricula does not promote understanding or interpretation. Instruction needs to focus on teaching the reasoning skills needed for a conceptual understanding of algebra. Our questions led us to develop the "iSolveIt," two prototype iPad apps that are designed to support struggling mathematics students based in the framework of Universal Design for Learning (UDL). This chapter will focus on an exploration of how the principles of UDL were applied to the development of a technology-based solution designed to improve outcomes for students who demonstrate difficulties in learning mathematics.

What is UDL?

Universal Design for Learning (UDL) is a means to provide opportunities for deep learning through the design of highly flexible instructional methods, materials and assessments. Specifically, the framework describes a set of principles for curriculum development which, when applied, allow for customization to individual needs. Design is focused on creating learning environments that are as inclusive of the variability present in the population as possible – learners are complex and variable, learning environments need to be flexible to support the needs of all learners and not simply some illusory average learner.

The UDL framework holds a broader conceptualization of what the term 'disability' means. Under UDL disability represents one form of variability within a given domain – in essence students with learning disabilities are representative of a set of outliers on a continuum where all students experience difficulty in mathematics to some degree. While many students' struggles with mathematics can be attributed to dyscalculia, which appears to impact basic number sense and the learning and remembering of arithmetic facts and procedures, there are other reasons why students have difficulty with mathematics, such as difficulty understanding and using representations, poor executive function, and affective issues. Students identified with mathematics disability represent one extreme of students who struggle with mathematics, and we believe these students can inform the ways in which approaches to mathematics education should be designed for all. UDL provides us with a framework for curriculum design that addresses students throughout the learning continuum. Three primary principles, based on research in the neurosciences and learning sciences, guide UDL:

- *Provide multiple means of representation* (the "what" of learning) – presenting information and content in different ways and making connections between them.
- *Provide multiple means of action and expression* (the "how" of learning) – providing different ways for students to work with information and content and to demonstrate what they are learning.
- *Provide multiple means of engagement* (the "why" of learning) – stimulate interest and motivation for learning (and persistence).

By applying the UDL framework to the design of technology-based mathematics instruction and materials we can significantly reduce the interference of construct-irrelevant barriers in learning for all students and provide just in time feedback with opportunities for practice through the provision of precise contextual support and scaffolding.

UDL and mathematics: applying the principles

Each UDL principle includes three guidelines that focus our thinking about ways to support students. The three guidelines are hierarchical, moving from supporting basic access to higher-order thinking, planning, and organizing.

Principle 1: multiple means of representation

If students do not have a basic, conceptual understanding of numbers, operations, patterns, and representations, they cannot fully grasp mathematics – even if they develop some skill following the procedures they learn in school. Representations play a major role in understanding mathematics concepts and relationships and in demonstrating that understanding. They help students to understand spatial relationships that are a part of geometry and to see the relationship between patterns in numbers and their representation in algebra. Representations also can help students to organize their thinking and provide contexts that make mathematics more complete.

Perception

At the most basic level, students need to be able to perceive a representation in order to interact with it and understand it. As representations in mathematics are generally presented visually, alternatives to this presentation, such as larger fonts, high contrast, and audio descriptions, might be needed for students with visual impairments. However, other students might also have difficulty understanding mathematics when too many representations are presented at once. For example, textbook pages may present multiple representations, through text, charts, illustrations, examples, in a format that makes it hard for a student to know where to begin. Issues with perception limit access to all aspects of mathematics, including algebra.

Language, mathematical expressions, and symbols

Much of mathematics is represented through mathematical expressions and symbols that students need to understand, interpret, and use. In addition, mathematics has specific vocabulary. Often words that are used commonly, such as difference, have specific meanings in mathematics. Other words, such as polynomial, are a part of a specialized mathematics vocabulary. Students need to understand these representations of mathematics concepts and use them appropriately. In algebra, students are introduced to more complex mathematical expressions and symbols, as well as new vocabulary, which can be an added burden for students who already struggle with mathematics.

Comprehension

At the highest level, representations in mathematics support understanding concepts and relationships. Concepts are taught using a variety of representations. For example, fractions might be taught using fraction bars, pie charts, mathematics expressions, and language. To truly grasp the concept, students need to see how these different representations relate to each other. They need to recognize the critical elements that represent the concept. In this way they learn structure and rules related to concepts and are able to generate and test hypotheses about them. Algebra is often taught as a series of abstract concepts. Many students struggle with the idea of a variable that can represent more than one number, and they have difficulty recognizing underlying patterns and functions that are critical to their understanding.

Principle 2: multiple means of action and expression

Just as representations play an essential role in understanding mathematics, learning is supported when students interact with materials and express what they are learning. Actions include skills that need to be performed fluidly and automatically, as well as higher-order thinking that requires goal-setting and monitoring progress.

In order to be an effective learner and problem-solver it is essential that basic skills and procedures become routine or automatic, allowing the learner to put more attention and effort into determining goals and developing strategies to meet them.

Physical action

Demonstrating knowledge in mathematics generally requires some form of physical action, such as writing, speaking, or pointing. Additionally, many concepts in mathematics are taught using manipulative materials. Special considerations are essential for students with a physical disability to ensure that they can be active participants through whatever actions are available to them. Other students might have more subtle motor problems that make fine motor actions more difficult. A student who must focus his or her effort on the physical action of producing written work will have little left for the higher level thinking required of algebra.

Expression and communication

Understanding mathematical language and symbols is an important aspect of representation; using this language and symbols to communicate about mathematics is an essential component of action and expression. Similarly, creating representations of mathematics concepts is a way to communicate understanding. Sharing thinking with others is a way to organize thinking and reflect on learning.

Just as effectiveness in written communication requires fluency in writing skills, effective communication in mathematics requires fluency in basic skills, such as recalling basic facts, the steps in algorithms, rules for estimation, creating data displays, or using a calculator; all skills needed for success in algebra. As with physical action, if a student puts extra effort into any of these, then less effort is available for the higher-order thinking that is a part of good communication in mathematics.

Executive function

Executive function is a set of mental skills that guide goal-setting, planning and strategy, organization of resources, monitoring progress, and reflecting on results. In mathematics several different strategies might be used to solve the same problem, and students use executive function to decide what approach might be best, given the resources that they have. The goal of these problems is not just to find a correct solution but to learn to apply their skills effectively, to reflect on their process as they work, and to see alternative approaches that might also be appropriate. In algebra, a thorough grounding in the underlying concepts can lead to the understanding that different strategies can be used to find solutions to problems.

Principle 3: multiple means of engagement

Within mathematics, reasoning and decision-making do not function as purely rational, cognitive systems. Emotional aptitude and processes play an important role in mathematics learning and especially in problem solving. More broadly, the accuracy and efficiency of thinking processes, perceptions, and effort are influenced by affective states; motivation and emotion substantially predict learning behavior and outcomes. Low motivation for, and negativity about, mathematics need not be inevitable consequences of mathematics education. Classroom experiences and instructional practices can be designed to enhance student motivation and engagement to improve mathematics achievement.

Interest

Learning experiences that do not foster engagement are inaccessible. Curricular materials do not typically offer the kinds of options, flexibility and choice that would be required to recruit the interests of diverse learners. There is *no single way* to engage all people. Individuals vary systematically in the ways in which they orient to the environment emotionally, are motivated, and engaged in learning processes. Within mathematics, negative emotion and anxiety can impact students' confidence and result in the belief that only "smart" people are good at mathematics. Disinterest or mathematics avoidance might manifest as visible consequences of the impact of years of stress associated with experiences with mathematics in school.

Effort and persistence

Learning skills and strategies within mathematics requires sustained attention and effort. Most students have the capacity to sustain the required effort and concentration, but learners differ substantially in their ability or desire to do so. Student emotions during mathematical problem solving are the product of conscious and subconscious cognitive evaluations or appraisals of their learning experience; students evaluate a problem-solving situation as good or bad, frustrating or challenging, constituting their emotions as negative or positive. The outcomes of these evaluations are highly variable and dependent on many factors not the least of which is students' prior experiences in mathematics. For example, many students come to attribute success in mathematics to innate ability, rather than their own efforts and persistence. These kinds of beliefs significantly diminish the probability that students will invest effort, use available supports, and persist with learning activities in the face of challenge. Providing options that allow students to experience "just-right" challenges in the presence of appropriate resources creates the conditions under which effort and persistence are likely to occur.

Self-regulation

Self-regulation, or strategic control over one's emotional state, is a critical human capacity and essential to any kind of complex or challenging learning scenario. Strong self-regulation skills allow learners to cope and engage with the environment in effective and efficient ways. Importantly, mathematics education is situated within a social-emotional context such that cognitive, motivational and affective factors interact to impact learning behaviors and outcomes. Many students do not implicitly develop strong self-regulation skills, and many classrooms do not address these skills explicitly.

Applying the principles: iSolveIt

While there are certainly many different ways to analyze the reasons students might do poorly in algebra, we used the UDL principles as a framework to guide our decision-making around why students who struggle with mathematics might have particular problems with algebra. These decisions led to three areas of focus. The first two are based in the principles of representation and action and expression. Algebra is highly symbolic, with its own specialized language. It involves reading, interpreting, and developing equations, as well as expressing and communicating their meaning. In addition, success in algebra is dependent on fluency in underlying mathematical skills. The second area is the reasoning needed to comprehend and apply algebraic concepts. This reasoning goes beyond working with numbers; it involves recognizing relevant patterns and relationships and using executive function skills to develop an approach to solving a problem, apply relevant strategies, monitor progress toward the solution and revise as needed, and reflect on the effectiveness of the approach. The third area is based on the engagement principle. Many students find mathematics in general and algebra in particular to be threatening. This negative affective reaction is exacerbated in students who are struggling. Along with the desire to avoid mathematics, they are often unwilling to persist when a problem is difficult or challenging and do not want to reflect on their success or failure.

We came to the conclusion that the underlying reasoning skills might help explain why success in algebra is predictive of future success in other areas – it could be the reasoning itself that is significant – and though there are many programs developed to address the needs of the struggling mathematics student, there are few if any programs that address reasoning skills specifically. We chose to apply the UDL principles to create a supportive environment in which students could isolate and practice reasoning skills through engaging and challenging activities. The result is the two proof-of-concept iSolveIt iPad apps, the prelude to an eventual suite of engaging tablet-based digital puzzles that focus on reasoning skills.

Creating puzzles in a digital format offers flexibility not available in pencil and paper puzzle versions. With digital puzzles students can select a specific puzzle that provides an appropriate challenge and can easily move through different levels of difficulty. Puzzles also can be developed with embedded supports that assist students when they need help without revealing the solution and can help isolate reasoning skills while supporting the construct-irrelevant pieces of the puzzle that might otherwise prevent students from moving forward within the puzzles. The tablet format makes it easy to try different strategies within a single puzzle and to correct errors without needing to start over. Most importantly, with a digital format every action taken by the student in solving each puzzle can be captured, as well as the order in which students choose to do the different puzzles available to them. These data can be used to analyze the different pathways that students take in reasoning through puzzles of different types

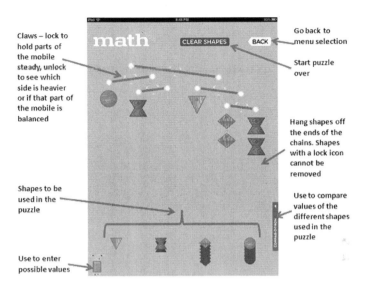

Claws – lock to hold parts of the mobile steady, unlock to see which side is heavier or if that part of the mobile is balanced

Go back to menu selection

Start puzzle over

Hang shapes off the ends of the chains. Shapes with a lock icon cannot be removed

Shapes to be used in the puzzle

Use to compare values of the different shapes used in the puzzle

Use to enter possible values

Figure 30.1 Features of MathematicsScaled

and varying levels of difficulty. With private funding, the two sets of puzzles we have developed to date are MathematicsScaled and MathematicsSquared.

MathematicsScaled

MathematicsScaled is based on a balance scale format, which is often used in algebra and pre-algebra classes to support understanding of equations. The goal is to place the shapes on the balance scale so that the scale is balanced. The weights of the shapes are not given. We have varied the level of difficulty through increasingly complex balance scales and different numbers of shapes used for balance. In the case of MathematicsScaled there is the visual representation of the balance beams that indicate equality such that coding the shapes being balanced to a numeric value is not required to solve the puzzle (Figure 30.1).

MathematicsSquared

MathematicsSquared is based on KenKen™ puzzles. These puzzles are often used as paper and pencil supplementary activities in mathematics classes in middle and high school. MathematicsSquared puzzles are grid-based puzzles that use the basic mathematics operations of addition, subtraction, multiplication, and division and require logic and problem-solving skills (see Figure 30.2). The grids have an equal number of rows and columns (e.g., 3 {x} 3, 4 {x} 4), and the goal of each puzzle is to fill a grid with numbers (e.g., 1 through 3 for a 3 {x} 3 grid) so that no number appears more than once in any row or column. Grids in MathematicsSquared range in size from 3 {x} 3 to 7 {x} 7. The grids are divided into heavily outlined groups of

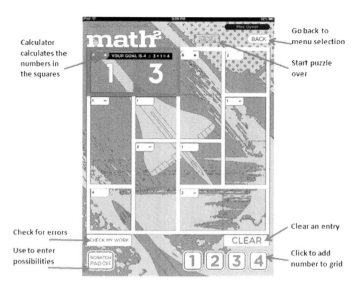

Figure 30.2 Features of MathematicsSquared

cells called "cages." The numbers in the cells of each cage must produce a certain "target" number when combined using a specified mathematical operation (either addition, subtraction, multiplication or division). There are alternate strategies on MathematicsSquared such as using the Sudoku rules that makes it such that calculation might not be required for every step along the puzzle.

UDL features in iSolveIt

We designed both puzzle sets using the UDL framework as a guide for our design decision-making. We applied the Representation Principle by having different types of puzzles that provide students with different representations of challenging situations. Also, both puzzles are solved more efficiently when students are able to discover underlying patterns or structure that leads to a solution.

Applying the Action and Expression Principle focused on helping students to develop strategies and analyze their performance. Students are supported in developing strategies through a scratch pad system that lets them try out possible strategies for solving. They also have the option of checking their work as they progress, so that they can analyze and correct errors as they go along. Students are encouraged to think about their strategies since the puzzles can be solved in different ways, and many have more than one solution. The research versions of MathematicsSquared and MathematicsScaled also include a back-end database that can be used to analyze how students approach the puzzles and how their strategies change over time.

As mentioned earlier, a major contribution of the Engagement Principle was the use of the puzzle format and the design of the apps as interesting and affectively pleasing puzzle challenges rather than typical mathematics practice. Both puzzle sets have multiple levels of difficulty, and students can select the level of challenge they want and move up or down through these levels, increasing the probability that students will independently choose to persist with practice on difficult problems. Students also can decide if and when they want to use the embedded UDL supports, such as the scratch pad.

One additional feature was added to MathematicsSquared as a result of our initial piloting. Although the mathematics required was minimal, some students still needed a calculator to determine possible target numbers, and even when given a calculator, many students did not know what numbers to calculate. To address these issues, we added a built-in "calculator" that highlights the target number for a cage. If numbers have been entered into the cage, the calculator function performs the calculation so that the student can see if he or she has made an error in calculation.

iSolveIt preliminary research

To date we have conducted two pilot studies on the iSolveIt puzzles with a total of 137 middle and high school students. The students used each puzzle for fifteen-minute blocks of time over a one-week period, resulting in each student engaging in about an hour's worth of hands-on time with each app. Researchers observed students and teachers as they interacted with the puzzle and conducted individual interviews with both after implementation. Additionally, all actions taken by the students when solving the puzzles were collected in a database and will be used for analysis.

Qualitative findings

The very first thing teachers noticed was how engaged their students were in solving the puzzles. Invariably, as soon as the iPads were in the students' and teachers' hands, the room would go silent as both worked to solve the puzzles. At the end of the fifteen-minute blocks of time, it was difficult to get them to stop solving the puzzles despite frequent prompts that they could return to it the next day. Teachers viewed the puzzles as helpful for having students see patterns, an important part of algebraic reasoning and mathematical thinking. Both teachers and students commented on how their strategies changed as they solved increasingly complex puzzles. The teachers described different ways in which they could be incorporated into their classrooms, including using them for longer sessions scattered throughout the year and having students work together to solve the puzzles and discuss their reasoning and strategies. They were interested in how they could access the information from the back-end database to better understand how their students were approaching the puzzles and how their strategies changed over time, in order to better guide their logical thinking.

Learning analytics

In order to use student data to support learning, students must be able to take record-able actions that can provide insight into the learning process. The research version of iSolveIt includes a back-end database that collects each action taken by a student when solving a puzzle, yielding a wealth of information that can be analyzed to gain a better understanding of different approaches to problem solving that students take, how these approaches may differ with more difficult puzzles, how they change over time, and, ultimately, how they vary among students with different learning challenges. We are at the early stages of these analyses and have begun with the question of how students decide which puzzles to select, with the goal of creating an environment that helps students to make good selections. According to the UDL guidelines, the role of the design should be to guide appropriate goal-setting so that "the students become adaptive, effective and intrinsically motivated." Using MathematicsSquared, we asked how we can create a design that adapts to the student's ability to choose. To explore this question the design started with a level selection screen that maximized choice. The student made two decisions: level selection and puzzle selection.

The level selection screen organized all puzzles to help inform the student about which puzzle to try next. Each puzzle was put into a category by size and level of difficulty. By showing which levels a student had already worked on, we supported their decision-making process. In Figure 30.3 the darker squares indicate the student has worked on puzzles in categories 3 {x} 3 – Level 1 and 4 {x} 4 – Level 2. Selecting 3 {x} 3 – Level 1 on this screen takes the student to the puzzle selection screen seen in Figure 30.4. It illustrates that the student has completed one puzzle at this level and has another puzzle in progress.

In the first pilot all fifteen categories of choice were available to students from the start. Some students indicated they would prefer to have levels unlock as they progressed. In the second pilot we adjusted the level selection screen to have gradual release, starting with six options available as seen in Figure 30.5. When the student

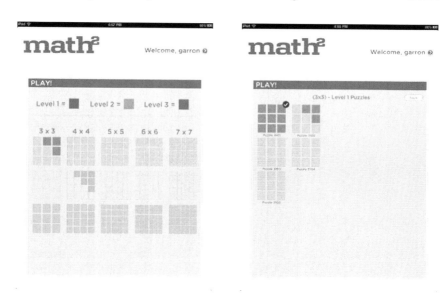

Figure 30.3 Level selection

Figure 30.4 Puzzle selection

solved five puzzles, an additional five options became available, as seen in Figure 30.6. After solving ten puzzles, all fifteen options became available, as seen in Figure 30.7.

When analyzing the data from the first pilot, where students had all fifteen options available from the beginning, we saw that some students would jump forward to

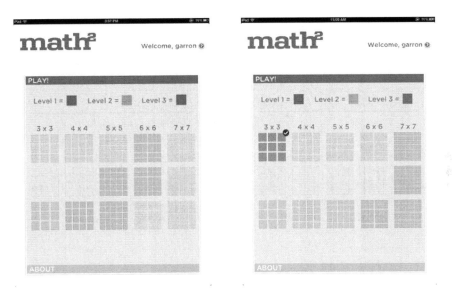

Figure 30.5 Six options

Figure 30.6 Eleven options

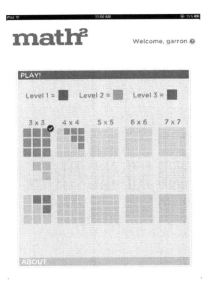

Figure 30.7 Fifteen options

difficult puzzles early in their exploration, sometimes selecting puzzles of size 7 {x} 7 early in their process. While the gradual release supported students who wanted levels to unlock, it simultaneously prevented students from jumping around early in their exploration. This raised a question: Is early exploration of difficult problems potentially helpful for learning?

Conclusion

Algebraic reasoning is a complex cognitive process that goes beyond proficiency in arithmetic. It includes skills such as the ability to manipulate variables, recognize patterns, develop functions, and create models, and use of these skills in making predictions and generalizations. Reasoning also requires flexibility and the ability to bring multiple strategies to problem solving, monitor the effectiveness of these strategies, and make changes when they appear to be ineffective or limited. Reasoning is not a skill that can be performed automatically but a complex process that requires persistence and reflection. Some students might struggle with specific acquired knowledge and skills (e.g., calculation, arithmetic concepts) while others might struggle with more general cognitive or affective processes (or both) resulting in difficulty with algebraic reasoning. With iSolveIt our goal is to work toward decoupling the algebraic reasoning from the calculation and symbolic components of algebra through digital tablet-based puzzles so as to allow for the customization of practice opportunities in the service of developing competence in algebra.

Creating iSolveIt in a digital format offered flexibility not available through pencil and paper materials and, thus, enabled inclusive design guided by UDL. With digital puzzles students were able to select a specific puzzle that provided an appropriate challenge and could easily move through different levels of difficulty. Puzzles were also developed with embedded supports that assisted students when they needed help without revealing the solution. The tablet format made it easy to try different strategies within a single puzzle and to correct errors without needing to start over. Within our digital, UDL format every action taken by students in solving puzzles could be captured, as well as the order in which students chose to do the different puzzles available to them.

The two pilot tests we describe here illustrate early stages of a bottom-up approach to adaptive systems with the explicit goal of adapting to student choice. While the initial pilots were small they raised a few questions to focus the next stages of work. Does autonomy in level selection allow students to gauge their skill set against the available challenge levels? Or does early selection of difficult challenges impact on the development of strategic thinking? Is it potentially harmful for some students to explore difficult puzzles early? Are there a variety of initial restrictions that could provide benefits for student choice? Might it help to provide recommendations on what puzzles we think they might benefit from trying next? Given people will have variable needs, how can we provide a flexible environment in order to design up-front for everyone? The exciting opportunity is to respond to the variation by leveraging data to explore evidence of the student's ability to choose as well as their perceived autonomy. Future work will need to explore how learning analytics can help us explore designs that balance the restriction and support of autonomy and evaluate the impact on engagement and strategic thinking. Finally, the full vision for this work suggest that the most robust innovation will emerge through the development of puzzle "micro-ecosystems" – that is, in the integration of multiple puzzles that vary in their relative demands so that students can start wherever they need, while having the opportunity to experience a variety of contexts for algebraic reasoning.

31

Dyscalculia in Higher Education

Systems, support and student strategies

Clare Trott

Systems in Higher Education (HE)

The legal context

In the UK in 2010 The Equality Act came into force. This carries forward the foundations laid down by previous legislation (The Special Educational Needs and Disability Act (SENDA) 2001, and The Disability Discrimination Act (DDA) 1995).

According to the legislation, there is a requirement for institutions to make 'reasonable adjustments' for disabled students to facilitate access to goods and services. As well as this, institutions are required to ensure disabled students do not receive less favourable treatment nor are unfairly disadvantaged due to a reason associated with their disability. Institutions are further entrusted to put in place 'anticipatory measures'. This might include materials produced in an appropriate and accessible format, provision of note-takers or alternative examination and assessment arrangements for students where required.

The duty is to make reasonable adjustments anticipatory. In terms of dyscalculia, Higher Education Institutions (HEIs) must consider the reasonable adjustments they may need to put in place in order to ensure the removal of unnecessary barriers in respect of the mathematical aspects of courses. HEIs must also promote best practice for inclusion at all levels.

Terms used in this chapter

Throughout this chapter, the terms 'SpLD' and 'neurodiversity' (Oliver, 1990) will be used. SpLD is the most frequently used and widely accepted term that refers to conditions such as dyslexia, dyscalculia and dyspraxia (Institute of Physics, 2013, p. 6).

It is preferred to define this as 'Specific Learning Difference' rather than 'Specific Learning Difficulty' since it moves away from the negative, deficit model and encompasses the idea that dyscalculic learners are likely to perceive mathematics in different ways to their non-dyscalculic peers. Exploration of these ways is still in its infancy.

'Neurodiversity' is 'an umbrella term for it encompasses a range of specific learning differences, including dyslexia, dyspraxia, dyscalculia, ADD, AD(H)D and Asperger's' (Grant, 2009, p. 35). The term neurotypical refers to the non-neurodiverse.

Disabled Students' Allowances

In the UK, Disabled Students' Allowances (DSA) provide extra financial help to students with a disability, mental health difficulty, medical condition or SpLD such as dyscalculia. The DSA is designed to help meet the extra costs students can face as a result of their disability or SpLD. This includes specialist equipment needed for studying and a non-medical helper, such as a study support tutor (Loughborough University, 2013).

Currently, specialist study support through DSA is predominantly focused on text-based material, time management and organisational skills. It is important to extend this practice to include study skills support that focuses on working with non-text material, such as numerical and symbolic notation in order to be able to fully support the dyscalculic student.

Current practice in HE for screening and assessment

Data from Drew and Trott (2011) found that 22% of dyscalculic students arrived at university with a pre-existing identification. If there exists a recent and valid assessment report from an Educational Psychologist or recognised assessor, then an application is made to the DSA body. Once approved, the student has an assessment of need and the agreed requirements are sent to the DSA body for final approval.

However, many dyscalculics are not identified until they reach HE level. Anecdotal evidence suggests that reliable and valid identification, both before entering HE and during the HE phase, is often difficult to obtain. Vouroutzidou (2011, p. 126) discusses the case of a student who was identified when she first came to university, through her own pro-active research. Trott (2010b, p. 71) cites the case of 'Liam', who was identified as dyscalculic during his first year at university. However, Liam attended an institution where screening and assessment procedures for dyscalculia were in place.

With increasing awareness of dyscalculia and greater consensus about its assessment, earlier identification of dyscalculia is likely.

From a survey of HEIs (Drew & Trott, 2011), the overall percentage of dyscalculic students in HE was found to be 0.04%. This is the number of students who have been formally identified as dyscalculic by a recognised assessor or Educational Psychologist. However, it is likely that there are dyscalculic students who have not sought help while at university and are coping with their learning difference (perhaps studying arts subjects), so this might not be a true reflection of the HE percentage. Furthermore, a grade C in GCSE mathematics is an entrance requirement for most

HE courses and this might act as a deterrent or seemingly insurmountable barrier for many dyscalculic students.

It is clear that, in comparison to the child-based dyscalculia prevalence data of 3–8% (Geary, 2004; Desoete et al., 2004; Butterworth, 2002), the majority of dyscalculic children fail to reach HE.

Screening

Screening generally precedes formal identification, which is followed by the assessment of need. 'Students with dyscalculia need to be identified and have their learning needs assessed' (Kirk & Payne, 2012, p. 16). The first step in the process is screening. This should indicate if the student is 'at risk' or not and if a formal assessment is therefore required.

In terms of dyslexia, Klein (1995) developed a structured in-depth diagnostic interview (DI), adopting a qualitative approach. Building up a detailed picture of the student's history and current situation enables a clear profile to emerge, highlighting the difficulties experienced as well as allowing for the elimination of some possible factors such as issues with reading or handwriting. Klein's work can be adapted and extended to cover mathematics.

In HE, the screening process is likely to consist of both a DI and a number-based understanding or operational mathematics test.

Drew and Trott (2011) noted that HEIs using a DI reported the identification of significantly more students at risk of dyscalculia. An interview component is seen as a necessary element in screening for dyscalculia since it reveals valuable data about childhood and everyday experiences that cannot be captured in a standardised test.

From their data, Drew and Trott (2011) found six of the HEIs in their sample had no screening procedure in place for dyscalculia. Participants' comments suggested that they were unhappy with their current screening and assessment process and were looking for guidance:

> We don't recognise dyscalculia as such. If they have comorbidity with another SpLD then they can access the support available to students with [that] SpLD . . . We have concerns over how dyscalculia is assessed (what tests are appropriate) and who has the expertise.

Within HE, specific screening tools used for dyscalculia are likely to include the Wide Ranging Achievement Test (WRAT; Wilkinson, 2006) or the Dyscalculia Screener (Butterworth, 2003).

DysCalculiUM (Iansyst/Tribal, 2011) is an age-appropriate first-line screening tool. It aims to provide an effective tool to identify those who might be at risk of dyscalculia, before referral to formal assessment.

The tool is designed to focus on the understanding of the number concepts and inter-relationships that are the key elements of dyscalculia. These are: number concepts, quantitative comparisons (subdivided into items that employ words, symbols or visual spatial representations) and operations. The operations category is further split into

Which sum gives the larger answer?

Select the correct answer

Sum A   2458 + 327
Sum B   2458 + 326

- Sum A
- Sum B
- Both the same
- Cannot tell

Figure 31.1 An exemplar item from DysCalculiUM

conceptual understanding of operations and the making of inferences from given results, as illustrated by the exemplar item in Figure 31.1.

The screening tool also includes several applications of these key elements, 'thus helping to identify what is conceptually understood and what can be effectively applied' (Trott, 2010a, p. 19). The model for DysCalculiUM is given in Figure 31.2.

DysCalculiUM provides an individual student profile based on the model given in Figure 31.2. In addition to an overall 'at risk' indicator, it provides a profile of the 11 categories showing the areas of relative strength and weakness. The indication of 'at risk' acts as guidance for referral to an Educational Psychologist or qualified assessor for a full and formal identification. Moreover, the resulting DysCalculiUM profile can provide a useful starting point for subsequent one-to-one learning support.

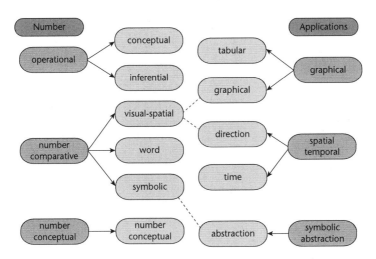

Figure 31.2 The model for DysCalculiUM: a first-line screening tool

DysCalculiUM provides an online delivery of the screening tool with results and student profile available to the tutor. Each individual will have a unique profile of strengths and weaknesses. Trott (in prep. for 2014) emphasises the importance of acknowledging and embracing the strengths and recognising and rewarding neurodiverse contributions and abilities.

Assessment

In HE in the UK, it is necessary to have a recent and valid assessment of dyscalculia in order to access DSA. Such an assessment should be carried out by an Educational Psychologist (EP) or recognised assessor.

Lauchlan and Boyle (2007) acknowledge that within the framework of UK legislation, positive opportunities are to be gained from the application of a label. Labels provide access to resources but caution should be exercised in order to consider the nature of those resources, including appropriate intervention. However, the 'label' frequently varies, depending on the assessor's nomenclature (Grant, 2013).

There are several issues that currently exist in assessments, particularly with regard to any clear consensus on the necessary profile for dyscalculia, specific maths weakness, mathematical difficulties or even mathematical anxiety. There is also an issue in the availability and selection of valid and reliable age-appropriate assessment tools.

There are various reasons why mathematical difficulties occur at HE level, one of which is dyscalculia. Consideration must be given to the other possible factors such as knowledge gaps through poor teaching or long periods of absence, mathematical anxiety, slow processing or reading difficulties. 'Different causes result in different diagnostic outcomes and different support needs' (Grant, 2013).

In moving the debate forward, Grant (2013) cites four key factors for an assessment of 'specific maths weakness'. These are: past history, current situation, a mathematics standardised test score less than perceptual reasoning scores and a low mathematics standardised test score that is primarily not the result of poor memory or slow processing speed. More importantly, Grant (2013) contends that a lack of numerosity is an essential element to reporting 'dyscalculia'. Gillam (2012) agrees: 'Based on the available neurological evidence, it does indeed seem appropriate to include a measure of numerosity in an assessment for dyscalculia' (p. 291).

What is needed is an unambiguous and clear agreement among professionals how identification such as: 'specific maths weakness', 'mathematical difficulty' or 'dyscalculia' is assessed and the respective constituent profiles.

Beyond the DSA, a formal and appropriate identification can help the student to understand the difficulties they will have experienced throughout school and in life. It can give the students a sense of their own mathematical and neurodiverse identity. Vouroutzidou (2011) cited the case of an HE dyscalculic student for whom identification 'came as a very positive experience because it confirmed that there is a professional explanation of the difficulties that the student had' (p. 127).

Research by Drew (2013) considered 14 case studies of dyscalculic students in HE. One of the students experienced similar feelings of relief that there was a reason for the mathematical difficulties: 'There was one side of me that was, "Oh, thank goodness; I'm not actually stupid, there is actually a reason for it"' (Rebecca) (Drew, 2013).

However, it should be noted that an identification of dyscalculia can, conversely, result in low self-esteem or a resignation factor. Rebecca went on to say: 'But then, the flip side was that the rug was pulled from underneath my feet, because that was my whole dream, all my goals, to be a nurse, was taken from me' (Rebecca) (Drew, 2013).

Another of the students in the research by Drew (2013) felt let down by the educational system that had not recognised her dyscalculia: 'school was so horrific. I was angry that it had taken that long for someone to go "This is what's going on"' (Nancy) (Drew, 2013).

Course of study

There are many courses in HE (e.g. Psychology, Sociology, Science and Engineering) that contain a mathematically based core component and where there will be an expectation of competency (Doyle, 2010, p. 56). When analysing the subject choices of dyscalculic students in HE, Drew and Trott (2011) found that almost 50% of the students in their sample had chosen courses in the 'subjects allied to medicine' category: nursing, midwifery and occupational therapy. Particular concerns in nursing have been raised (MacDougall, 2009; Kirk & Payne, 2012). Kirk and Payne (2012, p. 16) indicate that dyscalculia 'has significant implications for pre-registration nurse education'. 'Subjects allied to medicine' is an area that needs special attention with the specific issue of fitness-to-practise (MacDougall, 2009; Kirk & Payne, 2012) and where the mathematical elements such as drug-dose calculations are key.

The second highest category identified by Drew and Trott (2011) was 'Science'. This is another area with significant mathematical content. 'Science' includes many subject areas, including physical, bio and human sciences, with dyscalculic students likely to be in the latter two categories. Statistics is a key element of psychology, as well as social sciences. Dyscalculic students frequently enrol on such courses unaware of the level of statistical content in them. Similarly, another area containing sizeable mathematical content is 'Business and Management'.

Relatively few dyscalculic students were found to be in the 'humanities and languages' area (Drew & Trott, 2011) where mathematical content is minimal. They contend that this is likely to result from students not needing to seek help or identification. They further claim that courses with very high or very low mathematical content are unlikely to contain substantial numbers of identified dyscalculic students, but that dyscalculic students are most likely to be found on courses with moderate mathematical content.

Support

Support provision for dyscalculia

As discussed earlier, almost all HEIs in the UK have provision for one-to-one study skills support for dyslexia. Specialist support for dyscalculia must also be an essential element of the HEIs portfolio.

Kirk and Payne (2012) assert that tutorial support 'may be problematic if the educational institution does not have expertise in supporting people with dyscalculia' (p. 17). Trott (2009) agrees: 'for students with dyscalculia, appropriate support and practice is not often available in HE' (p. 139). She argues that dyscalculic students can benefit greatly from specialist support and makes the case for more specialist training in this area.

Support: general principles

McGahey and Szumko (2007, p. 1) state: 'beginning to work with a specialist tutor may be the first time they (the student) have really felt understood'. A dyscalculic student who reaches HE has already achieved much. They are likely to have experienced difficulties in school and perhaps, like Rebecca (Drew, 2013), been considered stupid or belittled in front of the rest of the class.

Blackburn (2003, p. 1) experienced this humiliation at a formative age:

> From the age of 6 when I stood stuttering and red-faced, yet again unable to recite my 3 times table and the class genius was invited to smugly recite his 13 times tables immediately after to show how easy it was, I thought something wasn't right. Not only was it not right, it wasn't ruddy fair. Hot tears would run down my cheeks and I'd creep away feeling stupid, angry, miserable and very, very alone.

The academic learning support tutor has an important role to play as 'change agent' (Hunter-Carsch & Herrington, 2001, p. 73). The Association of Dyslexia Specialists in Higher Education (ADSHE) (2009, pp. 12–13) state that one-to-one support focuses on the individual student and their evolving needs. The tutor and student should work in partnership. They further contend that the aim of support sessions is to reinforce and build on successful strategies, support the student in critical reflection to enable independent understanding of their working preferences and of how the interaction of SpLD and learning affects them, and to ensure that all sessions are student-centred (ADSHE, 2009, p. 14). Employing a multisensory approach will further support the needs of the dyscalculic student. This may be most effective as a hands-on approach, interacting with the real world and its numerical demands.

Neurodiverse students will clearly benefit from systematic support that places their individual needs at the heart of the process. It is essential to understand that there are differences in how they learn and adapt the teaching to each individual's needs, enabling the student to move towards independent learning.

Support: case studies

Dyscalculic students in HE are likely to struggle with number concepts and relationships. This will frequently include integers, but will certainly include fractions, decimals and percentages. Difficulties with placing numbers on the number line in a sequential order might be challenging. Consequently, reading graphical scales and understanding information presented graphically will be difficult.

It has already been mentioned that subjects such as psychology or social sciences contain modules of statistics. In nursing, charts of Body Mass Index or observations are required and therefore graphical literacy is important.

> I was there and I collected this data, I was on the ground. I can measure you out a quadrat of 100 metres squared and I can count the trees in it and I can measure the trees. You ask me to interpret the data and that's a whole different task.
>
> *(Fiona: Drew, 2013)*

The following two case studies serve to illustrate the impact of dyscalculia in HE.

Case study 1: Fiona (Trott et al., 2013)

Fiona is a mature student of Wildlife and Countryside Management at a rural agricultural college. She was identified with dyscalculia, but is otherwise very able and determined.

Fiona received learning support to help her understand why statistics is used to demonstrate real-life observed patterns. She needs to relate to data in a tangible and personal way, collecting the data herself and perceiving it with her own senses. This involves being in woodland counting fauna and flora and observing characteristics. Her understanding of the environment is as strong as her neurotypical peers.

However, Fiona struggles to quantify her data and to represent it graphically. While other students may find a bar chart or scatter graph useful to demonstrate a trend, Fiona does not visualise a graphical representation in the same way, and continues to question the need for it.

Case Study 2: Liam (Trott, 2010b)

'Liam' was a first year student studying transport management and was identified as dyscalculic during his first year at university.

Liam had always struggled with understanding basic mathematical concepts and had been placed in the lowest set for mathematics in school. However, he had excelled at other subjects, particularly languages. His dyscalculia meant he struggled with the conceptual understanding of number and with operations as well as the ability to understand graphical information. He had particular difficulty with sequencing numbers in the correct order and placing them on a number line.

On his HE course, Liam struggled, not only with number work, but also with the variety of tables, charts and graphs presented. This included tables of information that had to be interpreted and distance-time graphs that had to be both read and drawn.

Both Fiona and Liam struggled with the graphical aspects of their respective courses.

The issues appear to stem from difficulties in ordering a sequence of numbers on a number line. Since this is problematic in this one-dimension, when two number lines act as the axes of a graph, the problem compounds. Comprehending a simultaneous change in both variables becomes a complex task.

When the dyscalculic student is further faced with scales that include decimals, markers between the integers or scales that go up in fives, they will increasingly find graphical representations to be inaccessible to them (Drew, 2013).

Support for Liam initially focused on the sequential order of number. Numbers were written on post-its, one number on each, and Liam was encouraged to put them in order. Then he progressed to distance-time graphs.

> The graphs were re-drawn many times without the understanding being present. It was only by chance, that on one occasion he drew the graph with the vertical axis on the right hand side, and he had a 'eureka moment'. He said: 'It's climbing up the wall!'
>
> *(Trott, 2010b, p. 72)*

For Fiona, by keeping the charts as simple and uncluttered as possible and corresponding exactly to the question being asked (with as little interpretation as possible), she was able to start to understand how these graphs could represent real-life trends (Trott et al., 2013).

With regard to the tables of information, Liam was encouraged to use pieces of card to cover over the irrelevant information, in order to identify and focus on the appropriate data. The identification of key cells in tables of information or statistical output is an essential step to making them more manageable. As well as covering over those cells that are not relevant, colour coding can be useful. Indeed, the use of colour will make many aspects of the mathematics more user-friendly. Each variable can be written in a different colour, or each procedure assigned a colour. For example, one student always used blue for kilograms and green for grams. This must always be applied in a consistent way (Trott, 2009, p. 144).

Trott (2009) states that dyscalculic students bring into HE many varied strengths, including excellent literacy based skills. She argues that it is important to build on these strengths when attempting to make meaning in mathematics. 'Strong text based skills suggest that as much of the work as possible should be encapsulated in words' (Trott, 2009, p. 139).

Fiona found that talking through what the questions were asking for helped her to understand not only what was required of her, but also the statistical information itself. In the context of Non-verbal Learning Disorder, Zieman (2000) said: 'a thousand words is worth a lot more than two bar charts and a line graph'. A similar argument is valid for dyscalculia. The utilisation of strong literacy skills can, for the dyscalculic student, help offset the numerical difficulties. This appears in sharp contrast to the dyslexic student who is frequently a visual learner. A dyslexic student might approach a problem from a more visual perspective, make atypical connections and develop new ideas (Cooper, 2009, p. 66). Given the accompanying memory issues for dyslexic students, they are likely to favour a holistic approach based on sound conceptual understanding.

Thus, descriptions of procedures that can lead to solutions are, for the dyscalculic student, often more accessible than logical and notation-laden conceptual approaches to mathematics. The procedural or algorithmic approach is, for many dyscalculic students, a means to an end, fulfilling the mathematical course requirements. The student is likely to make extremely slow progress in their conceptual understanding and, coupled with time constraints, procedural learning is frequently the preferred mode for the dyscalculic student (Drew, 2013). Ramirez et al. (2012) argue that such algorithmic learners tend to rely on working memory intensive solution strategies and working memory is disrupted more by maths anxiety. The dyscalculic student is highly likely to be mathematically anxious. Therefore, the reliance on procedures or algorithms puts the dyscalculic student at high risk of failure.

Consequently, in supporting the dyscalculic student, emphasis needs to be placed on very small steps and successes that increase confidence and reduce the mathematical anxiety. A way forward for many dyscalculic students is through developing some limited conceptual understanding, reducing mathematical anxiety and building well-rehearsed procedures.

Dyscalculia: the social effects

There is still a long way to go to raise awareness of dyscalculia as an SpLD. Number and numeracy pervade our daily routines: household budgeting, checking change or telling the time. Anxious and frustrated dyscalculics face challenges every day, resulting in dysfunctional lives and low self-esteem.

Money

Financial management is a basic necessity for students living on a student loan (Trott, 2009). Many dyscalculic students are likely to rely on friends and family to work out their finances.

Trott (2010b, p. 71) recounts the scenario of one dyscalculic student who always paid with 'a purple' (£20 note), thereby ensuring that she had given enough money to cover the cost of her purchases. She was unable to count out the amount or check her change. Furthermore, she experienced difficulties in the café when she socialised there with her peers. Her embarrassment led her to stop going to the café and she became increasingly socially isolated.

Drew and Trott (2013) outlined some of the coping strategies that students employ when faced with financial situations. In addition to the use of large denominations of paper money, there is a reliance on technology. Strategies included shopping on the Internet (avoiding face-to-face embarrassment) and with debit cards. However, the latter involves keying in the PIN, which might be a barrier for many dyscalculics.

It is not surprising that many dyscalculic students experience anxiety about money. In HE in the UK, the student loan has to be managed carefully. Sound budgeting is necessary for students to pay for accommodation, food and materials required for their studies as well as numerous other competing demands on their finances.

One student commented: 'It's numbers so I am going to leave it alone so I've never really throughout university kind of like budgeted or anything like that' (Bradley) (Drew & Trott, 2013).

Time

Everyday life is time-dependent. Our daily routine is time-based and this creates a system to which everyone relates his or her lives.

To arrive at the correct location at the correct time involves calculating: the necessary arrival time, the travelling time involved and the correct time to set out. This is further complicated by the fact that the calculations are worked back from the end point. It is not surprising that some students adopt the strategy of arriving early and just waiting.

Bird (2007, p. xviii) notes that dyscalculia may result in 'a marked delay in learning to read a clock to tell the time'. The ability to read a clock relies on understanding numbers and difficulties can be life-long. Burny et al. (2012) claim the interpretation of numbers is especially difficult in clock reading as the clock does not make use of the base 10 structure, the meaning of a number depends on which clock hand is pointing at it and reading a clock involves the understanding of spatial and clockwise movements.

Results from Burny et al. (2012) show that complex clock reading tasks (reading the clock to 5-minute or 1-minute precision) remain difficult for children with mathematical difficulties on both analogue and digital clocks. They acknowledge that, while switching to digital clock will not resolve the difficulties, choosing between formats should be the child's preference.

Students appear to prefer digital clocks and, in particular, those based in the 12-hour system. Many rely on their mobile phone display for this. Moreover, mobile phones allow the student to set up alarms to signal different activities to be undertaken, thus avoiding the need to tell the time (Drew & Trott, 2013). There is also a reliance on Internet timetables and route planners (Drew & Trott, 2013). It should be noted too that university timetables are given in the 24-hour clock system so dyscalculic students are likely to struggle to read them.

Reasonable adjustments in HE frequently include extra time for examinations. This should be awarded for all examinations, not just those that include mathematics. An award of 25% extra time has to be calculated and distributed between each of the questions. Furthermore, this might need to be done in proportion to the number of marks allocated to each question. If a dyscalculic student struggles with time, then concentrating on an essay and keeping track of the time taken becomes a more severe test than for their non-dyscalculic peers (Trott & Drew, 2013).

With reference to examinations, one student commented: 'they always have big, round scary clocks' (Maggie) (Trott & Drew, 2013).

Conclusion

Within the context of current HE systems and procedures, it is important to understand the nature of dyscalculia and the barriers it creates. An understanding of how to make learning more accessible to the dyscalculic student, particularly through learning support, can help to ensure student progression and success.

Checklist

The following is a short checklist for Institutions of Higher Education. It aims to show the requirements for recognition and support of dyscalculia.

For dyscalculia: does your institution have . . .

- A screening procedure in place?
- A screening procedure that includes an in-depth interview to obtain a full history and current situation?
- Access to an Educational Psychologist or recognised assessor for a full assessment?
- Support provision with a qualified and/or experienced tutor?
- Provision for reasonable adjustments and anticipatory measures?

Does the support provided . . .

- Recognise and emphasise the students' strengths?
- Take a multisensory approach?
- Use colour coding in a consistent way?
- Focus on very small steps in conceptual understanding?
- Seek to reduce mathematical anxiety and increase confidence?
- Help and advise students with the social aspects such as telling the time, time management and money?

References

ADSHE (2009). *Guidelines for Quality Assurance in Specialist Support for Students with SpLDs in Higher Education.* http://adshe.org.uk/wp-content/uploads/ADSHE-Guidelines-June-20091.pdf (accessed 6 June 2013).

Bird, R. (2007). *The Dyscalculic Toolkit.* London: Sage.

Blackburn, J. (2003). Damn the Three Times Table. http://www.lboro.ac.uk/departments/mec/activities/maths-statistics-support/thedyscalculiaanddyslexiainterestgroup/personalperspectives/ (accessed 6 August 2012).

Burny, E., Vaicke, M., & Desoete, A. (2012). Clock reading. An underestimated topic in children with mathematics difficulties. *Journal of Learning Disabilities, 45*(4), 351–360.

Butterworth, B. (2003). *Dyscalculia Screener.* London: nferNelson Publishing Company Limited.

Butterworth, B. (2002). *Mathematics and the Brain.* Opening address to The Mathematical Association Conference, Reading, UK. http://www.mathematicalbrain.com/pdf/MALECTURE.PDF (accessed 2 February 2010).

Cooper, R. (2009). Dyslexia. In D. Pollak (ed.) *Neurodiversity in Higher Education: Positive Responses to Specific Learning Differences* (pp. 63–89). Chichester: Wiley and Sons.

Desoete, A., Roeyers, H., & De Clercq, A. (2004). Children with mathematics learning disabilities in Belgium. *Journal of Learning Disabilities, 37*(1), 50–61.

Doyle, A. (2010). *Dyscalculia and Mathematical Difficulties: Implications for Transition to Higher Education in the Republic of Ireland.* Disability Services, Trinity College, Dublin.

Drew, S. (2013). *Dyscalculia in Higher Education.* Presentation given to Mist, Haze and Shutters: Dyscalculia in FE/HE Conference, Loughborough University, April 2013.

Drew, S. & Trott, C. (2011). *An Initial Survey into Dyscalculia within Higher Education.* Presentation given to ADSHE 2011, Embracing Diversity – A Decade of Difference: Reflections on the Past and Looking to the Future, London.

Drew, S. & Trott, C. (2013). *Dyscalculia: Definitions, Screening, Support and Current Research.* Presentation given to PATOSS, 13 March 2013, West Bromwich College.

Geary, D.C. (2004). Mathematics and learning disabilities. *Journal of Learning Disabilities, 37*(1), 4–15.

Gillam, J. (2012). Dyscalculia: Issues for practice in educational psychology. *Educational Psychology in Practice: theory, research and practice in educational psychology, 28*(3), 287–297.

Grant, D. (2009). The psychological assessment of neurodiversity. In D. Pollak (ed.) *Neurodiversity in Higher Education: Positive Responses to Specific Learning Differences* (pp. 33–62). Chichester: Wiley and Sons.

Grant, D. (2013). *A Diagnostician's Dilemma: Dyscalculia? Specific Maths Weakness? Poor memory?* Keynote presentation given to Mist, Haze and Shutters: Dyscalculia in FE/HE Conference, Loughborough University, April 2013.

Hunter-Carsch, M. & Herrington, M. (2001). *Dyslexia and effective learning in secondary and tertiary education.* London: Whurr.

Iansyst/Tribal. (2011). *DysCalculiUM.* Available from https://shop.tribalgroup.co.uk/Assessment-screening/DyscalculiUM.html (accessed 14 August 2011).

Institute of Physics. (2013). *Supporting STEM Students With Dyslexia: A good practice guide for academic staff.* London: Institute of Physics.

Kirk, K. & Payne, B. (2012). Dyscalculia: awareness and student support. *Nursing Times, 108*(37), 16–18.

Klein, C. (1995). *Diagnosing Dyslexia* (2nd edn). London: The Basic Skills Agency.

Lauchlan, F. & Boyle, C. (2007). Is the use of labels in special education helpful? *Support for Learning, 22*(1), 36–42.

Loughborough University. (2013). Disabled Student Allowance. Loughborough University Counselling and Disability Service, http://www.lboro.ac.uk/services/cds/disability/dsa/ (accessed 30 June 2013).

MacDougall, M. (2009). *Dyscalculia, Dyslexia, and Medical Students' Needs for Learning and Using Statistics. Medical Education Online, 14*(2), 1087–2981. Available from http://www.med-ed-online.org (accessed 13 August 2013).

McGahey, P. & Szumko, J. (2007). Relationship at the Heart of Helping. Brain HE. Available from: www.brainhe.com/staff/types/documents/RelationshipattheHeartofSupportWork.doc (accessed 6 August 2013).

Oliver, M. (1990). *The Politics of Disablement.* Basingstoke: Palgrave Macmillan.

Ramirez, G., Gunderson, E., Levine, S. & Beilock, S. (2012). Math anxiety, working memory, and math achievement in early elementary school. *Journal of Cognition and Development, 14*(2), 187–202.

Trott, C. (2009). *Dyscalculia.* In D. Pollak (ed.) *Neurodiversity in Higher Education: Positive Responses to Specific Learning Differences* (pp. 125–148). Chichester: Wiley and Sons.

Trott, C. (2010a). Dyscalculia: A practitioner's view. *Assessment & Development Matters, 2*(2), 19–21.

Trott, C. (2010b). *Dyscalculia in Further and Higher Education,* CETL-MSOR Conference Proceedings 2010, University of Birmingham, 68–73. September 2010.

Trott, C. (in prep. for 2014). The neurodiverse mathematics student. In A.C. Croft, M.J. Grove, J. Kyle & D.A. Lawson (eds) *Transitions in Undergraduate Mathematics Education.* University of Birmingham.

Trott, C. & Drew, S. (2013). *Dyscalculia in Higher Education: Successful Interventional Support.* Presentation given to The 4th All-European Dyslexia Conference, Vaxjo, Sweden, September 2013.

Trott, C., Drew, S. & Maddocks, H. (2013). A Hub Service: extending the support provided by one institution to students of other local institutions. *MSOR Connections, 13*(1), 18–23.

Vouroutzidou, P. (2011). *The social organisation of learning difficulties at university: a qualitative study of four Higher Education Institutions in the North East Region of England.* PhD thesis, Durham University. Available from: http://etheses.dur.ac.uk/891/ (accessed 15 January 2013).

Wilkinson, G.S. (2006). *Wide Range Achievement Test: WRAT4.* Wilmington, DE: Wide Range Inc.

Zieman, G. (2000). *Nonverbal Learning Disability: The Math and Handwriting Problem. Parenting New Mexico,* February 2000. Available from: http://www.ziemang.com/pnm_articles/0002ld.htm (accessed 13 August 2013).

Index